P9-CZU-792

WITHDRAWN

824.8
Ar65c
v.7
c.2

Arnold

God and the Bible

66503

WITHDRAWN

LIBRARY
Northern Montana College
Havre, MT 59501

VII

God and the Bible

MATTHEW ARNOLD

GOD AND THE BIBLE

Edited by R. H. Super

ANN ARBOR   THE UNIVERSITY OF MICHIGAN PRESS

66503

Copyright © by The University of Michigan 1970
All rights reserved
ISBN 0-472-11657-6
Library of Congress Catalog No. 60-5018
Published in the United States of America by
The University of Michigan Press and simultaneously
in Don Mills, Canada, by Longmans Canada Limited
Manufactured in the United States of America

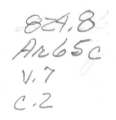

824.8
Ar65c
V. 7
C .2

Editor's Preface

In addition to the large work which gives the present volume its title, the reader will find herein two shorter essays on religious subjects ("A Persian Passion Play," subsequently added to the first series of *Essays in Criticism*, and the Introduction to Arnold's version of Isaiah XL–LXVI), three on education ("A Few Words about the Education Act," "Savings Banks in Schools," and "A Speech at Westminster"), two on France after the Franco-German war ("A French Elijah" and the review of Renan's *La Réforme intellectuelle et morale de la France*), and two on Anglo-Irish affairs (the Preface to the 1874 edition of *Higher Schools and Universities in Germany* and its supplement, the note on "Roman Catholics and the State"). The span of the volume is from January, 1871, to November, 1875, with one short essay of June, 1875, reserved for the next volume. "Savings Banks in Schools" and the essay on Renan's book were reprinted with notes by Fraser Neiman in *Essays, Letters, and Reviews by Matthew Arnold* (Cambridge: Harvard University Press, 1960); the former is Neiman's own discovery. "A Persian Passion Play" has recently been reprinted with notes in Sister Thomas Marion Hoctor's edition of *Essays in Criticism* (Chicago: University of Chicago Press, 1968). Dean Roger L. Brooks announced his discovery of "A Few Words about the Education Act" in *Modern Philology* for February, 1969—too late, obviously, for inclusion in its proper sequence in the sixth volume of this edition; it therefore takes its place here, out of proper order by only a few months. "A French Elijah" is a discovery of the present editor's; it must supplant the article on "University Reform" published as Arnold's in Neiman's volume but certainly not his. Arnold completed his version of the book of Isaiah with a second volume, *Isaiah of Jerusalem*, in 1883; the entire version will be reprinted with the Introduction of 1883 in the tenth volume of the present edition.

As with *Literature and Dogma*, Arnold greatly abridged his text of *God and the Bible* when he revised it for the "Popular Edition." And as with *Literature and Dogma*, the present edition uses the text of the Popular Edition, but includes (from the 1883 edition printed for the American market) all except the very briefest passages excised in the final revision, here marked off by square brackets at the beginning and end of each such passage and at the beginning of every paragraph within it. The use of single and double quotation marks has been made throughout consistent with the Popular Edition and the spelling of "connection," etc. (1883) has been altered to the "connexion," etc., of the Popular Edition. Scriptural references in footnotes have been normalized in a form somewhat between those of the two versions. "A Persian Passion Play" is printed from the 1883 edition of *Essays in Criticism*. The Introduction to Isaiah is printed from the edition prepared for the general market; variants from this version in the school text edition will be found in the Textual Notes: several are of considerable length and deserve the reader's attention. The other essays in this volume were not reprinted by Arnold and therefore present only a single authoritative text. The footnotes at the bottom of the page are Arnold's, very rarely augmented (in square brackets) by the editor. A few manifest errors in the text and Arnold's footnotes have been corrected and indicated in the Textual Notes, though simple misprints (as for example of Greek accents) have generally been silently corrected. The Textual Notes indicate all substantive differences between the present text and earlier versions of the works. Changes in italicizing, punctuation, and capitalization are ignored, but every change from a semicolon to a full stop, or the reverse, and every change in paragraphing is noted.

The Critical and Explanatory Notes aim at explaining Arnold's allusions, identifying his quotations, giving the background of the works, and (to a lesser extent) pointing out parallels in his other writings. Cross references to other parts of this volume are occasionally given; where they are not, the reader may find what he wants with the help of the Index. *God and the Bible* is a remarkable exercise in critical scholarship; the present editor lacked the resources to follow Arnold's every footstep as he traced a path through the nineteenth-century German critics of Scripture, but he hopes to have succeeded sufficiently to enable the reader to perceive what was going on. Nonetheless he is aware of some at least of his failures, in the present as in earlier volumes. It is especially regrettable when an editor's failure to find Arnold's source for a quotation is used (as has recently been done) as ground for supposing that Arnold invented the quotation; nothing, indeed, is less likely under any circumstances.

I am grateful to my friends Professors Stephen J. Tonsor and Sidney Warschausky for their help on particular matters that were troublesome to me. And at the moment of his retirement it cannot be amiss to express a sense of the debt of all users of this edition of Arnold to Mr. Walter Donnelly, Editor of the University of Michigan Press, who saw six volumes of the work through the press and began this seventh on its way. The present volume was assisted by a summer research fellowship from the Horace H. Rackham School of Graduate Studies at the University of Michigan.

Contents

A Few Words about
the Education Act

An immense deal of what is done, said, and written about the
Education Act has, and will continue to have, no real relation at
all to the design of getting the people of this country better educated, but turns, and will turn, entirely on certain points of political, social, and religious contention, interesting to the contend-   5
ers, but not to the genuine educationist. Careless of these points,
not even asking whether the Act, which has been so lately passed
and is not likely to be at once altered, is a good or a faulty piece
of legislation, the educationist will be disposed to take the Act as
it stands for his given instrument towards the work which he has   10
at heart, and to ask what use he can best make of it. That question we propose to try and answer here, with the same single eye
to the business in hand and the cause of education with which the
genuine educationist, we believe, will ask it.

People must be taken as we find them, and it is certain that the   15
dislike to rates, to ratepayers' management, and to a type of
school new and unfamiliar, will cause great efforts to be made to
supplement the existing school-provision, where it is defective,
with schools of the old kind, rather than have recourse to a
school board and rate-schools. The British and Foreign School   20
Society, which as a society has no denominational ends to serve
and does not work for such ends, may well think it finds in the
rate-school, such as under the Act it is likely to be, the sort of
school for which it has always contended, and be willing to transfer its schools to school boards. But with the clergy, the Wes-   25
leyans, and the Roman Catholics, the case will be different. They
may see the means of making the rate-school, if they are forced
to have it, something more to their mind than they at first feared
it must be; but they will certainly prefer to have their own

schools if they can. Accordingly we see prodigious efforts being
made by the Church of England to fill, while there is yet time,
the ground which is vacant and presents blots for the Act to hit.
Even in London the necessity for rate-schools is thus being much
5   reduced, and it is probable that the new school board for London
will find less to do in the way of having to provide new schools
out of the rates than is now imagined. In country districts the
necessity for rate-schools will, it seems likely, be by the efforts
now making done away almost entirely.

10   In the great majority of places, therefore, the educationist will
find that the case *necessitating* a school board and rate-schools
does not arise. There will be sufficient provision of schools of the
old type, with a conscience clause, and rate-schools will not be
wanted. Is he then to consider that a school board is not wanted
15   either, or that it is a machinery which cannot be applied where
there are no rate-schools? By no means. His great difficulty, that
of non-attendance and irregular attendance of children at school
remains in full force; a school board can alone give him the support of the 74th section of the Act,—the section which intro-
20   duces compulsion,—and it can give him this support without
rates and rate-schools. If parents know that the power of compulsion exists ready to be put in force, they will, in nine cases out
of ten, send their children to school without waiting for the law
to be applied against them; but it is essential they should see that
25   the power exists. The educationist, therefore, will, if he is wise,
in all cases seek to get school boards appointed, and to make existing school managers desire them, and work cordially with them
rather than be averse from them and jealous of them. The school
board in any parish will have the power to pass and enforce bye-
30   laws compelling attendance at *some* public elementary school
in the place (if there is more than one school, the choice between
them remains with the parent) even though the school be one
not provided by the board, a school of the old type and with a
private body of managers. In the cases where compulsion involves
35   free schooling, this likewise can easily be arranged with the managers, without having recourse to a rate. The burden of providing free schooling for children whom a school board pronounced
unable to pay (all who are able to pay, the school board will
make pay) would not be heavy, and would be gladly undertaken

by managers and subscribers if they were in cordial relations with the school board. The essential thing is that there should be these cordial relations; and it will be the aim of the educationist to produce and establish them.

These relations will be much promoted by perfectly fair deal- 5
ing, in country parishes and national schools, with Dissent; by the full observance of the conscience clause in the spirit as well as the letter. The educationist will certainly find that the Act, and the Department's working of the Act, help him to secure this fair dealing and full observance, on which so much depends. Dis- 10
senters said when the Act was under discussion, and they are say-ing still, that the conscience clause would prove a nullity in country parishes; that the squire and parson would make it un-derstood that they regarded as black sheep those who availed themselves of it; and that the dissenter would not venture to 15
withdraw his children from the religious instruction, however much he disliked it. The educationist will see that proceedings of this kind, if they took place, would inevitably kindle strife and heart-burnings, which would invade the school board, and mar those cordial relations between school board and managers, 20
which we have shown to be so fruitful of good for education. The educationist, therefore, will set his face against any such proceedings, of which, moreover, the dissenters much exagger-ate the probable prevalence; and it cannot be but that the Educa-tion Department, which in this matter has just the same interest 25
to guide it as the educationist, will certainly co-operate strenu-ously to prevent such proceedings. Complaints of a pressure put upon dissenters, to prevent their withdrawing their children from the religious instruction of the squire and parson's school, will be gone into, and the presence of dissenters' children at this 30
instruction, under circumstances at all calculated to excite suspi-cion, will occasion enquiry; and there can be no doubt that of managers and schools proved to have set at nought the intention of the law by unfair practices of this kind, the Department will make signal and deterrent examples. But it is probable, let us re- 35
peat, that the dissenters greatly exaggerate, to their own minds and to the public, the number of squires and parsons with a dis-position to have recourse to such practices.

An educationist such as we have supposed him (and many of

the managers of our existing schools will be of this type), inclined to reach his aim in the simplest manner by using the men
and the means already available, but using them in a pliant and
liberal manner, will certainly often wish to give a broader basis
5 to the committee of management of a national school than the
trust-deeds at present allow. One of the merits of a school board,
as a committee of management, will be, that it can have a broad
basis, representing all classes, and thus tending to spread, through
all, an interest in the school. Where the old committees of man-
10 agement remain, the educationist will naturally desire to give
them something of the advantage of this breadth of basis. But
there are many national schools with trust-deeds making the basis
for the committee of management very narrow; prescribing, for
example, that every manager shall be a communicant, and that
15 every manager shall be a yearly subscriber of at least twenty shillings, or even more. On these conditions, none but strict churchmen, and none of the working class, can be on the committee of
management. But here the Act gives no relief. Managers can get
rid of the obligations of their trust-deeds by transferring their
20 schools altogether to school boards; but this implies that the
schools come upon the rates and lose entirely their present character. The Act gives to managers no facilities for getting rid,
while their schools continue supported and managed as at present, of the obligations of their trust-deed, with a view to giving
25 to the management of their school a larger, a more public, and a
more useful character. Yet it might be contended that, in a mixed
parish, a single school-institution, with its managers necessarily
chosen on a very narrow and exclusive basis, cannot thoroughly
fulfil the requirement of section 8 of the Act, that the school for
30 a district shall be *suitable for the children of such district.* The
educationist will wish, therefore, that the management of existing
schools should have a power of liberalising itself beyond what is
given by the Act at present, and his wish seems well deserving of
consideration by the Education Department.
35   We have said that in general the educationist, wishing to see
the country educated, and employing for that purpose the men
and things readiest to his hand, will find that probably he has not
much to concern himself, in these first days at any rate, with

rates, rate-schools, and school boards managing them. Where he has to do with these, however, and where he is called to act whether as elector or member of such school boards, it is to be hoped that he will neither mistake their functions nor undervalue them. The Education Department, by reserving to itself the interpretation of the Act, has a good deal abridged the grounds for sectaries and politicians to wrangle over. If, for instance, the majority of a school board decide to have a school where the Bible is read and explained, and some of the school board contend that the exclusion of formularies implies the exclusion of explanation, this contention will be disposed of, not by interminable wrangling within the school board itself, nor yet by recourse to the delays and uncertainties of a court of law, but by recourse to the Education Department. But it is not the less true that there are left to the school boards questions of the highest interests to settle, questions of which the Education Department does not attempt the settlement, of which the old committees of management were quite unfit to attempt the settlement, and of which well composed school boards in our chief towns may attempt the settlement with the fairest hopes of doing great good, not only to their own schools, but to schools throughout the country; for throughout the country will their influence and example, if they are well composed and do their work well, extend. Questions of studies, school books, size of schools, hours of schooling, physical training, are questions of this kind; every educationist feels their importance, and how little there exists, at present, any school authority capable of dealing with them. To school boards and rate-schools he will look for help towards their solution. But whether his part in using the new Act is cast in town or country, with rate-schools or without them, he will himself try to use the Act, and to get it used by others in one interest and one interest only—the interest of education.

A French Elijah

The Paris correspondent of the *Times* tells us that "Gallia, a Lamentation," the symphonetic ode of M. Gounod just performed at Paris, is a sincere and profound work. It had need to be; for these qualities of sincerity and profoundness are just what the misfortunes of France demand of the artist who attempts to treat them. But these qualities are just those in which French artists are apt to fail, even when they have the most settled intention to exhibit them. There has just come into our hands a short dramatic piece given at the Odéon Theatre during the last month. The Odéon is a theatre for high and serious effort, and the author of this piece has the most evident conviction that he is making a high and serious effort. The title of the piece is, "Fais ce que Dois: Épisode Dramatique en un acte, en vers." To examine it will not take us long; and it is worth examining.

The author of "Fais ce que Dois" is a M. François Coppée, and his piece has reached a tenth edition. There are but three personages in it—Marthe, the widow of a French officer who has been killed in the late war with Prussia; Henri, a boy of fourteen, her son; and Daniel, a village schoolmaster, who had been a friend of Marthe's husband. Marthe is about to emigrate with her son; he is her only child, and she fears that if they stay in France he will have to enter the army, and will perish like his father. The boy is full of excitement at the thought of a sea voyage and a new world; his mother sends him to make sure that their berths are taken. When he is gone, Daniel enters. The village school children, he says, when they heard that their young acquaintance was going to emigrate—

> O Marthe, ils ont trouvé le mot qui déconcerte,
> Et, comme d'un soldat, ils ont dit, Il déserte.

The boy himself, he adds, is but a child, his mother can dispose of him; but is she doing her duty by him?—

> Connaît-il cette guerre infâme et notre haine?
> Sait-il qu'on nous a pris l'Alsace et la Lorraine,
> Que Metz et que Strasbourg ont dû courber leurs fronts
> Sous le joug allemand? ...
> Sait-il que dans nos mains on a brisé le fer,
> Et sait-il que son père est mort à Froeschwiller?

Marthe excuses herself by saying that the boy is her last hope, that if she loses him she must die, and that she hears her husband's voice telling her to depart with him. "Vous blasphémez!" answers Daniel. Henri re-enters, bringing word that all the arrangements are complete. Daniel begins to address him; Marthe bids the boy not to listen, tells him he will hear of the perils of the sea, will hear vain predictions of the reviving fortune of France. Then Daniel rejoins. No, he says "avec une profonde tristesse," no:—

> Nous sommes arrivés à notre âge de fer,
> Et ce pays descend une fatale pente.
> Espérer qu'il s'arrête un jour et se repente,
> Nourrir cette sublime et folle illusion
> *Qu'il redevienne encore la grande nation*,
> Qu'il se relève enfin, je ne l'ose plus guère.

But his countrymen, so full of faults, shall at least hear from him, he says, the bitter, wholesome truth:—

> Peuple qui dans l'orgueil et le mal persévères,
> Tes fils sauront de moi les vérités sévères.

He will tell his school-children the whole miserable history, down even to the abomination of desolation coming to plant itself in the queen of cities, down even—

> A l'heure du profond désespoir et des larmes
> Où Paris épuisé dut déposer les armes,
> A l'heure où, sous ses murs, ceux qui l'avaient vaincu,
> *Tristes que le géant eût encore survécu,*
> *N'osaient trop s'approcher et se disaient:*—Il bouge!

Yes, this excellent moralist cries:—

> Oui, je veux appliquer le fer qui cautérise
> Sur le mauvais orgueil, dans ces jeunes esprits.

But having thus lashed and cowed French vanity and presumption, he will turn and bring some comfort by recounting the mar-
5   vels of French heroism:—

> Je leur dirai qu'il fut encore des héros
> Chez nos pauvres soldats arrachés aux hameaux
> Lorsque nous inonda cette effroyable armée;
> Comme on a bien souffert dans la ville affamée,
10 Où pas un ne parlait de se rendre, pas un,
> Et comme on a bien su mourir à Châteaudun!

He will tell his school-children how the besieged in Paris—

> Mangèrent le pain dur, dormirent sous la toile,
> Et tombèrent, vaincus, mais frappés par devant;
15 Je leur raconterai ces histoires, enfant;
> *Je les enivrerai de haine et de souffrance,*
> *Et je préparerai des vengeurs à la France!*

Henri begins to take fire. Marthe interposes, appeals to Daniel not to rob her of her child for what must be, she feels, a hopeless
20 struggle.

> DANIEL.
> Marthe, écoutez-moi bien.
> Je suis simple d'esprit et n'ai rien d'un prophète,
> Et pourtant, malgré tout, malgré notre défaite,
25 Je crois que nous pouvons encore être sauvés.

> MARTHE.
> Mais un enfant? . . .

> DANIEL.
> Enfants, c'est vous qui le pouvez!

30 But you admit, says Marthe, how frivolous our nation is. Daniel answers:—

> Nous le transformerons, nous, les maîtres d'école;
> Oui, si ce peuple veut, et si tout son passé
> De folie et d'erreur est un jour effacé,
35 Si de son ignorance enfin il se délivre,
> S'il apprend à choisir la parole et le livre,

S'il cherche le progrès logique et régulier,
S'il se plie à la loi, s'il sait répudier
La révolution dont le monde s'effraie,
Et, prenant le chemin de la liberté vraie,
Qui n'est que le respect de soi-même et d'autrui,   5
S'il répare et maudit ses fautes d'aujourd'hui,
Il reprendra sa place à la tête du monde.

Make every citizen a soldier, he says, make—

De la patrie entière une famille armée
Et du seul sentiment du devoir enflammée,   10
Où le riche bourgeois coudoîra l'artisan,
Où le noble sera l'égal du paysan.

And then:

O mon pays en deuil, la chose sera mûre,
Et, poussant vers le ciel ton cri de conquérant,   15
Tu pourras les répandre alors comme un torrent,
Et planter, glorieux, les trois couleurs altières
De notre vieux drapeau sur nos vieilles frontières.

But if we succumb once more, Marthe asks; if the German once
more plunges his conquering steel into our hearts? The answer of   20
Daniel is sombre, Apocalyptic:—

Femme, nul ne connaît le destin des batailles;
Mais s'il doit les revoir couvrir son horizon,
Que Paris cette fois songe à son vieux blason.
    (*Avec enthousiasme.*)   25
O vaisseau qui du grand Paris portes le nom!
Dans l'ouragan hurlant plus haut que le canon
Nous t'avons vu souvent t'abîmer sous la brume;
Mais tu te relevais toujours, couvert d'écume,
Superbe et vomissant l'eau par les écubiers.   30
Si Paris doit périr, si c'est bien l'heure sombre
D'amener pavillon ou de couler à pic,
Souviens-toi de Jean-Bart et de Du Couëdic,
Navire, souviens-toi de Villaret-Joyeuse!
Lorsqu'après la bataille atroce et furieuse,   35
Rouge de sang, n'ayant plus de mâts, plus d'agrès,
Tu verras ces maudits face à face, tout près,
Et te jetant déjà les chaînes de l'esclave,
Meurs en volcan pour les engloutir sous ta lave!

Et que le monde entier convienne avec effroi,
Que le sort du *Vengeur* est seul digne de toi!

After this, can we wonder that Henri turns to Marthe and says?

O mère, *il a raison!* C'est un conseil funeste
Que te donnait tout bas ton désespoir.
                              (*A Daniel.*)
                                        Je reste.

                    MARTHE à Daniel.
Hélas! qu'avez-vous fait?

                         DANIEL.
                              Le devoir est ici.

                    MARTHE à Henri.
Tu l'exiges de moi, cruel enfant?

                    HENRI (*se jetant à son cou*).
                                        Merci!

                         MARTHE.
Soit, je cède, et je mets au ciel mon espérance.
Dieu, protége mon fils!

                         DANIEL.
                         Dieu, protége la France!

And so the curtain falls.

One might leave this piece to speak for itself; but to make one
or two remarks on it may be useful. First, let us remark the law—
the beneficent law—which, in the region of grave and serious
composition, connects bad poetry with false moral sentiments.
Good rhetoric may consist, in this region, with false moral sentiments, but good poetry, poetry which satisfies, never. The critic,
in many respects so ingenious, who in the last number of the
Fortnightly Review parallels M. Victor Hugo with Michael
Angelo, will do well to ponder this law, which is eternal. It is
also worth while to remark how, in the author of this piece,
moral sentiments utterly false go along with the most fixed intention to be sincere, profound and moral, with a copious use of the
words *Dieu* and *devoir*, with a bitter sense that the miserable situation of France has been made for her by her faults. The truth is,

that right moral sentiments are formed, not by an ardent intention to have and utter them, but by a long train of practical habits
in obedience to a high moral standard; and this is just the schooling Frenchmen not only do not give themselves thoroughly (few
people do), but seem to have hardly any conception of. Joubert   5
speaks of "a moral sense in ruins;" the moral sense of M. François
Coppée is not so much a moral sense in ruins as a moral sense
which has never been awakened and trained at all. People may
say of the Bible what they like, but its authoritative voice and
standard is the great awakener and trainer of this sense. M. Fran- 10
çois Coppée and the mass of his countrymen write and speak like
people who know of the Bible nothing at all, but who have a
quantity of tags of false classicism in its stead. In this respect
what France lost by the failure of the Reformation can hardly
be over-estimated. The Reformation failed in France mainly be-   15
cause France at large was, as M. Michelet most truly says, "éloig-
née de réforme morale." Let us convince ourselves of what she
lost by placing a Frenchman of 1569 side by side with our
Frenchman of 1871.

Coligny, after the battle of Montcontour, defeated, wounded,   20
and with the blame of all the failures of his party thrown upon
him, is retreating. The narrator is his contemporary, D'Aubigné:

L'amiral se voyant sur la tête, comme il advient aux capitaines des
peuples, le blâme des accidents, le silence de ses mérites, un reste
d'armée qui même avant le désastre désespérait déjà . . . ce vieillard, 25
pressé de la fièvre, endurait ces pointures qui lui venaient au rouge,
plus cuisantes que sa fâcheuse plaie. Comme on le portait en une litière, Lestrange, vieux gentilhomme, cheminant en même équipage et
blessé, fit avancer sa litière au front de l'autre, et puis passant la tête à
la portière regarde fixement son chef, et se sépare la larme à l'oeil avec   30
ces paroles: *Si est-ce, que Dieu est très-doux!* Là-dessus, ils se disent
adieu, bien unis de pensée, sans pouvoir dire davantage.

Coligny perished, and France had, instead, the *grand siècle*, 1789,
and M. Victor Hugo. The Reformation belonged to the sixteenth
century, and cannot come over again in the nineteenth. But how   35
well might Niebuhr say that to make a political revolution—a
1688 or a 1789—really fruitful, a 1517 must come first!

A Persian Passion Play

Everybody has this last autumn[1] been either seeing the Ammergau Passion Play or hearing about it; and to find any one who has seen it and not been deeply interested and moved by it, is very rare. The peasants of the neighbouring country, the great and
5 fashionable world, the ordinary tourist, were all at Ammergau, and were all delighted; but what is said to have been especially remarkable was the affluence there of ministers of religion of all kinds. That Catholic peasants, whose religion has accustomed them to show and spectacle, should be attracted by an admirable
10 scenic representation of the great moments in the history of their religion, was natural; that tourists and the fashionable world should be attracted by what was at once the fashion and a new sensation of a powerful sort, was natural; that many of the ecclesiastics present should be attracted there, was natural too. Roman
15 Catholic priests mustered strong, of course. The Protestantism of a great number of the Anglican clergy is supposed to be but languid, and Anglican ministers at Ammergau were sympathisers to be expected. But Protestant ministers of the most unimpeachable sort, Protestant Dissenting ministers, were there, too, and show-
20 ing favour and sympathy; and this, to any one who remembers the almost universal feeling of Protestant Dissenters in this country, not many years ago, towards Rome and her religion,—the sheer abhorrence of Papists and all their practices,—could not but be striking. It agrees with what is seen also in literature, in
25 the writings of Dissenters of the younger and more progressive sort, who show a disposition for regarding the Church of Rome historically rather than polemically, a wish to do justice to the undoubted grandeur of certain institutions and men produced by

[1] 1871.

that Church, quite novel, and quite alien to the simple belief of earlier times, that between Protestants and Rome there was a measureless gulf fixed. Something of this may, no doubt, be due to that keen eye for Nonconformist business in which our great bodies of Protestant Dissenters, to do them justice, are never wanting; to a perception that the case against the Church of England may be yet further improved by contrasting her with the genuine article in her own ecclesiastical line, by pointing out that she is neither one thing nor the other to much purpose, by dilating on the magnitude, reach, and impressiveness, on the great place in history, of her rival, as compared with anything she can herself pretend to. Something of this there is, no doubt, in some of the modern Protestant sympathy for things Catholic. But in general that sympathy springs, in Churchmen and Dissenters alike, from another and a better cause,—from the spread of larger conceptions of religion, of man, and of history, than were current formerly. We have seen lately in the newspapers, that a clergyman, who in a popular lecture gave an account of the Passion Play at Ammergau, and enlarged on its impressiveness, was admonished by certain remonstrants, who told him it was his business, instead of occupying himself with these sensuous shows, to learn to walk by faith, not by sight, and to teach his fellow-men to do the same. But this severity seems to have excited wonder rather than praise; so far had those wider notions about religion and about the range of our interest in religion, of which I have just spoken, conducted us. To this interest I propose to appeal in what I am going to relate. The Passion Play at Ammergau, with its immense audiences, the seriousness of its actors, the passionate emotion of its spectators, brought to my mind something of which I had read an account lately; something produced, not in Bavaria nor in Christendom at all, but far away in that wonderful East, from which, whatever airs of superiority Europe may justly give itself, all our religion has come, and where religion, of some sort or other, has still an empire over men's feelings such as it has nowhere else. This product of the remote East I wish to exhibit while the remembrance of what has been seen at Ammergau is still fresh; and we will see whether that bringing together of strangers and enemies who once seemed to be as far as the poles asunder, which Ammergau in such a remarkable way effected, does not hold good and find a parallel even in Persia.

Count Gobineau, formerly Minister of France at Teheran and at Athens, published, a few years ago, an interesting book on the present state of religion and philosophy in Central Asia. He is favourably known also by his studies in ethnology. His accomplishments and intelligence deserve all respect, and in his book on religion and philosophy in Central Asia he has the great advantage of writing about things which he has followed with his own observation and inquiry in the countries where they happened. The chief purpose of his book is to give a history of the career of Mirza Ali Mahommed, a Persian religious reformer, the original *Bâb*, and the founder of *Bâbism*, of which most people in England have at least heard the name. Bâb means *gate*, the door or gate of life; and in the ferment which now works in the Mahometan East, Mirza Ali Mahommed,—who seems to have been made acquainted by Protestant missionaries with our Scriptures and by the Jews of Shiraz with Jewish traditions, to have studied, besides, the religion of the Ghebers, the old national religion of Persia, and to have made a sort of amalgam of the whole with Mahometanism,—presented himself, about five-and-twenty years ago, as *the door*, *the gate* of life; found disciples, sent forth writings, and finally became the cause of disturbances which led to his being executed on the 19th of July, 1849, in the citadel of Tabriz. The Bâb and his doctrines are a theme on which much might be said; but I pass them by, except for one incident in the Bâb's life, which I will notice. Like all religious Mahometans, he made the pilgrimage to Mecca; and his meditations at that centre of his religion first suggested his mission to him. But soon after his return to Bagdad he made another pilgrimage; and it was in this pilgrimage that his mission became clear to him, and that his life was fixed. "He desired"—I will give an abridgment of Count Gobineau's own words—"to complete his impressions by going to Kufa, that he might visit the ruined mosque where Ali was assassinated, and where the place of his murder is still shown. He passed several days there in meditation. The place appears to have made a great impression on him; he was entering on a course which might and must lead to some such catastrophe as had happened on the very spot where he stood, and where his mind's eye showed him the Imam Ali lying at his feet, with his body pierced and bleeding. His followers say that he then passed through a sort of moral agony which put an end to all the hesitations of the natural man within him. It is certain that when he arrived at Shiraz, on his return, he was a changed man. No doubts troubled him any more: he was penetrated and persuaded; his part was taken."

This Ali also, at whose tomb the Bâb went through the spiritual crisis here recorded, is a familiar name to most of us. In general our knowledge of the East goes but a very little way; yet almost every one has at least heard the name of Ali, the Lion of God, Mahomet's young cousin, the first person, after his wife, who believed in him, and who was declared by Mahomet in his gratitude his brother, delegate, and vicar. Ali was one of Mahomet's best and most successful captains. He married Fatima, the daughter of the Prophet; his sons, Hassan and Hussein, were, as children, favourites with Mahomet, who had no son of his own to succeed him, and was expected to name Ali as his successor. He named no successor. At his death (the year 632 of our era) Ali was passed over, and the first caliph, or *vicar* and *lieutenant* of Mahomet in the government of the state, was Abu-Bekr; only the spiritual inheritance of Mahomet, the dignity of Imam, or *Primate*, devolved by right on Ali and his children. Ali, lion of God as in war he was, held aloof from politics and political intrigue, loved retirement and prayer, was the most pious and disinterested of men. At Abu-Bekr's death he was again passed over in favour of Omar. Omar was succeeded by Othman, and still Ali remained tranquil. Othman was assassinated, and then Ali, chiefly to prevent disturbance and bloodshed, accepted (A.D. 655) the caliphate. Meanwhile, the Mahometan armies had conquered Persia, Syria, and Egypt; the Governor of Syria, Moawiyah, an able and ambitious man, set himself up as caliph, his title was recognised by Amrou, the Governor of Egypt, and a bloody and indecisive battle was fought in Mesopotamia between Ali's army and Moawiyah's. Gibbon shall tell the rest:—"In the temple of Mecca three Charegites or enthusiasts discoursed of the disorders of the church and state; they soon agreed that the

deaths of Ali, of Moawiyah, and of his friend Amrou, the Viceroy of Egypt, would restore the peace and unity of religion. Each of the assassins chose his victim, poisoned his dagger, devoted his life, and secretly repaired to the scene of action. Their
5 resolution was equally desperate; but the first mistook the person of Amrou, and stabbed the deputy who occupied his seat; the prince of Damascus was dangerously hurt by the second; Ali, the lawful caliph, in the mosque of Kufa, received a mortal wound from the hand of the third."

10 The events through which we have thus rapidly run ought to be kept in mind, for they are the elements of Mahometan history: any right understanding of the state of the Mahometan world is impossible without them. For that world is divided into the two great sects of Shiahs and Sunis. The Shiahs are those who
15 reject the first three caliphs as usurpers, and begin with Ali as the first lawful successor of Mahomet; the Sunis recognise Abu-Bekr, Omar, and Othman, as well as Ali, and regard the Shiahs as impious heretics. The Persians are Shiahs, and the Arabs and Turks are Sunis. Hussein, one of Ali's two sons, married a Persian
20 princess, the daughter of Yezdejerd the last of the Sassanian kings, the king whom the Mahometan conquest of Persia expelled; and Persia, through this marriage, became specially connected with the house of Ali. "In the fourth age of the Hegira," says Gibbon, "a tomb, a temple, a city, arose near the ruins of
25 Kufa. Many thousands of the Shiahs repose in holy ground at the feet of the vicar of God; and the desert is vivified by the numerous and annual visits of the Persians, who esteem their devotion not less meritorious than the pilgrimage of Mecca."

But, to comprehend what I am going to relate from Count
30 Gobineau, we must push our researches into Mahometan history a little further than the assassination of Ali. Moawiyah died in the year 680 of our era, nearly fifty years after the death of Mahomet. His son Yezid succeeded him on the throne of the caliphs at Damascus. During the reign of Moawiyah Ali's two
35 sons, the Imams Hassan and Hussein, lived with their families in religious retirement at Medina, where their grandfather Mahomet was buried. In them the character of abstention and renouncement, which we have noticed in Ali himself, was marked

yet more strongly; but, when Moawiyah died, the people of
Kufa, the city on the lower Euphrates where Ali had been assassinated, sent offers to make Hussein caliph if he would come
among them, and to support him against the Syrian troops of
Yezid. Hussein seems to have thought himself bound to accept 5
the proposal. He left Medina, and, with his family and relations,
to the number of about eighty persons, set out on his way to
Kufa. Then ensued the tragedy so familiar to every Mahometan,
and to us so little known, the tragedy of Kerbela. "O death,"
cries the bandit-minstrel of Persia, Kurroglou, in his last song be- 10
fore his execution, "O death, whom didst thou spare? Were even
Hassan and Hussein, those footstools of the throne of God on the
seventh heaven, spared by thee? *No! thou madest them martyrs
at Kerbela.*"

We cannot do better than again have recourse to Gibbon's 15
history for an account of this famous tragedy. "Hussein tra-
versed the desert of Arabia with a timorous retinue of women
and children; but, as he approached the confines of Irak, he was
alarmed by the solitary or hostile face of the country, and suspected either the defection or the ruin of his party. His fears 20
were just; Obeidallah, the governor of Kufa, had extinguished
the first sparks of an insurrection; and Hussein, in the plain of
Kerbela, was encompassed by a body of 5000 horse, who inter-
cepted his communication with the city and the river. In a conference with the chief of the enemy he proposed the option of 25
three conditions:—that he should be allowed to return to Medina, or be stationed in a frontier garrison against the Turks, or
safely conducted to the presence of Yezid. But the commands of
the caliph or his lieutenant were stern and absolute, and Hussein
was informed that he must either submit as a captive and a crimi- 30
nal to the Commander of the Faithful, or expect the consequences of his rebellion. 'Do you think,' replied he, 'to terrify
me with death?' And during the short respite of a night he prepared, with calm and solemn resignation, to encounter his fate.
He checked the lamentations of his sister Fatima, who deplored 35
the impending ruin of his house. 'Our trust,' said Hussein, 'is in
God alone. All things, both in heaven and earth, must perish and
return to their Creator. My brother, my father, my mother,

were better than I, and every Mussulman has an example in the
Prophet.' He pressed his friends to consult their safety by a
timely flight; they unanimously refused to desert or survive their
beloved master, and their courage was fortified by a fervent
5   prayer and the assurance of paradise. On the morning of the fatal
day he mounted on horseback, with his sword in one hand and
the Koran in the other; the flanks and rear of his party were secured by the tent-ropes and by a deep trench, which they had
filled with lighted fagots, according to the practice of the Arabs.
10   The enemy advanced with reluctance; and one of their chiefs
deserted, with thirty followers, to claim the partnership of inevitable death. In every close onset or single combat the despair
of the Fatimites was invincible; but the surrounding multitudes
galled them from a distance with a cloud of arrows, and the
15   horses and men were successively slain. A truce was allowed on
both sides for the hour of prayer; and the battle at length expired
by the death of the last of the companions of Hussein."

The details of Hussein's own death will come better presently;
suffice it at this moment to say he was slain, and that the women
20   and children of his family were taken in chains to the Caliph
Yezid at Damascus. Gibbon concludes the story thus: "In a distant age and climate, the tragic scene of the death of Hussein
will awaken the sympathy of the coldest reader. On the annual
festival of his martyrdom, in the devout pilgrimage to his sep-
25   ulchre, his Persian votaries abandon their souls to the religious
phrenzy of sorrow and indignation."

Thus the tombs of Ali and of his son, the Meshed Ali and the
Meshed Hussein, standing some thirty miles apart from one another in the plain of the Euphrates, had, when Gibbon wrote,
30   their yearly pilgrims and their tribute of enthusiastic mourning.
But Count Gobineau relates, in his book of which I have spoken,
a development of these solemnities which was unknown to Gibbon. Within the present century there has arisen, on the basis
of this story of the martyrs of Kerbela, a drama, a Persian na-
35   tional drama, which Count Gobineau, who has seen and heard
it, is bold enough to rank with the Greek drama as a great and
serious affair, engaging the heart and life of the people who have
given birth to it; while the Latin, English, French, and German

drama is, he says, in comparison a mere pastime or amusement, more or less intellectual and elegant. To me it seems that the Persian *tazyas*—for so these pieces are called—find a better parallel in the Ammergau Passion Play than in the Greek drama. They turn entirely on one subject—the sufferings of the *Family of the* 5 *Tent*, as the Imam Hussein and the company of persons gathered around him at Kerbela are called. The subject is sometimes introduced by a prologue, which may perhaps one day, as the need of variety is more felt, become a piece by itself; but at present the prologue leads invariably to the martyrs. For instance: the 10 Emperor Tamerlane, in his conquering progress through the world, arrives at Damascus. The keys of the city are brought to him by the governor; but the governor is a descendant of one of the murderers of the Imam Hussein; Tamerlane is informed of it, loads him with reproaches, and drives him from his presence. 15 The emperor presently sees the governor's daughter splendidly dressed, thinks of the sufferings of the holy women of the Family of the Tent, and upbraids and drives her away as he did her father. But after this he is haunted by the great tragedy which has been thus brought to his mind, and he cannot sleep and cannot 20 be comforted. He calls his vizier, and his vizier tells him that the only way to soothe his troubled spirit is to see a *tazya*. And so the *tazya* commences. Or, again (and this will show how strangely, in the religious world which is now occupying us, what is most familiar to us is blended with that of which we know nothing): 25 Joseph and his brethren appear on the stage, and the old Bible story is transacted. Joseph is thrown into the pit and sold to the merchants, and his blood-stained coat is carried by his brothers to Jacob; Jacob is then left alone, weeping and bewailing himself; the angel Gabriel enters, and reproves him for his want of 30 faith and constancy, telling him that what he suffers is not a hundredth part of what Ali, Hussein, and the children of Hussein will one day suffer. Jacob seems to doubt it; Gabriel, to convince him, orders the angels to perform a *tazya* of what will one day happen at Kerbela. And so the *tazya* commences. 35

These pieces are given in the first ten days of the month of Moharrem, the anniversary of the martyrdom at Kerbela. They are so popular that they now invade other seasons of the year

also; but this is the season when the world is given up to them.
King and people, every one is in mourning; and at night and
while the *tazyas* are not going on, processions keep passing, the
air resounds with the beating of breasts and with litanies of "O
5   Hassan! Hussein!" while the Seyids,—a kind of popular friars
claiming to be descendants of Mahomet, and in whose incessant
popularising and amplifying of the legend of Kerbela in their
homilies during pilgrimages and at the tombs of the martyrs, the
tazyas, no doubt, had their origin,—keep up by their sermons
10 and hymns the enthusiasm which the drama of the day has excited. It seems as if no one went to bed; and certainly no one who
went to bed could sleep. Confraternities go in procession with a
black flag and torches, every man with his shirt torn open, and
beating himself with the right hand on the left shoulder in a
15 kind of measured cadence to accompany a canticle in honour of
the martyrs. These processions come and take post in the theatres
where the Seyids are preaching. Still more noisy are the companies of dancers, striking a kind of wooden castanets together,
at one time in front of their breasts, at another time behind their
20 heads, and marking time with music and dance to a dirge set up
by the bystanders, in which the names of the Imams perpetually
recur as a burden. Noisiest of all are the Berbers, men of a darker
skin and another race, their feet and the upper part of their body
naked, who carry, some of them tambourines and cymbals, others
25 iron chains and long needles. One of their race is said to have
formerly derided the Imams in their affliction, and the Berbers
now appear in expiation of that crime. At first their music and
their march proceed slowly together, but presently the music
quickens, the chain and needle-bearing Berbers move violently
30 round, and begin to beat themselves with their chains and to
prick their arms and cheeks with the needles—first gently, then
with more vehemence; till suddenly the music ceases, and all
stops. So we are carried back, on this old Asiatic soil, where beliefs and usages are heaped layer upon layer and ruin upon ruin,
35 far past the martyred Imams, past Mahometanism, past Christianity, to the priests of Baal gashing themselves with knives and to
the worship of Adonis.

The *tekyas*, or theatres for the drama which calls forth these celebrations, are constantly multiplying. The king, the great functionaries, the towns, wealthy citizens like the king's goldsmith, or any private person who has the means and the desire, provide them. Every one sends contributions; it is a religious act to furnish a box or to give decorations for a *tekya;* and as religious offerings, all gifts down to the very smallest are accepted. There are tekyas for not more than three or four hundred spectators, and there are tekyas for three or four thousand. At Ispahan there are representations which bring together more than twenty thousand people. At Teheran, the Persian capital, each quarter of the town has its tekyas, every square and open place is turned to account for establishing them, and spaces have been expressly cleared, besides, for fresh tekyas. Count Gobineau describes particularly one of these theatres,—a tekya of the best class, to hold an audience of about four thousand,—at Teheran. The arrangements are very simple. The tekya is a walled parallelogram, with a brick platform, *sakou*, in the centre of it: this *sakou* is surrounded with black poles at some distance from each other, the poles are joined at the top by horizontal rods of the same colour, and from these rods hang coloured lamps, which are lighted for the praying and preaching at night when the representation is over. The *sakou*, or central platform, makes the stage; in connection with it, at one of the opposite extremities of the parallelogram lengthwise, is a reserved box, *tâgnumâ*, higher than the *sakou*. This box is splendidly decorated, and is used for peculiarly interesting and magnificent tableaux,—the court of the Caliph, for example—which occur in the course of the piece. A passage of a few feet wide is left free between the stage and this box; all the rest of the space is for the spectators, of whom the foremost rows are sitting on their heels close up to this passage, so that they help the actors to mount and descend the high steps of the *tâgnumâ* when they have to pass between that and the *sakou*. On each side of the *tâgnumâ* are boxes, and along one wall of the enclosure are other boxes with fronts of elaborate woodwork, which are left to stand as a permanent part of the construction; facing these, with the floor and stage between, rise tiers of seats as in an amphitheatre. All places are free; the great people have generally provided and furnished the boxes, and take care to fill them; but if a box is not occupied when the performance begins, any ragged street-urchin or beggar may walk in and seat himself there. A row of gigantic masts runs across the middle of the space, one or two of them being fixed in the *sakou* itself; and 5 from these masts is stretched an immense awning which protects the whole audience. Up to a certain height these masts are hung with tiger and panther skins, to indicate the violent character of the scenes to be represented. Shields of steel and of hippopotamus skin, flags, and naked swords, are also attached to these masts. A 10 sea of colour and splendour meets the eye all round. Woodwork and brickwork disappear under cushions, rich carpets, silk hangings, India muslin embroidered with silver and gold, shawls from Kerman and from Cashmere. There are lamps, lustres of coloured crystal, mirrors, Bohemian and Venetian glass, porcelain 15 vases of all degrees of magnitude from China and from Europe, paintings and engravings, displayed in profusion everywhere. The taste may not always be soberly correct, but the whole spectacle has just the effect of prodigality, colour, and sumptuousness which we are accustomed to associate with the splendours 20 of the Arabian Nights.

In marked contrast with this display is the poverty of scenic contrivance and stage illusion. The subject is far too interesting and too solemn to need them. The actors are visible on all sides, and the exits, entrances, and stage-play of our theatres are impos- 25 sible; the imagination of the spectator fills up all gaps and meets all requirements. On the Ammergau arrangements one feels that the archaeologists and artists of Munich have laid their correct finger; at Teheran there has been no schooling of this sort. A copper basin of water represents the Euphrates; a heap of 30 chopped straw in a corner is the sand of the desert of Kerbela, and the actor goes and takes up a handful of it, when his part requires him to throw, in Oriental fashion, dust upon his head. There is no attempt at proper costume; all that is sought is to do honour to the personages of chief interest by dresses and jewels 35 which would pass for rich and handsome things to wear in modern Persian life. The power of the actors is in their genuine sense of the seriousness of the business they are engaged in. They are, like the public around them, penetrated with this, and so the

actor throws his whole soul into what he is about, the public
meets the actor halfway, and effects of extraordinary impressiveness are the result. "The actor is under a charm," says Count
Gobineau; "he is under it so strongly and completely that almost
always one sees Yezid himself (the usurping caliph), the   5
wretched Ibn-Said (Yezid's general), the infamous Shemer (Ibn-
Said's lieutenant), at the moment they vent the cruellest insults
against the Imams whom they are going to massacre, or against
the women of the Imam's family whom they are ill-using, burst
into tears and repeat their part with sobs. The public is neither   10
surprised nor displeased at this; on the contrary, it beats its breast
at the sight, throws up its arms towards heaven with invocations
of God, and redoubles its groans. So it often happens that the
actor identifies himself with the personage he represents to such
a degree that, when the situation carries him away, he cannot   15
be said to act, he *is* with such truth, such complete enthusiasm,
such utter self-forgetfulness, what he represents, that he reaches
a reality at one time sublime, at another terrible, and produces
impressions on his audience which it would be simply absurd
to look for from our more artificial performances. There is noth- 20
ing stilted, nothing false, nothing conventional; nature, and the
facts represented, themselves speak."

The actors are men and boys, the parts of angels and women
being filled by boys. The children who appear in the piece are
often the children of the principal families of Teheran; their ap- 25
pearance in this religious solemnity (for such it is thought) being
supposed to bring a blessing upon them and their parents. "Nothing is more touching," says Count Gobineau, "than to see these
little things of three or four years old, dressed in black gauze
frocks with large sleeves, and having on their heads small round   30
black caps embroidered with silver and gold, kneeling beside the
body of the actor who represents the martyr of the day, embracing him, and with their little hands covering themselves with
chopped straw for sand in sign of grief. These children evidently," he continues, "do not consider themselves to be acting;   35
they are full of the feeling that what they are about is something of deep seriousness and importance; and though they are
too young to comprehend fully the story, they know, in general,

that it is a matter sad and solemn. They are not distracted by the
audience, and they are not shy, but go through their prescribed
part with the utmost attention and seriousness, always crossing
their arms respectfully to receive the blessing of the Imam Hus-
5   sein; the public beholds them with emotions of the liveliest satisfaction and sympathy."

The dramatic pieces themselves are without any author's
name. They are in popular language, such as the commonest and
most ignorant of the Persian people can understand, free from
10   learned Arabic words,—free, comparatively speaking, from Oriental fantasticality and hyperbole. The Seyids, or popular friars,
already spoken of, have probably had a hand in the composition
of many of them. The Moollahs, or regular ecclesiastical authorities, condemn the whole thing. It is an innovation which they
15   disapprove and think dangerous; it is addressed to the eye, and
their religion forbids to represent religious things to the eye; it
departs from the limits of what is revealed and appointed to be
taught as the truth, and brings in novelties and heresies;—for
these dramas keep growing under the pressure of the actor's
20   imagination and emotion, and of the imagination and emotion
of the public, and receive new developments every day. The
learned, again, say that these pieces are a heap of lies, the production of ignorant people, and have no words strong enough to
express their contempt for them. Still, so irresistible is the vogue
25   of these sacred dramas that, from the king on the throne to the
beggar in the street, every one, except perhaps the Moollahs,
attends them, and is carried away by them. The Imams and their
families speak always in a kind of lyrical chant, said to have
rhythmical effects, often, of great pathos and beauty; their per-
30   secutors, the villains of the piece, speak always in prose.

The stage is under the direction of a choragus, called *oostad*,
or "master," who is a sacred personage by reason of the functions
which he performs. Sometimes he addresses to the audience a
commentary on what is passing before them, and asks their com-
35   passion and tears for the martyrs; sometimes, in default of a Seyid,
he prays and preaches. He is always listened to with veneration,
for it is he who arranges the whole sacred spectacle which so
deeply moves everybody. With no attempt at concealment, with

the book of the piece in his hand, he remains constantly on the stage, gives the actors their cue, puts the children and any inexperienced actor in their right places, dresses the martyr in his winding-sheet when he is going to his death, holds the stirrup for him to mount his horse, and inserts a supply of chopped straw 5 into the hands of those who are about to want it. Let us now see him at work.

The theatre is filled, and the heat is great; young men of rank, the king's pages, officers of the army, smart functionaries of State, move through the crowd with water-skins slung on their 10 backs, dealing out water all round, in memory of the thirst which on these solemn days the Imams suffered in the sands of Kerbela. Wild chants and litanies, such as we have already described, are from time to time set up by a dervish, a soldier, a workman in the crowd. These chants are taken up, more or less, 15 by the audience; sometimes they flag and die away for want of support, sometimes they are continued till they reach a paroxysm, and then abruptly stop. Presently a strange, insignificant figure in a green cotton garment, looking like a petty tradesman of one of the Teheran bazaars, mounts upon the *sakou*. He beck- 20 ons with his hand to the audience, who are silent directly, and addresses them in a tone of lecture and expostulation, thus:—

"Well, you seem happy enough, Mussulmans, sitting there at your ease under the awning; and you imagine Paradise already wide open to you. Do you know what Paradise is? It is a garden, 25 doubtless, but such a garden as you have no idea of. You will say to me: 'Friend, tell us what it is like.' I have never been there, certainly; but plenty of prophets have described it, and angels have brought news of it. However, all I will tell you is, that there is room for all good people there, for it is 330,000 cubits long. If 30 you do not believe, inquire. As for getting to be one of the good people, let me tell you it is not enough to read the Koran of the Prophet (the salvation and blessing of God be upon him!); it is not enough to do everything which this divine book enjoins; it is not enough to come and weep at the *tazyas*, as you do every day, 35 you sons of dogs you, who know nothing which is of any use; it behoves, besides, that your good works (if you ever do any, which I greatly doubt) should be done in the name and for the love of Hussein. It is Hussein, Mussulmans, who is the door to Paradise; it is Hussein, Mussulmans, who upholds the world; it is Hussein, Mussulmans, by whom comes salvation! Cry, Hassan, Hussein!"

5 And all the multitude cry: "O Hassan! O Hussein!"

"That is well; and now cry again." And again all cry: "O Hassan! O Hussein!" "And now," the strange speaker goes on, "pray to God to keep you continually in the love of Hussein. Come, make your cry to God." Then the multitude, as one man, throw 10 up their arms into the air, and with a deep and long-drawn cry exclaim: "*Ya Allah!* O God!"

Fifes, drums, and trumpets break out; the *kernas*, great copper trumpets five or six feet long, give notice that the actors are ready and that the *tazya* is to commence. The preacher descends 15 from the *sakou*, and the actors occupy it.

To give a clear notion of the cycle which these dramas fill, we should begin, as on the first day of the Moharrem the actors begin, with some piece relating to the childhood of the Imams, such as, for instance, the piece called *The Children Digging*. Ali 20 and Fatima are living at Medina with their little sons Hassan and Hussein. The simple home and occupations of the pious family are exhibited; it is morning, Fatima is seated with the little Hussein on her lap, dressing him. She combs his hair, talking caressingly to him all the while. A hair comes out with the comb; the 25 child starts. Fatima is in distress at having given the child even this momentary uneasiness, and stops to gaze upon him tenderly. She falls into an anxious reverie, thinking of her fondness for the child, and of the unknown future in store for him. While she muses, the angel Gabriel stands before her. He reproves her 30 weakness: "A hair falls from the child's head," he says, "and you weep; what would you do if you knew the destiny that awaits him, the countless wounds with which that body shall one day be pierced, the agony that shall rend your own soul!" Fatima, in despair, is comforted by her husband Ali, and they go together 35 into the town to hear Mahomet preach. The boys and some of their little friends begin to play; every one makes a great deal of Hussein; he is at once the most spirited and the most amiable child of them all. The party amuse themselves with digging, with mak-

ing holes in the ground and building mounds. Ali returns from
the sermon and asks what they are about; and Hussein is made
to reply in ambiguous and prophetic answers, which convey that
by these holes and mounds in the earth are prefigured interments
and tombs. Ali departs again; there rush in a number of big and   5
fierce boys, and begin to pelt the little Imams with stones. A
companion shields Hussein with his own body, but he is struck
down with a stone, and with another stone Hussein, too, is
stretched on the ground senseless. Who are those boy-tyrants
and persecutors? They are Ibn-Said, and Shemer, and others, the   10
future murderers at Kerbela. The audience perceive it with a
shudder; the hateful assailants go off in triumph; Ali re-enters,
picks up the stunned and wounded children, brings them round,
and takes Hussein back to his mother Fatima.

But let us now come at once to the days of martyrdom and to   15
Kerbela. One of the most famous pieces of the cycle is a piece
called the *Marriage of Kassem*, which brings us into the very
middle of these crowning days. Count Gobineau has given a
translation of it, and from this translation we will take a few extracts. Kassem is the son of Hussein's elder brother, the Imam   20
Hassan, who had been poisoned by Yezid's instigation at Medina.
Kassem and his mother are with the Imam Hussein at Kerbela;
there, too, are the women and children of the holy family, Omm-
Leyla, Hussein's wife, the Persian princess, the last child of Yezdejerd the last of the Sassanides; Zeyneb, Hussein's sister, the off-   25
spring, like himself, of Ali and Fatima, and the grand-daughter
of Mahomet; his nephew Abdallah, still a little child; finally, his
beautiful daughter Zobeyda. When the piece begins, the Imam's
camp in the desert has already been cut off from the Euphrates
and besieged several days by the Syrian troops under Ibn-Said   30
and Shemer, and by the treacherous men of Kufa. The Family of
the Tent were suffering torments of thirst. One of the children
had brought an empty water-bottle, and thrown it, a silent token
of distress, before the feet of Abbas, the uncle of Hussein; Abbas
had sallied out to cut his way to the river, and had been slain.   35
Afterwards Ali-Akber, Hussein's eldest son, had made the same
attempt and met with the same fate. Two younger brothers of
Ali-Akber followed his example, and were likewise slain. The

Imam Hussein had rushed amidst the enemy, beaten them from
the body of Ali-Akber, and brought the body back to his tent;
but the river was still inaccessible. At this point the action of the
Marriage of Kassem begins. Kassem, a youth of sixteen, is burning to go out and avenge his cousin. At one end of the *sakou* is
the Imam Hussein seated on his throne; in the middle are grouped
all the members of his family; at the other end lies the body of
Ali-Akber, with his mother Omm-Leyla, clothed and veiled in
black, bending over it. The *kernas* sound, and Kassem, after a
solemn appeal from Hussein and his sister Zeyneb to God and to
the founders of their house to look upon their great distress, rises
and speaks to himself:

Kassem.—"Separate thyself from the women of the harem,
Kassem. Consider within thyself for a little; here thou sittest, and
presently thou wilt see the body of Hussein, that body like a
flower, torn by arrows and lances like thorns, Kassem.

"Thou sawest Ali-Akber's head severed from his body on
the field of battle, and yet thou livedst!

"Arise, obey that which is written of thee by thy father; to be
slain, that is thy lot, Kassem!

"Go, get leave from the son of Fatima, most honourable among
women, and submit thyself to thy fate, Kassem."

Hussein sees him approach. "Alas," he says, "it is the orphan
nightingale of the garden of Hassan, my brother!" Then Kassem
speaks:

Kassem.—"O God, what shall I do beneath this load of affliction? My eyes are wet with tears, my lips are dried up with
thirst. To live is worse than to die. What shall I do, seeing what
hath befallen Ali-Akber? If Hussein suffereth me not to go forth,
oh misery! For then what shall I do, O God, in the day of the
resurrection, when I see my father Hassan? When I see my
mother in the day of the resurrection, what shall I do, O God, in
my sorrow and shame before her? All my kinsmen are gone to
appear before the Prophet: shall not I also one day stand before
the Prophet; and what shall I do, O God, in that day?"

Then he addresses the Imam:—

"Hail, threshold of the honour and majesty on high, threshold
of heaven, threshold of God! In the roll of martyrs thou art the

chief; in the book of creation thy story will live for ever. An orphan, a fatherless child, downcast and weeping, comes to prefer a request to thee."

Hussein bids him tell it, and he answers:—

"O light of the eyes of Mahomet the mighty, O lieutenant of Ali the lion! Abbas has perished, Ali-Akber has suffered martyrdom. O my uncle, thou hast no warriors left, and no standard-bearer! The roses are gone, and gone are their buds; the jessamine is gone, the poppies are gone. I alone, I am still left in the garden of the Faith, a thorn, and miserable. If thou hast any kindness for the orphan, suffer me to go forth and fight."

Hussein refuses. "My child," he says, "thou wast the light of the eyes of the Imam Hassan, thou art my beloved remembrance of him; ask me not this; urge me not, entreat me not; to have lost Ali-Akber is enough."

Kassem answers:—"That Kassem should live and Ali-Akber be martyred—sooner let the earth cover me! O king, be generous to the beggar at thy gate. See how my eyes run over with tears and my lips are dried up with thirst. Cast thine eyes toward the waters of the heavenly Euphrates! I die of thirst; grant me, O thou marked of God, a full pitcher of the water of life! it flows in the Paradise which awaits me."

Hussein still refuses; Kassem breaks forth in complaints and lamentations, his mother comes to him and learns the reason. She then says:—

"Complain not against the Imam, light of my eyes; only by his order can the commission of martyrdom be given. In that commission are sealed two-and-seventy witnesses, all righteous, and among the two-and-seventy is thy name. Know that thy destiny of death is commanded in the writing which thou wearest on thine arm."

This writing is the testament of his father Hassan. He bears it in triumph to the Imam Hussein, who finds written there that he should, on the death-plain of Kerbela, suffer Kassem to have his will, but that he should marry him first to his daughter Zobeyda. Kassem consents, though in astonishment. "Consider," he says, "there lies Ali-Akber, mangled by the enemies' hands! Under this sky of ebon blackness, how can joy show her face? Nevertheless if thou commandest it, what have I to do but obey? Thy commandment is that of the Prophet, and his voice is that of God." But Hussein has also to overcome the reluctance of the intended bride and of all the women of his family.

5   "Heir of the vicar of God," says Kassem's mother to the Imam, "bid me die, but speak not to me of a bridal. If Zobeyda is to be a bride and Kassem a bridegroom, where is the henna to tinge their hands, where is the bridal chamber?" "Mother of Kassem," answers the Imam solemnly, "yet a few moments, and in

10   this field of anguish the tomb shall be for marriage-bed, and the winding-sheet for bridal garment!" All give way to the will of their sacred Head. The women and children surround Kassem, sprinkle him with rose-water, hang bracelets and necklaces on him, and scatter bon-bons around; and then the marriage proces-

15   sion is formed. Suddenly drums and trumpets are heard, and the Syrian troops appear. Ibn-Said and Shemer are at their head. "The Prince of the Faith celebrates a marriage in the desert," they exclaim tauntingly; "we will soon change his festivity into mourning." They pass by, and Kassem takes leave of his bride.

20   "God keep thee, my bride," he says, embracing her, "for I must forsake thee!" "One moment," she says, "remain in thy place one moment! thy countenance is as the lamp which giveth us light; suffer me to turn around thee as the butterfly turneth, gently, gently!" And making a turn around him, she performs the an-

25   cient Eastern rite of respect from a new-married wife to her husband. Troubled, he rises to go: "The reins of my will are slipping away from me!" he murmurs. She lays hold of his robe: "Take off thy hand," he cries, "we belong not to ourselves!"

Then he asks the Imam to array him in his winding-sheet.

30   "O nightingale of the divine orchard of martyrdom," says Hussein, as he complies with his wish, "I clothe thee with thy winding-sheet, I kiss thy face; there is no fear, and no hope, but of God!" Kassem commits his little brother Abdallah to the Imam's care. Omm-Leyla looks up from her son's corpse, and says to

35   Kassem: "When thou enterest the garden of Paradise, kiss for me the head of Ali-Akber!"

The Syrian troops again appear. Kassem rushes upon them and they all go off fighting. The Family of the Tent, at Hussein's command, put the Koran on their heads and pray, covering themselves with sand. Kassem reappears victorious. He has slain Azrek, a chief captain of the Syrians, but his thirst is intolerable. "Uncle," he says to the Imam, who asks him what reward he wishes for his valour, "my tongue cleaves to the roof of my mouth; the reward I wish is *water*." "Thou coverest me with shame, Kassem," his uncle answers; "what can I do? Thou askest water; there is no water!"

Kassem.—"If I might but wet my mouth, I could presently make an end of the men of Kufa."

Hussein.—"As I live, I have not one drop of water!"

Kassem.—"Were it but lawful, I would wet my mouth with my own blood."

Hussein.—"Beloved child, what the Prophet forbids, that cannot I make lawful."

Kassem.—"I beseech thee, let my lips be but once moistened, and I will vanquish thine enemies!"

Hussein presses his own lips to those of Kassem, who, refreshed, again rushes forth, and returns bleeding and stuck with darts, to die at the Imam's feet in the tent. So ends the marriage of Kassem.

But the great day is the tenth day of the Moharrem, when comes the death of the Imam himself. The narrative of Gibbon well sums up the events of this great tenth day. "The battle at length expired by the death of the last of the companions of Hussein. Alone, weary, and wounded, he seated himself at the door of his tent. He was pierced in the mouth with a dart. He lifted his hands to heaven—they were full of blood—and he uttered a funeral prayer for the living and the dead. In a transport of despair, his sister issued from the tent, and adjured the general of the Kufians that he would not suffer Hussein to be murdered before his eyes. A tear trickled down the soldier's venerable beard; and the boldest of his men fell back on every side as the dying Imam threw himself among them. The remorseless Shemer —a name detested by the faithful—reproached their cowardice; and the grandson of Mahomet was slain with three and thirty strokes of lances and swords. After they had trampled on his body, they carried his head to the castle of Kufa, and the inhuman Obeidallah (the governor) struck him on the mouth with a cane. 'Alas!' exclaimed an aged Mussulman, 'on those lips have I seen the lips of the Apostle of God!' "

For this catastrophe no one *tazya* suffices; all the companies of actors unite in a vast open space; booths and tents are pitched round the outside circle for the spectators; in the centre is the Imam's camp, and the day ends with its conflagration.

Nor are there wanting pieces which carry on the story beyond the death of Hussein. One which produces an extraordinary effect is *The Christian Damsel*. The carnage is over, the enemy are gone. To the awe-struck beholders, the scene shows the silent plain of Kerbela and the tombs of the martyrs. Their bodies, full of wounds, and with weapons sticking in them still, are exposed to view; but around them all are crowns of burning candles, circles of light, to show that they have entered into glory. At one end of the *sakou* is a high tomb by itself; it is the tomb of the Imam Hussein, and his pierced body is seen stretched out upon it. A brilliant caravan enters, with camels, soldiers, servants, and a young lady on horseback, in European costume, or what passes in Persia for European costume. She halts near the tombs and proposes to encamp. Her servants try to pitch a tent; but wherever they drive a pole into the ground, blood springs up, and a groan of horror bursts from the audience. Then the fair traveller, instead of encamping, mounts into the *tâgnumâ*, lies down to rest there, and falls asleep. Jesus Christ appears to her, and makes known that this is Kerbela, and what has happened here. Meanwhile, an Arab of the desert, a Bedouin who had formerly received Hussein's bounty, comes stealthily, intent on plunder, upon the *sakou*. He finds nothing, and in a paroxysm of brutal fury he begins to ill-treat the corpses. Blood flows. The feeling of Asiatics about their dead is well known, and the horror of the audience rises to its height. Presently the ruffian assails and wounds the corpse of the Imam himself, over whom white doves are hovering; the voice of Hussein, deep and mournful, calls from his tomb: *"There is no God but God!"* The robber flies in terror; the angels, the prophets, Mahomet, Jesus Christ, Moses, the Imams, the holy women, all come upon the *sakou*, press round Hussein, load him with honours. The Christian damsel wakes, and embraces Islam, the Islam of the sect of the Shiahs.

Another piece closes the whole story, by bringing the captive women and children of the Imam's family to Damascus, to the presence of the Caliph Yezid. It is in this piece that there comes the magnificent tableau, already mentioned, of the court of the caliph. The crown jewels are lent for it, and the dresses of the ladies of Yezid's court, represented by boys chosen for their good looks, are said to be worth thousands and thousands of pounds; but the audience see them without favour, for this brilliant court of Yezid is cruel to the captives of Kerbela. The captives are thrust into a wretched dungeon under the palace walls; but the Caliph's wife had formerly been a slave of Mahomet's daughter Fatima, the mother of Hussein and Zeyneb. She goes to see Zeyneb in prison, her heart is touched, she passes into an agony of repentance, returns to her husband, upbraids him with his crimes, and intercedes for the women of the holy family, and for the children, who keep calling for the Imam Hussein. Yezid orders his wife to be put to death, and sends the head of Hussein to the children. Sekyna, the Imam's youngest daughter, a child of four years old, takes the beloved head in her arms, kisses it, and lies down beside it. Then Hussein appears to her as in life: "Oh! my father," she cries, "where wast thou? I was hungry, I was cold, I was beaten—where wast thou?" But now she sees him again, and is happy. In the vision of her happiness she passes away out of this troublesome life, she enters into rest, and the piece ends with her mother and her aunts burying her.

These are the martyrs of Kerbela; and these are the sufferings which awaken in an Asiatic audience sympathy so deep and serious, transports so genuine of pity, love, and gratitude, that to match them at all one must take the feelings raised at Ammergau. And now, where are we to look, in the subject-matter of the Persian passion-play, for the source of all this emotion?

Count Gobineau suggests that it is to be found in the feeling of patriotism; and that our Indo-European kinsmen, the Persians, conquered by the Semitic Arabians, find in the sufferings of Hussein a portrait of their own martyrdom. "Hussein," says Count Gobineau, "is not only the son of Ali, he is the husband of a princess of the blood of the Persian kings; he, his father Ali, the whole body of Imams taken together, represent the nation, represent Persia, invaded, ill-treated, despoiled, stripped of its inhabitants, by the Arabians. The right which is insulted and violated in Hussein, is identified with the right of Persia. The Arabians, the Turks, the Afghans,—Persia's implacable and hereditary enemies,—recognise Yezid as legitimate caliph; Persia finds therein an excuse for hating them the more, and identifies herself the more with the usurper's victims. It is *patriotism* therefore, which has taken the form, here, of the drama to express itself." No doubt there is much truth in what Count Gobineau thus says; and it is certain that the division of Shiahs and Sunis has its true cause in a division of races, rather than in a difference of religious belief.

But I confess that if the interest of the Persian passion-plays had seemed to me to lie solely in the curious evidence they afford of the workings of patriotic feeling in a conquered people, I should hardly have occupied myself with them at all this length. I believe that they point to something much more interesting. What this is, I cannot do more than simply indicate; but indicate it I will, in conclusion, and then leave the student of human nature to follow it out for himself.

When Mahomet's cousin Jaffer, and others of his first converts, persecuted by the idolaters of Mecca, fled in the year of our era 615, seven years before the Hegira, into Abyssinia, and took refuge with the King of that country, the people of Mecca sent after the fugitives to demand that they should be given up to them. Abyssinia was then already Christian. The king asked Jaffer and his companions what was this new religion for which they had left their country. Jaffer answered: "We were plunged in the darkness of ignorance, we were worshippers of idols. Given over to all our passions, we knew no law but that of the strongest, when God raised up among us a man of our own race, of noble descent, and long held in esteem by us for his virtues. This apostle called us to believe in one God, to worship God only, to reject the superstitions of our fathers, to despise divinities of wood and stone. He commanded us to eschew wickedness, to be truthful in speech, faithful to our engagements, kind and helpful to our relations and neighbours. He bade us respect the

chastity of women, and not to rob the orphan. He exhorted us
to prayer, alms-giving, and fasting. We believed in his mission,
and we accepted the doctrines and the rule of life which he
brought to us from God. For this our countrymen have persecuted us; and now they want to make us return to their idolatry."   5
The king of Abyssinia refused to surrender the fugitives, and
then, turning again to Jaffer, after a few more explanations, he
picked up a straw from the ground, and said to him: "Between
your religion and ours there is not the thickness of this straw
difference."   10

   That is not quite so; yet thus much we may affirm, that Jaffer's
account of the religion of Mahomet is a great deal truer than the
accounts of it which are commonly current amongst us. Indeed,
for the credit of humanity, as more than a hundred millions of
men are said to profess the Mahometan religion, one is glad to   15
think so. To popular opinion everywhere, religion is proved by
miracles. All religions but a man's own are utterly false and vain;
the authors of them are mere impostors; and the miracles which
are said to attest them, fictitious. We forget that this is a game
which two can play at; although the believer of each religion   20
always imagines the prodigies which attest his own religion to
be fenced by a guard granted to them alone. Yet how much
more safe is it, as well as more fruitful, to look for the main confirmation of a religion in its intrinsic correspondence with urgent
wants of human nature, in its profound necessity! Differing reli-   25
gions will then be found to have much in common, but this will
be an additional proof of the value of that religion which does
most for that which is thus commonly recognised as salutary
and necessary. In Christendom one need not go about to establish
that the religion of the Hebrews is a better religion than the reli-   30
gion of the Arabs, or that the Bible is a greater book than the
Koran. The Bible *grew*, the Koran *was made;* there lies the immense difference in depth and truth between them! This very inferiority may make the Koran, for certain purposes and for people at a low stage of mental growth, a more powerful instrument   35
than the Bible. From the circumstances of its origin, the Koran
has the intensely dogmatic character, it has the perpetual insistence on the motive of future rewards and punishments, the pal-

pable exhibition of paradise and hell, which the Bible has not. Among the little known and little advanced races of the great African continent, the Mahometan missionaries, by reason of the sort of power which this character of the Koran gives, are said to be more successful than ours. Nevertheless even in Africa it will assuredly one day be manifest, that whereas the Bible-people trace themselves to Abraham through Isaac, and the Koran-people trace themselves to Abraham through Ishmael, the difference between the religion of the Bible and the religion of the Koran is almost as the difference between Isaac and Ishmael. I mean that the seriousness about righteousness, which is what the hatred of idolatry really means, and the profound and inexhaustible doctrines that the righteous Eternal loveth righteousness, that there is no peace for the wicked, that the righteous is an everlasting foundation, are exhibited and inculcated in the Old Testament with an authority, majesty, and truth which leave the Koran immeasurably behind, and which, the more mankind grows and gains light, the more will be felt to have no fellows. Mahomet was no doubt acquainted with the Jews and their documents, and gained something from this source for his religion. But his religion is not a mere plagiarism from Judea, any more than it is a mere mass of falsehood. No; in the seriousness, elevation, and moral energy of himself and of that Semitic race from which he sprang and to which he spoke, Mahomet mainly found that scorn and hatred of idolatry, that sense of the worth and truth of righteousness, judgment, and justice, which make the real greatness of him and his Koran, and which are thus rather an independent testimony to the essential doctrines of the Old Testament, than a plagiarism from them. The world needs righteousness, and the Bible is the grand teacher of it, but for certain times and certain men Mahomet too, in his way, was a teacher of righteousness.

But we know how the Old Testament conception of righteousness ceased with time to have the freshness and force of an intuition, became something petrified, narrow, and formal, needed renewing. We know how Christianity renewed it, carrying into these hard waters of Judaism a sort of warm gulf-stream of tender emotion, due chiefly to qualities which may be

summed up as those of inwardness, mildness, and self-renouncement. Mahometanism had no such renewing. It began with a
conception of righteousness, lofty indeed, but narrow, and which
we may call old Jewish; and there it remained. It is not a *feeling*
religion. No one would say that the virtues of gentleness, mild-   5
ness, and self-sacrifice were its virtues; and the more it went on,
the more the faults of its original narrow basis became visible,
more and more it became fierce and militant, less and less was it
amiable. Now, what are Ali, and Hassan, and Hussein and the
Imams, but an insurrection of noble and pious natures against   10
this hardness and aridity of the religion round them? an insurrection making its authors seem weak, helpless, and unsuccessful
to the world and amidst the struggles of the world, but enabling
them to know the joy and peace for which the world thirsts in
vain, and inspiring in the heart of mankind an irresistible sym-   15
pathy. "The twelve Imams," says Gibbon, "Ali, Hassan, Hussein,
and the lineal descendants of Hussein, to the ninth generation,
without arms, or treasures, or subjects, successively enjoyed the
veneration of the people. Their names were often the pretence of
sedition and civil war; but these royal saints despised the pomp   20
of the world, submitted to the will of God and the injustice of
man, and devoted their innocent lives to the study and practice
of religion."

Abnegation and mildness, based on the depth of the inner life,
and visited by unmerited misfortune, made the power of the first   25
and famous Imams, Ali, Hassan, and Hussein, over the popular
imagination. "O brother," said Hassan, as he was dying of poison,
to Hussein, who sought to find out and punish his murderer, "O
brother, let him alone till he and I meet together before God!"
So his father Ali had stood back from his rights instead of snatch- 30
ing at them. So of Hussein himself it was said by his successful
rival, the usurping Caliph Yezid: "God loved Hussein, *but he
would not suffer him to attain to anything.*" They might attain
to nothing, they were too pure, these great ones of the world as
by birth they were; but the people, which itself also can attain   35
to so little, loved them all the better on that account, loved them
for their abnegation and mildness, felt that they were dear to
God, that God loved them, and that they and their lives filled

a void in the severe religion of Mahomet. These saintly self-deniers, these resigned sufferers, who would not strive nor cry, supplied a tender and pathetic side in Islam. The conquered Persians, a more mobile, more impressionable, and gentler race than
5   their concentrated, narrow, and austere Semitic conquerors felt the need of it most, and gave most prominence to the ideals which satisfied the need; but in Arabs and Turks also, and in all the Mahometan world, Ali and his sons excite enthusiasm and affection. Round the central sufferer, Hussein, has come to group
10 itself everything which is most tender and touching. His person brings to the Mussulman's mind the most human side of Mahomet himself, his fondness for children,—for Mahomet had loved to nurse the little Hussein on his knee, and to show him from the pulpit to his people. The Family of the Tent is full of women
15 and children, and their devotion and sufferings,—blameless and saintly women, lovely and innocent children. There, too, are lovers with their story, the beauty and the love of youth; and all follow the attraction of the pure and resigned Imam, all die for him. The tender pathos from all these flows into the pathos
20 from him and enhances it, until finally there arises for the popular imagination an immense ideal of mildness and self-sacrifice, melting and overpowering the soul.

Even for us, to whom almost all the names are strange, whose interest in the places and persons is faint, who have them before
25 us for a moment to-day, to see them again, probably, no more for ever,—even for us, unless I err greatly, the power and pathos of this ideal are recognisable. What must they be for those to whom every name is familiar, and calls up the most solemn and cherished associations; who have had their adoring gaze fixed all
30 their lives upon this exemplar of self-denial and gentleness, and who have no other? If it was superfluous to say to English people that the religion of the Koran has not the value of the religion of the Old Testament, still more is it superfluous to say that the religion of the Imams has not the value of Christianity. The charac-
35 ter and discourse of Jesus Christ possess, I have elsewhere often said, two signal powers: mildness and sweet reasonableness. The latter, the power which so puts before our view duty of every kind as to give it the force of an intuition, as to make it seem,—

to make the total sacrifice of our ordinary self seem,—the most simple, natural, winning, necessary thing in the world, has been hitherto applied with but a very limited range, it is destined to an infinitely wider application, and has a fruitfulness which will yet transform the world. Of this the Imams have nothing, except so far as all mildness and self-sacrifice have in them something of sweet reasonableness and are its indispensable preliminary. This they have, *mildness and self-sacrifice;* and we have seen what an attraction it exercises. Could we ask for a stronger testimony to Christianity? Could we wish for any sign more convincing, that Jesus Christ was indeed, what Christians call him, *the desire of all nations?* So salutary, so necessary is what Christianity contains, that a religion,—a great, powerful, successful religion,—arises without it, and the missing virtue forces its way in! Christianity may say to these Persian Mahometans, with their gaze fondly turned towards the martyred Imams, what in our Bible God says by Isaiah to Cyrus, their great ancestor:—"*I girded thee, though thou hast not known me.*" It is a long way from Kerbela to Calvary; but the sufferers of Kerbela hold aloft to the eyes of millions of our race the lesson so loved by the sufferer of Calvary. For he said: "Learn of me, that I am *mild*, and *lowly of heart;* and ye shall find *rest unto your souls.*"

La Réforme intellectuelle
et morale de la France

Par Ernest Renan.   Paris: 1871

Burke says, speaking of himself:—

"He has never professed himself a friend or an enemy to republics
or to monarchies in the abstract. He thought that the circumstances
and habits of every country, which it is always perilous and produc-
5 tive of the greatest calamities to force, are to decide upon the form
of its government. There is nothing in his nature, his temper, or his
faculties, which should make him an enemy to any republic, modern
or ancient. Far from it. He has studied the form and spirit of republics very early in life; he has studied them with great attention; and
10 with a mind undisturbed by affection or prejudice. But the result in
his mind from that investigation has been and is, that neither England
nor France, without infinite detriment to them, as well in the event as
in the experiment, could be brought into a republican form, but that
everything republican which can be introduced with safety into
either of them must be built upon a monarchy."
15

The name of Burke is not mentioned in M. Renan's book, but
it is difficult to believe that Burke's publications of eighty years
ago on the French Revolution, from which we have quoted the
foregoing passage, were not in M. Renan's hands when he wrote
20 his recent work. If it was so, it detracts nothing from M. Renan's
originality; a man of his powers cannot but be original in the
treatment of his subject, and to have read and agreed with Burke
will not make him less so. But the similarity of the point of view
strikes the reader in almost every page; and certainly it will be no
25 bad effect of M. Renan's book if it sends us back to those masterpieces of thinking and eloquence, the *Reflections on the Revolution in France*, the *Letter to a Member of the National Assembly*, and the *Appeal from the New to the Old Whigs*. They are
far too little read. They need to be received with discrimination

and judgment, and to common liberalism they can never be acceptable; yet so rich is their instructiveness that a serious politician could hardly make a better resolve than to read them through once every year.

"You have industriously destroyed all the opinions and prejudices, and, as far as in you lay, all the instincts which support government." "You might, if you pleased, have profited by our example. You had the elements of a constitution very nearly as good as could be wished. You possessed in some parts the walls, and in all the foundations, of a noble and venerable castle. You might have repaired those walls, you might have built on those old foundations. You had all these advantages in your ancient States; but you chose to act as if you had never been moulded into civil society, and had everything to begin anew." "Rousseau was your canon of holy writ."

These sentences are Burke's, and never surely could he have desired a better testimony to his wisdom than for a man like M. Renan to say eighty years afterwards, with the France of the present moment before his eyes:

"If no more had been done at the Revolution than to call together the States-General, to regularise them, to make them annual, all would have been right. But the false policy of Rousseau won the day. It was resolved to make a constitution *à priori*. People failed to remark that England, the most constitutional of countries, has never had a written constitution, drawn out in black and white." (P. 7.)

That the rights of its history do more for a society than the rights of man, that the mere will of the majority is an insufficient basis for government, that France was made by the Capets, that she ought never to have broken with them entirely, that she would even now do well to restore them, the younger branch of them, if the elder is impracticable, that with the monarchy she ought to form again aristocratic institutions, a second chamber, and, to some extent, a hereditary nobility—this is the main thesis of the new part of M. Renan's volume. If this is not done, France, he thinks, cannot hope to vie with Prussia, which owes its victory to its aristocratic organisation and to the virtues of endurance and discipline which this organisation fosters. France's only hope of revenge must then be in the International. The superficial ja-

cobinism, the vulgar republicanism, the materialism (for by all
these names and more does M. Renan call it), which the French
Revolution introduced, and which has brought France to her
present ruin, has fatal attractions for the crowd everywhere; it
has eaten far into the heart and life of England; it has overrun all
the Continent except Prussia and Russia. Prussia too is very probably doomed to enter into this "way of all flesh," to be forced
into "the whirl of the witches' sabbath of democracy;" and then
Prussia's day, too, is over, and France is revenged. At the same
time M. Renan suggests certain reforms in French education.
These reforms may at any rate, he thinks, go forward, whatever
else the future may have in store for us: whether a Capet at
Rheims or the International at Potsdam.

All this makes the new part of M. Renan's volume. He has reprinted here, besides, his two letters to Dr. Strauss and several
other publications occasioned by the late war; while the volume
ends with an essay on Constitutional Monarchy in France, and
another on the respective share of the family and the State in the
work of education, which appeared before the war began. These
two essays may rank with the best things M. Renan has written,
and to read them again heightens our admiration of them. The
new part of the book abounds with ingenious and striking
thoughts, eloquently expressed; yet this part will not entirely
satisfy the friends of M. Renan, nor does it quite answer, to say
the truth, to the impression left on us by the summary of its contents which we read in the *Times* before the book appeared. It
has not the usual consummate roundness of M. Renan's composition, the appearance of having been long and thoroughly prepared in the mind, and of now coming forth in perfect ripeness;
there are, or we seem to see, marks here and there of haste, excitement, and chagrin. This was perhaps inevitable.

Our business is not with politics, foreign or domestic; yet on
one or two of the political points where M. Renan does not quite
satisfy us, we must touch. We will not ask whether France in
general has not let the idea of dynastic attachment, as M. Renan
calls it, and the remembrance of its historic self before 1789, so
completely die out that it is vain to seek now to restore them, although, when Burke wrote, this might still have been possible.

But we will observe that this restoration has, in any case, an enemy more serious and more respectable than that vulgar jacobinism, with no higher aim than to content the envy and the materialistic cravings of the masses, which M. Renan assails with such scorn; it has against it the republicanism of men, for instance, like M. Quinet. This republicanism is a reasoned and serious faith, and it grows not out of a stupid insensibility to the historic life and institutions of a nation, nor out of a failure to perceive that in the world's progress, as M. Renan eloquently and profoundly urges, all cannot shine, all cannot be prosperous, some sacrificed lives there must be; but it grows out of the conviction that in what we call our civilisation this sacrifice is excessive. Our civilisation in the old and famous countries of Europe has truly been, as M. Renan says, in its origin an aristocratic work, the work of a few: its maintenance is the work of a few; "country, honour, duty, are things created and upheld by a small number of men amidst a multitude which, left to itself, lets them fall." Yes, because this multitude are in vice and misery outside them; and surely that they are so is in itself some condemnation of the "aristocratic work." We do not say that the historic life and continuity of a nation are therefore to be violently broken, or its traditional institutions abandoned; but we say that a case has been made out against our mere actual civilisation, and a new work given it to do, which were not so visible when Burke wrote, which would certainly have fixed the regards of Burke now, and which M. Renan too much leaves out of sight.

A mere looker-on may smile to read at p. 153, written before Alsace and Lorraine were ceded and when there was still hope of saving them, that France could not survive their loss, that she is like a building so compact that to pull out one or two large stones makes it tumble down, or like a living being with an organisation so highly centralised that to have an important limb cut off is death; and then to read at p. 58 and other passages, written since peace was made, that the immense resources of France are hardly at all altered or impaired, that she is *à peine entamée*. But of this kind of inconsistency a man of heart and imagination may well be guilty when his country is in question; Burke, assuredly, might have been guilty of it.

Our one serious point of difference with M. Renan, and where
we confess he somewhat disappoints us, is in his discussion of the
faults of France. The capital fault, the cherished defect of
France, is—what does the reader think?—want of faith in sci-
5 ence, *le manque de foi à la science.* In the same strain speaks
Mdme. Sand in the charming *Letters* she has lately published:
Nous voulons penser et agir à la fois, she says; and therefore we
are beaten. Nay our amiability itself puts us at a disadvantage, she
adds, in this bad actual world: *Nous ne sommes pas capables de*
10 *nous préparer à la guerre pendant vingt ans; nous sommes si in-*
capables de haïr! It is the head, *la tête,* which is so greatly in
fault; the heart, the sentiments are right; *le Français,* says M.
Renan, *est bon, étourdi;* yes, *étourdi* he may be, harum-scarum;
but he is *bon.* Burke, whom we have so much quoted, says of
15 Charles II.:

"The person given to us by Monk was a man without any sense of
his duty as a prince, without any regard to the dignity of his crown,
without any love to his people; dissolute, false, venal, and destitute of
any positive good quality whatsoever, except a pleasant temper and
20 the manners of a gentleman."

So far he, too, was *bon:* but his goodness had gaps which, though
certainly he was also without the scientific temper, would make
us hesitate to say that his chief fault was want of faith in science.
Of France we may say the same. It seems to us much more true
25 of England than of France that the national defect is want of
faith in science. In France the great defect lies, surely, in a much
simpler thing—want of faith in *conduct.* M. Renan's chief concern at the failure of the Reformation in France is for what *the*
head lost; for the better schools, the reading, the instruction,
30 which the Reformation would have brought with it. But M.
Michelet put his finger on the real cause for concern, when he
said that the Reformation failed in France because a *moral*
reformation France would not have. That sense of personal responsibility which is the foundation of all true religion, which
35 possessed Luther, which possessed also the great saints of Catholicism, but which Luther alone managed to convey to the popular
mind, earning thereby—little as we owe him for the theological
doctrines he imagined to be his great boon to us—a most true

title to our regard; *that* was what the Huguenots had, what the mass of the French nation had not and did not care to have, and what they suffer to this day for not having. One of the gifts and graces which M. Renan finds in France is her enmity to pedantry and over-strictness in these matters: and in his letter to Dr. Strauss he says that, although he himself has been sufficiently near holy orders to think himself bound to a regular life, he should be sorry not to see around him a brilliant and dissipated society. No one feels more than we do the harm which the exaggeration of Hebraism has done in England; but this is Hellenism with a vengeance! Considering what the natural propensions of men are, such language appears to us out of place anywhere, and in France simply fatal. Moral conscience, self-control, seriousness, steadfastness, are not the whole of human life certainly, but they are by far the greatest part of it; without them—and this is the very burden of the Hebrew prophets and a fact of experience as old as the world—nations cannot stand. France does not enough see their importance; and the worst of it is that no man can make another see their importance unless he sees it naturally. For these things, just as for the more brilliant things of art and science, there is a bent, a turn. "He showed his ways unto Moses, his works unto the children of Israel,"—to them, and to the heavy Germanic nations whom they have moulded; not, apparently, to the children of Gomer and to Vercingetorix. But this opens a troubled prospect for the children of Gomer.

But perhaps we English, too, shall be as the children of Gomer; for M. Renan has a theory that according to "that great law by which the primitive race of an invaded country always ends by getting the upper hand, England is becoming every day more Celtic and less Germanic;" in the public opinion and policy of England for the last thirty years he sees the *esprit celtique, plus doux, plus sympathique, plus humain.* We imagine our Irish neighbours by no means share his opinion. A more truly Germanic, or, at least, Anglo-Saxon, performance than the abolition of the Irish Church through the power of the Dissenters' antipathy to church-establishments, then telling ourselves in our newspapers we had done it out of a pure love of reason and justice, and then calling solemnly upon the quick-witted Irish, who

knew that the Dissenters would have let the Irish Church stand
for ever sooner than give a shilling of its funds to the Catholics
entitled to them, to believe our claptrap and be properly grateful to us at last, was never witnessed. What we call our Philistin-
5 ism, to which M. Renan might perhaps apply his favourite epithets of *dur et rogue*, may well bring us into trouble; but hardly,
we think, our *doux esprit celtique*.

It seems, indeed, as if, in all that relates to character and conduct strictly so called, M. Renan, whom at other times we fol-
10 low with so much sympathy, saw things with other eyes than
ours. In a parallel between the English Revolution of 1688 and
the French Revolution of 1830, he asks himself why the first succeeded and the second failed; and he answers that it cannot have
been owing to the difference between William of Orange and
15 Louis-Philippe, because the second had no faults as a ruler which
the first did not show in fully as great a degree. When we read
this, we are fairly lost in amazement. Surely the most important
point in a ruler is *character;* and William III., whatever were his
faults, had a character great and commanding; while Louis-
20 Philippe had, or gave the world the impression of having, a character somewhat (to speak quite frankly) ignoble.

We would fain stop here in our enumeration of matters of
difference; for to differ with M. Renan is far less natural to us
than to agree with him. But it is impossible not to notice one or
25 two assumptions respecting the French Revolution and the intellectual value of France to the world, because to these assumptions M. Renan, like almost all Frenchmen, seems to challenge
the assent of mankind, at least of all mankind except France's
rogue et jaloux enemy, Prussia. Greece and Judea, he says, have
30 had to pay with the loss of their national existence the honour
of having given lessons to all mankind; in like manner—

"France at this moment expiates her Revolution; she will perhaps one
day reap its fruits in the grateful ·memory of emancipated nations."

Just in the same strain writes Mdme. Sand, in the *Letters* we have
35 already quoted:

"Even though Germany should appear to conquer us, we shall remain the *peuple initiateur*, which receives a lesson and does not take
one."

In prosperity the French are incorrigible, so that a time like the present offers the only opportunity for disabusing them of notions of this kind, so obstructive to improvement; and M. Renan, one would have hoped, was the very man to do it. Greece has given us art and science, Judea has given us the Bible; these are   5
positive achievements. Whoever gives us a just and rational constitution of human society will also confer a great boon on us and effect a great work; but what has the French Revolution accomplished towards this? Nothing. It was an insurrection against the old routine, it furiously destroyed the medieval form of society;   10
this it did, and this was well if anything had come of it; but into what that is new and fruitful has France proceeded to initiate us? A colourless, humdrum, and ill-poised life is a baneful thing, and men would fain change it; but our benefactor and initiator is the poet who brings us a new one, not the drunkard who gets   15
rid of it by breaking the windows and bringing the house about his ears.

There seems to us a like exaggeration in the French estimate of their country's intellectual rank in the world. France is the *plat de sel*, the dish containing the salt without which all the other   20
dishes of the world would be savourless; she is (we will use M. Renan's own words, for a translation might easily do injustice to them)—

"la grande maîtresse de l'investigation savante, l'ingénieuse, vive et prompte initiatrice du monde à toute fine et délicate pensée;"   25

she alone has—

"une société exquise, charmante et sérieuse à la fois, fine, tolérante, aimable, *sachant tout sans avoir rien appris, devinant d'instinct le dernier résultat de toute philosophie*."

We wonder if it ever occurs to these masters *du goût et du tact*   30
that in an Englishman, an Italian, a German, this language provokes a smile. No one feels more than we do, and few Englishmen feel enough, the good of that amiability, even if it does not go very deep, of that sympathetic side in the French nature, which makes German and Protestant Alsace cling to defeated   35
France, while, mainly for the want of it, prosperous England cannot attach Ireland. No one feels more than we do, few En-

glishmen feel enough, the good of that desire for lucidity, ever apparent, in thought and expression, which has made the French language. But, after all, a nation's intellectual place depends upon its having reached the very highest rank in the very highest lines
5   of spiritual endeavour; this is what in the end makes its ideal; this is what fixes its scale of intellectual judgment, and what it counts by in the world. More than twenty years ago we said, lovers of France as we are, and abundant and brilliant as is her work of a lower order than the very highest:

10   "France, famed in all great arts, *in none supreme*"—

and this still seems to us to be the true criticism on her. M. Renan opposes living names, for or against which we will say nothing, to the best living names of Germany; but what is one generation? and what, directly we leave our own generation, are any names
15 but the greatest? And where, throughout all her generations, has France a name like Goethe? where, still more, has she names like Sophocles and Plato, Dante and Raphael, Shakespeare and Newton? That is the real question for her, when she is esteeming herself the salt of the earth. Probably the incapacity for seriousness
20 in the highest sense, for what the Greeks called τὸ σπουδαῖον, and Virgil calls *virtus verusque labor*, is here too what keeps France back from perfection. For the Greeks and Romans, and a truly Latin race like the Italians, have this seriousness intellectually, as the Hebrews and the Germanic races have it morally; and it may
25 be remarked in passing that this distinction makes the conditions of the future for Latin Italy quite different from those for Celtic France. Only seriousness is constructive; Latin Gaul was a Roman construction, old France was, as M. Renan himself says, a Germanic construction; France has been since 1789 getting rid
30 of all the plan, cramps, and stays of her original builders, and their edifice is in ruins; but is the Celt, by himself, constructive enough to rebuild?

We sincerely believe that France would do well, instead of proclaiming herself the salt of the earth, to ponder these things;
35 and sometimes it is hard to refrain from saying so. M. Renan tempted us; yet we see with regret our space nearly gone. Why could we not have kept to our own generation? and then we

might have given ourselves the pleasure of saying how high is M.
Renan's place in it. Certainly, we find something of a bathos in
his challenge to Germany to produce a living poet to surpass M.
Hugo; but in sober seriousness we might challenge Germany, or
any other country, to produce a living critic to surpass M. Renan.
We have just been reading an American essayist, Mr. Higginson,   5
who says that the United States are to evolve a type of literary
talent superior to anything yet seen in the mother country; and
this perhaps, when it is ready, will be something to surprise us.
But taking things as they now are, where shall we find a living
writer who so habitually as M. Renan moves among questions of   10
the deepest interest, presents them so attractively, discusses them
with so much feeling, insight, and felicity? Even as to the all-
importance of *conduct*, which in his irritation against the "chaste
Vandals" who have been overrunning France we have seen him
a little disposed just now to underrate, he is far too wise a man   15
not to be perfectly sound at bottom. *Le monde*, we find him saying in 1869, *ne tient debout que par un peu de vertu*. The faults
and dangers both of vulgar democracy and of vulgar liberalism
there is no one who has seen more clearly or described so well.
The vulgar democrat's "happiness of the greatest number" he   20
analyses into what it practically is—a principle *réduisant tout à
contenter les volontés matérialistes des foules*, of that "popular
mass, growing every day larger, which is destitute of any sort of
religious ideal and can recognise no social principle beyond and
above the desire of satisfying these materialistic cravings." The   25
esprit démocratique of this sort of democracy, *avec sa raideur,
son ton absolu, sa simplicité décevante d'idées, ses soupçons méti-
culeux, son ingratitude*, is admirably touched; but touched not
less admirably is another very different social type, the cherished
ideal of vulgar liberalism, the American type—   30

"*fondé essentiellement sur la liberté et la propriété, sans priviléges de
classes, sans institutions anciennes, sans histoire, sans société aristo-
cratique, sans cour, sans pouvoir brillant, sans universités sérieuses ni
fortes institutions scientifiques. Ces sociétés manquent de distinction,
de noblesse; elles ne font guère d'oeuvres originales en fait d'art et de*   35
science"—

but they can come to be very strong and to produce very good things, and that is enough for our Philistines. What can be better, and in the end more fruitful, than criticism of this force; but what constituency can accept a man guilty of making it? Let M. Renan continue to make it, and let him not fear but that in making it, in bringing thought into the world to oust claptrap, he fulfils a higher duty than by sketching paper constitutions, or by prosecuting electoral campaigns in the Seine-et-Marne. "*The fashion of this world passeth away,*" wrote Goethe from Rome in 1787, "and I would fain occupy myself only with the eternal."

Isaiah XL–LXVI: Introduction

At the very outset, the humbleness of what is professed in the present work cannot be set forth too strongly. With the aim of enabling English people to read as a connected whole the last twenty-seven chapters of Isaiah, without being frequently stopped by passages of which the meaning is almost or quite 5 unintelligible, I have sought to choose, among the better meanings which have been offered for each of these passages, that which seemed the best, and to weave it into the authorised text in such a manner as not to produce any sense of strangeness or interruption. This is all that I have attempted; not to translate or 10 to correct independently, for which my knowledge of Hebrew, —not more than sufficient to enable me in some degree to follow and weigh the reasons offered by others in support of their judgments,—and, indeed, my resources of all kinds, would be totally inadequate; but to use the work of more competent trans- 15 lators and correctors, to use it so as to remove difficulties in our authorised version which admit, many of them, of quite certain correction; and yet to leave the physiognomy and movement of the authorised version quite unchanged. Such a work of emendation may be, I hope, of a useful character, but it is certainly of 20 a humble one; and the reader is especially begged to note that to this, and no more, does the present work aspire.

With like prominency must be set in view its provisional character. It makes no pretensions to be permanent. Persons of weight and of proved qualifications are now engaged in revising 25 the Bible, and their revision must undoubtedly be looked to as that which, it is to be hoped, may obtain general currency. To have one version universally received is of the greatest advantage. And their corrections will, probably, be much more exten-

sive than those attempted here, and will extend far more to small points of detail; thus aiming at absolute correctness, at perfection. A version thus perfectly correct will most justly, if successful in other respects, supersede any private and partial attempts. Such a
5   partial attempt is mine; an attempt, not to present an absolutely correct version of the series of chapters treated, but merely to remove such cause of disturbance as now, in the authorised version, prevents their being read connectedly, with understanding of what they mean, and with the profit and enjoyment that
10 might else be drawn from them.

The present attempt was originally planned for the benefit of school-children. It appears in this larger form, because it has been found useful by many who are not school-children, and who find the small print of a school-book irk-
15 some. But it was intended in the first instance for the young and for the unlearned, and this its original design must not be forgotten.

The Hebrew language and genius, it is admitted by common consent, are seen in the Book of Isaiah at their perfection; this
20 has naturally had its effect on the English translators of the Bible, whose version nowhere perhaps rises to such beauty as in this Book. Whatever may be thought of the authorship of the last twenty-seven chapters, every one will allow that there comes a break between them and what goes immediately before them,
25 and that they form a whole by themselves. And the whole which they form is large enough to exhibit a prolonged development and connexion, and yet is of manageable length, and comes within fixed limits. Add to which, it is a whole of surpassing interest; so that, while Isaiah is styled the greatest of the prophets, the
30 evangelical prophet, and St. Jerome calls him not so much a prophet as an evangelist, and Ambrose told Augustine to read his prophecies the first thing after his conversion, and this prophet is of all Old Testament writers the one far most quoted in the New,—while all this is so, it is, moreover, in the last twenty-
35 seven chapters that the greatest interest is reached; insomuch that out of thirty-four passages from him which Gesenius brings together as quoted in the New Testament, there are twenty-one from these last chapters against only thirteen from the rest of the

Book. Finally, not only have the last twenty-seven chapters this poetical and this religious interest, but they have also an historical interest of the highest order; for they mark the very point where Jewish history, caught in the current of Cyrus's wars and policy, is carried into the great open stream of the world's history, never again to be separated from it. 5

The reader, therefore, may well be glad to have these chapters put by themselves, and made intelligible to him. I have also detached from their received place, and printed as an appendix to the last twenty-seven chapters, certain earlier chapters of the 10 Book of Isaiah:—the 13th with the 14th down to the end of the 23rd verse, the 21st down to the end of the 10th verse, the chapters from the beginning of the 24th to the end of the 27th, and the 34th and 35th chapters. These chapters are undoubtedly connected by their subject with the concluding series, and should be 15 read in connexion with them by every student who wishes to apprehend the concluding series fully. Evidently, as both they and this series now stand in his Bible, they are baffling to him; and this is due partly to their arrangement, partly to obscurities in the translation. To shew how this is so, let us take the 21st 20 chapter of Isaiah down to the end of verse 10. Thus it stands in our Bibles:—

The burden of the desert of the sea. As whirlwinds in the south pass through; *so* it cometh from the desert, from a terrible 25 land.

2. A grievous vision is declared unto me; the treacherous dealer dealeth treacherously, and the spoiler spoileth. Go up, O Elam: besiege, O Media: all the sighing thereof have I made to cease. 30

3. Therefore are my loins filled with pain: pangs have taken hold upon me, as the pangs of a woman that travaileth: I was bowed down at the hearing *of it;* I was dismayed at the seeing *of it.*

4. My heart panted, fearfulness affrighted me: the night of 35 my pleasure hath he turned into fear unto me.

5. Prepare the table, watch in the watch-tower, eat, drink: arise, ye princes, *and* anoint the shield.

6. For thus hath the LORD said unto me, Go set a watchman, let him declare what he seeth.

7. And he saw a chariot with a couple of horsemen, a chariot of asses, and a chariot of camels; and he harkened diligently with much heed:

8. And he cried, A lion: My lord, I stand continually upon the watch-tower in the daytime, and I am set in my ward whole nights:

9. And behold, here cometh a chariot of men, with a couple of horsemen. And he answered and said, Babylon is fallen, is fallen; and all the graven images of her gods he hath broken unto the ground.

10. O my threshing, and the corn of my floor: that which I have heard of the LORD of hosts, the God of Israel, have I declared unto you.

And then the chapter goes on without any interruption, in verses of just the same look, to a wholly different matter.

Now the general reader, who has the bare text of a common Bible and nothing more, may perceive that there is something grand in this passage, but he cannot possibly understand it; and this is due partly to the want of explanations, partly to the arrangement, partly to obscurity in the translation. He requires to be told first, as a reader would be told before reading an ode of Pindar, what it is all about; he requires to have the passage separated for him from that with which it has no connexion; and he requires to have the text made much clearer, both in its words and in its punctuation.

To supply explanations, it may be thought, is a matter which need not embarrass us much; but the same cannot be said of re-arranging and correcting. For it must always be remembered, that, in dealing with the English Bible, we are dealing with a work consecrated in the highest degree by long use and deep veneration.

With respect to the novel way of dividing, arranging, and pre-senting their single Psalms or single Chapters, which recent trans-lators, following Ewald, have adopted: in him and them, and for his and their purpose, we may acquiesce in it; but for an ordinary

reader it changes the face of the Bible too startlingly and entirely. The divisions in our common Bibles, however, do mark
too little the connexion of the sense, do often break it too arbi-
trarily, and of themselves create difficulties for the reader. This
will not be denied; but the question is, how to apply a remedy 5
without innovating overmuch. Now, it so happened that I had
for many years been in the habit of using a Bible[1] where the
numbers of the chapters are marked at the side and do not interpose a break between chapter and chapter; and where the divisions of the verses, being numbered in like manner at the side of 10
the page, not in the body of the verse, and being numbered in
very small type, do not thrust themselves forcibly on the attention. Breaks between the chapters, too, this Bible admits, but only
when the sense seems urgently to call for them; and sometimes,
from the same motive, it even breaks a verse in the middle. It had 15
always struck me how much more connected and comprehensible the sense of the Bible, and particularly of certain parts of
the Bible, such as the Prophetical Books and the Epistles, appeared in this arrangement than in that of our common Bibles;
insomuch that here things would often look comparatively 20
lucid and hanging together, which in our common Bibles looked
fragmentary and obscure. Well, then, it suggested itself to me to
try, for conveying to the general reader our series of chapters,
this mode of arrangement, extending it a little and simplifying it
a little; extending it by using breaks, if this seemed required by 25
the sense, a little more frequently; and simplifying it by getting
rid of italics, signs, references, and all apparatus of this sort,
which readers such as I have in view hardly ever understand,
and are more distracted than helped by. So one might hope to
exhibit this series of chapters in a way to give a clue to their 30
connexion and sense, yet without making them look too odd and
novel.

So far for the arrangement: but even a more important matter
was correction, since an unintelligible passage, baffling the reader
and throwing him out, will often, as I have said, spoil a whole 35

---

[1] Perhaps I may be allowed here to mention, what to me at least will always be very interesting, that this Bible was given to me by the late Mr.
Keble, my godfather.

chapter for him; and there are many such passages in the authorised version. To avoid this check in reading the grand series
of chapters at the end of Isaiah, I had gradually made for my
own use the corrections which seemed indispensable; these cor-
5 rections, after having been carefully revised, are adopted in the
text now offered. And by indispensable corrections I mean this:
corrections which enable us to read the authorised version without being baffled and thrown out. The urgent matter, of course,
is to get rid of the stoppage and embarrassment created by such
10 things as: 'He made his grave with the wicked . . . *because* he had
done no violence;' or as: 'That prepare a table for *that troop*, and
that furnish the drink-offering for *that number*[1].' A clear sense is
the indispensable thing. Even where the authorised version seems
wrong, I have not always, if its words give a clear sense, thought
15 it necessary to change them. When, however, the right correction seems to give a sense, either clearer, or higher in poetic propriety and beauty, than the authorised version, I have corrected.

For example. I think it certain that at verse 15 of the 65th chapter the right rendering is: 'And ye shall leave your name for a
20 curse unto my chosen, *So may the Lord God slay thee!*'—the
words in italics being the words of the curse, as in Jeremiah
xxix: 'Of them (Zedekiah and Ahab) shall be taken up a curse by
all the captivity of Judah which are in Babylon, saying, *The
Lord make thee like Zedekiah and Ahab!*' But the authorised
25 version gives a perfectly clear sense: 'And ye shall leave your
name for a curse unto my chosen; for the LORD God shall slay
thee;'—and I have therefore left this as it stands. Again, at verse
18 of the 66th chapter, I think the right rendering almost certainly is: 'But I —— their works and their thoughts!—it shall
30 come, that I will gather all nations,' &c.; the expression being, as
Ewald explains it, a broken, indignant one, with this sense:—
Utterly to confound and shame the expectations and practices of
the faithless, idol-seeking Jews (who have been the subject of
the preceding verse), idolatrous nations themselves shall come
35 and worship me. But the authorised version: 'For I know their
works and their thoughts' (referring to the idolatrous Jews of

[1] Isaiah liii. 9, and lxv. 11.

the preceding verse);—and then, after a pause, passing to another subjects: 'It shall come, that I will gather all nations,'—
gives, perhaps, a yet clearer sense, though, I am inclined to believe, not the right sense; but the sense given being good and
clear, I think it better to abstain from change. It may seem at   5
variance with this, that, for instance, in the last clause of the
46th chapter: 'I will place salvation in Zion for Israel my glory,'
which is quite clear, I have yet allowed myself to make a change,
and to substitute: 'I will give salvation to Zion; to Israel my
glory.' But this is because, while the change appears, from the   10
law of parallelism in Hebrew poetry, perfectly certain, the observance here of this law gives, at the same time, a decided gain
in poetic propriety and beauty. So, too, in verse 14 of the 43rd
chapter: 'I have sent to Babylon and have brought down all
their nobles, and the Chaldeans, whose cry is in the ships.' This   15
cannot be right, but it gives a sense which may be made out. We
may refer to what Heeren says of the maritime trade of Babylon
in the Persian Gulf, and explain the last clause of the Chaldean
fleets there, and of the joyful hailing and shouting of the sailors.
But we so little associate Babylon with a maritime trade and   20
fleets, that this sense for the passage is a strained and unaccept-
able one. Whereas the more correct rendering, 'I have sent to
Babylon, and do make them all to flee away, and the Chaldeans
upon the ships of their pleasure,' associates Babylon with her
great feature,—the river and the use of the river; and so gives   25
a sense, if not absolutely plainer, yet poetically much more natural and more pleasing. Here therefore is a case where our rules
justify a change.

But when a change, however pleasing and ingenious, depends
on taking license to alter by guess the original text, I have re-   30
garded it as quite forbidden. There is a difficult expression in
verse 17 of the 66th chapter, 'behind one tree in the midst,' where
the word *tree* is supplied by our English translators, and the original has only 'behind one in the midst.' Now, the Hebrew word
for *behind* nearly resembles the Hebrew word for *one*, and   35
Ewald proposes to read, in place of the word for *one*, the word
for *behind* repeated; so that the meaning will be: 'Back, back in
the innermost sanctuary!'—a cry of recoil of the idol-serving and

superstitious renegade Jews at the approach of their uninitiated, and, as they thought, profane countrymen. This suits well with the 'I am holier than thou!' attributed to the same renegades, and as a conjectural emendation it is highly plausible and attractive; still, a conjectural emendation it is, and therefore, as I consider, not permissible for our purpose here. All we may do is to supply a word giving a better sense than the word *tree*, and such a word is *chief*,—the ringleader or chief in the idolatrous processions and ceremonies held in the sacred gardens.

So it will be evident that our range for alteration is limited; indeed, it may almost be said, in general, to be restricted to those cases where in the authorised version there is unintelligibility or ambiguity baffling the reader and throwing him out. A translator whose aim is purely scientific, to render his original with perfect accuracy, will have much more latitude, and no one can blame him for taking it; but then the public he must propose to himself is different. And a body of Bible-revisers, probably, acting by public authority, ought, as I have already said, to take much more latitude, and to correct the old version not only where it is unintelligible, but also wherever they think it in error. But my object is such that to retain as far as possible the old text of the English Bible is very desirable, nay, almost indispensable. I want to enable the reader to apprehend, as a whole, a literary work of the highest order. And the Book of Isaiah, as it stands in our Bibles, is this in a double way. By virtue of the original it is a monument of the Hebrew genius at its best, and by virtue of the translation it is a monument of the English language at its best. Some change must be made for clearness' sake, without which the work cannot be apprehended as a whole; but the power of the English version must not be sacrificed, must, if possible, be preserved intact. And though every corrector says this, and pays his compliment to the English version, yet few proceed to act upon the rule, or seem to know how hard it is to act upon it when we alter at all, and why it is hard. Let us try and make clear to ourselves exactly what the difficulty is.

The English version has created certain sentiments in the reader's mind, and these sentiments must not be disturbed, if the new version is to have the power of the old. Surely this consid-

eration should rule the corrector in determining whether or not
he should put *Jehovah* where the old version puts *Lord*. Mr.
Cheyne, the recent translator of Isaiah,—one of that new band of
Oxford scholars who so well deserve to attract our interest, because they have the idea, which the older Oxford has had so far 5
too little, of separated and systematised studies,—Mr. Cheyne's
object is simply scientific, to render the original with exactness.
But how the Four Friends, who evidently, by their style of comment, mean their very interesting and useful book, *The Psalms
Chronologically Arranged*, for religious use, for habitual readers 10
of the Psalms, and who even take, because of this design, the
Prayer-Book version as their basis,—how they can have permitted themselves to substitute *Jehovah* for *Lord* passes one's
comprehension. Probably because they were following Ewald;
but his object is scientific. To obtain general acceptance by En- 15
glish Christians, who, that considers what the name in question
represents to these, what the Psalms are to them, what a place
the expression *The Lord* fills in the Psalms and in the English
Bible generally, what feelings and memories are entwined with
it, and what the force of sentiment is,—who, that considers all 20
this, would allow himself, in a version of the Psalms meant for
popular use, to abandon the established expression *The Lord* in
order to substitute for it *Jehovah? Jehovah* is in any case a bad
substitute for it, because to the English reader it does not carry
its own meaning with it, and has even, which is fatal, a mytho- 25
logical sound. *The Eternal*, which one of the French versions
uses, is far preferable. *The Eternal* is in itself, no doubt, a better
rendering of Jehovah than *The Lord*. In disquisition and criticism, where it is important to keep as near as we can to the exact
sense of words, *The Eternal* may be introduced with advantage; 30
and whoever has heard Jewish school-children use it, as they do,
in repeating the Commandments in English, cannot but have
been struck and satisfied with the effect of the rendering. In
his own private use of the Bible, any one may, if he will, change
The Lord into *The Eternal*. But at present, for the general reader 35
of the Bible or of extracts from it, *The Lord* is surely an expression consecrated. The meaning which it in itself carries is a meaning not at variance with the original name, even though it may be

possible to render this original name more adequately. But, besides the contents which a term carries in itself, we must consider
the contents with which men, in long and reverential use, have
filled it; and therefore we say that *The Lord* any literary cor-
5 rector of the English Bible does well at present to retain, because
of the sentiments this expression has created in the English reader's mind, and has left firmly fixed there.

It is in deference to these pre-established sentiments in the
reader that we prefer, so long as the sense is well preserved, for
10 any famous passage of our chapters which is cited in the New
Testament, the New Testament rendering, because this rendering will be to the English reader the more familiar, and touches
more chords. For instance, in the 2nd verse of the 42nd chapter,
He shall not cry nor lift up is the Old Testament rendering. *He
15 shall not clamour nor cry* might in itself be better; but *He
shall not strive nor cry* seems best of all, because the New Testament has made it so familiar. For the same reason, the change in
the first clause of the 53rd chapter[1] was originally made with the
utmost reluctance, and it has been now, after re-consideration,
20 abandoned. This is mentioned to shew what deference I really
feel to be due to the pre-established sentiments above spoken of.

But perhaps there would not be much difficulty if we had only
to avoid rash change in these marked cases. There is a far subtler
difficulty to be contended with. The English Bible is a tissue, a
25 fabric woven in a certain style, and a style which is admirable.
When the version was made, this style was *in the air*. Get a body
of learned divines, and set them down to translate, the right
meaning they might often have difficulty with, but the right
style was pretty well sure to come of itself. This style is in the
30 air no longer;—that makes the real difficulty of the learned divines now at work in Westminster. And exactly in what the
style consists, and what will impair it, and what sort of change
can be brought into it, and to what amount, without destroy-
ing it, no learning can tell them; they must trust to a kind of tact.
35 Every one agrees that in correcting the English Bible (we do not

---

[1] In the first editions, 'Who believed *what we heard*' was substituted for
'Who believed *our report*.'

now speak of re-translation in an aim of scientific exactness) you must not change its style. The question is, what kinds of altera- tion *do* change its style? By two kinds of alteration, it may be affirmed, you change its style; you change it if you destroy *the character of the diction*, and you change it if you destroy *the balance of the rhythm*. Either is enough; and one has only to state these two conditions to make it clear how entirely the observance of them must be a matter of tact, and cannot be ensured by any external rules. It is often said that no word ought to be used in correcting the English Bible which is not there already. This is pedantry; no word must be used which does not *suit* the Bible- diction, but plenty of words may suit it which do not happen to be there already. And after all, what have you gained, if you get a word which is ever so much a Bible-word, and put it in so as to spoil the rhythm? The style of the Bible is equally changed, whether it is the character of its diction that you destroy, or the balance of its rhythm.

Thus quite petty changes may have a great and fatal effect; the mass of a passage may be left (and this is what a corrector generally understands by shewing 'affectionate reverence for the Authorised Version'), and yet by altering a word or two the Bible-style may be more changed than if the passage had been half re-written. I name Bishop Lowth with the highest respect. He, Vitringa, and the Jewish commentator Aben-Ezra, are per- haps the three men who, before the labours of the Germans in our own century, did most to help the study of Isaiah. And what Lowth did was due mainly to fine tact and judgment in things of poetry and literature; this enabled him to make his just and fruit- ful remarks on the structure of the composition of the Hebrew prophets, and on the literary character of the whole Hebrew Scriptures. And he could point out, in Sebastian Castellio's Latin version, the fault of 'the loss of Hebrew simplicity, the affectation of Latin elegance,' and observe that 'to this even the barbarism of the Vulgate is preferable.' And he saw the merit, both in dic- tion and in rhythm, of our authorised English version: 'As to the style and language,' he says, 'it admits but of little improvement;' all he proposed to himself was to 'correct and perfect it.' But in good truth *style*, such as the beginning of the 17th century

knew it, was at the end of the 18th century no longer in the air.
Else how could a man of Lowth's sound critical principles and
fine natural tact have thought that he perfected 'Speak ye *com-*
fortably to Jerusalem,' by making it 'Speak ye *animating words*
to Jerusalem;' or '*Taught him knowledge*,' by substituting '*Im-*
part to him science;' or 'Hear now this, *thou that art given to*
pleasures, that dwellest carelessly,' by 'Hear now this, O *thou*
voluptuous, that sittest in security;' or 'Yet did we *esteem him*
stricken,' by 'Yet we *thought him judicially stricken*;' or 'When
thou shalt make his soul *an offering for sin*,' by 'If his soul shall
make *a propitiatory sacrifice*;' or 'My salvation is *near to come*,'
by 'My salvation is *near, just ready to come*?' Surely this is not to
be called perfecting but marring.

    So, too, Mr. Cheyne, who, scientific though his object be,
nevertheless talks of governing himself in making changes, by
'the affectionate reverence with which the Authorised Version is
so justly regarded,' may be rendering his original with more accuracy when he writes: 'He shall not fail nor be discouraged till
he have set religion in the earth, and the sea-coasts wait for his
doctrine.' But he must not imagine that he is making a slight
change in the rhythm of 'He shall not fail nor be discouraged,
till he have set judgment in the earth; and the isles shall wait for
his law;' for he destroys the balance of the rhythm altogether. He
may or may not be expressing the prophet's meaning in appropriate English, which he says is his design, when he puts 'Who
hath believed our *revelation*,' for 'Who hath believed our report,'
or 'He was *tormented, but he suffered freely, and* opened not his
mouth,' for 'He was *oppressed, and he was afflicted, yet he*
opened not his mouth;' but he is not governing himself by 'the
affectionate reverence with which the Authorised Version is so
justly regarded,' for he is changing its effect totally. And this,
though there may be only a word or two altered, or though the
new and imported words may be honest Bible-words like the old.

    Hence we see how delicate is the matter we are touching,
when we take in hand the authorised version to correct it. And as
there is so much risk, it seems the safest way, first indeed to be
very shy of correcting needlessly; but then, if there is need to
correct, to keep if possible the cast of phraseology and the fall of
sentence already given by the old version, and to correct within

the limits of these, transgressing the limits of neither. For instance: 'He was taken from prison and from judgment, and who shall declare his generation? for he was cut off out of the land of the living; for the transgression of my people was he stricken.' This needs correction, for it gives no clear sense; but it possesses 5 a cast of phraseology and a fall of sentence which are marked, which we all know well and should be loath to lose. Mr. Cheyne substitutes: 'From oppression and from punishment was he taken, —and as for his generation, who considered that he was cut off out of the land of the living, for the transgression of my people 10 he was stricken?' This is hardly clearer, indeed, than the old version; still, the old version's cast of phraseology is on the whole maintained, but what has become of its fall of sentence? Surely it is better to try and keep this too; and if we say: 'He was taken from prison and from judgment; and who of his generation re- 15 garded it, why he was cut off out of the land of the living? for the transgression of my people was he stricken!'—we do at least try to keep it. It would be easy to translate the verse more literally by changing its words and rhythm more radically; but what we should thus gain in one way is less than what we should 20 lose in another.

However, the safest way, of course, is to abstain from change; and the trial of the corrector is in deciding where to make change and where not. For the public and authorised corrector the latitude is greater, as I have said, than for an attempt like 25 mine. *I will destroy and devour at once*, in verse 14 of chapter 42, is clear and gives a tolerable sense, so I have kept it; but it can hardly be the sense of the original (although this sense is not quite certain), and public and authorised correctors might do well to change it. But I doubt whether any corrector should, merely 30 for the sake of being more exactly literal, change good words which give the general sense of the original. For example, in the second verse of the first chapter of our series, '*Her iniquity is pardoned*' sufficiently conveys the general sense; '*Her sin-offering is accepted*' is more exact, but there is no adequate reason for 35 change. But the next clause, '*She hath received at the Lord's hand double for all her sins*,' is ambiguous. It may mean, her punishments are twice as much as her sins, or it may mean, her blessings are twice as much as her punishments. It does mean the lat-

ter, but the words would lend themselves to the former meaning
more readily. Lowth substitutes, '*She shall receive at the hand of
Jehovah blessings double to the punishment of all her sins;*' the
right sense is given, but the rhythm of the old version is gone.

5 Whereas the changing only one word would have left the
rhythm as it was, and yet have made the meaning quite clear: '*She
shall receive at the Lord's hand double for all her* rue.'

   Lowth in this passage changes the tense of the verb, and here
too is a point where, it should be noticed, great heed is requisite.

10 Very often, in the Hebrew prophets and poets, the time is a
kind of indeterminate one, neither strictly present, past, nor future. They speak of God's action; and the time of God's action
is the time of a general law, which we can without impropriety
make present, past, or future, as we will. So in Horace's famous

15 lines declaring how regularly punishment overtakes the wicked:
'*Raro antecedentem scelestum deseruit pede poena claudo;*' the
verb here might almost equally well, as far as the sense is concerned, be *deseruit*, or *deseret*, or *deserit*,—hath abandoned, shall
abandon, or doth abandon. Very often, where the time is of this

20 kind, the form of the Hebrew verb does not make it certain for
us, as in Latin, how we shall render. The authorised version, having in view the nature, as popularly conceived, of prophetical
speech, always leans to the future. Some modern translators
uniformly lean the other way; but in all cases where the sense

25 is not certainly brought out better by one tense than another,
the corrector of the English Bible had better, in my opinion,
hold his hand; for to change the tense is, very often, to change
the rhythm. In the particular text of our prophet which we have
just been discussing, the authorised version has the verb in the

30 past tense: '*She hath received* at the Lord's hand double for all
her sins.' Lowth changes it to the future: '*She shall receive.*' The
present, however, is more vivid: '*She receiveth;*' for this represents the compensation as actually taking place and begun. But it
is the future tense in the authorised version which nine times out

35 of ten raises the question of change. Take as an example: 'The
isles *shall wait* for his law;' where I have rendered, 'Far lands *wait*
for his law.' For, surely, waiting is already prospective enough
without weakening it by making it more prospective still; so that

here, it seems to me, the meaning gains decidedly if we change the tense to the present. But except where there is a decided gain of this sort, I have let the futures of the old version stand.

So, too, as to that often recurring expression, *the isles, the islands.* This rendering is consecrated by its long and universal use; not only our Bibles have it, but the Septuagint and the Vulgate have it also, and Luther has it. And it is noble and poetical. *Coasts, strands,* is more literal, and is the rendering preferred by the modern German translators, and by Mr. Cheyne following them. But where the coasts and isles of the Mediterranean are alone intended, and no stress is meant to be specially laid on their remoteness, *isles,* which is more distinct and beautiful than *coasts,* seems preferable. Sometimes, however, remoteness is an important part of the idea, and then neither *isles* nor *coasts* quite satisfies. This is so in the passage quoted a little way back: 'The *isles* shall wait for his law.' The full meaning is not here brought out; nor does Mr. Cheyne bring it out any more by '*The sea-coasts* wait for his doctrine.' Lowth has: '*The distant nations* shall earnestly wait for his law;' and this is undoubtedly the meaning, only *distant nations* is prosaic, and breaks the character of the Bible-style. Therefore, where remoteness seems a prominent part of the idea, I have used the rendering *far lands;* as here: '*Far lands* wait for his law.' But in general I have retained the well-known *isles.*

And the same with those noble and consecrated expressions, *judgment, righteousness;* I have hardly ever meddled with them. To talk, indeed, like Mr. Cheyne, of setting *religion* in the earth, instead of setting *judgment* in the earth, seems to me wanton; but in our series of chapters there are several places where *saving health, salvation,* undoubtedly renders the original more truly than the *righteousness* of the English Bible. Here I have hesitated, and there was considerable inducement to change; still, the notions of *righteousness* and of *the salvation belonging to righteousness* do in our prophet so run into one another, and the word righteousness in the English Bible is so noble a word in itself, and so weighty an element of rhythm, that again and again, even after changing, I have gone back to it.

In short, I have had a most lively sense of the risk one runs in

touching a great national monument like the English Bible; and
how one is apt, by changes which seem small, to mar and destroy
utterly. If I am asked why I could not wait for the revision promised by Convocation, I answer that several years, probably, will
5   have yet to go by before the revision comes, and even then it will
not give us what is wanted,—this admirable and self-contained
portion of the Bible, detached to stand as a great literary whole.
But I will add, too, that I think there is a danger with any body
of modern correctors of changing too much, and of thinking that
10 little things, especially, may be freely changed without harm.
And I am conscious of an 'affectionate reverence' for the diction
and rhythm of the English Bible, greater even, perhaps, than that
of many of the official revisers,—a reverence which, while for
our purpose *some* change in the text is needed, makes me eager,
15 notwithstanding, to preserve its total effect unimpaired, and
binds me, in this aim, to a moderation in altering much more than
commonly scrupulous. After all, the total number of changes
made is considerable, for clearness required it; but nothing would
be so gratifying to me as to find that a reader had gone from
20 the beginning of the chapters to the end without noticing anything different from what he was accustomed to, except that he
was not perplexed and thrown out as formerly. No corrector
should wish to claim any property in the English Bible. That
work, and the glory of it, belongs to the old translators, and
25 theirs, even if their work is amended, it should remain. Even their
punctuation one would gladly retain; but this one finds oneself
more and more, the more one deals with it, obliged in the interest
of clearness and effect to alter.

I must still add a word about the notes and explanations. I have
30 no design in the present work to discuss, or even to raise, questions which are in dispute between different schools of Biblical
interpreters. There ought to be nothing in the book which should
hinder the adherent of any school of Biblical interpretation or of
religious belief from using it. The authorship of our series of
35 chapters is a vexed question; and undoubtedly I believe that the
author of the earlier part of the Book of Isaiah was not the author
of these last chapters. There is nothing to forbid a member of the
Church of England, or, for that matter, a member of the Church
of Rome either, or a member of the Jewish Synagogue, from

holding such a belief; but it is not a belief which a work like the present has to concern itself with. Our work ought simply to place itself, in presenting the last twenty-seven chapters of Isaiah, at the moment of history where the contents of them become simplest, most actual, most striking. Now, this moment evidently is the moment of Cyrus's attack on Babylon and contemplated restoration of the Jews. This is the moment when to the Jewish nation itself these chapters must undoubtedly have come out with far more clearness and fulness than could have been possible a hundred and fifty years earlier, when the matters handled must have been mere predictions of unknown future events. The greatness of Hebrew prophecy, or even its special character, are not concerned here. In my belief the unique grandeur of the Hebrew prophets consists, indeed, not in the curious foretelling of details, but in the unerring vision with which they saw, the unflinching boldness and sublime force with which they said, that the great unrighteous kingdoms of the heathen could not stand, and that the world's salvation lay in a recourse to the God of Israel. But, anyhow, the general prophecy that the great unrighteous kingdoms of the heathen could not stand was all that could in the time of Ahaz be fully effective; the full effect of all the particulars in our twenty-seven chapters must have been reserved for the time when these particulars began visibly to explain themselves by being produced and fulfilled. This every one must admit. Even those who believe that the prophecy existed in the reign of Ahaz, a century and a half before the conquests of Cyrus, will allow that at the moment of the conquests of Cyrus its significance would be brought out much more fully. And therefore we desire to place the reader in the position of a Jew reading the chapters at that critical moment, when the wars and revolutions with which they deal had a nearness, grandeur, and reality they could not have before or afterwards. But any one is free to suppose, if he likes, that these chapters, so apposite and actual at that moment, were an old prediction which had been in the possession of the Jews long before. Whether this was so or not, whether it is consistent with the true nature of Hebrew prophecy that this should have been so, are questions into which the present work does not enter, and ought not to enter.

Some persons will say, probably, that the notes and explanations confine themselves too much to the local and temporary side of these prophecies; that the prophecies have two sides, a side towards their nation and its history at the moment, and a
5 side towards the future and all mankind; and that this second side is by much the more important. I admit unreservedly that these prophecies have a scope far beyond their primary historical scope, that they have a secondary, eternal scope, and that this scope is the more important. The secondary application of the
10 53rd chapter of Isaiah to Jesus Christ, is much more important than its now obscure primary historical application. To deny this would, in my judgment, shew a very bad critic; but it would shew a very bad critic, also, to believe that the historical and literary substratum in the Bible is unimportant. Yet this belief
15 is wide-spread and genuine; but I answer,—and here is the justification of works like the present,—that it is of very high importance; that without this historical and literary substructure the full religious significance of the Bible can never build itself up for our minds, and that those who most value the Bible's religious
20 significance ought most to regard this substructure. Admirably true are these words of Goethe, so constant a reader of the Bible that his free-thinking friends reproached him for wasting his time over it: 'I am convinced that the Bible becomes even more beautiful the more one understands it; that is, the more one gets
25 insight to see that every word, which we take generally, and make special application of to our own wants, has had, in connexion with certain circumstances, with certain relations of time and place, a particular, directly individual reference of its own.'
30 So that though our series of chapters, like the Bible in general, contains more, much more, than what our notes chiefly deal with, yet this too, nevertheless, is of very high importance and leads up to that *more*. Moreover, it has the advantage of not offering ground for those religious disputes to which a more
35 extended interpretation of the Bible often gives rise. What disputes it offers ground for are of the sort which may arise out of any historical and literary enquiry, and they are the fewer the more the enquiry is conducted in an unassuming and truly scientific manner; when that only is called certain which is really cer-

tain, and that which is conjecture, however plausible, is allowed to be but conjecture. It sets Bible-readers against all historical and literary investigation of the Bible, when novelties are violently and arrogantly imposed upon them without sufficient grounds. No one who has been studying the Book of Isaiah 5 should close his studies without paying homage to the German critics who in this century have accomplished so much for that Book; and to two great names, perhaps, above all,—Gesenius and Ewald. Ewald, that ardent spirit,—whose death, the other day, may probably almost stand as marking a date in the history of 10 German learning, and as closing a period,—Ewald exhibited in a signal degree, over and above all his learning, two natural gifts: the historical sense and the poetical sense; the poetical sense, in my opinion, in a yet higher degree than the historical. But for both the literary and the historical investigation of the Bible he 15 has done wonders; yet perhaps no one has done more to offend plain readers with such investigation, by a harsh and splenetic dogmatism, as unphilosophical as it is unpleasing. His great fault is that he will insist on our taking as certainty what is and must be but conjecture. He knows just when each chapter and por- 20 tion of a chapter was written, just where another prophet comes in and where he leaves off; he knows it the more confidently the more another critic has known differently. But *know* in these cases he cannot, he can but guess plausibly; and sometimes his guess, which he gives as certain, has much to discredit even its 25 plausibility. Our series of chapters, for instance, he insists we shall believe was written in Egypt, not Babylon, because Persia is called in it *the north*, and Persia is north to Egypt, not to Babylon. How strange that it never occurred to him, before thus making a certainty where there can be none, that Persia is north 30 to *Zion;* and that for the Jewish exile in Babylon, Zion, the centre of his thoughts, may well also have been the centre of his geography!

The more we are content to let our text speak for itself, to try and follow its intentions and elucidate them without impos- 35 ing on it ours, the better critics we shall be certainly, but also the less risk we shall run of indisposing ordinary readers to sane Biblical criticism by rash changes, or by assertions pressed too far. There can hardly be a more interesting enquiry than who the

servant of God, so often mentioned in our series of chapters, really was. We all know the secondary application to Jesus Christ, often so striking; but certainly this was not the primary application. Who was originally meant? the purged idealised
5   Israel? or a single prophet, the writer of the book? or the whole body of prophets? or the pious and persisting part of the Jewish nation? or the whole mass of the Jewish nation? It may safely be said that *all* these are meant, sometimes the one of them, sometimes the other; and the best critic is he who does not insist on
10 being more precise than his text, who follows his text with docility, allows it to have its way in meaning sometimes one and sometimes the other, and is intelligent to discern when it means one and when the other. But a German critic elects one out of these several meanings, and will have the text decidedly mean that one
15 and no other. He does not reflect, that in his author's own being all these characters were certainly blended: the ideal Israel, his own personal individuality, the character of representative of his order, the character of representative of the pious and faithful part of the nation, the character (who that knows human nature
20 can doubt it?) of representative of the sinful mass of the nation. How then, when the prophet came to speak, could *God's servant* fail to be all these by turns? No doubt, the most important and beautiful of these characters is the character of the ideal Israel, and Ewald has shewn poetical feeling in seizing on it, and in elo-
25 quently developing its significance. Gesenius, Ewald's inferior in genius, but how superior in good temper and freedom from jealousy and acrimony! seizes in like manner on the character of representative of the order of prophets. But both of them make the object of their selection a hobby, and ride it too hard; and
30 when they come to the perilous opening of the 49th chapter, both of them permit themselves, in order to save their hobby, to tamper with the text. These are the proceedings which give rise to disputes, cause offence, make historical and literary criticism of the Bible to be regarded with suspicion. A faithful, simple,
35 yet discriminative following of one's author and his text might avoid them all.

I have been too long; but the present attempt is new, and needed explanation. One word of yet more special explanation has still to be added. A variety of interpretations of any passage is hardly ever given; one interpretation is adopted, and the rest are left without notice. This is not because I consider the interpretation to be in all cases certain, but because the notes are written for those who want not to occupy themselves with 5 weighing rival interpretations, but to get a clear view of the whole. I make no apologetic phrases about the faults of my own editing and annotating. It is not that I am unconscious of their defectiveness; but I know that the work for which they in some sort open a way is so important as far more than to make up for it. 10

To make a great work of soul pass into the general mind is not easy; but our series of chapters have one quality which facilitates this passage for them,—their boundless exhilaration. Much good poetry is profoundly melancholy; now, the life of the generality of people is such that in literature they require joy. And 15 if ever that 'good time coming,' for which we all of us long, was presented with energy and magnificence, it is in these chapters; it is impossible to read them without catching its glow. And they present it truly and with the true conditions. It is easy to misconceive it on a first view, easy to misconceive its apparent condi- 20 tions; but the more these chapters sink into the mind and are apprehended, the more manifest is their connexion with universal history, the key they offer to it, the truth of the ideal they propose for it. Many of us have a kind of centre-point in the far past to which we make things converge, from which our thoughts of 25 history instinctively start and to which they return; it may be the Persian War, or the Peloponnesian War, or Alexander, or the Licinian Laws, or Caesar. Our education is such that we are strongly led to take this centre-point in the history of Greece or Rome; but it may be doubted whether one who took the con- 30 quest of Babylon and the restoration of the Jewish exiles would not have a better. Whoever began with laying hold on this series of chapters as a whole, would have a starting-point and lights of unsurpassed value for getting a conception of the course of man's history and development as a whole. If but for a certain num- 35 ber of readers this could happen, what access would they thus gain to a new life, unknown to them hitherto! what an extending of their horizons, what a lifting them out of the present, what a

suggestion of hope and courage! 'It is a stingy selfishness,' says
Barrow, 'which maketh us so sensible of crosses and so uncapable
of comfort.' There are numbers whose crosses are so many and
comforts so few that to the misery of narrow thoughts they
5   seem almost driven and bound; what a blessing is whatever extri-
cates them and makes them live with the life of the race! Our acts
are, it is most true, infinitely more important than our thoughts
and studies; but the bearing which thoughts and studies may have
upon our acts is not enough considered. And the power of ani-
10 mation and consolation in those thoughts and studies, which, beginning by giving us a hold upon a single great work, end with
giving us a hold upon the history of the human spirit, and the
course, drift, and scope, of the career of our race as a whole, cannot be over-estimated. Not pathetic only, but profound also, and
15 of the most solid substance, was that reply made by an old Car-
thusian monk to the trifler who asked him how he had managed
to get through his life:—'*Cogitavi dies antiquos, et annos aeternos
in mente habui*[1].'

---

[1] Psalm lxxvii. 5 (in the Vulgate, lxxvi, 6).

Savings Banks in Schools*

It is too much to say that by legislative enactments little or nothing can be done to better the condition of the working-man. He does not believe this himself, and he will more and more show us that he does not believe it; it may be a pleasant doctrine for certain people to preach, but for him it is a depressing doctrine, and it is not true. Very much may be done, by laws removing what is old and instituting what is new, to create a form of society more favourable to the working-man than the form in which he now lives. Politics and politicians will have to address themselves to work of this kind going deeper and requiring more care and thought than any work with which they are now conversant. Nevertheless, it will always remain true that, though laws may do something for a man, the most that is to be done for him he must do for himself.

This it is which gives its interest to the little book or tract of which we are going to speak. Whatever laws we may for the working-man's benefit make or unmake, his acquiring the personal habit of self-command is what will always do most for his welfare. "Die Hauptsache ist," as Goethe says, "dass man lerne sich selbst zu beherrschen;" "the great matter is to learn to rule oneself;" it is and always will be so. Now, in order to save, the working-man must learn to rule himself; must set himself to this "great matter" of human life and succeed in it. M. Laurent's tract brings out strongly this moral and elevating side of the habit of saving, and by so doing acquires a special value.

A Dr. Guinard left, in 1867, his property to the town of

* "Conférence sur l'Épargne." Par F. Laurent, Professeur à l'Université de Gand. (Brussels. 1873.)

Ghent, on condition that every five years a prize of 10,000 f.
should be given "to whoever had produced the best work or the
best invention to improve the material or intellectual position of
the working class in general, without distinction." Last year the
5   two classes of letters and of sciences in the Royal Academy of
Belgium were asked to draw up, each of them, a list of candidates with claims to such a prize, and the King named a jury of
five members (among them the well-known publicist M. Émile
de Laveleye) to judge between the claims presented. The jury
10 decided in favour of a "Conférence sur l'Épargne," an address
delivered by M. Laurent to the normal school students of Ghent.
"Cet ouvrage," says their report, "ne compte qu'un petit nombre
de pages; mais l'idée qu'il développe est si juste, si féconde pour
l'avenir, et là où elle a été appliquée, notamment à Gand, elle a
15 donné des résultats si remarquables, qu'il a paru réunir toutes les
conditions voulues pour mériter les suffrages du jury." For to effect the improvement needed in the working-man's condition,
says the report, "il n'y a qu'un moyen, c'est de porter l'ouvrier à
l'épargne." Nowhere, it adds, is this more urgent than in Belgium,
20 where saving is so little the habit of the working-class that,
whereas Massachusetts has for every 1,000 of its population 200
depositors in savings banks, and England 110, and Switzerland
83, Belgium has only 10. But how to get the working-class to
save, where they have so little the habit of it? "L'écrit que nous
25 couronnons," says the report, "montre admirablement, et c'est
là son grand mérite, que c'est surtout par l'école qu'on y par-
viendra." It is vain to preach to the adult workman: he is past
the age when habits are formed. To take the child who is still
plastic, who has not yet acquired inveterate habits opposed to
30 saving, is the only chance. In his "Conférence" M. Laurent develops and defends a plan for effecting this, which had been
with signal success, thanks principally to him, introduced into
the elementary schools of Ghent. The jury adjudged the Guinard prize to M. Laurent for this production, which the Govern-
35 ment, also, has distributed through all the schools of Belgium.

In October, 1866, the school savings-bank was first instituted
in the communal schools of Ghent. The school savings-bank is
in connection with the Government savings-banks, which are

spread all over the country. These receive deposits of a franc and upwards, and pay interest at the rate of 3 per cent. per annum. Until a school-child's savings amount to one franc they are kept by the teacher, who receives deposits at the beginning of every school-time. They are entered upon a printed form furnished by the Government, of which the child has a duplicate. When they reach a franc they are paid into the nearest savings-bank, and the child has then a savings-bank book inscribed with his name, and treated by the savings-bank like the book of any other depositor; but his deposits are still received and forwarded by the teacher. In short, to receive and enter deposits is as much a part of the regular morning and afternoon business of a public elementary school in Ghent as to mark registers is with us.

In 1866 the work began in two communal schools; a third school came in to the plan in 1867, and in 1868 a fourth. The Government approved and recommended the plan, but did not enforce it; M. Laurent had to go about from school to school and from class to class, explaining its benefits. By the end of 1869 it had already so prospered that the Ghent school children had brought up the total number of savings-bank books for their town to 11,334, while for Antwerp, a town of nearly the same population, the number was only 564. In July, 1871, the Ghent schools alone, with 13,330 scholars, had 8,408 savings-bank books. What opposition there is comes from the parents and from the schools for adult workmen. In adult schools in 1871 more than half those who attended them refused to become depositors, while out of 3,741 scholars in the communal schools for boys all were depositors except 741. In the first six months of 1871 the number of fresh savings-bank books issued in the Ghent schools was 1,262. In June, 1872, these schools had altogether 12,420 books, and their deposits amounted to 430,227 f., giving an average of 34 f. 64 c. for each book. In the first six months of 1871 the savings-banks paid to the schools, in money withdrawn, very nearly 27,000 f. M. Laurent has a good right to say with exultation, as he does, "Un jour tout enfant de nos écoles aura un livret à la caisse d'épargne. Et ce qui se fait à Gand peut et doit se faire ailleurs. Déjà l'épargne est introduite à l'école dans presque toutes nos grandes villes; elle se répand dans les campagnes. C'est le premier pas fait dans la révolution qui est appelée à transformer les classes ouvrières."

It seems that it is the practice in Belgium for working people to give their children a couple of centimes every Sunday, and in this allowance, which used to be spent in sweet things, M. Laurent found a basis for his operations. Whether there is any such regular allowance to such children in this country or not, they come frequently, no doubt, into the possession of pence and halfpence, of which school savings-banks might get hold. What would probably be the chief obstacle to the institution of such banks is the doubt many of us might entertain as to the wholesomeness of setting children's minds upon acquisition and hoarding. In his address to the normal school students, M. Laurent meets this objection, and meets it well. It is the great merit, as we have said, of his address, and was probably the secret of his success in establishing his plan, that whereas his object is one which might easily be recommended on low and unworthy motives, he recommends it on high and worthy motives, and powerfully enlists the best side of human nature in its favour. Let us take his answer to the objection that the habit of saving is not one to inculcate upon children, that it will make them hard and calculating, and spoil the native generosity of their age. M. Laurent says:—

What illusions and what errors there are in this accusation! We think children are generous, whereas they are really full of themselves, selfish! Here is a child whose parents, though very poor, give him his couple of centimes on Sunday for his little indulgences. He runs off to buy some sweet thing with it; does he think of sharing this with anybody? He eats up his apple in a moment, and never even thinks that his parents have denied themselves an apple that he might have one. What are called a child's little indulgences are a mere apprenticeship to selfishness. To tell a child that he had better save his centimes is not, then, to give him a lesson in selfishness; it is, on the contrary, a lesson in going without what he likes; and to go without, what is it but the first step towards self-sacrifice, self-renouncement, self-devotion? This is no theory. The child soon gets to understand how his savings are employed; he draws out his money—why? In nine cases out of ten, to help provide for expenses at home; sometimes to bury his father, or to get bread for his widowed mother. Are these lessons of selfishness?

And M. Laurent gives a number of instances in which the savings of children have come into play at a critical moment and with dramatic effect. They generally serve, however, to purchase clothing for the child himself, or for members of his family.

The wealth, or, to use a more modest term, the command of resources, to which the habit of saving finally conducts the adult workman, M. Laurent treats in the same ethical way. He makes this command of resources a duty, as one of the means to man's perfection, and will not suffer the acquisition of money to remain a purposeless mania or a mere step to selfish indulgence. He says:—

We who preach saving, do we make riches an end in themselves? Riches are never more than means—an instrument of moral and intellectual development. There are outlays which are necessary; it requires an outlay to live, and man does not live by bread alone; his intelligence and his soul have also their wants to be satisfied. Here are legitimate calls for outlay, because their result is to make us reach the object of our life, which is intellectual and moral perfection.

This being so, "Why," asks M. Laurent, "are we not bound to train children to economy, just as we train them to obedience?" But what a dismal childhood, say some people, we thus make for the children of the poor!

How often have tender mothers and kind-hearted men reproached me for wanting to make the children miserable! Well, but it is just because I hold so much to human welfare, to giving to the children under our care all the happiness of which they are capable, that I insist so much upon the idea of sacrifice, which is at bottom identical with the idea of saving. Yes, it is a sacrifice which I demand; I ask the child to give up what he calls pleasures; but I maintain that my severe morality will make him far happier than he would be in gratifying his desires and fancies.

We are here on evangelical ground: *He that loveth his life shall lose it.*

We have thought that those interested in popular education would be glad to be informed of the attempt which M. Laurent and his friends are making, and in what spirit it is being made. The movement has, as we have seen, had already great success;

the one obstacle to its entire success is to be found in the early age at which children leave school. "What does a child of ten years old retain of its duties?" asks M. Laurent; "above all, of a duty so irksome as that of saving? He forgets his lessons of econ-
5   omy just as he forgets everything else that he has been taught. If we can succeed in keeping children at school till the age of four-teen, our cause will have been gained."

And it is hoped that in this, too, the philanthropists of Belgium will be successful. The savings-bank will then become as uni-
10 versal as the infant school is now; and then, perhaps, we shall see accomplished that saying of the economist Rossi, which M. Laurent has taken as the motto for his address:—"Les Salles d'Asile et les Caisses d'Épargne peuvent, à elles seules, changer la face de la société."

A Speech at Westminster

[The following address was made to an Association of Public Elementary Teachers in Westminster, at the Westminster Wesleyan Training College, on Saturday, December 6th.]

It is not at all in my line to attend meetings or make speeches, and when I was asked to come here this evening, my first impulse 5
was to decline. But when I found that the teachers of Westminster, my own district, were very desirous I should attend this first meeting of their association, and would be much disappointed if I did not, I felt that I could not refuse. Many of these teachers are very old friends of mine, and with the rest I hope 10
to become every year better acquainted. And now it is impossible, I think, for school teachers and a school inspector to come together at the present moment, without talking of the blame which is being so freely cast on their schools. Our schools, we are told, are "a miserable failure;" we are told that both the schools 15
and their system are bad, and that if we want a proper supply of "decent schools and decent teachers," we must imitate the United States and Australia. It most certainly behoves us to ask ourselves: Are these things really so? The inspectors' reports are quoted in proof of it. I am glad that no report of mine is quoted, 20
for the remarks of inspectors may easily be misused; and some of those which I see quoted seem to me, as they stand and divorced from their context, neither fair nor judicious. But you must remember what is the nature of the inspectors' reports. I believe ours is the only Government which publishes the reports 25
of its school inspectors; and certainly the practice, if on the whole expedient, which I think it is, has yet some disadvantages. For the inspectors' reports are addressed to the Education Department, which knows the circumstances of our schools, which

79

can supply the qualifications and make the allowances which
ought, and which the inspector himself means, to be supplied and
made. To such a department an inspector may speak of our
schools as they are relatively to the ideal of a thoroughly good
5   elementary school. Now, relatively to this ideal our schools fall
very short. But relatively to the American or Australian schools
and their system, are our schools and their system bad? Compared with the American and Australian schools and teachers, do
our schools and teachers deserve the blame which their inspec-
10   tors appear to cast on them? I entirely disbelieve it. It happens
that in the very last (the November) number of one of the most
seriously conducted and trustworthy reviews in Europe, the
Revue Suisse, an article caught my eye with *Public Instruction
in America* for its heading. I have had to concern myself so much
15   with education on the Continent that what they say there about
public instruction always interests me. And this article in the
Revue Suisse I found of special interest at the present moment.
For in this article a Swiss lady, who appears to have been a
teacher in America for some years, gives us her experience of the
20   American schools. "Suppose," she begins, "we were to attend a
meeting of American teachers and to tell them what their schools
really are?" Why, this is exactly what I, and the English teachers
I see gathered before me here, want to know. "As we cannot do
this," she continues, "we will say here what we know of them."
25   Well, she quotes official reports to show how the American
schools suffer, just as ours do, from irregular attendance. In the
state of Maine, she says, the average school time is but nineteen
weeks and two days in the year. Then the teachers, too, are said
on official authority to be, great numbers of them, incompetent;
30   in Michigan ninety-four per cent. of the schoolmasters are declared unfit for their function. Even the inspectors' reports have
not alleged such a rate of incompetency against you here. But it
is the lady's own remarks on the instruction which are the most
interesting, for a Swiss teacher well knows what sound instruc-
35   tion is. "Is the American school-child a bad pupil?" she supposes
people to ask; and she answers, "In most cases, yes!" The great
majority, though quick and sharp, "go through their school years
without any of their lessons taking real hold on them; irregular,

constantly changing school; ill-disciplined, a perpetual subject of astonishment to foreign teachers who have been accustomed to something better." This, it will be said, relates to higher instruction than the primary. Yes; but where is the root of the mischief? In the primary instruction. *The first stages are neglected*, says our informant—"on neglige les premiers degrés." As long as their primary instruction is not better, she continues, the Americans will never get a due return for their really great outlay on schools. Now Mr. Morley heard in America, that in one of the great towns of the West one of the best students at the professors' lectures there is a youth who goes down to the town every afternoon to earn a dinner by shaving at a barber's; and he was assured that it was the fault of any boy who had been at a common school if he had not picked up instruction enough for this. I put genius out of the account; Porson was the son of a parish clerk, and his first schoolmaster was his father. But I take the allegation that an American common school fits its pupils for going on to professors' lectures and higher instruction, while our schools cannot do as much. Now, professors' lectures and an ambitious programme of higher subjects are of little use if the foundations are unsound. At present, says our Swiss teacher, "for every twenty scholars, and even for every twenty teachers, who have studied geometry, *philosophy*, physiology, political economy, and much more, you will scarcely find two who can read really well, can write easily, correctly and legibly, or parse the simplest English sentence." So that when Mr. Morley was told by his American friends that it was the fault of any boy in an American common school if he had not picked up sufficient instruction to follow professors' lectures afterwards, he should have asked what this exactly amounted to; what the "professors' lectures" were, and what the "sufficient instruction" was. For how it stands with the primary instruction we have seen; but as to the professors' lectures also, as to the American pupil when he comes to higher instruction, our Swiss teacher gives us some very curious information. "The American pupil," says she, "imagines that the whole of knowledge is to be learnt in class by swallowing down bodily a certain number of manuals. Thus, as he is to know geometry, a treatise on geometry is learnt by heart,

and he knows geometry. It is the right thing to know history, so a history of the world is learnt in the same fashion, and one has settled one's accounts with that branch of human knowledge. The same with everything else—English literature, French, philosophy, physiology, political economy—a manual to be tossed off, nothing more." It is the same with pupils of both sexes. Young ladies are presented to a professor of foreign languages with an assurance that they know French. He speaks to them in French; they don't understand a word. Oh, but they read? Yes,
a great deal. Well, what have they read? A book of extracts and *Télémaque*. And a pupil who has done this is in America, says our informant, quoting in English the very phrase she has been accustomed to hear, "a fine French scholar." This sort of thing is not quite the higher instruction, perhaps, that Mr. Morley was
thinking of when he extols the American common schools for being able to pass on their pupils to it, and defies the English common schools to do the same. It is the sort of instruction we generally associate with our "Classical and Commercial Academies."

Now all this agrees, I must say, with what I have been told in
Germany; that something might be learnt from America as to providing and maintaining schools; but as to instruction, nothing. Good judges say that in countries without a real superior instruction, literary or scientific, countries without a learned class and a learned tradition to set the standard of thoroughness in
knowledge, primary or popular instruction can never be sound. The best Americans know the deficiencies of their country, deficiencies inseparable from its circumstances, and are bent on, with time, remedying them. The high praise of American schools comes to us from two sorts of people, philanthropists and politicians. A philanthropist, with a taste for institutions and no special knowledge of instruction, goes to America, sees great schools, great public interest in them, a great attendance of scholars; he sees a smart young lady of fourteen get up and rattle off an account of the organization of the ear or of the functions of di-
gestion, and he exclaims, "Bless me, how very beautiful! we cannot do these things in the old country." Then there is the politician, who, like Mr. Morley, thinks the Church of England "the ally of tyranny, the organ of social oppression, the champion

of intellectual bondage," and who is delighted with the secular
and free schools of a democratic country. I do full justice to Mr.
Morley's talents; and I must say that with what seems to be Mr.
Morley's governing feeling, impatience and indignation at the
state of the English labouring class, it is impossible, to me at any 5
rate, not to have great sympathy. But it is not well to warp facts
about schools to suit one's feelings about politics. It is, above all,
unjust to those who, like yourselves, are giving—and in general
honestly and ably giving—the work of their lives to our elementary schools. I will not speak positively of what I have not seen 10
with my own eyes; but I do not believe that your schools need
fear comparison with the common schools of America. I do not
believe that if you caught and examined all the boys of twelve in
Westminster and all the boys of twelve in New York, or all the
boys of twelve in Westmorland and all the boys of twelve in 15
Michigan, the Westminster and Westmorland boys would be
found to read and write worse than the New York and Michigan
boys. The difference comes later; the young American of eighteen or nineteen, who ploughs land or fells timber, is a very different person from the English agricultural labourer of the same 20
age. But this is due not to a difference in schools, but to a difference in the social condition of the two countries. The young
American has carried on his reading and reads the newspapers;
the English rustic has lost his and reads nothing. But let us be
careful, when we speak of instruction and of mental training, not 25
to rate reading the American papers as something higher and
more fruitful than it is. This great staple of American popular
reading, their newspapers and periodicals, our Swiss informant
(to take her testimony again) judges very severely. She says that
these are indeed devoured; but she describes scornfully "the un- 30
digested mixture offered by this ephemeral literature," politics,
poetry, advertisements, criticism, novels, scandal, horrors, mar-
vels; and she records her answer to an American friend who had
said to her, "It is the means of spreading a taste for instruction;"
"No," was her answer, "it is the means of spreading presump- 35
tuous ignorance!" I say, then: Our schools are a serious thing;
when we contrast their instruction with that of American
schools, let us have the real facts about these schools, and do not

let us warp the facts because we admire the political and social system of America.

It is the same case with that burning question which one hardly likes to approach, but which really we ought to approach, the question of religious instruction. For us it is, or ought to be, a question of education, and not a question of religious politics. We may take it as admitted at the present moment that some religious instruction school-children ought to have. Now, it is a real question in education, who can practically give the religious instruction best, the teacher or the minister of religion. I myself think that the facts and history of religion are one thing, the religious application of the facts and history another; to get acquainted with the parables is one thing, to have a sermon on them is another; and the facts and history of religion are, it seems to me, best taught by the person trained to teach, by the schoolmaster. It is vain, I admit, to try and restrict him to some bare outline which you call the facts and history as they stand simply: that cannot be done. You must leave him free, he will put his colour on the facts and history, and the colour will be that of his own religious persuasion. Still, while I fully allow this, I say the teaching the facts and history of religion, colouring and all, is a very different matter from preaching a sermon on them; and that while the minister can probably preach the best sermon, the schoolmaster can probably best give the teaching. Certainly the worst teaching I saw in Germany was the religious teaching given by a minister. But it is a fair matter for debate; only let us have the facts about it as they really are. Mr. Morley says, in his rhetorical way: "In Prussia the minister of the parish is personally charged with the religious instruction of the school. That is not added to the proper duties of the schoolmaster, nor, I believe, is the function of digging graves." That is astounding! I say, on the other hand, that at this moment in every public elementary school in Prussia the religious instruction is given by the teacher. It is given by the minister to the dissenting minority only, who are withdrawn from the religious instruction of the majority. What probably misled Mr. Morley was that the minister of the parish is in Germany the local school inspector of all elementary schools. Would Mr. Morley like to introduce that here?

Nor is it Mr. Morley alone of whom the schools have a right to complain in this matter. Almost all public writers and speakers treat those questions, which for us are practical, in the same unsatisfactory manner. I read the other day a leading article of the *Daily News* on Mr. Forster's recent speech at Liverpool. It complained of Mr. Forster for alleging that anyone proposed to exclude religious instruction from our schools. "He can hardly have been so unobservant," said the *Daily News*, "as not to know that the question is not whether religion shall be taught, but who shall teach it. The undenominational party ask that the schoolmaster shall be limited to his own province, and provision be made for authorized teachers of every Church and denomination to give voluntary instruction in religion to the children of their respective adherents." The *authorized teacher* means, I take for granted, the minister; at any rate, he it is who will almost always be the authorized teacher in these matters. Well, this is the demand of the earnest and intelligent Liberal who writes the leading article. But in the very same newspaper I find a speech by another earnest and intelligent Liberal, Mr. Rogers, the well-known Nonconformist minister of Clapham, and what does he say? He, too, denies that the party with which he acts advocate the exclusion of the Bible from schools. Of course; but how does he go on? "But what they desired was that in any teaching given from the Bible care should be taken that religious instruction should not be placed in the hands of the priests." "The present struggle," says Mr. Rogers, "is, whether the education of the children of the poor shall be in the hands of the priests or of the people." That was loudly cheered. Now I know, of course, that Mr. Rogers would repudiate the title of priest for himself and his brother dissenting ministers. But how, if religious instruction is to be given in our schools, and the schoolmaster is not to give it, you are to give it without admitting the ministers of religion, and of course the priest, Roman or Anglican, among them, it really passes my wits to discover. So that our earnest and intelligent Liberalism demands two incompatible things, and our poor unfortunate schools may well say to its professors: "What are we to be at, gentlemen? which cry do you really mean to go in for, *The intrusive Schoolmaster* or *The intrusive Clergyman?* because you cannot well go in for both at once. Or rather, you both can and do; but we cannot practically comply with both at once." Why really, I must say, and I am sure you feel the same as I do, what unprofitable, insincere, rhetorical stuff all this sort of talk about the religious instruction in our schools is!

5   But the question remains for us, nevertheless, however rhetorically and inaccurately people may talk about the instruction in our schools, however rhetorically and inaccurately they may compare other schools with our own, the question, I say, remains: What *is* the truth about our own schools, what *is* their

10   character? Better, a great deal, than Mr. Morley supposes; not at all inferior, probably, to that of the American and Australian schools. Better, far better, than that of the schools of our middle-class; but then, the schools for our middle-class, which no one talks about because no political or politico-religious capital is to

15   be made out of them, are probably the worst in Europe. Ten years ago I should have said that our inspected elementary schools, in their way, might very well be matched with what are commonly called our public schools, that is, those secondary schools which have got publicity and the stimulus and advan-

20   tages of publicity. Both left much to be desired, but the instruction in both had the same sort of faults and the same sort of merits, and the merits were considerable. Since the Revised Code, I should say that our inspected elementary schools correspond very well, in their way, with what our public schools

25   would be, if for ten years their income had depended on an annual examination, in which each individual boy was to construe a sentence of Latin and a sentence of Greek, and to write a sentence of Latin prose. But if we are to match our elementary schools with schools of their own class, such as the elementary

30   schools of the continent, what are we to say? Mr. Fitch, who has just done good service by picking to pieces some extravagant statistics used in condemnation of our schools, gives these schools higher praise, I confess, than I, when I compare them with the continental schools, can quite agree to. I agree with Mr. Mun-

35   della, that our schools are far inferior to the schools, for example, of Prussia, Saxony, or Zurich. And from what cause? One great cause, of course, is the irregularity and brevity of our school attendance. This is not the fault of you teachers; it has come from

the condition of our people, from the want of care for instruction in our people itself. The people of England, with all its splendid qualities, has long remained a people mentally untouched and unawakened. This it is, even, which gives a peculiar character to what we, as a nation, have done; that it has been done with a people mentally untouched and unawakened. If so much has been done with a people even in this state, what may not be done with the same people awakened? And now our people is waking up, is beginning to feel its own mental life. Well, and now, therefore, we shall get their children to school, we shall get schooling made obligatory. The great obstacle, however, here in England, to this, is one which is in general left out of sight; it is, that whereas everywhere on the Continent you have the municipality, the *Gemeinde*, the *Commune*, in all rural England, and in nearly all our small towns, you have still only the ecclesiastical organization of the middle ages—the parish. The other great cause of the inferiority of our schools to the best continental schools is, I agree with Dr. Abbott, the Revised Code. I incurred some danger, perhaps, by freely blaming this Code in its day of triumph; I shall speak of it with great moderation now that it has been succeeded by another. It was just the sort of measure which it would have occurred to a very clever man, not practically conversant with schools, to introduce. *Payment by results* sounds extremely promising; but payment by results necessarily means payment for a minimum of knowledge: payment for a minimum of knowledge means teaching in view of a minimum of knowledge; teaching in view of a minimum of knowledge means bad teaching. George Herbert well said:

"Who aimeth at the sky
Shoots higher much than he that means a tree."
The teacher's high aim, the formation, out of his regularly attending scholars, of a good first class, to be a sort of nucleus of light, came to be forgotten; the instruction of his irregularly attending scholars remained imperfect still, for it could not, so long as they attended irregularly, be otherwise. The mere introduction of extra subjects could not cure the defects of the Revised Code; payment by results on individual examination in extra subjects involves the same bad teaching as in the case of

elementary subjects; it is an educational law, this; the thing cannot but turn out so. Most of us who are here present know, by
sad experience, that piece of futility, the map of Middlesex,
which our scholars in the fifth standard learn to draw, and learn
5   to draw nothing else. Where is the remedy? In general, in giving
greater freedom to the teacher, greater freedom to the inspector;
in particular, I am inclined to think the remedy lies in retaining
the present examination for only the first, second, and third standards, and beyond that point, paying grants, not on individual
10 examination, but on the report that the classes have been properly instructed. In that direction, I myself think, the particular
remedy lies; but you teachers should turn your own minds to
these matters, they can only be settled by experience and reflection. There is now no distinction of schools before the State.
15 Teachers have a common ground on which they can unite in
associations like this of the Westminster teachers, and the united
experience of teachers, if they are reasonable, must have great
weight, as the school synods have in Switzerland. We must be
patient, however; things cannot move as fast as our wishes would
20 have them move. Our schools will not in our lifetime be what we
could wish to see them; we shall not live to do more than a very
small part of what has to be done for them. What, however, we
can all do, each in our measure, is to set ourselves against having
our schools and their system governed by clap-trap of any kind
25 —educational clap-trap, or political clap-trap, or politico-religious clap-trap, the worst of all. For the rest, let us not deceive
ourselves; the science of teaching is still in its infancy, the right
programme of studies has yet to be discovered. Give your pupil
a whole of some important kind for his thoughts to crystallize
30 around; that is the best advice I can give you. The reason why I
have taken such interest, as you know, in introducing the exercise, so novel to our schools, of learning passages of standard
poetry by heart, is this: that to give a child the possession of two
or three hundred lines of sterling poetry is to give something to
35 nature to work upon, something that we cannot manipulate by
our codes and schedules, but are obliged to permit nature to
work upon freely. For a child's mind is a soil with its own
powers; a soil which we did not make, but into which we have to

put the right thing. Our best art consists in enabling the powers of the soil to act, instead of thwarting and perverting them. The seed we sow we should sow with this thought before our eyes; a thought as true in education as it is in religion, and admirably conveyed in one of the most profound verses of the New Testa- 5 ment, with which I will conclude these remarks that you have listened to so kindly. "So is the kingdom of God, as a man may cast seed on to the earth, and may go to bed and get up night and day, and the seed will shoot and extend he knoweth not how."

Higher Schools and Universities
in Germany:
Preface to the Second Edition

The book on 'Schools and Universities on the Continent,' which
I published in 1868, has long been out of print; I now republish
that part of it which relates to Germany. The historical interest
of tracing the development of the French school-system, from
5   the University of Paris and its colleges down to the lyceums and
faculties of the present day, is extremely great; the practical
value of this school-system, in affording lessons for English people's guidance at the present moment, is small. The German
schools and universities, on the other hand, offer an abundance
10 of such lessons.

During the debates in Parliament this last spring on Irish university education, a foreign critic remarked that the ignorance
which foreigners are accused of displaying when they talk of
England could not possibly exceed the blundering into which
15 the English debaters fell when they talked of universities on the
Continent. And a good deal of ignorance about these there certainly, among English public men, is; while some of the lessons
to be got from a right knowledge of them are, as we have said,
very valuable. Now of German higher schools and universities,
20 in particular, there exist for the use of people outside Germany
scarcely any clear and trustworthy accounts; my account was
found useful both in England and on the Continent, and I have
ascertained that the description it gives of German public instruction still holds good. I therefore reprint it, and in reprinting
25 it I will take the opportunity to point out, by way of preface,
one or two things which at this moment in England have especial
significance for us in the German way of dealing with public
instruction.

Laws in Germany about public instruction come from statesmen, and so too, it may be said, do laws in England. Now, a statesman can hardly rise to power without being superior in range of experience and largeness of judgment to the mass of mankind; at least, if he can, it speaks ill for those who employ him. And, in Germany, a law about public instruction may be taken to be the best which a statesman, superior to the bulk of the community in experience and judgment, and free to use these unhampered, can devise. But we in England are, as is well known, a self-governing people. This is probably in the long run the best possible training for a nation, but let us observe how it acts on our statesmen and on our law-making. A statesman having to make a law about public instruction is not, with us, free to make it according to the best lights of his own experience and judgment; he is hampered by the likes and dislikes of the bulk of the community, or of some large body or bodies in the community which are necessary to his support. And of the men in general who compose these the judgment and experience are, by the supposition we follow, and indeed by the very nature of things, inferior to his own. Probably at the very best it will be a give and take between him and them; he will concede something to their prejudices, and will try, along with this concession, to slip in as much of what he judges to be really right and expedient as he can. But the more he slips in of this the less he will tell the body of his supporters that their prejudices are prejudices; he will even make out, in passing, the best case for these he can, and will soothe and humour them, in order that what he does gain he may gain safely. Therefore in any matter which, like education, touches many passions and prejudices, we do not get the best our statesmen would naturally devise; and what we do get is given in a manner not to correct popular prejudices, but rather to humour them. Our statesmen, therefore, and their measures, do directly hardly anything to check and set right widespread errors amongst the community. Our most popular newspapers do even less; because, while they have all the temptations of statesmen to coax popular prejudices rather than counteract them, they have not the same chance of being, by experience and strength of judgment, raised really above them. But it is evident that the whole value of its training, to a nation which gets the training of self-government,

depends upon its being told plainly of its mistakes and prejudices; for mistakes and prejudices a large body will always have, and to follow these without let or hindrance is not the training we want, but freedom to act, with the most searching criticism of our
5   way of acting.

Now a criticism of our way of acting, in any matter, is tacitly supplied by the practice of foreign nations, in a like matter, put side by side with our practice; and this criticism by actual examples is more practical, more interesting, and more readily at-
10 tended to than criticism by speculative arguments. And the practice of Germany supplies a searching criticism of this kind; for we know how German practice is governed by the notion that what is to be done should be done *scientifically*, as they say; that is, according to the reason of the thing, under the direction of
15 experts, and without suffering ignorance and prejudice to intrude. But this criticism our politicians and newspapers,—having always, as we have seen, to consider the prejudices of those bodies on which they lean for support,—will never apply stringently and unflinchingly. The practice of foreign nations they
20 will always try to exhibit by a side which may make their own supporters feel proud and comfortable, rather than humiliated and uneasy; and perhaps it is to this cause, even more than to simple carelessness and ignorance, that those inaccurate assertions about foreign universities by our public men, on which
25 foreigners comment, are attributable. Therefore we have always said that in this country the functions of a disinterested literary class—a class of non-political writers, having no organised and embodied set of supporters to please, simply setting themselves to observe and report faithfully, and looking for
30 favour to those isolated persons only, scattered all through the community, whom such an attempt may interest—are of incalculable importance.

Such men may well be dissatisfied with the accounts and criticisms of what is in Germany done for public education which
35 often pass current here. Germany makes laws, for instance, which affect the education of Roman Catholics and the condition of the Roman Catholic church and clergy. We, likewise, in Ireland have to deal with the Roman Catholic church and Ro-

man Catholic education. Naturally, therefore, we must all look
with interest to see what they are doing in Germany. Some of us
give praise to what is being done there, others give blame. Both
praise and blame are generally made to turn to our own credit, to
commend what we have done in England, and to make English 5
people comfortable; but neither by him who praises nor by him
who blames are the German proceedings ever presented just as
they really stand, nor is the lesson ever drawn out from them
which, for the people of this country, they really convey. What
is done to Roman Catholics in Germany is based on the best con- 10
sideration and judgment of statesmen, free of popular prejudice
and clap-trap; what is done to Roman Catholics in Ireland is
based, if we tell the real truth, on popular prejudice and clap-trap.
This constitutes an immense difference. The Roman Catholics
will cry out against the policy pursued by the Prussian Govern- 15
ment towards them, but they cannot help having a respect for it,
because it is based on principles of reason which an able statesman
sincerely holds, can plainly avow, and has power to follow. But
for the policy pursued by the English Government towards the
Roman Catholic church in Ireland, no Roman Catholic can have 20
any respect; for it does not represent the real mind of able statesmen, but the mind of a quantity of inferior people controlling
the action of statesmen, whose ability goes to putting the best
colour they can upon the action so controlled. And the policy of
the Prussian Government may succeed. I speak with caution, be- 25
cause, in the first place, a foreigner cannot well have a thorough
knowledge of the circumstances; and, in the second place, what
is right and reasonable does not always succeed, or the best judgment of the ablest statesman may fail to hit truly what is right
and reasonable, or he may shew temper and indiscretion in de- 30
tails even where he is right in his main drift. However, I think
that Prince Bismarck's policy will succeed, and that he may hope
to see the great body of the German Catholics finally come in to
it. But I am sure that the English Government's policy towards
the Irish Catholics never can succeed; for it does not even follow 35
in its main drift that Government's best notions of what is right
and reasonable. As much as these may not always be enough for
success; but less than these, never.

Now wherein lies the essential point of difference between the English and the German Governments, in their practical dealings with Roman Catholic education and kindred matters? That is just what from English public speakers and writers one would
5 never learn. Exeter Hall praises Prince Bismarck because, like England at its best moments, he sternly restrains Romanism. On the other hand, the *Spectator* says that Prince Bismarck adopts towards Roman Catholics the illiberal policy of England before Catholic emancipation; the *Standard* says that what he does is as
10 if an English Minister forced all Roman Catholics, wanting to take orders, to come to Oxford and Cambridge to be educated. Is it really so? and if it is not so, where is the difference?

It is here:—that Prussia, before proceeding to regulate in certain points the course of Roman Catholics, *first established and*
15 *endowed their religion.* Before compelling Roman Catholic candidates for orders to attend universities, *she gave them Roman Catholic universities to go to.* Has England, when it was restraining Romanism, stood towards it as Prussia stands? Before Catholic emancipation, was the Roman Catholic religion in Ireland estab-
20 lished and endowed, or was it encompassed by prohibitions and penalties? At this moment, have the Roman Catholics of Ireland a Roman Catholic university, or are they in the condition of having vainly asked England to give them one? And when the English Government at last offered them a university without the-
25 ology, philosophy, or history, was not even this offer cried out against in England as 'a plan of endowment however mitigated and disguised,' and are we not told to rejoice at the offer having failed because even so much as this will never be offered to the Catholics again?

30 Now the treatment to which Prince Bismarck is subjecting Roman Catholicism may be wise or unwise, just or unjust; to this we will come presently. But in all that he does, he stands on a vantage-ground which we do not occupy. One thing that Protestants have, and that Catholics think they have a right, where
35 they are in great numbers, to have too, this thing to the Prussian Catholics Prussia has given. What the Irish object to in Trinity College, Dublin, is, they say: 'the settlement in the metropolis of a Catholic country and for a Catholic nation of a non-Catholic

college and university backed up by all the prestige of the antiquity, the wealth, and the learning of Trinity College.' For my part, I have not a word to say against Trinity College; its distinguished past and honourable present, and the large proportion of the wealth and property of Ireland which belong to Protestants, amply justify its continuance. But the Catholic bishops have reason in what they say, nevertheless. In short, they want a Catholic university for a Catholic country, just as Oxford and Cambridge are Protestant universities for a Protestant country. They may be told by Mr. Lowe that all a man ought to wish for is an Examining Board, and that faculties and professors are a great mistake; but they hold to the old notion, that a regular university is a better thing. They may be told that they ought to be satisfied with an university where theology and the matters akin to it are not taught; or where theology is not taught, and history and philosophy are taught without reference to religion, without any one asking of what religion are the persons who teach them. That is not their opinion; they prefer that their sons should be taught theology, philosophy, and history at the university as well as other things; and that they should be taught theology, philosophy, and history by persons of their own religion. This is no extravagant claim of theirs, they say; they are only asking for what the majority of people desire elsewhere for their children, and what elsewhere is given. In England and Scotland Protestants choose to make their universities places where their children can learn theology, philosophy, and history, and can learn them from Protestants; why may not Roman Catholics do the same, where they are the bulk of the population? And in Germany they may; but in Ireland they are told by the English Government: 'Oh, no, that is impossible; we have a *principle* that for the future we must not, in Ireland, endow religion in any way whatever.' But Prince Bismarck has not this principle; he gives Roman Catholic universities to the Roman Catholics. Only he insists that Roman Catholic priests, paid by the State, shall have passed through the studies and examinations of the university, instead of remaining satisfied with the studies and examinations of their own seminaries. That is his principle; and the Roman Catholics find fault with it, as they do with ours. But evi-

dently it is quite a different principle from ours; indeed, it can only be reached by first rejecting our principle altogether. Yet the *Times*, as is natural for a leading English newspaper, talks as if by our principle we generously conferred on the Irish Roman
5 Catholics a precious boon, and a great advantage over their Prussian brethren. 'We feel,' it says, 'that however inconsistent Ultramontane principles may be with the general tendency of English life, we are strong enough to leave them to be encountered by the natural influences of free discussion.' This is just the sort of col-
10 our which the mass of Englishmen like to see given to our Irish policy,—liberal and rosy. And certainly, if we do not grant to our Roman Catholics any university, we cannot force them to take degrees there. However, the party affected is not content with what we do any more than with what Prince Bismarck does;
15 in Ireland they want an university, and in Prussia they do not want to have their clergy made to pass through university studies and examinations. So the Roman Catholics dislike both what our Government does and what Prince Bismarck does; but there the likeness between the German and the English policy ends. The
20 two go upon wholly different principles; and if one policy is right the other hardly can be, if the one is likely to succeed the other must be likely to fail. Which is right, which is likely to succeed, will depend on the comparative truth and worth of the principles at the bottom of each.
25   Prince Bismarck's principle is, that a man who exercises an important public function in dealing with men's minds, should exercise it with the light, help, and discipline of the best culture which the nation has to give. This culture is given by the national universities. The man may, it is true, go through it without
30 being benefited by it; but it is likely he will be benefited by it, and so much benefited as to make it worth while to insist on his going through it. This is really what Prince Bismarck's principle, stated simply, comes to; he holds it, we may well believe, quite honestly and sincerely, for it seems reasonable in itself, and what
35 reasonable Roman Catholics might themselves be brought to admit. How far, in this or that detail, he may have applied it injudiciously, how far his adversaries' resistance may have provoked him to show temper and self-will, and to go beyond what was reasonable, a foreigner cannot well judge, and I do not

mean here to inquire. People for the most part so respectable as are the Catholic hierarchy in Germany, people who can plead such a long prescription for their independence of the State, who so sincerely think this independence their right, should, one would think, when innovations are made and they resist them, be treated with the greatest possible indulgence and long-suffering. As to attempts to cut the tie between the Catholic priest and Rome, and to substitute for it State-appointment or popular election, this may be very desirable in itself; and, if the Catholic community wishes it, well and good. But so long as the Catholic community sees in its priest a functionary to whose religious ministrations his tie with Rome gives their whole virtue, to forbid this tie is to forbid the Catholic community the exercise of its religion. If Prince Bismarck suffers his new legislation to run into excesses of this kind, they may easily be fatal to it. Anything, too, like a direct prohibition of the ecclesiastical schools, or a direct regulation of studies and control of books in them, seems to me a harsh and ill-advised measure. To interpose, somewhere between the private seminary and the public cure of souls, the studies and examinations of the university, seems to me all that is really required; and to require thus much is reasonable. It is true, the Roman Catholics have the right to certain guarantees in the matter. They have a right to demand that the university shall not be made an engine of Protestant or of antireligious propagandism, that the seminarist shall not be put in the hands of the enemies of his faith, that his university, therefore, shall be a Roman Catholic university, and his professors for theology, philosophy, and history, Roman Catholics. This being guaranteed, I think the State may reasonably impose university studies as a preliminary to orders, and that it may fairly hope to obtain, with time, the approbation of its Roman Catholic members themselves to its doing so. The reasonable ones will be brought to approve first, but the mass will come in time.

It is true, also, the Roman Catholic hierarchy will claim to have more guarantees than those mentioned, and will make an outcry at first if it does not get them. A body of this kind will always try to make the best terms for itself it can. The Irish bishops claimed from Lord Mayo the government of their Irish university, the right of veto on the appointment of professors, the

right of dismissing professors. This would make the university
simply a continuation of the seminary with a State payment. But
what is the object of an university? To diffuse the best culture by
means of the best professors. And it is granted, that since with
so many and great parts of culture religion is concerned, Roman
Catholics may fairly wish to have, in an university where they
send their sons, Roman Catholic professors; the question is, who
is likely to choose them best, the State or the bishops. A minister
of State will choose them with a wider view, and with a more
public, a fuller, and a more concentrated responsibility,[1] than the
bishops can; therefore the State is likely to choose them best.
This is so agreeable to reason that one certainly need not despair
of bringing the Roman Catholic laity to admit it; indeed, even at
this moment, given a Roman Catholic university either in Prussia
or in Ireland, and suppose you polled the Roman Catholic fathers
of families, whose sons are to use it, to say whether the State or
the bishops should appoint the professors, I doubt if a majority
would not say the State. It is an excellent principle in government to believe that to what is reasonable one may always hope
to make the majority of men at last come in. And reasonable it
seems that the national clergy should be required to have gone
through university studies under the control of university professors; professors of their own faith, chosen, however, not by
any close corporation, but by the whole nation in its collective
and corporate character, by the State acting through a responsible minister. This is what the policy of Prince Bismarck, in that
part of it which we are at present considering, aims, I believe, at
bringing about; and therefore I say it is a reasonable policy he
follows, and he may look for success in it in due course, although
he may be called a demon-minister on the way.

   But now we come to the principle of the English Government

---

[1] It cannot be too often repeated that this is the real unanswerable argument for State intervention; the whole community is supposed to govern,
and in a minister of State the whole community gets, better than anywhere
else, *a centre in which to fix responsibility*. Experience, by palpably showing the defectiveness of such substitutes as, for instance, the new governing bodies of our public schools, will bring us finally to the simple truth, to
which so many of us wish to shut our eyes.

in regard to university education in Ireland. This principle is, as we have seen, that for the future we must not, in Ireland, endow religion in any way whatever. Now it is remarkable that in the soundness of this their principle many of the chief members of the English Government appear, if we may judge by their own admissions, not to believe; whereas in the soundness of *his* Prince Bismarck appears to believe heartily. However, a principle may no doubt be sound, even though its upholders do not themselves believe in it; the question is, does the principle of the English Government, when we examine it, turn out to be sound in itself? Because if it is not, it can never be likely to succeed, much as it may be written up and called a great and necessary principle. So much written up, indeed, it is, and asserted so confidently, that it has come to be treated by a great many people as almost a truism, as something which in its general form, that the State ought to have nothing to do with religion, one must begin by admitting as a matter of course, though circumstances may here and there prevent our as yet shaping our action in conformity to it. A truism, as is well known, is something true and trite. Now, the principle in question is not exactly a truism, but it is next door to it; it is what Archbishop Whately used to call a *falsism*. A truism is something true and trite, and a falsism is something trite and false; and that is just what the maxim we are now dealing with is: something trite but false, a *falsism*. We will endeavour to make this clear by analysing the maxim in the grounds on which its maintainers base it.

For manifestly it is not a principle which carries its own proof on the face of it, like the self-evident truths in mathematics; it is collected from other propositions. In the same way, Prince Bismarck's principle that the Roman Catholic clergy should pass through university studies is not a self-evident truth in itself: it depends on the truth of a proposition behind it, that a nation's public ministers in mental and spiritual things should have passed through the best culture of the nation. So also the principle that the State should have nothing to do with religion depends on further propositions advanced respectively by those two powers in this country which we have elsewhere called Millism and Miallism. These nicknames give offence, and we will not employ

them here; one of them, besides, might turn out to be not strictly
accurate. For Mr. Mill, who was not, perhaps, the great spirit
that some of his admirers suppose, but who was a singularly
acute, ardent, and interesting man, was capable of following
lights that led him away from the regular doctrine of philosophical radicalism, and on no question was he more capable of doing
this than in one where the Catholics of Ireland were concerned.
We will say then, instead of Millism and Miallism, Secularist
Radicalism and Nonconformity. Both call themselves Liberal,
both unite in the proposition that the State should have nothing
to do with religion; but they take different grounds. We hear
most in this country of the ground taken by Nonconformity;
but out of England, on the Continent, hardly anyone takes this
ground. Secularist Radicalism, on the other hand, is a great
power on the Continent as well as with us; and its reason for
severing all connection of the State with religion you hear
perpetually.

This reason is, that religion, as it exists, is merely another
name for obscurantism and superstition; that it keeps out light
and prevents improvement of every kind; that the State, therefore, ought on no account to recognise it, to give it a public character and allow it to hold public property, all of them advantages
which tend to make it honourable in the eyes of men, and to render it more stable and lasting. It is a sort of malady, think the
Continental Liberals, which was bred in times of suffering, darkness, and ignorance, but with which a number of purifying influences are now at war; let the State stand aside and give it no
artificial aid, and it will gradually die out like the black death or
the sweating sickness. This is what Liberalism, thoroughgoing
Liberalism, which knows its own mind and is therefore a serious
power, really means by saying that the State has nothing at all
to do with religion: and it is in this sense that it adopts the cry:
A free Church in a free State! Liberalism of this sort objects
strongly to the State's interference in Switzerland or Germany
between the Old Catholics and the ecclesiastical authority; in
Italy it is for sweeping religion out of the schools and theology out of the universities, and leaving the Church to deal with

these by herself and just as she likes. The nonsense cannot go all at once, they say, but in time it will go; and it will go the sooner the less you encourage it by taking any public notice of it whatever.

Now these enlightened people fall into error, because there is really more in religion than they imagine. True, all sorts of ignorance and superstition have fastened themselves on to religion; true, all sorts of inconvenience and damage have come from religion as we see it existing. But this is because religion,—the rule and sanctions of conduct,—interests all the world, and has thus become the mixed and strange-shapen thing which the practice and opinions of great multitudes of men were likely to fashion. Particularly has this been so with that form of Christianity which has most penetrated the societies where it lived, most laid hold on the multitude and been reacted on by the multitude,— Roman Catholicism. But religion is not on that account like the black death or the sweating sickness, a mere disease out of which, if we do nothing to foster it and will let the influences of modern civilisation work, we may hope mankind will grow; it is a natural human need which will manage to satisfy itself. To this matter we shall return presently; we will now only point out that the nations of Europe have all provided themselves with an organisation of religion just as they have provided themselves with an organisation of society; the one was made a public affair for the same reason as the other, because both were felt to interest the public profoundly, as human needs of primary importance. And when it is said that this or that thing has not been made a matter of public organisation, and why should religion be, we shall always find, if we look close enough, that this was because the thing in question did not interest the public profoundly, was not held (whatever its real merits may have been) to be a thing worth instituting publicly, a public need of primary importance; whereas religion was. Religion has been publicly instituted because it is a recognised public need; it has not been made a public need by being publicly instituted. Naturally the publicly instituted religion in Ireland would be that of the immense majority of the people, the Roman Catholic religion. But this has not been

allowed to institute itself publicly, because it was not the religion
of the minority who conquered Ireland; Irish Catholicism, therefore, has been entirely dissociated from the public life of the
country, and been left to be an entirely private concern of the
5   persons attached to it. Well, but what has been the consequence?
Has it died out because of this wholesome neglect by the State?
Among no people is their religion so vigorous and pervasive.
Has it fewer faults and disadvantages than the same religion in
countries where the nation institutes it? In no country, probably,
10   is Roman Catholicism so crude, blind, and unreasoning as in
Ireland. It seems, then, that by dissociating religion from the
public life of a country, you do not get rid of it, and you do not
abate what is faulty and mischievous in it; you only make this
stronger than ever. And so far, perhaps, philosophic Liberalism
15   hits the truth in its comparison of religion to a disease; what there
is hurtful and virulent in religion, as men have corrupted religion, becomes worse when it is driven in and when the light and
air are shut off from it. Roman Catholicism does not disappear
in Ireland, where it has no public organisation, any more than
20   in Germany, where it has; but it is a thousand times more superstitious and unprogressive. So that the maxim of Secularism, that
the State must have nothing to do with religion, a maxim which
is grounded on the notion that the inconveniences of religion will
dissappear quicker if the State treats it as if it did not exist, turns
25   out to be, as we say, a *falsism;* that is, it is false because the notion on which it is grounded is false, at the same time that it is
trite because so many Liberals are constantly saying it.

But it is from the Nonconformists that we hear loudest, in
England, the maxim that the State must have nothing to do with
30   religion; indeed, so loud do they say it, that they frighten many
of us into assenting to it, whether we believe in it or no. With
the Nonconformists, also, the maxim depends for its truth upon
the truth of another maxim behind it. This maxim is not by any
means that of Secularist Radicalism, that religion with all its
35   inconveniences will die out if not artificially sustained. The Nonconformists think religion a thing most precious and imperishable. Their notion, however, is that religion will thrive best if
the State lets it alone, and if it is not publicly instituted. At least,

this is the notion which at the present moment they wish to pro-
claim as their principle, and to stand or fall by.

Now, this principle is a puzzling matter to deal with, because
its truth or falsehood cannot be seen on the face of it, but depends upon an immense experience which we have not had. On
the one hand is the fact that men, so far as we see, when they
were left to themselves and acted naturally, have almost always
made religion a public institution. True, the world is far from
being perfect. But if religion, or, to limit ourselves to what our
experience can better deal with, if Christianity, ever since its first
appearance, had been left to itself as a concern for individuals
and private congregations only, would the world, men being
what they are, have been any better? It is really impossible to
say. The modern Dissenters tell us it would, but what experience
have they to go upon? They have this: that at the Reformation,
many of the English middle class, discontented with the shape
which the public institution of religion then took amongst us,
renounced it for themselves, and made their religion a thing of
private congregations and individuals. Then these same people,
with their habits of separatism established, crossed the sea, and
founded English America with the same 'dissidence of dissent'
pervading its religion as pervaded the religion of its founders.
For as soon as they had given in to separatism they found it was
a thing that grew upon them, and they began to differ and separate from one another as much as from the religion publicly
instituted in England. Now, then, has religion thriven more with
the English Dissenters, and in America, than it has thriven under
the common conditions? Of course the Dissenters say it has, and
they are fond of pointing to the number of chapels and churches
they build, and to the number of chapels and churches built in
America, and to the salaries paid to ministers, to prove that religion thrives best on their plan. But the real question is, which
produces, not the most churches and the best salaries, but *the best
type of religion*, the public institution of it or the leaving it to
private handling? Here, too, the Dissenters will confidently answer that they and their plan produce the best type of religion.
We differ from them; we are strongly of opinion that neither in
Great Britain nor in America have the separatist churches pro-

duced so good and lovely a type of religion as that which is suggested by the name of Fénelon, for instance, in the Roman Catholic Church, or by the names of Ken or Wilson in our own.
There is another thing. A swarm of private religious sects wastes
5 power; it absorbs for its machinery, squabbles, and gossip, force
of brain which might be better employed, and is not good, therefore, for mental progress. Not much of English thought comes
from the Dissenters. America, occupied in the material installa-
tion of society over a vast continent, gets most of her thinking
10 done for her in Europe; but if she had to depend on herself for
it, she would find, I suspect, her religious organisation unfavourable to her growth in thought and knowledge. But we do not
offer all this as a certainty so evident that everyone must admit
it, nor do we allege that it settles the question between private
15 and national churches absolutely. Appearances are, we think,
against the private churches, but data for deciding positively
against them are wanting. But even more, or at any rate, surely,
just as much, are they wanting for deciding in their favour. So in
a matter where there is no self-evident certainty, and no cer-
20 tain proof from experience, but where general practice has gone
one way, and the majority prefer it, surely it is a case for com-
pliance, for letting them institute religion publicly if they like,
for *pleasing one's neighbour*, as St. Paul says, *for becoming to the
weak as weak, that we may gain the weak*. To deny him and
25 scuffle with him for such a thing is to be contentious, and to
incur the same apostle's sentence: *If any think good to be contentious, we have no such habit, nor the churches of God*. For
this is the Nonconformist's endeavour: to take away or deny
what the majority like, on the plea that religion will thrive best
30 if the State has nothing to do with it. In England they have not
yet succeeded, but in Ireland they succeed; there they prevent
all public institution of Catholicism, any formation of a public Catholic university, though the vast majority of the Irish
would like it. And they prevent it on a ground which has and
35 can have no positive certainty, and carries for mankind at large
no conviction.

We may safely say that if this alleged ground of the modern
Dissenters was their only and their real ground in refusing, for

instance, the Catholic university wished for in Ireland, they would be powerless. The absurdity and injustice of refusing on a ground so inconclusive such a wish of the majority of Irishmen would be too glaring. But it is not the real ground. Most certainly it is not the real ground with the rank and file of the Nonconformists; and we take the liberty of doubting, we who make it our business to try and see things as they really are, whether it is the actual motive even with the leaders, although no doubt they have now persuaded themselves that it is so. Their natural and first thought was that to which Pym gave utterance when he said that it was the business of legislators to establish true religion and to punish false. The Church of England's was not the true religion, therefore the Nonconformists repelled it. But the bulk of them long hoped to establish the true religion, that is, their own, in its stead. This was hopeless, because of the many and ever-multiplying differences amongst themselves. The Nonconformist minorities had to put forward the plea of religious equality, to free themselves from risk of persecution by the Nonconformist majority. The Independents' denial of the right of the civil magistrate to interfere in matters of religion was to bar the claim of the Presbyterian ministers to invoke the civil magistrate's arm to punish what they thought heresy. But John Goodwin, the greatest name among the Independents and an interesting and remarkable man, expressly says that he does not quarrel with the setting up of Presbyterianism by the Government, but with the directing of the Government, in the punishment of heresy, by the Presbyterian ministers. The contention was for *toleration;* that religious bodies had no authority, as the Savoy Confession says, 'to impose their opinions upon one another.' The same was the contention of the Baptists.

But all this was rested on the ground that in matters of conscience Christ is king, and the magistrate ought not to meddle; and this ground, taken originally with an eye to toleration, easily suggested to the Nonconformist minorities a new departure. It was, that there should be no public institution of religion at all; and thus that, though any separatist's own religion might not be first, yet nobody's should. This would rescue them from a mortifying position of inferiority, while it would at the same time in-

flict a mortifying loss of rank upon their rivals. Nonconformists
have since come to see all manner of fine aspects in the idea of religious equality, and they love to think that they have embraced
it for these; but the real reasons why they embraced it are those
5 we have given. They adopted it first to get toleration; they insist
on it now to bring their publicly instituted neighbours to their
own level.

However, to this day, what imparts real strength to the opposition of the rank and file of them to the Church of England,
10 what procures them whatever real sympathy they get from the
public outside, is the belief, not in the virtue and excellency of
the idea of religious equality, but the belief that the Church of
England teaches *false religion*. Still more does the strength of the
opposition to all endowment of Roman Catholicism come from
15 the belief that the Church of Rome teaches *false religion*. The
Nonconformist leaders know where their strength lies, and freely
use invectives against Ritualism or Popery to move the common
public; it is for select audiences that the philosophical beauty of
the idea of religious equality is exhibited. Mr. Miall has mused on
20 this beauty till he has got sincerely enamoured of it and can exhibit it to the best advantage; still, one need not go beyond his
own newspaper to see that it is not this beauty which inflames his
supporters, but the ugliness of what they consider false religions.
A supporter writes to Mr. Miall's newspaper to inveigh against
25 permitting the fees of pauper children in Roman Catholic schools
to be paid out of public rates. What reason does he give? 'The
consciences of three-fifths of the populations of the United Kingdom rise up and cry: You, the State, are being generous with our
money. By force of the tax-gatherer you are compelling us to
30 teach as truth that which *we before God assert without the
slightest misgiving to be dismal error.* You make us parties to *a
lie.* If the conscience of the pauper parent be violated by the
omission of his peculiar religious tenets in the teaching of his
child, how do you appraise the injury inflicted on ours by forc-
35 ing us to pay money in support of *heathenish superstitions?*' This,
this is the notion really behind the Nonconformist maxim that the
State must have nothing to do with religion, the notion which
gives to this abstract maxim nearly all the power it has. The State

paying for Ritualism in England is bad enough, but the State paying for Roman Catholicism in Ireland is making Protestant England and Scotland parties to *a lie*, to *heathenish superstitions*. The majority in England and Scotland like for themselves a public institution of religion: but for Ireland, because the religion of 5 the majority there is a lie and heathenish superstition, we adopt the Nonconformist maxim that the State must have nothing to do with religion.

Now we do not speak to the representatives of the dissidence of dissent, and the Protestantism of the Protestant religion. Their 10 divisions cannot all of them be instituted publicly; while, at the same time any other form of religion which does get instituted publicly, appears thereby to acquire an advantage which they have not. Therefore, to reinforce their objection on the score of its falsehood and superstitiousness to publicly instituting Roman 15 Catholicism, the Nonconformists have the further objection that this would be giving to the Roman Catholics an advantage which they themselves cannot have. The two objections together make them proof against conviction. But we appeal to the majority in England, who have given to their own religion its public institu- 20 tion, which they still maintain. They are the majority,[1] or it would not be maintained. Well, what is it which made them, and which makes men in general, wish to give to their religion this public institution? Is it not the desire to give more weight, solemnity and grandeur to religion, to make it less like a thing of 25 private fancy or invention? The Roman Catholics, where they are the majority, have just the same desire; why are they not to follow it? Because the Roman Catholic religion is so false and dangerous! that is really the English answer. Now, quixotic as the attempt may seem, I am sure we ought boldly to confront 30 this answer, and to show its hollowness. The time has come for doing it, and the attempt is not, perhaps, so quixotic as it looks.

[1] It is to be hoped we shall now be permitted to ascertain to what extent they are the majority. I believe they are the overwhelming majority. At any rate, it was not creditable to the late House of Commons, and it leaves 35 a serious gap in the religious statistics of Europe, that the Nonconformists should have been able at the last census to prevent the fact being ascertained.

We shall not be thought to deny that Roman Catholicism contains much that is false and hurtful, and that Protestantism has many points of advantage over it. But Protestantism has not so much advantage over it as to be entitled to present itself as abso-
5   lutely true, and to brand Roman Catholicism as absolutely false; its doing so must appear to every wise man, even, as an extravagant pretension, and to every Roman Catholic as insolence and outrage. It is no answer to say that Catholicism sets up the same sort of pretension against Protestantism. For the question is not,
10 how is a Catholic country to govern a Protestant appendage, but how is a Protestant country to govern a Catholic appendage. If England were an appendage of Ireland, and Ireland legislated for England on the ground that Protestantism is false and dangerous, then the Catholics would be in the same false position that we are
15 in now. But the case is not so; the present case is, that we treat Irish Catholicism as something false and dangerous which we must not institute publicly. Therefore it is to our own people and to English Protestantism that we must say, and must use every effort to make the idea intelligible and convincing: All forms of
20 religion are but *approximations* to the truth. Your own is but an approximation; Catholicism, whatever it may pretend, is but an approximation. It is true, one approximation may be better than another. But all great forms of Christianity are aimed at the truth, and it is by this their good side that they exhibit them-
25 selves to the view of their adherents and engage their affections. We shall always appear insolent and unjust in the sight of a religion's adherents, so long as we look at it from the negative side only, and not on that attractive side by which they see it themselves. Yet Catholicism we are always looking at from the nega-
30 tive side.

Nevertheless of no religion, one may say, is the favourable side so easy to find or so proper to inspire indulgence. The Roman Catholic religion is the religion which has most reached the people. The bulk of its superstitions come from its having really
35 plunged so far down into the multitude, and spread so wide among them. The two great ideas of religion are the idea of conduct and the idea of happiness; and no religion has equalled

Catholicism in giving on a great scale publicity to the first and reality to the second. The Pope tells a French deputation that the virtuous woman is the salt of society and the depraved woman its bane; he tells an American deputation that industry and energy are fine things, but that the care for riches narrows and hardens the heart; and the sentences are telegraphed round Europe like a king's speech, read with reverence in every Catholic family as the words of the head of Catholicism, forced upon the eye of careless thousands who never think a moral thought by the very newspapers which never utter one. Who, again, has seen the poor in other churches as they are seen in Catholic churches, or common soldiers in churches as they are seen in the churches of Rome? And why? Because the attaching doctrine of the equal share of Christians in the beauty and glory of religion, which all churches preach, the Church of Rome makes palpable; and the poor find in church, and free to them as to the rich, the 'gilded saloons' which with us they hear of but can never enter. It is so vast, too, this old popular religion of Christendom, that in the repertory of its history you may find almost anything; a good for every bad, the condemnation of every folly and crime which it has itself committed. It has the Inquisition on the one hand, and on the other is has Gregory the Great saying: 'The Church, formed in the school of humility, does not command its erring children by authority but persuades them by reason.' It has one Pope proclaiming his infallibility; it has another Pope crying: 'Why should you wonder at our being mistaken, we who are men? Prophets have been misled; is it strange that we should be misled who are no prophets? The multiplicity of our business overwhelms us; and our minds, having to attend to so many things, can attend the less to each single thing, and are the easier in some one thing deceived.' We upbraid it, with much show of justice, as making the word of God of none effect by its tradition; yet all the while it is saying in a popular manual: 'True conversions are very rare, because nothing under a total and thorough change will suffice. Neither tears, nor good desires, nor intentions, not the relinquishment of some sins, nor the performance of some good works will avail anything, but *a*

new creature.'[1] Such is the range of this religion. We know only
the tyranny and folly, and therefore we call the religion *a lie;*
but the Catholic's attachment to his religion is bred of all the
mildness and wisdom which are there also, though we do not see
them, and a successful management of him can never be dictated
by Protestant antipathy which will know nothing of them.

The Catholic sees, too, what the Protestants who call his religion *a lie* do not, that an enemy reproaching Protestantism can
say much the same things against it which Protestants say against
Catholicism; and for people who thus live themselves in a glass
house to be throwing stones at him cannot but appear to him
both very unjust and very ridiculous. Mr. Fitzjames Stephen,
whose strong understanding seems clouded by his dislike when
he speaks of Catholicism, as Mr. John Morley's is when he speaks
of the Church of England,[2] said the other day, upbraiding Catholics with their enmity to modern science: 'You cannot serve God
and Mammon, neither can you believe in your heart and with
any intelligence in modern science and in the Roman Catholic
creed. Does anyone suggest that the doctrine of transubstantiation, for instance, rests on anything like as good grounds as the
doctrine that the earth moves round the sun?' Alas! does he not
see that just the same thing may be said of the Protestant doctrine, so familiar to his own youth, of justification, of *pleading
the blood of the covenant;* and that a Catholic must keenly feel
the injustice of having it said of transubstantiation exclusively?
Science professes to assert nothing which it cannot positively
verify. 'Does anyone suggest that the doctrine of the atonement
rests on anything like as good grounds as the doctrine that the
earth moves round the sun?' The same persons, the Catholic
might retort, would say this both of the atonement and of our
doctrine of transubstantiation, and with just the same degree of

---

[1] See Alban Butler's *Lives of the Saints;* SS. Philemon and Appia, November 22.

[2] But Ireland is not England, and Mr. Morley, alone, so far as I can remember, of English Liberals, has boldly contended that Ireland has a right
to a Catholic university, if she desires it. Mr. Fitzjames Stephen, on the
other hand, so hard upon the Catholics, is in general fair as between the
Church of England and Dissent.

reason in both cases. Science, he might add, has plenty to say against Protestant as well as Catholic. Even Puritan ministers have maintained that the laying on of hands gave them power to cast out devils. Protestant ministers cried out against Galileo's assertion of the earth's movement just as loudly as Catholic priests; 5 indeed, it was observed that here, for the first time, ministers and priests agreed, and Descartes wrote that there was a good time coming for the theory of the earth's motion, as the priests would probably begin to allow it now that all the ministers condemned it. But Protestants in general, it is urged, are favourable to mod- 10 ern science. And so too, to a Catholic, it seems that Catholics in general are favourable to modern science; because he looks at Catholicism by the good side, and treats untoward incidents as the exception, not the rule. But we treat them as the rule for his religion, never for our own. Now, how such a proceeding 15 must strike *him*, is what we ought to ask ourselves.

No, Protestantism and Catholicism are alike mere approximations, but tolerable approximations they both of them are, and all public institution of its religion cannot fairly or rationally be refused by Protestants to a Catholic country on the sort of plea 20 one might use against the worship of Juggernaut, that Catholicism is *a lie* and *heathenish superstition*. It is true, however, that Catholicism does seem to us, as we have already said, to have certain points of grave disadvantage if we compare it with Protestantism. These, however, are of a kind to be lessened rather 25 than aggravated by a public institution of religion. The gravest disadvantage is undoubtedly the dependence on Rome; the establishment, through this dependence, of a foreign power in the country. It was this which chiefly made the English Reformation; and almost everywhere, as the individuality of the Euro- 30 pean nations ripened, and unity in one's nation became a dominant habit and idea, collisions were found to arise between this unity and that old unity in Rome which belonged naturally to a time when all the nations were englobed in the Roman Empire. Such collisions between allegiance to the nation and allegiance 35 to Rome are to the English spirit intolerable; Great Britain got rid of them by the Reformation, and that Ireland should still offer a field for them is to English people an irritating and alarm-

ing thought. And the double allegiance is undoubtedly a source
of danger and difficulty. But here, too, we shall deal best with
our cause of difficulty if we regard it, not as a monstrous and
perverse aberration, but as the thing presents itself to the Irish
5   Catholics themselves, and as in its nature it really is. To the Irish
Catholics, to Catholics everywhere, the attractiveness of union
with Rome is not in the dependence on a government of foreigners, which is naturally attractive to no man, but in the
greater solidity, settledness, and unity which religion by means
10   of this common centre seems to them to acquire. If there is a
thing specially alien to religion, it is divisions; if there is a thing
specially native to religion, it is peace and union. 'The unity of
the spirit,' 'the unity of the faith;' 'be of one mind, live in peace;'
'let us walk by the same rule, let us mind the same thing;' these
15   evangelical injunctions, the eternal rule of Christianity, give to
Ultramontanism its power. In the prologue to the Savoy Confession, the very Independents lamented that their churches were
'like so many ships launched singly, and sailing apart and alone
in the vast ocean of these tumultuous times;' it is the sense how
20   alien is this isolation and separation to the nature of Christianity
which makes Catholics imagine even a church coextensive with a
man's nation too narrow, and seek a common centre in Rome. 'If
we consider the Church as unity,' said Pascal, no friend to papal
usurpation, 'the Pope is its head; *the multitude which is not re-*
25   *duced to unity is confusion.*' That, I say, is the Catholic sentiment, natural and attractive, lying hid beneath that creation of
'a State within a State' which is often found in practice so baneful. Practically, no doubt, no body of clergy can be reckoned
upon, wise enough and temperate enough to fill, without being
30   intoxicated by it, the mighty part which, in the Catholic scheme,
is reserved for Rome; practically, a church as wide as his nation,
suited to his nation, nationally governed, is what a man should
seek, and he does ill to run after the shadow of more and lose the
substance of this. But the national sense is strong in every nation,
35   and may be trusted to assert itself as time goes on. What hinders
it from asserting itself in Irish Catholicism? What keeps Irish
Catholicism Ultramontane? Our policy and our policy only. We
will not let Irish Catholicism be instituted publicly; we will not

suffer it to be national, to have the sense of being the Church of Ireland, and independent; we keep it a private thing, and its only way of being great and public is by being Ultramontane. We will not allow a Catholic university with a charter from the Crown, so Ireland will have a Catholic university with a charter from the 5
Pope. What admirable, what successful management! Granted that Catholicism has really, as compared with Protestantism, grave elements of inconvenience and danger; the worst of these dangers, the Ultramontane tendency, we do not abate by our 'principle' of not endowing in any shape religion in Ireland; we 10
aggravate and exasperate it a thousand-fold.

Ultramontanism is a *political* disadvantage connected with Catholicism. But we will go further and say that Catholicism has, as compared with Protestantism, an intellectual and spiritual disadvantage likewise. We must always remember what Catholi- 15
cism has been,—the great popular religion of Christendom, with all the accretions and superstitions inseparable from such a character. Long before the Reformation serious and intelligent Catholics could, for their single selves, separate these accretions from their religion. They could see, for instance, that the papal sys- 20
tem, or that the worship of the Virgin and of saints, had taken dimensions quite out of proportion with what is said or indicated of them in the New Testament, and could go back nearer to the foundations of the whole matter. Serious and intelligent Catholics can do for their single selves the same thing still; with 25
them, the essentials of religion are much what they are with a pious Protestant; they can hold this or that accretion very cheap, and talk of it very lightly. But at the Reformation the mass of the community, in Protestant countries, adopted, in breaking with Rome, this rejection of what was evidently accretion and 30
superstition, and got a freedom and a new point of departure, in subjects of thought the most widely and deeply interesting that are known, which, in Catholic countries, was reserved for the superior few alone. Protestantism had dangers and drawbacks of its own, and its criticism of the Bible was not *the truth* any more 35
than Catholicism's. But by the mere getting rid of an immense baggage of erroneous ideas,—the most evidently unsound part of Catholicism, and felt to be so by the best Catholics themselves,

yet the part the most naturally attractive to the multitude,—the breach with Rome did certainly accomplish, for the nations which became Protestant, a popular education of very considerable value. And this education Catholic countries must also with
5 time go through, though certainly they need not and will not adopt the forms of Protestantism as we now see it. But the very resolve, natural and praiseworthy as it is, to remain Catholics still, to avoid the sectarian dissensions of Protestants, to keep the unity of the spirit and the unity of the faith, creates for Catholic com-
10 munities a great intellectual difficulty. Much that has to be got rid of, and that Protestants, by breaking unity, made a clean sweep of, they cannot get rid of so easily. We see for instance how the Old Catholics, as they are called, rejecting the extravagant papal pretensions admitted by other Catholics, are all the
15 more anxious on that account, are almost nervously anxious, to profess that all the system of Catholic dogma they still embrace, that in this they wish for no change. Yet in this, too, there must and will be great change, whether they wish it or not; the continuance of religion depends upon it, and continue religion will.
20 Protestants, who see the necessity of this change and have themselves advanced some way in it, must surely desire to facilitate it for Catholics. And the change is in the air, all the influences of the time help it; wherever the pressure of the time and of collective human life can make themselves felt, and therefore in all
25 public and national institutions for education, Catholic as well as Protestant, the change works. The one way to prevent or adjourn its working, is to keep education what is called a hole-and-corner affair, cut off from the public life of the nation and the main current of its thoughts, in the hands of a clique who have
30 been thus narrowly educated themselves. And this is precisely what we are doing in Ireland by refusing to institute Catholic education publicly. We keep it a hole-and-corner thing, with its teachers picked by the Catholic bishops, and neither of public appointment nor designated by public opinion as eminent men;
35 we prevent all access of the enlarging influences of the time to either teachers or taught.

In short, Roman Catholicism is not *a lie;* it is, like Protestantism itself, an essay in religion, an approximation. But it has two special disadvantages in its load of popular error, and in its Ultra-montanism; and our policy is precisely calculated to maintain and increase both.

Influences of the time! national influences! but these are just what the Roman Catholic hierarchy are afraid of! In Ireland you would have to negotiate with the Roman Catholic hierarchy the settlement of Roman Catholic education; and they would reject your overtures, and entertain no plan except such as puts education entirely in their hands. This is often said; I disbelieve it altogether. At present, indeed, the Roman Catholic hierarchy know very well that the Government cannot seriously negotiate with them, because it is controlled by popular prejudice and unreason; therefore any parleyings are a mere game of brag, in which there is nothing sincere on either side, and in which the Catholic bishops may freely advance pretensions the most exorbitant, because they know that nothing reasonable can be done. But clear the unreason away; let it be evident that the Government can and will treat with the Irish Catholics for the only public institution of their religion asked for, the institution of a Catholic university, such as they have a right to, and such as in the Catholic parts of Germany Catholics possess. If the Irish bishops proved impracticable then, at any rate we should have offered what is reasonable, and our conscience would be clear. But would the Irish bishops then be found impracticable, or would Ireland allow them to be so, even if they were so inclined? Certainly a wise and firm negotiator would be needed to deal with them; but that fair terms might be come to if the Government were really free, I have no doubt. And why? Because behind the bishops there is *the people* concerned in this matter, the Irish nation. A wise Government will always regard the nation, and rely on its reasonableness, if its genuine wants and wishes are fairly met, for controlling the unreasonableness or ambition of individuals or corporations. The Roman Catholic priesthood in Ireland is a corporation of which I shall speak with no disrespect, but it is naturally interested in securing its own paramount authority if it can. The Irish nation has no such interest. It is itself a corporation wider than the Roman Catholic priesthood, and including them. It desires such an university as England and Scotland have.

So long as we refuse Ireland this because its religion is *a lie* and *heathenish superstition*, the Roman Catholic priesthood have free play, they may talk as extravagantly of their claims as they like; we have been so utterly unreasonable that we can call forth no reason in the Irish people to control them. But give Ireland the university to which it has a right, and say at the same time: Experience proves that the appointment and dismissal of professors is best in the hands of no corporation less large and public than the nation itself; your professors shall be nominated and removed,[1] not by the bishops, but by a responsible Minister of State acting for the Irish nation itself; and see if Ireland would give you no support, even if the bishops were contrary.

This is not Caesarism, as Archbishop Manning might probably call it; it is something the very opposite of Caesarism. Caesarism is imposing an individual's wishes upon a nation; this is trying to observe a nation's real wants and to follow them. There have been instances of Liberalism, as it calls itself, seeking to impose by enactment its own enlightenment, as it calls it, upon an unwilling and unprepared people; that, too, is a sort of Caesarism, and vain, unspeakably vain are such efforts. Very different is the course which we are suggesting for the English Government in Ireland. This course has for its object not to constrain the people, but to give the people free play. It proceeds on the notion that religion is a matter universally interesting, which follows, like human society itself, a law of progress and growth, and that this law manifests itself in the whole community rather than in any religious hierarchy. The hierarchy may be necessary, may be venerable, may possess great virtues; but it inevitably prizes too high what favours its own authority, its traditions, its discipline. The hierarchy may claim to stand as the proctor and plenipotentiary of the whole community in all that may concern religion; but this is a claim not to be admitted by Governments, Catholic any more than Protestant; and a Catholic Government the English Government in Ireland ought to all intents and purposes to

[1] In the first instance. But the body of professors once formed, and constituting the Academical Senate, might present names to the minister for vacant professorships. With the minister, however, the ultimate responsibility of appointment and dismissal should always rest.

be. The proctor for a nation is the national government. The community will show its real wants most truly and naturally, and secure them best, if it acts for itself, through its proper adequate representative. And the only adequate representative of the whole community is its executive government. While the bishops, if they have the appointment of professors in a Catholic university, will inevitably ask: 'Who will suit the bishops? who will be convenient to the bishops?' the community is interested in asking solely: 'Who is the best and most distinguished Catholic for the chair?' And this is the very question which, if the professors are of State appointment, it is always the Government's duty, and will in general (allowing for human imperfection) be its practice, to ask and to rule itself by.

The truth is, religion is too great a thing, too universal a want, to be well dealt with except nationally. Men in general may think little and feel bluntly; but the chief exercise of their higher thought and emotion which they have, is their religion. Their conduct may be very imperfect, but the chief guide and stay of conduct, so far as it has any at all, is their religion. Nothing, therefore, is of so much importance to them. This is where the philosophical Liberals, who think that religion is a noxious thing and that it must die out, make so great a mistake. Their mistake is so great, indeed, that they themselves cannot persistently keep to it, and we find even the acutest of them contradicting themselves flatly. Mr. Mill tells us, in a passage where he is adopting his father's words, that his father 'looked upon religion as the greatest enemy of morality.' Eighteen pages further on, where he is descanting on the lamentable absence, in English society, of any high and noble standard of conduct, he adds that this absence prevails everywhere '*except among a few of the stricter religionists.*' The little that *is* done for morality is done, then, by morality's greatest enemy! A statesman in any Christian country will be nearer the truth in thinking that religion is morality's greatest friend and that therefore it is mankind's greatest friend. Men want religion, a rule and sanctions of conduct which enlist their feelings; and the actual forms of Christianity are approximations to this. And men want it public and national, to prevent religion, the proper source of all solidity and union, from being precar-

ious and divided. Hence the national churches. The philosopher may talk of over-strong churches, *les églises trop fortes;* he may point out that public institution makes them so, that without this a church will roll from one schism to another—*roulera de*
5   *schisme en schisme*—until it disappears. That may be a charming prospect for the philosopher, but it is just what the bulk of the community want to guard against. 'Church history,' says M. Renan, with a wistful gaze towards that happy time, 'was one tissue of schisms till the Christian Emperors stopped them;' to an
10   ordinary mortal, that is just the merit of Constantine's work.

But some nations, in their attachment to religion, have come to allow the corporation of its priests to govern the whole State. This, as we have seen, is inevitably bad government; the State, the corporation which contains all others, ought not to be gov-
15   erned by one of the corporations which it contains. And in Italy Cavour, to stop this, raised the cry: A free Church in a free State! Liberals have taken this as the last word of the great stateman's philosophy in these matters. It was no such thing. It applied, as Cavour meant it, simply to countries where the
20   Church had hitherto ruled the State; this usurpation it stopped, and to accomplish thus much was a great gain, a great progress. Church and State were left to go each its own road; the clergy's sway of the State was stopped. Cavour did not pause to ask, it was not then the moment for asking, what the Church really was;
25   he took the Church as he found it, the Church represented by the clergy, and he left them perfectly free to manage what are called their own affairs, on condition they left the State to manage itself. But who are interested in the Church, that is, in the society formed of those concerned about religion? The clergy only?
30   No, as we have seen, the whole people. And who are really the Church? Evidently the whole religious society, and not its ministers only. The ministers exist for the sake of the community to which they minister; the clergy are for the people, not the people for the clergy. A national church is what is wanted; but a
35   clergy, as the clergy in Italy now are, disparaged, irritated, and isolated, treated very rigorously as to church property, yet treated as the sole depositaries of religion, give to religion a form narrower and narrower, make it a thing which less and less corre-

sponds to the wants of the nation and of the time, and communicate their own discontent to all with whom they come in contact.

This is what is happening in Italy; this is what comes of taking a catchword, like *a free Church in a free State*, absolutely, instead of using it, as wise men do, only for the precise moment and circumstances which it suits. The Secularist Liberals so little know what religion really is, they so sincerely think that religion if wisely neglected will die out, that they keep on advising any treatment of the difficulty rather than the right one. They can see that religion in Italy is in an unsatisfactory state, and that, on the other hand, the sectarianism of Protestant countries is baneful; but 'in religious matters,' says the *Progresso Educativo*, 'our traditional indifferentism will save us from sectarian divisions.' This traditional indifferentism is not what needs encouraging; a severe judge might say that the traditional indifferentism of the Italians in religion was probably the secret of their traditional impotence. What educated Italians need is to be less indifferent in religion, and to know that it is a matter which concerns themselves also, not the clergy only. M. de Molinari, a writer who is always worth reading, is eloquent in the *Journal des Débats* on the injustice of attempts such as are being now made in Switzerland, attempts by the community to control the organisation of religion to meet their own wants. 'The Church is free,' says he, 'and the State is free;'—and for him the clergy are the Church and the community are the State. 'The Church has the right to change, if it chooses, its symbol or its discipline, without asking leave of cantonal or federal councils, just as the State has the right to change its constitution without asking leave of bishops or clergy.' He forgets that the community, whom these cantonal and federal councils represent, is the Church; that they have religious wants and have formed themselves into a religious society to satisfy them; that the bishops and clergy are but the ministers to the society, and a small fraction of it; and that the whole design of the society is frustrated if the wants of the mass are to be of no account, but the fraction of ministers is to rule everything. As well might he say that the ministers and magistrates in the State have a right to change its constitution, without asking leave of the community. He speaks in this way because he

has no conception of religion as of a real want of the community
which the community have to satisfy: he has not this conception,
and it would be a great embarrassment to him to admit it into his
calculations and to have to adjust things to it. But it is a conception which may be found working, more or less clearly, in the
mind of communities, of nations, wherever we turn; and our age
will have to deal with it.

   In Italy it is beginning to fix the attention of intelligent men,
who a few years ago thought that *a free Church in a free State*
was all they wanted. Signor Bonghi, one of these persons, made
last year a remarkable speech on the subject in the Italian Parliament, and has since published it. He blames the suppression of
the theological faculties in the national universities; he says that
the clergy is more and more being cut off from the life and
thought of the nation, and that this is not good for the clergy,
not good for religion, not good for the nation. A national church
in harmony with the community's wants is what he drives at.
But above all does this conception manifest itself in the serious
Germanic, or partly Germanic nations, where the sense that religion is a genuine concern of the community is native, and
where the indifferentism of philosophical Liberalism is a plant of
artificial growth. What is passing in Switzerland and Germany
shews the desire to give effect to the idea of national churches, to
the idea that religion is an affair of the community, against the
difficulties which the peculiar constitution and relations of the
Roman Catholic clergy throw in the way of its working. The
governments are not trying to impose a religion of their own,
some modern enlightenment or other congenial to governments
and discouraging to religion; they are, at bottom, trying to give
effect to this sincere desire of the community. In one place there
is some new dogma which the community do not want to receive, but which the clergy want to force upon them; in another
place there is some religious reform for which the community
are ripe, but to which the clergy oppose a stubborn resistance; in
another, there is some cherished national aim of the community
on which the clergy frown. And the clergy retain, from the
times when they were the Church and the Church ruled the
State, all sorts of means of thwarting and punishing the commu-

nity which sticks to its own view and does not comply with theirs. To remove all these means, to make the community the Church, and self-ruling; above all, to transform the clergy itself, to bring the clergy, a body in many respects so excellent, into closer sympathy with the community by bringing it to share 5 the community's best culture,—this, I believe, is in general the sincere intention of the religious policy of the German and Swiss governments, although in particular points they may have acted harshly and unadvisedly. The community, in Switzerland and Germany, wishes religion a public institution and yet a thing 10 which may grow according to their needs and be administered according to their needs. This is what Prince Bismarck has to meet; it is a wish which in modern communities will more and more make itself felt, and which governments will have to meet more and more. And neither the wish nor the trying to meet it is 15 Caesarism.

Well, but when we English praise Prince Bismarck for what he is doing and sympathise with him, we pass judgment on ourselves. We have not clean hands in the matter for which we praise him. He is doing what our mind has not been clear enough, 20 our prejudices not enough under the control of our reason, to put us in a position for doing. Some people say he is following our Tudor legislation. If he followed our Tudor legislation, he would establish Protestantism throughout Prussia, and pass an act of uniformity to make Catholics conform to it. If he fol- 25 lowed the policy of our modern Liberals, he would withhold from the Catholic community any public institution of their religion or any Catholic university to send either their laymen or clergy to. He does nothing of the kind. He is following a course which has its difficulties, indeed, but which approves itself to 30 reason. Our modern Liberals, on the other hand, are for governing Ireland in obedience to a maxim which turns out, when we examine it, to be a falsism; current enough, certainly, but unsound; trite and false;—the maxim that a modern State must not endow religion in any shape. So that really the right thing to 35 do is not to go about saying: 'The Liberal party has emphatically condemned religious endowment, the Protestants of Great Britain are implacably hostile to the endowment of Catholicism in

any shape or form,' if in this both the Liberal party and the Protestants of Great Britain are proceeding upon a falsism. For
Ireland can never be successfully governed so long as, in a matter
which deeply interests her and in which her wishes differ from
ours, we proceed, however resolutely, upon a falsism. The right
thing is rather, if we believe in the power of reason, and that the
Liberal party and the Protestants of Great Britain have faculties
for being persuaded of reason, to labour diligently to convince
them that it is a falsism they are going upon. And the Liberal
party so much values itself upon its intelligence that with them
we ought to begin, and show them, as we have been trying to
show them here, that this favourite old stock maxim of theirs:
'The State (that is, the nation in its collective and corporate character) is of no religion,' is quite unsound. In exchange for it we
ought to solicit them, with a persistency which never tires, to
take a better: 'It is false to say the State is of no religion; *the
State is of the religion of all its citizens without the fanaticism
of any of them.*'

Surely for getting this kind of return made upon our minds
and maxims there could not well be a more favourable moment
than the present! The country is profoundly Liberal; that is, it is
profoundly convinced that a great course of growth and transformation lies before it; and whoever should try to make it think
that this is not so, but that all must stay where it is, would soon
find out his mistake. Still the actual policy and principles of our
Liberal friends do seem, if we may judge by the recent elections,
to be profoundly uninteresting to the country, or at any rate, to
have lost their charm for it. So instead of being angry with us
for having long said that their performance was not quite what
they supposed, that their doings wanted more thought to direct
them, that for the religious difficulty in Ireland the abolition
of the Protestant establishment by the power of our Dissenters'
antipathy to State churches was really no solution, that for the
difficulties arising out of the way in which the land in England
is held, bills like the Real Estates Intestacy Bill were no solution;
that even marriage with one's deceased wife's sister was not a
staff to help one far on one's road;—instead of being angry with
us for saying this, and declaring still, like the *Daily Telegraph*,

that 'there is no such thing as conquering the principles of which Mr. Gladstone has been these five years the triumphant exponent,' surely our Liberal friends would do well to consider whether there may not have been some truth in what we said, and to use the leisure they seem likely to have for reviewing their ideas a little.

The Secularist Radicals, especially the younger and more ardent among them, who have been brought up to think that religion is dying out, and who are all of them, perhaps, more or less in the same case as Hume, who confessed that he had never read the New Testament with attention, might well improve their present opportunity by acquainting themselves a little with the nature and history of religion, and to this end studying, among other books, the Bible. But the benefit which we may expect from the Secularist Radicals, during the present lull, thus revising their ideas, is as nothing compared to what may accrue from the Dissenters performing the same process. It is not too much to say that the chief hope of progress, in the next five years, for true Liberalism, lies in the conversion of the Protestant Dissenters; or to speak more correctly, as well as, perhaps, more agreeably, in their *nationalisation.*

They can hardly be ignorant that a very strong light has been turned lately upon them and upon their proceedings, and that the general impression left with the public has not been favourable. They have offended, any clear-sighted looker-on can see that they have offended, what Burke well calls 'the ancient and inbred integrity, piety, good nature and good humour of the English people.' We shall not affect to regret this, for we have long said, and the Dissenters have been very angry with us for saying, that they are an obstacle to civilisation. They are indeed; our greatest. But we say this so resolutely because we see so clearly of what good elements their body is composed; how signal an example they furnish of a false tendency given to admirable forces and of the grievous waste of power caused thereby. We have never forgotten, too, although perhaps we have never said with emphasis enough that we remembered it, how many of them have inherited their position of conflict with the national church, not made it for themselves. Such persons are like men

who have inherited, not originated, a vexatious lawsuit; a wise man, however, when he has inherited such a lawsuit, does not persist in it because he has inherited it, but gets out of it as fast as possible. That it is a vexatious lawsuit, a suit causing a fatal
5   exasperation of temper, with a vain and most lamentable waste of life and power, in which the Protestant Dissenters are engaged, is more and more forcing itself upon the mind both of the public in general, and of religious people in particular. As far as religion is concerned, that course cannot be a wholesome one
10   which has produced a sort of temper so opposite to peace, that even in Barrow's time the great evangelical injunction to *follow peace* had among the Nonconformists come, as he remarked, to be 'by many esteemed an impossiblity, by others a wonder, by some a crime;' a temper which has grown now to be more in-
15   tense and fiercer than ever. That course cannot, moreover, be for the advancement of religion, which ends by setting up as its great mark an object in no way religious: religious equality. The cry, the watchword of the modern Dissenters, the eternal burden of Mr. Miall's song, is *religious equality*. But the evangel-
20   ical watchword is religious submission; *submitting yourselves one to another in the fear of God.* Nay, and the very Pope, the representative of the religion which is, as the *Nonconformist's* correspondent says, 'heathenish superstition,' has at least the grace to call himself by predilection the servant of servants,
25   *servus servorum.*

        This, I say, so far as religion is concerned, is clear. The general public, however, is getting indisposed to the Dissenters not on grounds of religion only; its good sense and reflection are beginning to tell against them too. It has begun to dawn upon the
30   general public, the Dissenters being of late perpetually before it with the cry that their conscience constrains them to do this and will not let them do the other, it has dawned upon the public, the question having become thus practical, that after all one must ask, where the public action is concerned in what a man's
35   conscience commands or forbids, whether the conscience commands or forbids *reasonably*. And it has come very much to the conclusion that a man's conscience commanding himself is reasonable, but that his conscience forbidding his neighbours is un-

reasonable. It is agreed that a man is not to be made to say a thing is right if he does not think so; when his conscience protests against this, it protests reasonably. A man is free to say he thinks monarchy wrong, he is free to say he thinks an Established Church wrong; he is not to be compelled to accept the ministrations of bishops, he is not to be compelled, even, to take off his hat to the Queen. Positive approval and adherence are matters of conscience. But the majority wish for a monarchy, the majority wish for the public institution of religion known as the Church of England. Public funds, we will suppose, are applied directly or indirectly to the support of both. Well, but a man objects; he feels his conscience violated by his contributing to maintain an institution which he thinks wrong. Well, now, what the public are more and more coming to perceive is that this objection is *not* reasonable, and that the proper answer to it, instead of turning up one's eyes and saying 'How very grievous!' is: 'Then you *ought not* to feel your conscience violated by it.' No one has a right to oblige you to say you approve of monarchy if you disapprove of it, or to conform to the Church of England if you differ from it; but you, on the other hand, have no right to prevent the majority from instituting monarchy or instituting a national church, and providing for them directly or indirectly, partially or entirely, out of public funds. To profess an opinion or adopt a practice for *oneself*, can reasonably be said to engage one's conscience; to pay a tax laid by the majority for an institution which the opinion or practice of the majority leads them to adopt, can engage the conscience only if what is instituted is plainly flagitious. Violent men easily allege, no doubt, that all opinion or practice at variance with their own is flagitious and pernicious. But here, again, the public at large is the judge, and more and more assumes the right of judging, whether this allegation is fairly sustainable. Direct support Dissenters have to give to the Church of England none; but a school rate, suppose, may in some cases make them give an indirect support to it. Well, for this to engage their conscience, the church-school and what it teaches must be something plainly flagitious. Many violent Nonconformists have alleged in the past and do allege in the present against the Church of England, that its opinion and prac-

tice are plainly flagitious and pernicious; but this allegation all reasonable people, and the public at large also, feel to be unsustainable. Pretensions that for their support require this allegation to be true, are felt, therefore, to be unsustainable also. And a dis-
5 satisfaction and impatience, founded on an increasingly clear perception of all this, is beginning to pervade the nation at large in respect to the action of the Dissenters.

No doubt the Dissenters will be slow to see this themselves. They will be slow to yield, they are not apt at yielding. Their
10 first thought, their first effort, will be to unite the discomfited Liberal party again in a programme of their own dictating. They have settled ideas, the Liberal party has not; they know clearly what they seek, the Liberal party does not. Political Dissent will for a time become more prominently political than ever, and
15 contend more fiercely; but the more it does this, the more will its inherent faults make themselves felt, the more will its unattractiveness, its bitter narrowness, its essential unreligiousness become apparent, and the more dissatisfied will the public grow with it. Mr. Miall does not charm; but the lead will pass from
20 Mr. Miall to men like Mr. Leatham, a spokesman whom really, when one hears or reads some of his deliverances, a moralist might be almost tempted to call the drunken Helot of Protestant Dissent, an example set up to show the temper and tone Dissent, or the championing of it, at last leads to. Or there will be efforts
25 like Mr. Chamberlain's to win the working men to the cause of Nonconformity by making their jealousy of the Church, as a Conservative institution, combine its force with the Dissenters' jealousy of the Church as a religious rival; such efforts will have a certain measure of success, and the confluence of two jealousies
30 may produce a considerable stream. But Dissent is a *religious* cause: it has to stand or fall as a religious cause. And the more partisans it has like Mr. Leatham or Mr. Chamberlain, the more these partisans take the lead, the more their efforts are crowned with success, so much the more will Dissent as a religious cause
35 be discredited, so much the more will it lose ground in the esteem of the nation. More and more it will shock the 'integrity, piety, good nature and good humour of the English people.' It will lose

ground in the attachment of its own best men for the same reason. On all its best men the dissatisfaction with its temper will operate; on the younger amongst them, the growing modern perception that all the forms of Christianity are approximative only, that one's own sect has not got the truth, *the gospel*, while all other religious communities are in error, will act in concert with the other ground for dissatisfaction. Already this is manifest, already these causes of dissolution are beginning to act. Twenty years hence, Dissent will have no such group to present as the group of its best men is now; these will have passed away, and the younger men of like worth will be elsewhere. Mr. Miall seems making preparation to retire, and he will retire at the right time, for the part which he has played will not be possible for a man of his good qualities in the future. May he, and Mr. Carvell Williams, and the rest of these men of war, who have talked so much of religion, who have really cared for it so much, and have stood so much in its way, may they in the evening of their day, before they close their eyes for ever, be allowed at least one short glimpse of what *the way of peace* really is!

Yes, the cause of the Nonconformists is destined to suffer eclipse, not to be the rallying-point of the Liberalism of the future. And religious history's final sentence on this cause, whatever praise political history may bestow on it, will be a severe one. It will say of it, even after all its advocates have been heard and everything has been weighed which tells in its favour, that in temper and contentiousness it began, by temper and contentiousness it perished. It was originally embraced by the strong and serious middle part of a somewhat hard, a high-tempered, and a self-willed nation. Of these qualities of the nation, its strong middle part had naturally most; and these qualities are not religious. They have given to Nonconformity a fatal ply; so far one must speak unfavourably. Then, however, comes the worthier side of Nonconformity into view. Seriousness and strenuousness and manliness and uprightness *are* religious; and the English Nonconformists have been eminent for them, and they can never be lost. They will avail to give their possessors a victory for good, though not for evil. They will not give them a victory for

sectarianism over the national church, but they will enable them
to transform the national church as it needs transformation. All
the faults of the Church come not from its being a public institution, but from its not being enough a public institution. There
is, even at present, far more of popular sentiment and sympathy
among the clergy than is commonly supposed; but all the faults
with which the Church is now reproached, its close dependence
upon the landed gentry, its sale of livings, its disregard, in the
choice of incumbents, of the wants and wishes of the people, its
retention of worthless ministers, its over-ritualism and fantasticality, all are to be remedied not by making the Church a private institution but a more truly public one, and by pouring into
it that large portion of the middle class, with its popular sentiment and its robust energy, which the Dissenters constitute. If
the Church has effeminacy, they are the people to do it good; if it
has silliness and formalism, they are the people to cure it. A
majority of the nation desire a public institution of religion and a
national church; how great a majority we cannot tell, for the Dissenters have hindered our ascertaining, but I believe an immense
majority. Not to keep up a jealous and angry struggle against
this wish, but to adopt it, to impress their stamp upon the national church, and to aid in developing that religion of the future, which, as all living things follow the law of growth and
change, will not in a great and living people be the religion of
to-day, is the new aim to which, in the next five years, the Dissenters should have their thoughts and wishes turned.

But in this and all the matters most important to us, progress,
at the point where our nation now stands, depends on our getting just, clear, well-ordered thoughts about them, and setting
at defiance clap-trap and catchwords. We have seen that Ireland
has a right to a Catholic university, and that it is really expedient
she should have one. We cannot expect her to be satisfied, any
quantity of agitation for Home Rule is justified, so long as we
refuse one to her. But she is governed in deference to the British
Protestant's clap-trap and catchwords, which find their expression in such sayings as that 'the Protestants of Great Britain are
implacably hostile to concurrent endowment in any shape or

form;' and if she is to be governed aright, it can only be in defiance of such clap-trap. But for an active politician to go counter
to clap-trap is, as we have seen, hard; and, indeed, by the nature
of things it must be hard. And therefore it is that we rejoice to
see a moment of lull in their active political life come to so many   5
of our Liberal friends, because they thus escape from great
temptation, and are set free to use their intelligence. For the active politician can hardly get on without deferring to clap-trap
and even employing it. Nay, as Socrates amusingly said, the man
who defers to clap-trap and the man who uses his intelligence   10
are, when they meet in the struggle of active politics, like a doctor and a confectioner competing for the suffrages of a constituency of schoolboys; the confectioner has nearly every point in
his favour. The confectioner deals in all that the constituency
like; the doctor is a man who hurts them, and makes them leave   15
off what they like and take what is disagreeable. And accordingly
the temptation, in dealing with the public and with the trade of
active politics, the temptation to be a confectioner is extremely
strong, and we see that almost all our leading newspapers and
leading politicians do in fact yield to it. What our policy towards   20
Irish Catholicism has, in deference to British Protestant feeling,
really been, we now know; but the *Daily Telegraph* calls it 'a
great and genial policy of conciliation,' and the *Times* says that
'English Liberals demanded, in 1868, that the grievances which
alienated the Irish Catholic should be removed.' This is to speak   25
like a confectioner; for we know, and the Irish, alas! know, that
the words 'so far as this was compatible with Protestant prejudice, and could be made to fall in with Nonconformist ends,' require to be understood. And Mr. Lowe is even bolder than the
newspapers, and declares that by their Irish policy the ministry   30
resolved 'to knit the hearts of the empire into one harmonious
concord,' and knitted they were accordingly. What could be
more fitted to delight the public? But this is really to speak like a
confectioner; and just as Mr. Lowe calls Mr. Disraeli a teratologist, so one may call Mr. Lowe, in his turn, a confectioner, a   35
brilliant and accomplished confectioner. Only the confectioner
is not at this moment what we most require. Our wants are the

same as those which made Socrates, again, say, that though himself no confectioner and taking quite another line from the active politicians round him, indeed, just because of this, he, or any
man who held the same course as to current clap-trap that he did,
5   was 'the only true politician of men now living.'

Roman Catholics and the State

To the Editor of the PALL MALL GAZETTE.

SIR,—An assertion made in the preface to my account of German Higher Schools, that "before Prussia compelled Roman Catholic students to attend university instruction she gave them Roman Catholic universities to go to," has met and still meets with so much denial, and the matter at issue is so important, that I will ask you to afford me space for an explanation.

In my preface I was contrasting the position of the university student in Ireland, if he is a Roman Catholic, with the position of university students in Prussia and Great Britain. I remarked that, whereas in England and Scotland Protestants had public universities where religion and philosophy and history were taught by Protestants, and in Prussia both Catholics and Protestants had public universities where these matters were taught by professors of the student's own confession, in Ireland Catholics had no such university, and we would not let them have one. Writing for the general reader, I applied the term Catholic or Protestant to universities as he himself, I thought, would be likely to apply it; meaning by a Roman Catholic university not a university where no Protestant might enter, and where even botany and mineralogy must be taught by Catholics, but a university where the Catholic student would find religion taught by Catholics, and matters where religion is interested, such as philosophy and history, taught by Catholics too. In speaking of a university as Protestant I meant the same limitation to be understood.

Again and again I find it triumphantly urged in answer to the remark in my preface, "Oh no, you are quite wrong; the Prussian universities are undenominational." To use our English phraseology, they are undenominational in this sense—that they have

concurrent endowment. Where there are both Catholics and
Protestants, there are both Catholic and Protestant professors of
theology, and both Catholic and Protestant professors of philosophy and history. At Bonn, for instance, this is the case. I will
relate an incident which happened in the faculty of philosophy
at Bonn. The Senatus Academicus, as is well known, nominates
professors; the Government appoints them. At Bonn the Academical Senate nominated a Catholic professor of philosophy
who was himself a Catholic certainly, but who was married to a
Protestant, and who allowed his wife to bring up their children as
Protestants. The Minister pointed out to the Senate that this
was a cause of objection to their nominee; that a Catholic professor of philosophy who was so lax a Catholic that he suffered
his children to be brought up as Protestants did not give the guarantees which Catholic parents had a right to expect. And the
nomination was dropped.

The universities of Bonn and Breslau have thus a double theological faculty and double professorships in philosophy and history. Münster and Braunsberg have in theology a Catholic faculty only, and in philosophy and history Catholic professors
only. It is true in Germany the name of university is reserved to
those places of instruction which have all four faculties of theology, arts, law, and medicine, and supply instruction in all of
them. Münster and Braunsberg are not, therefore, called universities. But their instruction in the two faculties which they have
counts for just the same as university instruction, and in these
two faculties they confer degrees just as the full universities do.
Münster and Braunsberg are, in short, exactly what we in England—who by university studies mean in general theology and
arts, and who give the name of university to places like Durham,
which have not professors for all the four faculties of theology,
arts, law, and medicine—should call sheer Catholic universities.

I had a right, then, to say, speaking to English people, that before Prussia compelled Roman Catholic students to attend university instruction, she gave them Roman Catholic universities
to go to.

I had also a right, I think, to say that while we would not
give the Irish a public university where religion, philosophy, and

history were taught by Catholics, we English and Scotch had for ourselves public universities where religion, philosophy, and history are taught by Protestants. This is indisputably so as to religion; the only question can be whether it is so too as to philosophy and history. Can any one think that a Catholic could be appointed to a chair of history or philosophy at Oxford or Cambridge? No one. But a distinguished Scotch Liberal—eminent alike by rank, office, talents, and character—assured me that as to all chairs of philosophy and history the Scotch universities were now perfectly un-Protestantized. In law, no doubt; but in fact? In fact, they remain exclusively Protestant. My Scotch informant himself supplied me with the best possible proof of it. For when I went on to ask him, "Would it be possible, then, for the Government to appoint an eminent Catholic metaphysician —Father Dalgairns, for instance—to a chair of metaphysics in Scotland?" my informant answered instantly, "Of course not; it would be a national outrage." But really the Irish Catholics could hardly desire for themselves anything more agreeable than a national Irish university where it should be a national outrage for the Government to appoint Mr. Bain, or any one except a Catholic, to a chair of mental philosophy.

It is most needful to insist on the essential difference between Germany and ourselves in the treatment of Roman Catholicism, and to suffer no convenient clouding or suppressing of the truth, no self-deception. The difference itself, indeed, is undeniable; the great need is to mark plainly wherein the difference consists. We like to flatter ourselves that it consists in Protestant England's dispassionate equitableness towards an adversary whom Protestant Germany persecutes with passionate unfairness. Says the *Times*:—"It is precisely because we dissent so strongly from all that is especially characteristic of Rome, that we would be careful to allow to Roman Catholics the same measures of freedom that we should claim for ourselves if they were masters of a national Government to which we were subject." What could be more beautiful? The more we differ from the Roman Catholics the more scrupulous we are to be perfectly just to them! And it is certain that the Prussian Government are dealing with Roman Catholicism very stringently, and that their proceedings

are regarded with considerable dissatisfaction in England. What
is the real cause of this dissatisfaction? A dislike of any interference with conscience, a sympathy for the weaker party sternly
pressed by a powerful adversary, a jealousy of all high-handed
5   proceedings on the part of the State, a distaste for that crudeness
and unattractiveness which there really is in the Prussians and in
their way of doing things? All these go for something in producing a coldness here towards Prince Bismarck's policy, but they
are not the real cause of the coldness. The real cause is the aver-
10   sion of the Protestant public in Great Britain to that recognition
of Catholicism which is implied in the State's dealing with it,
making terms with it, intervening in its appointments, in its education. For all this is treating Catholicism as a religion serious and
permanent; but the Protestant public of Great Britain wishes to
15   regard Catholicism as an idolatry which we cannot stamp out indeed, but with which we must have no dealings, and which will
sooner or later die of its own abominations.

    On the details of Prince Bismarck's treatment of Roman Cathol-
icism I pass no judgment. A foreigner, as I have said elsewhere,
20   cannot well judge them. Some of them may exhibit harshness
and passion, want of temper and want of wisdom. I will not pronounce that they do or do not, but let us even suppose that they
do. That may well prove a hindrance to Prince Bismarck's succeeding, but it does not affect the character of his general scope.
25   His general scope is determined by a conception of Catholicism
far more statesmanlike, far more just, far more appreciative of
the life and virtue in Catholicism itself, than any which obtains
in this country. It proceeds on a conception of it as a great natural fact, as a serious religion with a profound basis in history and
30   in the habits and workings of man's spirit, existing over a large
part of the world, and certainly destined still to exist for a great
while to come. Such is the conception—a conception as unlike
that of the Protestant public of Great Britain as possible. And the
general scope of policy determined by this conception is, to *na-*
35   *tionalize* the religion in question, to bring it into contact with
public, national influences, that to the thought and growth of
the whole nation it may not be a stranger. Therefore its education must not be in the hands of an unnational or anti-national
clique; the appointment of its officers must not be in the hands of

an unnational or anti-national clique. But its hierarchy at present happens to be in great measure an unnational or anti-national clique; therefore it vehemently resists a change which menaces its own constitution and rule. If the British public would dismiss from their minds, as the mere fringes of the matter, all discussion of the incidents of Prince Bismarck's policy, and would get clearly before their minds this its general scope, they would understand why, in spite of all that our daily and weekly political lecturers may preach on the other side, in spite of the faults of the Prussian character and of Prince Bismarck himself, his policy will very likely in the end succeed. This they would understand; and they would get into their minds, moreover, by means of the true view of his policy, just the very ideas which it is good for them to meditate as regards Ireland.

Irish Catholicism is a natural, existing fact, and certain to exist for a great while to come. It is not going to disappear because it is not so enlightened as the religion of the *Fortnightly Review*, or so pure as the religion of Messrs. Moody and Sankey. For a very long while yet, our only course will be to take Irish Catholicism as a fact and to do the best we can with it;—now, the worst we can do with it is to shut it up in itself. True, Catholicism has political inconveniences in its Ultramontanism, social inconveniences in its confessional, intellectual and moral inconveniences in its denial of the necessity and the duty of private judgment. All these incidents of the religion of Catholics, however, Catholics have accepted because their religion itself was so attractive to them. They will not drop these things because we dislike them; and most certainly they will not drop their religion to get rid of these things. They will get rid of them, or of what is bad in them, not by a sudden change, not by a wholesale conversion, not by ceasing to profess themselves Catholics, but only by the slow advance of culture in the body of the Catholic community itself, only by the general widening and clearing of European thought being felt through this community. This is a truth which statesmen cannot lay too much to heart; and it is the gravest possible condemnation of our policy towards Catholicism in Ireland.

For what are we doing in Ireland? Forcing Catholicism to remain shut up in itself because we will not treat it as a national

religion. And why will we not? In deference to two fanaticisms:
a Secularist fanaticism which holds religion in general to be noxious, and, above all, a Protestant fanaticism which holds Catholicism to be idolatry. But Catholicism will not disappear, and at
5   this rate it can never improve. Mr. Lyon Playfair made an excellent speech the other day on the defects of the Irish schools.
The *Times* had an excellent article remonstrating against these
schools being treated with a slack indulgence unknown in England; against grants without examination, and teachers without
10   certificates. But Mr. O'Reilly says that what the Irish ask for is
training schools as in England and Scotland, Catholic training
schools as there are Protestant training schools here, and aided
on just the same terms as the English and Scotch training schools;
then we shall be quite ready, says Mr. O'Reilly, to forego grants
15   without examination, and teachers without certificates. And
really there is no answering Mr. O'Reilly, supposing the facts to
be as they are stated; the Irish have a right to training schools like
those in England and Scotland, and it is our fanaticism which
retards education in Ireland by refusing them.

20   It is the same thing as to universities for Irish Catholics. Mr.
Gladstone's Irish University Bill is spoken of as the extreme of
concession ever to be offered by England to Irish Catholicism.
Yet that famous bill was in truth—if one may say so without
disrespect to Mr. Gladstone, who had to propound his Univer-
25   sity Bill under the eye of his Secularist and Nonconformist supporters—simply ridiculous. Religion, moral philosophy, and
modern history are probably the three matters of instruction in
which the bulk of mankind take most interest; and this precious
university was to give no instruction in any one of them! The
30   Irish have a right to a university with a Catholic faculty of theology, and with Catholic professors of philosophy and history.
By refusing them to Ireland our fanaticism does not tend to make
one Catholic the less, it only tends to make Irish Catholicism
unprogressive.

35   So long as we refuse them, Sir, I persist, instead of congratu-
lating myself with the *Times* on our admirably fair and wise
treatment of Catholicism—I persist in thinking that, where we
are put to the test, our treatment of Catholicism is dictated solely

by that old friend of ours—strong, steady, honest, well-disposed, but withal somewhat narrow-minded and hard-natured—the British Philistine.—Your obedient servant,

MATTHEW ARNOLD

April 6.

God and the Bible

A Sequel to
'Literature and Dogma'

'Im Princip, das Bestehende zu erhalten, Revolutionären vorzubeugen, stimme ich ganz mit den Monarchisten überein; nur nicht in den Mitteln dazu. Sie nämlich rufen die Dummheit und die Finsternis zu Hülfe, ich den Verstand und das Licht.' GOETHE.

'In the principle, to preserve what exists, to hinder revolutionists from having their way, I am quite at one with the monarchists; only not in the means thereto. That is to say, they call in stupidity and darkness to aid, I reason and light.'

God and the Bible

Introduction

Modern criticism will not allow us to rely either on the Epistle of Polycarp, or on the narrative of his martyrdom, as certainly authentic. Nevertheless, a saying from the latter we will venture to use. As Polycarp stood in the amphitheatre at Smyrna just before his martyrdom, with the heathen multitude around crying out against him as an atheistical innovator, the Roman proconsul, pitying his great age, begged him to pronounce the formulas which expressed adherence to the popular religion, and abhorrence of Christianity. 'Swear,' said he, 'by the fortune of Caesar; cry: *Away with the atheists!*' Whereupon Polycarp, says the letter of the Church of Smyrna which relates his martyrdom, looking round with a severe countenance upon the heathen clamourers who filled the amphitheatre, pointed to these with his hand, and with a groan, and casting up his eyes to heaven, cried: 'Away with the atheists!' This did not give satisfaction, and Polycarp was burnt.

Yet so completely has the so-called atheism of Polycarp prevailed, that we are almost puzzled at finding it called atheism by the popular religion of its own day, by the worshippers of Jupiter and Cybele, of Rome and the fortune of Caesar. On the other hand, Polycarp's retort upon these worshippers, his flinging back upon their religion the name of atheism, seems to us the most natural thing in the world. And so most certainly will it be with the popular religion of our own day. Confident in its traditions and imaginations, this religion now cries out against those who pronounce them vain: *Away with the atheists!* just as the heathen populace of Asia cried out against Polycarp. With a groan, and casting up his eyes to heaven, the critic thus execrated might well, like Polycarp, point to his execrators and retort: *Away with the*

atheists! So deeply unsound is the mass of traditions and imaginations of which popular religion consists, so gross a distortion
and caricature of the true religion does it present, that future
times will hardly comprehend its audacity in calling those who
5 abjure it atheists; while its being stigmatised itself with this hard
name will astonish no one.

Let us who criticise the popular theology, however, show a
moderation of which our adversaries do not always set us the
example. [We may not indeed, like the *Times* newspaper, call
10 this established theology 'an English, a Protestant, and a reasonable religion.' But let us never forget that it professes, as we ourselves have again and again repeated, along with all its pseudo-
science and all its popular legend, the main doctrine of the Bible:
the pre-eminence of righteousness and the method and secret of
15 Jesus;—professes it and in some degree uses it. Let us never forget that our quarrel with its pseudo-science and its popular legend is because they endanger this main doctrine, this saving truth,
on which our popular religion has in some degree hold. Let us
gladly admit that the advance of time and of knowledge has even
20 begun to shake the overweening confidence of our established
theology in its own pseudo-science and popular legend, and that
its replies to the impugner of them, if still too apt to be intemper-
ate, are yet fast freeing themselves from the insolence and invec-
tive of thirty years ago. The strictures on *Literature and Dogma*
25 have certainly not been mild; yet, on the whole, their moderation has surprised me. An exception ought to be made, perhaps,
for the *Dublin Review*. But an Englishman should always ask
himself with shame: If Irish Catholicism is provincial in its violence and virulence, whose fault is it?]
30   To retort[, therefore,] upon those who have attacked *Literature and Dogma* as anti-christian and anti-religious, to recapitu-
late their hard words and to give them hard words in return, is
not our intention. It is necessary, indeed, to mark firmly and
clearly that from our criticism of their theology,—that grotesque
35 mixture, as we have called it, of learned pseudo-science with
popular legend,—their outcry does not make us go back one
inch; that it is they who in our judgment owe an apology to
Christianity and to religion, not we. But when this has once been

clearly marked, our business with our assailants is over. Our business is henceforth not with them, but with those for whose sake *Literature and Dogma* was written.

These alone we have in view in noticing criticisms of that book, whatever may be their nature. And there have appeared criticisms of it very different from those blind and angry denunciations of which we have spoken, those denunciations from the point of view of popular and official theology. There have been criticisms deserving our high respect and our careful attention. But nothing is more tiresome to the public than an author's vindication of his work and reply to his critics, however worthy they may be of attention; and certainly nothing of this kind should we in most cases think of proposing to ourselves. To weigh what his critics say, to profit by it to the best of his judgment, and either to amend or to maintain his work according to his final conviction, is the right course for a criticised author to follow. It is in general all that the public want him to do, and all that we should wish to do ourselves.

But let us recall the object for which *Literature and Dogma* was written. It was written in order to win [access for the Bible and its religion to many of those who now neglect them. It was written to restore the use of the Bible to those (and they are an increasing number) whom the popular theology with its proof from miracles, and the learned theology with its proof from metaphysics, so dissatisfy and repel that they are tempted to throw aside the Bible altogether. It was written to convince such persons that they cannot do without the Bible, that the popular theology and the learned theology are alike formed upon a profound misapprehension of the Bible; but that, when the Bible is read aright, it will be found to deal, in a way incomparable for effectiveness, with facts of experience most pressing, momentous, and real.

[This conviction of the indispensableness of the Bible, which in *Literature and Dogma* we sought to impart to others, we ourselves had and have. In England the conviction has long prevailed and been nearly universal, but there are now signs of its being shaken. To maintain it, to make it continue to prevail, to hinder its giving way and dying out, is our object. It seemed to us that

the great danger to the Bible at present arises from the assumption that whoever receives the Bible must set out with admitting
certain propositions, such as the existence of a personal God, the
consubstantiality of Jesus Christ with this personal God who is
5   his Father, the miraculous birth, resurrection, and ascension of
Jesus. Now, the nature of these propositions is such that we cannot possibly verify them. It seemed to us that with the unin-
structed or ill-instructed masses of our people this obstacle to
the Bible's reception, which for a long time was an obstacle not
10 existent for them at all, is, as things now stand, an obstacle almost
insuperable. Therefore we sought and seek to show that the Bible
is really based upon propositions which all can verify.

[It is true, some deny that there exists the danger which we
apprehend for the Bible. The masses, say they, the working men,
15 are not hard-headed, reasoning people at all; they are eminently
people led by their feelings and passions. Yes, led by their feelings and passions towards what flatters their feelings and passions; but religion and the Bible do not flatter their feelings and
passions. Towards religion and the Bible, which fill them with
20 superstitious awe no longer, but which claim to check and control their feelings and passions, they have plenty of suspiciousness, incredulity, hard-headed common-sense to oppose. At most,
they will make religion into something which flatters their feelings and passions. Thus one hears from those who know them,
25 and one can see from their newspapers, that many of them have
embraced a kind of revolutionary Deism, hostile to all which is
old, traditional, established and secure; favourable to a clean
sweep and a new stage, with the classes now in the background
for chief actors. There is much to make the political Dissenters,
30 on their part, fall in with this sort of religion, inasmuch as many
of its ends are theirs too. And we see that they do incline to fall
in with it, and to try to use it.

[A revolutionary Deism of this kind may grow, not improbably, into a considerable power amongst us; so habituated are
35 the people of this country to religion, and so strongly does their
being vibrate to its language and excitements. The God of this
religion of the future will be still a magnified and non-natural
man indeed, but by no means the magnified and non-natural man

of our religion as now current. He may be best conceived, perhaps, as a kind of tribal God of the Birmingham League. Not
by any means a *Dieu des Bonnes Gens*, like the God of Béranger,
a God who favours garrets, grisettes, gaiety, and champagne;
but a *Dieu des Quatre Libertés*, the God of Free Trade, Free   5
Church, Free Labour, and Free Land;—with a new programme,
therefore, and with Birmingham for his earthly headquarters
instead of Shiloh or Jerusalem, but with the old turn still preserved for commanding to hew Agag in pieces, and with much
even of the Biblical worship and language still retained; Mr. Jesse   10
Collings and Mr. Chamberlain dancing before his ark, and Mr.
Dale and Mr. George Dawson, in the Birmingham Town Hall,
offering up prayer and sacrifice. All this is possible, and perhaps
not improbable.

[But a revolutionary Deism, based on the supposed rights of   15
man and ardently destructive, is not the real religion of the Bible.
It will fail; and its failure, the failure of that attempted application of the Bible which made the Bible flatter their feelings and
passions, will discredit the Bible with the masses more than ever,
will make them more than ever confront it with a suspiciousness,   20
a hard incredulity, which take nothing upon trust. And fail the
application must, for it is just one of those attempts at religion,
at setting up something as righteousness which is not, that inevitably as often as we try them break down, and that by breaking
down prove the grandeur and necessity of true religion, and tes-   25
tify to what it is. Nothing but righteousness will succeed, and
nothing is righteousness but the method and secret and sweet reasonableness of Jesus Christ. But these have nothing to do with
the gospel of the rights of man, of the natural claim of every man
to a certain share of enjoyment. Political science may create   30
rights for a man and maintain them, may seek to apportion the
means of enjoyment. Such is not the function of the Christian
religion. Man sincere, man before conscience, man as Jesus put
him, finds laid down for himself no rights; nothing but an infinite
dying, and in that dying is life.   35

[We persevere therefore in thinking, both that danger,
whether from active hostility or from passive indifference, to the
continued authority and almost universal use of the Bible in this

country there is; and also that the only safe way of meeting this danger is to find, as grounds for men's continued veneration and use of the Bible, propositions which can be verified and which are unassailable. This, then, has been our object: to find sure and
5   safe grounds for the continued use and authority of the Bible.

[2.]

[It will at once be evident how different a design is this, and how much humbler and more limited, from that of those Liberal philosophers whose design is in general to discover and to lay down *truth*, as (after Pilate)[1] they call it. For we start with ad-
10   mitting that truth, so far at least as religion is concerned, is to be found in the Bible, and what we seek is, that the Bible may be used and enjoyed. All disquisitions about the Bible seem to us to be faulty and even ridiculous which have for their result that the Bible is less felt, followed, and enjoyed after them than it was
15   before them. The Bible is in men's hands to be felt, followed, and enjoyed; this conviction we set out with. Men's instinct for self-preservation and happiness guided them to the Bible; now, it is of the essence of what gives safety and happiness to produce enjoyment and to exercise influence. And] the Bible has long been
20   widely used, deeply enjoyed, and powerfully influential; its summons to *lay hold of eternal life*, to *seek the kingdom of God*, has been a trumpet-call bringing life and joy to thousands. They have regarded the Bible as a source of life and joy, and they were right in so regarding it; we wish men to be able so to regard it still.
25   All that we may say about the Bible we confess to be a failure, if it does not lead men to find the Bible a source of life and joy still.

[Liberal philosophers reproach us with treating the Bible like an advocate; with assuming that Israel had a revelation of ex-

---

[1] See John xviii. 37. Pilate asks Jesus: 'Art thou a king?' Jesus answers:
30   'Yes, I am a king; a king of whom all who love the truth are the subjects.' Jesus says, '*the* truth.' He means the doctrine of righteousness as set forth in the Old Testament first, and then interpreted and developed by himself. Pilate catches at the word *truth;* takes it (as if he had been a member of the British Association) in the sense of *universal knowledge;* drops the arti-
35   cle, and asks his disconsolate question: 'What is truth?'

traordinary grandeur, that Jesus Christ said wonderfully profound things, and that the records of all this are something
incomparably delightful and precious. Now, we say that no inquiries about the Bible can be fruitful that are not filled with a
sense of all this, which Christendom has always felt and rightly   5
felt, only it has justified its feelings on wrong grounds. But Liberal investigators of truth think, some of them, that the Bible
often offends against morality, and at its best only utters in an old-
fashioned and ineffective way the commonplaces of morality
which belong to all ethical systems; therefore, say they, the Bible   10
had better be dropped, and we should try to enounce in modern
congenial language the new doctrines which will satisfy at once
our reason and our imagination. Other investigators of truth
destroy to the best of their ability all the grounds on which
people have accustomed themselves to receive the Bible as some-   15
thing divine and precious: and then they think to save everything by a few words of general respect and esteem for the Bible,
or for religion in the abstract. Their negative criticism has great
fulness, ardour, and effect; their positive commendation of the
Bible or religion is such as to have no effect at all. It was this   20
which we blamed in the Bishop of Natal's treatment of the Bible,
now several years ago. We have no wish to revive a past controversy; but we thought then, and we think still, that it was a signal
fault in Dr. Colenso's book that it cut away men's usual ground
for their religion and supplied really no other in its place;—for   25
his prayer of Ram, and his passage from Cicero's *Offices*, and his
own sermon, we must be permitted to regard as being, under the
circumstances, quite comically insufficient. Mr. Greg, who took
up arms for Dr. Colenso, did not understand this; he does not
understand it now. And no wonder; for his own original book   30
on the Creed of Christendom, acute and eloquent as his writing
often is, had on the whole the same fault as Dr. Colenso's work.
The upshot of the matter, after reading him, seemed to be that
the Bible was a document hopelessly damaged, and that the new
doctrines which are to satisfy our reason and our imagination   35
must be sought elsewhere.

[The same is to be said of a very learned and exact book which
has appeared lately, having for its title *Supernatural Religion*.

Hereafter we shall have occasion to criticise several things in
this work, but we now will remark of it only that it has the fault
of leaving the reader, when he closes it, with the feeling that the
Bible stands before him like a fair tree all stripped, torn, and de-
5   faced, not at all like a tree whose leaves are for the healing of the
nations. No doubt this is not the author's design, and no doubt
the current notions assailed by him, the popular view of the
Bible-books and of their composition, are full of error. But attacking these throughout two thick volumes with untiring vig-
10   our and industry, and doing nothing more, he simply leaves the
ordinary reader, to whom the Bible has been the great, often the
only, inspirer of his conduct, his imagination, his feelings,—he
leaves him with the sense that he sees his Bible with a thousand
holes picked in it and fatally discredited as an authority.

15   [These investigators go upon the supposition that a man's first
concern is to know *truth*, and that to know *truth* about the Bible
is to know that much of it is legendary and much of it of uncertain authorship. We say, on the other hand, that no one knows
the truth about the Bible who does not know how to enjoy the
20   Bible; and he who takes legend for history and who imagines
Moses or Isaiah or David or Paul or Peter or John to have written
Bible-books which they did not write, but who knows how to
enjoy the Bible deeply, is nearer the truth about the Bible than
the man who can pick it all to pieces but who cannot enjoy it.

25   [Perhaps, however, we ought to say that the author of *Supernatural Religion*, like Dr. Colenso, tries to provide a substitute
for what he destroys. After declaring that 'there is little indeed
in the history and actual achievements of Christianity to support
the claim made on its behalf to the character of a scheme divinely
30   revealed for the salvation of the human race,' he tells us that after
getting rid of Jewish mythology 'we rise to higher conceptions
of an infinitely wise and beneficent Being,' that 'all that we do
know of the regulation of the universe being so perfect and wise,
all that we do not know must be equally so,' and that 'here enters
35   the true and noble faith which is the child of reason.' Alas, for
our part we should say rather: 'Here enter the poor old dead
horses of so-called natural theology, with their galvanic move-
ments!' But this is our author's prayer of Ram, his passage from
Cicero's *Offices*, his sermon; and he promises us, so far as we

understand him, more at a future time in the same style. We say
that it is ludicrously insufficient, all of it, to fill the place of that
old belief in Christianity's claim to the character of a scheme divinely revealed for the salvation of the human race, which he
seeks to expel. We say it is a string of platitudes, without the   5
power of awakening religious emotion and joy, and not a whit
more provable, moreover, as scientific fact, than the miracle of
the resurrection, or the Johannine authorship of the Fourth
Gospel.

[We, on the other hand, think that there is everything in the   10
history and actual achievements of Christianity to support its
claim to the character of a religion divinely revealed for the salvation of the human race. We look with apprehension on all that
diminishes men's attachment to the Bible. But that the Bible is
not what men have fancied it, and that to be divinely revealed is   15
not what men have supposed, time and experience are beginning
to bear in upon the human mind. Many resist vehemently these
intimations from time and experience. This resistance we believe
to be utterly vain. We counsel men to accept them, but we seek
to show that the Bible and the Christian religion subsist, all the   20
while, as salutary, as necessary, as they ever were supposed to
be; and that they now come out far more real, and therefore far
more truly grand, than before.

[Our adversaries will say, perhaps, that this attempted demonstration is *our* prayer of Ram. And the test of our work does   25
really lie here. If the positive side in *Literature and Dogma*, if its
attempt to recommend the Bible, to awaken enthusiasm for the
Bible, on new grounds, proves ludicrously insufficient, weak and
vain; if its negative side, its attempt to apply to popular religion
the confutations and denials which time and experience suggest,   30
proves the more prominent, the only operative one,—if this is
so, then our work is, by our own confession and with our own
consent, judged; it is valueless, perhaps mischievous. We can
scarcely, however, be expected ourselves to admit that this is
already proved. The time for the book's wide working, as we   35
said on first publishing it, has hardly yet fully come. At its first
appearance it was sure to be laid hold of by those for whom it
was not written, by the religious world as it is called, the unhesitating recipients of the Christianity popularly current, and to

occasion scandal. But it was not written for those who at present
receive the Bible on the grounds supplied either by popular or
by metaphysical theology. It was written for those who from
dissatisfaction with such grounds for the Bible are inclined to
5   throw the Bible aside.]

Now, into the hands of not a few readers has *Literature and
Dogma* fallen, both here and abroad, who have found it of service to them. They have been enabled by it to use and enjoy the
Bible, when the common theology, popular or learned, had al-
10   most estranged them from it.

But then the critics interpose. Grave objections are alleged
against the book which many readers have found thus service-
able. Its conclusions about the meaning of the term *God*, and
about man's knowledge of God, are severely condemned; strong
15   objections are taken to our view of the Bible-documents in general, to our account of the Canon of the Gospels, to our estimate
of the Fourth Gospel. What are the readers, who believed they
had derived benefit from our book, to think of these objections
to it, or at least of the more important among them? what weight
20   are they to attach to them? Are they to go back from the way of
reading and interpreting the Bible which we had counselled them
to follow, and which they had begun to find profit in, or are they
still to pursue it steadfastly? Puzzled and shaken by some of the
objections we may suppose them to be; and yet, if they give ear
25   to the objections, if they do not get the better of them and put
them aside, they will lose, we believe, all sure hold on the Bible,
they will be more and more baffled, distressed, and bewildered
in their dealings with religion.

To the extent, therefore, necessary for enabling such readers
30   to surmount their difficulties, and to enjoy the Bible, we propose
to deal with some reproaches and objections brought against
Literature and Dogma.

[3.]

[But first there is one reproach to be noticed, not so much for
the reader's sake as for our own: the reproach of irreverent lan-
35   guage, of improper and offensive personalities. The parable of
the three Lord Shaftesburys, the frequent use of the names of

the Bishops of Winchester and Gloucester to point a moral,—
every one will remember to have heard of these as serious blem-
ishes in *Literature and Dogma*. To have wounded the feelings of
the religious community by turning into ridicule an august doctrine, the object of their solemn faith; to have wounded the 5
feelings of individuals either by the wanton introduction of their
names in a connexion sure to be unpleasing to them, or else by
offensive ridicule and persistent personal attack, is a crime of
which the majority of English reviewers have found us plainly
guilty, and for which they have indignantly censured us. The 10
Guardian has even been led by our mention of the Archbishop
of York, and by our remarks on the Bishops of Winchester and
Gloucester, to conclude that the order of bishops has upon us
the effect of a red rag upon a bull, and that we cannot contem-
plate it without becoming infuriated. A word of notice these 15
censures seem to demand.

[As regards the three Lord Shaftesburys, we say boldly that
our use of that parable shows our indulgence to popular Christianity. Polycarp sternly called the disfigured religion he saw
prevalent around him, *atheism*. We have said, and it is important 20
to maintain it, that popular Christianity at present is so wide of
the truth, is such a disfigurement of the truth, that it fairly deserves, if it presumes to charge others with atheism, to have that
charge retorted upon itself; and future ages will perhaps not
scruple to condemn it almost as mercilessly as Polycarp con- 25
demned the religion of heathen antiquity. For us, the God of
popular religion is a legend, a fairy-tale; learned theology has
simply taken this fairy-tale and dressed it metaphysically. Clearly
it is impossible for us to treat this fairy-tale with solemnity, as a
real and august object, in the manner which might be most ac- 30
ceptable to its believers. But for the sake of the happiness it has
given, of its beauty and pathos, and of the portions of truth mixed
up with it, it deserves, we have said, and from us it has received
and always will receive, a nearly inexhaustible indulgence. Not
only have we not called it atheism; we have entirely refused to 35
join our Liberal friends in calling it a degrading superstition.
Describing it under the parable of the three Lord Shaftesburys,
we have pointed out that it has in it, as thus represented, nothing
which can be called a degrading superstition; that it contains, on

the contrary, like other genuine products of the popular imagination, elements of admirable pathos and power. More we could
not say of it without admitting that it was not a legend or fairy-
tale at all, and that its personages were not magnified and non-
5   natural men. But this we cannot admit, although of course its
adherents will be satisfied with nothing less. It was our object to
carry well home to the reader's mind what a fairy-tale popular
Christianity really is, what a trio of magnified and non-natural
men is its Trinity. The indulgence, however, due from us to
10   popular Christianity has been shown, if we have admitted that
its fairy-tale, far from being a degraded superstition, is full of
beauty and power, and that its divinities are magnifications of
nothing unworthy, but of a sort of character of which we have
an eminent example amongst ourselves, in a man widely beloved
15   and respected, and whom no one respects more than we do.

[As to the bishops, whose sacred order is supposed to fill us
with rage and hatred, it must be modern bishops that have this
effect, for several bishops of past times are mentioned in *Literature and Dogma* with veneration. Of three modern bishops, how-
20   ever, the deliverances are criticised: of the Archbishop of York,
the late Bishop of Winchester, and the Bishop of Gloucester and
Bristol. But the deliverances of all the three are by no means criticised in the same manner. Logical and metaphysical reasonings
about essence, existence, identity, cause, design, have from all
25   time been freely used to establish truths in theology. The Archbishop of York early acquired distinction in the study of logic;
that he should follow in theological discussion a line of which
St. Anselm, Descartes, Leibnitz, and Locke have set him the example, is a matter neither for surprise nor for ridicule. Certainly
30   we hold that this line can lead in theology to nothing but perplexity and disappointment. We believe that religion could
never have been originated by it, can never be confirmed by it.
We say this freely when we see the Archbishop of York adopting it. But we say it without a thought of ridicule or disrespect
35   towards the Archbishop of York, either for his adoption of such
a line of argument, or for his management of the line of argument which he has thus chosen to employ.

[The case is different with regard to that brilliant and well-
known personage, who since the publication of *Literature and*

Dogma has passed away from amongst us. We feel more restraint
in speaking of the late Bishop of Winchester now that he is dead
than we should have felt in speaking of him in his lifetime. He
was a man with the temperament of genius; and to his energy,
his presence, his speech, this temperament could often lend   5
charm and power. But those words of his which we quoted, and
his public deliverances far too frequently, had a fault in which
men of station and authority who address a society like ours,
deserve at all times as severe a check as either blame or ridicule
can inflict upon them. To a society like ours, a society self-regu-   10
lating, which reads little that is serious and reflects hardly at all,
but which desires to pursue its way comfortably and to think
that it has in its customary notions and beliefs about religion,
whenever it may be driven to fall back upon them, an impreg-
nable stronghold to which it can always resort; to such a society   15
men of eminence cannot do a worse service than to confirm and
encourage it, with airs of superior knowledge, profound certainty, and oracular assurance, in its illusion. A man of Bishop
Wilberforce's power of mind must know, if he is sincere with
himself, that when he talks of 'doing something for the honour of   20
Our Lord's Godhead,' or of 'that infinite separation for time and
for eternity which is involved in rejecting the Godhead of the
Eternal Son,'—he must know that by this singular sort of mixture of unction and metaphysics he is solemnly giving a sem-
blance of conceivability, fixity, and certainty to notions which   25
do not possibly admit of them. He must know this, and yet he
gives it, because it suits his purpose, or because the public, or a
large body of the public, desire it; and this is clap-trap.

[The *Times*, it is true, speaks of the current Christianity of
this country as 'an English, a Protestant, and a reasonable reli-   30
gion.' The *Times*, however, is a popular newspaper; and the public, when it reads there things which suit its wishes, is always
half-conscious at least that to suit its wishes they are written. But
the late Bishop of Winchester was a man in high office and dignity, a man at the same time of great gifts; he spoke to the En-   35
glish public with authority, and with responsibility proportion-
ate to that authority; yet he freely permitted himself the use of
clap-trap. The use of clap-trap to such a public by such a man
ought at least to be always severely treated before the tribunal of

letters and science, for it will be treated severely nowhere else. Bishop Wilberforce was a man of a sympathetic temper, a dash of genius, a gift of speech, and ardent energy, who professed to be a guide in a time, a society, a sphere of thought, where the
5 first requisite for a guide is perfect sincerity;—and he was signally addicted to clap-trap. If by ridicule or by blame we have done anything to discredit a line such as that which he adopted, we cannot regret it. Those who use clap-trap as the late Bishop of Winchester used it, those who can enthusiastically extol him
10 as an ideal bishop, only prove their valuelessness for the religious crisis upon which we are now entering. No talents and acquirements can serve in this crisis without an absolute renunciation of clap-trap. Those who cannot attain to this have no part in the future which is before us. Real insight and real progress are impos-
15 sible for them; Jesus would have said of them: *They cannot enter into the kingdom of God.*

[With regard to the Bishop of Gloucester and Bristol, we feel an esteem for him as one of the very few public men who in any degree carry on serious studies after having left the University.
20 But he certainly joined himself with the Bishop of Winchester in holding the language on which we have animadverted above, and he laid himself open, therefore, to the same criticism.

[Perhaps we ought, finally, to say one word of a remark concerning the late Mr. Maurice, which has given great umbrage to
25 some of his friends. We cannot say that anything Mr. Maurice touched seems to us to have been grasped and presented by him with enough distinctness to give it a permanent value. But his was a pure and fine spirit, perpetually in a state of ferment and agitation. On many young men of ability, agitated by the un-
30 settled mental atmosphere in which we live, he exercised a great attraction. Some of them have cleared themselves; and as they cleared themselves they have come to regard Mr. Maurice as the author of all the convictions in which after their ferment and struggle they have found rest. This is generous in them, and we
35 say with pleasure that to Mr. Maurice it does honour to have made such disciples.

[And now we have done with these personal matters, and can address ourselves to our main purpose.]

Chapter I

The God of Miracles

To people disposed to throw the Bible aside *Literature and Dogma* sought to restore the use of it by two considerations: one, that the Bible requires for its basis nothing but what they can verify; the other, that the language of the Bible is not scientific, but *literary*. That is, it is the language of poetry and emotion, approximate language thrown out, as it were, at certain great objects which the human mind augurs and feels after, and thrown out by men very liable, many of them, to delusion and error. This has been violently impugned. What we have now to do, therefore, is to ask whoever thought he found profit from what we said, to examine with us whether it has been impugned successfully; whether he and we ought to give it up, or whether we ought to hold by it firmly and hopefully still.

First and foremost has been impugned the definition which, proceeding on the rule to take nothing as a basis for the Bible but what can be verified, we gave of God. And of this we certainly cannot complain. For we have ourselves said, that without a clear understanding in what sense this important but ambiguous term *God* is used, all fruitful discussion in theology is impossible. And yet, in theological discussion, this clear understanding is hardly ever cared for, but people assume that the sense of the term is something perfectly well known. 'A personal First Cause, that thinks and loves, the moral and intelligent governor of the universe,' is the sense which theologians in general assume to be the meaning, properly drawn out and strictly worded, of the term God. We say that by this assumption a great deal which cannot possibly be verified is put into the word 'God'; and we propose, for the God of the Bible and of Christianity, a much less pretentious definition, but which has the advantage of

containing nothing that cannot be verified. The God of the Bible
and of Christianity is, we say: *The Eternal, not ourselves, that
makes for righteousness.*

Almost with one voice our critics have expostulated with us
5   for refusing to admit what they call a personal God. Nothing
would be easier for us than, by availing ourselves of the ambiguity natural to the use of the term God, to give such a turn to
our expressions as might satisfy some of our critics, or might enable our language to pass muster with the common religious
10   world as permissible. But this would be clean contrary to our
design. For we want to recommend the Bible and its religion by
showing that they rest on something which can be verified.
Now, in the Bible God is everything. Unless therefore we ascertain what it is which we mean by God, and that what we mean
15   we can verify, we cannot recommend the Bible as we desire. So
against all ambiguity in the use of this term we wage war. Mr.
Llewelyn Davies says that we ourselves admit that the most
proper language to use about God is the approximative language
of poetry and eloquence, language thrown out at an object which
20   it does not profess to define scientifically, language which cannot, therefore, be adequate and accurate. If Israel, then, might
with propriety call God 'the high and holy one that inhabiteth
eternity,' why, he asks, may not the Bishop of Gloucester with
propriety talk of 'the blessed truth that the God of the universe
25   is a person'? Neither the one expression nor the other is adequate; both are approximate. We answer: Let it be understood,
then, that when the Bishop of Gloucester, or others, talk of the
blessed truth that the God of the universe is a person, they mean
to talk, not science, but rhetoric and poetry. In that case our
30   only criticism on their language will be that it is bad rhetoric and
poetry, whereas the rhetoric and poetry of Israel is good. But
the truth is, they mean it for science; they mean it for a more formal and precise account of what Israel called poetically 'the high
and holy one that inhabiteth eternity;' and it is false science be-
35   cause it assumes what it cannot verify. However, if it is not
meant for science, but for poetry, let us treat it as poetry; and
then it is language not professing to be exact at all, and we are
free to use it or not to use it as our sense of poetic propriety may

dictate. But at all events let us be clear about one thing: Is it meant for poetry, or is it meant for science?

If we were asked what in our own opinion we had by *Literature and Dogma* effected for the benefit of readers of the Bible, we should answer that we had effected two things above all. First, that we had led the reader to face that primary question, so habitually slurred over, what 'God' means in the Bible, and to see that it means the Eternal not ourselves that makes for righteousness. Secondly, that we had made him ask himself what is meant by 'winning Christ,' 'knowing Christ,' 'the excellency of the knowledge of Christ,' and find that it means laying hold of the method and secret and temper of Jesus. And of these two things achieved by us, as we think, for the Bible-reader's benefit, the first seems to us the more important. Sooner or later he will find the Bible fail him, unless he is provided with a sure meaning for the words 'God,' 'Deity.' Until this is done, and to keep steadily before his mind how loosely he and others at present employ the word, we even recommend him to allow to the word 'Deity' no more contents than by its etymology it has, and to render it 'The Shining.' Archbishop Whately blames those who define words by their etymology, and ridicules them as people who should insist upon it that sycophant shall mean 'fig-shewer' and nothing else. But etymological definition, trifling and absurd when a word's imported meaning is sure, becomes valuable when the imported meaning is unfixed. There was at Athens a practice, says Festus, of robbing the fig-orchards; a law was passed to check it; under this law vexatious informations were laid, and those who laid them were called *sycophants*, fig-informers, or, if Archbishop Whately pleases, fig-shewers. Then the name was transferred to vexatious informers or to calumniators generally, and at last to cheating impostors of other kinds. The wider new meaning thus imported into the word was something quite clear, something on which all were agreed; and thenceforward to insist on limiting *sycophant* to its old etymological sense of fig-informer would have been ridiculous.

But the case is different when the fuller meaning imported into a word is something vague and loose, something on which people are by no means agreed. It is then often an excellent discipline to revert to the etymology; and to insist on confining ourselves to the sense given by this, until we get for our word a larger sense clear and certain. 'The Shining is our hope and strength.' 'O Shining, thou are my Shining, early will I seek thee!' 'My soul, wait thou only upon The Shining, for my expectation is from him!' 'The fool hath said in his heart: There is no Shining!'[1] This will not give us satisfaction. But it will thereby stimulate us all the more to find a meaning to the word 'God' that does give us satisfaction; and it will keep vivid in our minds the thought how little we ourselves or others have such a meaning for the word at present.

The late Lord Lyttelton published in the *Contemporary Review* a disquisition on 'Undogmatic and Unsectarian Teaching,' which signally illustrates the utility of this etymological discipline. Lord Lyttelton is very severe upon those whom he calls 'the shallow sciolists and apostles of modern Unsectarianism;' and very favourable to dogma, or the determined, decreed and received doctrine of so-called orthodox theology. He draws out a formal list of propositions beginning with: 'God is, God made the world, God cares for men, God is the Father of men,' and ending with: 'The Deity of God is in one sense One in another Threefold, God is One in Three Persons.' He defies any one to show where in this list that which is universal ends and that which is dogmatic begins. And his inference apparently is, that therefore the last propositions in the series may be freely taught. But if he had examined his thoughts with attention he would have found that he cannot tell where the character of his propositions changes because he has been using the word 'God' in the same sense all through the series. Now, the sense given to this word governs the sense of each and all of his propositions, but this sense he omits to furnish us with. Until we have it, we may agree that his latter propositions are dogmatic, but we cannot possibly concede to him that his earlier propositions have universal validity. Yet the whole force of his series of propositions, and of the argument which he founds upon it, depends on this: whether his definition of God, which he does not produce, is un-

---

[1] *Psalm* xlvi. 1; lxiii. 1; lxii. 5; xiv. 1.

challengeable or no. Till he produces it, his readers will really best enable themselves to feel the true force of Lord Lyttelton's propositions by substituting for the word Deity its bare etymological equivalent Shining,—the only definition to which, until the fuller definition is produced and made good, the word has 5 any right. The propositions will then run: 'The Shining is, The Shining made the world, The Shining cares for men, The Shining is the Father of men;' and so on to the final and fantastic proposition: 'The Shining is One in Three Persons.' That entire inconclusiveness, of which we are by these means made fully 10 aware, exists just as much in Lord Lyttelton's original propositions, but without being noticed by himself or by most of his readers.

Resolutely clear with himself, then, in using this word 'Deity,' 'God,' we urge our reader to be, whatever offence he may give 15 by it. When he is asked in a tone of horrified remonstrance whether he refuses to believe in a personal God, let him steadily examine what it is that people say about a personal God, and what grounds he has for receiving it.

People say that there is a personal God, and that a personal 20 God is a God who thinks and loves. That there is an Eternal not ourselves which makes for righteousness and is called God, is admitted; and indeed so much as this human experience proves. For the constitution and history of things show us that happiness, at which we all aim, is dependent on righteousness. Yet certainly 25 we did not make this to be so, and it did not begin when we began, nor does it end when we end, but is due, so far as we can see, to an eternal tendency outside us, prevailing whether we will or no, whether we are here or not. There is no difficulty, therefore, about an Eternal not ourselves that makes for righ- 30 teousness, and to which men have transferred that ancient high name, *Deus*, the Brilliant or Shining, by which they once adored a mighty object outside themselves, the sun, which from the first took their notice as powerful for their weal or woe.

So that God is, is admitted; but people maintain, besides, that 35 he is a person, and thinks and loves. 'The Divine Being cannot,' they say, 'be without the perfection which manifests itself in the human personality as the highest of which we have any knowl-

edge.' Now, 'the deeper elements of personality are,' they add, 'existence, consciousness of this existence and control over it.' These therefore, they say, God must have. And that the Eternal that makes for righteousness has these, they account (though
5 their language is not always quite consistent on this point) a fact of the same order and of as much certainty as that there is an Eternal that makes for righteousness at all. 'It is this power itself,' says M. Albert Réville, 'this not ourselves which makes for righteousness, that constantly reveals to us the fact that it is a
10 Spirit, that is to say, not merely an influence, but life, consciousness, and love.' Religion, it is affirmed, religion, which is morality touched with emotion, is impossible unless we know of God that he is a person who thinks and loves. 'If the not ourselves which makes for righteousness,' says M. Réville, 'is an unconscious force,
15 I cannot feel for it that sacred emotion which raises morality to the rank of religion. Man no longer worships powers of which he has discovered the nature to be impersonal.' All this sort of argumentation, which M. Réville manages with great delicacy and literary skill, is summed up in popular language plainly and well
20 by a writer in the *Edinburgh Review*. 'Is the Power around us not a person; is what you would have us worship a thing? All existing beings must be either persons or things; and no sophistries can deter us from the invincible persuasion which all human creatures possess, that *persons* are superior to *things*.'

25   Now, before going farther, we have one important remark to make upon all this. M. Réville talks of those who *have discovered* the nature of God to be impersonal. In another place he talks of *denying* conscious intelligence to God. The Edinburgh Reviewer talks of those who would have us worship a *thing*. We
30 assure M. Réville that we do not profess to have discovered the nature of God to be impersonal, nor do we deny to God conscious intelligence. We assure the Edinburgh Reviewer that we do not assert God to be a *thing*. All we say is that men do not know enough about the Eternal not ourselves that makes for
35 righteousness, to warrant their pronouncing this either a person or a thing. We say that no one has discovered the nature of God to be personal, or is entitled to assert that God has conscious intelligence. Theologians assert this and make it the basis of religion. It is they who assert and profess to know, not

we. We object to their professing to know more than can be known, to their insisting we shall receive it, to their resting religion upon it. We want to rest religion on what can be verified, not on what cannot. And M. Réville himself seems, when he lets us see the bottom of his thoughts, to allow that a personal God   5
who thinks and loves cannot really be verified, for he says: 'It is in vain to ask how we can verify the fact that God possesses consciousness and intelligence.' But we are for resting religion upon some fact of which it shall not be in vain to ask whether we can verify it. However, the theologians' conception of God is repre-   10
sented as a far more satisfying one in itself than ours, and as having, besides, much to make its truth highly probable, at any rate, if not demonstrable. And the reader of *Literature and Dogma* may think, perhaps, that we have been over-cautious, over-negative; that we are really, as M. Réville says, 'decidedly too   15
much afraid of the idea of the personality of God.' He may think, that though we have given him as his foundation something verifiable and sure, yet that what we have given him is a great deal less than what the theologians offer, and offer with such strong and good reasons for its truth, that it becomes almost   20
certain if not quite, and a man is captious who will not accept it.

Descartes, as is well known, had a famous philosophical method for discovering truths of all kinds; and people heard of his method and used to press him to give them the results which this wonderful organ had enabled him to ascertain. Quite in a   25
contrary fashion, we sometimes flatter ourselves with the hope that we may be of use by the very absence of all scientific pretension, because we are thus obliged to treat great questions in such a simple way that any one can follow us, while the way, at the same time, may possibly be quite right after all, only over-   30
looked by more ingenious people because it is so very simple.

Now, proceeding in this manner, we venture to ask the plain reader whether it does not strike him as an objection to our making God a person who thinks and loves, that we have really no experience whatever, not the very slightest, of persons who think   35
and love, except in man and the inferior animals. I for my part am by no means disposed to deny that the inferior animals, as they are called, may have consciousness, that they may be said to think and love, in however low a degree. At any rate we can see

them before us doing certain things which are like what we do
ourselves when we think and love, so that thinking and loving
may be attributed to them also without one's failing to understand what is meant, and they may conceivably be called persons
5   who think and love. But really this is all the experience of any
sort that we have of persons who think and love,—the experience afforded by ourselves and the lower animals. True, we
easily and naturally attribute all operations that engage our notice to authors who live and think like ourselves. We make per-
10 sons out of sun, wind, love, envy, war, fortune; in some languages every noun is male or female. But this, we know, is
figure and personification. Being ourselves alive and thinking,
and having sex, we naturally invest things with these our attributes, and imagine all action and operation to proceed as our
15 own proceeds. This is a tendency which in common speech and
in poetry, where we do not profess to speak exactly, we cannot
well help following, and which we follow lawfully. In the language of common speech and of poetry, we speak of the Eternal
not ourselves that makes for righteousness, as if he were a person
20 who thinks and loves. Naturally we speak of him so, and there
is no objection at all to our so doing.

But it is different when we profess to speak exactly, and yet
make God a person who thinks and loves. We then find what
difficulty our being actually acquainted with no persons superior
25 to ourselves who think and love brings us into. Some, we know,
have made their God in the image of the inferior animals. We
have had the God Apis and the God Anubis; but these are
extravagances. In general, as God is said to have made man in his
own image, the image of God, man has returned the compliment
30 and has made God as being, outwardly or inwardly, in the image
of man. What we in general do is to take the best thinking and
loving of the best man, to better this best, to call it *perfect*, and
to say that this is God. So we construct a magnified and non-
natural man, by dropping out all that in man seems a source of
35 weakness, and by heightening to the very utmost all that in man
seems a source of strength, such as his thought and his love.
Take the account of God which begins the Thirty-nine Articles,
or the account of God in any Confession of Faith we may

choose. The same endeavour shows itself in all of them: to construct a man who thinks and loves, but so immensely bettered that he is a man no longer. Then between this magnified man and ourselves we put, if we please, angels, who are men etherealised. The objection to the magnified man and to the men etherealised is one and the same: that we have absolutely no experience whatever of either the one or the other.

Support, however, is obtained for them from two grounds;—from metaphysical grounds, and from the ground of miracles. Let us take first the ground said to be given by miracles. Interferences and communications of such a kind as to be explainable on no other supposition than that of a magnified and non-natural man, with etherealised men ministering to him, are alleged to have actually happened and to be warranted by sure testimony. And there is something in this. If the alleged interferences and communications have happened, then by this supposition they may fairly be explained. If the progress of the natural day was really stopped to enable the chosen people to win a great victory over its enemies, if a voice out of the sky really said when Jesus was baptized: *This is my beloved Son*,—then the magnified and non-natural man of popular religion, either by himself or with angels, etherealised men, for his ministers, is a supposition made credible, probable, and even almost necessary, by those incidents.

2.

Thus we are thrown back on miracles; and the question is, are we to affirm that God is a person who thinks and loves because miracles compel us? Now, the reader of *Literature and Dogma* will recollect that perhaps some half-a-dozen pages of that book, and not more, were taken up with discussing miracles. The *Guardian* thinks this insufficient. It says that solid replies are demanded to solid treatises, and that I ought to have taken Dr. Mozley's Bampton Lectures on Miracles, and given, if I could, a refutation to them. It tartly adds, however, that to expect this 'would be to expect something entirely at variance with Mr. Arnold's antecedents and with his whole nature.' Well, the au-

thor of *Supernatural Religion* has occupied half a thick volume
in refuting Dr. Mozley's Bampton Lectures. He has written a
solid reply to that solid treatise. Sure I am that he has not convinced the *Guardian*, but that journal ought at least to be pleased
5   with him for having so far done his duty. For my part, although
I do justice to Dr. Mozley's ability, yet to write a refutation of
his Bampton Lectures is precisely, in my opinion, to do what
Strauss has well called 'going out of one's way to assail the paper
fortifications which theologians choose to set up.' To engage in
10 an *à priori* argument to prove that miracles are impossible, against
an adversary who argues *à priori* that they are possible, is the
vainest labour in the world. So long as the discussion was of this
character, miracles were in no danger. The time for it is now
past, because the human mind, whatever may be said for or
15 against miracles *à priori*, is now in fact losing its reliance upon
them. And it is losing it for this reason: as its experience widens,
it gets acquainted with the natural history of miracles, it sees
how they arise, and it slowly but inevitably puts them aside.

Far from excusing ourselves for the brevity and moderation
20 with which the subject of miracles is in *Literature and Dogma*
treated, we are disposed to claim praise for it. It is possible to
spend a great deal too much time and mental energy over the
thesis that miracles cannot be relied on. The thesis, though true,
is merely negative, and therefore of secondary importance. The
25 important question is, what becomes of religion,—so precious,
as we believe, to the human race,—if miracles cannot be relied
on? We ought never so to immerse ourselves in the argument
against miracles, as to forget that the main question lies beyond,
and that we must press forward to it. As soon as we satisfy our-
30 selves that on miracles we cannot build, let us have done with
questions about them and begin to build on something surer.
Now, it is in a much more simple and unpretending way than
controversialists commonly follow that we satisfy ourselves that
we cannot build upon miracles.

35 For it is possible, again, to exaggerate untruly the demonstra-
tive force of the case against miracles. The logical completeness
of the case for miracles has been vaunted, and vaunted falsely;
some people are now disposed to vaunt falsely the logical com-

pleteness of the case against miracles. Poor human nature loves the pretentious forms of exact knowledge, though with the real condition of our thoughts they often ill correspond. The author of *Supernatural Religion* asserts again and again that miracles are contradictory to a complete induction. He quotes Mr. Mill's rule: 'Whatever is contradictory to a complete induction is incredible,' and quotes Mr. Mill's account of a complete induction: 'When observations or experiments have been repeated so often and by so many persons as to exclude all supposition of error in the observer, a law of nature is established;' and he asserts that a law of nature of this kind has been established against miracles. He brings forward that famous test by which Paley seeks to establish the Christian miracles, his 'twelve men of known probity and good sense relating a miracle wrought before their eyes, and consenting to be racked and burned sooner than acknowledge that there existed any falsehood or imposture in the case,' and he asserts that no affirmation of any twelve men would be sufficient to overthrow a law of nature, or to save, therefore, the Christian miracles.

Now, these assertions are exaggerated and will not serve. No such law of nature as Mr. Mill describes has been or can be established against the Christian miracles; a complete induction against them, therefore, there is not. Nor does the evidence of their reporters fail because the evidence of no men can make miracles credible. The case against the Christian miracles is that we have an induction, not complete, indeed, but enough more and more to satisfy the mind, and to satisfy it in an ever increasing number of men, that miracles are untrustworthy. The case against their reporters is, that more and more of us see, and see ever more clearly, that these reporters were not and could not be the sort of picked jury that Paley's argument requires, but that, with all the good faith in the world, they were men likely to fall into error about miracles, to make a miracle where there was none, and that they did fall into error and legend accordingly.

This being so, we have no inclination, even now, either to dwell at excessive length on the subject of miracles, or to make a grand show of victoriously demonstrating their impossibility. But we have to ask ourselves, if necessary, again and again, when-

ever anything is made to depend upon them, how their case really and truly stands, whether there can be any prospect, either for ourselves or for those in whose interest *Literature and Dogma* was written, of returning to a reliance upon them. And
5 the more we consider it the more we are convinced there is none; and that the cause assigned in *Literature and Dogma* as fatal to miracles,—that the more our experience widens, the more we see and understand the process by which they arose, and their want of solidity,—is fatal to them indeed. The time has
10 come when the minds of men no longer put as a matter of course the Bible-miracles in a class by themselves. Now, from the moment this time commences, from the moment that the comparative history of all miracles is a conception entertained and a study admitted, the conclusion is certain, the reign of the Bible-
15 miracles is doomed.

3.

Let us see how this is so. Herodotus relates, that, when the Persian invaders came to Delphi, two local heroes buried near the place, Phylacus and Autonous, arose, and were seen, of more than mortal stature, fighting against the Persians.[1] He relates,
20 that before the onset at Salamis the vision of a woman appeared over an Aeginetan ship, and cried in a voice which all the Grecian fleet heard: 'Good souls, how long will ye keep backing?'[2] He relates, that at Pedasus, in the neighbourhood of his own city Halicarnassus, the priestess of Athene had a miraculous sprouting
25 of beard whenever any grievous calamity was about to befall the people around; he says in one place that twice this miraculous growth had happened, in another, that it had happened thrice.[3] Herodotus writes here of times when he was himself alive, not of a fabulous antiquity. He and his countrymen were not less acute,
30 arguing, critical people than the Jews of Palestine, but much more. Herodotus himself, finally, is a man of a beautiful character and of pure good-faith.

[1] Herodotus viii. 38, 39.   [2] Herod. viii. 84.
[3] Herod. viii. 104, [i. 175].

But we do not believe that Phylacus and Autonous arose out
of their graves and were seen fighting with the Persians; we
know by experience, we all say, how this sort of story grows up.
And that after the Crucifixion, then, many dead saints arose and
came out of the graves and went into the holy city and appeared   5
unto many, is not this too a story of which we must say, the moment we fairly put it side by side with the other, that it is of the
same kind with it, and that we know how the sort of story grows
up? That the phantom-woman called to the Aeginetan crew at
Salamis, *How long will ye keep backing?* we do not believe any   10
the more because we are told that all the Grecian fleet heard it.
We know, we all say, by experience, that this is just the sort of
corroboration naturally added to such a story. But we are asked
to believe that Jesus after his death actually cried to Paul on his
way to Damascus: *It is hard for thee to kick against the pricks*,   15
because the bystanders are said to have heard it, although to be
sure in another place, with the looseness natural to such a story,
the bystanders are said *not* to have heard this voice. That the
Salamis story and the Damascus story are of one kind, and of
what kind, strikes us the moment that we put the two stories   20
together.

The miraculous beard of the priestess of Pedasus, again, is
really just like the miraculous dumbness of Zacharias, the father
of John the Baptist. The priestess of Pedasus, however, is said
by Herodotus in one place to have twice had her marvellous   25
beard, in another to have had it thrice; and the discrepancy
proves, we all say, how loose and unhistorical this kind of story
is. But yet when Jesus is in the Second Gospel said to have healed
as he departed from Jericho one blind man who sate by the wayside, and in the First Gospel to have healed as he departed from   30
Jericho two blind men who sate by the wayside, there is here, we
are asked to believe, no discrepancy really at all. Two different
healings are meant, which were performed at two different visits
to Jericho. Or perhaps they were performed at one and the
same visit, but one was performed as Jesus entered the city,   35
and the other as he left it. And the words of St. Mark: 'And
he came to Jericho; and as he went out of Jericho blind Bartimaeus sate by the wayside,' really mean that Bartimaeus sate

there as Jesus went *in* to Jericho, and two other blind men sate
by the wayside as he went *out*. How arbitrary, unnatural and
vain such an explanation is, what a mere device of our own
to make a solid history out of a legend, we never feel so irresistibly as when we put the Jericho story by the side of others
like it.

[Yet still, in new and popular books, this precious device for
reconciling inconsistent accounts of the same thing,—the hypothesis that the incident did really happen more than once,—
is furbished up and brought out afresh. So strong, so persistent,
so desperate is the endeavour to make that wonderful mixture of
truth and fiction, which the Four Gospels give us, into one uniform strain of solid history. The attempt must fail. It will impair
the understanding of all who make it, it will mar the reputation
of every critic who makes it, and yet will disappoint them after
all.The kindest thing one can do to an intelligent reader of the
Bible is to convince him of the utter hopelessness of any such attempt, to bring him speedily and once for all to a state of settled clearness on the subject. And this will be done, not so well
directly, by arguing how improbable such an hypothesis as that
incidents should exactly repeat themselves in itself is, as indirectly, by showing from examples how very prone is the human
imagination to reproduce striking incidents a second time, although the incidents have in truth occurred only once.

[To save the exactness of the Gospel narratives, the stories of
the healing of the blind men at Jericho are made to pass, we have
seen, for the stories of two separate miracles. But a more remarkable instance still of the actual production of an incident twice, is
alleged in regard to the clearing the Temple of buyers and sellers.
The Fourth Gospel, as is well known, puts the clearance at the
beginning of Christ's career. The Synoptics put it at the end,
shortly before his arrest. Probably the Synoptics are right; for
the act was one which, coming from an unknown man, would
have merely seemed extravagant and exasperating, whereas, coming from Jesus after his line of teaching and reforming had become familiar, it would have had significance and use. But be this
as it may; at any rate, if the act was done at the outset of the
career of Jesus, then the Synoptics, one would say, must have

made a mistake; if at the close, then the author of the Fourth Gospel. Not at all! The same striking incident with all its circumstances really happened, we are told, twice: first at the outset of Christ's career, and then again at its close. Neither the Synoptics, therefore, nor the author of the Fourth Gospel are in error. 5

[Now, this seems surprising. But some who are lovers of the Bible may be inclined to try and believe it, may seek to cling to such an explanation, may argue for its possibility *à priori*. Crumble to bits, sooner or later, such explanations will. That which may convince a man, once and for ever, of their hollowness, and 10 save him much loss of time and distress of mind, is the application of such a piece of experience as the following:—

[Some years ago a newly-married couple were during their honeymoon travelling in the Alps. They made an excursion on Mont Blanc; the bride met with an accident there, and perished 15 before her husband's eyes. The other day we had, strange to relate, just this touching story over again. Again a newly-married couple were in the Alps during their honeymoon, again Mont Blanc was the scene of an excursion, again the bride met with an accident, again she perished in her husband's sight. Surprising, 20 but there was the fact! People talked of it, the telegraph spread it abroad. But ours is a time of broad daylight and searching inquiry. The matter drew attention, and in a few days the telegraph announced that the second accident had never really happened at all, that it was a mere doubling and reflexion of the 25 first. Men's imagination reiterates in this way things which strike it, and loose relation narrates the doubled fact seriously. As our experience widens, it brings us more and more proof that this is so; and one day a signal example is decisive with us. The Mont Blanc story, or some story of the kind, comes with a sort of 30 magic to make the scales fall from our eyes. It is still possible *à priori* that the Temple may have been cleared twice, and that there is no mistake in the Gospel reports. The induction against it is not a complete induction. But it is henceforth complete enough to serve; it convinces us. In spite of the *à priori* possibil- 35 ity, we cannot any longer believe in the double clearance of the Temple, and in the exactitude of both the accounts in the Gospels, even though we would.]

4.

It is this impossibility of resting religion any more on grounds
once supposed to be safe, such as that the Gospel narratives are
free from mistake and that the Gospel miracles are trustworthy,
which compels us to look for new grounds upon which we may
5 build firmly. Those men do us an ill turn, and we owe them no
thanks for it, who compel us to keep going back to examine the
old grounds, and declaring their want of solidity. What we need
is to have done with all this negative, unfruitful business, and to
get to religion again;—to the use of the Bible upon new grounds
10 which shall be secure. The old grounds cannot be used safely
any more, and if one opens one's eyes one must see it. Those who
inveigh against us could see it, if they chose, as plainly as we do;
and they ought to open their eyes and see it, but they will not.
And they want us to go on trusting foolishly to the old grounds
15 as they do, until all tumbles in, and there is a great ruin and confusion. Let us not do so. Let those who have read *Literature and
Dogma* with satisfaction be sure that what is in that book said
against miracles, kept though it be within the narrowest limits
possible, is indispensable, and requires so little space just because
20 it is so very certain. Let them accustom themselves to treat with
steadiness, with rigorous simplicity, all the devices to save those
unsaveable things, the Bible miracles.

To reduce the miraculous in them to what are thought reasonable dimensions is now a favourite attempt. But if anything
25 miraculous is left, the whole miracle might as well have been left;
if nothing, how has the incident any longer the proving force of
a miracle? Let us treat so absurd an attempt as it deserves. Neander supposes that the water at the marriage-feast at Cana was
not changed by Jesus into wine, but was only endued by him
30 with wine's brisk taste and exhilarating effects. This has all the
difficulties of the miracle, and only gets rid of the poetry. It is as
if we were startled by the extravagance of supposing Cinderella's
fairy godmother to have actually changed the pumpkin into a
coach and six, but should suggest that she did really change it
35 into a one-horse cab. Many persons, again, feel now an insur-

mountable suspicion (and no wonder) of Peter's fish with the tribute-money in its mouth, and they suggest that what really happened was that Peter caught a fish, sold it, and paid the tribute with the money he thus got. This is like saying that all Cinderella's godmother really did was to pay a cab for her godchild by selling her pumpkins. But then what becomes of the wonder, the miracle? Were there ever such apologists as these? They impair the credit of the Evangelists as much as we do, for they make them transform facts to an extent wholly incompatible with trustworthy reporting. They impair it more; for they make them transform facts with a method incompatible with honest simplicity.

Simple, flexible common-sense is what we most want, in order to be able to follow truly the dealings of that spontaneous, irregular, wonderful power which gives birth to tales of miracle,— the imagination. It is easy to be too systematic. Strauss had the idea, acute and ingenious, of explaining the miracles of the New Testament as a reiteration of the miracles of the Old. Of some miracles this supplies a good explanation. It plausibly explains the story of the Transfiguration, for instance. The story of the illumined face of Jesus,—Jesus, the prophet like unto Moses, whom Moses foretold,—might naturally owe its origin to the illumined face of Moses himself. But of other miracles Strauss's idea affords no admissible explanation whatever. To employ it for these cases can only show the imperturbable resolution of a German professor in making all the facts suit a theory which he has once adopted.

Every miracle has its own mode of growth and its own history, and the key to one is not the key to others. Such a rationalising explanation as that above quoted of the money in the mouth of Peter's fish is ridiculous. Yet a clue, a suggestion, however slight, of fact, there probably was to every miracle; and sometimes, not by any means always, this clue may be traced with likelihood.

The story of the feeding of the thousands may well have had its rise in the suspension, the comparative extinction, of hunger and thirst during hours of rapt interest and intense mental excitement. In such hours a trifling sustenance, which would commonly serve for but a few, will suffice for many. Rumour and imagination make and add details, and swell the thing into a miracle. This sort of incident, again, it is as natural to conceive repeating itself, as it is unnatural to conceive an incident like the clearance of the Temple repeating itself. Or to take the walking on the Sea of Galilee. Here, too, the sort of hint of fact which may have started the miracle will readily occur to every one. Sometimes the hint of fact, lost in our Bibles, is preserved elsewhere. The Gospel of the Hebrews,—an old Gospel outside the Canon of Scripture, but which Jerome quotes and of which we have fragments,—this Gospel, and other records of like character, mention what our Four Gospels do not: a wonderful light at the moment when Jesus was baptized. No one, so far as we know, has yet remarked that in this small and dropped circumstance,—a weird light on Jordan seen while Jesus was baptized, —we not improbably have the original nucleus of solid fact round which the whole miraculous story of his baptism gathered.

He does well who, steadily using his own eyes in this manner, and escaping from the barren routine whether of the assailants of the Bible or of its apologists, acquires the serene and imperturbable conviction, indispensable for all fruitful use of the Bible in future, that in travelling through its reports of miracles he moves in a world, not of solid history, but of illusion, rumour, and fairy-tale. Only, when he has acquired this, let him say to himself that he has by so doing achieved nothing, except to get rid of an insecure reliance which would inevitably some day or other have cost him dear, of a staff in religion which must sooner or later have pierced his hand.

One other thing, however, he has done besides this. He has discovered the hollowness of the main ground for making God a person who thinks and loves, a magnified and non-natural man. Only a kind of man magnified could so make man the centre of all things and interrupt the settled order of nature in his behalf as miracles imply. But in miracles we are dealing, we find, with the unreal world of fairy-tale. Having no reality of their own, they cannot lend it as foundation for the reality of anything else.

Chapter II

The God of Metaphysics

There remain the grounds for asserting God to be a person who thinks and loves which are supplied by metaphysics.

'Continuo auditae voces, vagitus et ingens.'

At the mention of that name *metaphysics*, lo! essence, existence, substance, finite and infinite, cause and succession, something $\quad$ 5 and nothing, begin to weave their eternal dance before us; with the confused murmur of their combinations filling all the region governed by *her*, who, far more indisputably than her late-born rival, political economy, has earned the title of the Dismal Science. Yet even into this region we ask the reader of *Literature* $\quad$ 10 *and Dogma*, if he does not disdain an unsophisticated companion, to enter with us. And here, possibly, we may after all find reason to retract, and to own that the theologians are right. For metaphysics we know from the very name to be the science of things which come after natural things. Now, the things which come $\quad$ 15 after natural things are things not natural. Clearly, therefore, if any science is likely to be able to demonstrate to us the magnified and non-natural man, it must be the science of non-naturals.

2.

Professor Huxley's interesting discourse at Belfast drew attention to a personage who once was in the thoughts of everybody $\quad$ 20 who tried to think,—René Descartes. But in this great man there were, in truth, two men. One was the anatomist, the physicist, the mechanical philosopher who exclaimed: 'Give me matter and motion, and I will make the world!' and of whom Pascal said that the only God he admitted was a God who was useless. This $\quad$ 25 is the Descartes on whom Professor Huxley has asked us to turn once more our eyes; and no man could ask it better or more persuasively.

But there is another Descartes who has of late years been much more known, both in his own country and out of it, than Descartes the mechanical philosopher, and that is the Descartes who is said to have founded the independence of modern philosophy and to have founded its spiritualism. He began with universal doubt, with the rejection of all authority, with the resolve to admit nothing to be true which he could not clearly see to be true. He ended with declaring that the demonstration of God and the soul was more completely made out than that of any other truth whatever; nay, that the certitude and truth of every science depended solely on our knowledge of the true God![1]

Here we have the Descartes who is commonly said to have founded modern philosophy. And who, in this our day of unsettlement and of impatience with authority, convention, and routine, who, in this our day of new departures, can fail to be attracted by the author of the 'Méthode,' and by his promises? '*Je n'admets rien qui ne soit nécessairement vrai;* I admit nothing which is not necessarily true.' '*Je m'éloigne de tout ce en quoi je pourrais imaginer le moindre doute;* I put aside everything about which I can imagine there being the smallest doubt.' What could we, who demand that the propositions we accept shall be propositions we can verify, ask more? '*Il n'y a que les choses que je conçois clairement et distinctement qui aient la force de me persuader entièrement; je ne puis me tromper dans les jugements dont je connais clairement les raisons;* Only those things which I conceive clearly and distinctly have the power thoroughly to persuade me; I cannot be mistaken in those judgments of which I clearly know the reasons.' What can be better? We have really no other ground for the certainty of our convictions than this clearness.

[Will it be said, however, that there is here an opening, at any rate, for unsoundness, and that in the following sentence, for

---

[1] Je reconnais très clairement que la certitude et la vérité de toute science dépend de la seule connaissance du vrai Dieu.

example, we can plainly see how? '*Toutes les choses que nous concevons clairement et distinctement sont vraies de la façon dont nous les concevons;* All things that we conceive clearly and distinctly are true as we conceive them.' There is an ambiguity, is there not, about 'clearly and distinctly;' a man may say or fancy he sees a thing clearly and distinctly, when he does nothing of the kind? True, this is so; a man may deceive himself as to what constitutes clearness and distinctness. Still, the test is good. We can only be sure of our judgments from their clearness and distinctness, though we may sometimes fancy that this clearness and distinctness is present when it is not.]

The rule of Descartes, therefore, not to receive anything as true without having clearly known it for such, is for us unchallengeable. How vain and dangerous did we find Butler's proposal that we should take as the foundation of our religion something for which we had a low degree of probability! In this direction, assuredly, Descartes does not err. 'Inasmuch as my reason convinces me,' says he, 'that I ought to be as careful to withhold my belief from things not quite certain and indubitable as from those which I plainly see to be false, it will be a sufficient ground to me for rejecting all my old opinions if I find in them all some opening for doubt.' Certainly this is caution enough; to many it will even seem excess of caution.

It is true, the doubts which troubled Descartes and which have troubled so many philosophers,—doubts, whether this world in which we live, the objects which strike our senses, the things which we see and handle, have any real existence,—are not exactly the doubts by which we ourselves have been most plagued. Indeed, to speak quite frankly, these are doubts by which we have never been tormented at all. Our trouble has rather been with doubts whether things which people assured us really existed or had really happened, but of which we had no experience ourselves and could not satisfy ourselves that anyone else had had experience either, were really as those people told us. Descartes could look out of his window at Amsterdam, and see a public place filled with men and women, and say to himself that he had yet no right to be certain they were men and women, because they might, after all, be mere lay figures dressed up in hats and cloaks. This would never have occurred, perhaps, to the generality of mankind; to us, at any rate, it never would have occurred. But if this sort of scrupulosity led Descartes to establish his admirable rules: 'I admit nothing which is not necessarily true;' 'Only those things which I conceive clearly and distinctly have the power to convince me;' we cannot regret that he was thus scrupulous. Men, all of them, as many as have doubts of any kind and want certainty, find their need served when a great man sets out with these stringent rules to discover what is really certain and verifiable. And we ourselves accordingly, plain unphilosophical people as we are, did betake ourselves once to Descartes with great zeal, and we were thus led to an experience which we have never forgotten. And perhaps it may be of use to other plain people, for the purpose of the enquiry which at present occupies us,—the enquiry whether the solid and necessary ground of religion is the assurance that God is a person who thinks and loves,—to follow over again in our company the experience which then befell us.

Everyone knows that Descartes, looking about him, like Archimedes, for a firm ground whereon he might take his stand and begin to operate, for one single thing which was clearly certain and indubitable, found it in the famous '*Cogito, ergo sum;* I think, therefore I am.' If I think, said he, I am, I exist; my very doubting proves that I, who doubt, am. 'After thinking it well over and examining it on all sides, to this conclusion I cannot but come; I cannot but consider it settled that this proposition, *I am, I exist*, is necessarily true every time that I pronounce it or that I conceive it in my mind.' The discovery of this axiom appears to have filled Descartes with a profound sense of certitude and of satisfaction. And the axiom has been hailed with general approval and adopted with general consent. Locke repeats it as self-evident, without taking the trouble to assign to Descartes the authorship of it: 'If I doubt of all other things, that very doubt makes me perceive my own existence and will not suffer me to doubt of that.' Thinker after thinker has paid his tribute of admiration to the axiom; it is called the foundation of modern philosophy.

Now we shall confess without shame,—for to the prick of shame in these matters, after all the tauntings and mockings we have had to undergo, we are by this time quite dead,—we shall confess that from this fundamental axiom of Descartes we were never able to derive that light and satisfaction which others de- 5 rived from it. And for the following reason. The philosopher omits to tell us what he exactly means by to *be*, to *exist*. These terms stand for the most plain, positive, fundamental of certainties, which is established for us by the fact that we think. Now what to *think* means we all know; but even if we did not, Des- 10 cartes tells us. 'A thing which thinks,' says he, 'is a thing which doubts, which understands, which conceives, which affirms, which denies, which wishes, which declines, which imagines also, and which feels.' So far so good. But Descartes does not tell us what those other terms *be* and *exist* mean, which express that 15 fundamental certainty established for us by the fact of our think- ing; and this we do not so clearly know of ourselves without be- ing told. Philosophers know, of course, for they are always using the terms. And perhaps this is why Descartes does not trouble himself to explain his terms, I *am*, I *exist*, because to him they 20 carry an even more clear and well-defined sense than the term, I *think*. But to us they do not; and we suspect that the majority of plain people, if they consented to examine their minds, would find themselves to be in like case with us.

To get a clear and well-defined sense for the terms, I *am*, I 25 *exist*, in the connexion where Descartes uses them, we are obliged to translate them at a venture into something of this kind: 'I feel that I am alive.' And then we get the proposition: 'I think, there- fore I feel that I am alive.' This asserts our consciousness to de- pend upon our thinking rather than upon anything else which 30 we do. The assertion is clear, it is intelligible, it seems true; and perhaps it is what Descartes meant to convey. Still, it is disap- pointing to a plain man, who has been attracted to Descartes by his promises of perfect clearness and distinctness, to find that his fundamental proposition, his first great certainty, is something 35 which we cannot grasp as it stands, but that we have to translate it into other words in order to be able to grasp it.

Perhaps, too, this translation of ours does not, after all, represent what Descartes himself meant by 'I am, I exist.' Perhaps he
really did mean something more by the words, something that we
fail to grasp. We say so, because we find him, like philosophers
5   in general, often speaking of essence, existence, and substance,
and in speaking of them he lays down as certain and evident
many propositions which we cannot follow. For instance, he says:
'We have the idea of an infinite substance, eternal, all-knowing, all-powerful, the creator of all things, and with every pos-
10 sible perfection.' Again, he says: 'The ideas which represent substances to us are undoubtedly something more, and contain in
themselves, so to speak, more objective reality,—that is to say,
they partake by representation in more degrees of being or perfection,—than those which represent to us modes or accidents
15 only.' 'Undoubtedly,' says he, this is so; he introduces it, too,
with saying: 'It is evident.' So our guide, who admits nothing
which is not necessarily true, and puts aside everything about
which he can imagine there being the smallest doubt, lays down
that we have the idea of an *infinite substance;* and that of *sub-*
20 *stances* we have ideas distinguished from ideas of modes or accidents by their possessing more *being*, and this is equivalent to
possessing more perfection. For when we assert that one thing
is more *perfect* than another, this means, Descartes informs us,
that it has more reality, more *being*.

25 All this, I say, our guide finds certain and not admitting of the
least doubt. It is part of the things which we conceive with clearness and distinctness, and of which, therefore, we can be persuaded thoroughly. Man is a finite substance, that is, he has but
a limited degree of being, or perfection. God is an infinite sub-
30 stance, that is, he has an unlimited degree of being, or perfection.
Existence is a perfection, therefore God exists; thinking and loving are perfections, therefore God thinks and loves. In short,
we have God, a perfect and infinite Being, eternal, all-knowing,
all-powerful, the creator of all things, and having every perfec-
35 tion we can think of for him. And all this turns upon the words
is, being. Infinite being, necessary being, being in itself, as opposed to our own finite, contingent, dependent being, is something, says Descartes, that we clearly conceive. Now something

cannot come from nothing, and from us this infinite being could never have come; therefore it exists in itself, and is what is meant by God.

Not Descartes only, but every philosopher who attempts a metaphysical demonstration of God, will be found to proceed in this fashion, and to appeal at last to our conception of *being*, *existing*. Clarke starts with the proposition that something must have existed from eternity, and so arrives at a self-existent cause, which must be an intelligent *Being;* in other words, at God as a person who thinks and loves. Locke lays it down that 'we know there is some real being, and that non-entity cannot produce any real being,' and so brings us to an eternal, powerful, knowing *Being;* in other words, God as a person who thinks and loves. Of the God thus arrived at, Locke, like Descartes, says that 'the evidence is, if I mistake not, equal to mathematical certainty.' St. Anselm begins with an essential substantial good and great, whereby, he says, it is absolutely certain, and whoever likes can perceive it, that all the multifarious great and good things in the world get their goodness and greatness; and thus again we come to a one *Being* essentially great and good, or Divine Person who thinks and loves.

Now here it is, we suppose, that one's want of talent for abstract reasoning makes itself so lamentably felt. For to us these propositions, which we are told are so perfectly certain, and he who will may perceive their truth,—the propositions that we have the idea of an infinite substance, that there is an essential substantial good and great, that there is some real being, that a self-existent cause there must have been from eternity, that substances are distinguished in themselves and in our ideas of them from modes or accidents by their possessing more being,—have absolutely no force at all, we simply cannot follow their meaning. And so far as Descartes is concerned, this, when we first became aware of it, was a bitter disappointment to us. For he had seemed to promise something which even *we* could understand, when he said that he put aside everything about which he could imagine there being the smallest doubt, and that the proof of things to us was in the perfect clearness and distinctness with which we conceived them.

However, men of philosophical talents will remind us of the truths of mathematics, and tell us that the three angles of a triangle are undoubtedly equal to two right angles, yet very likely from want of skill or practice in abstract reasoning we cannot see the force of *that* proposition, and it may simply have no meaning for us. And let us suppose this may be so. But then the proposition in question is a deduction from certain elementary truths, and the deduction is too long or too hard for us to follow, or, at any rate, we may have not followed it or we may have forgotten it, and therefore we do not feel the force of the proposition. But the elementary assertions in geometry even we can apprehend; such as the assertion that two straight lines cannot enclose a space, or that things which are equal to the same are equal to each other. And we had hoped that Descartes, after his grand promises of clearness and certainty, would at least have set out with assertions of this kind, or else with facts of the plainest experience; that he would have started with something we might apprehend as we apprehend that three and two make five, or that fire burns. Instead of this, he starts with propositions about *being*, and does not tell us what *being* is. At one time he gives us hopes we may get to know it, for he says that to possess more being is to possess more perfection; and what men commonly mean when they talk of perfection, we think we can discover. But then we find that with Descartes to possess more perfection means to possess, not what men commonly call by that name, but to possess more being. And this seems to be merely going round in a circle, and we have to confess ourselves fairly puzzled and beaten.

So that when even Fénelon says, that most attractive of theologians: 'It is certain that I conceive a Being, infinite, and infinitely perfect,'—that is to say, infinitely *being*, we have to own with sorrow and shame that we cannot conceive this at all, for want of knowing what *being* is. Yet it is, we repeat, on the clearness and certainty of our conceptions of *being*, that the demonstration of God,—the most sure, as philosophers say, of all demonstrations, and on which all others depend,—is founded. The truth of all that people tell us about God, turns upon this question what *being* is. Philosophy is full of the word, and some philosophies are concerned with hardly anything else. The scholastic

philosophy, for instance, was one long debate about *being* and its conditions. Great philosophers, again, have established certain heads, or 'categories' as they call them, which are the final constitutive conditions of things, into which all things may at last be run up; and at the very top of these categories stands *essence*   5
or *being*.

Other metaphysical terms do not give us the same difficulty. Substance, for example, which is the Latin translation of essence or being, merely means *being* in so far as *being* is taken to be the subject of all modes and accidents, that which stands under them   10
and supplies the basis for them. Perhaps *being* does really do this, but we want first to know what *being* is. Spirit, which they oppose to matter, means literally, we know, only breath, but people use it for a *being* which is impalpable to touch as breath is. Perhaps this may be right, but we want first to know what *being* is.   15
Existence, again, means a standing or stepping forth, and we are told that God's essence involves existence, that is, that God's *being* necessarily steps forth, comes forth. Perhaps it does, but we require first to know what *being* is.

Till we know this, we know neither what to affirm nor what   20
to refuse to affirm. We refused to affirm that God is a person who thinks and loves, because we had no experience at all of thinking and loving except as attached to a certain bodily organisation. But perhaps they are not attached to this, but to *being*, and we ourselves have them, not because we have a bodily organisation,   25
but because we partake of *being*. Supreme *being*, therefore, *being* in itself, which is God, must think and love more than any of us. Angels, too, there may be, whole hierarchies of them, thinking and loving, and having their basis in *being*. All this may be so; only we cannot possibly verify any of it until we know what   30
being is; and we want to rest religion upon something which we can verify. And we thought that Descartes, with his splendid promises, was going to help us here; but just at the very pinch of the matter he fails us.

After all, plain, simple people are the great majority of the   35
human race. And we are sure, as we have said, that hundreds and thousands of people, if their attention were drawn to the matter, would acknowledge that they shared our slowness to see

at once what *being* is, and, when they found how much depended on seeing it, would gladly accompany us in the search
for some one who could give us help. For on this we ourselves,
at any rate, were bent:—to discover some one who could tell
us what *being* is. And such a kind soul we did at last find. In these
days we need hardly add, that he was a German professor.

3.

But not a professor of logic and metaphysics. No, not Hegel,
not one of those great men, those masters of abstruse reasoning,
who discourse of being and non-being, essence and existence,
subject and object, in a style to which that of Descartes is merely
child's play. These sages only bewildered us more than we were
bewildered already. For they were so far advanced in their
speculations about being, that they were altogether above entertaining such a tyro's question as what *being* really is.

No, our professor was a mere professor of words, not of ontol-
ogy. We bethought ourselves of our old resource, following the
history of the human spirit, tracking its course, trying to make
out how men have used words and what they meant by them.
Perhaps in the word *being* itself, said we to ourselves, there may
be something to tell us what it at first meant and how men came
to use it as they do. *Abstracta ex concretis*, say the etymologists;
the abstract has been formed out of the concrete. Perhaps this
abstract *being*, also, has been formed out of some concrete, and
if we knew out of what, we might possibly trace how it has come
to be used as it has. Or has indeed the mystic vocable no natural
history of this sort, but has dropped out of heaven, and all one
can say of it is that it means *being*, something which the philosophers understand but we never shall, and which explains and
demonstrates all sorts of hard problems, but to philosophers only,
and not to the common herd of mankind? Let us enquire, at any
rate.

So, then, the natural history of the word was what we wanted.
With a proper respect for our Aryan forefathers, first we looked
in Sanscrit dictionaries for information. But here, probably from
our own ignorance and inexperience in the Sanscrit language,

we failed to find what we sought. By a happy chance, however, it one day occurred to us to turn for aid to a book about the Greek language,—a language where we were not quite so helpless as in Sanscrit,—to the 'Principles of Greek Etymology,' by Dr. George Curtius, of Leipsic.[1] He it was who succoured a poor soul whom the philosophers had driven well-nigh to despair, and he deserves, and shall have, our lasting gratitude.

In the book of Dr. Curtius we looked out the Greek verb *eimi, eis, esti*, the verb which has the same source as the English verb *is*. Shall we ever forget the emotion with which we read what follows:—'That the meaning, addressed to the senses, of this very old verb substantive was *breathe*, is made all but certain by the Sanscrit *as-u-s*, life-breath, *asu-ra-s*, living, and the Sanscrit *âs*, mouth, parallel with the Latin *os*. The Hebrew verb substantive *haja* or *hawa* has, according to M. Renan (*De l'Origine du Langage*, 4th ed., p. 129), the same original signification. The three main meanings succeed one another in the following order: *breathe, live, be*.' Here was some light at last! We get, then, for the English *is*,—the French and Latin *est*, the Greek *estin* or *esti*,—we get an Indo-European root *as*, breathe.

To get even thus much was pleasant, but what was our joy to find ourselves put by Dr. Curtius, in some words following those we have quoted, on the trace of a meaning for the mysterious term *being* itself? Dr. Curtius spoke of a root synonymous with *as*, the root *bhu*, in Greek φυ, and referred his readers to No. 417. To No. 417 we impatiently turned. We found there the account of the Greek verb φύω, φύομαι, I beget, I grow. This word is familiar to us all in our own words *future* and *physics*, in the French *fus*, in the Latin *fui*. All these are from an Indo-European root *bhu*, 'be,' which had primarily that sense of 'grow,' which its Greek derivative has kept. 'The notion *be* attaches to this root,' says Dr. Curtius, 'evidently on the foundation only of the more primitive *grow*.' If the root *as*, breathe, gives us then our *is, essence*, the root *bhu*, grow, gives us our *be, being*. This was indeed a discovery. *Is, essence* and *entity*, *be* and *being*, here we

---

[1] *Grundzüge der Griechischen Etymologie*, von Georg Curtius; 3rd edit., Leipzig, 1869.

have the source of them all! as in another Indo-European root, *sta*, stand, we have, as everybody knows, the source of our words *existence, substance*. Our composite verb substantive in English, like the verb substantive in Latin, employs both the root
5 *as* and the root *bhu;* we have *is* and *be*, as the Latin has *est* and *fui*. The French verb substantive manages to employ,—so M. Littré in his admirable new dictionary points out,—the roots *as, bhu*, and *sta*, all three.

Now then it remained for us to ask, how these harmless con-
10 cretes, *breathe, grow*, and *stand*, could ever have risen into those terrible abstracts, *is, be*, and *exist*, which had given us so much torment. And really, by attending to the natural course followed by the human mind, to men's ways of using words and arriving at thoughts, this was not so very hard to make out. Only, when
15 once it was made out, it proved fatal to the wonderful perform-ances of the metaphysicians upon their theme of *being*. How-ever, we must not anticipate.

Men took these three simple names of the foremost and most elementary activities in that which they knew best and were
20 chiefly concerned with,—in themselves,—they took *breathing, growing, standing forth*, to describe *all* activities which were re-marked by their senses or by their minds. So arose the verb sub-stantive. Children, we can observe, do not connect their notions at all by the verb, the word expressing activity. They say, 'horse,
25 black,' and there they leave it. When man's mind advanced be-yond this simple stage, and he wanted to connect his notions by representing one notion as affecting him through its appearing or operating in conjunction with another notion, then he took a figure from the activity that lay nearest to him and said: 'The
30 horse breathes (is) black.' When he got to the use of abstract nouns his verb still remained the same. He said: 'Virtue breathes (is) fair; Valour growing (being) praiseworthy.' Soon the sense of the old concrete meaning faded away in the new employment of the word. That slight parcel of significance which was re-
35 quired had been taken, and now this minimum alone remained, and the rest was left unregarded and died out of men's thoughts.

We may make this clearer to ourselves by observing what has happened in the French and Dutch words for our common word *but*. *But* is in French *mais*, the Latin *magis*, our word *more;* in Dutch it is *maar*, our word *more* itself. *Mais* and *maar* were originally used, no doubt, with the sense of their being a check, or stop, given to something that had been said before, by the *addition* to it of something fresh. The primitive sense of addi- 5 tion faded away, the sense of check remained alone. And so it was with *as* and *bhu*, the primitive *breathe* and *grow*. What- ever affected us by appearing to us, or by acting on us, was at first said by a figure to breathe and grow. The figure was forgot- ten; and now *as* and *bhu* no longer raised the idea of breathing 10 and growing, but merely of that appearance or operation,—a kind of shadow of breathing and growing,—which these words *as* and *bhu* had at first been employed to convey. And for breath- ing and growing other words than *as* and *bhu* were now found, just as, in French, *mais* now no longer means *more*, but for *more* 15 another word has been found: the word *plus*. Sometimes, how- ever, as in the case of the Greek verb γίγνομαι, ἐγενόμην, we see the same word continuing to be used both in its old full sense and in its new shrunk sense; γενέσθαι may mean both *to be born* and *to be*. But the user employed it, probably, in the two different ac- 20 ceptations, as if he had been employing two different words; nor did its use as hardly more than a copula necessarily raise in his mind the thought of its originally fuller significance.

Nor indeed were these primitive verbs, *as* and *bhu*, used only as a copula, to connect, in the manner we have described, the 25 attribute with its subject. They were also used as themselves ex- pressing an attribute of the subject. For when men wanted strongly to affirm that action or operation of things, that image of their own life and activity, which impressed itelf upon their mind and affected them, they took these same primitive verbs 30 and used them emphatically. Virtue *is*, they said; Truth does not cease to *be*. Literally: Virtue *breathes;* Truth does not cease to *grow*. A yet more emphatic affirmation of this kind was sup- plied by the word *exist*. For to exist is literally to step forth, and he who steps forth gives a notable proof of his life and activity. 35 Men said, therefore: Duty *exists*. That is, according to the origi- nal figure: Duty steps forth, stands forth.

And the *not ourselves*, mighty for our weal or woe, which so

soon by some one or other of its sides attracted the notice of
man, this also man connected with whatever attributes he might
be led to assign to it, by his universal connective, his now established verbs *as* and *bhu*, his *breathe* and *grow* with their blunted
5 and shadowy sense of breathing and growing. He said: God
breathes angry; our God *breathes* a jealous God. When he
wanted to affirm emphatically that this power acts, makes itself
felt, lasts, he said: God *exists*. In other words: God *steps forth*.

Israel conceived God with a solemnity and a seriousness un-
10 known to other nations, as, 'The not ourselves that makes for
righteousness.' 'When I speak of this unique God of Israel,' asked
Moses, 'how shall I name him?' And the answer came (we will
give it in the words of the literal Latin version, printed under the
Hebrew in Walton's noble Polyglot Bible): 'Dixit Deus ad
15 Mosen: *Ero qui ero*. Et dixit: Sic dices filiis Israel: *Ero* misit me
ad vos.' '*I will breathe* hath sent me unto you;' or, as the Arabic
version well renders this mystic name: *The Eternal, that passeth
not*. For that this is the true meaning of the name there can be
no doubt:—The *I will go on living, operating, enduring*. 'God
20 here signifies of himself,' says Gesenius, 'not simply that he is *he
who is*, for of this everyone must perceive the frigidity, but he
signifies emphatically that he is *he who is always the same*, that is,
the Immutable, the Eternal.' To the like effect Dr. Kalisch, in his
valuable Commentary, after reciting the series of more fanciful
25 and metaphysical interpretations, rests finally in this, the simple
and the undoubtedly true one: 'He that changeth not, and that
faileth not.'

'*I will breathe* hath sent me unto you!' Still the old sensuous
image from the chief and most striking function of human life,
30 transferred to God, taken to describe, in the height and perma-
nency of its beneficent operation, this mighty *not ourselves*,
which in its operation we are aware of, but in its nature, no.

And here is, indeed, the grand conclusion to be drawn from
this long philological disquisition, from our persistent scrutiny of
35 the primitives *as* and *bhu*, breathe and grow: that by a simple
figure they declare a perceived energy and operation, and nothing more. Of a *subject*, as we call him, that performs this operation, of the nature of something outside the range of plants and

of animals who do indeed grow and breathe, and from whom the figure in *as* and *bhu* is borrowed, they tell us nothing. But they have been falsely supposed to bring us news about the primal nature of things, to declare a subject in which inhered the energy and the operation we had noticed, to indicate a fontal category or supreme constitutive condition, into which the nature of all things whatsoever might be finally run up.

For the original figure, as we have said, was soon forgotten; and *is* and *be*, mysterious petrifactions, remained in language as if they were autochthons there, and as if no one could go beyond or behind them. Without father, without mother, without descent, as it seemed, they yet were omnipresent in our speech, and indispensable. Allied words in which the figure was manifest, such as existence and substance, were thought to be figures from the world of sense pressed into the service of a metaphysical reality enshrined in *is* and *be*. That imposing phrase of the metaphysicians for summing up the whole system of things, *substance and accident*,—phenomena, and that which stands under phenomena and in which they inhere,—must surely, one would think, have provoked question, have aroused misgivings,—people must surely have asked themselves what the *that* which stands under phenomena was,—if the answer had not been ready: *being*. And *being* was supposed to be something absolute, which stood under all things. Yet *being* was itself all the while but a sensuous figure, *growing*, and did not of necessity express anything of a thing's nature, expressed only man's sense of a thing's operation.

But philosophers, ignorant of this, and imagining that they had in *being* a term which expressed the highest and simplest nature of things, stripped off (to use a phrase of Descartes), when they wanted to reach the naked truth of a thing, one of the thing's garments after another, they stripped away this and that figure and size for bodies, this and that thought and desire for mind, and so they arrived at the final substances of bodies and of mind, their *being* or *essence*, which for bodies was a substantial essence capable of infinite diversities of figure and size, for mind a substantial essence capable of infinite diversities of thought and desire. And that for bodies and for mind they thus got a highest reality merely negative, a reality in which there was less of reality than in any single body or mind they knew, this they did not heed, because in *being* or *essence* they supposed they had the supreme reality.

Finally, in considering God they were obliged, if they wanted to escape from difficulties, to drop even the one characteristic they had assigned to their substance, that of admitting modes and accidents, and thus to reduce, in fact, their idea of God to nothing at all. And this they themselves were much too acute, many of them, not to perceive; as Erigena, for instance, says: '*Deus non immerito nihilum vocatur;* God may be not improperly called nothing.' But this did not make them hesitate, because they thought they had in pure *being*, or *essence*, the supreme reality, and that this *being* in itself, this *essence* not even serving as substance, was God. And therefore Erigena adds that it is *per excellentiam*, by reason of excellency, that God is not improperly called nothing: '*Deus per excellentiam non immerito nihilum vocatur.*'

To such a degree do words make man, who invents them, their sport! The moment we have an abstract word, a word where we do not apprehend both the concrete sense and the manner of this sense's application, there is danger. The whole value of an abstract term depends on our true and clear conception of that which we have abstracted and now convey by means of this term. *Animal* is a valuable term because we know what breathing, *anima*, is, and we use animal to denote all who have this in common. But the *être* of Descartes is an unprofitable term, because we do not clearly conceive what the term means. And it is, moreover, a dangerous term, because without clearly conceiving what it means, we nevertheless use it freely. When we at last come to examine the term, we find that *être* and *animal* really mean just the same thing: *breather*, that which has vital breath.

How astounding are the consequences if we give to *être* and its cognates this their original sense which we have discovered! *Cogito, ergo sum*, will then be: 'I think, therefore I breathe.' A true deduction certainly; but *Comedo, ergo sum*, 'I eat, therefore I breathe,' would be nearly as much to the purpose! Metaphysics, the science treating of *être* and its conditions, will be the science treating of breathing and its conditions. But surely the

right science to treat of breathing and its conditions is not metaphysics, but physiology! 'God *is*,' will be, God *breathes;* exactly
that old anthropomorphic account of him which our dogmatic
theology, by declaring him to be without body, parts, or passions, has sought to banish! And even to adore,—like those men   5
of new lights, the French revolutionists, haters of our dogmatic
theology,—even to adore, like Robespierre, the *Être Suprême*,
will be only, after all, to adore the Supreme Animal! So perfidi-
ously do these words *is* and *be*,—on which we embarked our
hopes because we fancied they would bring us to a thinking and   10
a loving, independent of all material organisation,—so perfidi-
ously do they land us in mere creature-worship of the grossest
kind. Nay, and perhaps the one man who uses that wonderful
abstract word, *essence*, with propriety, will turn out to be, not
the metaphysician or the theologian, but the perfumer. For   15
while nothing but perplexity can come from speaking of the essence or *breathing* of the Divine Nature, there is really much
felicity in speaking of the essence or *breathing* of roses.

4.

   Dismayed, then, at the consequence of a rash use of *being*
and *essence*, we determined henceforth always to subject these   20
vocables, when we found them used in a way which caused us
any doubt, to a strict examination. Far from remaining, as formerly, in helpless admiration of the philosophers, when upon the
foundation of these words they built their wonderful cloud-
houses and then laughed at us for not being able to find our   25
way about them, we set ourselves to discover what meaning
the words, in men's use of them, really did and could contain.
And we found that the great thing to keep steadily in mind
is that the words are, as we have shown, figure. Man applied
this image of breathing and growing, taken from his own life,   30
to all which he perceived, all from which he felt an effect;
and pronounced it all to be living too. The words, therefore,
which appear to tell us something about the life and nature of all
things, do in fact tell us nothing about any life and nature except
that which breathing and growing go in some degree to consti-   35
tute;—the life and nature, let us say, of men, of the lower animals,

and of plants. Of life or nature in other things the words tell us nothing, but figuratively invest these things with the characters of animal and vegetable life. But what do they really tell us of these things? Simply that the things have an effect upon us, oper-
5   ate upon us.

The names themselves, then, *being* and *essence*, tell us something of the real constitution of animals and plants, but of nothing else. However, the real constitution of a thing it may happen that we know, although these names convey nothing of it
10 and help us to it not at all. For instance, a chemist knows the constitution, say, of common ether. He knows that common ether is an assemblage of molecules each containing four atoms of carbon, ten of hydrogen, and one of oxygen, arranged in a certain order. This we may, if we please, call the being or es-
15 sence, the *growing* or *breath*, of common ether. That is to say, to the real constitution of a thing, when we know it, we often apply a figurative name originally suggested by the principal and prominent phenomena of our own constitution.

This in the case of bodies. When we speak of the being or es-
20 sence of bodies, it may be that we know their real constitution and give these names to it. But far oftener men say that bodies have *being*, assert that bodies *are*, without any knowledge, either actual or implied, of the real constitution of the bodies, but merely meaning that the bodies are seen, heard, touched, tasted,
25 or smelt by us, affect our senses in some way or other. And to bodies, thus acting upon us and affecting us, we attribute being or *growing*, we say that they are or *breathe*, although we may know nothing of their constitution. But we apply to their action a figurative name originally suggested by the principal and
30 prominent activities of our own constitution.

And we proceed just in the same way with what are not bodies. Men come by abstraction to perceive the qualities of courage and self-denial, and then talk of the *being* of the qualities at which they have thus come; they say that courage and duty
35 have *growing* or being, they assert that courage and duty *breathe* or are. They apply to the working of their abstraction figurative names, drawn originally from the principal and prominent workings of their own life.

Or, again, they become aware of a law of nature, as it is called, —of a certain regular order in which it is proved, or thought to be proved, that certain things happen. To this law, to the law, let us suppose, of gravitation, they attribute *being;* they say that the law of gravitation is, exists, *breathes, steps forth.* That is, they 5 give to the regularly ordered operation which they perceive, figurative names borrowed from the principal and prominent functions of their own life.

Or, finally, they become aware of a law of nature which concerns their own life and conduct in the highest degree,—of an 10 eternal not ourselves that makes for righteousness. For this is really a law of nature, collected from experience, just as much as the law of gravitation is; only it is a law of nature which is conceived, however confusedly, by very many more of mankind as affecting them, and much more nearly. But it has its origin in 15 experience, it appeals to experience, and by experience it is, as we believe, verified. [A writer whom we name with esteem because he has so firmly grasped the truth, that what Jesus Christ cared for was to change the inner man of each individual, not to establish organisations of any sort, Mr. Dunn says, that the God of 20 popular religion, the personal God who thinks and loves, is as much verifiable by experience as our eternal power that makes for righteousness. Possibly he imagines us to mean by *power* some material agent, some body, some gas; and such a divine agent making for righteousness is no more verifiable by experi 25 ence, we confess, than a divine person, who thinks and loves, making for it. We no more pretend to know the origin and composition of the power that makes for righteousness than of the power that makes for gravitation. All we profess to have ascertained about it is, that it has effect on us, that it operates. 30

[Some deny that it operates. *The fool hath said in his heart: There is no God.* But we maintain that experience is against the fool, that righteousness is salvation. As far as man's experience reaches, it comes out, and comes out ever more clearly, both by the operation of the law itself and by man's inward 35 sense of affinity and response to it, that our welfare, which we cannot but pursue, is inextricably and unalterably, and by no procuring of ours but whether we will or no, dependent on con-

duct. Mr. Dunn does not surely think that we have the same
experience of God as a person who thinks and loves, which we
have of this? He says that a great many people have believed that
God is a person who thinks and loves. Undoubtedly they have;
5 just as a great many people have believed this or that hypothesis
about the system of nature. But the question is, whether they had
any such good grounds from experience for accepting these
things as true, as there are for accepting as true the law of gravitation and the law of righteousness, the Eternal that makes for
10 righteousness.

[It is said, again, that *eternal*,—that which never had a beginning, and can never have an end,—is a metaphysical conception
not given by experience. Yes indeed, *eternal*, as that which never
had a beginning and can never have an end, is, like the final sub-
15 stance or subject wherein all qualities inhere, a metaphysical conception to which experience has nothing to say. But eternal, *aevi-
ternus*, the age or life-long, as men applied it to the Eternal that
makes for righteousness, was no metaphysical conception. From
all they could themselves make out, and from all that their fathers
20 had told them, they believed that righteousness was salvation,
and that it would go on being salvation from one generation of
men to another. And this is the only sound sense in which we
can call the law of righteousness, or the law of gravitation, or
any other law which we may perceive, eternal. From all that we
25 hear or can make out it holds good; and we believe, therefore,
that it will go on holding good.

[Well, then,] men become aware from experience,—that
source of all our knowledge,—they become aware of a law of
righteousness. And to this law they attribute *being*. They say
30 that the law of conduct, the eternal not ourselves which makes
for righteousness, is, exists,—*breathes, steps forth.* That is to say,
they give to the stedfast, unchanging, widely and deeply working operation which they perceive, figurative names borrowed
from the principal and prominent operations of their own life.

35   *Being* and *essence* men in this way attribute to what they perceive, or think they perceive, to be a law of nature. But often,
long before they perceive it as a law of nature, they are conscious
of its working; they feel its power by many a sharp lesson. And
imagination coming in to help, they make it, as they make every-

thing of which they powerfully feel the effect, into a human agent, at bottom like themselves, however much mightier,—a human agent that feels, thinks, loves, hates. So they made the Sun into a human being; and even the operation of chance, Fortune. And what should sooner or more certainly be thus made into a human being, but far mightier and more lasting than common man, than the operation which affects men so widely and deeply, —for it is engaged with conduct, with at least three-fourths of human life,—the *not ourselves* that makes for righteousness?

Made into a human being this was sure to be, from its immense importance, its perpetual intervention. But this importance does not make the personifying, anthropomorphic process, the less the explanation of the attributed human qualities in this case, than it is the explanation of them in others. Yet we will have it, very many of us, that the human qualities are in the one case really there and inherent, but in all the other cases they are the mere work of man's plastic and personifying power. What was the Apollo of the religion of the Greeks? The law of intellectual beauty, the eternal not ourselves that makes for intellectual beauty. By a natural and quite explicable working of the human spirit, a heightened, glorified human being, thinking and loving, came to stand for the operation of this power. Who doubts this? But the thinking and loving Apollo of the Greeks, and every other example of the like kind except one, this natural working of the human spirit is supposed to explain; only the thinking and loving Jehovah of the Hebrews shall not be explained by this working, but a person who thinks and loves he really is!

To return, then, to our much abused primitives. They were supposed to give us for conscious intelligence, for thinking and loving, a basis or subject independent of bodily constitution. They do in fact give us nothing beyond bodily phenomena; but they transfer by a figure the phenomena of our own bodily life to all law and operation. On a fine and subtle scale they still carry on that personifying anthropomorphic process, native in man and ineradicable, which in all the early religions of the world we can see going forward on a scale gross and palpable.

So it appears, that even when we talk of the *being* of things, we use a fluid and literary expression, not a rigid and scientific one. [And in every case where anything is made to depend upon

the use of the words *is* and *be*, we ought to examine what is said,
and see what sense they can really, in that particular case, bear.
For instance, Descartes says, that what makes him certain of the
truth of his fundamental proposition, 'I think, therefore I am,
5   *Je pense, donc je suis*,' is that he sees quite clearly that in order to
think one must be:—'*Pour penser il faut être*.' And *être* really
means to breathe; and we do, indeed, see quite clearly that, in
order to think, we must breathe. And this is the clearest sense
the words can have. Nevertheless, it is not the sense Descartes
10   meant to give them. Well, then, they can also bear the sense that
because we think, we feel ourselves to be alive. And probably
this is what Descartes alleges that he and all of us can see quite
clearly. So when philosophers tell us, in their grand language,
that 'from our actual thought we affirm our actual existence,' let
15   us simple people interpret, and say, that this means that because
we think, we feel ourselves to be alive; and let us concede, with
due admiration for those who clothe the thing in such imposing
language, that we can clearly see this also to be true. Only let us
remember exactly what it is that we have seen to be true. And
20   when the philosophers go on to tell us, further, that 'as we affirm
our actual existence from our actual thought, similarly, the idea
we have of the infinite and infinitely perfect Being, that is, of
God, clearly involves his actual existence;' let us again put the
thing into easier language, and propound it to ourselves that as,
25   because we think, we feel ourselves to be alive, similarly, because
we think of God, God feels himself to be alive. Probably we shall
not be disposed to concede that we can clearly see this to be true;
nor, perhaps, would the philosophers allege it as certain, if they
had accustomed themselves to inquire in all cases what *being*,
30   *existing*, really mean.]

5.

Armed with this key of the real signification of our two poor
little words, *is* and *be*, let us next boldly carry the war into the
enemy's country, and see how many strong fortresses of the
metaphysicians, which frown upon us from their heights so defi-
35   antly, we can now enter and rifle. For *is* and *be*, we have learnt,
simply mean, in reality, *breathe* and *grow*, while in mankind's

use of them they simply mean *operate*, or *appear to man to operate*. But when the metaphysicians start with their at least certainly knowing that *something is*, they always have in their minds:—'Something thinks which neither breathes nor grows, and we know of a subject for thinking which neither breathes 5 nor grows, and that subject is *being*, *être*.' They are unaware that *being*, *être*, are two words which in reality simply mean breathing and growing. And then, with two supposed data of a cogitative substance and an incogitative substance, the metaphysicians argue away about the necessary mutual relations of these two in 10 the production of things, and form all manner of fine conclusions. But all the knowledge they do really set out with in their *something is* amounts to this: 'We are aware of *operation*.' And this neither tells them anything about the nature and origin of things, nor enables them to conclude anything. 15

Now, if we keep this in mind, we shall see the fallacy of many reasonings we meet with. The *Edinburgh Review* says: 'All existing beings must be persons or things; persons are superior to things; do you mean to call God a thing?' [The ambiguity is in *beings*. He who asserts this or that to be a person or a thing,— 20 endued, that is, with what we call life or not endued with it,— pronounces something concerning its constitution. And when we pronounce that God has *being*, that God *is*, we may mean by this that God has growth, that God breathes; and then we do assert something concerning God's constitution, and affirm God 25 to be a person not a thing. But we may also mean, when we pronounce that God has *being*, that God *is*, simply that God operates, that the Eternal which makes for righteousness has operation. And then we assert nothing about God's constitution whatever, we neither affirm God to be a person nor to be a thing. 30 And, indeed, we are not at all in a position to affirm God to be either the one or the other.] But he who pronounces that God must be a person or a thing, and that God must be a person because persons are superior to things, talks as idly as one who should insist upon it that the law of gravitation must be either a 35 person or a thing, and should lay down which of the two it must be. Because it is a law, is it to be pronounced a thing and not a person, and therefore inferior to persons? and are we quite sure that a bad critic, suppose, is superior to the law of gravitation?

The truth is, we are attempting an exhaustive division into things and persons, and attempting to affirm that the object of our thought is one or the other, when we have no means for doing anything of the kind, when all we can really say of our object
5   of thought is, that it *operates*.

Or to take that favourite and famous demonstration of Anselm and Descartes, that if we have the idea of a perfect being, or God,—that is to say, of an infinite substance, eternal, all-knowing, all-powerful, the creator of all things, and with every pos-
10 sible perfection,—then this perfect being must exist. Existence, they argue, is a perfection, and besides, our imperfect finite being could never have given to itself the idea of a perfect infinite being. But we have this idea, they say, quite clearly and distinctly, and therefore there must exist some other being besides ourselves
15 from whom we must have received it. All this, again, tumbles to pieces like a house of cards the moment we press it. The ambiguity lies in the words *perfect being, infinite substance*. Of a *not ourselves* we are clearly aware;—but a clear idea of an infinite substance, a perfect being, knowing and thinking and yet
20 not breathing and growing? And this idea we could not have given to ourselves, because it is a *clear idea* of an infinite substance, full of perfection; and we are a finite substance, full of imperfection? But the idea which men thus describe is not a clear idea, and it is an idea which, in the only state wherein they really
25 have it, they may perfectly well have given to themselves. For it is an idea of a man hugely magnified and improved.

The less and more in ourselves of whatever we account good, gives us a notion of what we call perfection in it. We have degrees of pleasure, and we talk of perfect, infinite pleasure; we
30 have some rest, and we talk of perfect, infinite rest; we have some knowledge, and we talk of perfect, infinite knowledge; we have some power, and we talk of perfect, infinite power. What we mean is, a great deal of pleasure, rest, knowledge, power; as much of them as we can imagine, and without the
35 many lets and hindrances to them which we now experience. Our idea of a perfect being, all-knowing, all-powerful, is just like that idea of a myriagon, of which Descartes himself speaks somewhere. Of a pentagon, or five-sided figure, we have a distinct

idea. And we talk of our idea of a myriagon, or ten-thousand-sided figure, too; but it is not a clear idea, it is an idea of something very big, but confused. Such is our idea of an infinite substance, all-knowing, all-powerful. Of a bounded man, with some knowledge and some power, we have a distinct idea; of an unbounded man, with all knowledge and all power, our idea is not clear; we have an idea of something very wise and great, but a confused idea. And even granting that clear ideas prove themselves, this alleged clear and distinct idea of an infinite substance, all-knowing and all-powerful, is one of those cases where an idea is fancied to be clear and distinct when it is not.

But people still insist that our truly perfect ideas, at any rate, must have being quite independently of us and our experience, and must inhere, therefore, in a source, a subject, an infinite substance, which is God. For we have, say they, the idea of a perfect circle; yet this idea cannot be given us by experience, because in nature there is no such thing as a perfect circle. We have the idea of a perfect good; yet this idea cannot be given us by experience, because in nature there is no such thing as a perfect good. But let us ask ourselves whether even the circle and the triangle were first, probably, pure conceptions in the human mind, and then applied to nature? or whether these forms were not first observed in nature, and then refined into pure conceptions? And was perfect good, in like manner, or perfect beauty, first a pure conception in the human mind, and then applied to things in nature? or were things more or less good and beautiful first observed in experience, and goodness and beauty then refined into pure conceptions? Because, in that case, our ideas of a perfect circle and a perfect good are simply the imagination of a still rounder circle and a still better good than any which we have yet found in experience. But experience gave us the ideas, and we have no need to invent something out of experience as the source of them.

Finally, let us take the grand argument from design. Design, people say, implies a designer. The ambiguity lies in the little termination *er*, by which we mean a *being* who designed. We talk of a being, an *être*, and we imagine that the word gives us conscious intelligence, thinking and loving, without bodily organisation; but it does not. It gives us one of two things only;—

either it gives us breathing and growing, or it gives us effect and
operation. Design implies a designer? Human design does; it implies the presence of a being who breathes and thinks. So does
that of the lower animals, who, like man himself, breathe, and
5   may be said to think. A very numerous class of works we know,
which man and the lower animals make for their own purposes.
When we see a watch or a honeycomb we say: It works harmoniously and well, and a man or a bee made it. But a yet more numerous class of works we know, which neither man nor the
10   lower animals have made for their own purposes. When we see
the ear, or see a bud, do we say: It works harmoniously and well,
and a man or one of the lower animals made it? No; but we say:
It works harmoniously and well, and an infinite eternal substance, an all-thinking and all-powerful being, the creator of all
15   things, made it. Why? Because it works harmoniously and well.
But its working harmoniously and well does not prove all this;
it only proves that it works harmoniously and well. The well and
harmonious working of the watch or the honeycomb is not what
proves to us that a man or a bee made them; what proves this to
20   us is, that we know from experience that men make watches and
bees make honeycombs. But we do not know from experience
that an infinite eternal substance, all-thinking and all-powerful,
the creator of all things, makes ears and buds. We know nothing
about the matter, it is altogether beyond us. When, therefore, we
25   are speaking exactly, and not poetically and figuratively, of the
ear or of a bud, which we see working harmoniously and well,
all we have a right to say is: It works harmoniously and well.

6.

We besought those who could receive neither the miracles of
popular theology nor the metaphysics of learned theology, not
30   to fling away the Bible on that account, but to try how the Bible
went if they took it without either the one or the other, and
studied it without taking anything for granted but what they
could verify. But such indignant and strenuous objection was
made in the religious world to this proposal, and in particular
35   it was so emphatically asserted that the only possible basis for

religion is to believe that God is a person who thinks and loves, that the readers of *Literature and Dogma* who had taken our advice and had begun to find profit from it, might well be supposed to feel alarm and to hesitate, and to ask whether, after all, they were doing well in following our recommendation. So we have had to look again at the reasons for laying down as the foundation of religion the belief that God is a person who thinks and loves. And we found reasons of two kinds alleged: reasons drawn from miracles, and reasons drawn from metaphysics. But the reasons from miracles we found, after looking at miracles again, that we could not rely on, that fail us sooner or later they surely must. And now we find the same thing with the reasons drawn from metaphysics.

The reasons drawn from miracles one cannot but dismiss with tenderness, for they belong to a great and splendid whole,—a beautiful and powerful fairy-tale, which was long believed without question, and which has given comfort and joy to thousands. And one abandons them with a kind of unwilling disenchantment, and only because one must.

The reasons drawn from metaphysics one dismisses, on the other hand, with sheer satisfaction. They have convinced no one, they have given rest to no one, they have given joy to no one. People have swallowed them, people have fought over them, people have shown their ingenuity over them; but no one has ever enjoyed them. Nay, no one has every really understood them. No one has ever fairly grasped the meaning of what he was saying, when he laid down propositions about finite and infinite substance, and about God's essence involving existence. Yet men of splendid ability have dealt in them. But the truth is, the reasons from metaphysics for the Divine Personality got their real nourishment and support out of the reasons from miracles. Through long ages the inexperience, the helplessness, and the agitation of man made the belief in a magnified and non-natural man or men, in etherealised men,—in short, in preternatural personages of some sort or other,—inevitable. And, the preternatural having been supposed to be certainly there, the metaphysics, or science of things coming after natural things and no longer natural, had to come in to account for it. But the miracles proving to

be an unsubstantial ground of reliance, the metaphysics will certainly not stand long. Now, an unsubstantial ground of reliance
men more and more perceive miracles to be; and the sooner they
quite make up their mind about it, the better. But if it is vain
5   to tamper with one's understanding, to resist one's widening experience, and to try to think that from miracles one can get
ground for asserting God to be a person who thinks and loves,
still more vain is it to try to think one can get ground for this
from metaphysics.

10   And perhaps we may have been enabled to make this clear to
ourselves and others, because we, having no talent for abstruse
reasoning and being known to have none, were not ashamed,
when we were confronted by propositions about essence and
existence, and about infinite substance having undoubtedly more
15   objective reality than finite substance, we were not ashamed, I
say, instead of assenting with a solemn face to what we did not
understand, to own that we did not understand it, and to seek
humbly for the meaning of the little words at the bottom of it all;
and so the futility of all the grand superstructure was revealed
20   to us. If the German philosopher, who writes to us from Texas
reproaching us with wasting our time over the Bible and Christianity, 'which are certainly,' says he, 'disappearing from heart
and mind of the cultured world,' and calling us to the study of
the great Hartmann, will allow us to quote the Bible yet once
25   more, we should be disposed to say that here is a good exempli-
fication of that text: '*Mansueti delectabuntur;* The meek-spirited
shall be refreshed.'

But to our reader and to ourselves we say once again, as to
the metaphysics of current theology, what we said as to its mir-
30   acles. When we have made out their untrustworthiness, we have
as yet achieved nothing, except to get rid of an unsafe stay which
would inevitably have sooner or later broken down with us. But
to use the Bible, to enjoy the Bible, remains. We cannot use it,
we cannot enjoy it, more and more of us, if its use and enjoyment
35   require us first to take for granted something which cannot possibly be verified. Whether we will or not, this is so; and more and
more will mankind, the religious among them as well as the profane, find themselves in this case. 'In good truth,' said Pascal to

the Jesuits, 'the world is getting mistrustful, and no longer believes things unless they are evident to it.' In the seventeenth
century, when Pascal said this, it had already begun to be true;
it is getting more widely true every day. Therefore we urge all
whom the current theology, both popular and learned, dissatis-   5
fies (for with those whom it does not dissatisfy we do not meddle), we urge them to take as their foundation in reading the
Bible this account of God, which can be verified: 'God is the
eternal power, not ourselves, which makes for righteousness,'
instead of this other: 'God is a person who thinks and loves,'   10
which cannot. We advise them to eschew as much as possible,
in speaking about God, the use of the word *Being*, which even
strict thinkers are so apt to use continually without asking themselves what it really means. The word is bad, because it has a false
air of conveying some real but abstruse knowledge about God's   15
nature, while it does not, but is merely a figure. *Power* is a better
word, because it pretends to assert of God nothing more than
effect on us, operation. With much of the current theology our
unpretending account of God will indeed make havoc; but it
will enable a man, we believe, to use and enjoy the Bible in secur- 20
ity. Only he must always remember that the language of the
Bible is to be treated as the language of letters, not science, language approximative and full of figure, not language exact.
   Many excellent people are crying out every day that all is
lost in religion unless we can affirm that God is a person who   25
thinks and loves. We say, that unless we can verify this, it is impossible to build religion successfully upon it; and it cannot be
verified. Even if it could be shown that there is a low degree of
probability for it, we say that it is a grave and fatal error to imagine that religion can be built on what has a low degree of prob-   30
ability. However, we do not think it can be said that there is even
a low degree of probability for the assertion that God is a person
who thinks and loves, properly and naturally though we may
make him such in the language of feeling; the assertion deals
with what is so utterly beyond us. But we maintain, that, start-   35
ing from what may be verified about God,—that he is the Eternal
which makes for righteousness,—and reading the Bible with this
idea to govern us, we have here the elements for a religion more

serious, potent, awe-inspiring, and profound, than any which
the world has yet seen. True, it will not be just the same religion
which prevails now; but who supposes that the religion now current can go on always, or ought to go on? Nay, and even of that
5   much-decried idea of God as *the stream of tendency by which
all things seek to fulfil the law of their being*, it may be said with
confidence that it has in it the elements of a religion new, indeed,
but in the highest degree hopeful, solemn, and profound. But our
present business is not with this. Our present business is with
10 the religion of the Bible; to show a new aspect of this, wherein it
shall appear true, winning, and commanding.

And if our reader has for a time to lose sight of this aspect
amid negations and conflicts,—necessary negations, conflicts
without which the ground for a better religion cannot be won,—
15 still, by these waters of Babylon, let him remember Sion! After
a course of Liberal philosophers proposing to replace the obsolete Bible by the enouncement in modern and congenial language of new doctrines which will satisfy at once our reason and
imagination, and after reading these philosophers' grand con-
20 clusion that there is little indeed in the history and achievements
of Christianity to support the claim made on its behalf to the
character of a scheme divinely revealed for the salvation of the
human race, a man may of a truth well say: '*My soul hath long
dwelt among them that are enemies unto peace!*' and may with
25 longing remember Sion. But we will not quarrel with him if he
says and does the same thing after reading us, too, when we
have kept him so long at the joyless task of learning what not to
believe. But happily this part of our business is now over. In
what follows, we have to defend ourselves, and secure him,
30 against the Liberal philosophers who accuse us of teaching him
to believe too much.

Chapter III

The God of Experience

Among German critics of the Bible, a sort of criticism which we may best, perhaps, describe as a *mechanical* criticism, is very rife. For negative purposes this criticism is particularly useful. It takes for granted that things are naturally all of a piece and follow one uniform rule; and that to know that this is so, and to judge things by the light of this knowledge, is the secret for sure criticism. People do not vary; people do not contradict themselves; people do not have under-currents of meaning; people do not divine. If they are represented as having said one thing to-day and its seeming opposite to-morrow, one of the two they are credited with falsely. If they are represented as having said what in its plain literal acceptation could not hold good, they cannot have said it. If they are represented as speaking of an event before it happened, they did not so speak of it,—the words are not theirs. Things, too, like persons, must be rigidly consistent, must show no conflicting aspects, must have no flux and reflux, must not follow a slow, hesitating, often obscure line of growth. No, the character which we assign to them they must have always, altogether, and unalterably, or it is not theirs.

This mechanical character strongly marked a certain review of *Literature and Dogma* of which the line was as follows:— 'Israel's first conception of God was that of an unseen but powerful foe, whose enmity might be averted by the death of victims;' therefore the God of Israel cannot have been, as we represent him, the Eternal which makes for righteousness. 'The original and current idea of righteousness in Israel was largely made up of ceremonial observances;' we must not say, therefore, that to Israel was revealed the Eternal that loveth righteousness. We, again, had said that the world cannot do without the Bible,

and we desire to bring the masses to use the Bible. But no! Israel
went to ruin, and Christendom is far from perfect; therefore the
Bible cannot be of much use. 'Take,' says the reviewer, 'the commentary afforded by Israel's history on the value of the Bible!
5 The Bible failed to turn the hearts of those to whom it was addressed; how can it have an efficacy for the regeneration of our
masses?' In a like strain the author of *Supernatural Religion:*
'There is little, indeed, in the history and actual achievements of
Christianity to support the claim made on its behalf to the char-
10 acter of a scheme divinely revealed for the salvation of the human race.'

On persons and their sayings this sort of criticism does execution in very short and sharp fashion. Jesus said of the daughter
of Jairus: 'She is not dead, but sleepeth.' Well, then, 'we have
15 here, by the express declaration of Jesus, a case of mere suspension of consciousness.' Jesus said, *sleepeth;* and how, then, *can*
the girl have been more than asleep? If Jesus is reported to have
said: 'Before Abraham was, I am,' or to have said: 'Therefore
doth my Father love me because I lay down my life that I may
20 take it again,' these speeches *must* have been invented for him
after his death, when the Resurrection had become a matter of
Christian belief, or when the dogma of the Godhead of the
Eternal Son wanted proving. That they should have arisen in
any other way is 'wholly inexplicable.' Men do not foresee their
25 own death, or conceive the virtue in themselves as operating long
before they were born. It is 'wholly inexplicable' to this kind of
criticism that Jesus should have both said of the Gentile cen-
turion: 'I have not found so great faith in Israel,' and also said to
the Canaanitish woman: 'It is not meet to take the children's
30 bread and cast it to the dogs,' because the two sayings show a
different tendency, and the same man does not utter two sayings
showing a different tendency. Either the first saying must have
been put into the mouth of Jesus by a Pauline universalist, or the
second by a Judaic particularist. If Jesus speaks of the destruc-
35 tion of Jerusalem, then the speech must have been invented for
him after Jerusalem was destroyed; for it is 'wholly inexplicable'
that a man should speak of a thing before it happens. To suppose
otherwise, to suppose, as we do, that Jesus foretold to his disciples

that they should see Jerusalem destroyed, that he varied his line
according to the occasion and the hearer, that he foresaw his own
death, and that he dealt with the terms *living* and *dying* in a profound manner easily misapprehended,—to suppose all this is to
'invest Jesus with attributes of prescience and quasi-omniscience   5
which we can only characterise as divine,' and is therefore inad-
missible.

One of the many reproaches brought against *Literature and
Dogma* is, that its conception of the development of our religion
is wanting in vigour and rigour. Certainly the sort of criticism   10
we are now noticing does not err by want of vigour and rigour.
It has abundance of both, and does its work with great thoroughness. The only thing to be said against it is, that the growth of
human things, and above all of immense concerns like religion,
does not exactly proceed with vigour and rigour; rather it fol-   15
lows an order of development loose and wavering. And to impose, therefore, on the growth of religion and Christianity a
method of development of great vigour and rigour, to criticise
its productions and utterances with the notion that we shall reach
the truth about them by applying to them such a method, is most   20
probably to criticise them all wrong.

And it would not be difficult to show that this method is, in
fact, fallacious in each of the points where we have been just now
seeing it draw its conclusions. But we are here solely concerned
with whatever may be supposed to check and disconcert the   25
reader of *Literature and Dogma* after that book had seemed to
put him in a way of reading the Bible with profit. Now certainly
nothing could check and disconcert him so much as to find that
the God of Israel, the God of the Bible, cannot be taken to be the
Eternal that loveth righteousness. For in place of the magnified   30
and non-natural man given by miracles and metaphysics, but
who cannot be verified, we had advised our reader to take as the
God of the Bible, and the foundation of the whole matter of his
Christianity, the Eternal that loves righteousness, makes for righteousness. This Eternal can be verified indeed, but now we are   35
told that he is not the God of the Bible. Or, at any rate, he is not
the God of Israel and of the Old Testament; the God of Israel
and of the Old Testament is something quite different. This ob-

jection then, we must deal with, and we must establish against it, if we can, our assertion that the God of Israel and of the Bible is the Eternal that makes for righteousness.

2.

The above-mentioned reviewer objects to us that 'Israel must
5 have had a faculty for abstract thought quite unparalleled if his conception of a God came to pass as Mr. Arnold describes it. A people in a very early stage of civilisation is so deeply absorbed in the study and practice of morality that they discover that there is a law which is not themselves, that makes for it, which
10 law they proceed to worship! Can improbability go further!' This, says the reviewer, is the *à priori* argument against 'the opinion that Israel's God was not a person, but the deification of a natural law.' But certainly we do not opine,—and the reader of *Literature and Dogma* will hardly have supposed us to opine,—
15 that Israel's God was the *conscious* deification of a natural law. To attack, therefore, the improbability of this, is merely to tilt against a phantom of one's own creating. Unquestionably, that Israel, as we see him in the earliest documents of the Old Testament, should have been likely to sit down and say to himself: 'I
20 perceive a great natural law, the law of righteousness, ruling the world; I will personify this law as a God,—the one and only God; I will call it Jehovah, build a sanctuary for it, and invent a worship for it';—that this should have happened is utterly improbable. One can almost as well conceive Israel saying that he
25 was aware of the law of gravitation, and felt disposed to deify it and to erect a temple to it.

But if one has certain facts before one, one naturally asks oneself how they can have come about. Israel is always saying that in the Eternal he puts his trust, and that this Eternal is righteous,
30 and loves righteousness. He is always saying that among the gods of other people there is no God like the Eternal, none that can do what the Eternal does, and that whoever runs after another God shall have great trouble. These are his ruling thoughts. Where did he get them? They were given him, says popular the-
35 ology, by a magnified and non-natural man, who was in constant

communication with him, walked in the garden where he was, talked to him, showed him even, on one occasion, his bodily parts, and worked miracle after miracle for him. And this is Israel's own account of the matter. But how many other religions also, besides Israel's, present us with personages of this kind! And we hold that 5 the personages are not real, but have their origin in the play of the human imagination itself. How, then, did the God of Israel, with the special characters that we find in him, actually arise?

Now, it may be contended either that these special characters, which we assign to him, are not really there; or that they have 10 come there by chance, and nothing can be inferred from them; or, finally, both that the characters are there, and that it was their pressure upon the mind of Israel which made him give to his religion, and to his Eternal, that unique type which we profess to find in them. Let us examine these alternatives, so important to 15 the reader of *Literature and Dogma*.

We must go to Sir John Lubbock or to Mr. Tylor for researches concerning what is called 'pre-historic man,' human nature in its inchoate, embryo, and as yet unformed condition. Their researches concerning this are profoundly interesting. But 20 for our present business we have not to go back higher than historic man,—man who has taken his ply, and who is already much like ourselves. With inchoate, pre-historic man, the great objects of nature and the pleasure or pain which he experienced from them may probably enough have been the source of religion. In 25 those times arose his name for Deity: *The Shining*. So may have originally commenced the religion of even the most famous races,—the religion of Greece, the religion of Israel. But into the thoughts and feelings of man in this inchoate stage we cannot, as we now are, any longer fully enter. We cannot really participate 30 in them; the religion of man in this stage does not practically concern us. Man's religion practically concerns us from that time only when man's real history has commenced; when moral and intellectual conceptions have invaded the primordial nature-worship, have, in great measure, superseded it and given a new 35 sense to its nomenclature. The very earliest Bible-religion does not go higher than a time of this kind, when already moral and intellectual conceptions have entered into religion. And no one will deny, that, from the first, those conceptions which are moral rather than intellectual,—the idea of conduct and of the regulation of conduct,—appear in Bible-religion prominently.

To bring out this, let us for a moment leave Bible-religion, and let us turn to the people who, after the Hebrews, have had most influence upon us,—to the Greeks. Greek history and religion begin for us, as do the religion and history of the Hebrews, at a time when moral and intellectual ideas have taken possession of the framework given originally, it may be, by nature-worship. The great names of Hellenic religion, Zeus and Phoebus, come, as every one knows, from the sun and air, and point to a primordial time of nature-worship. But Greek history and religion begin with the sanctuaries of Tempe and of Delphi, and with the Apolline worship and priesthood which in those sanctuaries under Olympus and Parnassus established themselves. The northern sanctuary of Tempe soon yielded to Delphi as the centre of national Hellenic life and of Apolline religion. Now, we all are accustomed to think of Apollo as the awakener and sustainer of genius, as the power illuminating and elevating the soul through intellectual beauty. And so from the very first he was. But in those earliest days of Hellas, Apollo was not only the nourisher of genius,—he was also the author of every higher moral effort. He was the prophet of his father Zeus, in the highest view of Zeus, as the source of the ideas of moral order and of right. For to this higher significance had Zeus and Phoebus,—those names derived merely from sun and air,—by this time risen. They had come to designate a Father, the source of the ideas of moral order and of right; and a Son, his prophet, purifying and inspiring the soul with these ideas, and also with the idea of intellectual beauty.

But it is with the ideas of moral order and of right that we are at this moment concerned. These ideas are in human nature; but they had, says the excellent historian of Greece, Dr. Curtius, 'especially been a treasure in the possession of the less gay and more solitary tribes in the mountains of Northern Greece.' These were Delphi's first pupils. And the graver view of life, the thoughts which give depth and solemnity to man's soul,—the moral ideas, in short, of conduct and righteousness,—were the main elements of early Greek religion. *Soberness* and *righteousness*, to which

the words written up on the temple at Delphi called all comers,[1]
were thus the primal rule of Hellenic religion. For a long while,
in the great poets of Hellas, the power of this influence shows
itself. From Pindar, Aeschylus, and Sophocles, may be quoted
sentences as religious as those which we find in Job or Isaiah.
And here, in this bracing air of the old religion of Delphi,—this
atmosphere of ideas of moral order and of right,—the Athenians,
Ionian as they were, imbibed influences of character and steadiness, which for a long while balanced their native vivacity and
mobility, distinguished them profoundly from the Ionians of
Asia, and gave them men like Aristeides and Pericles.

Every one knows, however, that this archaic severeness of
Hellenic religion, this early pre-occupation with conduct and
righteousness, did not last. There were elements of mobility and
variety in men's dispositions which proved fatal to it. The manner in which this came about we have not here to trace; all we
are now concerned with is the fact that it was so. It had come
to be so even by the time when, with the Persian War, the brilliant historic period of Greece begins. Even by this time the living influence of Delphi had ceased. Bribes had discredited its
sanctity; seriousness and vital power had left it. Delphi had come
to be little more than a name, and what continued to exist there
was merely a number of forms. The predominance, for Hellas,
of a national religion of righteousness, of grave ideas of conduct, moral order, and right, outweighing all other ideas, disappeared with the decline of Delphi, never to return. Still, indeed, these ideas inspired poetry; and Greek poetry was now
more religious than Greek religion, and partly supplied its place.
Finally, they ceased even to inspire poetry, and took refuge with
philosophic thinkers.

We by no means say that they disappeared from life. They
are, we repeat, in human nature; they cannot disappear wholly.
But a religion founded on them, a religion of soberness and righteousness, ceased to be set up before the eyes of all men, ceased
to stand in the minds of all men for the great primary concern

---

[1] See Plato, *Erastae*, cap. vii. τοῦτ᾽ ἄρα, ὡς ἔοικε, τὸ ἐν Δελφοῖς γράμμα
παρακελεύεται, σωφροσύνην ἀσκεῖν καὶ δικαιοσύνην.

of human life, as it had stood before the minds of the grave forefathers of Hellas in the shadow of their Parnassian sanctuary.
And to this extent, of course, the ideas were weakened and effaced in Greek life;—that they were no longer impressively
5   presented as life's first concern by a national religion, itself the
great and solemn centre of men's thoughts. We by no means,
again, say that for this there were no compensations. Other aspects of life presented themselves than the aspect in which life
appears exclusively concerned with soberness and righteousness.
10 Many a line of activity did these new aspects suggest to the Hellenic genius, and with what brilliant success it followed them we
all know. Still, the fact remains, that in Greece, as the national
history went on, the all-importance of conduct and righteousness pressed no longer upon the Hellenic spirit and upon Hel-
15 lenic religion as their omnipresent and central idea. In the later
days of the national life of Hellas, it was a religious solemnity,
witnessed by the public with transport, and celebrated by the
first artist of the time, to see the courtesan Phryne enter the sea
at Eleusis, and represent there, to an innumerable multitude
20 of spectators, *Venus Anadyomene*,—Venus issuing from the
waves.[1] To this had come the religion of Delphi and the art of
Olympia. And it was at Eleusis that this happened, the old seat of
the mysteries;—those highest means possessed by Greek religion
for deepening and ennobling men's thoughts about life and death.
25 The time had been when the religious solemnities at Eleusis were
of a character to draw from Pindar a strain such as we now call
Biblical,—a strain like that of Job, or Isaiah, or the Psalms.
'Blessed is the man who hath beheld these things before he goeth
under the earth! he knoweth the end of man's life, and he know-
30 eth its God-given beginning.'

3.

Not long after Phryne's religious performance at Eleusis came
the last days, too, of the national life of the Jews, under the suc-

---

[1] See Athenaeus, lib. xiii, p. 590.

cessors of Alexander. The religious conceptions of the Jews of
those days are well given by the Book of Daniel. How popular
and prevalent these conceptions were, is proved by their vitality
and power some two centuries later at the Christian era, and by
the large place which they fill in the New Testament. We are   5
all familiar with them; with their turbid and austere visions of the
Ancient of Days on his throne, and the Son of Man coming with
the clouds of heaven to give the kingdom to the saints of the Most
High, and to bring in everlasting righteousness. Here, then, is the
last word of the religion of the Hebrews, when their national life   10
is drawing to an end, when their career has been, for the most
part, run; when their religion has had nearly all the development which, within the limits of their national life, belonged
to it. This, we say, is its last word: *To bring in everlasting
righteousness.*[1]   15

Let us now go back to the commencement of Hebrew history.
The beginnings of Hebrew national life may not inaptly be par-
alleled with the beginnings of Greek national life,—with that
epoch when the infant Hellenic tribes met in federation under
the religious shadow of Tempe or Delphi, and set before their   20
eyes the law of 'soberness and righteousness.' Such an epoch in
the career of the Hebrew race is well given by the history of
Abraham. The religion of Abraham, this founder and father of
the Hebrew people, is a religion, as King Abimelech says, of 'integrity of heart and innocency of hands.'[2] The God of Abraham   25
has chosen Abraham and his race, because, God says: 'I know
Abraham, that he will command his children and his household
after him, and they shall keep the way of the Eternal to do righteousness and judgment.'[3] So that the Hebrew people and Hebrew history, when they begin, begin, like the Hellenic people   30
and like Hellenic history, with a religion of soberness and righteousness. And the after-decline of this religion in Greece we
have seen. But in Judaea, at the close of the national history, what
do we find to be the condition of this religion? Has it weakened,
has it grown obsolete, has it fallen out of sight and out of mind?   35

[1] Daniel ix. 24.   [2] *Genesis* xx. 5.   [3] *Gen.* xviii. 19.

So far from it, that it has grown into an enthusiasm, turbid, passionate, absorbing and all-pervasive, to *bring in everlasting righteousness.*

How was the long intervening period filled between the call of Abraham at the beginning of Israel's national history, and the Book of Daniel at its close? Let us take, as a mid-point, that wonderful collection, ranging over so many years, reflecting so many experiences, contributed by so many voices, and answering so profoundly to the religious consciousness of Israel: the Book of Psalms. Two things are equally manifest, on the very face of the Book of Psalms,—Israel's attachment to his religion, and that religion's character. One may dip into the Psalms where one will, and be sure to find them not far off.

First, as to the attachment and strong reliance with which Israel's religion inspired him. 'In the Eternal put I my trust,'[1] is the constant burden of his song. 'My hope hath been in thee, O Eternal; I have said, Thou art my God!' 'Blessed are the people whose God is the Eternal!' 'They who run after another God shall have great trouble.'[2]

And then as to the character, expressed briefly and generally, of this God of Israel, this Eternal. There is really no doubt about it. 'The Eternal loveth the thing that is *right!*'[3] Ten thousand variations are played on the one theme, but the theme is that. 'The Eternal alloweth the *righteous*, but the *wicked* his soul hateth,'[4] says David. 'Unto the ungodly saith God: Why dost thou take my covenant in thy mouth, whereas thou hatest to be *reformed?*'[5] 'My help cometh of God, who preserveth them that are *true of heart*.'[6] 'I will wash my hands in *innocency*, O Eternal, and so will I go to thine altar.'[7] As in the days of Abimelech, so it was still; the religion of the Hebrew people was a religion of integrity of heart and innocency of hands. This is the essential character of Israel's Eternal: to love the thing that is *right*, to abhor that which is *evil*.

[1] *Ps.* xi. 1.   [2] *Ps.* xxxi. 14; xxxiii. 12; xvi. 4.
[3] *Ps.* xxxvii. 28.   [4] *Ps.* xi. 5.   [5] *Ps.* l. 16, 17.
[6] *Ps.* vii. 10.   [7] *Ps.* xxvi. 6.

Do we want a somewhat fuller account of what *right* is, that we may be sure it does not mean a mere performance of ceremonies? Here it is:—'Come, ye children, and hearken unto me; I will teach you the fear of the Eternal. Keep thy tongue from evil, and thy lips that they speak no guile; eschew evil and do good, seek peace and pursue it.'[1] Or of what *evil* is,—what is the course of those who do not 'understand and seek after God;' that we may be sure evil does not mean a mere omission of ceremonies, or a sparing to smite God's enemies who happen to be also one's own? 'Their mouth is full of cursing and bitterness, their feet are swift to shed blood, destruction and unhappiness is in their ways, and the way of peace have they not known.'[2] In a plain way, all this points well enough, and with perfect clearness, to just what we universally mean by right and wrong, good and evil. It points to morals, conduct; to a man's behaviour, way and walk in life. And this was what Israel meant by religion: to attend to one's way and walk in life, and to regulate them according to the commandments of the Eternal that loveth righteousness. 'I called mine own ways to remembrance,' he says, 'and turned my feet unto Thy testimonies.'[3] And they who do so, maintains he, 'shall want no manner of thing that is good.'[4] '*That* shall bring a man peace at the last.'[5] 'To him that ordereth his conversation right shall be shown the salvation of God.'[6]

But our reviewer says that we are not to rely much on what comes from prophets and psalmists, 'on the most spiritual utterances of the most spiritual part of the nation, of men who were at once reformers and poets.' 'They were,' says he, 'innovators, unorthodox free-thinkers.' What they alleged about righteousness by no means proves that righteousness was the religion of Israel.

And perhaps this sort of argument can, in some cases, be used fairly enough. Pindar may have lofty passages about the end and

---

[1] *Ps.* xxxiv. 11, 13, 14.
[2] *Ps.* xiv (Prayer Book Version). 6, 7; and *Rom.* iii. 14–17.
[3] *Ps.* cxix. 59.　　　　　　　　　[4] *Ps.* xxxiv. 10.
[5] *Ps.* xxxvii. 38.　　　　　　　　[6] *Ps.* l. 23.

the God-given beginning of man's life. Socrates and Plato may
have their minds still bent on those ideas of moral order and of
right which were the treasure of the primitive and serious tribes
of early Hellas. They may harp still upon the old-fashioned doctrines recommended from the temple at Delphi. Yet, if the Greek
nation and its religion have taken quite another line, these utterances of philosophers and poets will not justify us in saying that
the religion of Greece was a religion of righteousness. But we
have a right to give Israel the benefit of the utterances of its
prophets and psalmists. And why? Because the nation adopted
them. So powerfully did the inmost chords of its being vibrate
to them, so entirely were they the very truth it was born to and
sought to find utterance for, that it adopted them, made them its
standards, the documents of that most profound and authentic
expression of the nation's consciousness, its religion. Instead of
remaining literature and philosophy, isolated voices of sublime
poets and reforming free-thinkers, these glorifications of righteousness became Jewish religion, matters to be read in the synagogue every Sabbath-day. So that while in Greece it was a religious solemnity to behold a handsome courtesan enter the sea,
in Judaea it was a religious solemnity to hear that 'the righteous
Eternal loveth righteousness.'

What we claim, then, for Israel, when we say that he had the
intuition of the Eternal Power, not ourselves, that makes for
righteousness, when we say that to him our religion was first
revealed, is this:—that the ideas of moral order and of right,
which are in human nature, which appear in a recognisable shape,
whatever may be their origin, as soon as man is sufficiently
formed for him to have a history at all, to be intelligible to us at
all, to stand related to us as showing a like nature with ourselves,
—that these ideas so laid hold upon Israel as to be the master-
element in his thoughts, the sheet-anchor of his life. [And these
ideas have such a range that they take in at least three-fourths
of human life.] It matters nothing that Israel could give no satisfying and scientific account of the way in which he came by
these ideas; that he could only give legendary and fanciful accounts of it. It matters nothing that the practical application he
gave to these ideas was extremely crude and limited, that they

were accompanied in him by gross imperfection. It matters nothing that there may be shown to have hung about them any number of waifs and strays from an earlier and unripe stage, survivals from a time of nature-worship, or of any other passage which preceded, with Israel, the entrance upon his real history. If from the time he was formed, and distinguishable, and himself, if from one end of the Bible to the other, we find him, far more than any other race known to us, impressed, awe-struck, absorbed by the idea of righteousness, whatever alloys he may mix with it, and however blindly he may deal with it; if we find him, —and it is indisputable that we do find him,—thus fascinated, it is enough, and he has the intuition, the revelation.

[His very shortcomings prove the force of the intuition within him, since all the wear and tear of them could not rase it out. '*Cogitavi vias meas, et converti pedes meos in testimonia Tua;* I called mine own ways to remembrance, and turned my feet unto Thy testimonies.'[1] Israel is the great, standing, unsilenceable, unshaken witness to the necessity of minding one's ways, of conduct. And whatever else he may have done, or not done, he can assuredly plead: *Cogitavi vias meas.* 'Sacrifices mark a conception in which morality has no part,' says the *Westminster* Reviewer; 'sacrifices existed in Israel *ab origine.*' Even in his historic time there hung about Israel traces of an inchoate and dark stage, remains of an early 'conception of God as an unseen but powerful foe, whose enmity might be averted by the death of victims.' It may have been so; but, 'Still,' Israel can answer, 'still, all hampered with these survivals of a lower world: *Cogitavi vias meas!*' 'Though righteousness,' pursues the *Westminster* Reviewer, 'entered largely into Israel's conception of the Eternal, yet that conception contained much that conflicts with righteousness. The God of Israel often appears as more patriotic than righteous; blesses Jael, for instance, for the treacherous murder of Sisera.' True; but true, also, that with all this mixture: *Cogitavi vias meas!* 'Israel's God,' the objector goes on, 'is a magnified and non-natural man, not impassive and uniform like a law of nature, but angry and then repenting him, jealous and then

---

[1] *Ps.* cxix. 59.

soothed.' Nevertheless, with this crude anthropomorphic conception of God: *Cogitavi vias meas!* 'Israel's religion deals in
ecstasy, enthusiasm, evocations of the dead.' *Cogitavi vias meas!*
'The current idea of righteousness in Israel was largely made
5   up of ceremonial observances.' *Cogitavi vias meas!* Finally, in
spite of all this thinking upon his ways, Israel misdirected them.
'The Bible,' cries the *Westminster* Reviewer, 'failed to turn the
hearts of those to whom it was addressed; the commentary afforded by Israel's history on the value of the Bible!' True, as
10 Israel managed his profession of faith, it did not save him; but
did he on that account drop it? *Cogitavi, cogitavi vias meas!*]

4.

Our reviewer will now, perhaps, understand what we mean
by saying that the Hebrew people had the revelation and intuition of the Eternal that makes for righteousness. We do not
15 mean that this people had a clear and adequate idea of rightness
in conduct as a law of nature, that they then proceeded to personify this law and deify it, and that they deified it in their Jehovah. If this were what we meant, all the criticisms of the
reviewer upon the shortcomings of Jehovah and Jahvism in the
20 Old Testament would take effect. We do not mean it, however.
But perhaps our saying that Israel had the *revelation* of the
Eternal that makes for righteousness is the stumbling-block. Let
us try, then, so to draw out what we mean by this, that to the
reviewer and to others it may appear as simple and certain as it
25 does to ourselves.

For let us now conceive man, so far as this is possible for us,
just as the investigation of his beginnings and the actual observation of the state of certain savages shows him to us, in his inchoate, pre-historic, almost pre-human condition. In this time of
30 ignorance his gods have their origin. We are accused of introducing in the *not ourselves* which presses, we say, upon man's
spirit, a refined metaphysical conception. It is so far from this,
that it is one of the first pieces of man's experience, and dates
from the most primitive time. It is whatever appears to man as

outside himself, not in his own power, and affecting him whether he will or no. Now, the more helpless and inexperienced man is, the greater is the number to him of things not in his own power. Who can trace or divine all the possibilities of hope and fear in this wide field? But we know and can easily understand how on 5 certain great and prominent objects of nature, exercising a powerful influence on human life,—such as the sun, for instance,—hope and fear fastened, and produced worship. And we know, too, and can well understand, how by a natural impulse men were moved to represent in a human form like their own, the 10 powers which attracted their hope, fear, and worship; as Xenophanes says that if horses, oxen, and lions could paint or model, they would certainly make gods in their own image,—horses in that of horses, oxen in that of oxen, lions in that of lions. And even when men did not represent their gods in human form, they 15 still supposed in them human thoughts and passions.

In those times arose names like Eloah, Elohim, *The Mighty;* or Deva, Deus, *The Shining.* And then, too, in those days of bounded view and of apprehensive terror, grew up and prevailed 'the conception of God,' to use our reviewer's words, 'as a foe 20 whose enmity might be averted by the death of victims.' Such, he asserts, was Israel's first conception of God; and although here he speaks positively of things beyond the ken of any certain knowledge, yet we are not concerned to dispute the probability of his conjecture, that with the inchoate and primordial Israel it 25 may have been so. For 'the gods,' as Xenophanes again says, 'did not from the first show to men all things; but in time, by searching, men came to a discovery of the better.'

Such a 'better' was reached at a point where human history and human religion, in the only sense which our race can now 30 attach to the word *religion*, first began. It was reached when the ideas of conduct, of moral order and of right, had gathered strength enough to declare and establish themselves. Long before, indeed, during man's chaotic and rudimentary time, these ideas must have been at work; and as they were no conscious 35 creation of man's will, but solicited him and ripened in him whether he would or no, we may truly and fitly call them the

Spirit of God brooding over chaos, moving silently upon the human deep. Then these ideas found and took possession of the framework of the older, and,—for so we may call them,—the as yet irreligious religions. [In many an imagining and legend men
5 gave voice to their half-recollection of stages and moments in man's dim ante-natal time, mixing it and colouring it with their later experience.]

From these older religions were handed on ceremonial and rite, which have, in truth, their proper origin, not in the moral
10 stirrings of man's nature at all, but in the stirrings which we call aesthetic. Many practices, even, were not at once dropped, which had their proper origin in darkness and disease of the moral feelings, in blind and pusillanimous terror. Of this kind were human sacrifices, such as Abraham's sacrifice of Isaac. Nevertheless
15 God, by the very cradle of Hebrew history, the God of Abraham, the God of 'integrity of heart and innocency of hands,' is no longer 'a foe whose enmity might be averted by the death of victims.' The God of Abraham is a *friend;* and the intended sacrifice is no longer an act of selfish terror to avert a powerful
20 foe's enmity, it is an act of faithful devotion to the supposed will of an all-wise and all-good friend. To this extent in its very cradle did the one true religion, Israel's religion, the religion of righteousness, succeed in transforming the baneful and false usage which clung to it from the times of darkness out of which
25 it emerged, until the day came for the disappearance of the usage altogether.

In a like 'better' did the history and religion of Hellas also, as we have seen, take their rise; a 'better' brought about by the ideas of moral order gathering strength and making themselves
30 felt. Then the nature-deities of ruder times, Zeus and Phoebus, became the Father of judgment and of right, and his Prophet-Son. At that moment, therefore, the Eternal who makes for righteousness, the God of Israel, who is, as St. Paul said to the Athenians, *not far from every one of us,* seemed offering to reveal
35 himself to Greece also. But it was for a moment only. Other aspects of life than the moral aspect came into view and into favour with the Greeks; other tendencies than the tendency

which disposes men to preoccupy themselves with conduct, and with its divine sanctions, prevailed. 'They did not like,' says the Hebrew Paul austerely, 'to retain God in their knowledge, and so God gave them over to a reprobate mind.'[1] This is, no doubt, a stern sentence. What the Greeks were and what they accomplished, and how brilliant a course they ran after their religion had passed out of its brief moment of accord with that of Israel, we know; and with that knowledge we shall not be forward to utter against them harsh censures. But thus much, at least, we may say, notwithstanding all the glory and genius of Greece, notwithstanding all the failure and fanaticism of Israel;—thus much we may well say, whenever we contrast the heart and mind of the Graeco-Roman world in its maturity with the interior joys of Israel: *They that run after another God shall have great trouble.*

Israel advanced from the God of Abraham, the Mighty who requires integrity of heart and innocency of hands, to the God of Moses, the Eternal who makes for righteousness unalterably. Then the law in its primitive shape, an organism having for its heart the Ten Commandments, arose. It formulated, with authentic voice and for ever, the religion of Israel as a religion in which ideas of moral order and of right were paramount. And so things went on from Moses to Samuel, and from Samuel to David, and from David to the great prophets of the eighth century and to the Captivity, and from that to the Restoration, and from the Restoration to Antiochus and the invasion of Greek culture, to the Maccabees and the Book of Daniel, and from thence to the Roman conquest, and from that to John the Baptist; until all the wonderful history received its solution and consummation in Jesus Christ. Through progress and backsliding, amid infectious contact with idolatry, amid survival of old growths of superstition, of the crude practices of the past; amid multiplication of new precepts and observances, of formalism and ceremonial; amid the solicitation of new aspects of life; in material prosperity, and in material ruin;—more and more the

[1] *Rom.* i. 28.

great governing characteristics of the religion of Israel accentuated and asserted themselves, and forced themselves on the world's attention: the God of this religion, with his eternal summons to keep judgment and do justice; the mission of this
5   religion, to bring in everlasting righteousness.

And this native, continuous, and increasing pressure upon Israel's spirit of the ideas of conduct and of its sanctions, we call his intuition of the Eternal that makes for righteousness, the revelation to him of the religion of this Eternal. Really, we do not
10 know how else to account for the evident fact of the pressure, than by supposing that Israel had an intuitive faculty, a natural bent for these ideas; that their truth was borne in upon him, revealed to him. How else are we to explain their pressure on him? We put aside all the preternatural;—a magnified and non-natural
15 man, walking in gardens, speaking from clouds, sending dreams, commissioning angels. We give an explanation which is natural. But we say that this natural explanation is yet grander than the preternatural one.

Some people, however, when they have got rid of the preter-
20 natural in religion, seem to think that they are bound to get rid, as much as they can, of the notion of there being anything grand and wonderful in religion at all; at any rate, to reduce this element of what is grand and wonderful to the very smallest dimensions. They err. They impede the acceptance of even the real
25 truths which they have to tell the world, because the world feels that on the main matter they are wrong. They act imprudently, therefore; but they really fail, besides, to appreciate and explain their facts. We have already, in *Literature and Dogma*, mentioned Professor Kuenen's explanation of the morality in Bible-
30 religion from the simple and severe life of the primitive Beni-Israel as nomads of the desert. But whoever will read in M. Caussin de Perceval's Arabian History the Moàllacas of the poets among the Arabs before Mahomet, will find this poetry extremely licentious, in spite of the nomad life led in the desert by
35 the Arab tribes. And the reformation of Mahomet is undoubtedly a reformation largely inspired by the Bible of the Beni-Israel. On the other hand, we find Semitic people without the nomad

life,—the Semitic people of great cities,—developing a worship such as Herodotus has described to us in that of Mylitta.[1]

Professor Kuenen's excellent History is now published in English. We may all read there of a religious revival in Hebrew religion under Samson and Samuel, and how by degrees Jahvism grew in spirituality, and the age of ecstasy and of the Witch of Endor gave place to the prophets of the eighth century, conscious of a real inner call. Well, but what is the reason of all this advance, this 'development of monotheism,' as people call it? Professor Kuenen thinks that it is largely due to 'the influence of the war between Baal and Jahveh upon the minds of those who had remained loyal to Jahveh.' So, we are told, arose the deep gulf of separation between Jahveh and the heathen 'nonentities,' as the Hebrew prophets call them.

So?—but how? Not out of mere blind obstinacy, not from having fought for a God called Jahveh, against a God called Baal, so long and so hard that his champions grew bent on sticking to Jahveh and found out all manner of perfections for him. Israel adhered to Jahveh for the same reason which had at first made him take to the worship of Jahveh:—that Jahveh was the Eternal Power that makes for righteousness, was the centre and source of those ideas of moral order and of conduct which are, we repeat, in human nature, but which pressed on Israel's spirit with extraordinary power. This alone gives us a natural, intelligible clue to the development of the religion of the Bible.

[But even suppose that we reject all notion of a special bent or intuition in Israel determining the course of his religion. Suppose that we allow him to have had not one whit more bent than other people for the ideas of moral order and of right, but that his religion came to be what it was by the mere force of external circumstances and from accident. Still we shall have a religion insisting on the idea of righteousness with an energy and impressiveness absolutely unparalleled. We shall have a fact which cannot be accounted for through any intelligible process of cause and effect, and which is due to mere chance;—but we shall have

[1] Herod., i, 199.

the fact all the same. In Israel's religion, far and away more than in the religion of any other ancient people, the Eternal Power that makes for righteousness is impressive and paramount. And of Israel, therefore, the distinction assigned by the word of this Eternal will hold true:—*You only have I known of all the families of the earth.*[1]]

5.

But now, as if it were not enough to have one vigorous and rigorous reviewer on our hands, there comes a second such reviewer besides, and strikes his blow at *Literature and Dogma.* After some animadversions on our weak reasoning faculty, which no doubt are just, and some compliments to the clearness of our diction, which we hesitate to accept, because it is the very simplicity of our understanding that incapacitates us for the difficult style of the philosophers, and drives us to the use of the most ordinary phraseology,—after these preliminaries, this second reviewer says that we have no right to call our 'enduring power, not ourselves, which makes for righteousness,' a verifiable fact at all, or to talk of Israel's intuition of it. And why? 'Because,' says the reviewer, 'the origin of the moral perceptions in man is assigned by some to intuition, by others to education, and by Mr. Darwin to a social instinct, arising out of evolution and inheritance.'

Let us assure this reviewer that, for our purpose, whether a man assigns the origin of the moral perceptions to intuition, or to education, or to evolution and inheritance, does not matter two straws. And really we are almost astonished at having to explain this, so clear does it seem to us. For surely, because we may choose to say that the English people have an intuitive sense for politics, we are not therefore to be understood as settling the question about the origin of political perceptions, whether they proceed from intuition, or from education, or from evolution and inheritance. Nay, and we thought that on this very point we had said in *Literature and Dogma* all that was necessary; but

[1] Amos iii. 2.

we find it is not so. We find a great many people imagining that if Mr. Darwin is right in assigning the origin of the moral perceptions to evolution and inheritance, in that case everything we have said about an enduring power which makes for righteousness, and about Israel's recognition of this power, must necessarily fall to the ground. Come, then, let us make it clear to the reader of *Literature and Dogma*, that these imaginations are quite vain, and that he would do very ill to be moved by them.

So let us take Mr. Darwin's doctrine and see how innocent it is, and how entirely unaffected religion is by it. But we will not take it from the mouth of that illustrious philosopher himself, because to many religious people he is a bugbear. Neither will we take it from M. Littré, as we did in *Literature and Dogma*, for the sake of softening a little the stern hearts of the Comtists; for M. Littré's name is not more acceptable to the religious world than Mr. Darwin's. No, we will take it from one of the clearest of thinkers, and one of the most religious of men,— Pascal. 'What is nature?' says Pascal. 'Perhaps a first habit, as habit is a second nature.' *Qu'est-ce que la nature? Peut-être une première coutume, comme la coutume est une seconde nature.* Here, briefly and admirably expressed, is the famous doctrine of Mr. Darwin.

And now suppose that our moral perceptions and rules are all to be traced up, as evolutionists say, to habits due to one or other of two main instincts,—the reproductive instinct and the instinct of self-preservation. Let us take an example of a moral rule, due to each instinct. For a moral rule traceable, on our present supposition, to the instinct of self-preservation, we cannot do better than to take 'the first Commandment with promise:' *Honour thy father and thy mother.* We say that it makes not the smallest difference to religion whether we suppose this commandment to be thus traceable or not.

For let it be thus traceable, and suppose the original natural affection of the young to their parents to be due to a sense of dependence upon them and of benefit from them; and then, when the dependence and benefit end, when the young can shift for themselves, the natural affection seems in the lower animals,

as they are called, to pass away. But in man it is not thus evanescent. For at first, perhaps, there were some who from weakness or from accident felt the dependence and received the benefit longer than others, and in such was formed a more deep and
5 strong tie of attachment. And while their neighbours, so soon as they were of adult vigour, heedlessly left the side of their parents and troubled themselves about them no more, and let them perish if so it might happen, these few remained with their parents and grew used to them more and more, and finally even fed and
10 tended them when they grew helpless. Presently they began to be shocked at their neighbours' callous neglect of those who had begotten them and borne them, and they expostulated with their neighbours, and entreated and pleaded that their own way was best. Some suffered, perhaps, for their interference; some had
15 to fight for their own parents, to hinder their neighbours maltreating them; and all the more fixed in their new feelings did these primitive gropers after the Fifth Commandment become.

Meanwhile this extending of the family bond, this conquering of a little district from the mere animal life, this limiting of the
20 reign of blind, selfish impulse, brought, we may well believe, more order into the homes of those who practised it, and with more order more well-doing, and with both more happiness. And when they solicited their more inhuman neighbours to change their ways, they must always have had to back them the remem-
25 brance, more or less alive in every man, of an early link of affection with his parents; but now they had their improved manner of life and heightened well-being to back them too. So the usage of the minority gradually became the usage of the majority. And we may end this long chapter of suppositions by supposing
30 that thus there grew at last to be communities which honoured their fathers and mothers, instead of,—as perhaps, if one went back far enough, one would find to have been the original practice,—eating them.

But all this took place during that which was, in truth, a twi-
35 light ante-natal life of humanity, almost as much as the life which each man passes in the womb before he is born. The history of man as man proper, and as distinguished from the other

animals,—the real history of our race and of its institutions,—
does not begin until stages such as that which we have been describing are passed, and feelings such as that of which we have
been tracing the growth are already formed. Man and his history
begin, we say, when he becomes distinctly conscious of feel-   5
ings which, in a long preparatory period of obscure growth, he
may have been forming. Then he calls his habit,—acquired by a
process which he does not recollect,—*nature*, and he gives effect
to it in fixed customs, rules, laws, and institutions. His religion
consists in acknowledging and reverencing the awful sanctions   10
with which this right way for man has, he believes, been invested by the mighty *not ourselves* which surrounds us; and the
more emphatically he places a feeling under the guardianship of
these sanctions, the more impressive is his testimony to the hold
it has upon him. When Israel fixed the feeling of a child's natural 15
attachment to its parents by the commandment: *Honour thy father and thy mother, that thy days may be long in the land
which the Eternal thy God giveth thee*, he showed that he had
risen to regard this feeling,—slowly and precariously acquired
though by our supposition it may have been,—as a sure, solid,   20
and sacred part of the constitution of human nature.

But as well as the supposition of a moral habit and rule evolved
out of the instinct of self-preservation, we are to take the supposition of a moral habit and rule evolved out of the reproductive instinct. And here, indeed, in the relations between the sexes, 25
we are on ground where to walk right is of vital concern to
men and where disaster is plentiful. Who first, in the early and
tentative up-struggling of our race, who first discerned them,
this peril of disaster, this necessity for taking heed to one's steps?
Who was he that, amid the promiscuous concubinage of man's   30
commencements,—if we are to suppose that out of the sheer
animal life human life had to evolve itself and rise,—who was
he who first, through attachment to his chance companion or
through attachment to his supposed offspring, gathered himself
together, put a bridle on his vague appetites, marked off himself 35
and his, drew the imperfect outline of the circle of home, and
fixed for the time to come the rudiments of the family? Who

first, amid the loose solicitations of sense, obeyed (for create it
he did not) the mighty *not ourselves* which makes for moral
order, the stream of tendency which was here carrying him, and
our embryo race along with him, towards the fulfilment of the
5   true law of their being?—became aware of it and obeyed it?
Whoever he was, he must soon have had imitators; for never
was a more decisive step taken towards bringing into human
life greater order, and with greater order greater well-doing and
happiness. So the example was followed, and a habit grew up,
10   and marriage was instituted.

And thus, again, we are brought to the point where history
and religion begin. And at this point we first find the Hebrew
people, with polygamy still clinging to it as a survival from the
times of ignorance, but with the marriage-tie solidly established,
15   strict and sacred, as we see it between Abraham and Sara. Presently this same Hebrew people, with that aptitude which, we
say, characterised it for being profoundly impressed by ideas of
moral order, placed in the Decalogue the marriage-tie under the
express and solemn sanction of the Eternal, by the Seventh
20   Commandment: *Thou shalt not commit adultery.*

Now, we might jump at once from here to the end of Jewish
history, and show Jesus Christ renewing by his method the Seventh Commandment, as he did also the Fifth, renewing them
and extending them, clearing casuistry and formalism away from
25   them, and making them look as fresh and impressive in this new
light as in their old light they had in Israel's best days looked to
him. But let us first, after hearing Israel in the Decalogue on the
relation of the sexes, take Israel in the middle of his career, as the
Book of Proverbs discovers him to us. There the author touches
30   on that great and often-arising theme in what our philosophers
call 'sociology': *the strange woman.* And this is his sentence on
the man who is bewitched by her: *He knows not that the dead
are there, and that her guests are in the depths of hell.*[1]

Now, we ask our reviewer to consider this saying of the Book
35   of Proverbs, led up to by the Seventh Commandment in the ear-

[1] *Proverbs* ix. 18.

lier days of Israel's history, and consummated by such things as
the review of the Seventh Commandment by the well-known
sentence of Jesus in the later.[1] Religion, we know, arises when
moral ideas are touched with emotion. And this may be the case
with moral ideas from whatever source they were at first derived. And that people, amongst whom it is the case eminently,
are the chosen people of religion. We have granted the supposition that moral perceptions and habits in what concerns the relation of the sexes may have been originally formed for Israel,
and for everybody else, by evolution and inheritance. We will
grant, besides, that religious worship and many of its names and
ceremonies arose out of ignorant hope and fear in man's rudimentary time. But, for us now, religion is, we say, morality
touched with emotion, lit up and enkindled and made much
more powerful by emotion. And when morality is thus touched
with emotion, it is equally religion, whether it have proceeded
from a magnified and non-natural man in the clouds, or arisen
in the way we have supposed. And those in whom it appears thus
touched with emotion most, are those whom we call endued
with most bent for religion, most feeling, most apprehension; as
one man and one race seem to turn out to have more gift, without any conscious intending and willing of it, for one thing, and
another man and another race for another. Now such a bent,
such a feeling, when it declares itself, we call an intuition. And
we say that Israel had such an intuition of religion, that he shows
it in the matter with which we are now dealing, and in other matters of like kind, and that this people is, therefore, the chosen
people of religion.

For how does a special bent or feeling of this kind for moral
perceptions declare itself, when it has grown strong enough to
declare itself? It declares itself by the accent and power with
which its utterances are made;—the accent of conviction in the

---

[1] Matth. v. 27, 28. Compare: 'Not in the lust of concupiscence, *as the
Gentiles who know not God;*' 'The time past may suffice us *to have
wrought the will of the Gentiles* when we walked in lasciviousness,' &c.—
I *Thessalonians* iv. 5; I Peter iv. 3.

speaker himself, the power of impressiveness on those who hear
him. Moral perceptions, and rules securing and establishing them,
take, on the supposition we are here following, a long while to
build up. There is a backwards and forwards with them; often it
looks as if they would never have strength to get established at
all. However, at last there comes some one like Israel, and lays
down a sentence like the Seventh Commandment, and reinforces
it by such deliverances as that of the Book of Proverbs, and that
of the Sermon on the Mount. He thus, we say, takes a lead in
what vitally concerns conduct and religion, which for ever remains to him and for ever is proving its reality.

For, again, a moral perception does not always, and for all persons, retain the vividness it had at the moment when it established itself in a rule like the Seventh Commandment. Human
nature has many sides, many impulses; our rule may seem to
lose ground again, and the perception out of which it grew may
seem to waver. Practice may offer to it a thousand contradictions, in what M. Taine calls the *triste défilé*, the dismal procession of the Haymarket, and in what a sage or a saint might, perhaps, in like manner call the dismal procession of the Bois de
Boulogne. Not practice alone is against the old strictness of rule,
but theory; we have argumentative systems of free love and of
re-habilitation of the flesh. Even philosophers like Mr. Mill, having to tell us that for special reasons they had in fact observed
the Seventh Commandment, think it right to add that this they
did, 'although we did not consider the ordinances of society
binding on a subject so entirely personal.' So arises what these
same philosophers would call a disintegration of that moral perception on which the Seventh Commandment is founded. What
we have to ask, then, is: Was this perception, and the rule
founded on it, really a conquest for ever, placing human nature
on a higher stage; so that, however much the perception and rule
may have been dubious and unfounded once, they must be taken
to be certain and formed now? And whatever now makes the
perception or the rule fluctuating, does it tend, so far, not to
emancipate man, but to replace him in the bondage of that old,
chaotic, dark, almost ante-human time, from which slowly and

painfully he had emerged when the real history and religion of our race began? And whatever, on the other hand, reinvigorates the perception, does it tend to man's freedom, safety, and progress? Because, if this is so, the incomparably impressive accent of clear and decisive conviction in Israel's comment on the theory of Free Love marks him as a seer and divinely inspired guide, gives him a lead in religion.

Here, then, let us summon the most naturalistic, the freest, the calmest of observers on these matters,—Goethe. He is speaking to the Chancellor von Müller against over-facility in granting divorce. He says: 'What culture has won of nature we ought on no account to let go again, at no price to give up. In the notion of the sacredness of marriage, Christianity has got a culture-conquest of this kind, and of priceless value, although marriage is, properly speaking, unnatural.' Unnatural, he means, to man in his rudimentary state, before the fixing of moral habits has formed the right human nature. Emancipation from the right human nature is merely, therefore, return to chaos. Man's progress depends on keeping such 'culture-conquests' as the Christian notion of the sacredness of marriage. And undoubtedly this notion came to Christianity from Israel. Such was Israel's genius for the ideas of moral order and of right, such his intuition of the Eternal that makes for righteousness, that he felt without a shadow of doubt, and said with the most impressive solemnity, that Free Love was,—to speak, again, like our modern philosophers,—fatal to progress. *He knows not that the dead are there, and that her guests are in the depths of hell.*

And now, perhaps, our second reviewer will suffer us to speak of Israel's 'intuition' of the Eternal that makes for righteousness, even though moral perceptions and habits may have originally been evolved as Mr. Darwin supposes. And our first reviewer will let us repeat that the word of this Eternal concerning Israel, as distinguished from every other nation of antiquity, is true, in spite of Israel's sacrifices and polygamy: *You only have I known of all the families of the earth.*[1]

---

[1] Amos iii. 2.

6.

Again, a third and very Biblically disposed reviewer is at one with our first and anti-Biblical reviewer in denying the possibility of basing on experimental grounds the claim of the Bible and of its religion to our acceptance. 'The Power making for righteousness,' says this third reviewer, 'the Secret of Jesus, are not really experimental notions which any man can verify. The contrary is true. The Secret and the Power are objects of *faith* only. Experience offers every day abundant contradictions to the reality of the Power.'

Now on this point it is certainly indispensable that the reader of *Literature and Dogma* should be in no doubt. For the fundamental thesis of that book is, that righteousness is salvation verifiably, and that the secret of Jesus is righteousness verifiably; and that the true faith which the Bible inculcates is the faith that this is so. But unquestionably the common notion among religious people is our reviewer's: that experience is altogether against the saving power of righteousness or of the secret of Jesus, but that their saving power will be proved to a man after he is dead by a great judgment, and by a system of rewards and punishments in accordance with them; and that faith is the belief that this will really happen. And unquestionably all this is taken from Israel himself, who in his latter days consoled himself, as we can see in the Book of Daniel, by the idea of a resurrection, judgment, and recompence of this sort, and for whom faith came to be the belief that it all would certainly happen.

But Jesus Christ, we say, made it the great object of his teaching to clear and transform this *extra-belief* of his countrymen. Upon that, however, we will not insist now. Neither will we now set about proving that experimentally righteousness is salvation, and experimentally the secret of Jesus is righteousness, independently of the soundness or unsoundness of the *extra-belief* of Jews or Christians. On the experimental character of these truths, which are the undoubted object of religion, we have elsewhere said what is necessary. But they are the matter of an immense experience which is still going forward. It is easy to dispute them, to find things which seem to go against them; yet, on the whole, they prove themselves, and prevail more and more. And the idea of their truth is in human nature, and everyone has some affinity for them, although one man has more and another less. But if any man is so entirely without affinity for them, so subjugated by the conviction that facts are clean against them, as to be unable to entertain the idea of their being in human nature and in experience, for him *Literature and Dogma* was not written.

We suppose, therefore, the reader of *Literature and Dogma* to admit the idea of these truths being in human nature and in experience. Now, we say that the great use of the Bible is to animate and fortify faith in them, against whoever says that 'experience offers every day abundant contradictions to their reality.' The truth that righteousness is salvation has double power upon mankind through the inspiration of the sublime witness borne to it by Israel in his best days. This is why these Scriptures are truly said to be 'written for our learning, that we through patience and comfort of the Scriptures might have hope.'[1] True, in his later days Israel had taken refuge in an ideal world to ensure the triumph of righteousness; had imagined his apocalyptic Ancient of Days to be necessary, and his Son of Man coming in the clouds; his *crisis*, his *anastasis*, and his Messianic reign of the saints. All this was, in a certain way, a testimony to the ideas of moral order and of right. But Israel's best, his immortal testimony to them, is the testimony borne in his earlier days and in his prime, when his faith is in the triumph of the ideas themselves, not in a phantasmagoric restitution of all things to serve them. *As the whirlwind passeth, so is the wicked no more, but the righteous is an everlasting foundation. As righteousness tendeth to life, so he that pursueth evil pursueth it to his own death.*[2]

This imperishable faith of the true Israel, clouded in his later days, resumed and perfected by Jesus Christ, but from the first only half understood and mixed with natural errors by his disciples, makes the glory and the grandeur of the Old Testament. It has an answer,—a far better answer than any we could give,—to every objection of our third reviewer. 'The power making

---

[1] *Rom.* xv. 4.   [2] *Prov.* x. 25; xi. 19.

for righteousness is not really,' says this reviewer, 'an experimental notion, which any man can verify; the contrary is true.'
Let Israel answer. *I have been young and now am old, and yet
saw I never the righteous forsaken. I have seen the wicked in*
5 *great power, and flourishing like a green bay-tree; I went by,
and lo, he was gone!*[1] ['Experience,' pursues M. Secrétan, 'offers
every day abundant contradictions to the reality of this power.'
What says Israel? *I should utterly have fainted, but that I believe verily to see the goodness of the Eternal in the land of the*
10 *living.*[2] Israel would not allow time enough for the demonstration of his truth that righteousness is salvation; hence his later
disappointments and illusions. But] for anyone who believes that
the saving power of righteousness is a profound law of human
nature, Israel's faith in it during his best days opens a boundless
15 source of joy, courage, and enthusiasm; and it is a source such as
no other people of antiquity offers. So that here, again, is confirmation of that unique rank emphatically assigned to Israel by
the Eternal that makes for righteousness: *You only have I
known of all the families of the earth.*

7.

20   Another reviewer asks: 'How are we to know that Israel's
words had any solidity when he pronounced righteousness to be
salvation, if we contend that they have no solidity when he
brings in God talking, thinking, and loving?' Surely because in
the one case he is on ground of experience where we can follow
25 him, but in the other he is not. Therefore, when he says: *There
ariseth light for the righteous,*[3] his words present no difficulty,
and we can take them as they stand; but when he speaks of God
walking in a garden, we are driven to find for the words some
other origin than his actual experience. And whoever attends to
30 the history of the human spirit, will soon see that such an origin
is not hard to find.

The same reviewer asks, again, where in Wordsworth, whose
personifying language about nature we produced to illustrate

---

[1] *Ps.* xxxvii. 25, 35, 36.   [2] *Ps.* xxvii. 13.   [3] *Ps.* xcvii. 11.

Israel's personifying language about God, we can point to language which speaks of nature in the 'mood of real expectation
and confidence common in the Psalms.' Why, where Wordsworth says: *Nature never did forsake the heart that loved her.*
Or where, asks the reviewer, can we find language which 'treats   5
distrust in the promises of nature as a sin?' Why, in plain prose,
without going to the poets for it at all; in one of the profoundest
and most impressive passages to be found in Butler, in his sermon on *The Ignorance of Man.* 'If things afford to man,' says
Butler, 'the least hint or intimation that virtue is the law he is   10
born under, scepticism itself should lead him to the most strict
and inviolable performance of it; *that he may not make the
dreadful experiment of leaving the course of life marked out
for him by nature, whatever that nature be, and entering paths
of his own, of which he can know neither the danger nor the*   15
end.' What can be more solemn and grand? it is grand with
the grandeur of Greek tragedy. But Israel had more than a hint
or intimation that virtue is the law man is born under. He had
an irresistible intuition of it. Therefore he breaks into joy, which
Butler and Greek tragedy do not. Nevertheless, the greatness of   20
Butler, as I have elsewhere shown, is in his clear perception and
powerful use of a 'course of life marked out for man by nature,
whatever that nature be.' His embarrassment and failure is in his
attempt to establish a perception as clear, and a use as powerful,
of the popular theology. But from Butler, and from his treatment   25
of *nature* in connexion with religion, the idea of following out
that treatment frankly and fully, which is the design of *Literature and Dogma*, first, as I am proud to acknowledge, came to
me; and, indeed, my obligations of all kinds to this deep and
strenuous spirit are very great.   30

Finally, from our use of the proof from happiness, accusations
have been brought against us of eudaemonism, utilitarianism.
We are reproached by a foreign critic with utilitarianism,—with
making, 'conformably to the tradition of the English school, self-
interest the spring of human action.' Utilitarianism! Surely a   35
pedant invented the word; and oh, what pedants have been at
work in employing it! But that joy and happiness are the magnets to which human life inevitably moves, let not the reader of

Literature and Dogma for a moment confuse his mind by doubting. The real objection is to low and false views of what constitutes happiness. *Pleasure* and *utility* are bad words to employ,
because they have been so used as to suggest such views. But *joy*
and *happiness*, on the whole, have not. We may safely say, then,
that joy and happiness are the magnets to which human life irresistibly moves. The men of positive experience are for us here,
but so are the chief men of religion too. St. Augustine:—'Act we
must in pursuance of that which gives most delight.' Pascal:—
'However different the means they employ, all men without exception tend towards one object,—happiness.' Barrow:—'The
sovereign good, the last scope of our actions, the top and sum of
our desires,—happiness.' Butler:—'It is manifest that nothing
can be of consequence to mankind, or any creature, but happiness.' This truth cannot be gainsaid; and to reject the truth itself, because of frequent perversions of it, is a fatal error. [From
theologians of the Unitarian school the cry against eudaemonism
comes loudest. To champion anti-eudaemonism, and to champion the metaphysical personality of God, are tasks to which this
school at the present moment appears to have especially addressed
itself. Hardly could it give a stronger sign of that sterility in
religion, to which, in spite of all its benevolence and intelligence,
it seems perpetually doomed.]

8.

The objections most likely to make an untoward impression
on the reader of *Literature and Dogma* we have now, we believe,
noticed, and done our best to remove. On others we will not
linger, because they can hardly occasion any real difficulty. A
reviewer complains of our talking of the *secret* of Jesus, because, says the reviewer, Jesus made no secret of it himself.
Neither did the Eternal make a secret to Israel of righteousness,
and yet Israel talks of the *secret* of the Eternal. The truth which
its holder is supposed alone or in especial to have the clue to and
to deal in, men call his *secret*. Again, we are told that we must
not suppose an element of genuine curativeness in the exorcising
of unclean spirits by Jesus, because the Jewish thaumaturgists

are represented exorcising them also. But what? because there are charlatans who play upon the nervous system for their own purposes, can there be no doctor who plays upon it beneficently? Again, we have said that it can be verified that Jesus is the son of the Eternal that makes for righteousness, and a reviewer objects that 'to say that any man is the son of a natural law is absurd.' But the Bible never speaks of the Eternal as a natural law, but always as if this power lived, and breathed, and felt. Speaking as the Bible speaks, we say that Jesus is verifiably the Son of God. Speaking as our reviewer speaks, and calling God a natural law, we say that of this natural law Jesus is verifiably the offspring or outcome. [Finally, the *Quarterly* Reviewer will not allow us to pronounce it verifiable that righteousness is only possible by the method of Jesus, because, says he, there was righteousness in the world before the Christian era. Really, the Fourth Gospel answers him, where Jesus says: *Before Abraham was, I am.*[1] But, perhaps, though a *Quarterly* Reviewer, he has been dallying with the Tübingen school, and pronounces the Fourth Gospel a fancy-piece. Let us try him, then, with St. Augustine:—*Res ipsa, quae nunc religio Christiana nuncupatur, erat apud antiquos, nec defuit ad initio generis humani.*]

We pass to a quite different line of objection with another reviewer, who lays it down that the weakest part of *Literature and Dogma* is its reliance on sayings of Jesus from the Fourth Gospel. On his death-bed Baur pleasantly remarked that to his Tübingen school, so often reported vanquished, might with truth be applied the words of St. Paul: *As dying, and behold we live.* Well might Baur say so. He and his school live, above all, in the strong and growing acceptance of their criticism of the Fourth Gospel. Already Liberal reviewers in this country begin to treat that criticism as certain. Discussions of it have hitherto not been frequent amongst us, but the vogue for such discussions will certainly increase. What I think of this class of questions, and of its fundamental character, I have said in *Literature and Dogma*. But to return for a little to the subject, to treat it a little more closely, may be well. Probably, too, the reader of *Literature and Dogma*

[1] John viii. 58.

will expect us to make good our free use, in that work, of the Fourth Gospel. Although the method, the secret, and the *epiei-keia* or temper of Jesus are independent of the Fourth Gospel, still from that Gospel they receive most important illustration.

5   But the question concerning the Fourth Gospel raises the whole question concerning the Canon of the New Testament, and, indeed, concerning the Canon of Scripture generally. On this larger question also, then, we cannot but touch; we shall, however, particularly address ourselves to considering the

10 Fourth Gospel, and the criticisms which have been directed against it. To invalidate it two tests are employed: the test of external evidence, and the test of internal evidence. We will, after saying what seems needful on the general question of the Canon of Scripture, proceed to take first the external evidence

15 in the case of the Fourth Gospel, the questions of dates and of texts. But the internal evidence, the test of literary criticism, is above all relied on as decisive by Baur and his school. So we will, finally, try the Fourth Gospel by that test too. *Caesarem appel-lasti, ad Caesarem ibis.*

Chapter IV

The Bible-Canon

We said in *Literature and Dogma*, that all our criticism of the Four Evangelists who report Jesus had this for its governing idea: *to make out what, in their report of Jesus, is Jesus, and what is the reporters.* We then went on to speak as follows:—'Now, this excludes as unessential much of the criticism which is be- 5 stowed on the New Testament. What it excludes is those questions as to the exact date, the real authorship, the first publication, the rank of priority of the Gospels, on which so much thought is by many bestowed,—questions which have a great attraction for critics, which are in themselves good to be enter- 10 tained, which lead to much close and fruitful observation of the texts, and in which very high ingenuity may be shown and very great plausibility reached, but not more; they cannot really be settled, the data are insufficient. And for our purpose they are not essential.' And we concluded by saying:—'In short, to know 15 accurately the history of our documents is impossible; and even if it were possible, we should yet not know accurately what Jesus said and did; for *his reporters were incapable of rendering it, he was so much above them.'*

As to the character of the documents, however, we added 20 this:—'It must be remembered that of none of these recorders have we, probably, the very original record. The record, when we first get it, has passed through at least half a century, or more, of oral tradition, and through more than one written account.'

Nevertheless, we thought that in the Fourth Gospel we found, 25 after all these deductions had been made as to the capacity of the Gospel-reporters and the quality of the Gospel-documents, a special clue in one most important respect to the line really taken by Jesus in his teaching. A Gospel-writer, having by nature his

head full of the external evidence from miracles would never, we
said, have of his own invention insisted on internal evidence as
what, above all, proves a doctrine. 'Wherever we find what en-
forces this evidence, or builds upon it, there we may be especially
5 sure that we are on the trace of Jesus; because turn or bias in
this direction the disciples were more likely to omit from his
discourse than to import into it, they were themselves so wholly
preoccupied with the evidence from miracles.' But we find in the
Fourth Gospel a remarkable insistence upon the internal evi-
10 dence for the doctrine promulgated by Jesus. Here then we certainly come, we said, upon a trace, too little marked by the reporters in general, of the genuine teaching of Jesus; and this gives
a peculiar eminency and value to the Fourth Gospel.

All this is contested; some of it by one set of critics, some of it
15 by another. Some critics will not allow that Jesus was over the
heads of his reporters. The author of *Supernatural Religion*, far
from thinking that the Fourth Gospel puts us in a special way on
the trace of Jesus, declares that it 'gives a portrait of Jesus totally
unlike that of the Synoptics,' contrasts 'the dogmatic mysticism
20 and artificial discourses of the one' with 'the sublime morality
and simple eloquence of the other,' assigns, in short, the entire
superiority to the Synoptics. On the other hand, the critics
in the opposite camp,—critics of so-called orthodox views,—
will by no means allow that in our Four Gospels we have not
25 the very original record; or that they went through the period
of incubation and of gradual rise into acceptance which we suppose. From the end of the first century of our era there was,
according to these critics, a Canon of the New Testament, and
our Four Gospels formed the Gospel-part of it.

30 But, above all, it is contested, and in the most practical way
possible, that inquiries as to the exact date, the real authorship,
the first publication, the rank of priority, and so forth, of our
Four Gospels, can with any truth be called, as we have called
them, unessential, or that the data are insufficient, as we have
35 said they are, for ever really settling such questions. Whoever
reads German will know that there exists a whole library of
German theological works addressed to these questions; and
that, far from being treated as questions which cannot really be
settled, they are in general settled in these works with the great-

est vigour and rigour. Gradually these works are getting known here, partly by translation, partly by their influence upon English writers. The author of *Supernatural Religion* has nourished himself upon them, and has thrown himself with signal energy, and with very considerable success, into that course of inquiry 5 which these works pursue. He occupies a volume and a half with this line of inquiry, and he has at any rate succeeded, one can see, in giving unbounded satisfaction to the Liberal world, both learned and unlearned. [He huddles up into a page a declaration of adherence to 'an infinitely wise and beneficent Being,' and to 10 'the true and noble faith which is the child of Reason;' and the claims of religion being thus satisfied, with all the difficult and troublesome questions which they open, he is free to devote his volume and a half to a negative examination of the current notions about the date and authorship of the Bible-documents. And 15 so doing, and doing it with much effectiveness, he is, we say, in the eyes of the Liberal world, almost the ideal of what 'an able critic' on Biblical matters, 'a profound critic,' ought to be. Liberals say to one another, with an air of thankful conviction: 'Surely, Superstition is at last doomed; it can never survive this 20 blow!' Liberal newspapers, Liberal reviews, Liberal philosophers, and the scientific gentlemen in strong force besides (some of the latter being inclined, however, to substitute the word 'Christianity' for the word 'Superstition'), have with wonderful unanimity been moved to blend their voices, ever since the book called 25 *Supernatural Religion* became known to the public, in this new and strange kind of Hallelujah Chorus.]

What, then, is the reader of *Literature and Dogma* to think? That on these points, which we treated as not admitting of complete settlement, one can, on the contrary, attain full and abso- 30 lute certainty? That the Fourth Gospel, which we treated as affording a special clue to the line of evidence insisted on by Jesus, is, on the contrary, a guide utterly misleading? And, finally, that the investigations which we treated as unessential, are, on the contrary, all-important, and that it behoves him to go 35 eagerly into them?

In determining his answer to these questions, he will do well to keep in mind what is the one object we set before him in the present inquiry: *to enjoy the Bible and to turn it to his benefit.*

Whatever else he may propose to himself in dealing with the
Bible, this remains his one proper object. In another order of interest, the poetry of Homer supplies here a useful illustration for
us. Elaborate inquiries have been raised as to the date, author-
5   ship, and mode of composition of the Homeric poems. Some
writers have held, too, and have laboriously sought to prove, that
there is a hidden, mystical sense running all through them. All
this sort of disquisition, or at any rate some department of it, is
nearly sure to catch at one time or other the attention of the
10   reader of Homer, and to tempt and excite him. But, after all, the
proper object for the reader of the Homeric poems remains this:
to enjoy Homer, and to turn him to his benefit. In dealing even
with Homer, we say, this is found true, and very needful to be
borne in mind;—with an object where yet the main interest is
15   properly intellectual. How much more does it hold true of the
Bible! where the main interest is properly not intellectual, but
practical.

Therefore our reader has still his chief work with the Bible
to do, after he has settled all questions about its mode of com-
20   position, if they can be settled. This makes it undesirable for him
to spend too much time and labour on these questions, or indeed
on any collateral questions whatever. And he will observe, moreover, that as to the rules with which he starts in setting himself
to feel and apply the Bible, he is practically just in the same posi-
25   tion when he has read and accepted our half dozen lines about
the composition of the Gospels, as when he has read the volume
and a half devoted to it in *Supernatural Religion.* For the result is
the same: that the record of the sayings and doings of Jesus,
when we first get it, has passed through at least half a century,
30   or more, of oral tradition, and through more than one written
account. So, too, a man is practically in the same position when
he has read and accepted our half dozen pages about miracles, as
when he has read the half volume in which the author of *Supernatural Religion* professes to establish a complete induction
35   against them. For the result reached is in both cases the same:
that miracles do not really happen. And we suppose our reader
to be ready enough to admit what we say both of miracles and of
the condition in which the Gospel-record reaches us. For our
book is addressed to those inclined to doubt the Bible-testimony,

and to attribute to its documents and assertions not too much
authority, but too little.

When, however, our reader has accepted what we say about
the untrustworthiness of miracles and the looseness of the
Gospel-record, his real work has still to begin. [Whereas when   5
the author of *Supernatural Religion* has demonstrated the same
thing to him in two volumes, his work is over. Or, at most, he has
still to edify himself with the page saying how 'from Jewish
mythology we rise to higher conceptions of an infinitely wise
and beneficent Being;' or perhaps, to retire into the 'one unas-   10
sailable fortress' of the Duke of Somerset. With us at this stage,
on the contrary, his work only begins.] His work, in our view,
is to learn to enjoy and turn to his benefit the Bible, as the Word
of the Eternal. It would be inexcusable in us, therefore, to give
him more preliminary trouble than we can help, by the elaborate   15
establishment of conclusions where he is with us already, or
which he is quite disposed to take from us on trust.

No; for the reader whom *Literature and Dogma* has in view,
learned discussions of the date, authorship, and mode of composition of this or that Bible-document,—whether complete   20
certainty can be attained in them or whether it cannot,—are, as
we called them, unessential. Even the question of the trust-
worthiness of the Fourth Gospel is not an essential question for
him. For the value of the Fourth Gospel, as we think, is that
whereas Jesus was far over the heads of all his reporters, he was   25
in some respects better comprehended by the author of this
Gospel than by the Synoptics; the line of internal evidence
which Jesus followed in pressing his doctrines is better marked.
But still the all-important thing to seize in Jesus is his method,
and his secret, and the element of mildness and sweet reasonable-   30
ness in which they both worked; and these are perfectly well
given in the Synoptics. [In the Synoptics are the great marking
texts for all three. For the method: 'Cleanse the *inside* of the cup;
what comes from within, *that* defiles a man.' For the secret: 'He
that will save his life shall lose it; he that will lose his life   35
save it.' For the sweet reasonableness and mildness: 'Learn of me
that I am mild and lowly in heart, and ye shall find rest unto your
souls.' So that] if we lose the Fourth Gospel, we do not lose
these. All we lose is a little lifting up of that veil with which the

imperfection of the reporters, and their proneness to demand miracles, to rely on miracles, have overspread the real discourse and doings of Jesus.

2.

Nevertheless, according to the buoyant and immortal sentence
5   with which Aristotle begins his Metaphysics, *All mankind natu-rally desire knowledge*. When discussions about the Canon of the New Testament are so rife, the reader of *Literature and Dogma* may well wish to know what he may most reasonably think touching the origin and history of those documents to which he is
10   so often referred by us. More particularly may he wish to know this about that wonderful document which has exercised such a potent fascination upon Christendom, the Fourth Gospel. Luther called it 'the true head-gospel;' it is hardly too much to say that for Christendom it has been so. The author of *Supernatural Re-*
15   *ligion* speaks contemptuously of its dogmatic, mysterious, and artificial discourses; but its chief opponents have spoken of it with more respect. Strauss is full of admiration of the Fourth Gospel for the artistic skill of its composition; Baur, for its spiritual beauty. The reader of *Literature and Dogma* cannot but be
20   interested in getting as near as he can to the truth about such a document, the object of criticisms so diverse.

We will take him, then, by the same road which we travelled ourselves, when we sought to ascertain how stood the truth about the New Testament records, so far as it could be known.
25   We shall suppose him to come to this inquiry as we did ourselves; —absolutely disinterested, with no foregone conclusion at the bottom of one's mind to start with, no secondary purpose of any kind to serve; but with the simple desire to see the thing, so far as this may be possible, as it really is. We ourselves had not, indeed,
30   so much at stake in the inquiry as some people. For whenever the Gospels may have been written, and whether we have in them the very words of Matthew, Mark, Luke, and John, or not, we did not believe the reporters of Jesus capable, in either case, of rendering Jesus perfectly; he was too far above them.
35   In England the evidence as to the Canon of the Gospels ought

to be well judged, if it be true, as Sir Henry Maine thinks, that
the English law of evidence by its extreme strictness has formed
English people to be good judges of evidence. Two things, however, must everywhere, if they are found present, impede men
in judging questions of evidence well. One is, a strong bias   5
existing, before we try the questions, to answer them in a certain manner. Of Biblical criticism with this bias we have abundance in England. In examining the evidence as to the literary history of the New Testament, our orthodox criticism
does not, in fact, seek to see the thing as it really is, but it holds 10
a brief for that view which is most convenient to the traditional
theology current amongst us. We shall not blame this criticism.
The position of the critic, the circumstances under which he
writes, are perhaps such as to make his course inevitable. But his
work, produced under such conditions, cannot truly serve men's 15
need, cannot endure long; it is marked with death before it is
born. [Great learning it may have, or great ingenuity, or great
eloquence; but the critic is all the time holding a brief, and these
advantages are then, in fact, of use only to serve the side for
which his brief is held. To be seriously useful, they should be 20
employed solely to exhibit and recommend the truth of the
things investigated, as this truth really is.]
    The other obstacle to a sound judgment of the evidence re-
specting the Canon arises when people make too much of a
business of such inquiries, give their whole life and thoughts too 25
exclusively to them, and treat them as if they were of paramount
importance. One can then hardly resist the temptation of establishing certainties where one has no right to certainty; of introducing into the arrangement of facts a system and symmetry of
one's own, for which there are no sufficient data. How many a 30
theory of great vigour and rigour has in Germany, in the Protestant faculties of theology, been due to this cause! A body of
specialists is at work there, who take as the business of their lives
a class of inquiries like the question about the Canon of the Gospels. They are eternally reading its literature, reading the theories 35
of their colleagues about it; their personal reputation is made
by emitting, on the much-canvassed subject, a new theory of
their own. The want of variety and of balance in their life and

occupations impairs the balance of their judgment in general. Their special subject intoxicates them. They are carried away by theorising; they affirm confidently where one cannot be sure; and, in short, prove by no means good and safe judges of the evi-
5   dence before them.

In France and England people do not, certainly, in general err on the side of making too great a business of this particular specialty. In general we too much neglect it, and are in consequence either at the mercy of routine, or at the mercy of the first bold
10   innovator. Of Biblical learning we have not enough. Yet it remains true, as we have said already, and a truth never to be lost sight of, that in the domain of religion, as in the domain of poetry, the whole apparatus of learning is but secondary, and that we always go wrong with our learning when we suffer our-
15   selves to forget this. The reader of *Literature and Dogma* will allow, however, that we did not there intrude any futile exhibition of learning to draw off his attention from the one fixed object of that work—religion. We did not write for a public of professors; we did not write to interest the learned and curious.
20   We wrote to restore the use and enjoyment of the Bible to plain people, who might be in danger of losing it. We hardly subjoined a reference or put a note; for we wished to give nothing of this kind except what a plain reader, busy with our main argument, would be likely to look for and to use. Our reader will trust us,
25   therefore, if we now take him into this subject of the criticism of the Canon, not to bury him in it, not to cozen him with theories of vigour and rigour, not to hold a brief for either the Conservative side or the Liberal, not to make certainties where there are none; but to try and put him in the way of forming a plain
30   judgment upon the plain facts of the case, so far as they can be known.

[Thus he will see the grounds for what we said in *Literature and Dogma* about the Canon of the Gospels, and about the Fourth Gospel's peculiar character, without having himself to
35   plunge into the voluminous literature of the subject. In our search for a sure standing-ground in the use of the Bible, we have had to go through a great deal of this literature in our time; of how much of it may we not exclaim with Themistocles: *Give*

me, not to remember, but to forget! If Goethe could say that all
which was really worth knowing in all the sciences he had ever
studied would go into one small envelope, how much more may
one say this of the harvest to be gathered from the literature now
in question! That may be no reason for neglecting it, indeed; 5
light and adjustment often come insensibly to us from labours
of which the direct positive result seems small. Nevertheless, in
these days of multifarious studies soliciting us let us keep a
wholesome dread, and let our reader share it with us, of spend-
ing too much of our life and time over the wrong ones. We have 10
quoted in *Literature and Dogma* the day's prayer given in a
short sentence of the Imitation: '*Utinam per unum diem bene
simus conversati in hoc mundo!* Would that for one single day
we may have lived in this world as we ought!' He who adds to
that sentence this other from the same book: '*Da mihi, Domine,* 15
scire quod sciendum est! Grant that the knowledge I get may be
the knowledge that is worth having!'—and sets the two sentences together before him for his daily guidance, will not have
prayed amiss.]

Let us, then, come to the Canon. And as the New Testament 20
follows the Old and depends upon it, and since about the Old
Testament, too, we had in *Literature and Dogma* a great deal to
say, our reader will wish, perhaps, before going into the question of the New Testament, to see brought together first, in the
shortest possible summary, what he may reasonably think of the 25
Canon of the Old.

3.

The Law and the Prophets are often mentioned in the New 30
Testament. But we also find there a threefold division of the Old
Testament Scriptures: *Law, Prophets, Psalms.*[1] And the Greek
translator of the lost Hebrew book of the Wisdom of the Son of
Sirach, or, as we call it, Ecclesiasticus, who writes in the latter
half of the second century before Christ, speaks of *the law, and* 35

---

[1] Luke xxiv. 44. τὰ γεγραμμένα ἐν τῷ νόμῳ Μωυσέως καὶ τοῖς προφήταις καὶ
ψαλμοῖς.

the prophecies, and the rest of the books.[1] Here we have the
Bible of the Old Testament Scriptures. And, indeed, the writer
calling himself Daniel,—whose date is between the translator of
the Book of Ecclesiasticus, and this translator's grandfather, who
5   composed it,—in a passage wrongly translated in our version,
designates the body of Old Testament Scriptures by a word answering to our very word *Bible.*[2] Can we trace, without coming
down below the Christian era to late and untrustworthy Jewish
traditions, how this Bible came together?

10   We can. In the second Book of the Maccabees, dating probably from much the same time as our Greek Ecclesiasticus, the
writer, telling the Egyptian Jews of the purification of the Temple at Jerusalem after the Maccabean victories, and of the revival
of Jewish religion, says that Nehemiah,—who with Ezra had ac-
15   complished the famous restoration of Jewish religion three
centuries before,—that Nehemiah, as was related in his writings
and commentaries, *founding a library, brought together in addition the things concerning the kings and prophets, and David's
things, and letters of kings about offerings.*[3] Offerings to the
20   Temple are here meant, such as those of King Seleucus which the
Maccabean historian mentions in his next chapter.[4] At the re-
building of the Temple, gifts of this kind from friendly foreign
kings had a peculiar importance. The letters concerning them
could not, however, merit a permanent place in the Bible, and
25   they dropped out of it. But the other writings which Nehemiah
is said to have 'brought together in addition' to the stock of already recognised Scriptures, that is, to the Law, answer to that
second instalment of Scriptures, which did really, from Nehemiah's time onwards, obtain authority at Jerusalem. They com-
30   prise the Books of Judges, Samuel, and Kings, for the 'things
concerning the kings;' the Books of Isaiah, Jeremiah, Ezekiel, and

---

[1] ὁ νόμος, καὶ αἱ προφητεῖαι, καὶ τὰ λοιπὰ τῶν βιβλίων. Prologue to *Ecclesiasticus*, in the Septuagint.

[2] Daniel ix. 2.

35

[3] καταβαλλόμενος βιβλιοθήκην, ἐπισυνήγαγε τὰ περὶ τῶν βασιλέων καὶ
προφητῶν, καὶ τὰ τοῦ Δαυίδ, καὶ ἐπιστολὰς βασιλέων περὶ ἀναθημάτων. II *Maccabees* ii. 13.

[4] II *Maccabees* iii. 3.

the twelve Minor Prophets, for 'the prophets;' and the collection
of the Psalms,—called in general after the famous name of the
royal Psalmist, David,—for 'David's things.'

But the Maccabean historian then proceeds:—'In like manner
also Judas (Maccabeus) brought together in addition all the
things that were lost by reason of the war we had, and they
remain with us.'[1] Now, this further addition to the stock of
recognised Scriptures corresponds to the third instalment of
Scriptures,—some of them of then recent date, like the Book of
Daniel, others much older, like the Book of Job,—which was
received and authorised at Jerusalem. It comprehended exactly
the same books, and no more, that our Bibles add to the books
said to have been 'brought together' by Nehemiah, and to the
Pentateuch and the Book of Joshua. But the order of the later
books in the Hebrew Bible was by no means the same as it is in
ours, and to this we shall return presently.

The Law itself, the Thora, the first of the three great divisions
of the Hebrew Bible, whom shall we call as evidence for it? The
founder of the second division, Nehemiah himself. He has told
us how at Jerusalem, after the restoration, 'the people gathered
themselves together as one man into the street that was before the
water-gate, and they spake unto Ezra the scribe to bring the
book of the law of Moses; and Ezra the priest brought the law,
and he read therein from the morning until mid-day, before the
men and the women and those that could understand; also day
by day, from the first day unto the last day, he read in the book
of the law of God.'[2] This book was Israel's history from its first
beginning down to the conquest of the Promised Land, as this
history stands written in the Pentateuch and the Book of Joshua.
To that collection many an old book had given up its treasures
and then itself vanished for ever. Many voices were blended
there; unknown voices, speaking out of the early dawn. In the
strain there were many passages familiar as household words,
yet the whole strain, in its continuity and connexion, was to the

---

[1] II *Maccabees* ii. 14. ὡσαύτως δὲ καὶ Ἰούδας τὰ διαπεπτωκότα διὰ τὸν πόλεμον
τὸν γεγονότα ἡμῖν ἐπισυνήγαγε πάντα, καὶ ἔστιν παρ' ἡμῖν.
[2] Nehemiah viii. 1, 2, 3, 18.

mass of the people at that time new and affecting. 'All the people
wept when they heard the words of the law.'[1] And the Levites,
in stilling them, gave in one short sentence the secret of Israel's
religion and of the religion of the Bible: 'Mourn not, nor weep,'
they said; *'the joy of the Eternal is your strength.'*[2]

Now, this revival of religion in Jerusalem, under Ezra and
Nehemiah, had had its counterpart in a former revival, two centuries earlier, under King Josiah. In Josiah's discovery of the
book of the law, and his solemn publication of it to the people,
we have the original consecration of a written historic record
embodying the law; we have the nucleus of our existing Bible.
In repairing the Temple, 'Hilkiah the priest found a book of the
law of the Lord by the hand of Moses. Then Hilkiah delivered
the book to Shaphan; Shaphan the scribe told the king, saying:
Hilkiah the priest hath given me a book. And Shaphan read it
before the king. And it came to pass, when the king had heard
the words of the law, that he rent his clothes. And the king
went up into the house of the Lord, and all the men of Judah, and
the inhabitants of Jerusalem, and the priests and the Levites, and
all the people great and small, and he read in their ears all the
words of the book of the covenant that was found in the house
of the Lord. And he caused all that were present in Jerusalem and
Benjamin to stand to it.'[3] The centre-piece of Josiah's reading
was, in all probability, a new book, Deuteronomy; as an edifying
summary, from the point of view of the time then present,[4] of
the chosen people's early history and of its covenant with God.
Around Deuteronomy the rest of the Pentateuch and the story
of Joshua's conquest gathered. Many old books of the Hebrew
nation contributed, as we have said, their contents to them. Of
some of the books we have still the names; but when once their
substance had been secured for ever in the Thora, their function

---

[1] Nehem. viii. 9.   [2] Nehem. viii. 9, 10.

[3] II *Chronicles* xxxiv. 14, 15, 18, 19, 30, 32. See also II *Kings* xxii, xxiii.

[4] Chapters xxxi and xxxii of *Deuteronomy*, if we read them with attention, tell us the book's date. They belong to the revival under Josiah in the
seventh century, nearly a hundred years after the ruin and captivity of the
house of Israel, and with 'the line of Samaria and the plummet of the house
of Ahab' threatening also Jerusalem and the royal house of Judah.

was at an end, and they perished. Among the devout Jews of the Captivity, severed from the Holy Land and the Temple services, this first instalment of the Bible, this 'volume of the book' of which a Psalmist of the exile speaks,[1] became firmly established. It came back with them at the Return, a consecrated authority; and from this book it was that Ezra read to the people.

Do we inquire for the original nucleus of the Thora itself, for the Law as in its earliest written form it existed, in the primitive times when writing was scarce and difficult, and documents were short, and readers were few? This also we can find. It was the 'Book of the Law,' consisting probably of the Decalogue, and of some other portions besides the Decalogue of what we now find in Exodus, 'put in the side of the ark of the covenant of the Lord.'[2] The 'testimony' thus laid up before the Lord and guarded by the priests and Levites, was given to the kings at their accession and solemnly accepted by them.[3]

The arrangement of the Hebrew Bible corresponds with this its history and confirms it. Only we must add, that from each of the two earlier collections the last book was taken, and was employed to serve as an introducer to the collection which followed. Thus the Pentateuch, or five books of Moses, stood alone as the 'Thora.' This first great instalment of the Bible Samaria, as is well known, received from Jerusalem, but would receive nothing more. The Book of Joshua stood at the head of the second instalment of the Bible,—the eight books of Prophets, 'Nebiim,' as they were called. For, indeed, prophecy and the prophet were the force and glory of Israel's religion; and the Books of Joshua, Judges, Samuel, and Kings, which we call historical, were at Jerusalem prized chiefly as the records of many a word and deed of prophets anterior to the age of literary prophetic compositions, and went by the name of *Earlier Prophets*. Isaiah, Jeremiah, Ezekiel, and the book of the Minor Prophets, were called the four *Later Prophets*.

The third division of the Bible, received from the time of Judas Maccabeus onward, had the name of 'Ketubim,' translated

---

[1] *Ps.* xl. 7. [2] *Deuteronomy* xxxi. 26.

[3] II *Kings* xi. 12; *Deut.* xvii. 18.

by Jerome *Hagiographa*, but simply meaning *Writings, Scriptures*. These are 'the rest of the books,' mentioned by the translator of Ecclesiasticus. They were nine in number, and the twenty-two books of the now completed Canon thus answered
5   to the twenty-two letters of the Hebrew alphabet. At the head of the nine was placed the last book of the second formation of authorised Scriptures,—'the things of David,' the Psalms. This admirable book with its double merits,—merit prophetic and religious, and merit poetic and literary,—might well serve to
10 usher in and commend a series of mixed character. Early works of the highest poetical value, not hitherto included in the Canon, such as the Book of Job, this series adopted and saved; early works, also, of the highest ethical value, such as the Book of Proverbs. It adopted contemporary works also, like the Book of
15 Daniel;—works which reflected and powerfully engaged, as we can see by the prominence of the Book of Daniel at the Christian era, the feelings of the time. It adopted works like the Book of Ezra, which glorified Jerusalem, and deeply interested the Temple-hierarchy whose sanction made the books canonical. But in
20 gravity and indispensableness for the proper religion of the Old Testament, this late instalment of 'the remaining writings,' 'the rest of the books,' cannot, after we leave the Psalms, in general quite rank with the two earlier instalments of Law and Prophets. Simply to recite the last names in the Hebrew Canon is to mark
25 sufficiently this somewhat inferior character of the final gleanings. The last books in the Hebrew Bible are not, as in ours, the Minor Prophets; they are Esther, Daniel, Ezra, Nehemiah, and Chronicles.

During the two centuries between Judas Maccabeus and the
30 fall of Jerusalem, materials for a fourth instalment of Scriptures accumulated. In the deep spiritual agitation of those times, religious books which met the needs of the moment, and which spoke a modern language easy to be read and to be understood, were greatly in request. Particularly was this the case among the
35 Greek Jews, and at a distance from Jerusalem. The hierarchy at Jerusalem had its authorised list; but at Alexandria or in the provinces additional Scriptures were freely read and became popular. The additions to Daniel and Esther, the Book of Baruch, the Book of Tobit, Wisdom, Ecclesiasticus,—almost all the books

which we find in our Apocrypha,—were Scriptures of this class. Into the Greek Bible, the Bible for the great world and in the then universal language, they made good their entrance. Other new Scriptures, which did not make their way into the Greek Bible, we find elsewhere. The Aethiopian Bible preserved the Book of Enoch. Some of these books were earlier than books admitted to the Hebrew Canon. Some, like the Book of Wisdom, were very late, and existed in Greek only. But they answered to the wants of their time, and they spoke its language. *Resurrection*, the great word of the New Testament, never appears in the canonical books of the Old; it appears in the Apocrypha. Many of these works were edifying and excellent. We can trace in the New Testament their popularity and their strong influence; indeed, the Book of Enoch is quoted in the New Testament as a genuine Scripture.[1] At the Christian era, then, these books were knocking, we may say, for admission into the Hebrew Canon. And, undoubtedly, if Christianity had not come when it did, and if the Jewish state had endured, the best of them would have been (and with good reason) admitted. But with Christianity came the end of the Jewish state, the destruction of Jerusalem; and the door was shut.

For the stronghold on Mount Moriah was now gone; the Bible of the ancient people remained the one stronghold of its religion. It is well known with what rigidity Rabbinism established itself in this stronghold. At first it even bethought itself of sacrificing what might seem weak points in the received Scripture, like the Book of Ecclesiastes and the Song of Solomon. They were retained, however, and the worship of the letter of Scripture, which then set in with full force, was extended to them also. But that worship extended not to Scriptures outside the Hebrew Canon, as this Canon had been for the last time formally approved in the days of Judas Maccabeus. The enlarged Greek Bible was the Bible of Christians, and Greek was the language of Christianity. Rabbinism now deplored the day when the Bible had been translated into Greek. It retranslated it into Greek in an anti-Christian sense; it sternly rejected the Greek additions; it mocked at the ignorant Christians who re-

---

[1] Epistle of Jude, verse 14.

ceived them. But the Greek Bible, with all its books, had become
dear to Christians, and was by the Christian Church preserved.
Learned men, like Origen and St. Jerome, knew well the difference between the books of the Apocrypha and the books of the
5 Hebrew Canon. But this difference was by the mass of Christians
unregarded or unknown, and the Latin Bible inevitably repro-
duced the books of the Greek. The African Synods, at the end
of the fourth century, mark the time when the distinction between the Apocrypha and the Hebrew Canon had become so
10 generally obliterated in the West, that the books of both were
stamped by the Church as having one and the same canonical
authority.

At the Reformation, Protestantism reverted to the Hebrew
Canon. But the influence of the Latin Vulgate, and of the Greek
15 Bible, still shows itself in the order of the books. The Greek,
and the Vulgate following it, had adopted, in place of the old
and significant tripartite division into Law, Prophets, and Writings, a division into prose books and poetical books, the prophets
being counted with the latter; and in arranging the books of each
20 class, the order of date was followed.[1] This innovation our Bibles
retain; and therefore our Old Testament ends with the last of the
poetical books, Malachi, instead of ending with the last of the
Ketubim, Chronicles.

4.

Thus we have summarised, for the benefit of the reader of
25 *Literature and Dogma*, the history of the Canon of that Old
Testament to which we are so often sending him. The points in
the history of the Canon of the New Testament require to be
treated with more of detail, for our positions have here to be
made good against objectors.
30 We know how the Scriptures of the Old Testament are appealed to in the New. They are appealed to as an authority established and recognised, just as the Bible is now appealed to by
us. But when did the New Testament, in that form in which we

[1] The *Maccabees* only, though a prose book of history, is in the Vulgate
35 printed by itself at the end of the poetical books.

possess it, come to be recognised as *Scripture* like the Old Testament? Clearly the documents composing it appeared at different times, and were not first published to the world as one authorised whole called the New Testament. Clearly there was a time when they had not acquired the authority they possessed afterwards; when people preferred, for instance, to any written narrative, the oral relations of eye-witnesses. One of the earliest and most important witnesses to the written narratives, Papias, is a distinct witness, at the same time, to this preference for oral relations. 'I did not consider,' he says, speaking in the first half of the second century after Christ, about the year 140,—'I did not consider things from books to be of so much good to me, as things from the living and abiding voice.'[1] And he goes on to mention his communications with those who had actually heard 'the disciples of the Lord.' For Papias, then, there was not yet a body of Scriptures fully answering to our New Testament, and having like authority with the Old; if there had been, he would hardly have spoken in this fashion. And no man can point to any exact moment and manner in which our body of New Testament Scriptures received its authority. But we can point to a moment after which we find our present New Testament Canon in possession of undisputed authority in the Church of the West, and before which we do not.

We have mentioned the African Synods. The two Synods of Carthage,—the first of them held in the year 397 of our era, the second in the year 419,—deliver the Canon of the New Testament as we have it now.[2] All its books, and no others, are *canonical;* that is, they furnish the rule of faith, they form a class by themselves, they are authorised for public use. And so, as every

---

[1] See Papias in Eusebii *Historia Ecclesiastica* iii. 39. οὐ γὰρ τὰ ἐκ τῶν βιβλίων τοσοῦτόν με ὠφελεῖν ὑπελάμβανον, ὅσον τὰ παρὰ ζώσης φωνῆς καὶ μενούσης. The latter words are commonly taken to mean merely the voice of living speakers, but they almost certainly contain a reminiscence of I Peter i. 23, and of Isaiah xl. 8, and mean speakers who had heard the voice of Jesus.

[2] The earlier Synod mentions the Epistle to the Hebrews apart, though as Paul's; the second Synod drops this distinction, and speaks of Paul's 'Fourteen Epistles.' The New Testament Canon of the two Synods is in other respects the same.

one knows, they have continued. For the Eastern Church, a similar authoritative enunciation of our Canon of the New Testament is first found in the Festal Letter of St. Athanasius, of which
the date is probably A.D. 365. But an absence of fixed consent as to
5 certain books goes on showing itself amongst Greek Christians
for long afterwards. Our present business, however, is with our
own Western Christianity.

St. Jerome died in 420, the year after the second Synod of
Carthage. His Biblical labours and learning are celebrated; he
10 knew more about the Bible than any of his contemporaries.
Cavillers he had, as have all men who bring new criticism to
disturb old habits; but his orthodoxy was undoubted. His Biblical publications were undertaken at a Pope's request; and the first
instalment of them, a corrected Latin version of the Four Gos-
15 pels, appeared in the year 383 with a prefatory letter addressed
to the Pope himself. This great churchman has left us his remarks
on several of the works which the African Synods were presently to include in the Canon of the New Testament, and which
have stood there ever since, possessing in the eyes of Christen-
20 dom a like sacredness and authority with the rest of the Canon.
In reading him, we are to bear in mind the character of the
speaker. It is as if Dr. Pusey, with the reputation for learning and
orthodoxy which we know him to have, and commissioned, besides, by the heads of the Church to revise the Bible, were speak-
25 ing of the Canon. St. Jerome, then, says of the Epistle to the
Hebrews:—'The custom of the Latin Christians does not receive
it among the Canonical Scriptures.'[1] Of the Apocalypse he says:
—'The Greek Churches use the same freedom in regard to John's
Apocalypse.'[2] Of the so-called Second Epistle of Peter he says:—
30 'It is denied by most to be his.'[3] Of the Epistle of James he says:
—'It is asserted to have been brought out by somebody else under his name.'[4] Of the Epistle of Jude he says:—'Inasmuch as the
author appeals to the Book of Enoch, which is apocryphal, the

---

[1] Latinorum consuetudo non recipit inter scripturas canonicas.
35 [2] Nec Graecorum quidem ecclesiae Apocalypsin Joannis eadem libertate
suscipiunt.
[3] Secunda a plerisque ejus esse negatur.
[4] Ab alio quodam sub nomine ejus edita asseritur.

Epistle is rejected by most.'[1] Of the three Epistles attributed to
St. John, Jerome says:—'He wrote one Epistle which is acknowledged by all churches and scholars, but the remaining two are
asserted to be by John the Elder.'[2]

Now, all Jerome's sympathies were with what was orthodox,
ecclesiastical, regular. The works on which he has here been
remarking seemed to him good and edifying; they had been
much used, and had inspired attachment. The tendency in the
Church was to admit them to canonicity, as the African Synods
did. Jerome wished them to be admitted. He helped forward
their admission by arguments in its favour, some of them not a
little strained. But what we want the reader to observe is the
entire upset which Jerome gives to our popular notion of the
Canon of the New Testament; to the notion of a number of
sacred books, just so many and no more, all alike of the most
indisputable authenticity, and having equal authority from the
very first. It is true, they were about to get invested with this
character, but through the authority of the Church, and because,—while this authority was on the increase,—learning and
criticism, amidst the miseries of the invasions and general break-
up then befalling Europe, languished and died nearly out. Already the African Synods, which may be said to have first laid
down authoritatively for our Western Europe the Canon of the
New Testament, imagined that Wisdom and Ecclesiasticus were
by Solomon, although Wisdom was composed in Greek hardly
half a century before the Christian era. St. Augustine, who died
ten years after St. Jerome, was far too accomplished a man not to
know, although his studies had not lain in this special direction,
how, in general, the Canon of the New Testament had arisen,
and how great was the difference between the evidence for some
books and for others. But the authority of the Church was
enough for him. In a sentence, which for Paul would have been
inconceivable, he shows us how the idea of this authority had by
his time grown:—'*I believe the Gospel itself*,' he says, '*only*

---

[1] Quia de libro Enoch, qui apocryphus est, in ea assumit testimonium, a
plerisque rejicitur.

[2] Reliquae autem duae Joannis presbyteri asseruntur.

upon the authority of the Catholic Church.[1] The Reformation
arrived, and to Protestants the authority of the Church ceased
to appear all-sufficient for establishing the canonicity of books of
Scripture. Then grew up the notion that our actual New Testa-
5 ment intrinsically possessed this character of a Canon, the notion
of its having from the first been one sure and sacred whole as it
stands, a whole with all its parts equipollent; a kind of talisman, as
we have elsewhere said, that had been handed to us straight out
of heaven.

10   Therefore the other day, when there was published for the use
of the young a Bible in which some parts of the Scriptures were
taken and others left out, the late Dean of Carlisle, Dr. Close,
wrote an indignant letter in blame of this audacious attempt, as
he thought it, to make distinctions in what was all alike the Word
15 of God. To very many his blame will have seemed perfectly just.
Nay, all that mechanical employment of Scripture texts which
is so common in the religious world, and so unhesitating, is due
to just such a notion of Scripture as the venerable Dean's. Yet
how evidently is the notion false! Four hundred years after
20 Christ we have the last representative of Biblical learning before
the setting-in of mediaeval ignorance,—we have the Dr. Pusey
of his time, a great churchman, orthodox, learned, trusted,—declaring, without the least concealment, the essential difference in
authority between some documents in our New Testament and
25 others! For manifestly the difference in authority is great between a document like the so-called Second Epistle of Peter,
rejected by most, and a document like the Epistle to the Romans,
which every churchman accepted.

And the more we ascend to the times before St. Jerome, to
30 the primitive times, as they are called,—the more does this difference between the documents now composing the Canon become
visible. Churchmen like Eusebius and Origen testify as clearly as
Jerome to the non-acceptance, in their time, of books now in
the Canon, and do not, as Jerome, plead for their acceptance. So

35   [1] Ego evangelio non crederem, nisi me catholicae ecclesiae auctoritas
commoveret.

that really, when one comes to look into the thing, the common notion about the Canon is so plainly false, that to take it for granted, as the Dean of Carlisle did, and to found indignant denunciations upon it, will one day be resented as an outrage upon common sense and notorious facts. It is like the Bishop of Lincoln's allegation that 'episcopacy was an institution of God Himself;' an allegation which might make one suppose that in Genesis, directly after God had said *Let there be light* (or, perhaps, even before it), he had pronounced, *Let there be bishops!* There are plenty of true reasons for the existence of bishops without invoking false ones; and the time will come when thus to invoke the false ones solemnly and authoritatively will shock public opinion.

As to the Canon of the New Testament, then, we see that consent determined it; that after the beginning of the fifth century this consent may be regarded as established in favour of the books of our actual Canon; that before the fifth century it was not yet fully established, and the most eminent doctors in the Church did not hesitate to say so. Consent depended on the known or presumed authenticity of books as proceeding from apostles or apostolic men, from the Apostles of Christ themselves or from their personal followers. Some books of our Canon had not this consent, even in Jerome's time; and of its not being certain in primitive times that these books are what they are now commonly said to be, we have thus the clearest evidence. If the Christian Church of the fourth century had believed it to be absolutely certain that the Johannine Apocalypse was by the Apostle John, or the second Petrine Epistle by the Apostle Peter, no churchman would have rejected them. Some books, then, in our New Testament Canon there plainly are of which the authenticity is doubtful.

We have given cases in which the want of consent is grave. It is grave when we find it in churchmen; it has its weight even when it is found in heretics. Marcion did not use St. Paul's Epistles to Timothy and Titus, while he used the others. It is something against the genuineness of the Pastoral Epistles that a fervent admirer of St. Paul in the first half of the second century,

should not have received them. It is possible that Marcion may have rejected these epistles because they did not suit him. It is possible; but we know that he and his party complained of the adulteration of the rule of Christianity, and professed to revert
5   to what was genuine; it may be, therefore, that Marcion rejected the Pastoral Epistles because he really thought them spurious. Or he may have not used the Pastoral Epistles because they were in his time not yet written. It is a case in which the internal evidence for or against the authenticity of the documents in ques-
10 tion becomes of peculiar importance. The Alogi, again, heretics of the second century, rejected the Fourth Gospel. The authenticity of this Gospel, therefore, cannot be said to have such a security in general consent as the authenticity of the First Gospel, which not even heretics challenged.

15   Now to be indignant with those who, under such circumstances, will not take for granted the authenticity of books in the New Testament Canon, is really unreasonable. We have for the books in the Canon, it is sometimes said, as good evidence as we have for the history of Thucydides; why not require the
20 history of Thucydides to prove its authenticity? This will not bear a moment's examination. The history of Thucydides tells us itself, in the most explicit way possible, the name of its author, and what he was, and what he designed in writing his work. Its authenticity no one has challenged. To forge it under the
25 name of Thucydides no one had any interest. But not one of our Four Gospels says anywhere who its author was. Heretics challenged the authenticity of the Fourth Gospel, and we have seen how documents now in the Canon, which purport to be by this or that Apostle, were gravely suspected in the Church itself. St.
30 Paul himself, in the Second Epistle to the Thessalonians, warns his converts not to let themselves be 'troubled *by letter as from us*,' thus indicating that forgery of this kind was practised as to epistles. As to gospels and acts it was practised too. Tertullian mentions a detected case of it,—forged Acts of Paul, authorising
35 a woman to baptize. The practice of forgery and interpolation was notorious, and the temptation to it was great. One explicit witness is as good as twenty, and we will again take for our

witness a churchman, the ecclesiastical historian Eusebius, bishop of Caesarea, who died in the year 340. He says that scriptures were current 'put forth by the heretics in the name of the Apostles, whether as containing the Gospels of Peter and Thomas and Matthias, or those also of any others besides these, or as containing the Acts of Andrew and John and the other Apostles.'[1]

The Gospels give us the sayings and doings of Jesus himself, and are therefore of the highest importance. How far back can we certainly carry the chain of established consent in favour of our four canonical Gospels? Let us begin with St. Jerome, whom we have already quoted, and from him let us go backwards. For St. Jerome our canonical four are already established:—'Four Gospels whereof the order is this: Matthew, Mark, Luke, John.'[2] That was at the end of the fourth century. In the earlier part of the same century, for Eusebius likewise, whom we have just now cited to show the existence of spurious gospels, the canonicity of our four was established. Let us follow back the chain of great churchmen to the third century and to Origen. He died A.D. 254. For him, too, our four canonical Gospels are 'alone undisputed in the Church of God upon earth.'[3] Let us ascend to the second century. Irenaeus wrote in the last quarter of it, and no testimony to the Four Gospels of our Canon can be more explicit than his. 'Matthew it was who, among the Hebrews, brought out in their own language a written Gospel, when Peter and Paul were preaching in Rome, and founding the Church. Then, after their departure, Mark, the disciple and interpreter of Peter, he too delivered to us in writing what Peter preached; and Luke, moreover, the follower of Paul, set down in a book the Gospel preached by Paul. Then John, the disciple of the Lord, who

---

[1] Eusebius *Hist. Eccles.* iii. 25. γραφὰς ... ὀνόματι τῶν ἀποστόλων πρὸς τῶν αἱρετικῶν προφερομένας, ἤτοι ὡς Πέτρου καὶ Θωμᾶ καὶ Ματθία ἢ καί τινων παρὰ τούτους ἄλλων εὐαγγέλια περιεχούσας, ἢ ὡς Ἀνδρέου καὶ Ἰωάννου καὶ τῶν ἄλλων ἀποστόλων πράξεις.

[2] *Praefat. ad Damasum.* Quatuor Evangelia quorum ordo est iste: Matthaeus, Marcus, Lucas, Johannes.

[3] Quoted by Eusebius *Hist. Eccles.* vi. 25. τῶν τεσσάρων εὐαγγελίων, ἃ καὶ μόνα ἀναντίρρητά ἐστιν ἐν τῇ ὑπὸ τὸν οὐρανὸν ἐκκλησίᾳ τοῦ θεοῦ.

also lay on his breast, John too published his Gospel, living at
that time at Ephesus, in Asia.'[1] And for Irenaeus this number of
four, which the Gospels exhibit, has something fixed, necessary, and sacred, 'like the four zones of our world, and the four
5 winds.'

Here then, about the year 180 of our era, we have from a
great churchman the most express testimony to the Four Gospels
of our Canon. Higher than this we cannot find a great churchman
who gives it us. Ignatius does not give it, nor Polycarp, nor Justin
10 Martyr. But a famous fragment, discovered by Muratori, the
Italian antiquary, in the monastery of Bobbio in North Italy, and
published by him in the year 1740, carries us, perhaps, to an age
a little higher than that of Irenaeus. The manuscript containing
this fragment is said to be of the eighth century, and is in barbar-
15 ous Latin. The monastery at Bobbio was founded by St. Columban, and it has been alleged that the barbarisms in our fragment
are due to the Irish monks who copied it from the original.
Others have assigned to these barbarisms an African source;
others, again, have supposed that the fragment is a translation of
20 a Greek original, Greek having been the language of the Roman
Church at the time when the author of the fragment lived. However this may be, the important matter is that the fragment,—
called, from its finder and first publisher, the *Fragment of Muratori*, the *Canon of Muratori*,—gives us with tolerable nearness its
25 own date. It says that the *Pastor* of Hermas, a work received as
Scripture by many in the early Church, was written '*quite lately,
in our own times*, while Pius, the brother of Hermas, was filling
the episcopal chair at Rome.' Pius died in the year 157 of our era.
If we believe what the author of the fragment here tells us, we
30 have only to ask ourselves, therefore, what '*quite lately, in our*

---

[1] Quoted by Eusebius *Hist. Eccles.* v. 8. ὁ μὲν δὴ Ματθαῖος ἐν τοῖς Ἑβραίοις
τῇ ἰδίᾳ αὐτῶν διαλέκτῳ καὶ γραφὴν ἐξήνεγκεν εὐαγγελίου, τοῦ Πέτρου καὶ τοῦ
Παύλου ἐν Ῥώμῃ εὐαγγελιζομένων καὶ θεμελιούντων τὴν ἐκκλησίαν. μετὰ δὲ τὴν
τούτων ἔξοδον, Μάρκος ὁ μαθητὴς καὶ ἑρμηνευτὴς Πέτρου, καὶ αὐτὸς τὰ ὑπὸ Πέτρου
35 κηρυσσόμενα ἐγγράφως ἡμῖν παραδέδωκε, καὶ Λουκᾶς δὲ, ὁ ἀκόλουθος Παύλου, τὸ
ὑπ᾽ ἐκείνου κηρυσσόμενον εὐαγγέλιον ἐν βίβλῳ κατέθετο. ἔπειτα Ἰωάννης ὁ
μαθητὴς τοῦ κυρίου, ὁ καὶ ἐπὶ τὸ στῆθος αὐτοῦ ἀναπεσὼν, καὶ αὐτὸς ἐξέδωκε τὸ
εὐαγγέλιον, ἐν Ἐφέσῳ τῆς Ἀσίας διατρίβων.

own times' means. And the words can hardly, one must allow, mean a time more than thirty years back from the time of the person uttering them. This would give us the year 187 as the latest date possible for the original of the fragment in question; and as there is no reason why we should put it at the latest date possible, it seems fair to assign it to a time some ten or twelve years, perhaps, before A.D. 187; that is, to a date rather earlier than the date of the testimony of Irenaeus.

But the author of *Supernatural Religion* will not allow the Canon of Muratori to be authentic, any more than he will allow to be authentic two fragments of Claudius Apollinaris, bishop of Hierapolis, quoted in the Paschal Chronicle, which show that Apollinaris, about the year 170 of our era, knew and received the Fourth Gospel. The author of *Supernatural Religion* has a theory that the Fourth Gospel, and, indeed, all the canonical Gospels, were not recognised till a particular time. This theory the Canon of Muratori and the fragments of Apollinaris do not suit; so he rejects them. There is really no more serious reason to be given for his rejection of them. True, Eusebius gives a list of some works of Apollinaris; and the work on the Paschal controversy, from which the two fragments are taken, is not among them. But Eusebius expressly says that there were other works of Apollinaris of which he did not know the titles. True, Greek was the language of the Roman Church in the second century; but must we think a document forged sooner than admit that a single Roman Christian may have chanced to write in Latin, or that a document written in Greek may have got translated? No; the one real reason which the author of *Supernatural Religion* has for rejecting these three pieces of evidence is, that they do not suit his theory. And this leads us to say a word as to the difference between the practice which we impose on ourselves in dealing with evidence, and the practice followed by critics with a theory.

For we suppose the reader of *Literature and Dogma*, for a while suspicious of the Bible, but now convinced that (to use Butler's famous phrase with a slight alteration) *there is something in it*, nay, that there is a great deal in it,—we suppose him to find that there is a hot controversy about the age and authen-

ticity of many of the chief documents of the New Testament,
and to wish to know what to think about them. Soon he will perceive that the controversy is in general conducted by people
who, in the first place, think that for every question which can
5   be started the answer can be discovered, and who, in the second
place, have a theory which all things must be made to suit. Evidence is dealt with in a fashion that no one would ever dream
of who had not a theory to warp him. In the so-called Epistle of
Barnabas, a work of the end of the first century, the words *many*
10 *called, but few chosen*, are quoted with the formula, *as it is
written*,[1] implying that they are taken from Scripture. The
Greek words are the very same that we find in St. Matthew, and
no one without a theory to warp him would doubt that the
writer of the epistle quotes, not, indeed, necessarily from our
15 Gospel of St. Matthew, but from a collection of sayings of Jesus.
Dr. Volkmar, however, maintains that what is here quoted as
Scripture must be a passage of the Apocrypha: *There be many
created, but few shall be saved*.[2] Strauss applauds him, and says
that 'beyond all doubt' this is so. And why? Because, to cite a
20 third well-known critic, Dr. Zeller, 'if in a work of earlier date
than the middle of the second century we find a passage quoted
as *Scripture*, we may be sure that either the quotation is not
from the New Testament, or else the work is not genuine; because *Scripture* is not used for the New Testament till long after
25 the middle of the second century.' That is to say, because the
New Testament is not *generally* called Scripture till after the
middle of the second century, that it should *occasionally* have
been called so before is impossible. But the New Testament did
not begin in one day to be called Scripture by an Order in Coun-
30 cil. There must have been a time when to find it called so was
comparatively rare; a time, earlier still, when it was exceedingly
rare. But at no time, after the written sayings of Jesus were first
published, can it have been *impossible* for a Christian to call them
Scripture.
35   The innovating critics are certainly the most conspicuous of-
fenders in this way, but the conservative critics are not to be

---

[1] ὡς γέγραπται.   [2] II Esdras, viii, 3.

trusted either. Neander rejects, like the author of *Supernatural Religion*, a fragment of Apollinaris, and rejects it for the very same reason: that it fails (though from a different cause) to suit him. Bunsen (unaware that by the Epistle to the Alexandrians, named in the Canon of Muratori and stigmatised as apocryphal, the Epistle to the Hebrews is probably meant) lays it down that 'it is quite impossible this Epistle could have been omitted,' and supposes that 'there is, in the middle of this barbarous translation or extract of the Greek original, a chasm, or omission, respecting the Epistle to the Hebrews.' What may we not put in or leave out when we take license to proceed in this fashion?

Sick of special pleading both on one side and on the other, the reader of *Literature and Dogma*, after a brief experience of the impugners of the Canon and of its defenders, will probably feel that what he earnestly desires, and what no one will indulge him in, is simply to be permitted to have the fair facts of the case, and to let them speak for themselves. Here it is that we sympathise with him and wish to aid him, because we had just the same earnest desire ourselves after a like experience. And we treat the evidence about the Canon with a mind resolutely free and straightforward, determined to reject nothing because it does not suit us, and to proceed as we should proceed in a literary inquiry where we were wholly disinterested. In the first place, we confess to ourselves that a great many questions may be asked about the New Testament Canon to which it is impossible to give an answer. In the second place, we own that it is *something* in favour of a fact that it has been asserted, and that tradition delivers it. Men do not, we acknowledge, in general use language for the purpose of falsehood, but to communicate a matter faithfully. Of course, many things may be said which we yet must decline to receive, but we require substantial reasons for declining, and not fantastic ones. The second Petrine Epistle calls itself St. Peter's. But we find the strongest internal evidence against its being his; we know that epistles were forged, and we find that its being his was in the early Church strongly disputed. On the other hand, a writer at the end of the first century quotes words of Jesus as Scripture, and a writer towards the year 175 gives a list of works then received in the Catholic Church as apos-

tolical. We see no strong natural improbability in their having done so; there is no external evidence against it, no suspicious circumstance. And the criticism which, because it finds what they say inconvenient, pronounces their words spurious, inter-
5 polated, or with a drift quite other than their plain apparent drift, we call fantastic.

So we receive the witness of the Fragment of Muratori to the canonicity, about the year 175, of our four canonical Gospels, and of those Gospels only.[1] We receive the witness of Claudius
10 Apollinaris, a year or two earlier, to the same effect. He denies that St. Matthew assigns the Last Supper and the Crucifixion to the days which the Judaising Christians supposed, and to which St. Matthew, it seems certain, does assign them; but to make him do so, says Apollinaris, is to make 'the Gospels be at variance.'
15 Whatever we may think of his criticism, let us own that most probably the Bishop of Hierapolis has here in his eye the three Synoptics and St. John.

But he is really our last witness. Ascending to the times before him, we find mention of *the gospel*, of *gospels*, of *memorabilia*[2]
20 and *written accounts*[3] of Jesus by his Apostles and their fol-lowers. We find incidents given from the life of Jesus, sayings of Jesus quoted. But we look in vain in Justin Martyr, or Poly-carp, or Ignatius, or Clement of Rome, either for an express recognition of the four canonical Gospels, such as we have given
25 from churchmen who lived later, or for a distinct mention of any one of them. No doubt, the mention of an Evangelist's name is unimportant, if his narrative is evidently quoted, and if we recognise, without hesitation, his form of expression. Eusebius quotes words about John baptising in Aenon, near to Salim,
30 and continues his quotation: 'For John was not yet cast into

---

[1] The Fragment begins with a broken sentence relating to the Second Gospel, and continues: *Tertio, evangelii librum secundum Lucam.* It gives St. John's Gospel as the fourth, and there can be no room for doubt that it named Mark and Matthew before coming to Luke.
35   [2] ἀπομνημονεύματα ἅ φημι ὑπὸ τῶν ἀποστόλων αὐτοῦ καὶ τῶν ἐκείνοις παρακο-λουθησάντων συντετάχθαι.

[3] συγγράμματα.

prison.' Whether Eusebius expressly mentioned the Fourth Gospel or not, we might be sure that here he was quoting from it. But the case is different with 'sayings of the Lord.' These may be quoted either from oral tradition or from some written source other than our canonical Gospels. We have seen from Papias how strong was at first the preference for oral tradition; and we know that of written sources of information there were others besides our canonical Gospels. Learned churchmen like Origen and Jerome still knew them well; they mention them, quote from them. The Gospel of the Hebrews or according to the Hebrews, the Gospel according to the Aegyptians, the Gospel according to the Twelve Apostles, are thus mentioned. Again, there were the writings of which we quoted some way back a list from Eusebius.

The Gospel of the Hebrews was of great antiquity and currency; it was held to be the original of our St. Matthew, and often confounded with it. The Ebionites are said indifferently to receive no Gospel but that of *the Hebrews*, and to receive no Gospel but that of *Matthew*. Jerome found in Syria, and translated, an Aramaic version of this old Gospel of the Hebrews, which he was at first disposed to think identical with our St. Matthew; afterwards, however, he seems to have observed differences. From this Gospel are quoted incidents and sayings which we do not find in the canonical Gospels, such as the light on Jordan at Christ's baptism, already mentioned in our first chapter; the appearance of the Lord after his resurrection to James, expressly recorded by Paul, but not in our Gospels; the words of Jesus to his startled disciples after the *Handle me and see* of our Gospels: 'For I am not a bodiless ghost.'[1] We know that this Gospel of the Hebrews was used by the first generation of Christian writers after the apostolic age, by Ignatius, Justin Martyr, and Hegesippus. From it, or from old gospels attributed to Peter or James, come other sayings and stories strange to our Gospels, but in the earliest times current as authentic. Such a story is that of the birth of Jesus in a cave, mentioned by Justin,

---

[1] οὐκ εἰμὶ δαιμόνιον ἀσώματον.

and familiar to Christian art; and such a saying is the saying of
Christ, *Be ye approved bankers*,[1] quoted in the pseudo-Clemen-
tine Homilies and the Apostolic Constitutions, quoted by the
Church historians Eusebius and Socrates, and by Clement of
Alexandria, Origen, Ambrose, and Jerome.

Well, then, how impossible, when the Epistle of Barnabas simply applies the verse of the 110th Psalm, *The Lord said unto
my Lord*, as Jesus applied it, or when it quotes simply as 'Scripture' the words *Many called, but few chosen*,—how impossible
to affirm certainly that it refers to our canonical Gospels, and
proves that by the end of the first century our Gospel-Canon
was established! Yet this is how Tischendorf proceeds all through
his book on the Canon. Wherever he finds words in an early
writer of which the substance is in our canonical Gospels, he
assumes that from our canonical Gospels the writer took them,
and that our Canon must already have existed. We will not speak
of Tischendorf without remembering the gratitude and respect
which, by many of his labours, he has merited. But his treatment
of the question proposed by him, *When were our Gospels composed?* is really, to anyone who reads attentively and with a fair
mind, absurd. It is as absurd on the apologetic side, as Dr. Volkmar's treatment of the quotation in the Epistle of Barnabas, *Many
called, but few chosen*, is on the attacking side. Tischendorf assumes that the Epistle of Barnabas, in applying the 110th Psalm
and in quoting *Many called, but few chosen*, must needs be referring to our canonical Gospels. But the writer of the Epistle
of Barnabas gives no reference at all for his application of the
words of the 110th Psalm. For the words, *Many called, but few
chosen*, he refers simply to Scripture; and he elsewhere calls, let
us add, the apocryphal Book of Enoch also *Scripture*. In applying the 110th Psalm he may have been going upon oral tradition
merely. In quoting *Many called, but few chosen*, as Scripture,
he was certainly quoting some written and accepted authority,
but what we cannot possibly say.

[1] γίνεσθε τραπεζῖται δόκιμοι, or γίνεσθε δόκιμοι τραπεζῖται. In Jerome's
Latin: 'Estote probati nummularii.'

In the times with which we are now dealing, there is no quotation from any one of our Evangelists with his name, such as in Irenaeus and from his time forward is usual. There is no quotation from the narrative of any one of the Synoptics in which the manner of relating or turn of phrase enables us to recognise with certainty the author. Sayings and doings of Jesus are quoted, but there is nothing to prove that they are quoted from our Gospels. Moreover, almost always, however briefly they may be quoted, they are not quoted quite as they stand in our Gospels. But it is supposed that they are quoted from memory, freely and loosely. The question then arises, is a *Canon* habitually and uniformly quoted in this way? If our Four Gospels had existed in the time of Clement of Rome or of Justin Martyr as the canonical Four, of paramount authority and in the state in which we now have them, would these writers have uniformly quoted them in the loose fashion in which now, as is alleged, they do quote them?

Here we will give, for the benefit of the reader of *Literature and Dogma*,—who by this time is convinced, we hope, that we endeavour to let the facts about the Gospel-Canon fairly and simply speak for themselves,—we will give for his benefit a piece of experience which on ourselves had a decisive effect. The First Epistle attributed to Clement of Rome is, as everyone knows, of high antiquity and authority. It probably dates from the end of the first century. Jerome tells us that it was publicly read in church as authorised Scripture. It is included in the Alexandrian manuscript of the New Testament, and one may say that it was within an inch of gaining, and not undeservedly, admission to our Canon. A good while ago, in reading this Epistle with the disputes about the Canon of the Gospels perplexing our mind, we came upon a quotation of the beginning of the fifty-first Psalm. We read on, and found that as much as the first sixteen verses, or nearly the whole Psalm, was quoted. The Bible of Clement of Rome was the Greek Bible, the version of the Seventy. 'Well, then, here,' said we to ourselves, 'is a good opportunity for verifying the mode of quoting the canonical Scriptures which is followed by an early Christian writer.' So we took the Septuagint, and went through the first sixteen verses of the fifty-first Psalm. We found that Clement followed his canonical original with an exactness which, after all we had heard of the looseness with which these early Christian writers quote Scripture, quite astonished us. Five slight and unimportant variations were all that we could find—variations so slight as the omission of an *and* in a place where it was not wanted. One knows, from Origen and his labours of reformation, into how unsure a state the text of the Greek Vulgate had in the second century fallen; so that this exactitude of Clement was the more surprising.

Now, shortly before we came upon the fifty-first Psalm, we had remarked, in the thirteenth chapter of Clement's Epistle, a cluster of sayings from the Sermon on the Mount. We turned back with eagerness to them, and compared them with the like sayings in St. Matthew and in St. Luke.[1] Neither in wording nor in order did the Epistle here correspond with either of these Gospels; the difference was marked, although in such short, notable sayings, there seems so little room for it. We turned to a longer cluster of quotations from the Sermon on the Mount in Justin Martyr's first Apology. It was with Justin Martyr precisely as with Clement; the wording and order in what he quoted differed remarkably from the wording and order of the corresponding sayings in our Gospels. The famous sentence beginning, *Render to Caesar*, was quoted by Justin. Words so famous might well have been expected to be current in one form only, and their tallying in Justin with our Gospels would not at all prove that Justin quoted them from our Gospels. But even these words, as he quotes them, run differently from the version in our Gospels. So that these early writers could quote canonical Scriptures correctly enough when they were Scriptures of the Old Testament, but when they were Scriptures of the New they quoted them in quite another fashion.

We examined a number of other passages, and found always the same result, except in one curious particular. Certain proph-

---

[1] We give the passage from Clement, which the reader can compare with the counterparts in Matthew and Luke for himself. ἐλεεῖτε ἵνα ἐλεηθῆτε· ἀφίετε ἵνα ἀφεθῇ ὑμῖν. ὡς ποιεῖτε, οὕτω ποιηθήσεται ὑμῖν. ὡς δίδοτε, οὕτως δοθήσεται ὑμῖν· ὡς κρίνετε, οὕτως κριθήσεται ὑμῖν. ὡς χρηστεύεσθε, οὕτως χρηστευθήσεται ὑμῖν· ᾧ μέτρῳ μετρεῖτε, ἐν αὐτῷ μετρηθήσεται ὑμῖν.

etic passages of the Old Testament were quoted, not as they stand in the Septuagint, but exactly, or almost exactly, as they stand in our Gospels; at least, the variations were here as slight as those of Clement quoting from the Greek the fifty-first Psalm. Thus Justin quotes the passage from Micah, *And thou, Bethlehem*, &c., almost exactly as it is given in St. Matthew, although in the Septuagint it stands otherwise; and the passage from Zechariah, *They shall look on him whom they pierced*, as it is given in St. John, although in the Septuagint it stands otherwise. But this one point of coincidence, amid general variation, indicates only that passages of prophecy where the Greek Bible did not well bring out the reference to Christ, were early corrected among Christians, so as to let the reference appear; and that the Messianic passages are given in this corrected form both in our Gospels and in Justin. For it is in these passages that a literal, or almost literal, correspondence between them occurs, and in no others.

This satisfied us, and we were henceforth convinced that in the first two centuries, up to about the time of Irenaeus, there existed beyond doubt a body of canonical Scripture for Christian writers, and that they quoted from it as men would naturally quote from canonical Scriptures. Often they quote it literally and unmistakably; and therefore their variations from it, though they are sometimes greater, sometimes less, are yet no more than what may be naturally explained as loose quoting, quoting from memory. But this body of canonical Scripture was the Old Testament. The variations from our Gospels we found to be quite of another character, and quite inexplicable in men quoting from a Canon, only with some looseness occasionally. And we felt sure, and so may the reader of *Literature and Dogma* feel sure, that either no Canon of the Gospels, in our present sense, then existed, or else our actual Gospels did not compose that Canon.

However, the author of *Supernatural Religion*, who has evidently a turn for inquiries of this kind, has pursued the thing much further. He seems to have looked out and brought together, to the best of his powers, every extant passage in which, between the year 70 and the year 170 of our era, a writer might be supposed to be quoting one of our Four Gospels. And it turns

out that there is constantly the same sort of variation from our
Gospels, a variation inexplicable in men quoting from a real
Canon, and quite unlike what is found in men quoting from our
Four Gospels later. It may be said that the Old Testament, too, is
often quoted loosely. True; but it is also quoted exactly; and
long passages of it are thus quoted. It would be nothing that
our canonical Gospels were often quoted loosely, if long passages from them, or if passages, say, of even two or three verses,
were sometimes quoted exactly. But from writers before Irenaeus
not one such passage of our canonical Gospels can be produced
so quoted. And the author of *Supernatural Religion*, by bringing
all the alleged quotations forward, has proved it.

[This, we say, the author of *Supernatural Religion* has proved;
and here, at any rate, if not against miracles, he may claim to
have been successful in establishing his complete induction. We
call him a learned and exact writer from the diligence and accuracy with which he has conducted this investigation. He deserves the title, and we take the liberty to maintain it. His con-
struing of Greek and Latin may leave something to be desired.
His conception of the Bible and its religion seems to us quite
inadequate. His rejection of evidence which does not suit his
purpose makes him,—as it makes so many another critic, besides
him, both among those who attack popular Christianity, and
among those who defend it,—an untrustworthy guide. But this,
which it is the main object of his book to show: that there is no
evidence of the establishment of our Four Gospels as a Gospel-
Canon, or even of their existence as they now finally stand at all,
before the last quarter of the second century,—nay, that the
great weight of evidence is against it,—he has shown, and in the
most minute and exhaustive detail. We should say, with unnecessary detail; because a reader whose eyes and mind were open
would satisfy himself with much less. But the mass of Englishmen enjoy pounding away at details long after it ceases to be
necessary. What they hate is having to face the new ideas which
await them when the detail-hunt is done with, and to re-make
and re-settle their minds. Probably, for producing an impression
on the public, the style in which the author of *Supernatural Religion* has done his work is well chosen. We attach too,—for

reasons which we shall give when we come to sum up the case as to the New Testament Canon, after we have dealt with the Fourth Gospel,—much less importance to the point he seeks to prove, than he and perhaps most people do. But his point, we say, he has proved. No fineness of accomplishment, no pursuit of the author of *Supernatural Religion* into side-issues, no discrediting of him in these, will avail to shake his establishment of his main position, where the facts are for him and he has collected them with pertinacious industry and completeness.]

The upshot of all this for the reader of *Literature and Dogma* is, that our original short sentence about the record of the life and words of Jesus holds good. *The record*, we said, *when we first get it, has passed through at least half a century, or more, of oral tradition, and through more than one written account.*

Chapter V

The Fourth Gospel from Without

[Sometimes a youthful philosopher, provoked at our disrespect towards metaphysics, tells us that he has been reading Hegel, and would greatly like to have a word with us about *being*. Our impulse is to reply that he had much better have been reading
5   Homer, and that about Homer we, at any rate, had much rather he should talk to us. That divine poet is always in season, always brings us something suited to our wants. And now, when we have finally, after making good our general description of the Gospel-records, to make good our special estimate of the Fourth
10 Gospel, and when, approaching the closer consideration of this Gospel, we are confronted by the theorisings of ingenious professors about it and might well be overawed by their exceeding vigour and rigour, a saying of Homer comes to our mind and raises our courage, and emboldens us to scrutinise the vigorous
15 and rigorous theorisings with coolness. Yet the saying is not at all a grand one. We are almost ashamed to quote it to readers who may have come fresh from the last number of the *North American Review*, and from the great sentence there quoted as summing up Mr. Herbert Spencer's theory of evolution:—'Evo-
20 lution is an integration of matter and concomitant dissipation of motion during which the matter passes from an indefinite incoherent homogeneity to a definite coherent heterogeneity, and during which the retained motion undergoes a parallel transformation.' Homer's poor little saying comes not in such formidable
25 shape. It is only this:—*Wide is the range of words! words may make this way or that way*.[1]

    [But really, of nine-tenths of the theorising about the Gospels

---

[1] ἐπέων δὲ πολὺς νομὸς ἔνθα καὶ ἔνθα. *Iliad* xx. 249.

which comes to us from Germany, these few words of Homer
give us just the right criticism. There stand the Gospel words.
It is possible to put a certain construction upon them. Off starts
the German professor whose theory this construction suits, and
puts it. Presently he forgets that this was only a *possible* con-   5
struction for the words to bear, and often, though a possible, not
even a probable one. He assumes it to be the certain, necessary
construction for the words. He treats it as such in all his arguments thenceforward; and his theory is certain, because, for-
sooth, the construction certainly to be placed on the Gospel   10
words proves it.

[How many a vigorous and rigorous theory owes its force
to this process! The Third Gospel is the Gospel of Paulinism,
composed with a view to exalt Paul's teaching and to disparage
the older apostles. Where are the proofs? The famous words to   15
Peter, *Thou art Peter, and upon this rock will I build my church*,
are not given in the Third Gospel. Well, it is a possible inference
from that omission, that the writer meant to disparage Peter.
But it is not the necessary inference, there is not even ground
for saying that it is the probable inference. And yet, when Baur   20
says that the words 'are completely ignored in the Third Gospel
because the writer could not possibly recognise such a primacy
of Peter,' all he really has to go upon is the supposed necessity
of his inference.

[In the same Gospel, Peter has been fishing all night, and has   25
caught nothing. Jesus appears, and at his command the net is
once more let down, and 'they inclosed a great multitude of
fishes, and the net brake.' Here, says Dr. Volkmar, the writer
meant to contrast the barren result of preaching the Gospel to
the Jews with the fruitful result of preaching it to the Gentiles.   30
If we concede to Dr. Volkmar, not that the writer certainly
meant this, but that it is a not absolutely impossible construction
to put on his words, we make him a very handsome admission.
Yet the absolute *certainty* of this sort of construction is the proof
for the Universalist and anti-Petrine character of the Third   35
Gospel!

[Finally, it is 'an ingenious conjecture' of Dr. Schwegler, that
by the two crucified thieves, the one converted, the other im-

penitent, the writer of the Third Gospel intended to contrast
Jew and Gentile, the obstinate rejection of Christ by the former,
the glad acceptance of him by the latter. No doubt this may be
called 'an ingenious conjecture,' but what are we to think of the
5   critic who confidently builds upon it?

[The Fourth Gospel, again, is an advance beyond the Third; it
is composed with 'a profoundly calculated art,' as the Gospel of
Universalism in the highest degree. How is this proved? It is
proved because in relating the miraculous draught of fishes,—a
10   miracle borrowed, we are told, from Luke, but placed by the
borrower after the Resurrection,—the author of the Fourth Gospel declares that the net was not broken, whereas Luke says that
it was. What can be clearer? The advanced Universalist means
to indicate that the multitudes of the heathen world may be
15   brought in to Christianity without any such disruption of the
Christian Church as to his faint-hearted predecessor had seemed
inevitable. The Third Gospel, again, speaks of two boats engaged in fishing, the Fourth of but one. What a progress, cries
Strauss, is here! The peaceable co-existence of a Jewish and a
20   Gentile Christianity no longer satisfies the religious consciousness; it will be satisfied with nothing less than a Catholic Church,
one and indivisible.

[The Dutch are determined not to be beaten at this sort of
criticism by the Germans. For the Germans, the artistic Uni-
25   versalist who composed the Fourth Gospel is still a writer wishing to pass himself off as the Pillar-Apostle John. For Dr.
Scholten, in Holland, this is insufficient. For him, the disciple
whom Jesus loved is an ideal figure representing the free Christian consciousness of a later time; corresponding to none of the
30   original narrow-minded Jewish disciples, but in a designed contrast with them. This ideal figure it is who starts with Peter
for the sepulchre and outruns him,—arrives first at his Lord. To
be sure, Peter is the first to enter the sepulchre. What does that
matter, when the ideal disciple, who enters after him, has the
35   advantage over him that he 'saw and believed?' And what is
meant, again, by Jesus saying to Peter of this same disciple: 'If I
will that he tarry till I come, what is that to thee?' Any reference
to John and to the advanced age to which he went on living?

Not at all. Jesus means that the free spiritual Gospel of the idealising artist, his latest expounder, is the true one and shall stand;
that it shall endure indestructible until his own coming again.

[Now, if it were positively established on other grounds that
the case is with the author of the Third Gospel, or with the author of the Fourth, just as these critics say, then we might have
no such great difficulty, perhaps, in putting on the texts above
quoted the construction proposed for them. But really it is only
by placing this construction on the texts that the case as to their
authors can be made out to be what these critics say. And when
we are summoned to admit the construction as if it were the necessary, or even most probable one, we demur, and answer with
the good Homer: *Wide is the range of words! words may make
this way or that way*.

[Sometimes the construction which is to prove the critic's
theory has against it not only that it is but one possible construction out of many;—it has even more against it than this. The
Paulinian author of the Third Gospel has for his great object,
we are told, to disparage the older apostles. See, says Baur, how
he relates the story of the raising of Jairus's daughter![1] If it
were not his main object to disparage the Twelve, how could he
have made their three eminent representatives, Peter, James, and
John, figure in a situation which seems expressly designed to
show them in an unfavourable light? 'When Jesus came to the
house of Jairus,' says Luke, 'he suffered no man to go in save Peter
and James and John, and the father and the mother of the
maiden.' Now, Matthew does not mention this; and why? Because he does not write with Luke's object. For what follows?
'And all wept and bewailed her; but he said, Weep not; she is
not dead but sleepeth. *And they laughed him to scorn*, knowing
that she was dead. *And he put them all out.*'[2] Who are here, asks
Baur, the laughers at Jesus, that are put out by him? 'Evidently
the three apostles are of the number; who consequently here, in
spite of their having been a considerable time in close intimacy

---

[1] Baur, *Kritische Untersuchungen über die kanonischen Evangelien*
(Tübingen, 1847), pp. 458 and 469.
[2] Luke viii. 51–54. Compare Matt. ix. 23–25.

with Jesus, only give a new proof of their spiritual incapacity!'
And again: 'That the three most trusted of the disciples of Jesus
behaved to him in such a way as to occasion his ordering them
to leave him, *is the main point, which the whole representation*
5 *of our Evangelist is directed to bring out!*' Was ever anything
so fantastical? And to think that Baur should have found a
brother critic of the Gospels, 'The Saxon *Anonymus*,' more fantastical than himself, whom he has to take seriously to task for
his flights! In the first place, there is nothing whatever to show
10 that the laughers in Luke's narrative, whom Jesus puts out, are his
own three apostles and the father and mother of the maiden. It
is far more likely that they are, as in St. Matthew, 'the people.'
But there is not only this against the sense imposed by Baur on
the passage. The all-important words, *He put them all out*, are
15 wanting in the two oldest and best manuscripts of the New
Testament![1] They have probably crept into the text through a
remembrance of corresponding words in St. Matthew: 'But
when the people were put out.' And this is positively the evidence for 'the main point which the whole representation of our
20 Evangelist is directed to bring out,'—the point that *the three*
most trusted of the disciples of Jesus behaved to him in such a
way as to occasion his ordering them to leave him. A precious
main point indeed!

[The sort of reasoning which proves this to be the Evangelist's
25 main point is not reasoning at all, it is mere playing at reasoning.
But how much of Baur's Biblical criticism is of this nature! We
will try him once more. 'Pauline Universalism is recognisable as
the view which prevails throughout the Third Gospel.'[2] Well,
Baur has told us this again and again; we want some real proof
30 of it. He proceeds to give his proof:—'Those declarations of
Jesus in the First Gospel which have a particularistic turn are
absent from the Third.' Certainly this is important, if true; is it
true? See how Baur proves it:—'That saying which is so characteristic of Matthew's Gospel,—the saying about the fulfilment

35   [1] The Vatican and the Sinaitic.
     [2] 'Gibt sich der Paulinische Universalismus als die Grundanschauung des
Evangeliums zu erkennen.'—Baur, *Geschichte der christlichen Kirche*, vol.
i. p. 74.

of the law and its enduring validity,—Luke's Gospel has not. What Matthew's Gospel says of the indestructibility of the very smallest part of the law, Luke's Gospel says,[1] *according to the original reading*, of the words of Jesus.' According to the original reading? Do, then, our earliest manuscripts of the New Testament, or does one of them, or does any manuscript, read 'one tittle of *my words*,' instead of 'one tittle of *the law?*' Not a manuscript, old or new, important or unimportant. Only Marcion quotes Jesus as having said *one tittle of my words;* Marcion, who is handed down to us as having 'mutilated' Luke, and whose profound antipathy to Judaism and its law would just have led him to alter such a sentence as this. Let us allow all possible weight to Tertullian's admission that Marcion complained of the adulteration of the rule of Christianity, and professed to revert to what was genuine. Still there is nowhere a syllable to show that this *reverting* consisted in a return to the original, genuine text of Luke, whereas the common text and all the other Gospels were adulterated. Not one syllable is there to this effect; yet the most explicit assurance to this effect would be requisite to make Baur's assertion even plausible. As the evidence stands, his *according to the original reading* is monstrous.

[To put one's finger on the fallaciousness of the criticism in these cases will make us suspect it in others. There are questions of literary criticism where positive proof is impossible; where the assertor appeals to critical tact, and not to formal evidence. Still, when we have found a man arbitrary and fantastic in those judgments where he professes to go by formal evidence, there is likelihood that he will be arbitrary and fantastic in those also where he professes to go by critical tact. 'Mark was no epitomator,' says Baur; 'he was a man with a special turn for adding details of his own, in order to give the *rationale* of things, and to supply the logical explanation of them.' What sort of example does Baur bring of this? 'Mark,' says Baur,[2] 'prefixes to the words with which, in the other Synoptics, the story of the disciples taking the ears of corn concludes, *The Son*

---

[1] Luke xvi. 17.
[2] *Kritische Untersuchungen über die kanonischen Evangelien*, p. 554.

of Man is Lord also of the Sabbath, Mark prefixes to these words
a proposition to give the reason for them: *The Sabbath was made
for man, not man for the Sabbath.*[1] One would think that Mark's
motive for inserting these words might be, that there was a
tradition of their having been really spoken by Jesus, in whose
manner they exactly are. But no, this is the very last explanation
which ever occurs to a critic of the Tübingen School. All our
Gospels are more or less *Tendenz-Schriften*, tendence-writings,
—writings to serve an aim and bent of their several authors; and
a Tübingen critic is for ever on the look-out for tendence in
them. The words in Mark *cannot* be authentic, says Baur, because they *must* be an addition inserted to give the rational explanation of the words following them. But the ground for this
must is really not in any necessary law of criticism, but only
that it pleases Baur to say so. Mark's turn for little circumstantial
details is indeed curious; but it is a thing to be noticed in passing,
not to be pressed to this extravagant extent.

[It is just the same with Baur's proof of another assertion: the
assertion that the Sermon on the Mount in the First Gospel is a
work of 'artistic reflexion,' a body of sayings on different occasions, grouped by the Evangelist 'in one logically ordered whole,
to produce a certain calculated total-effect.' The proof of this is
that the Sermon on the Mount follows throughout 'a methodical
march from point to point according to a determined idea.' That
is to say, Baur determines an idea for the Sermon on the Mount,
and makes it follow that idea methodically. But the idea, and
the Sermon's conformity to it, are neither of them given by the
necessary laws of criticism, they are not facts commending themselves to every sound judgment. They are merely a construction
which it is possible to put upon the words. But *wide is the range
of words!* Very likely there may be in the Sermon on the Mount
sayings belonging to more than one occasion; but very likely,
nevertheless, the Sermon may not at all be a work of 'artistic
reflexion,' and not at all follow 'a methodical march from point
to point.']

Evidence has three degrees of force: demonstration, probability, plausibility. On very many questions which German critics

---

[1] Mark ii. 27, 28.

of the Gospel-record raise, and treat as if they were matter for
demonstration, demonstration cannot really be reached at all.
The data are insufficient for it. Whether there was one original
written Gospel, a single *schriftliches Urevangelium*, or whether
there was a plurality of written sources, a *Mehrheit von Quellen-* 5
Schriften,—a favourite question with these critics,—is a question
where demonstration is wholly out of our power. Whether the
co-existence in the First Gospel of passages which 'bear the
stamp of Jewish Particularism,' and of passages which breathe
'another, freer spirit,' is due, as Dr. Schwegler maintains, to an in- 10
corporation of new and later elements with the original Gospel,
is a question not really admitting of demonstration one way or
the other. Whether the Second Gospel, as Dr. Hilgenfeld asserts
and Baur denies, is 'an independent Petrine Gospel representing
the transition from the strict Judaic Christianity of Matthew to 15
the law-emancipated Paulinism of Luke;' whether, as Dr. Volkmar contends, all our canonical Gospels are 'pure tendence-
writings of the at first kept under, at last victorious Pauline spirit,'
can never be settled to demonstration, either in the affirmative
or in the negative. Whether, as Baur and Strauss confidently 20
declare, the substitution by Luke, in reporting a speech of Jesus,
of *adikia* for Matthew's *anomia*, of *unrighteousness* for *iniquity*,
'metamorphoses a Judaic outburst against Paul into a Paulinian
outburst against Judaic Christianity;' whether Luke's Sermon in
the *Plain* is meant to be opposed to the Sermon on the *Mount* 25
of Matthew, no one can ever prove, and no one can ever disprove. The most that can be reached in these questions is probability or plausibility; and plausibility,—such a display of ingenuity as makes people clap their hands and cry *Well done!*
but does not seriously persuade them,—is not much worth a wise 30
man's ambitioning.

There remains probability. But the probability of such a thesis
as that our four Gospels are 'pure tendence-writings of the at
first kept under, at last victorious Pauline spirit,' does not depend
on the demonstrable certainty of inferences from any text or 35
texts in them. It depends on considerations drawn from experience of human nature, and from acquaintance with the history
of the human spirit, which themselves guide our inferences from
these texts. And what is the great help for interpreting aright the

experience of human nature and the history of the human spirit, for getting at the fact, for discovering what is fact and what is not? Sound judgment and common sense, bred of much conversance with real life and with practical affairs.

5   [Now, 'nowhere else in the world,' declares, as we have already seen, Sir Henry Maine, 'is there the same respect for a fact as in England, unless the respect be of English origin.' He attributes this to the habits of strictness formed by the English law of evidence; but the English law of evidence is itself due, probably, to

10   the practical character of the people. Faults this character has, and plenty of them. Much may be said against its indifference to learning and study, its neglect of organising research;] much may well be said in praise of the lives and labours of German professors. Yet, after all, shut a number of men up to make study and

15   learning the business of their lives, and how many of them, from want of some discipline or other, seem to lose all balance of judgment, all common sense! [Hear the amenities of organised research in Germany, hear Dr. Volkmar on Tischendorf:—'Of every sovereign in the world he has begged decorations; in vain!

20   people would not treat him seriously. Renan, in his life of the Messiah Jesus, never once names the Messiah Tischendorf!' Hear Tischendorf on Dr. Volkmar:—'The liedom which tramples under foot Church and science indifferently! stuck full of lying and cheating!' But indeed, for fear we should lose these flowers of

25   learned compliment, Professor Max Müller,—who has a foot in both worlds, the English and the German,—transplants into an English review this criticism by Professor Steinthal on a rival:— 'That horrible humbug! that scolding flirt! that tricky attorney! whenever I read him, hollow vanity yawns in my face, arrogant

30   vanity grins at me.' And only the other day the newspapers brought us an address of Dr. Mommsen, in which the new Rector of the University of Berlin, with a charming crudity, gravely congratulated his countrymen on not being modest, and adjured them never to fall into that sad fault! These are the in-

35   temperances and extravagances which men versed in practical life feel to be absurd. One is not disposed to form great expectations of the balance of judgment in those who commit them. Yet what is literary and historical criticism but a series of most deli-

cate judgments on the data given us by research,—judgments requiring great tact, moderation, and temper? These, however, are
what the German professor who has his data from research, and
makes his judgments on them, is so often without, not having
enough of the discipline of practical life to give it to him. We
speak of judgments, be it observed, not in the exact sciences, but
in matters where we deal with the experience of human nature
and with the history of the human spirit.

[Goethe seems to have strongly felt how much the discipline
of a great public life and of practical affairs had to do with intelligence. 'What else is *cultur*,' he asks, in a remarkable passage,
'but a higher conception of political and military relations?
Everything depends, for a nation, upon the art of bearing itself
in the world, and of striking in when necessary.'[1] And he adds in
a more remarkable sentence still: 'Whenever and wherever the
French lay aside their Philistinism, they stand far above us in
critical judgment, and in the comprehension of original works
of the human spirit.'[2] He means that in France the practical life
of a great nation quickened the judgment, and prevented fumbling and trifling. And we shall see what Germany does, now
that she, too, has 'struck in' with signal effect, and has the practical life of a great nation to correct and balance her learning.
But hitherto her learning has lacked this counter-weight.]

2.

We have led the reader thus gradually to the consideration of
German theories about the Fourth Gospel, because these theories, coming to us without our having any previous acquaintance with their character and their authors, are likely at first,
though not in the long run, to make a powerful impression here.
In the first place, they have great vigour and rigour, and are

---

[1] 'Was ist Cultur anderes als ein höherer Begriff von politischen und
militärischen Verhältnissen? Auf die Kunst sich in der Welt zu betragen,
und nach Erfordern dreinzuschlagen, kommt es bei den Nationen an.'

[2] 'So oft die Franzosen ihre Philisterei aufgeben und wo sie es thun,
stehen sie weit über uns im kritischen Urtheil und in der Auffassung origi-
neller Geisteswerke.'

confidently presented to us as certain, demonstrated fact. Now an Englishman has such a respect for fact himself, that he can hardly imagine grave people presenting him with anything as fact when they have absolutely no right to do so whatever. Then, in the next place, the theories are presented and vouched for by English importers; and they seem to feel no misgivings about them. But then the very last English people to have misgivings about them would naturally be their importers, who have taken the trouble to get them up, translate them, and publish them. Finally, there is a fashion in these things; and no one can deny that the fashion just now is in favour of theories denying all historical validity to the Fourth Gospel. [One can see it by the reviews and newspapers. To reject the Fourth Gospel bids fair even to become, like disestablishment, or like marriage with a deceased wife's sister, a regular article of our Liberal creed, asserting its place in the programme of the future, compelling Mr. Gladstone to think once, twice, and thrice about it, and setting Sir William Harcourt to consider whether it may not be possible for him to build a new Liberal party of his own upon some safer basis.]

Sooner or later, however, these theories will have to confront the practical English sense of evidence, the plain judgment as to what *is* proved matter of fact and what is not. So long as the traditional notion about the Bible-documents was accepted in this country, people allowed the conventional defences of that notion to pass muster easily enough. The notion was thought certain in itself, was part of our life. That the conventional defences should be produced was very proper. Whether or not they were exactly right did not much matter; they were produced in favour of what was a certainty already. But the old notion about the Bible-documents has given way. The result is that no theories about them will any longer be allowed by English people to pass muster as easily as the old conventional defences did. All theories, the old and the new, will have to stand the ordeal of the Englishman's strong and strict sense for fact. We are much mistaken if it does not turn out that this ordeal makes great havoc among the vigorous and rigorous theories of German criticism concerning the Bible-documents. The sense which English people have for fact and for evidence will tell them, that as to demonstration, in most of those cases wherein our critics profess to supply it to us, *wide*, as Homer says, *is the range of words*, and demonstration is impossible. As to probability, which in these cases is as much as can be reached, we shall discover that the German Biblical critics are in general not the likeliest people to reach it, and that their theories do, in fact, attain it very seldom.

Let us take the performance of the greatest and most famous of these critics,—Ferdinand Christian Baur,—upon the Fourth Gospel. 'It is Baur's imperishable glory,' says Strauss, himself in some respects a rival of Baur, 'to have succeeded in stripping the Fourth Gospel of all historical authority.' Baur has *proved*, it is said, that the Fourth Gospel was composed about the year 170 after Christ, in the heat of a conflict between Jewish and anti-Jewish Christianity, and to help the anti-Jewish side. It has a direct dogmatic design from beginning to end. With a profoundly calculated art, it freely treats the Gospel-story and Gospel-personages in the interests of this design. It develops the Logos-idea, and its Christ is a dogma personified. Its form is given by the Gnostic conception of an antithesis of the principles of light and darkness,—an antithesis found both in the physical and in the moral world, and in the moral world exemplified by the contrast of Jewish unbelief with true faith. The author does not intend to deliver history, but to deliver his idea in the dress of history. No sayings of Jesus are authentic which are recorded in the Fourth Gospel only. The miracles of the Fourth Gospel are not, like those of the Synoptics, matter given by popular report and legend. They are all, with deliberate art, 'made out of the carver's brain,' to serve the carver's special purposes.

For example.[1] The first miracle in the Fourth Gospel, the change of water into wine, is invented by the artist to figure Jesus Christ's superiority over his precursor, and the transition and progress from the Baptist's preparatory stage to the epoch of Messianic activity and glory. The change of water into wine

[1] For what follows, see *Kritische Untersuchungen über die kanonischen Evangelien*, pp. 114–184.

indicates this transition. Water is the Baptist's element; Jesus
Christ's element is the Holy Ghost. But in the First Gospel the
antithesis to the Baptist's element is not called Holy Ghost only,
it is also called fire. In the Fourth Gospel this antithesis is, by
5   means of the Cana miracle, figured to us as wine. 'Why,' asks
Baur, 'should not the difference and superiority of Jesus Christ's
element be indicated by wine as well as fire? *Geist*, fire, wine, are
all allied notions.'

    Then come Nicodemus in the third chapter, the woman of
10 Samaria in the fourth. They are created by the artist to typify
two opposite classes of believers. Nicodemus, who holds merely
to miracles, is the representative of Judaism,—Judaism which
even in its belief is unbelieving. The woman of Samaria represents the heathen world, susceptible of a genuine faith in Christ.
15 The same capacity for a true faith is observable in the nobleman
of Capernaum; he must therefore be intended by the author
for a heathen, and not, as is commonly thought, for a Jew.

    We proceed, and come to the healing of the impotent man at
the pool of Bethesda. Now the Jesus of the Fourth Gospel is the
20 principle of life *and* light in contrast to the principle of death
and darkness. The healing of the impotent man is a miracle designed to exhibit Jesus as the principle of life. Presently, therefore, it is balanced by the miracle wrought on the man born
blind, in order that Jesus may be exhibited as the principle of
25 light. The reader sees what an artistic composition he has before
him in the Fourth Gospel. As Baur says, this is indeed a work
where all is intention and conformity to plan; nothing is mere
history, but all is idea moulding history! Everything in the work
is strictly, to speak like the artists, *motived*. To say that anything
30 in the Fourth Gospel is not strictly motived, 'is as good,' says
Baur, 'as calling the Evangelist a very thoughtless writer.'

    Here, then, we have a theory of genuine vigour and rigour.
Already we feel its power, when we read in one of our daily
newspapers that 'the author of the Fourth Gospel stands clearly
35 revealed as the partisan and propagandist of a dogma of trans-
cendental theology.'

    Now, Baur himself would have told us that the truth of his
theory was certain, demonstrable. But we have seen what these
critics call *demonstration*. That wine *may* figure the Holy Spirit

is with them a proof that in the Cana miracle it *does*, and that the true account of that miracle is what we have seen. Demonstrably true Baur's theory of the Fourth Gospel is not, and cannot be; but is it probably true? To try this, let us, instead of imposing the theory upon the facts of the case and rejecting whatever facts do not suit it,—let us, in our plain English way, take the evidence fairly as it stands, and see to what conclusions it leads us about the Fourth Gospel.

3.

What is the earliest piece of evidence we can find concerning the composition of this Gospel? It is a piece of evidence given us in the already mentioned Canon of Muratori, dating, probably, from about the year 175 after Christ. This fragment says:— 'The fourth of the Gospels is by the disciple John. He was being pressed by his fellow disciples and (fellow) bishops, and he said: "Fast with me this day, and for three days; and whatsoever shall have been revealed to each one of us, let us relate it to the rest." In the same night it was revealed to the Apostle Andrew that John should write the whole in his own name, and that all the rest should revise it.'

This is the earliest tradition; and in Clement of Alexandria, who died A.D. 220, we find[1] the same tradition indicated. 'John last,' says Clement, 'aware that in the other Gospels were declared the things of flesh and blood, *being moved thereto by his acquaintances*, and being inspired by the Spirit, composed a spiritual Gospel.' To the like effect Epiphanius, in the latter half of the fourth century, says that John wrote *last*, wrote *reluctantly*, wrote because he was *constrained* to write, wrote in Asia at the age of ninety.[2]

Such is the tradition: that the Fourth Gospel proceeded from the Apostle John; that it was the last written, and that it was revised by the apostle's friends. The theory, on the other hand,

---

[1] In his *Hypotyposes*, quoted by Eusebius *Hist. Eccles.* vi. 14:—Τὸν μέντοι Ἰωάννην ἔσχατον, συνιδόντα ὅτι τὰ σωματικὰ ἐν τοῖς εὐαγγελίοις δεδή- λωται, προτραπέντα ὑπὸ τῶν γνωρίμων, πνεύματι θεοφορηθέντα, πνευματικὸν ποιῆσαι εὐαγγέλιον.

[2] See Epiphanii *Panarium*, *Haer.* LI. 12.

says that the Gospel proceeds from a consummate artist unknown, who wrote it during or after the Paschal controversy
in Asia Minor in the year 170, in order to develop the Logos-
idea, and to serve other special purposes. Which are we to incline
5   to, the theory or the tradition?

Tradition may be false; yet it is at least something, as we have
before remarked, in a thing's favour, that men have delivered it.
But there may be reasons why we cannot believe it. Let us see,
then, what there is to make us disbelieve the tradition of Epi-
10   phanius, of Clement of Alexandria, and of the Fragment of
Muratori. There is the miraculous form of the story, the machinery of dream and revelation; that, we know at once, cannot
be historical. But it is the form in which a matter of fact was
nearly sure, under the circumstances of the case, to have got
15   delivered; and the gist of the tradition,—the Fourth Gospel's
having its source in the Apostle John,—may be matter of fact
still. What is there, then, against St. John's authorship of the
Fourth Gospel?

We shall not touch questions of language, where the reader,
20   in order to be able to decide for himself, must know other languages than his own, and where, if he does not know them, he
must take upon trust what is said. Our points shall be all such
that an ordinary reader of plain understanding can form an opinion on them for himself. And we shall not concern ourselves
25   with every point which may be raised, but shall be content with
what seems sufficient for the purpose in view.

Now, a plain reader will certainly, when his attention is called
to the matter, be struck with the extraordinary way in which the
writer of the Fourth Gospel, whom we suppose a Jew, speaks
30   of his brother Jews. We do not mean that he speaks of them with
blame and detestation; this we could quite understand. But he
speaks as if they and their usages belonged to another race from
himself,—to another world. The waterpots at Cana are set 'after
the manner of *the purifying of the Jews;*' 'there arose a question
35   between some of John's disciples *and a Jew about purifying;*'[1]
'now *the Jews' Passover* was nigh at hand;' 'they wound the
body of Jesus in linen clothes with spices, *as the manner of the*

[1] The text followed is that of the Vatican manuscript.

Jews is to bury;' 'there they laid Jesus, because of *the Prepara-tion of the Jews.*' No other Evangelist speaks in this manner. It seems almost impossible to think that a Jew born and bred,—a man like the Apostle John,—could ever have come to speak so. Granted that he was settled at Ephesus when he produced his Gospel, granted that he wrote in Greek, wrote for Greeks; still he could never, surely, have brought himself to speak of the Jews and of Jewish things in this fashion! His lips and his pen would have refused to form such strange expressions, in what-ever disposition he may have written; nature and habit would have been too much for him. A Jew talking of *the Jews'* Pass-*over,* and of a dispute of some of John's disciples *with a Jew about purifying?* It is like an Englishman writing of the Derby as *the English people's* Derby, or talking of a dispute between some of Mr. Cobden's disciples *and an Englishman* about free-trade. An Englishman would never speak so.

When once the reader's attention has been called to this peculiarity in the Fourth Gospel, other things will strike him which heighten it. The solemn and mystical way in which John the Baptist is introduced: 'There was a man sent from God whose name was John,'—how unlike the matter-of-fact, histor-ical way in which John the Baptist is introduced by Jewish writers who had probably seen him, like the writer of the First Gospel; who at any rate were perfectly familiar with him, knew all about him! 'In those days came John the Baptist, preaching in the wilderness of Judaea.' How much more is the Fourth Gos-pel's way of speaking about John the Baptist the way that would be used about a wonderful stranger, an unknown! Again: twice the Fourth Gospel speaks of Caiaphas as 'high-priest of that year,' as if the Jewish high-priesthood had been at that time a yearly office, which it was not. It is a mistake a foreigner might per-fectly well have made, but hardly a Jew. It is like talking of an American President as 'President of that year,' as if the American Presidency were a yearly office. An American could never adopt, one thinks, such a way of speaking. Again: the disciple who, at the high priest's palace, brings Peter in, is called by the writer of the Fourth Gospel 'an acquaintance of the high priest.' One of the poor men who followed Jesus *an acquaintance* of a grandee like Caiaphas! A foreigner, not intimate by his own experience

with the persons and things of Palestine, but seeing through a
halo the disciples who were with Jesus in the great tragedy,
might naturally have written so. But a Jew, a fisherman of Galilee, who knew quite well the distance and difference between
5   the humble people in the train of Jesus and the rich, haughty,
aristocratical priesthood at Jerusalem,—could it ever have occurred to *him* to commit an exaggeration, which is like the exaggeration of calling a London working-man, who is in the throng
round a police-court during an exciting inquiry and has interest
10   enough to get a friend in, 'an acquaintance of the Secretary of
State'?

As the social distinctions of Palestine are confounded, so are
its geographical distinctions. 'Bethany beyond Jordan'[1] is like
'Willesden beyond Trent.' A native could never have said it.
15   This is so manifest, indeed, that in the later manuscripts *Bethany*
was changed into *Bethabara*, and so it stands in our version. But
the three earlier and authoritative manuscripts all agree in *Bethany*, which we may pronounce certainly, therefore, the original
reading. Nevertheless, the writer knew of the Bethany near
20   Jerusalem; he makes it the scene of the raising of Lazarus. But his
Palestinian geography is so vague, it has for him so little of the
reality and necessity which it would have for a native, that when
he wants a name for a locality he takes the first village that comes
into his remembrance, without troubling himself to think
25   whether it suits or no.

Finally,—and here, too, the plainest reader will be able with
a little reflexion to follow us, although to the reader of considerable literary experience the truth of what we say will be most
evident,—the lofty strain of the prologue to the Gospel is nearly
30   inconceivable as the Apostle John's. Neither form nor matter
can well have come from him. At least, to suppose them his we
must place ourselves in the world of miracle,—in the world
where one is transported from Bagdad to Cairo by clapping
one's hands, or in which one falls asleep, and wakes understand-
35   ing the language of birds and hearing the grass grow. To this
world we do not permit ourselves to have recourse. But in the

[1] John i. 28.

world of fact and experience it is a phenomenon scarcely conceivable that a Galilean fisherman, changing his country and his
language after fifty, should have compassed the ideas of the introduction to the Fourth Gospel, and the style which serves as
organ to those ideas, and, indeed, to the Gospel throughout. Paul 5
was a highly educated man, and yet Paul never compassed ideas
and a style of which the cast was Greek. The form in which the
Fourth Gospel presents its ideas is Greek,—a style flowing, ra-
tiocinative, articulated. The ideas of the introduction are the
ideas in which Gnosticism worked, and undoubtedly there were 10
Jewish Gnostics as well as Greek. But the strange and disfigured
shape which the genuine Jewish mind, the mind of a Jew with
the sort of training of the Apostle John, gave to Gnostic ideas
when it worked among them, is well shown in the fragments of
the Book of Elxai.[1] Not so are Gnostic ideas handled in the in- 15
troduction to the Fourth Gospel. They are there handled with
all the ease and breadth which we find in the masters of Greek
Gnosticism, in Valentinus or Basileides.

Well, then, the reader will say, the Tübingen critics are right,
and the tradition is wrong. The Fourth Gospel has not its source 20
in the Apostle John; it is a fancy-piece by a Greek literary artist.
But stop; let us look at the tradition a little more closely. It
speaks of a *revision* of what the Apostle John produced. It speaks
of a pressure put upon him, of his being *moved by his friends* to
give his recollections, and of his friends having a hand in the 25
work which stood in John's name. And if we turn to the Gospel
itself, we find things which remarkably suit with this account
of the matter. We find things which seem to show that the person who was the source of the Fourth Gospel did not produce
his work himself, but that others produced it for him, and guar- 30
antee what is said, and appeal to his authority. They say: 'This
is the disciple who testified these things and who wrote these
things: and *we know* that his testimony is true.'[2] They say again:
'He who hath seen, hath borne witness, and his witness is true:

[1] See the fragments collected in Hilgenfeld's *Novum Testamentum* 35
extra Canonem receptum, vol. iii, pp. 153–167.

[2] John xxi. 24. οὗτός ἐστιν ὁ μαθητὴς ὁ καὶ μαρτυρῶν περὶ τούτων καὶ ὁ γράψας
ταῦτα, καὶ οἴδαμεν ὅτι ἀληθὴς αὐτοῦ ἡ μαρτυρία ἐστίν.

and that man knoweth that he saith true, that ye may believe.'[1]
That man knoweth that he saith true!—surely the actual composer of a work would never refer to himself so strangely. But
if we suppose that the editors of a work are speaking of the man
5   who supplied them with it, and who stands as their authority for
it, the expression is quite natural.

And then we shall find that all things adjust themselves. In his
old age St. John at Ephesus has *logia*, 'sayings of the Lord,' and
has incidents in the Lord's story, which have not been published
10   in any of the written accounts that were beginning at that time
to be handed about. The elders of Ephesus,—whom tradition
afterwards makes into apostles, fellows with St. John,—move
him to bestow his treasure on the world. He gives his materials,
and the presbytery of Ephesus provides a redaction for them and
15   publishes them. The redaction, with its unity of tone, its flow-
ingness and connectedness, is by one single hand;—the hand of a
man of literary talent, a Greek Christian, whom the Church of
Ephesus found proper for such a task. A man of literary talent,
a man of soul also, a theologian. A theological lecturer, perhaps,
20   as in the Fourth Gospel he so often shows himself,—a theological
lecturer, an earlier and a nameless Origen; who in this one short
composition produced a work outweighing all the folios of all
the Fathers, but was content that his name should be written only
in the Book of Life. And, indeed, what matters literary talent
25   in these cases? Who would give a care to it? The Gospel is
John's, because its whole value is in the *logia*, the sayings of the
Lord, which it saves; and by John these *logia* were furnished.
But the redaction was not John's, and could not be; and at the
beginning of the second century, when the work appeared, many
30   there would be who knew well that John's the redaction was
not. Therefore the Church of Ephesus, which published the
work, gave to it that solemn and singular *imprimatur:* 'He who
hath seen hath borne witness, and his witness is true; *and that
man knoweth that he saith true*, that ye may believe.' The Asiatic

---

35   [1] John xix. 35. ὁ ἑωρακὼς μεμαρτύρηκεν, καὶ ἀληθινὴ αὐτοῦ ἐστιν ἡ μαρτυρία.
καὶ ἐκεῖνος οἶδεν, ὅτι ἀληθῆ λέγει, ἵνα καὶ ὑμεῖς πιστεύητε.

public, to whom the document originally came, understood what this *imprimatur* meant, and were satisfied. The Fourth Gospel was received in that measure in which alone at that early time,—in the first quarter of the second century,—any Gospel could be received. It was read with love and respect; but its letter did not and could not at once acquire the sacredness and fixity of the letter of canonical Scripture. For at least fifty years the Johannine Gospel remained, like our other three Gospels, liable to changes, interpolations, additions; until at last, like them, towards the end of the second century, by ever increasing use and veneration, it passed into the settled state of Holy Scripture.

Now, this account of the matter explains a great deal of what puzzles us when we try to conceive the Fourth Gospel as having its source in the Apostle John. It explains the Greek philosophy and the Greek style. It explains the often inaccurate treatment of Palestinian geography, Palestinian usages, Jewish feelings and ideas. It explains the way in which the Jews are spoken of as strangers, and their festivals and ceremonies as things *of the Jews*. It explains, too, the unsure and arbitrary way in which incidents of the Gospel-story are arranged and handled. Apologists say that the first chapter bears the very stamp of a Palestinian Jew's authorship. Apologists will say anything; they say that the Fourth Gospel must be St. John's, because it breathes the very spirit of the Apostle of Love, forgetting that our whole conception of St. John as the Apostle of Love comes from connecting him with this Gospel, and has no independent support from the testimony of writers earlier than Clement of Alexandria and Jerome, for whom the belief in the Johannine authorship was firmly established. In like manner, it is to set all serious ideas of criticism at defiance, to talk of the version of the calling of Peter in the first chapter, any more than the version of the clearing of the Temple in the second, as having the very stamp of a Palestinian Jew's authorship upon them. They have not. They have, on the contrary, the stamp of a foreigner's management of the incidents, scenes, and order of a Palestinian history.

The writer has new *logia*, or sayings of the Lord, at his disposal; and he has some new incidents. But his treasure is his *logia;*

the important matter for him is to plant his *logia*. His new incidents are not, as Baur supposes, inventions of the writer's own,
any more than the incidents of the other three Evangelists; but
all his incidents stand looser in his mind, are more malleable, less
5 impose themselves on him in a definite fashion than theirs. He is
not so much at home amongst the incidents of his story; but then
they lend themselves all the better on that account to his main
purpose, which is to plant his *logia*. He assigns to incidents an
order or a locality which no Jew would have assigned to them.
10 He makes Jews say things and feel things which they could
never have said or felt; but, meanwhile, his *logia* are placed. As
we observed in *Literature and Dogma*:—'The narrative,—so
meagre, and skipping so unaccountably backwards and forwards between Galilee and Jerusalem,—might well be thought,
15 not indeed invented, but a matter of infinitely little care and
attention to the writer of the Gospel; a mere slight framework,
in which to set the doctrine and discourses of Jesus.'

Now there is nothing which the vigorous and rigorous critics
of Germany, and their English disciples like the author of *Super-*
20 *natural Religion*, more detest than the endeavour to make two
parts in the Fourth Gospel,—a part belonging to John, and a part
belonging to somebody else. Either reject it all, cries Strauss, or
admit it all to be John's! By what mark, he adds, by what guide,
except mere caprice, is one to distinguish the hand of the Apostle
25 from the hand of the interpolator? No, aver these critics; the
whole Gospel, without distinction, must be abandoned to the
demolishing sweep of inexorable critical laws!

But that there went other hands as well as John's to the making of the Fourth Gospel the tradition itself indicates, and what
30 we find in the Gospel seems to confirm. True, to determine
what is John's and what is not is a delicate question; nay, it is a
question which we must sometimes be content to leave unde-
termined. Results of more vigour and rigour are obtained by a
theory which rejects the tradition, and which lays down either
35 that John wrote the whole, or that the whole is a fancy-piece.
But that a theory has superior vigour and rigour does not prove
it to be the right account how a thing happened. Things do not

generally happen with vigour and rigour. That it is a very difficult and delicate operation to separate the different elements in
the Fourth Gospel does not disprove that only by this operation
can we get at the truth. The truth has very often to be got at
under great difficulty.   5

No; but what makes the strength of those critics who deride
the hypothesis of there being two parts, a Johannine part and
another, in the Fourth Gospel, is the strange use of this hypothesis by those who have adopted it. The discourses they have almost all assigned to John;—the discourses, and, from its theolog-   10
ical importance, the prologue also. The second hand was introduced in order to account for difficulties in the incidents and
narrative. With the exception of some bits in the narrative, the
whole Gospel is, for Schleiermacher, 'the genuine biographical
Gospel of the eye-witness John.' Far from admitting the tradi-   15
tion which represents it as supplementing the other three,
Schleiermacher believed that it preceded them all. Weisse regarded the prologue as the special work of the Apostle. Ewald
supposed that in the discourses we have the words of Jesus trans-
figured by 'a glorified remembrance,' after lying for a long time   20
in the Apostle John's mind. All this is, indeed, open to attack.
No difficulties raised by the narrative can be greater than the
difficulty of supposing the discourses of the Fourth Gospel to
be St. John's own 'glorified remembrance' of his Master's words,
or the prologue to be the special work of the Apostle, or the   25
Gospel to be, in general, the record at first hand of pure personal
experience (*lauter Selbsterlebtes*). The separation of elements is
not to be made in this fashion. But, made as it should be, it will be
found to resolve the difficulties of the case, not in a way demonstrably right indeed (for demonstration is here out of our reach),   30
but in a way much more probably right than the theory of Baur.

4.

Baur's theory, however, relies not only on its own internal certainty, but on external evidence. It alleges that there is proof
against the existence of the Fourth Gospel during the first three-

quarters of the second century. It is undeniably quoted, and as
John's, by Theophilus, Bishop of Antioch,[1] who wrote in the
year 180. This, it is said, is the earliest proof of its existence; and
it cannot have existed earlier.

5   But why? Let us put aside the Fragment of Muratori, of which
the date and authority are disputed, and let us take facts which
are undisputed. There is no doubt that Justin Martyr, in his first
Apology, written probably in the year 147, says, speaking of
Christian baptism and its necessity: 'For Christ said, *Except ye be*
10 *born again, ye shall not enter into the kingdom of heaven.* Now
to all men it is manifest that it is impossible that they who are
once born should enter into the wombs of them that bare them.'[2]
Every one will be reminded of the words to Nicodemus in the
Fourth Gospel: 'Except a man be born again, he cannot see the
15 kingdom of God;' and of the answer of Nicodemus: 'How can a
man be born when he is old? can he enter a second time into his
mother's womb and be born?' Justin does not quote the Fourth
Gospel; he never expressly quotes any one of our Gospels. He
does not quote word for word in such a manner that we can at
20 once say positively: 'He is quoting the passage in our Gospel!'
But then he never does quote in such a manner as to enable us
to say this. All a candid yet cautious reader will affirm is, that
Justin here has in his mind the same sayings as those given in the
conversation between Jesus and Nicodemus in our Fourth Gos-
25 pel. He may have quoted from some other source. Almost certainly, if he is quoting from our present Fourth Gospel, this
Gospel was not a canonical Scripture to him, or he would have
quoted it more correctly. But to no candid reader will it occur
to think that what Justin has here in his eye is not at all the con-
30 versation with Nicodemus about being born again and its difficulties, but quite another matter, this passage from the First
Gospel: 'Except ye be converted, and become as little children,

---

[1] *Ad Autolycum* ii. 22. The first and third verses of the first chapter are
quoted, and as John's, and exactly.
35   [2] καὶ γὰρ ὁ Χριστὸς εἴπεν, "Ἂν μὴ ἀναγεννηθῆτε, οὐ μὴ εἰσέλθητε εἰς τὴν βασιλείαν τῶν οὐρανῶν. ὅτι δὲ καὶ ἀδύνατον εἰς τὰς μήτρας τῶν τεκουσῶν τοὺς ἅπαξ
γεννωμένους ἐμβῆναι, φανερὸν πᾶσίν ἐστιν. Compare John iii. 3, 4.

ye shall not enter into the kingdom of heaven.'[1] This is what
critics of the Tübingen school advance. But to no plain reader
would it ever occur to advance it; to no one except a professed
theological critic with a theory. If our Fourth Gospel is to be a
fancy-piece, and a fancy-piece not composed before the year   5
170, sayings and incidents peculiar to it must pass for inventions
of its own, cannot be real traditional sayings known and cited by
Justin long before. No; but on the other hand, if they *are* so
known and cited, the Fourth Gospel cannot well be a mere
fancy-piece, and we lose a vigorous and rigorous theory. If they   10
are, and to any unbiassed judgment they clearly are,—then it is
probable, surely, that Justin, who used written records, had in
his eye, when he cited the sayings in question, the only written
record where we find them,—the Fourth Gospel, only this Gospel not yet admitted to the honours of canonicity. But at any   15
rate, it is now certain that all sayings and incidents not common
to this Gospel with the Synoptics are not to be set down as pure
inventions.

But we can go back farther than Justin. Some twenty-five years
ago there was published at Oxford, under the title of Origen's   20
Philosophumena, a newly-discovered Greek work. Origen's it is
not; but because, besides giving the *Philosophumena* or doctrines
of heathen philosophy, from which all heresies are supposed to
spring, the work purports also to be *a Refutation of all Heresies*,
and because Hippolytus, Bishop of the Port of Rome in the early   25
part of the third century, wrote a work with this title, of which
the description in Photius well agrees with the so-called *Philosophumena*, Bunsen and others pronounced that here was certainly
the missing work of Hippolytus. Against this we have the difficulty that the Paschal Chronicle, professing to cite textually in 30
reference to the Quartodeciman controversy this work of Hippolytus, cites a passage which is not in our *Philosophumena*, although the Quartodeciman heresy is there refuted.[2] Bunsen is
ready with the assertion that 'this passage *must* have existed in

---

[1] Matth. xviii. 3.   35
[2] *Chronicon Paschale* (edition of Bonn), vol. i, p. 13.

our work,' exactly as he was sure that in the Canon of Muratori
the Epistle to the Hebrews *must* have been mentioned. But this is
just the sort of assertion we will not allow ourselves to make;
and we refrain, therefore, from pronouncing the *Philosophu-*
5   *mena* to be certainly the *Refutation of all Heresies* by Hippolytus. Still the work is of the highest importance, and it gives its
own date. The author was contemporary with Zephyrinus, and
tells us of having had controversy with him. Zephyrinus was
Bishop of Rome from the year 201 of our era to the year 219. To
10 the heretics and heresies of the second century our author comes,
therefore, very near in time, and his history of them is of extraordinary value.

In his account of the Gnostic philosopher Basileides, who
flourished at Alexandria about the year 125 after Christ, he re-
15 cords the comments of Basileides on the sentence in Genesis, *Let
there be light*, and quotes as follows from Basileides, whose name
he has mentioned just before:—'This, says he (Basileides), is that
which is spoken in the Gospels: *That was the true light which
lighteth every man that cometh into the world*.'[1] The words are
20 quoted exactly as they are given in the Fourth Gospel;[2] and if
we cannot pronounce certainly that *logia* of Jesus are quoted
from one of our Gospels because they are to be found there, yet
no one will dispute that if we find the reflexions of one of our
Evangelists quoted, they must surely have been taken from that
25 Evangelist. Therefore our Fourth Gospel, not necessarily just as
we have it now, not necessarily yet regarded as canonical Scripture, but in recognisable shape, and furnished with its remarkable prologue, already existed in the year 125.

[The Tübingen critics have an answer for this. The writer of
30 the *Philosophumena*, say they, mixes up the deliverances of the
founder of a school with those of his followers,—what comes
from Basileides or Valentinus with what comes from disciples of
their school who lived long afterwards. The *he says* of the quotation from the Fourth Gospel is really, therefore, subjectless;

35   [1] *Philosophumena* vii. 22. We follow, for the passage in St. John, the
rendering of our version, although ἐρχόμενον probably belongs to φῶς and
not to ἄνθρωπον.
                          [2] John i. 9.

it does not mean Basileides in particular. And of this *subjectless he says* the author of *Supernatural Religion*, following the German critics, makes a grand point. If Basileides is not meant, but only one of his school, then the quotation from the Fourth Gospel will not date from A.D. 125, but from some fifty years later, when no doubt the Gospel had appeared.

[Now it is true that the author of the *Philosophumena* sometimes mixes up the opinions of the master of a school with those of his followers, so that it is difficult to distinguish between them. But if we take all doubtful cases of the kind and compare them with our present case, we shall find that it is not one of them. It is not true that here, where the name of Basileides has come just before, and where no mention of his son or of his disciples has intervened since, there is any such ambiguity as is found in other cases. It is not true that the author of the *Philosophumena* habitually wields the *subjectless he says* in the random manner alleged, with no other formula for quotation both from the master and from the followers. In general, he uses the formula *according to them*[1] when he quotes from the school, and the formula *he says*[2] when he gives the dicta of the master. And in this particular case he manifestly quotes the dicta of Basileides, and no one who had not a theory to serve would ever dream of doubting it. Basileides, therefore, about the year 125 of our era, had before him the Fourth Gospel. Schleiermacher talks wildly, no doubt, when in defiance of the tradition he claims for the Fourth Gospel a date earlier than that of the other three. But it is true that we happen to have an earlier testimony to words which can be verified as belonging certainly to the Fourth Gospel, than to any words which can be verified as belonging certainly to any one of the other three.]

But this is not all the evidence afforded by the *Philosophumena*. The first heresies described are those of Oriental Gnostics, who preceded the Greek. The line of heretics commences with the Naasseni and the Peratae, both of them 'servants of the snake;'—not the Old Serpent, man's enemy, but 'the Catholic snake,' the principle of true knowledge, who enables his votaries

---

[1] κατ’ αὐτούς.   [2] φησί.

to pass safely through the mutability and corruption which comes of birth. The Naasseni are the Ophites of Irenaeus and Epiphanius. Their name is taken from the Hebrew word for the Greek *ophis*, a snake, and together with other Hebrew names in
5   the account of them indicates, what we might expect, that as Jewish Christianity naturally preceded Greek Christianity, so Jewish Gnosticism preceded Greek Gnosticism. Moreover, the author of the *Philosophumena*, passing from this first batch of Gnostics to a second, in which are Basileides and Valentinus, ex-
10 pressly calls this second batch of Gnostics *the subsequent ones*.[1] So we must take the Naasseni and the Peratae, whom the author of *Supernatural Religion* dismisses in a line as 'obscure sects towards the end of the second century,' we must take them as even earlier than Basileides and the year 125.

15   These sects we find repeatedly using, in illustration of their doctrines, the Fourth Gospel. We do not say that they use it as John's, or as canonical Scripture. But they give sayings of Jesus which we have in the Fourth Gospel and in no other, and they give passages from the author's own prologue to the Fourth
20 Gospel. Both the Naasseni and the Peratae are quoted as using the opening verses of the prologue, though with a punctuation for certain clauses which is different from ours.[2] Both sects know of Jesus as *the door*. 'I am the door,' one of them quotes him as saying; the other, 'I am the true gate.'[3] The Peratae have the sen-
25 tence, 'As Moses lifted up the serpent in the wilderness, even so must the Son of Man be lifted up,' with only one slight verbal change.[4] With somewhat more of change they give the saying to the woman of Samaria: 'If thou hadst known,' is their version, 'who it is that asketh, thou wouldst have asked of him and he
30 would have given thee living water springing up.'[5] The Naasseni have, without any alteration, the famous sentence to Nicodemus

---

[1] *Philos.* vi. 6. νυνὶ δὲ καὶ τῶν ἀκολούθων τὰς γνώμας οὐ σιωπήσω.

[2] ὃ γέγονεν is joined to ἐν αὐτῷ ζωή ἐστιν, not to οὐδὲ ἕν. The Naasseni insert a δέ before γέγονεν. *Philos.* v, 8, 16.

[3] *Philos.* v. 8, 17.

[4] ὃν τρόπον for καθώς. *Philos.* v. 16; compare John iii. 14.

[5] *Philos.* v. 9. εἴρηκεν ὁ σωτήρ, Εἰ ᾔδεις τίς ἐστιν ὁ αἰτῶν, σὺ ἂν ᾔτησας παρ' αὐτοῦ καὶ ἔδωκεν ἄν σοι πιεῖν ζῶν ὕδωρ ἀλλόμενον. Compare John iv. 10.

in the Fourth Gospel: 'The Saviour hath said, *That which is born of the flesh is flesh, and that which is born of the spirit is spirit.*'[1] Again, they attribute to Jesus these words: 'Except ye drink my blood, and eat my flesh, ye shall not enter into the kingdom of heaven. Howbeit, even if ye do drink of the cup which I drink of, whither I go, thither ye cannot enter.'[2] A mixture, one must surely confess,—a mixture, with alterations, of the same sayings that we find in the sixth and thirteenth chapters of St. John, and in the twentieth chapter of St. Matthew.

Any fair person accustomed to weigh evidence, and not having a theory to warp him, will allow that from all this we have good grounds for believing two things. First, that in the opening quarter of the second century the Fourth Gospel, in some form or other, already existed and was used. We find nothing about its being John's, it is not called Scripture, its letter is not yet sacred. It is used in a way which shows that oral tradition, and written narratives by other hands, might still exercise pressure upon its account of Jesus, might enlarge its contents, or otherwise modify them. But the Gospel in some form or other existed. Secondly, we make out that Baur and Strauss go counter to at least the external evidence, when they declare that all sayings of Jesus appearing in the Fourth Gospel, and not appearing in one of the Synoptics also, are late inventions and spurious. The external evidence, at any rate, is against that being so. And this point,—to ascertain whether the sayings are genuine or spurious, —is the point which mainly interests the reader of *Literature and Dogma;* for in that book we assured him that the special value of the sayings of Jesus in the Fourth Gospel is, that they explain Jesus and the line really taken by him. This they cannot do if they are spurious; and here, therefore, is the centre of interest for us in all these questions about the Fourth Gospel. Not whether or no John wrote it, is for us the grand point, but whether or no Jesus said it.

---

[1] *Philos.* v. 7. Compare John iii. 6.

[2] *Philos.* v. 8. ἐὰν μὴ πίνητέ μου τὸ αἷμα καὶ φάγετέ μου τὴν σάρκα, οὐ μὴ εἰσέλθητε εἰς τὴν βασιλείαν τῶν οὐρανῶν. ἀλλὰ κᾶν πίητε, φησί, τὸ ποτήριον ὃ ἐγὼ πίνω, ὅπου ἐγὼ ὑπάγω, ἐκεῖ ὑμεῖς εἰσελθεῖν οὐ δύνασθε. Compare John vi. 53; xiii. 33; and Matth. xx. 22.

And that the sayings in the Fourth Gospel, at least the chief and most impressive of them, are genuine *logia* of Jesus, the external evidence goes to prove with a force, really, of which what we have hitherto said quite fails to give an adequate notion. The
5 Epistle to the Hebrews,—which undoubtedly existed at the end of the first century, for it is so much used by Clement of Rome that he has been conjectured to be its author,—has the Johannine phrase, 'the shepherd of the sheep.'[1] Probably the Fourth Gospel did not yet exist when the Epistle to the Hebrews was written;
10 but what the use of the phrase in the Epistle to the Hebrews proves is, that the phrase was early current, and does not, therefore, come from an inventor late in the second century. Other phrases, connected with this one, have also the strongest confirmation of their authenticity. We have already seen how the
15 earliest Jewish Gnostics were familiar with the saying: *I am the door*. Hegesippus, in the middle of the second century, relates that the Jews asked James the Just: 'What is the door of Jesus?'[2] and it requires a very vigorous and rigorous theory to make a man suppose that the Jews were here thinking of something in
20 the Old Testament, and not of the saying of the Lord: *I am the door*. We have the testimony of the Canon of Muratori, that Hermas, the author of the *Pastor*, was brother to Pius, Bishop of Rome; and that he wrote his *Pastor* at Rome, while his brother Pius was sitting in the episcopal chair of the church of that city,[3]
25 —that is, between year 141 and the year 157. In the *Pastor* we find it written, that *the new gate* was manifested in the last days, 'in order that they which shall be saved might enter into the kingdom of God by it;' and it is added: 'Now the gate is the Son of God.'[4] The pseudo-Clementine Homilies cannot be accurately
30 dated; but from their mode of quoting New Testament sayings and incidents,—which is that of Justin, and never alleges the name of a Gospel-writer,—we know that the work must have been written before 170 and the age of Irenaeus. In the third

---

[1] *Heb.* xiii. 20.   [2] Euseb. *Hist. Eccles.* ii. 23.
35 [3] In urbe Roma Hermas conscripsit, sedente cathedra urbis Romae ecclesiae Pio episcopo fratre ejus.
[4] Hermae *Pastor, Similitudo* ix. 12.

Homily, Jesus is quoted as saying: 'I am the gate of life; he that entereth by me entereth into life.'[1] Presently, after the saying, *Come unto me all that travail*, another (a Johannine) saying of Jesus is quoted: 'My sheep hear my voice.'[2] Irenaeus relies upon the authority of certain 'elders, disciples of the Apostles;' and he says that his elders taught that in the Messianic kingdom the saints should have different habitations in proportion to the fruit borne by them, and that they confirmed this by quoting the Lord's saying: 'In my Father's house are many mansions.'[3]

Finally, everyone has heard of the dispute about the Epistles of Ignatius, martyred in the year 115. Of his seven Epistles, mentioned by Eusebius, there exist a longer and a shorter recension; —the longer recension amplifying things much in the same way in which the later manuscripts used for our version of the Gospels have amplified, in the sixth chapter of the Fourth Gospel, Peter's confession of faith into *Thou art that Christ the Son of the living God*, from the original *Thou art the holy one of God* preserved by the Vatican and Sinaitic manuscripts. But a still shorter Syriac recension of the Epistles of Ignatius was found by Mr. Cureton, and this recension, besides, gives only three of the seven Epistles mentioned by Eusebius. We will not enter into the question whether the Syriac three do really annul the Greek seven; for our purpose it is sufficient to take the Syriac three only. For even in these three we have more than once the Johannine expression, *the prince of this world*.[4] We have: 'The bread of God I want, which is Christ's flesh, and his blood I want for drink, which is love incorruptible.'[5] We agree that we are not compelled to suppose that Ignatius took these expressions and ideas from the Fourth Gospel; but that *the prince of this world*, and *the bread which I will give is my flesh*, of the Fourth Gos-

---

[1] *Clementis Romani quae feruntur Homiliae, Hom.* iii. 52.

[2] *Clementis Romani quae feruntur Homiliae*, Hom. iii. 52.

[3] Irenaeus *Adv. Haereses* v. 36.

[4] Ignatius *Ad Ephesios* xix; *Ad Romanos*, at the end.

[5] *Ad Romanos* vii. ἄρτον θεοῦ θέλω, ὅς ἐστιν σὰρξ Χριστοῦ, καὶ τὸ αἷμα αὐτοῦ θέλω πόμα, ὅ ἐστιν ἀγάπη ἄφθαρτος. The Greek recensions, both the longer and the shorter, after [the first] θέλω add ἄρτον οὐράνιον, ἄρτον ζωῆς.

pel, are expressions and ideas of Jesus, and not inventions of a
Greek literary artist after the year 170, the employment of these
ideas and expressions by Ignatius does compel us to suppose.

Again, Baur maintained that it was impossible to produce testimony outside the Fourth Gospel to a legend of any single Fourth
Gospel miracle not common to it with the Synoptics. Soon
afterwards the conclusion of the pseudo-Clementine Homilies
was discovered; and in the nineteenth Homily, speaking of sins
of ignorance, the author says: 'Our Master being asked concerning the man afflicted from his birth and who was restored to
sight by him, whether this man sinned or his parents, that he was
born blind, made answer: "Neither this man sinned nor his parents, but that the power of God should be made manifest
through him." '[1] The miracle is clearly the one recorded in the
Fourth Gospel, and in the answer of Jesus there is hardly the
slightest verbal difference.

We may say, indeed, if we like, that the pseudo-Clementine
Homilies were composed in the third or fourth century. We
may say that not one word of Ignatius is genuine, that Irenaeus
did not mean to quote his elders, or that he misquoted them; we
may say that the author of the Epistle to the Hebrews stum-
bled by chance on the expression *the great shepherd of the sheep;*
that Hermas, author of the *Pastor,* was not brother to Pius,
Bishop of Rome, and did not write the *Pastor* during his brother's
episcopate. All this we may say if we like, and may bring ingenious reasons to support it. But no plain man, taking facts
fairly, would ever say so;—only some professor with a theory
to establish, a theory of vigour and rigour.

But if the Johannine sayings are in great part genuine, then a
plain man will surely be disposed to accept the tradition that the
Fourth Gospel is supplementary to the others, and that in John
it had its source. The sayings form a class distinct from the sayings of the Synoptics. They must have come from some one who
had been with Jesus, and who spoke with authority. Tradition

---

[1] *Hom.* xix, 22 (Dressel's edition). οὔτε οὗτός τι ἥμαρτεν, οὔτε οἱ γονεῖς
αὐτοῦ, ἀλλ' ἵνα δι' αὐτοῦ φανερωθῇ ἡ δύναμις τοῦ θεοῦ. Compare John ix. 2, 3.

says that they came from John at Ephesus; and the form of the Johannine Gospel suits well enough, as we have seen, with this tradition. To be sure, we have the famous argument that the Fourth Gospel cannot have existed in the time of Papias, between the years 130 and 140 of our era, or Papias would have made mention of it; and if Papias had made mention of it, Eusebius, from whom we get our knowledge of Papias, would have quoted the mention. Eusebius declares, says the author of *Supernatural Religion*, that he 'will carefully intimate' every early testimony to the Christian Scriptures, both to the Scriptures received and to the Scriptures disputed. But in the first place, the words used by Eusebius do not mean: *I shall carefully intimate*.[1] They mean: *I shall be glad to indicate; I shall think it an advantage to indicate*. And to suppose that to even as much as is here promised Eusebius would closely stick, because he had promised it, is to know Eusebius very ill. Never, perhaps, was there any writer who told us so much that was interesting, and told it in so loose a fashion and with so little stringency of method, as the Bishop of Caesarea. In the second place, it is quite certain that another Gospel, the Third, existed in some shape in the time of Papias, for Marcion about the year 140 used it. And yet on the subject of the Third Gospel, as well as the Fourth, Papias as quoted by Eusebius is wholly silent.

But then, again, there is the vigorous and rigorous theory of Professor Scholten that John never was at Ephesus at all. If he had been, Papias and Hegesippus must have mentioned it; if they had mentioned it, Irenaeus and Eusebius must have quoted them to that effect.[2] As if the very notoriety of John's residence at Ephesus would not have dispensed Irenaeus and Eusebius from adducing formal testimony to it, and made them refer to it just in the way they do! Here, again, we may be sure that no one, judging evidence in a plain fashion, would ever have arrived at Dr. Scholten's conclusion; above all, no one of Dr. Scholten's

[1] See Eusebius *Hist. Eccles.* iii, 3. προΰργου ποιήσομαι ὑποσημήνασθαι.

[2] See Dr. [J. H.] Scholten's treatise in the German translation, *Der Apostel Johannes in Kleinasien* (Berlin, 1872); pp. 24, 36.

great learning and ability. It is just an hypothesis for a man professorially bound to accomplish a feat of ingenuity, what the French call a *tour de force;*—to produce a new theory of vigour and rigour. [We gladly make Professor Lightfoot a present of such foreign theories to put along with our home-grown theory of the One Primeval Language. The only distinction to be drawn, perhaps, is, that whereas the foreign theories, German or Dutch, come from having too much criticism, from an hypertrophy, as the doctors might say, of the critical organ; our British-born theory comes rather from not having criticism enough, from an absence of the critical organ altogether.]

And now, in conclusion, for the internal evidence as to the Fourth Gospel.

Chapter VI

The Fourth Gospel from Within

To any fair judge of evidence, the external evidence is in favour
of the belief that the Fourth Gospel had its source in the Apostle
John. But what is relied on, as above all fatal to this belief, is the
internal evidence. The internal evidence is supposed to lead us
with overpowering force to the conclusion that the Fourth Gos- 5
pel is a fancy-piece by a Gnostically disposed Greek Christian, a
consummate literary artist, seeking to develop the Logos-idea, to
cry up Greek Christianity and to decry Jewish, and taking for
the governing idea of his composition the antithesis between
light and darkness. Everything in the Fourth Gospel, we are 10
told, is profoundly calculated in this sense. So many miracles, and
in such a graduation, as were proper to bring out fully the contrast between light and darkness, life and death, Greek willing-
ness to believe and Jewish hardness of heart, so many miracles,
and no more, does the Fourth Gospel assign to Jesus. The whole 15
history of the Last Supper and of the Crucifixion is subtly
manipulated to serve the author's design. Admirable as is his art,
however, he betrays himself by his Christ, whose unlikeness to
the Christ of the Synoptics is too glaring. His Christ 'is a mere
doctor; morality has disappeared, and dogma has taken its place; 20
for the sublime and pregnant discourses of the Sea of Galilee and
the Mount of Olives, we have the arid mysticism of the Alexandrian schools.' So that the art of our Greek Gnostic is, after
all, not art of the highest character, because it does not manage to
conceal itself. It allows the Tübingen critics to find it out, and 25
by finding it out to pull the whole of the Fourth Gospel to
pieces, and to ruin utterly its historical character.

Now here, again, in what these critics say of the internal evidence offered by the Fourth Gospel, the external evidence in

some respects makes it hard for a plain man to follow them. The Gnostic author, they say, governed by his idea of the antithesis between light and darkness, assigns to Jesus no more miracles than just what are required to bring out this antithesis. There-
5 fore the last two verses of the twentieth chapter, which speak of the 'many other signs which are not written in this book,' are spurious. Like the whole twenty-first chapter which follows, they are a later addition by some one ignorant of the artist's true design. Well, but in the seventh chapter we find the Jewish peo-
10 ple asking:[1] 'When the Christ comes, will he do more miracles than this man does?' and in the sixth chapter it is implied[2] that the miracles of Jesus were, as the Synoptics represent them, numerous. Did the artist forget himself in these places; or is it the Tübingen critics who have forgotten to tell us that in these
15 places, too, the text is spurious? In the eleventh chapter we have a like oversight on the part of somebody, either the artist or (which one would hardly have thought likely) his German in- terpreters. The chief priests and Pharisees are, by some mistake, allowed to say: 'This man doeth many miracles.'[3] In the twelfth
20 chapter matters are even worse; it is there said that the Jews would not believe in Jesus 'though he had done so many miracles before them.'[4] No doubt this is spurious, and in omitting to tell us so the critics fail a little in vigour and rigour. But, on the whole, what admiration must we feel for the vigour and rigour
25 which in spite of these external difficulties can see so far into a millstone, and find such treasures of internal evidence there, as to be able to produce a theory of the Fourth Gospel like Baur's?

The internal evidence, then, is what the rejectors of the Fourth Gospel confidently rely on. But to us the internal evidence seems
30 to point by no means to a speculative genius, a consummate artist, giving to Christianity a new form of his own, adopting a certain number of sayings and doings of the real Jesus from the Synoptics, but inventing for Jesus whatever he did not thus adopt. Much more it seems to us to point to a sincere Christian,
35 a man of literary talent certainly and a Greek, but not a consum- mate artist; having traditions from John, having, above all, *logia* from John, sayings of the Lord, and combining and presenting

---

[1] Verse 31.   [2] Verse 2.   [3] Verse 47.   [4] Verse 37.

his materials in the way natural to him. The Evangelist's literary procedure is that of a Greek of ability, well versed in the philosophical speculation of his time, and having the resources of Greek style and composition at his command. But when one hears of a consummate artist, an idealising inventor, when one 5 hears of a gifted writer arranging his hero's life for effect, and freely making discourses for him, one thinks of Plato. Now, the writer of the Fourth Gospel is no Plato. The redaction and composition of this Gospel show literary skill, and indicate a trained Greek as their author, not a fisherman of Galilee. But it 10 may be said with certainty, that a literary artist, capable of inventing the most striking of the sayings of Jesus to Nicodemus or to the woman of Samaria, would have also made his composition as a whole more flawless, more artistically perfect, than the Fourth Gospel actually is. Judged from an artist's point of view, 15 it has blots and awkwardnesses which a master of imaginative invention would never have suffered his work to exhibit. Let us illustrate this by examples, taking, as our rule is, no case which is not clear, and where the plain reader may not be expected, if he will only take the trouble to look carefully for 20 himself at the passages we quote, to follow us without doubt or difficulty.

2.

Our Evangelist has, we say, to place and plant records of Jesus supplied to him by John. But he has to place them without a personal recollection of the speakers and scenes, and without a 25 Jew's instinct for what, with such speakers and scenes, was possible and probable. He combines and connects, but his connexion is often only exterior and apparent, not real.

For example. No artist of Plato's quality would have been satisfied with the connexion in the discourse of Jesus reported 30 at the end of the fourth chapter, from the thirty-fifth verse to the thirty-eighth: 'Say not ye, There are yet four months, and then cometh harvest? behold, I say unto you, Lift up your eyes, and look on the fields, that they are white already to harvest: and he that reapeth receiveth wages, and gathereth fruit unto life 35 eternal, that he that soweth and he that reapeth may rejoice together. *For herein is that saying true: One soweth and another reapeth. I sent you to reap that whereon ye have bestowed no labour; other men have laboured, and ye are entered into their labours.'* Surely there are here two parts, of which that one which we have given in italics has a motive quite different from the motive of the other which precedes it. The motive of the first is the ripeness of the harvest and the guerdon of the reapers. The motive of the second is the admission of the disciples to reap what they had not sown. Both have all the character of genuine sayings of Jesus, but there is no real connexion between them, only they coincide in pairing a sower with a reaper. Jesus did not make continuous speeches, jointed and articulated after the Greek fashion. He uttered pregnant sentences, gnomic sayings; and two sets of such sayings, quite distinct from each other, which were among the Greek editor's store of *logia*, we have here. But to this editor the continuous and jointed form of Greek discourse seemed the natural one; and therefore, caught by the verbal coincidence, he blends the two sets of sayings into one, and claps a *for* in between them to establish a connexion. It is a matter of no great importance. The two *logia* of Jesus are safely there, and the real relation between them was sure to be brought out by time and scrutiny. It is only of importance as a gauge of the Evangelist's artistic faculty. A consummate artist, inventing for Jesus, could not have been satisfied with such a merely seeming and verbal connexion.

More striking is the artistic failure at the beginning of the tenth chapter. We will remark, that on any supposition of a consummate artist and of perfect motiving, the mode of introducing all the lovely group of sayings about 'the good shepherd' and 'the door' is quite unaccountable. But let that pass, and let us look at the sayings themselves. Who can doubt that here, again, we have two separate sets of *logia* of Jesus:—one set which have *I am the good shepherd* for their centre, and another set which have for their centre *I am the door;* and that our Evangelist has thrown the two together and confused them? Beautiful as are the sayings even when thus mixed up together, they are far more beautiful when disentangled. But the Evangelist had a door-keeper and a door and sheep in his first parable; and he had another parable, in which was a 'door of the sheep.' Catching again at an apparent connexion, he could not resist joining the two parables together, and making one serve as the explanation of the other.

To explain the first parable, and to go on all fours with it, the second ought to run as follows: 'I am the door of the sheep. All that *climb up some other way* are thieves and robbers; but the sheep *do not hear* them. I am the door; by me if any man enter, *he is the shepherd of the sheep.*' The words in italics must be substituted for the words now in the text of our Gospel;[1] and Jesus must stand, not as the door of salvation in general, but as the door by which to enter is the sign of the true teacher. There can be no doubt, however, that the words now in the text are right, and that what is wrong is the connexion imposed on them. The seventh and ninth verses are a *logion* quite distinct from what precedes and follows, and ought to be entirely separated from it. Their *logion* is: 'I am the door of the sheep. I am the door; by me if a man enter he shall be saved, and shall go in and out and find pasture.' The eighth verse belongs to the first parable, the parable of the shepherd; not to the parable of the door. It should follow the fifth verse, and be followed by the tenth. Jesus says of the sheep: 'A stranger will they not follow, but will flee from him, for they know not the voice of strangers. All that ever came before me are thieves and robbers, but the sheep did not hear them. The thief cometh not but to steal and to kill and to destroy; I am come that they might have life, and that they might have it more abundantly. I am the good shepherd.'

Piecing his *logia* together, seeking always a connexion between them, the Evangelist did not see that he was here injuring his treasures by mixing them. But what are we to think of a consummate artist, inventing freely, and capable of producing, by free invention, such things as the most admirable of the sayings attributed to Jesus in the Fourth Gospel; what are we to think of such an artist, combining in cold blood his invented sayings of

[1] See John x. 7, 8, 9. Instead of ἦλθον πρὸ ἐμοῦ we must read ἀναβαίνουσιν ἀλλαχόθεν, instead of ἤκουσαν we must read ἀκούουσιν, and ποιμήν ἐστιν τῶν προβάτων instead of σωθήσεται καὶ εἰσελεύσεται καὶ ἐξελεύσεται καὶ νομὴν εὑρήσει.

Jesus so ill, that any one with eyes in his head can detect a better
combination for them?

The reader, probably, will follow us without much difficulty
here. But certainly he will have no difficulty in following us if
we take the last words of the fourteenth chapter, *Arise, let us
go hence*, and assert that no consummate artist, no Plato, would
ever have given us that. Beyond all manner of doubt, Jesus never
said in one connexion: 'As the Father gave me commandment,
even so I do; arise, let us go hence; I am the true vine, and my
Father is the husbandman,' and so on, without the least sign of
rising or going away, but with the discourse continuing throughout three more chapters. How the Evangelist could have come
to make him say it, is the question. Probably, with the commencement of our fifteenth chapter the writer passed to a fresh
set of notes, containing another set of sayings of Jesus; and he
marked the transition by inserting between the end of one set
and the beginning of the next the words: 'Arise, let us go hence.'
They were traditional words of Jesus, as we see from the 'Rise,
let us be going,'[1] of St. Matthew; and the composer of the Fourth
Gospel may have thought they would come in serviceably at
this point. What he thought, we can only conjecture; but that no
man freely inventing, not arranging and combining, and above
all, that no consummate artist, would ever have dreamed of placing those words at that point, we may affirm with the utmost
confidence. Certainly there needed an imaginative intellect not
less fine than Plato's to invent for Jesus such a saying as: 'The
hour cometh and now is, when the true worshippers shall worship the Father in spirit and in truth.' But conceive a Plato ordering the march of his composition thus: 'Arise, let us go hence; I
am the true vine, and my Father is the husbandman!'"

To the same category of defects of composition, inexplicable
on the theory of a consummate artist freely inventing, but quite
intelligible if we suppose a literary arranger sometimes embarrassed in dealing with his materials, for which he has the profoundest reverence, belong those curious jolts in the narrative
which are occasioned, as we believe, by the author having John's

---

[1] Matth. xxvi. 46.

very words in his memory, and being determined to preserve them. Such a jolt occurs in introducing the dialogue with the woman of Samaria. 'Jesus, tired with his journey, sat *thus*[1] by the well.' Thus? how? There has not been a word to tell us, and the expression as it stands is incongruous. But the writer, prob- bly, had in his mind John's own words: 'Jesus, tired with his journey, sat, *as I have been telling you*, by the well;' and he could not forbear using them. The same formula appears in two other places, and in both it probably is a relic of John's own narrative. 'He, lying *as I am telling you* on Jesus' breast, saith unto him: Lord, who is it?'[2] And again: 'After these things, Jesus mani- fested himself again to his disciples at the Sea of Tiberias; and he manifested himself *as I am going to tell you*.'[3] In these two cases to preserve John's words does not create any awkwardness; but the writer still preserves them even when it does.

He preserves them, again, without duly adjusting the context to them, in the forty-fourth verse of the fourth chapter. 'After the two days he departed thence into Galilee. *For Jesus himself testified that a prophet hath no honour in his own country*.' That was a reason for staying away from Galilee, not for going there. But the writer has John's words about the testimony of Jesus in his mind, and hastens to give them without preparing their way by saying: 'And this he did, notwithstanding his own testimony.' The embarrassed sentences about the return to Capernaum, in the sixth chapter, owe their embarrassment, not improbably, to the same cause: to John's words sticking in the writer's mem- ory, and not being properly fused by him with his own narrative.

In like manner, who can read without a shock of surprise, in the relation of the feeding of the five thousand among the hills beyond the Sea of Galilee, that abrupt and motiveless sentence: 'Now the passover, the feast of the Jews, was nigh?'[4] The most fanciful and far-fetched explanations are offered. But who would not prefer the simple and natural explanation, that the words are a relic of John's original narrative which had been brought in by him to date his story; that they were fast lodged in our

[1] οὕτως. John iv. 6. [2] John xiii. 25.
[3] John xxi. 1. [4] John vi. 4.

Evangelist's memory, and that he was loath to lose them? They
are a little touch of detail, just like: 'These things he said in the
treasury as he taught in the temple;' or like: 'It was then the feast
of dedication at Jerusalem; it was winter, and Jesus walked in the
5   temple in Solomon's porch.'[1] They are exactly the expressions
which a man telling a story would be likely to use; but our author preserves them in his regular composition, whether they
suit the context or no. And an author such as we suppose our
Evangelist to be was likely enough to do this; but a consummate
10 artist, freely following his invention, does not do things thus
negligently.

3.

These are grounds for the improbability of Baur's theory
which suggest themselves from a defectiveness of artistic construction in the Fourth Gospel. Other grounds of improbability
15 are suggested by defects of philosophical grasp. It is alleged that
our Evangelist improves on the Jesus of the Synoptics, invents
his profoundest things for him. But it can be made as clear as
light, to any unbiased and attentive reader, that this wonderful
inventor does not always himself fully understand the very
20 things he is supposed to be inventing, obscures them by unintelli-
gent comment on them. One instance of this we have given in
Literature and Dogma. Jesus says: 'If any man thirst, let him
come unto me and drink.'[2] Then, with a reminiscence of a passage in Isaiah he adds: 'He that believeth in me, as the Scrip-
25 ture saith, there shall flow out of his belly rivers of living water.'
Who can doubt that Jesus here meant to say that the believer's
faith,—the faith of the follower of Christ,—should be an eternal
source of refreshment? But the Evangelist proceeds to comment
on the saying of Jesus, and to give what is, in his view, the
30 proper explanation of it. And the explanation he gives is as follows: 'But this spake he of the Spirit (*Pneuma*) which they that
believe on him should receive; for the Holy Spirit was not yet

[1] John viii. 20; x. 22, 23.
[2] John vii. 37–39. Compare Isaiah lviii. 11.

given, because Jesus was not yet glorified.' Nothing can be more natural than that a Christian of the first or second century should wish to date all comforts of the Spirit from after the famous effusion of *Pneuma* subsequent to Christ's death. But surely the true sense of this saying of Jesus is clear; and it is clear, too, that it is narrowing and marring of his words to put our Evangelist's mechanical construction upon them. The reporter who puts it fails to grasp the words fully, deals with them unintelligently. And how incredible that a writer should fail to seize rightly the clear sense of a saying invented by himself!

Again, take a like case from the eighteenth chapter. Jesus had said of his disciples: 'None of them is lost but the son of perdition.'[1] Then comes the arrest, and the speech of Jesus to the band which arrested him: 'I have told you that I am he; if therefore ye seek me, let these go their way.'[2] He gives up himself, but puts his disciples out of danger. His speech is just what we might have expected; but instantly our Evangelist adds that he made it *'in order that the saying might be fulfilled which he spake: Of them whom Thou hast given me have I lost none.'* Can anything be more clear than that the two sayings have nothing at all to do with one another, and that it is a mechanical and narrowing application of the second-mentioned saying which makes it lead up to the first? In the second, eternal salvation is the theme; in the first, safety from a passing danger. And could the free and profound inventor of the second saying have been so caught by the surfaces of things, as to make it the mere prophecy of the first?

Jesus over the heads of all his reporters!—this idea is for us a constant guide in reading the Gospels. It is, we are convinced, the only safe one. But the Tübingen professors reverse the idea, and say that in the Fourth Gospel it is the reporter who is over the head of Jesus. In the concluding chapters of this Gospel the philosophical author, they say, so frames the discourse of Jesus that his resurrection is presented 'as an internal phenomenon continually being accomplished in the believer's consciousness.' No doubt this view of the resurrection is indicated in the Fourth Gospel, as it is indicated also by St. Paul. But the question is, does

[1] John xvii. 12. [2] John xviii. 5–9.

it come from Jesus himself, or was it invented by the more spiritual among his followers to give a profounder sense to the physical miracle of his resurrection? We confine ourselves at present
to the Fourth Gospel, and we say: 'True, the resurrection of
5   Christ is there suggested as a phenomenon accomplishing itself
in the believer's consciousness. The idea is a profound one; it
needed a great spirit to conceive it. If the author of the Fourth
Gospel conceived it, we may allow that he carries the significance of the resurrection higher than the Synoptics carry it;
10   higher than the Jesus of the Synoptics visibly carries it. But if
he is the author of this idea, he will present it firmly and clearly.
If he presents it confusedly, then he probably got the idea from
Jesus, and did not quite understand it.' How, in fact, does he
present it?

15   All through the discourses of Jesus in the Fourth Gospel, the
attentive reader may perceive that there are certain fundamental
themes which serve as *nuclei* or centres, appearing repeatedly
and in several connexions, with a form sometimes shorter, sometimes more expanded. It is of great importance to a right under-
20   standing of the Fourth Gospel that we should discover in such
cases the primitive theme, the original *logion* of Jesus. Now this,
or at least the nearest approach to it, will in general be given by
the theme in its shorter and less expanded form. Very likely
Jesus may himself have used a theme on several occasions, and
25   himself have sometimes given to it a more expanded form; still,
from the theme in its simplest and shortest form, we probably
get our best clue to what was actually said by Jesus.

      Two such primitive themes in the long discourse of Jesus be-
fore his arrest are these:—*I go to the Father*,[1] and: *I go away,*
30   *and come again to you.*[2] Let us add to these two a third: *A little*
while and ye see me not, and again a little while, and ye shall see
me.[3] These three sayings appear and reappear, they come in dif-

---

[1] ὑπάγω πρὸς τὸν πατέρα, John xvi. 17. This is probably the primitive
theme; we have also: ὑπάγω πρὸς τὸν πέμψαντά με (vii. 33, and xvi. 5); πρὸς
35   τὸν πατέρα μου ὑπάγω (xvi. 10); ἀφίημι τὸν κόσμον καὶ πορεύομαι πρὸς τὸν
πατέρα (xvi. 28).

[2] ὑπάγω καὶ ἔρχομαι πρὸς ὑμᾶς. John xiv. 28.

[3] μικρόν, καὶ οὐ θεωρεῖτέ με, καὶ πάλιν μικρόν, καὶ ὄψεσθέ με. John xvi. 17.

ferent connexions, they take forms somewhat varying. But they are primitive themes; they give us probably the nearest approach now possible to the words actually uttered by Jesus.

This, then, is what we have:—*I go to the Father. I go, and come again to you. A little while and ye see me not, and again a little while and ye shall see me.* Now it is alleged, and truly, that the Fourth Gospel suggests a view of the resurrection of Jesus as an internal phenomenon accomplishing itself in the believer's consciousness. The basis on which this allegation must rest is supplied by the three *logia* which we have quoted.

But the three *logia* lend themselves either to the announcement of a physical resurrection or to the announcement of a spiritual resurrection. Everything depends on their context and connexion. And by piecing things together, by putting these *logia* in the front, by connecting them immediately with other *logia* given by our Evangelist, by dropping out things he inserts between, we can get at a resurrection announced by Jesus which is clearly spiritual. 'I go to the Father; I go, and come again to you. A little while and ye see me not, and again a little while and ye shall see me. I will not leave you desolate, I will come to you. Yet a little while and the world seeth me no more; but ye see me, because I live and ye shall live.' A disciple here asks how it is that they shall see him, and that the world shall not. Jesus answers: 'If a man love me, he will keep my word; and my Father will love him, and I will love him, and we will come to him and make our abode with him. Let not your heart be troubled, neither let it be afraid. I go away and come again to you.'[1] And this resurrection of Jesus is connected by him with the coming of the Paraclete, the Spirit of truth, the new light, who should bring out in the hearts of the disciples the real significance of Jesus and of what he had said.[2]

Thus placed and connected, the primitive ἔρχομαι, the *I come again* of Jesus, gives to us, no doubt, the resurrection of Christ as 'an internal phenomenon accomplishing itself in the believer's consciousness.' It gives it to us as being this in Jesus Christ's own

---

[1] John xvi. 10; xiv. 28; xvi. 16; xiv. 18, 19, 23, [21,] 27, 28.
[2] John xiv. 23–26.

view and prediction of it. The same idea is preserved for us by
the First Epistle of St. John, an Epistle which cannot well have
been written by our Evangelist, its style is so unlike his. But the
Epistle deals with many of the ideas dealt with by our Gospel;
5 and it presents the *abiding* in Jesus, and in his Father, as the accomplishment of the promise of eternal life made by Jesus to his
followers.[1]

The idea is so fruitful and profound a one, that if our Evangelist
had ever fairly grasped it, still more if he had conceived and in-
10 vented it, he could hardly have so dealt with it as to leave us in
doubt whether he himself entertained it or not. He could no
more do this than Paul could have left us in doubt whether he
himself entertained his great idea of the *necrosis*,—of the dying
and resurrection of Jesus accomplishing themselves in this life
15 in the believer's personal experience. The mind which, although
accepting the physical miracle of the resurrection, could yet
discern that the phenomenon, to be made fruitful, must have a
moral and a spiritual significance given to it,—such a mind would
certainly have been impressed deeply by such an idea, and have
20 had it distinct and firm. But our Evangelist so arranges his materials as to make the reference of ἔρχομαι and ὄψεσθε to a spiritual
resurrection very dubious, to overlay it with other things, and to
obscure it; while their reference to a physical resurrection is
brought out distinctly. 'In my Father's house are many mansions;
25 if it were not so, I would have told you. For I go to prepare a
place for you, and if I go, I will prepare a place for you. I come
again, and will take you unto myself, that where I am ye may be
also.'[2] There can be little doubt that the primitive theme of
ἔρχομαι πρὸς ὑμᾶς, *I come again unto you*, is here so used and con-
30 nected as to make it point decisively to a physical resurrection.
And this key for the whole strain being once given, the impression left by that other primitive theme, μικρὸν καὶ ὄψεσθέ με, *a little
while and ye shall see me*, is in the main an impression to the same
effect. 'A little while and ye see me not, and again a little while
35 and ye shall see me. Ye shall weep and lament; ye shall be sorrowful, but your sorrow shall be turned into joy. Ye have sorrow

---

[1] I John ii. 24, 25.
[2] John xiv. 2, 3. The text followed is that of the Vatican manuscript.

now; but I will see you again, and your heart shall rejoice, and your joy no man shall take from you.'[1] Here the whole wording and connexion are such that it seems clear the commentators have rightly interpreted the mind of the Evangelist, when they make this passage, and the theme μικρὸν καὶ ὄψεσθέ με, a prophecy of the approaching physical resurrection and reappearance of Jesus.

Must we then suppose that to a spiritual resurrection such sayings as the three primitive themes which we have quoted do not really refer, but may be made to signify it only as a secondary and after-meaning, brought in for purposes of edification, and originally hidden in them, perhaps, for those purposes? This, no doubt, will be the character assigned to the words both by official theology and by popular religion. To us, however, it seems certain that to a spiritual resurrection the words primarily and really point, and that our Evangelist has obscured their true scope.

For him, as for Christendom long after him, Jesus Christ's physical resurrection stood, and could not but stand, a phenomenon fixed, immense, overpowering; a central sun attracting everything to it. But experience slowly and inevitably reveals that phenomena of this kind do not actually happen. Romulus does not mount into heaven, Epimenides does not awake, Arthur does not return. Their adoring followers think they do, think they have promised it;—but they do not, have not. We have, then, to account for the firm belief of the first Christians in the physical resurrection of Jesus, when this resurrection did not actually happen. We can only account for it from things really said by Jesus, which led them to expect it. That Jesus was a fanatic, expecting and foretelling his own physical resurrection, —deceived like his followers, but so filling them with his own belief that it prevailed and triumphed with them when he died,— is an explanation which the whole account we have of Jesus, read seriously, shows to be idle. His disciples were misled, therefore, by something Jesus did actually say, which had not really the sense that he should physically rise from the dead, but which was capable of lending itself to this sense, and which his disciples misunderstood and imagined to convey it.

[1] John xvi. 19, 20, 22.

And, indeed, they themselves as good as tell us that this is what actually happened. Only, what was in truth *misunderstanding*, they call *understanding*. They themselves as good as tell us that they unconsciously exercised a creative pressure, long after the time when they were going about with Jesus and hearing him, on sayings and doings of their Master. 'When he was risen from the dead,' they tell us, after recording one of his prophetic speeches, '*his disciples remembered that he had said this.*'[1] Even if one had not known beforehand that from the nature of the case it was impossible for the records of Jesus in our Gospels to have been notes taken down day by day, as by a Saint-Simon or a Boswell, here is an Evangelist himself telling us in so many words that they were not. 'These things understood not his disciples at the first,' he tells us again, after relating an incident which afforded a remarkable fulfilment of prophecy, 'but when Jesus was glorified *then remembered they* that these things were written of him, and *that they had done these things unto him.*'[2] They recorded, then, the sayings of Jesus about his resurrection long after they had been uttered, and when the belief in his physical resurrection was firmly fixed in their minds.

But even after his death, 'as yet,' they tell us of themselves, 'they knew not the Scripture that he must rise again from the dead.'[3] This affords the most irrefragable proof that the sayings of Jesus about his resurrection cannot originally have been just what our Gospels report; that these sayings, as they now come to us, must have been somewhat moulded and accentuated by the belief in the resurrection. If Jesus had simply said to the Twelve the very words our Gospels report him to have said, the Twelve could have been in no ignorance at all of 'the Scripture that he must rise again from the dead,' and in no doubt at all that they were to count on his rising. 'He took unto him the Twelve, and said unto them: Behold we go up to Jerusalem, and all things that are written by the prophets concerning the Son of Man shall be accomplished. For he shall be delivered unto the Gentiles, and shall be mocked and spitefully entreated, and spitted on; and they shall scourge him, *and put him to death; and the third day*

---

[1] John ii. 22. [2] John xii. 16. [3] John xx. 9.

he shall rise again.'[1] It is in vain that the Evangelist adds: 'And they understood none of these things, and this saying was hid from them, neither knew they the things which were spoken.'[2] If Jesus had spoken just merely as he is here reported, if what he said had had no peculiar connexion and significance given to it by something else which he also said, if he had simply thus laid down in black and white, as the phrase is, his death and resurrection as going to happen, the disciples could not have helped understanding him. It would have been quite impossible for them to make that astounding declaration, which yet is evidently the plain truth, that even up to the days which followed his death, 'as yet they knew not the Scripture that he must rise again from the dead.' Something was no doubt said by Jesus not unlike what the Evangelist reports, something which easily adapted itself to the character of a simple and literal prophecy of the resurrection, when that event had, as was believed, taken place. But the precise speech put into the mouth of Jesus, that speech and nothing more at all upon the subject, he cannot have uttered.

The Third Gospel, which reports the speech just quoted, is the Gospel which guides us to the discovery of what Jesus can have originally and actually said about his rising again on the third day. He was told that if he did not leave Jerusalem Herod would put him to death. He made answer: 'Go ye and tell that fox, Behold, I cast out devils and I do cures to-day and to-morrow, *and the third day I shall be perfected.*'[3] Having for ever before his mind the humble and suffering Servant of our fifty-third chapter of Isaiah, and labouring for ever to substitute this in his disciples' minds as the Messias-ideal instead of the brilliant and triumphing Conquerer of popular Jewish religion, Jesus here, beyond all doubt, following the prophet,[4] spoke of his violent and ignominious end as his perfection and victory. That

[1] Luke xviii. 31–33.　　　　　[2] Luke xviii. 34.

[3] τῇ τρίτῃ ἡμέρᾳ τελειοῦμαι. Luke xiii. 32. The text of the Vatican manuscript is followed.

[4] See Isaiah liii. 10, 11. 'It pleased the Eternal to bruise him, he hath put him to grief. When he hath made his soul an offering for sin, he shall see his seed, he shall prolong his days, and the pleasure of the Eternal shall prosper in his hand; he shall see of the travail of his soul and be satisfied.'

violent end he, as was natural, could plainly foresee and often predicted. Here he predicts it in this wise: 'On the third day I shall be perfected.' On other occasions he said instead: 'The third day I shall rise again.' What made him say: *The third day?*[1] We
5 know how he loved to possess himself of locutions of the prophets and to use them. For instance, in that well-known saying, 'Take my yoke upon you, and learn of me that I am mild and lowly in heart, and ye shall find rest unto your souls,' the concluding phrase, *Ye shall find rest unto your souls*, is a reminis-
10 cence of Jeremiah.[2] And in like manner his phrase, *On the third day I shall be perfected, The third day I shall rise again*, is a reminiscence of the prophet Hosea. Amid the ruin of Israel, in the eighth century before Christ, Hosea had said: 'Come and let us return unto the Eternal; for he hath torn and he will heal us;
15 *after two days will he revive us, on the third day we shall rise again.*'[3] 'We shall be restored *presently*,' Hosea means; and, 'I shall be perfected *presently*,' is what Jesus means.

Here we lay our finger, almost certainly, upon the veritable foundation for the belief that Jesus had himself announced he
20 would rise from the dead on the third day. Let us seek to combine the scattered *logia*, transposed, some of them, to the time after his death, which in a certain degree enable us, through the cloud of his disciples' inadequate apprehension and of legend and marvel, to follow the line of light of the Divine Master.

25 The root of everything with Jesus is, as we just now said, the effort, the incessant effort, to substitute as the Messias-ideal in the mind of his followers the Servant, mild and stricken, for the regal and vengeance-working Root of David. And he knew, that the victory of this right Messias-ideal his own death, and that

---

30 [1] He talked, also, of his rising from the dead, without the addition of the words *on the third day*, or *in three days*. See Mark, ix, 9, 10, where the disciples are represented as puzzled, and as συζητοῦντες τί ἐστιν τὸ ἐκ νεκρῶν ἀναστῆναι.

[2] Jeremiah vi. 16.

35 [3] Hosea vi. 1, 2. In the Greek Bible of the Seventy the words are: ἐν τῇ ἡμέρᾳ τῇ τρίτῃ ἀναστησόμεθα, *on the third day we shall rise again.* Compare this with the words in Luke: τῇ τρίτῃ ἡμέρᾳ τελειοῦμαι; and again, τῇ ἡμέρᾳ τῇ τρίτῃ ἀναστήσεται. Luke xiii. 32, and xviii. 33.

only, could found. 'O fools and slow of heart at taking in all that the prophets have spoken! *must not* the Messiah suffer these things, and enter into his glory? Behold, we go up to Jerusalem, and the Son of Man shall be betrayed unto the chief priests and scribes, and they shall deliver him to the Gentiles to crucify. Nevertheless, I do cures to-day and to-morrow; we must work the works of him that sent me while it is day, the night cometh when no man can work. I must walk to-day and to-morrow and the day following, and the third day I shall be perfected. All things written by the prophets for the Son of Man shall be accomplished. He shall be delivered to the Gentiles, and mocked and outraged and spit upon; and they shall scourge him and put him to death; and the third day he shall rise again. Except a grain of corn fall and die, it abideth alone; but if it die, it bringeth forth much fruit. As Moses lifted up the serpent in the wilderness, so must the Son of Man be lifted up; and I, if I be lifted up from the earth, will draw all men unto me.'[1]

Yes, *thus it was written that the Christ should suffer, and rise from the dead the third day*.[2] Inevitably the disciples materialised it all, wrested it all into a prophesying of bodily reappearance and miracle. And they did the like also with the words: 'I go to the Father; I go away and come again to you; a little while and ye see me not, and again a little while and ye shall see me.' To these words the disciples gave a turn, they placed them in a connexion, to suit the belief which alone, after the death of Jesus, could reassure and console them;—the belief in his speedy resuscitation and bodily reappearance on earth, his temporary re-withdrawal and ascension into heaven, to be followed soon by his triumphal bodily advent to avenge and judge.

It could not but be so. *It was written that in his name should be preached to all nations repentance unto remission of sins*;[3] and

---

[1] Luke xxiv. 25, 26; Matth. xx. 18, 19; Luke xiii. 32; John ix. 4 (in the Vatican manuscript); Luke xiii. 33, and xviii. 31–33; John xii. 24, iii. 14, and xii. 32. For *mocking*, see *Psalm* xxii. 7; for *scourging* and *spitting*, see Isaiah l. 6. The traits used by prophet and psalmist in delineating the stricken Servant are to be conceived as always vividly present to the mind of Jesus.

[2] Luke xxiv. 46. The Vatican manuscript is followed.

[3] Luke xxiv. 47.

only in this way could the work proceed. Only in this way, through profound misapprehension, through many crude hopes, under the stimulus of many illusions, could the method and secret, and something of the temper and sweet reason and bal-
5 ance of Jesus, be carried to the world. Only thus, through natural and national *extra-belief* reinforcing their real love to their Master and zeal to propagate his doctrine, could the weak arm of the disciples acquire energy enough to hold aloft the word of life, set up the kingdom of Christ, found the true Israel, and
10 bring in everlasting righteousness.

But the promises and predictions of their Master were, nevertheless, not what they fancied. He had said: 'Ye shall see me again, because I live and ye shall live; if a man keep my saying he shall never see death. If ye love me and keep my words, I
15 will come unto you and make my abode with you.'[1] They construed this into: 'Ye shall see me, because I will come again and take you unto myself to reign in the kingdom of the saints in the New Jerusalem.'[2] The genuine promise of Jesus was the promise of a spiritual resurrection; and this promise his disciples
20 misapprehended, misconnected, and obscured. Only on this supposition is even their own version of the history intelligible.

Far, therefore, from inventing the idea of the resurrection as an internal phenomenon accomplishing itself in the believer's consciousness, the author of the Fourth Gospel transmits the
25 idea, indeed, but obscures it. He saved it for us, as in that second harvest of the *logia* of Jesus he saves for us so much which is precious. He saved it from being lost, and added it to the indications which survive for us of the line truly taken by Jesus. But from his very mode of delivering it, we can see that he is not an
30 artist inventing it, but a reporter transmitting it imperfectly.

4.

Furthermore, Baur's theory of the artistic Greek Christian inventing all things with a deep-laid design to damage Jewish Christianity, and to exalt Christ's divinity, is upset by the admis-

---

[1] John xiv. 19; viii. 51; xiv. 23.   [2] John xiv. 3; Matth. xix. 28.

sion of things contrary to the alleged design. A free inventor, inventing with the express aim of doing damage to Jewish Christianity, would never have made Jesus say: *'Salvation is of the Jews.'*[1] A free inventor, inventing to impair the credit of Peter and the original Apostles, would never have made Peter enter the sepulchre first, or throw himself into the sea, or receive the charge: *Feed my sheep.*[2] A free inventor, inventing from a zeal to establish the dogma of Christ's personal divinity, would never have made Jesus give the turn to his calling himself *the Son of God* which is given in the tenth chapter, when Jesus appeals to the authority of the Old Testament for those being called *Gods* to whom the word of God came, and asks why he too, then, may not call himself the Son of God?[3] 'Why haggle about words and definitions in these matters?' he in fact asks; 'all you can say about them is approximate merely.' And the whole question of the dogma of Christ's personal divinity is a question of words and definitions in the very sphere where Jesus pronounces such questions to be vain. All these things may be ingeniously explained by Baur now that they stand there in the Gospel, and challenge explanation from him. But, had Baur's theory of the Fourth Gospel been true, they would never have stood there for him to explain.

Finally, the theory of the consummate artist implies that the Fourth Gospel is a work proceeding from the imaginative intellect. But we deny (and here, too, the attentive reader will not, we think, find it hard to follow us), we deny that the Fourth Gospel has the character of a work proceeding from the imaginative intellect. It has the character of a work proceeding from the soul. It is profoundly and solemnly religious. It is the work of a man who, we grant, like all the reporters of Jesus, understood him but imperfectly; who gives us much which is not Jesus, much which comes from himself and his time, much which is addition and legend. But it is the work of a man who gives us this seriously and in good faith, and whose attitude of mind is not that of a freely inventing artist. He is too much subjugated

[1] John iv. 22.   [2] John xx. 6; xxi. 7, 16.
[3] John x. 34–36.

by Jesus to feel free to deal with him in this fashion, as a mouthpiece for his own purposes and his own ideas. He does sometimes attribute his own ideas to Jesus, but unconsciously; and
when he does, we can perceive that he is doing so. If he had attempted it consciously all through his Gospel, he would have
produced something quite different from what we have, and we
should easily have found him out. He would have given us a
work where Jesus would have spoken, all through, as he now
speaks from the sixteenth verse of the third chapter to the
twenty-first,—a passage in which our theological lecturer evidently lectures us through the mouth of Jesus. For his mind did
not hold itself so easily and independently towards Jesus,—no
serious Christian's did or could,—as to suffer him to play freely
with Jesus, to throw himself into his character, to use him as a
vehicle for saying,—but in character and with verisimilitude,—
whatever the user wanted to convey. Plato might do this with
Socrates, but the author of the Fourth Gospel could not do it
with Jesus. And the safe analogy to take, in considering what for
our Evangelist in dealing with his subject could and did happen,
is the analogy not of Plato but of Paul.

The old school of apologists was fond of urging that the
Fourth Gospel could only have been the work of one of the original chief Apostles, it is so excellent. Baur had no difficulty in
replying to this, that in Paul we have a Christian who had probably never even seen Jesus, who was certainly not one of the
original chief Apostles; and who yet is at least equal to any of
them, and whose productions surpass theirs. Why, therefore,
may we not have, he argued, in the author of the Fourth Gospel
a second gifted outsider like Paul, but whose name has remained unknown, because it was essential for his purpose that it
should do so, and that his work should point mysteriously to the
Apostle John as its author?

Certainly we, for our part, feel no backwardness in admitting
that outside of the primitive circle of the Apostles there might
arise Christians, like Paul, capable of making invaluable contributions to the New Testament. But we think that none of them
could have done what Baur's theory supposes the author of the
Fourth Gospel to have done. Paul himself could not have done

it. The attitude of their minds towards Christianity and its Founder was too earnest and reverential to allow it. When Paul quotes a *logion* like that exquisite *logion* quoted by him at Miletus, but not found in any one of our Evangelists, *It is more blessed to give than to receive*,[1] he is clearly quoting Jesus, as he says he is, not artistically inventing for Jesus, not original. His manner when he is original we know, and it is quite different. Imagine St. Paul sitting down to recommend the dogma of justification by faith, through means of a fancy Gospel composed of *logia* invented for Jesus, and suiting his character as *It is more blessed to give than to receive* suits his character! Paul could not have done it; any sound critic will feel that he could not. So, too, with the author of the Fourth Gospel. Where the *logia* are suited to the character of Jesus, they come from Jesus. Where they are not, there we have the theological lecturer merely expanding a theme given by Jesus, developing or thinking that he develops it. But he remains himself in doing so. To possess himself as a dramatist of the personage of Jesus, to fix his sentiments and his whole part for him, as would be implied by inventing the fundamental themes instead of merely developing them, he would not have felt himself free.

The question for us will be, then: *Are* there fundamental themes discoverable in the Fourth Gospel, and peculiar to it, which are quite according to the character of Jesus, and to his recognised habit of speech? Because, if there are, our Evangelist has not invented them, but they must come from Jesus.

Now that there are *logia* peculiar to the Fourth Gospel, which entirely suit the character and the habit of Jesus as these are known to us from the Synoptics, we can hardly conceive any one denying; except, indeed, he have a thesis to make good which constrains him. Let us bring forward a few of them: *'My kingdom is not of this world.—In my Father's house are many mansions.—The good shepherd giveth his life for the sheep.—Other men laboured, and ye are entered into their labours.—The night cometh, when no man can work.—The servant abideth not in the house for ever, the son abideth for ever.—A woman when*

---

[1] *Acts* xx. 35.

*she is in travail hath sorrow because her hour is come; but as
soon as she is delivered of the child she remembereth no more
her anguish, for joy that a man is born into the world.*[1] Except
a man be, we say, in the clutches of some tyrannous theory, we
5 can hardly conceive his denying that these *logia* are as perfectly
and naturally in the character of Jesus as are the most characteristic *logia* found in the Synoptics, such as: *Render Caesar's things
to Caesar, and God's things to God;* or, *No man having put his
hand to the plough, and looking back, is fit for the kingdom of
10 God;* or, *Foxes have holes and the birds of the air have nests, but
the Son of Man hath not where to lay his head.*[2]

5.

Yet the Tübingen professors and our Liberal newspapers must
surely have something to go upon, when they declare that the
Jesus of the Fourth Gospel speaks quite differently from the
15 Jesus of the Synoptics, and propound their theory of the Gnostic
philosopher inventing, with profoundly calculated art, his fancy
Gospel. No doubt they have. Jesus never can have delivered the
long connected harangues, or entered into the formal development of his own nature and dignity, or made the endless repeti-
20 tions, which are in the Fourth Gospel attributed to him. All this
is so absolutely contrary to his manner, which we know both
from his sayings in the Synoptics and from express testimony,
that every rule of criticism bids us suspect it. The sayings in the
Synoptics will be present to every one's mind; two or three of
25 them, indeed, characteristic specimens, we have just brought
forward. Justin's famous sentence has been again and again
quoted: 'Short and concise are the sayings that came from him,
for he was no sophist, but his word was power divine.'[3] And
equally express is the following testimony, perhaps not so fa-
30 miliar, given by the pseudo-Clementine Homilies: 'His wont
was to make concise utterances touching the things of concern-

---

[1] John xviii. 36; xiv. 2; x. 11; iv. 38; ix. 4; viii. 35; xvi. 21.
[2] Matth. xxii. 21; Luke ix. 62; Matth. viii. 20.
[3] βραχεῖς δὲ καὶ σύντομοι παρ' αὐτοῦ λόγοι γεγόνασιν, οὐ γὰρ σοφιστὴς ὑπῆρ-
35 χεν, ἀλλὰ δύναμις θεοῦ ὁ λόγος αὐτοῦ ἦν.

ment to the truth.'[1] A better description of the style of his sayings could hardly be given. They were *concise utterances touching the things of concernment to the truth*. The character of his
parabolic and figured teaching tells its own story, and needs no
describing; what distinguished his direct teaching was this its
gnomic or maxim-like character.

These gnomic sayings of Jesus the Evangelists had to place in
their narrative, and to provide for them a setting and a connexion. The Greek editor of the Fourth Gospel provides this setting in a very different style from the Synoptics, just because he
is a Greek, a man of literary skill and philosophical acquirements,
and with an intellect trained in the Greek fashion. The gnomic
form of teaching was not unknown in Greek philosophy, but
at the Christian era this form was to Greek writers an archaic
one. They had come to dovetail their thoughts into each other,
to join their sentences by articulations, and so to frame their matter into one continuous discourse, just as we do now with ours;
indeed, it is from the Greeks that the world has learnt to do it.
And in this Greek fashion the Fourth Gospel was composed.

The author of the First Gospel, on the other hand, was a
Hebrew; and to a Semitic people the gnomic form, the delivering one's thought in detached sentences, was always natural. To
the author of the First Gospel, therefore, this form was natural,
as it was to Jesus himself. And there can be no doubt, that the
form of the utterances of Jesus the First Gospel reproduces more
faithfully than the Fourth. Still, it is incredible that the Sermon
on the Mount, or the prediction in the twenty-fourth chapter
of the final troubles and of the coming of the Son of Man, should
have been spoken straight off by Jesus just as they are given in
the First Gospel. No sane critic will maintain that they were. In
both passages the Evangelist has had a number of *logia* to place,
and has given to them, as well as he could, a setting and connexion in accordance with their subject-matter and with the
occasion to which he knew them generally to belong. But he, for
the most part, gives them their setting and connexion simply by

---

[1] *Hom.* xvii. 6. περὶ τῶν τῇ ἀληθείᾳ διαφερόντων συντόμως τὰς ἀποφάσεις
ἐποιεῖτο.

juxtaposing them; whereas the editor of the Fourth Gospel, having to give this setting and connexion to his *logia*, gives it by articulating them. Therefore he changes the look of the *logia* which he reports more than either of the three Synoptics changes
5   it. He less faithfully reproduces the fashion in which each separate *logion* was originally said by Jesus.

Furthermore, the editor of the Fourth Gospel had to deal with a second harvest of *logia*, gathered from John after the first harvest of sayings had been reaped and had made men eager for
10 what might yet remain. The mass of the first harvest was sure to consist of the more picturesque, simple, and practical sayings of the Lord. In the nature of things it was probable that this should be so; from the character of the first reporters it was certain that it would be so. There remained a number of *logia* somewhat pro-
15 founder and more obscure, more over the heads of the disciples than the simpler *logia*, and therefore less interesting to them. Of this kind were sayings in which Jesus spoke of his relation to the Father, and of life and death in the sense that he loved to give to those words. '*I came forth from the Father.—The Father sent*
20 *me.—My doctrine is not mine, but his that sent me.—The Father is greater than I.—I can of mine own self do nothing.—The Son can of himself do nothing, but only what he seeth the Father doing.—He that hateth me hateth my Father also.—I and the Father are one.—He that believeth on me hath everlasting life.—*
25 *If a man keep my word he shall never see death.—I am the resurrection and the life.*'[1]

That sayings of this kind were from the first known and reported is proved by our finding in the First Gospel such a *logion* as the following:—'All things are delivered unto me by my Fa-
30 ther, and no one knoweth the Son but the Father, neither knoweth any one the Father save the Son, and he to whomsoever the Son will reveal him.'[2] We need hardly say that here the Tübingen professors smell *Tendenz*, and affirm that a piece of Greek Gnosticism must have got thrust into the Gospel of the

35   [1] John xvi. 28; xvii. 8, 18, 21, 23, 25; vii. 16; xiv. 28; v. 30; v. 19; xv. 23; x. 30; vi. 47; viii. 51; xi. 25.

[2] Matth. xi. 27.

old Jewish Evangelist. But these solutions we do not permit to ourselves; and the *logion*, famous in the history of the criticism of the New Testament text, is given by two out of the three Synoptics,—by St. Luke[1] as well as by St. Matthew. We receive it, therefore, as giving clear proof of the existence of sayings of the Lord on that class of subjects which the *logia* of the Fourth Gospel touch so frequently, subjects such as the relation of Jesus to the Father, and the like. Indeed, we do not see how Jesus could have pursued his design of transforming the popular ideal of the Messiah, who was described by prophecy as the Son of God, without touching on such subjects. And it is in part to the prominence in the Fourth Gospel of sayings on them that the tradition points, when it so early distinguishes this as the *spiritual* Gospel.[2]

To the Greek editor of John's materials these *logia* naturally assumed a transcendent interest and importance. He was plainly a man, as we have said, of philosophical acquirements. True, religion was uppermost with him, not speculation. The tone of his prologue, though from Jesus such a perfomance is inconceivable, is profoundly religious, penetrated by the grace and truth of the religion of Jesus. Whoever compares it with what remains to us of the great Greek Gnostics, of Basileides or Valentinus, will feel that the difference between them and the writer of the Fourth Gospel lies here: that while they are above all men of speculative thought, he is above all a man of religion. Still, in this world of speculative thought he had lived, in this world of ceaseless questions, as Tertullian says: '*Unde malum et quare, et unde homo et quomodo, et unde Deus?*—whence and why is evil, and whence and how is man, and whence is God?' Such questions had in his eyes an infinite interest and importance; sayings of Jesus which bore upon them could not but rivet and fascinate his mind. In his redaction of John's materials we see that he cannot make too much of such *logia*. He returns to them again and again, and avails himself of every occasion for re-introducing them.

---

[1] Luke x. 22.

[2] πνευματικὸν εὐαγγέλιον. See Eusebius *Hist. Eccles.* vi. 14.

Well, then, to change the gnomic form of his fundamental themes, the sayings of Jesus, and to connect these into an articulated and flowing discourse, was a rule, as we have seen, of our Evangelist's redaction, and of itself necessitated a considerable change in his primitive data. A yet further change was caused by affection for certain themes, leading him to present these themes again and again, slightly varied. Moreover, in his whole redaction, in his presentment of sayings of Jesus as well as of incidents in his life, he laboured, in spite of his superiority to the Synoptics in literary skill and in philosophical thought, under one disadvantage. He had the disadvantage of a foreigner who presents manners, locutions, localities, not his own, but alien to him. He could not be warned by that instinct which perpetually, on points of detail, keeps a native straight, and makes him feel certain things to be improbable and impossible.

We have seen that the internal evidence, to be drawn from the Gospel itself, contradicts Baur's theory of the consummate artist at the end of the second century freely inventing all the Fourth Gospel. But the internal evidence suits very well with the supposition of a Greek Christian editing a second harvest, for which the materials were furnished by John, of sayings and doings of the Lord, arranging them in his own fashion, and giving to the *logia* an interdependence and connexion which originally they had not; moreover, amplifying and repeating certain *logia*, and making developments from them. Now, the tradition gives us John, in Asia, supplying the materials of this second harvest, but not himself editing them. If another edited them in Asia, for the benefit of the Asiatic Churches, this other was surely a Greek Christian; and if a Greek Christian edited them, he was likely to proceed in the way alleged, and of which the Gospel bears, surely, strong marks.

For according to all the rules, we will not say of criticism, but of common sense,—according to all rules of probability, and of speakers speaking in character, and not violently and unaccountably deserting it,—can anything be more incredible than that Jesus should have actually spoken to Nicodemus, or John the Baptist to a disciple, the latter part of the speeches attributed to them in the third chapter of our Gospel? Let us take first the speech to Nicodemus. It is probable that the real end of the dialogue is to be found in the tenth verse: 'Art thou Israel's teacher, and knowest not these things?' But our Evangelist had two other *logia* of Jesus:—'We speak that we do know, and testify that we have seen, and ye receive not our testimony;'[1] and, 'If I tell you earthly things and ye believe not, how shall ye believe if I tell you heavenly things?'[2]—which admitted of being placed in this connexion. So here he places them. This, we say, is probable; but what is certain is, that Jesus did not speak the verse which follows these two *logia*, the thirteenth: 'And no man hath ascended up into heaven save he that came down from heaven, the Son of Man.' That is a variation on a primitive theme of Jesus, *I am the bread that came down from heaven*,[3] inserted here by our theological lecturer, because he knew that it was a theme dwelt upon by Jesus, and thought that he saw here a natural place for it. A genuine *logion* of Jesus follows, bearing every mark of being still quite or almost in its original form, but woven into this context by our lecturer, and owing its connexion with what precedes simply to his conjunction *and:* 'As Moses lifted up the serpent in the wilderness, so must the Son of Man be lifted up, that whosoever believeth on him may have everlasting life.' Then enters the theological lecturer, and continues (one may almost say) lecturing in his own proper person till the end of the speech, from the sixteenth verse to the twenty-first. For who, that has studied the sayings of Jesus well, can ever believe that Jesus said: 'For God so loved the world that he gave his only-begotten Son, to the end that whosoever believeth in him should have everlasting life,'[4] and the rest? Our Evangelist does not, however, in these verses, think he is inventing; for he is going all the time upon three primitive themes of Jesus: *He that believeth on me hath everlasting life; I came not to judge the world, but to save the world; I am come a light into the world, that whosoever believeth on me should not abide in darkness.*[5] On these genuine *logia* he is going, and he merely amplifies and

---

[1] John iii. 11.   [2] John iii. 12.   [3] John vi. 41.
[4] The text of the Vatican manuscript is followed.
[5] John vi. 47; xii. 47, 46.

repeats them; developing them, in his own judgment, naturally, and as it was to be supposed Jesus himself did.

Let us now pass to the speech of John the Baptist, at the end of the same chapter. The real sayings assigned to John the Baptist by our Evangelist's tradition ended, one can hardly doubt, with the words: 'He must increase, but I must decrease.'[1] The rest, down to the end of the thirty-sixth verse, is our theological lecturer. That criticism only which sees no impossibility in Jesus having spoken the sixteenth verse of this chapter will see no impossibility in John the Baptist's having spoken the thirty-sixth. But again our Evangelist is not inventing, but developing. He has certain genuine *logia* of Jesus as his basis, the chief of them being that which we have already quoted: 'He that believeth on me hath everlasting life.'[2] He has these *logia* with several variations of phrase, indicating that they were used more than once, in more connexions than one, perhaps by more than one speaker. The speech of John the Baptist seems to him a connexion eminently proper for them. The Baptist's real words appear to him to imply their adoption and addition; it appears to him natural and certain that the Baptist adopted and added them. So we come to have John the Baptist saying: 'He that believeth on the Son hath everlasting life; but he that believeth not the Son hath not life, but the wrath of God abideth on him.'[3]

All that is said of 'the dogmatic mysticism, and artificial, prolix discourses' of the Fourth Gospel, all the complaints of its substituting 'for the sublime and pregnant discourses of the Sea of Galilee and the Mount of Olives the arid mysticism of the schools of Alexandria,' will be found, we think, so far as they are just, to be best met by the supposition of a Greek editor connecting, repeating, and amplifying themes of Jesus; not by the supposition of a consummate artist inventing the whole Gospel. The kernel of the work, the fundamental themes of Jesus, we

---

[1] John iii. 30.
[2] John vi. 47. The true sense is given by Jesus in a *logion* quoted v. 24: but the theme itself, in its most concise and authentic form, is probably the verse at vi. 47, in the reading of the Vatican manuscript, which omits *on me*, and has simply, ὁ πιστεύων ἔχει ζωὴν αἰώνιον.
[3] John iii. 36.

maintain to be no 'arid mysticism' at all, but to be in profound unison with 'the sublime and pregnant discourses of the Sea of Galilee and the Mount of Olives.' And we do not see who was capable of uttering them but Jesus. Unless our Evangelist invented them, we do not see from whom he can have got them, except from Jesus through John; and, indeed, it is not even contended that he got them from anyone else. But it is contended, in defiance of all the tradition, that he himself invented them. But to us it seems incredible, even on grounds of literary criticism solely, that the man who was such a consummate artist as to invent for Jesus the first part of his conversation with Nicodemus should have followed it up by the second. It seems incredible, again, that a dramatic genius capable of inventing for John the Baptist: 'He that hath the bride is the bridegroom, but the friend of the bridegroom, who standeth and heareth him, rejoiceth greatly because of the bridegroom's voice; this my joy therefore is fulfilled,'[1]—it seems incredible that such a genius should have finished the Baptist's speech by making him say: 'He that believeth not the Son shall not see life, but the wrath of God abideth on him.'[2] And the question, whether this is incredible or no, we would cheerfully consent to submit to the judgment of any competent tribunal; only the judges constituting the tribunal ought not to be the professors of the theological faculties of Germany, but Germans like Lessing, Herder, and Goethe.

It seems certain, then, that what is theological lecture in the speeches of Jesus comes not from him or from John, but from John's editor. But a treasure of *logia* remains, which have all the characters of genuine sayings of Jesus, and which are invaluable as indicating the line really taken by him. The *bread of life*, the *true vine*, the *good shepherd*, the *light of the world*, are all of them images from the Old Testament, such as the hearers of Jesus were familiar with and gladly heard, such as philosophers like Philo were at that time copiously employing for their allegorical theology, such as Jesus himself loved naturally and used instinctively, and such as he could and did make admirably helpful to his main design. That design was, it cannot be too

---

[1] John iii. 29.   [2] John iii. 36.

often repeated, to change the popular Messias-ideal; and what
stroke towards such an end could be at once more happy and
more characteristic of Jesus than when, for example, calling himself *the light of the world*,[1] he in a moment identified for his fol-
5 lowers his ideal of mildness and self-renouncement with the famous world-light of Messianic prophecy: 'It is a small thing that
thou shouldest be my servant to raise up the tribes of Jacob, and
to restore the preserved of Israel: I will also give thee for *a light
to the Gentiles, that my salvation may be unto the ends of the
10 earth*.'[2] Strokes like these belong essentially to Jesus, and it is an
unsound criticism which can think of assigning them to our
theological lecturer.

Many, too, of the objections brought against *logia* of the
Fourth Gospel are frivolous, and merely show the bringer's want
15 of imagination. It is objected that Jesus cannot have said: 'As
Moses lifted up the serpent in the wilderness, so shall the Son of
Man be lifted up,'[3] because he could not have foreseen the manner of his own death. But he fixed on the most miserable kind of
death as his fitting and sure climax; and Plato, following up a
20 supposed sufferer to his climax of misery, fixes, we shall find,
upon the very same:—'Finally,' says he, 'we will suppose him
crucified.'[4] It is objected that Jesus cannot have said to his
disciples things like: *He that eateth me shall live by me*,[5] because
the disciples were certain to misunderstand them, and he would
25 not have said things they must misunderstand. This is a most extraordinary objection. One can account for it only by the strong
reluctance of mankind to recognise the gulf between every great
spirit and themselves. To this day, whoever reads a controversy
about the Real Presence, will find Christians,—and learned Chris-
30 tians,—misapprehending the words of Jesus about eating him,
even after he himself has supplied the plain explanation of them,[6]
as totally as did the Jews; will find the Christian theologians
stumbling and fumbling, just like the Jewish theologians, in their
gross, dark, narrow materialism. Half of what any great spirit

35   [1] John viii. 12.   [2] Isaiah xlix. 6.   [3] John iii. 14.
               [4] Plato *Gorgias* cap. xxviii.
      [5] John vi. 57.   [6] John vi. 63.

says is sure to be misapprehended by his hearers; much more than half of what Jesus said was sure to be misapprehended by his disciples. If he talked to them at all, he could not but talk to them as he did. And if he talked to them as he did, taking their language about God, the Messiah, bread from heaven, life and death, and translating it into that of his higher ideal, they could not but misunderstand him. Yet he could not but talk to them, and they could not but reap some benefit from it. What Christianity has done up to this time is the measure of the benefit which Jesus, even imperfectly apprehended, could produce; and that benefit has been something immense. But such are the necessary conditions on which a great spirit speaks to those who hear his word. They understand him imperfectly; nevertheless they appropriate what they can of him, and get helped along by it somehow.

Let us look closer at the very *logion*, the famous *logion*, last quoted, and observe how in itself it is an entirely probable saying of Jesus, and how its improbability all comes from its editor's treatment of it. The *logion* is exactly what we call a primitive theme, a nucleus. Our Evangelist composed, of course, his sixth chapter with the institution of the Last Supper full in his view, and with the words, *This is my body*, *This is my blood*, ever present to his thoughts. But he had anterior incidents and words to go upon. He had a story from John, how the Jews, with the multitude's faith in miracles and desire to get them worked for its benefit, had required Jesus, as the alleged 'prophet like unto Moses,' to feed them miraculously as Moses did. Was it not written in the Scriptures: 'He gave them bread from heaven to eat?'[1] Our Evangelist, we say, had a tradition from John of sayings and answers which this demand of the Jews had called forth. Jesus had said: 'Labour not for the meat that perisheth, but for the meat that endureth unto everlasting life.'[2] He had said: 'Not Moses gave you the bread from heaven, but my Father giveth you the true bread from heaven.'[3] 'Give us then this bread,'[4] was the Jews' rejoinder. Jesus had answered: 'He that

[1] *Ps.* lxxviii. 24.
[2] John vi. 27.
[3] John vi. 32.
[4] John vi. 34.

believeth hath everlasting life; he that heareth my word, and believeth him that sent me, hath everlasting life. I am the bread of
life! I am the bread that came down from heaven! He that
cometh to me shall never hunger, and he that believeth on me
5 shall never thirst. Not as your fathers did eat manna in the wilderness and are dead; he that eateth this bread shall live for ever.'[1]
The Jews, with their keen sensuousness, were familiar with the
image of God's word as something to feed on, something good
to eat and pleasant to taste. It is written in the Psalms: 'How
10 sweet are thy words unto my taste, yea, sweeter than honey unto
my mouth!'[2] But they exclaimed, when Jesus called himself the
bread from heaven: 'Is not this Jesus the son of Joseph, whose
father and mother we know? how saith he that *I am come down
from heaven?* how can he give us his flesh to eat?'[3] Then Jesus
15 had answered: 'As the living Father sent me, and I live by the
Father, so he that eateth me, he also shall live by me.'[4]

These we may take as the primitive themes out of which our
Evangelist's sixth chapter is built up. Other genuine *logia* are
worked into it. But they are worked into it; they are not its es-
20 sential elements. Most probably, too, the primitive themes were
several times reiterated by Jesus, not without some variation.
But we shall hardly err if we take the primitive themes above
given, as our nearest possible approach to what Jesus and his
interlocutors did actually say. And this substratum being com-
25 mitted to our combining and amplifying Greek editor, how
natural and explicable becomes the apparition, in the chapter, of
those sayings which now stagger every serious critic! It is almost
inconceivable, if one thinks of it, that Jesus should have actually
said in the conversation in question: 'Except ye eat the flesh of
30 the Son of Man and drink his blood, ye have no life in yourselves; he that eateth my flesh and drinketh my blood hath everlasting life, and I will raise him up in the last day; for my flesh
is meat indeed, and my blood is drink indeed.'[5] But it is perfectly

---

[1] John vi. 41, 47 (compare v, 24), 48, 35, 58, and 49.
35   [2] *Ps.* cxix. 103.   [3] John vi. 42, 52.
[4] John vi. 57.   [5] John vi. 53–55.

conceivable that he should have said, the image of the bread from heaven being once started: '*I am the bread of life! he that eateth me shall live by me!*'[1] and that our editor being such a man as we suppose, and having the words of institution of the Last Supper swaying his mind, should by his mode of combining, reiterating and developing these primitive themes, when he had them to place, have turned them into such speeches of Jesus as now puzzle us.

For, again, it is almost inconceivable that Jesus should have really said: 'For the bread of God is he *that cometh down from heaven*, and that giveth life unto the world;' or that he should have said: '*I am come down from heaven*, not to do mine own will, but the will of him that sent me!'[2] But it is entirely natural that our editor, having such primitive themes of Jesus as: 'I am the bread that came down from heaven! I am the bread of life! I came not to do mine own will, but the will of him that sent me!'[3] should have combined them and developed them in the way he does. It is almost inconceivable that after saying, 'It is written in the prophets: *And they shall be all taught of God!* Every one that heareth and learneth from the Father cometh unto me,'—Jesus should have subjoined the remark: 'Not that any man hath seen the Father, save he who is from God; he hath seen the Father.'[4] An addition of this kind is inconceivable from Jesus, because both the matter and the manner of it are the clean opposite of his. But it was in entire conformity with our theological lecturer's notion and style, after giving the genuine *logia* of Jesus, to complete and guard the sense of them, as he fancied, by the amplifying clauses.

---

[1] John vi. 48, 57. For the current conception of the word of God as a bread of life, see Jesus himself quoting *Deuteronomy* (viii. 3) in Matth. iv. 4: 'Man shall not live by bread alone, but by every word that proceedeth out of the mouth of God;' and see, too, Philo, in his *Sacrarum Legum Allegoriae* (Mangey's edit., vol. i, p. 120): ὁρᾷς τῆς ψυχῆς τροφὴν οἵα ἐστίν; λόγος θεοῦ συνεχής, ἐοικὼς δρόσῳ κ. τ. λ. Only it is to be observed, in general, that while an allegorising theologian, such as Philo, uses images of this kind like a pedant, Jesus uses them like a poet.

[2] John vi. 33, 38.　　　[3] John vi. 41, 48, 38.　　　[4] John vi. 45, 46.

6.

We might go through the Fourth Gospel chapter by chap-
ter, and endeavour to assign to each and all of the *logia* in it their
right character,—to determine what in them is probably Jesus,
and what is the combining, repeating, and expanding Greek
5   editor. But this would be foreign to our object. We seek, not to
produce a complete work of ingenious criticism on the Bible,
or on any one document in it, but to help readers, sick of popular
and conventional theology, and resolved to take the Bible for
nothing but what it really is,—to help such readers to see what
10 the Bible really is, and how very much, seen as it really is, it concerns them. So we sought to show that the Old Testament is
really a majestic homage to the grandeur of righteousness, or
conduct, and a sublime witness to its necessity; while the New
Testament, again, is really an incomparable elucidation by Jesus
15 Christ of what righteousness in fact and in truth is. And there
can be no question that books of which this is the real character
do concern men vitally. So, again, we seek to show that of Jesus
Christ's incomparable elucidation of what righteousness is, several main elements are really to be found in the Fourth Gospel.
20 In that case it urgently concerns people to study the Fourth
Gospel, instead of tossing it aside as a Gnostic forgery, crammed
with 'the arid mysticism of the schools of Alexandria.' But to
lead men to study it, and to clear out of their way objections
which might for ever prevent their studying it, is our aim; when
25 we have accomplished this, we have accomplished as much as we
intend.

But to restore perfectly the Jesus of the Fourth Gospel, or
indeed of any Gospel, is impossible. The data are insufficient, and
the alteration, often important though perhaps verbally slight,
30 which his sayings have undergone from the pressure of other
minds upon them, is too considerable. Our restoration must frequently be conjectural, and we may be wrong in our conjectures. We do not pretend that we could establish as clear and
certain our criticism of every passage, or nearly every passage,
35 in the Fourth Gospel, supposing we were to go through it with

our reader. And even if we could save him from one or two mistakes by not merely giving him the guiding ideas with which to
read the Gospel for himself, but by going through it with him,
our object is not to make as faultless a critic of him as possible,
but to keep him in contact with a book which will do him good,   5
and to make him study it for himself. If he thinks it spurious, he
is not likely to study it; but we try to show him that it is full of
genuine things, and to give him the guiding ideas by which to
account for the things that made the charge of spuriousness seem
plausible, and by which to extricate the things that are genuine.   10

[Nor let this be esteemed a slight assistance, or the abandon-
ing him to uncertainty. What is uncertain, what a reader may
frequently not determine right, and what we might not determine right if we came to help him, is the occasion on which each
particular saying was uttered and the connexion to which it   15
belongs. But the main doubt as to the Gospel's genuineness arose
from the occasion assigned and the connexion given by our
Evangelist to his stock of 'Sayings of the Lord.' Now, we show
that his circumstances and literary procedure were such that the
occasion and connexion imposed by him on his *logia* are not to   20
be trusted. We may be tempted to try and restore the right
occasion and connexion, and in this work there must necessarily
be some uncertainty. But if we stop quite short of this, if we
simply set aside our Evangelist's combinations as untrustworthy,
then we leave to the *logia* of Jesus in the Fourth Gospel,—those 25
of them which are not manifestly theological developments and
exercitations by our lecturer,—the character of maxim-like, isolated sayings, complete in themselves. Now, the teaching of
Jesus, as of the nation and race to which he belonged, really
had in general this character. His deliverances were 'concise ut- 30
terances touching the things of concernment to the truth.' And
for practical use among Christians it is in this way,—as maxims,
detached sayings,—that they are in fact generally employed;
and it is when they are employed in this way that their practical usefulness is greatest. As single sayings the mind ruminates 35
them, turns them over and over, feeds upon them. For a critical
curiosity, then, we may not yet have done enough, when we
have established that instead of taking the sayings of Jesus in

that connexion wherein the Fourth Gospel places them, it is far
safer to take them as detached sayings. But for the practical use
of the contents of the Fourth Gospel we have by this means done
very much.

5   [Jesus, no doubt, did not in his discourse deliver sentences
articulated in the Greek fashion one to another. He delivered
sentences juxtaposed in the Semitic fashion one to another. Because in the Fourth Gospel his sentences are articulated in the
Greek fashion, those sentences have been confidently pro-
10   nounced not to be sayings of Jesus. But the *logion* of Jesus is
there; and often, in order to get at it, we have only to drop the
Greek editor's conjunctions. For instance; suppose we take the
sayings which form the speech of Jesus at the end of the twelfth
chapter, from the forty-fourth verse to the fiftieth. As a con-
15   nected speech Jesus did not deliver those sayings; our Evangelist
has made them into one speech for him. But drop the conjunctions and the connecting clauses, and there is not a *logion*
there to offend, singly, even a jealous criticism; there is not one
which does not show the characteristic and satisfying mark of
20   Jesus.]

Our great point[, then,] as to the Fourth Gospel is this: the
Evangelist is a combiner, not an inventor. It is his forms of
connecting and articulating which obscure the gnomic character of the sayings of the Lord in this Gospel; get rid of those
25   forms, and the gnomic and genuine character reappears. Our
Evangelist had a number of *logia* to plant. He did not, he could
not, know their true connexion; and the connexion he imposes
on them is not to be depended upon. Often we, studying quietly
his work as it lies before us complete, can perceive a better con-
30   nexion for certain *logia* than that which he has devised for them.
[Almost certainly, the last half of the fourteenth verse and the
first half of the fifteenth, in the tenth chapter, have their right
place not where we now read them but in the twenty-seventh
verse of the same chapter. The twenty-seventh verse should run:
35   'My sheep hear my voice, and I know them, and they know me, as
the Father knoweth me, and I know the Father; and they follow
me.' The thirtieth verse of the same chapter ('I and the Father
are one') has almost certainly its right place, not where it stands,

but side by side with the *logion* in the fourteenth chapter, 'He that hath seen me hath seen the Father,'[1] and in a similar connexion. Almost certainly the fourteenth verse of the twentieth chapter, 'He that receiveth whomsoever I send receiveth me, and he that receiveth me receiveth him that sent me,' is misplaced where it stands, and should go with the sixteenth verse of the fifteenth chapter, the eighteenth verse of the seventeenth, and the twenty-first of the twentieth,[2] and in a similar connexion. Almost certainly the four verses from the twenty-second to the twenty-fifth, in the fifteenth chapter, belong to a connexion such as that in the eighth chapter, were said to the Jews not to the Apostles, and are a mere unseasonable repetition, put by our Evangelist into the mouth of Jesus speaking to his disciples, of things which he had previously said to the Jews.] But we can never be absolutely sure of having found the real original connexion for them; the safe thing is to distrust our Evangelist's connexion, and to take the *logia* singly. Even where they have a dramatic propriety and beauty as joined together by our Evangelist, it is often very questionable whether Jesus thus joined them, whether we are not more on the trace of Jesus when we take them singly. Nothing can well be finer or more impressive than the speech formed by the series of *logia*[3] attributed to Jesus after Andrew tells him of the Greeks desiring to see him. But it is highly improbable that Jesus did actually thus deliver these *logia* as a series, and in one speech, and on one occasion; although we may grant every *logion* in the series to be in itself authentic, and of the very highest value.

Now, it is wonderful how the likelihood of our having as the substance of the Fourth Gospel genuine sayings of Jesus will be found to gain, and the unlikelihood of it to dwindle, the moment we come to disregard our Evangelist's combinations, and to suppress his repetitions and lecturings. Let us take the series of chapters against which so much of objection has been brought,

---

[1] John xiv. 9.

[2] 'I have appointed you that ye should go and bring forth fruit, and that your fruit should remain.' 'As Thou sentest me into the world, so send I them into the world.' 'As my Father hath sent me, even so send I you.'

[3] John xii. 23–26.

the series from the twelfth chapter to the end of the seventeenth.
They form almost one continuous speech, and most certainly
they were not spoken as such. They contain, also, repetitions
which Jesus, to judge from everything that we know of his man-
5   ner, cannot have made, and some things which he cannot have
said at all. It is easy to see this, and to reject the whole series of
chapters as unauthentic. But a little attention will show us a
number of primitive themes, or *nuclei*, on which our Evangelist
is operating; and that these themes,—to judge, again, from every-
10 thing that we know of the manner of Jesus,—have all the marks
of being authentic. And we may with profit try to get back to
what Jesus can have actually said; only we must be careful, in
attempting this, to distinguish between what is certain, and what
can only be called probable.

15   [For example. The governing word of our series of chapters
is certainly the word ὑπάγω, *I go away*. And the chapters have
their reason for existence, certainly, in a development by Jesus
of this governing word. And that development is: συμφέρει ἵνα
ἀπέλθω,[1]—*It is expedient that I depart*. And the form of this de-
20 velopment is certainly twofold at least: συμφέρει ἐμοί, συμφέρει ὑμῖν,
—*It is expedient for me, It is expedient for you*. It is expedient
for *me*, because I go to the Father.[2] It is expedient for *you*, because the Paraclete's coming to you depends on my going from
you.[3] This, we say, seems certain. And to us it seems probable
25 that there is also a third development given by Jesus to his *I go
away;* and that this development is: συμφέρει τῷ κόσμῳ,—*It is expedient for the world*. We find this third development in the
words of Jesus: 'Ye shall weep and lament, but the world shall
rejoice; ye shall be sorrowful, but your sorrow shall be turned
30 into joy. A woman when she is in travail hath sorrow, because
her hour is come; but as soon as she is delivered of the child she
remembereth no more her anguish, for joy that a man is born
into the world.'[4] Combined as our Evangelist combines them,
these words appear to mean, no doubt, that the world, the

35   [1] John xvi. 7.   [2] John xiv. 28.   [3] John xvi. 7.
                                    [4] John xvi. 20, 21.

wicked world, shall exult in the sufferings and death of Jesus;
and so the commentators take them. But we cannot help thinking, that, as Jesus spoke them, they were words to be classed
with the texts: 'I am come a light into the world, that whoso believeth on me should not abide in darkness:' 'A light to lighten   5
the Gentiles;' 'One flock, one shepherd.'[1] We believe that they
really mean, not, *The world shall exult at my death*, but, *My
death is good for the world as well as for you and me;* and that
they are a third and admirable development given to the ground-
motive of our chapters, ὑπάγω. This we believe; and perhaps if   10
we were in a professor's chair at Tübingen, we should say that
we could and did demonstrate it. But being what we are, we
say that it is not demonstrable, indeed, nor yet with such overwhelming probability in its favour as to seem certain;—the evidence is not such as to admit of its being either the one or the   15
other. But we say that it is probable; and that it has so much to
recommend it that we ourselves believe it.]

That Jesus, however, uttered a great deal of what is attributed
to him in the series of chapters from the twelfth to the seventeenth, that he gave the primitive themes which are the basis of   20
them, that the combination of the themes is the Evangelist's, and
that by the Evangelist Jesus is made to repeat himself over and
over again, to connect things as he never connected them, and to
say things which he never said, we regard as so probable that it
becomes certain. For the primitive themes are in the character-   25
istic manner of Jesus, and we do not see from whom else they
can have proceeded. The combination, repetition and development of the themes are in the characteristic manner of the
Evangelist.

[The governing word of the chapters under review has been   30
just now mentioned.] In a former part of our argument, we had
occasion to single out one or two of the primitive themes. [Be-
sides] these[, which] we showed to be the nucleus of sayings
delivering Jesus Christ's own real doctrine about his own resurrection, [there is the parable of the heavenly house with its many   35

---

[1] John xii. 46; Luke ii. 32; John x. 16.

mansions, a parable which is the Evangelist's authentic nucleus
for unauthentic combinations and developments favourable to
the popular doctrine of the resurrection.[1] There is the parable of
the vine and the branches, illustrating that primitive theme of
5 Jesus: *Abide in me and I in you*.[2] There are the new commandment; the promise of the Paraclete; the promise that the disciples'
requests should be heard; the exhortation not to fear the world's
hatred; the prayer for the disciples; the sayings of Jesus about
his glory; the sayings about his relation to the Father. All of these
10 have their primitive theme or themes; all of them are connected,
introduced and reintroduced, and more or less developed by our
Evangelist.] Now, if the reader simply takes all the sayings belonging to each theme, and puts them together, he will do what is
very conducive both to a right enjoyment of this series of chap-
15 ters, and to a right criticism of them. [On the one hand, he will
bring out the beauty and significance of the genuine sayings of
Jesus; on the other, he will bring out how much is evidently
repetition, serving to introduce our Evangelist's developments.]
We should like our reader to distribute under [the] heads [or
20 themes indicated] all the sayings on each theme, and then to
judge them for himself. We will, however, taking one or two
themes not hitherto touched by us, show at least how true it is
that by the process we recommend both objects are served: the
right enjoyment of our Evangelist's materials, and the right criti-
25 cism of them.

First, as to the enjoyment of what our Evangelist has, in these
chapters, saved for us. We will simply put together the scattered
logia having for their theme the 'new commandment,' and make
the subject begin where it naturally does begin, with the sayings
30 of Jesus after he has washed the disciples' feet at the Last Supper. 'Know ye what I have done unto you? Ye call me Master
and Lord, and ye say well, for so I am. If I then, your Master and
Lord, have washed your feet, ye also ought to wash one another's
feet. For I have given you an example that ye also should do as I
35 have done to you. Verily I say unto you, the servant is not

[1] John xiv. 2, 3; compared with xvi. 22, and xvii. 24.
[2] John xv. 4.

greater than his lord, neither is he that is sent greater than he that sent him. A new commandment give I unto you, that ye love one another; as I have loved you, that ye also love one another. Hereby shall all men know that ye are my disciples, if ye have love one to another. This is my commandment, that ye love one another as I have loved you. Greater love hath no man than this, that a man lay down his life for his friends. Ye are my friends, if ye do that which I command you. Ye have not chosen me, but I have chosen you. Henceforth I call you not servants, for the servant knoweth not what his lord doeth; but I have called you friends, for all things that I hear of my Father I make known unto you. These things I command you, that ye love one another.'[1] All these sentences we may take as genuine *logia* having the 'new commandment' for their theme. Relieved from the separation which the Evangelist, for the purposes of his long discourse and its developments, inflicts on them, simply put together again as by their subject they belong together, how their effectiveness and impressiveness increases, how heightened is our enjoyment of them!

And next, as to the right criticism of our Evangelist's mode of procedure. Let us take the sayings on another theme, the primitive theme for all which is said about the disciples' prayers being granted, the words: 'Whatsoever ye shall ask in my name, I will do it.'[2] Let us put with these words all the scattered repetitions of this same theme, some of them with a little variation, others in words almost identical with the *logion* we have quoted. When we see them all together, we see that by all the repetitions nothing is really added, either in the substance or in the form of expression, to the primitive theme;—nothing is gained. The primitive theme, then, alone is from Jesus. The repetitions are our Evangelist's, to enable Jesus to make a long, connected speech, such as Jesus never dealt in, such as is quite alien to his manner. Now, it is argued that the *logia* proper to the Fourth Gospel are all of them inventions, because they are unmeaningly and vainly repeated. But is the ineffective repetition, several

[1] John xiii. 12–16, 34, 35; xv. 12–17.
[2] John xiv. 13.

times, of a *logion*, any reason why Jesus should not have given it with effect once?

The same with the sayings of Jesus about his glory. It is argued that the frequent and earnest insistence on his glory, particularly in the long prayer of the seventeenth chapter, is not at all in the style of Jesus and cannot be his. As the Evangelist presents and develops it, we will own it cannot. But let us put together all the sayings of Jesus about his glory, going back for this purpose as far even as the eleventh chapter, where is the first apparition of them, and we shall be able to see, both what Jesus may probably have said on the subject, and how the Evangelist has probably dealt with it. To begin with, we find a primitive theme entirely in the style of Jesus, in his exclamation when he heard from Andrew and Philip of the Gentiles, or Greeks, present at his last Passover and desirous to see him: 'The hour is come that the Son of Man should be glorified!'[1] In all the Four Gospels there is not a saying of Jesus more safe to accept than this, more perfectly in character. To Jesus, these foreigners desiring to see him were the Gentiles, the nations. The Messiah, of whom the Jews had their minds full, he steadfastly identified, we know, with the mild and stricken Servant of prophecy, 'his visage so marred more than any man, and his form more than the sons of men,'[2] and himself with this Messiah. He knew that the victory of this Messiah and of his cause could only come when he had 'poured out his soul unto death.'[3] What was that victory? It was the foundation, and henceforth unconquerable institution for the world at large, of the kingdom of God, the reign of righteousness. 'The Eternal will cause righteousness and praise to spring forth before all nations; I will set my glory among the heathen; from the rising of the sun even unto the going down of the same my name shall be great among the Gentiles.'[4] But to bring in the reign of righteousness, was to bring in the Eternal's glory; and the Servant who brought in this, founded his own by doing so. We may conceive of many and various texts as contributing here. Texts originally proper to the despised Servant, the

---

[1] John xii. 23.   [2] Isaiah lii. 14.   [3] Isaiah liii. 12.
[4] Isaiah lxi. 11; Ezekiel xxxix. 21; Malachi i. 11.

Messias-ideal of Jesus: 'So shall many nations exult in him; kings shall shut their mouths before him.'[1] Texts originally proper to the renewed Israel: 'The Gentiles shall see thy righteousness, and all kings thy glory.'[2] Texts originally proper to the righteous man in general: 'Thou shalt guide me with thy counsel, and afterwards receive me to glory.'[3] Texts originally proper to the conquering Root of David, the Messias-ideal of the Jews: 'His rest shall be glory.'[4] All these we may conceive as present and contributory in the mind of Jesus, when, seeing his death imminent, and hearing at the same time of the Gentile strangers desirous to see him, he said: 'The hour is come that the Son of Man should be glorified!'

But once this primitive theme given, how natural that our Evangelist should harp upon it, recur to it, develop it! The whole seventeenth chapter may be called a development of this theme. It is as much in character for a disciple to love to prolong the theme of Christ's glory and dilate upon it, as it is little in character for Jesus himself to do so. And the mode of development followed is just the mode tempting to a disciple,—Jew or Greek, —of Jesus, but never adopted or encouraged by Jesus himself.

Jesus checked questions of theosophy. He contented himself with taking the conception of God as the Jews had it, and as the Old Testament delivered it, as the eternal and righteous Father; and with saying of himself: 'I came forth from God,' 'God sent me.' But questions of theosophy had and have, as we see by the history of Gnosticism, and, indeed, by the whole history of religion, an irresistible attraction for the human mind. Men asked themselves, as Tertullian says, *Unde Deus?*—and they loved to inquire, in like manner, precisely how Jesus was related to his Father who sent him. In a famous passage in the Book of Proverbs, Wisdom says of herself: 'The Lord possessed me in the beginning of his way before his works of old; I was set up from everlasting. I was by him as one brought up with him, and I was daily his delight.'[5] The Book of Wisdom, a late work, but for that very reason more likely to be popular, and

---

[1] Isaiah lii. 15.   [2] Isaiah lxii. 2.   [3] *Psalm* lxxiii. 24.
[4] Isaiah xi. 10.   [5] *Prov.* viii. 22, 23, 30.

of which in the Epistle to the Hebrews we can see the influence,
added these striking traits: 'Wisdom is the breath of the power of
God, and a pure influence flowing from the glory of the Almighty. She is the brightness of the everlasting light, the un-
5   spotted mirror of the power of God, and the image of his goodness.'[1] Eagerly did theosophy possess itself of these images, and
spin its fancies by the help of two supposed personages, *Sophia*
and *Logos*, the Wisdom and Word of God. Jesus spoke of himself as uttering the word of God; but that he called himself the
10 *Logos*, there is neither indication nor probability. There is, however, some trace of his having perhaps called himself the *wisdom*
of God. At least, a saying of the First Gospel, 'Wherefore, behold, *I* send unto you prophets and wise men and scribes,'[2] is
given in the Third Gospel in the following different and remark-
15 able form: 'Wherefore also *the wisdom of God* said, I will send
unto them prophets and apostles.'[3] It is just possible that we have
here a trace of Jesus having really and naturally, on at least one
occasion, called himself 'the wisdom of God,' and having to that
extent seemed to give countenance to the personifying lucubra-
20 tions upon these terms *Sophia* and *Logos*,—the Wisdom, Reason,
or Word, of God,—of both Jewish and Greek theosophy. It is
just possible, I say, that our Evangelist, in developing what Jesus
said of his glory, had thus much to go upon.[4] But at any rate, the
glory of Jesus was made to accord with that of the *Sophia* or
25 *Logos* of theosophical speculation, and with the attributes assigned to them by Scripture. And so we have Jesus made to say:
'And now, Father, glorify thou me beside thine own self with
the glory which I had beside thee before the world was.'[5] We

[1] *Wisdom* vii. 25, 26. Compare ἀπαύγασμα φωτὸς ἀϊδίου . . . καὶ εἰκὼν τῆς
30 ἀγαθότητος αὐτοῦ, in this passage, with *Heb.* i. 3: ἀπαύγασμα τῆς δόξης καὶ
χαρακτὴρ τῆς ὑποστάσεως αὐτοῦ.
[2] Matth. xxiii. 34.
[3] Luke xi. 49.
[4] Probably, however, Jesus was simply referring to a well-known phrase
35 of prophecy: 'I have sent unto you all my servants the prophets, rising up
early and sending them; but ye have not inclined your ear nor hearkened
unto me' (see Jeremiah xxxv. 15), and did not mean either *the Wisdom of
God* or the *I* to stand for himself.
[5] John xvii. 5.

have him saying: 'Father, that which thou hast given me, I will that they also be with me where I am, that they may see my glory which thou gavest me because thou lovedst me before the foundation of the world.'[1] These things are not at all in the manner of Jesus. Jesus, as we have said, never theosophised. Not thus did he employ Scripture, not thus did he establish his divinity, not thus did he conceive his glory. But it is entirely in the manner of our Evangelist. And this is the good of putting together everything which relates to a primitive theme; because we then are enabled to perceive clearly, both how simple and characteristic was the original nucleus given by Jesus, and also how naturally the additions to it which perplex us may have arisen from the manipulation by the Evangelist of this given nucleus, from his expansions and developments of it.

7.

The seventeenth chapter is one where these expansions and developments appear to exceed greatly in amount the original nucleus. This is by no means always the case in our Evangelist's report of the sayings of Jesus. But in his report of miracles, and indeed in all reports of miracles, we may safely take it that the additions exceed the original nucleus of fact very largely. We said in our first chapter, that the suspension or diminution of hunger, when the attention is absorbed and the interest excited, was quite basis enough for the story of the miraculous feeding of the thousands. The answer has positively been hazarded, that no absorption or excitement could enable five thousand people to satisfy themselves upon five loaves and two fishes, and to leave twelve baskets full of fragments. As if the details of a miraculous story had the sort of solidity which would warrant one in thus gravely arguing upon them! as if any one who has come to distrust miracles trusts all the circumstances related for them and only distrusts the miraculousness! It is in the circumstances that the legend consists, that the creative power of the imagination shows itself active. Granted that a starting-point and a hint of

---

[6] John xvii. 24. The Vatican manuscript is followed.

fact for the miracles related in our Gospels there has nearly always been, yet in nine cases out of ten we shall probably err if we imagine we can now seize even this hint of fact; it was so slight in the first instance, and has been so buried under the additions.

5   We have already remarked how perhaps the sole nucleus of solid fact for the miraculous incidents at Christ's baptism was that weird light on Jordan mentioned in the Apocryphal Gospels. Sometimes the nucleus for a miracle was afforded, not improbably, by some saying of Jesus. Perhaps this is the true way of
10   accounting for the miracle of the raising of Lazarus. The miracle of the raising of Lazarus has been the theme of endless disquisition; every detail of it has been canvassed with elaborate minuteness. What part of the details is solid we shall never know. But it may safely be said, that, the human mind being what it is, and
15   stories of miracle arising as they do, the juxtaposition of one or two sayings of Jesus is sufficient, to an investigator willing to look at things simply, to account for the whole miracle. Let us try to effect this juxtaposition.

The crowning moment in the career of Jesus, as Jesus him-
20   self construed and connected his own career, had arrived,—the moment for 'the Messiah to suffer and to enter into his glory.'[1] At this moment Jesus is told of the death of a faithful disciple and friend. He says to his followers: *Our friend Lazarus sleepeth; I go to awake him.*[2] To the eye of Jesus, the kingdom of God,
25   the reign of the saints, the introduction and triumph of everlasting righteousness,—that triumph in which re-live all the saints who are dead, and the saints who are yet alive live for evermore, —was at this moment beginning. The sisters of the departed are plunged in weeping and lamentation; Jesus says to Martha: *Thy*
30   *brother shall rise again.*[3] Not with the bodily resurrection which Martha and the popular religion of Palestine then expected, and which the popular religion of Christendom expects now;—this materialism Jesus had to transform, as he had to transform the materialism of the Messias-ideal. Martha, however, imagines that
35   Jesus is speaking of the resurrection in the sense of popular religion; but Jesus corrects her. Vain gleam of illumination in that

---

[1] Luke xxiv. 26.   [2] John xi. 11.   [3] John xi. 23.

moment of early and darkling dawn! He corrected her; but his correction was a gleam of light destined slowly to brighten, not of force at that time to pierce the darkness. His words were: *I am the resurrection and the life; he who believeth on me, though he die, shall live, and he who liveth and believeth on me shall never die.*[1] The *logion* is of like kind with this other: *If a man keep my saying, he shall never see death.*[2] 'If a man uses my method and my secret,' Jesus means, 'uses them as I do, uses them *in me*, he cannot die, he is passed from death to life.' But premature and vain, we repeat, was this ray of illumination then. Out of the very *logion* which thus points to a wholly new ideal of resurrection,—out of that *logion*, passed from hearer to hearer, repeated, brooded over, misapprehended,—grew up, not improbably, the story of the great miracle of resurrection according to the old ideal, the miracle of the raising of Lazarus. That *logion*, together with the saying to Martha, *Thy brother shall rise again*, together with the saying to the disciples, *Our friend Lazarus sleepeth, I go to awake him*, were the materials out of which was built up a miraculous tale exactly effacing the truth which Jesus wished to convey. [*Sed nondum est finis*, should always be our reflexion in these cases. 'The end is not yet;'[3] the space and scale required for working out the truths of the Bible are very large.]

The developing of miracle out of slight materials is, however, common to our Evangelist with the Synoptics. Baur opposes these to our Evangelist in such a fashion, that one is sometimes tempted to ask whether he supposes, then, that the Synoptics are historical. They have, indeed, over our Evangelist certain advantages already noticed; but historical they are no more than he is. A creative pressure on incidents they all alike exercise. A creative pressure on the sayings, too, of Jesus, the Synoptics as well as our Evangelist exercise, though in a different manner from his. Nay, sometimes he is more historical than the Synoptics. If we think of it seriously, for the words spoken by Jesus during his agony in the garden[4] the Synoptics could not possibly have had

---

[1] John xi. 25, 26.
[2] John viii. 51.
[3] Matth. xxiv. 6.
[4] Matth. xxvi. 39, 42.

evidence, since the only companions of Jesus were asleep when the reported words were spoken. Their real source, probably, the Fourth Gospel discovers to us. This Gospel gives us two utterances of Jesus, made, one of them shortly before his arrest,
5 the other at the moment of it. 'Now is my soul troubled, and what shall I say: Father, save me from this hour? But for this cause came I unto this hour.'[1] And again: 'The cup which my Father hath given me, shall I not drink it?'[2] We have here, probably, the true original of the words assigned by the Synoptics to
10 the prayer of agony in the garden.

    Where the Synoptics are more historical than our Evangelist is in cases where knowledge of Jewish localities and usages is required. When he varies from them in such matters, however, it is because this sort of knowledge is lacking to him, not because
15 he is warping facts to suit a design. Baur and his Tübingen school are confident that the truth of their theory about the Fourth Gospel is quite established by our Evangelist's account of the Last Supper and of the Crucifixion. Baur found design in the whole of it: design to discountenance any observance of the
20 Passover supper by Christians, design to identify the Passover sacrifice with the death of Christ, design to prove the ending of all things Jewish, the coming-in of the reign of *Pneuma*, or spirit. But how slight are his grounds when we examine them!

    True, the Synoptics represent the Last Supper as eaten on the
25 day when the Passover was eaten. This day was 'the fourteenth day of the first month at even,'[3]—the 14th of the Jewish month of Nisan; and the Crucifixion the Synoptics represent as taking place on the day following, the 15th. True, the Fourth Gospel represents the Crucifixion as happening on the very same day on
30 which the Passover was eaten,—on the 14th of Nisan, therefore, not on the 15th. On the morning of the Crucifixion, the Jews, says our Evangelist, would not enter the Praetorium, 'in order that they might not be defiled, but might eat the Passover';[4]— that Passover which, according to the Synoptics, had been eaten
35 the evening before! The Last Supper, then, must, according to

---

[1] John xii. 27.   [2] John xviii. 11.
[3] *Exodus* xii. 18.   [4] John xviii. 28.

our Evangelist, have been eaten on the 13th of Nisan, not on the 14th; not on the day appointed for eating the Jewish Passover.

There can be little doubt that the Synoptics, and not our Evangelist, are right, although the growing estrangement from things Jewish caused the Christian Church to explain their testimony away, and to assign the Crucifixion to the 14th of Nisan. *Christ did not eat the Paschal Lamb, he suffered as the Paschal Lamb,*[1] was the view which prevailed. In the latter half of the second century, we find a keen controversy turning, in fact, upon this,— whether the 14th of Nisan was the day on which Jesus ate the Last Supper, as the Passover Supper, with his disciples. The Asiatic Churches contended that he did; and Polycrates, the aged Bishop of Ephesus, appealed[2] to the practice of the Apostle John, who, he said, had always observed the 14th as the day on which Jesus, keeping the Passover Supper, had eaten his last meal with the Twelve. But the Fourth Gospel puts this last meal on the 13th. It cannot, then, argues Baur, have proceeded from St. John. It was written by one of the anti-Jewish party, during the Paschal controversy, to put a stop to the identification of the Last Supper with the Jewish Passover.

It is certain that Rome, and the Christian Church at large, adopted the view that the 14th was the day of the Crucifixion, not of the Last Supper. There was, however, for the Church one cause of doubt and difficulty in the matter. How could it be that St. John, the author of the Fourth Gospel, kept the 14th as the day on which Jesus ate the Last Supper? This difficulty was got over by supposing that John, having to do with a number of Jewish Christians, had accepted, for the sake of peace, their identification of the Last Supper with the Passover, although he knew better all the time. In Bede's History, we find our English St. Wilfrid offering to doubters this explanation.[3]

Nothing can be be more improbable than that St. John, know-

---

[1] See *Paschal Chronicle* (edition of Bonn), vol. i, p. 12. οὐκ ἔφαγεν τὸν νομικὸν ἀμνὸν ἐν ἐκείνῃ τῇ ἡμέρᾳ ὁ κύριος, ἀλλ᾽ αὐτὸς ἔπαθεν ὡς ἀληθὴς ἀμνός.

[2] In his letter to Victor and the Church of Rome, quoted by Eusebius *Hist. Eccles.* v. 24.

[3] Bede *Hist. Eccles.* iii. 25.

ing the observance of the 14th of Nisan as the day of the Last
Supper to be an error, should nevertheless have countenanced
the error by complying with it in his practice. The tradition that
he kept the 14th may well be believed; but then he must have
5 kept it with the sincere conviction that it was the day of the Last
Supper. And so, no doubt, it was. John, then, cannot have written
the eighteenth chapter of the Fourth Gospel, cannot have put
the Crucifixion on the day when the Passover Supper was to be
eaten. This we freely concede to Baur. But does the chapter aim,
10 as Baur imagines, at marking, and marking with a controversial
and anti-Jewish intention, an error of the Synoptics about the
respective days of the Last Supper and of the Crucifixion? Is
this the reason why John, who shared the error of the Synoptics
if it was an error, cannot have written the chapter? By no means.
15 St. John cannot have written it for the same reason that he cannot have talked of *Bethany beyond Jordan*, or made the high-
priesthood of Caiaphas a yearly office. He cannot have written
it because he was a Jew, and exactitude about Jewish days and
ceremonies came natural to him. Now, it is simply for want, as it
20 seems to us, of this exactitude, that the Fourth Gospel varies from
the Synoptics in dating the Last Supper and the Crucifixion; not
from any controversial design.

John's Greek editor knew Jewish usages, and liked to import
them into his narrative. But he knew them loosely, as a foreigner,
25 and he sometimes placed them incoherently. He is like Michelet
enlivening his account of things English with traits of detail, and
meaning to say that at a financial crisis in London there was 'con-
sternation in Change Alley.' That would have been all very well.
But Michelet says, instead of Change Alley, *Alley Change*. Per-
30 haps neither a Greek nor a Frenchman could ever bring himself
to learn with minute accuracy the details of any civilisation not
his own. John's Greek editor knew the Jewish scrupulosity, and
that a Jew in a state of defilement could not eat the Passover. He
takes the occasion of Jesus being carried before Pilate to exhibit
35 this piece of knowledge, and says that the Jews could not enter
the Praetorium with Jesus, for fear they should be defiled and
hindered from eating the Passover. He does not observe that he

is thus contradicting the common tradition and the Synoptics, who represent the Passover as being eaten, not on the evening of the day of Christ's Crucifixion, but on the evening of the day before. Yet it may surely be seen, except by people bent on finding mountains in mole-hills, that he does not *mean* to contradict the Synoptics; for he calls the day of the Crucifixion the Preparation Day,[1] as they do. The Preparation Day was the day intervening between the 14th of Nisan and the Sabbath. If Jesus was crucified on the 14th of Nisan, the day for eating the Passover, that day could not at the same time be the Preparation Day, the day subsequent to the day for eating the Passover, and coming between that day and the Sabbath.

The truth is, on these topics of Jewish doings and ceremonies, our Greek editor is rather in a haze. Thus he talks of putting *a sponge on hyssop*[2] where the Synoptics talk of putting *a sponge on a cane.*[3] Hyssop is the Hebrew name for a plant something like our marjoram, with a close, bunching head of flowers, which can serve for a mop or a sponge. To talk of putting a sponge on hyssop is, therefore, like talking of putting a sponge on sponge. But our Greek editor knew the connexion of hyssop with 'the blood of sprinkling,' and did not clearly know what hyssop was; so he makes it do duty for the cane of the Synoptics. He has no profound dogmatic design to represent the death of Christ otherwise than as the Synoptics represented it; but his hold on Jewish details is less firm than theirs, and his use of Jewish details more capricious.

Again, the whole story of the soldier piercing the side of Jesus with his spear is said by Baur to be an invention of our Evangelist with the design of identifying Jesus with the Paschal Lamb (*a bone of him shall not be broken!*), and of mystically representing, by the effusion of water and blood, the apparition of the new powers of *Logos* and *Pneuma*. No other Evangelist mentions the incident, argues Baur. The quotation from Exodus[4] shows what was in the writer's mind; and Apollinaris of Hierapolis, taking

---

[1] John xix. 31.   [2] John xix. 29.

[3] Matth. xxvii. 48; Mark xv. 36.   [4] *Exod.* xii. 46.

part in the Paschal controversy soon after the year 170 of our era, marks the figurative character of the incident, identifies Christ with the Paschal Lamb slain on the 14th of Nisan, and the water and blood with *Logos* and *Pneuma*.[1]

5   Now, the argument, that if an important thing in the Fourth Gospel is not found in the Synoptics also, it must be a mere invention of our Evangelist's, is always pressed by Baur against our Evangelist only. But why is it more incredible that the piercing of the side, though given in the Fourth Gospel alone, should
10   yet really have been matter of tradition, than that the last words of Jesus: *Father, into thy hands I commend my spirit*, which are in Luke only,[2] should proceed, not from Luke's own invention, but from a real tradition? Nor has the quotation: *A bone of him shall not be broken*,[3] in all probability the reference alleged. Not
15   Exodus or the Paschal Lamb is probably here in our Evangelist's mind, but one of the Psalms on the preservation of the righteous: *Thou keepest all his bones, so that not one of them is broken*.[4] The form of the Greek verb corresponds with the form used in this passage from the Psalms,[5] not in the passage from
20   Exodus; which latter runs: 'Ye shall not break a bone thereof.' Besides, the Evangelist is heaping together instances of the fulfilment of predictions made by Prophet and Psalmist, and to suppose him suddenly turning to the Law and its precepts is not natural.

25   It is most probable that the side-piercing, followed by the appearance of something thought to resemble blood and water, was really, like our Evangelist's incidents in general, given by tradition. As early as Justin's time, nay, as early as the date of the

---

[1] ἡ ιδ′ τὸ ἀληθινὸν τοῦ κυρίου πάσχα, says Apollinaris; and presently after-
30   wards: ὁ ἐκχέας ἐκ τῆς πλευρᾶς αὐτοῦ τὰ δύο πάλιν καθάρσια, ὕδωρ καὶ αἷμα, λόγον καὶ πνεῦμα.

[2] Luke xxiii. 46.
[3] John xix. 36.
[4] *Psalm* xxxiv. 20.

35   [5] συντριβήσεται, and not συντρίψετε. Some later manuscripts of the New Testament show the pressure to connect John xix. 36, with *Exod.* xii. 46, rather than with *Ps.* xxxiv. 20. See in Sabatier, *Bibliorum Sacrorum Latinae Versiones Antiquae*, his note on the verse in John.

Apocalypse, the passage from Zechariah,[1] which in the Greek
Bible was mis-translated to mean: *They shall turn their eyes
towards me in exchange for their insulting*,[2] had been altered to
its true meaning: *They shall look on him whom they pierced*, as
it stands in the Fourth Gospel.[3] This proves, it is true, nothing   5
as to the antiquity of the Fourth Gospel. Passages of the Old
Testament which had a Messianic sense were early, as we have
said already, corrected to bring this sense out, if before they
obscured it. But it proves the antiquity of some tradition of a
piercing which the passage in Zechariah suited. If the piercing   10
had been merely that of the hands and feet by the nails, as given
by one of the Messianic Psalms, the Greek verb of that Psalm
would probably have been used for the prophecy of Zechariah
also; now, a different verb is taken.[4]

We do not at all deny that the identification of Christ's sacri-   15
fice with the Paschal sacrifice was a conception entertained by
our Evangelist, who speaks of *the Lamb of God that taketh away
the sin of the world*.[5] It was a conception familiar also to Paul,[6]
and a conception just and natural. What we deny is that it has
become with our Evangelist, any more than with Paul, the nu-   20
cleus of a theory for which he combines, arranges, invents. In
the Paschal controversy in the latter part of the second century,
the idea had become a nucleus of this kind. There is no doubt as
to what Apollinaris makes our Evangelist's words mean, any
more than there is doubt as to what Baur makes our Evangelist's   25
words mean. But, if our Evangelist had really meant what Apollinaris and Baur find in his words, he would have expressed himself somewhat as they do, he would have shown his intention as
they do. But he expresses himself so very differently! Therefore
we cannot credit him with the mystic meaning and design they   30
suppose for him. 'The 14th is the true Passover of the Lord,'
says Apollinaris; 'the great sacrifice, the Son of God in the lamb's

---

[1] Zechariah xii. 10.

[2] ἐπιβλέψονται πρός με ἀνθ' ὧν κατωρχήσαντο.

[3] John xix. 37. ὄψονται εἰς ὃν ἐξεκέντησαν.   35

[4] ἐξεκέντησαν instead of ὤρυξαν. See, in the Greek Bible, *Psalm* xxi. 16.

[5] John i. 29.   [6] See I *Cor.* v. 7.

stead.' Again: 'His holy side was pierced, and he shed back out
of his side the two cleansers, water and blood, *word and spirit*.'[1]
There is no uncertainty about the writer's intention, here; and if
our Evangelist had invented his Gospel to serve the same intention, that intention would have been as manifest. Probably, however, what the water and blood figured to our Evangelist's mind
was not *logos* and *pneuma* at all, but,—as the First Johannine
Epistle indicates, and as Theophylact interpreted,[2]—the union
of the human and divine natures in Christ. The water was a kind
of celestial ichor, the blood was the blood of mortal man.

8.

Tried fairly, then, and without a preconceived theory to warp
our criticism, the Fourth Gospel comes out no fancy-piece, but a
serious and invaluable document, full of incidents given by tradition and of genuine 'sayings of the Lord.'

Sayings are not to be rejected as inventions too easily. They
are not to be rejected because they seem strong and harsh, and
we do not like them. For example, there is the saying of Jesus
to the Jews about *their father the devil:* 'He was a manslayer
from the beginning.'[3] Its violence is objected to. But the Peratae
quote it in substance, and that is an external testimony to its genuineness; the invectives against the scribes and Pharisees in the
Synoptics make it a not improbable saying in itself.

Neither are sayings to be rejected because they are profound,
and over their hearers' heads; as, for example, the saying: 'Before
Abraham was, I am.'[4] Ever since man appeared upon earth, the
clearing and saving influences, which constitute the very being
of Jesus, have been present and at work amongst mankind; often
they have been latent, but they have been always there. And

---

[1] See the fragment of Apollinaris in Otto, *Corpus Apologetarum Christianorum Saeculi Secundi*, vol. ix, p. 487; with the notes in that work both
to the fragments of Apollinaris and to those of Melito of Sardis.

[2] In his Commentary on the Fourth Gospel. His words are: τὸ μὲν αἷμα
σύμβολον τοῦ εἶναι ἄνθρωπον τὸν σταυρωθέντα, τὸ δὲ ὕδωρ ὑπὲρ ἄνθρωπον, τοῦ
εἶναι θεόν.

[3] John viii. 44.   [4] John viii. 58.

always has this gentle and healing virtue saved, and always has it been sacrificed; therefore Jesus was well called by Apostle and Seer, and well too might he have called himself: *The Lamb slain from the foundation of the world*.[1] When he said to the Jews, 'Before Abraham was, I am,' Jesus did but pursue, as he pursued on so many other occasions also, his lofty treatment of the themes of life and immortality, while his hearers stuck fast in their materialistic notions of them and failed to follow his real meaning. In this there is nothing strange or incredible.

Nor, finally, are sayings to be rejected because they accommodate themselves to the materialism of the disciples. Only under these familiar figures of a bodily resurrection and a visible judgment-assize, of sitting on thrones to try the twelve tribes of Israel, of a heavenly Father's house with many mansions, could Jesus convey the ideas of happiness and recompense to these materialistically trained children of the new birth, whom yet to raise out of their materialism he for ever strove. If he was to say to them nothing but either what they could perfectly follow, or what they could not possibly misunderstand, he could not, as we have more than once said, have spoken to them at all. The only sayings we are called upon to reject are those which contradict the known manner and scope of Jesus, as his manner and scope are established for us by the mass of the evidence existing.

But we do not even require our reader to be so chary as we ourselves have been, about admitting sayings of the Fourth Gospel as genuine. If he finds himself disposed to receive as genuine some sayings of Jesus at which we hesitate, so be it. For we have sought merely to establish a minimum of what must be received, not a maximum; to show, that after the most free criticism has been fairly and strictly applied, and all deductions, to the very outside of what such a criticism can require, have been fully made, there is yet left an authentic residue comprising all the profoundest, most important, and most beautiful things in the Fourth Gospel.

We have found, however, in our study of the Fourth Gospel, nothing to shake our opinion about the canonical Gospels in

---

[1] *Revelation* xiii. 8; I Pet. i. 19, 20.

general and their history, but everything to confirm it. For at
least fifty years after its production the Fourth Gospel appears
not to have been in the settled state of Holy Scripture. There was
a long period during which this Gospel yielded more easily to
5   pressure, whether for altering its first contents or for interpolat-
ing additions to them, than it did afterwards. And so with our
other three Gospels also.

The rudiments of all four Gospels were probably in existence
and current by the year 120 of our era, at the very latest. As we
10   accept the evidence of Basileides, to show that the Fourth Gospel in some shape or other already existed in the early years of
the second century, so we accept the evidence of Marcion to
show the same thing for the Third Gospel, and that of Papias
for the Second and First.[1] True, the description given by Papias
15   does not accurately characterise our present Gospels either of
Mark or Matthew.[2] But the hypothesis of other works of theirs
being meant is extremely improbable, while it is not at all improbable that between the first appearance of a Gospel and its
admission to canonicity it should have undergone alterations.
20   The final admission of a Gospel to canonicity proves that it has
long been in men's hands, and long been attributed to a venerable
authority; that it has had time to gain their affections and to establish its superiority over competing accounts. To suppose as
the originals of our First and Second Gospels such collections by
25   Matthew and Mark as are described by Papias; to suppose as the
original of our Third Gospel (which in its prologue tells us itself that in its present form it is not the work of an eye-witness
but of a writer with two stages, even, between him and the eye-
witnesses[3]) a work by the same hand from whence proceed those
30   records in the first person which crop out in the Acts; to suppose
as the original of our Fourth Gospel data furnished by John at

---

[1] See Eusebius *Hist. Eccles.* iii. 39.

[2] Papias says of Matthew: τὰ λόγια συνεγράψατο. Of Mark he says that he
wrote, ἀκριβῶς, οὐ μέντοι τάξει, τὰ ὑπὸ τοῦ Χριστοῦ ἢ λεχθέντα ἢ πραχθέντα.
35   See the chapter of Eusebius just cited.

[3] The first stage is from the writer of our Third Gospel to the πολλοί,
whose διηγήσεις he criticises; the second from these πολλοί to the αὐτόπται,
the original eye-witnesses.

Ephesus,—is at once agreeable to what traditions we have, and also the most natural way of accounting for the facts which present themselves.

But to suppose that in our present Four Gospels we have the original works as they at first stood, that they were at their first birth formed into a Canon and thereby protected from altera- tion, is contrary both to the direct evidence we have and to prob- ability. The descriptions of Papias do not, as we have said, at all well describe our present Gospels of St. Matthew and St. Mark. And we see that our Gospels had gradually to establish them- selves, because before the time of Irenaeus they are hardly ever quoted as Scripture, but after his time constantly. We know, too, that there were several other Gospels besides these, and that works not in our present Canon enjoyed such favour among Christians of the second century that even Irenaeus quotes the *Pastor* of Hermas as 'Scripture,'[1] and a so-called Gospel of Peter was publicly read in church with episcopal sanction.[2] We know, above all, that there is no instance,—not one,—before the age of Irenaeus and the last quarter of the second century, of even two or three consecutive verses being anywhere quoted just as we now read them in our Gospels.

Nay, so little were our Gospels documents sacred from the very first against all change and interpolation, that the habit of interpolation went on long after the Canon was formed, and the difference between the received text and that of the earliest manuscripts shows it. If the Vatican and Sinaitic manuscripts of the Fourth Gospel contain neither the story of the woman taken in adultery nor the account of the angel troubling the water in the pool of Bethesda; if, where the later manuscripts which our received text follows make Peter say: 'Thou art the Christ, the Son of the living God,' the Vatican and Sinaitic make him

---

[1] And in remarkably emphatic language: καλῶς οὖν εἶπεν ἡ γραφὴ ἡ λέγ- ουσα, κ. τ. λ. The words of Irenaeus are quoted by Eusebius *Hist. Eccles.* v. 8.

[2] The bishop was Serapio, Bishop of Antioch from A.D. 191 to 213; the church was that of Rhossus in Cilicia. Serapio discovered afterwards that there was Docetism in the gospel of which he had inadvertently permitted the public reading. See Eusebius *Hist. Eccles.* vi. 12.

say merely: 'Thou art the holy one of God;'[1] and if this sort of
change could befall a Gospel-text between the fourth century
and the tenth, while it was Holy Scripture beyond question; how
strong must have been the original bent to additions and interpolations, and how much more must the text have been exposed
to them in its earlier and less closely watched period, when the
settled stamp of Holy Scripture it as yet had not!

To suppose, therefore, that we have in our Gospels documents
which can stand as the very original, strictly drawn up, strictly
authenticated and strictly preserved depositions of eye-witnesses,
is absurd. They arose not in the sort of world where depositions
are taken, nor in the sort of world where manuscripts are
guarded. They arose, and they passed many years, in the immense, underground, obscure, fluctuating world of the common
people. Probably even neighbours and contemporaries never
knew, or cared to know, quite accurately, the literary history of
a document like one of our Gospels; and beyond question the
knowledge, if it ever existed, was soon lost irrecoverably. The
important inference to be drawn from this is, that the internal
evidence must, in sayings and doings of Jesus which are given us
in our Gospels, be considered with great care. Jesus was far over
the heads of his reporters; he is not to be held responsible for
their notions, or for all that they may make him do or say. And
the way in which our Gospels arose and grew up was such, that
pressure upon the stock of data furnished by the original eye-
witnesses, and additions to this stock, and insertions, were extremely natural and extremely easy.[2]

[1] John vi. 69.

[2] Nothing can be more vain, therefore, than attempts to *reconcile* our
Four Gospels with one another, to make one exact, concordant and trustworthy history out of them. Griesbach, to whom the improvement of the
New Testament text owes so much, has, in some remarks directed simply
at the chronology of the Gospels, passed an excellent general criticism on
all such attempts. He says: 'Valde dubito, an ex Evangelistarum libellis har-
monica componi possit narratio: quid enim, si nullus Evangelistarum ordi-
nem temporis accurate ubique secutus est; et si sufficientia non adsunt in-
dicia e quibus constare possit quisnam et quibusnam in locis a chronologico
ordine recesserit? Atque in hac me esse haeresi fateor.'

In each of the chief Epistles of St. Paul, we have, much more indubitably than in any other New Testament documents, the real original production of the assumed author. Letters like his, with the strong stamp of the author's individuality, and following in general a continuous argument, lend themselves to additions and interpolations far less readily than works like the Gospels. We know, however, that forged epistles, covering themselves with the authority of apostolic names, were early current; and here too, therefore, the internal evidence must have great weight. The exact literary history of our documents is irrecoverable; and in the absence of it we cannot but have recourse to the test of internal evidence. But we ought, also, to resign ourselves to be ignorant of much, we ought to be sparing of vigorous and rigorous theories, to allow something to tradition, to dismiss the notion of sheer, designed forgery and imposture, to admit that for each and every Epistle, perhaps, in our Canon of the New Testament, there is something of a genuine basis.

Striking phrases from apostolic letters or addresses were likely to survive and to float in men's memories, though the context had been lost. Here was the hint and at the same time the defence for an imitator, speaking in an Apostle's name, and, as he imagined, in that Apostle's sense. Everything is against the genuineness of the Second Petrine Epistle as a whole. But things like the phrase: 'Give diligence to make your calling and election sure,' in the first chapter,[1] and the passage beginning at the eighth verse of the third chapter and ending with the words: 'Nevertheless we, according to his promise, look for new heavens and a new earth, wherein dwelleth righteousness,' may well have been Peter's, and their incorporation would have, probably, quite served to justify the Epistler both in his own eyes and in those of his public.

It is easy to be too sweepingly negative in these matters; easy, also, to think we can know more about them, and more certainly, than we can. To me it appears very rash to pronounce confidently against the first Johannine Epistle being St. John's. Cer-

---

[1] II Pet. i. 10.

tainly there is the difficulty of a Galilean fisherman learning to
write Greek after the age of fifty; but, with this exception, almost all the difficulties are absent which make it so hard to think
that St. John can have written the Fourth Gospel. The style is
5 not flowing and articulated; the sentences come like minute-
guns, as they would drop from a natural Hebrew. The writer
moves, indeed, amidst that order of religious ideas which meets
us in the Fourth Gospel, and which was that of the Greek world
wherein he found himself. He moves amongst these new ideas,
10 however, not with the practised facility of the Evangelist, but
with something of helplessness, although the depth and serene
beauty of his spirit give to all he says an infinite impressiveness
and charm. Save one ambiguous expression of Eusebius,[1] there
is nothing to indicate that John's authorship of the First Epistle
15 was in the early Church ever questioned. Papias used the Epistle,[2]
and it may fairly be inferred from what Epiphanius says[3] that
even the Alogi received it, although they rejected both the
Fourth Gospel and the Apocalypse.

Of the authorship of the Apocalypse all we can safely assert is
20 what we learn from the book itself,—that the author was named
John, and wrote in Asia. It was natural that this John in Asia, the
recipient of so weighty a revelation, should be identified with
the Apostle John; and as early as the middle of the second century we find Justin Martyr thus identifying him.[4] But there was
25 so little sureness about the matter, that for Eusebius, in the
fourth century, the Apocalypse was no more than a disputed
and doubtful book of Scripture, which a Christian might receive
or not as he thought good. And to us it seems impossible to make

[1] *Hist. Eccles.* vi. 14. μηδὲ τὰς ἀντιλεγομένας παρελθών, τὴν Ἰούδα λέγω καὶ
30 τὰς λοιπὰς καθολικὰς ἐπιστολάς. The word λοιπάς is not certain, and even if
it were, we could not be sure from the sentence, Eusebius being the sort
of writer he is, that the First Johannine Epistle was disputed, or that Eusebius meant to say that it was.

[2] *Hist. Eccles.* iii. 39.

35 [3] *Haer.* LI. xxxiv. Epiphanius conjectures that the Alogi *must* have rejected the Epistles because they rejected the Gospel and the Apocalypse.
If they *had* rejected the First Epistle, he would almost certainly have heard
of it.

[4] *Dialogus cum Tryphone*, cap. 81.

out more than that the Apocalypse was written by a John, but by what John there is nothing to show.[1]

[1] M. Renan's confident conclusion that the author was the Apostle John is one of the few points in his admirable criticism of the Apocalypse where he fails to carry us with him. His only serious argument is, that no one but an Apostle would have ventured to speak so authoritatively. But surely the recipient of this grand revelation would, as such, have felt himself entitled to be authoritative to any extent in delivering it.

Conclusion

The Canon of the New Testament, then, is not what popular religion supposes; although, on the other hand, its documents are in some quarters the object of far too aggressive and sweeping negations. The most fruitful result to be gained from a sane criti-
5 cism of the Canon is, that by satisfying oneself how the Gospel-records grew up, one is enabled the better to account for much that puzzles us in the representation of Jesus,—of his words more especially. There were facilities for addition and interpolation, for adding touches to what the original accounts made Jesus
10 do, for amplifying, above all, what they made Jesus say. Evidence such as apologists always imagine themselves to be using when they appeal to the Gospels,—the pure, first-hand, well-authenticated evidence of discriminative eye-witnesses,—our Gospels are not.
15 Such evidence is, indeed, remarkably wanting for the whole miraculous side in the doings recorded of Jesus. Sometimes we seem to be near getting such evidence, but it vanishes. Jerome tells us that Quadratus, in the second century, declared that there were yet living in his time persons who had beheld with their
20 own eyes Jesus raise the dead to life, and that he himself had seen them and spoken with them. It happens that the declaration of Quadratus is preserved by Eusebius, in whose History Jerome probably read it. Quadratus undoubtedly says that in his time there were yet alive those who had witnessed the raising of the
25 dead by Jesus; but the important addition which alone takes this statement out of the category of hearsay, and makes it personal evidence,—the addition that these alleged witnesses he himself

had seen and known,—Quadratus does not make. The addition is merely a rhetorical flourish of Jerome's.[1]

No doubt this is so; yet the importance of it all is greatly diminished by one consideration. *If we had the original reports of the eye-witnesses, we should still have reports not essentially differing, probably, from those which we now use.* Certain additions which improved a miraculous story as it grew, certain interpolations which belong to the ideas and circumstances of a later age, would be absent. But we should most likely not have a miracle the less, and we should certainly find a similar misapprehension of Jesus and of what he intended. The people who saw Jesus were as certain to seek for miracles, and to find them, as the people who lived a generation or two later, or as the people who resort to Lourdes or to La Salette now. And this preoccupation with miracles was sure to warp their understanding of Jesus, and their report of his sayings and doings. The recurrence, so much talked of and recommended, either to the Apostles, or to the first three centuries, for the pure rule of faith and the genuine doctrine of Jesus, is in truth therefore, however natural an expedient, an utterly futile one. There were indeed, as we have shown in *Literature and Dogma*, certain prominent points in the teaching of Jesus which his immediate followers had not yet lost sight of, and which fell more out of view afterwards. But the pure and genuine work and doctrine of Jesus neither his immediate followers, nor those whom they instructed, could seize; so immured were they in the ideas of their time and in the belief of the miraculous, so immeasurably was Jesus above them.

2.

But our opponents say: 'Everything turns upon the question whether miracles do or did really happen; and you abstain from all attempt to prove their impossibility, you simply assume that they never happen.' And this, which our opponents say, is true,

---

[1] See Eusebius *Hist. Eccles.* iv. 3; and Routh, *Reliquiae Sacrae*, vol. i, pp. 71, 74. Routh quotes Jerome, and points out his exaggeration.

and we have repeatedly admitted it. At the end of this investigation we admit it once more, and lay stress upon it. That miracles *cannot* happen we do not attempt to prove; the demonstration is too ambitious. That they *do not* happen,—that what are called
5 miracles are not what the believers in them fancy, but have a natural history of which we can follow the course,—the slow action of experience, we say, more and more shows; and shows, too, that there is no exception to be made in favour of the Bible-miracles.
10 Epiphanius tells us, that at each anniversary of the miracle of Cana, the water of the springs of Cibyra in Caria and Gerasa in Arabia was changed into wine; that he himself had drunk of the transformed water of Cibyra, and his brothers of that of Gerasa.[1] Fifty years ago, a plain Englishman would have had no difficulty
15 in thinking that the Cana miracle was true, and the other two miracles were fables. He is now irresistibly led to class all these occurrences in one category as unsubstantial tales of marvel. Scales seem to have fallen from his eyes in regard to miracles; and if he is still to hold fast his Christianity, it must no longer depend
20 upon them.

It was not to discredit miracles that *Literature and Dogma* was written, but because miracles are so widely and deeply discredited already. And it is lost labour, we repeat, to be arguing for or against them. Mankind did not originally accept miracles
25 because it had formal proof of them, but because its imperfect experience inclined it to them. Nor will mankind now drop miracles because it has formal proof against them, but because its more complete experience detaches it from them. The final result was inevitable, as soon as ever miracles began to embarrass people,
30 began to be relegated,—especially the greater miracles,—to a certain limited period long ago past and over. Irenaeus says, that people in his time had arisen from the dead, 'and abode with us a good number of years.'[2] One of his commentators, embarrassed by such stupendous miracles occurring outside of the Bible,

35 [1] Epiphanius *Haer.* LI. xxx.
[2] See Irenaeus, *Adv. Haer.*, lib. II, cap. xxxii. 4; with the note on the passage in Stieren's edition.

makes an attempt to explain away this remarkable allegation; but the most recent editor of Irenaeus points out, with truth, that the attempt is vain. Irenaeus was as sure to want and to find miracles as the Bible-writers were. And sooner or later mankind was sure to see how universally and easily stories like this of Irenaeus arose, and that they arose with the Bible-writers just as they arose with Irenaeus, and are not a whit more solid coming from them than from him.

A Catholic imagines that he gets over the difficulty by believing, or professing to believe, the miracles of Irenaeus and Epiphanius, as well as those of the Bible-writers. But for him, too, even for him, the *Zeit-Geist* or Time-Spirit is gradually becoming too strong. As we may say in general, that, although an educated Protestant may manage to retain for his own lifetime the belief in miracles in which he has been brought up, yet his children will lose it; so to an educated Catholic we may say, putting the change only a little farther off, that (unless some unforeseen deluge should overwhelm European civilisation, leaving everything to be begun anew) his grandchildren will lose it. They will lose it insensibly, as the eighteenth century saw the gradual extinction, among the educated classes, of that belief in witchcraft which in the century previous a man like Sir Matthew Hale could affirm to have the authority of Scripture and of the wisdom of all nations,—spoke of, in short, just as many religious people speak of miracles now. Witchcraft is but one department of the miraculous; and it was comparatively easy, no doubt, to abandon one department, when men had all the rest of the region to fall back upon. Nevertheless the forces of experience, which have prevailed against witchcraft, will inevitably prevail also against miracles at large, and that by the mere progress of time.

The charge of presumption, and of setting oneself up above all the great men of past days, above 'the wisdom of all nations,' which is often brought against those who pronounce the old view of our religion to be untenable, springs out of a failure to perceive how little the abandonment of certain long-current beliefs depends upon a man's own will, or even upon his sum of powers, natural or acquired. Sir Matthew Hale was not inferior in force of mind to a modern Chief Justice because he believed in

witchcraft. Nay, the more enlightened modern, who drops errors of his forefathers by help of that mass of experience which his forefathers aided in accumulating, may often be, according to the well-known saying, 'a dwarf on the giant's shoulders.' His merits
5   may be small compared with those of the giant. Perhaps his only merit is, that he has had the good sense to get up on the giant's shoulders, instead of trotting contentedly along in his shadow. Yet even this, surely, is something.

3.

We have to renounce impossible attempts to receive the leg-
10 endary and miraculous matter of Scripture as grave historical and scientific fact. We have to accustom ourselves to regard henceforth all this part as poetry and legend. In the Old Testament, as an immense poetry growing round and investing an immortal truth, 'the secret of the Eternal:'[1] *Righteousness is salva-*
15 *tion.* In the New, as an immense poetry growing round and investing an immortal truth, the secret of Jesus: *He that will save his life shall lose it, he that will lose his life shall save it.*

The best friends of mankind are those who can lead it to feel animation and hope in presence of the religious prospect thus
20 profoundly transformed. The way to effect this is by bringing men to see that our religion, in this altered view of it, does but at last become again that religion which Jesus Christ really endeavoured to found, and of which the truth and grandeur are indestructible. We should do Christians generally a great injus-
25 tice, if we thought that the entire force of their Christianity lay in the fascination and subjugation of their spirits by the miracles which they suppose Jesus to have worked, or by the materialistic promises of heaven which they suppose him to have offered. Far more does the vital force of their Christianity lie in the boundless
30 confidence, consolation, and attachment, which the whole being and discourse of Jesus inspire. Whatever Jesus, then, himself thought sufficient, Christians too may bring themselves to accept with good courage as enough for them. What Jesus himself dis-

[1] *Psalm* xxv. 14.

missed as chimerical, Christians too may bring themselves to put aside without dismay.

The central aim of Jesus was to transform for every religious soul the popular Messias-ideal of his time, the Jewish people's ideal of happiness and salvation; to disengage religion, one may say, from the materialism of the Book of Daniel. Fifty years had not gone by after his death, when the Apocalypse replunged religion in this materialism; where, indeed, it was from the first manifest that replunged, by the followers of Jesus, religion must be. It *was* replunged there, but with an addition of inestimable value and of incalculable working,—the figure and influence of Jesus. Slowly this influence emerges, transforms the turbid elements amid which it was thrown, brings back the imperishable ideal of its author. To the mind of Jesus, his own 'resurrection' after a short sojourn in the grave was the victory of his cause after his death and at the price of his death. His disciples materialised his resurrection, and their version of the matter falls day by day to ruin. But no ruin or contradiction befalls the version of Jesus himself. He *has* risen, his cause has conquered; the course of events continually attests his resurrection and victory. The manifest unsoundness of popular Christianity inclines at present many persons to throw doubts on the truth and permanence of Christianity in general. Creeds are discredited, religion is proclaimed to be in danger, the pious quake, the world laughs. Nevertheless, *the prince of this world is judged;*[1] the victory of Jesus is won and sure. Conscience and self-renouncement, the method and the secret of Jesus, are set up as a leaven in the world, nevermore to cease working until the world is leavened. That this is so, that the resurrection and re-emergent life of Jesus are in this sense undeniable, and that in this sense Jesus himself predicted them, may in time, surely, encourage Christians to lay hold on this sense as Jesus did.

So, too, with the hope of immortality. Our common materialistic notions about the resurrection of the body and the world to come are, no doubt, natural and attractive to ordinary human nature. But they are in direct conflict with the new and loftier

---

[1] John xvi. 11.

conceptions of life and death which Jesus himself strove to establish. His secret, *He that will save his life shall lose it, he that will lose his life shall save it*, is of universal application. It judges, not only the life to which men cling here, but just as much the life we love to promise to ourselves in the New Jerusalem. The immortality propounded by Jesus must be looked for elsewhere than in the materialistic aspirations of our popular religion. *He lived in the eternal order, and the eternal order never dies;*—this, if we may try to formulate in one sentence the result of the sayings of Jesus about life and death, is the sense in which, according to him, we can rightly conceive of the righteous man as immortal, and aspire to be immortal ourselves. And this conception we shall find to stand us in good stead when the popular materialistic version of our future life fails us. So that here again, too, the version which, unfamiliar and novel as it may now be to us, has the merit of standing fast and holding good while other versions break down, is at the same time the version of Jesus.

People talk scornfully of 'a sublimated Christianity,' as if the Christianity of Jesus Christ himself had been a materialistic fairy-tale like that of the Salvation Army or of Messrs. Moody and Sankey. On the contrary, insensibly to lift us out of all this sort of materialism was Jesus Christ's perpetual endeavour. His parable of the king, who made a marriage for his son, ends with the episode of the guest who had not on a wedding-garment, and was therefore cast out.[1] And here, as usual, the Tübingen critics detect *tendence*. They see in the episode a deliberate invention of the Evangelist; a stroke of Jewish particularism, indemnifying itself for having had to relate that salvation was preached in the highways. We have disagreed often with the Tübingen critics, and we shall venture finally to disagree with them here. We receive the episode as genuine; but what did Jesus mean by it? Shall we not do well in thinking, that he, whose lucid insight was so incomparable, and who indicated so much which was to be seized not by the present but by the future, here marked and meant to indicate, although but incidentally and in passing, the profound, the utter insufficiency of popular religion? Through the

---

[1] Matth. xxii. 1–14.

turbid phase of popular religion his religion had to pass. Good and bad it was to bear along with it; the gross and ignorant were to be swept in by wholesale from the highways; *the wedding was to be furnished with guests*. On this wise must Christianity needs develop itself, and the necessary law of its development was to be accepted. Vain to be too nice about the unpreparedness of the guests in general, about their inevitable misuse of the favours which they were admitted to enjoy! What must have been the end of such a fastidious scrutiny? To turn them all out into the highways again! But the king's design was, that *the wedding should be furnished with guests*. So the guests shall all stay and fall to;—popular Christianity is founded. But presently, almost as if by accident, a guest even more unprepared and gross than the common, a guest 'not having on a wedding-garment,' comes under the king's eye, and is ejected. Only one is noted for decisive ejection; but ah! how many of even the remaining guests are as really unapt to seize and follow God's designs for them as he! *Many are called, few chosen*.

The conspicuous delinquent is sentenced to be bound hand and foot, and taken away, and cast into outer darkness. In the severity of this sentence, Jesus marks how fatally those who are gathered to his feast may fail to know him. The misapprehending and materialising of his religion, the long and turbid stage of popular Christianity, was, however, inevitable. But to give light and impulsion to future times, Jesus stamps this Christianity, even from the very moment of its birth, as, though inevitable, not worthy of its name; as ignorant and transient, and requiring all who would be truly children of the kingdom to rise beyond it.

Preface

[In reading through the following [i.e., preceding] chapters, I
see that the faults, as I think them, of German critics of the Bible
are marked with an emphasis which renders necessary some acknowledgment of the other, the meritorious, side in those critics,
5   and of the much gratitude due to them. Their criticism, both
negative and constructive, appears to me to be often extremely
fanciful and untrustworthy. But in collecting, editing, and illustrating the original documents for the history of Christianity,
those critics now perform for the benefit of learning an honour-
10 able and extremely useful labour, once discharged by Paris, Oxford, and Cambridge, but discharged by them no longer;—perform it with modern resources, and for the most part admirably.
Some of them are men of great ability. Ferdinand Christian Baur,
whose theories respecting the Fourth Gospel are controverted in
15 the following pages, was a man of pre-eminent ability. His exegesis is often full of instruction and of light. Whoever wishes to
be convinced of it has only to turn to his remarks on the phrase
poor in spirit,[1] or to his exposition of the parable of the unjust
steward.[2] Nevertheless Baur is, on the whole, an unsafe guide,
20 for a reason which makes the generality of critics of the Bible,
in the Protestant faculties of theology in Germany, unsafe guides.
These professors are under strong temptations to produce new
theories in Biblical criticism, theories marked by vigour and rigour; and for this purpose to assume that things can be known
25 which cannot, to treat possibilities as if they were certainties, to
make symmetry where one does not find it, and so to land both
the teacher, and the learner who trusts to him, in the most fanci-

---

[1] *Geschichte der christlichen Kirche*, vol. i. p. 26.
[2] *Kritische Untersuchungen über die kanonischen Evangelien*, p. 450.

ful and unsound conclusions. There are few who do not succumb to their temptations, and Baur, I think, has succumbed to
them.

[Even while acknowledging the learning, talents, and services
of these critics, I insist upon their radical faults; because, as our
traditional theology breaks up, German criticism of the Bible is
likely to be studied here more and more, and to the untrained
reader its vigorous and rigorous theories are, in my opinion, a
real danger. They impose upon him by their boldness and
novelty. To his practical hold on the Bible they conduce nothing,
but rather divert from it; and yet they are often really farther
from the truth, all the while, than even the traditional view
which they profess to annihilate.

[The alleged bitter hatred of St. Peter and the other *pillar-*
apostles against St. Paul, and St. Paul's reciprocation of it, is a case
in point. This hatred is supposed to have filled the first years of
the Christian Church, and to give the clue to its history. The invectives in the Apocalypse against Balaam and his followers are
said to be aimed at Paul and Pauline Christianity. The Simon
Magus of the pseudo-Clementine Homilies is taken to be Paul,
and Peter's unwearying war against Simon Magus and his false
doctrine represents Peter's war against Paul.[1] The Acts, finally,
are a late work designed to wipe out the memory of this hatred,
and to invent a harmony between Paul and the pillar-apostles
which never existed. Now, it is easy to dress up this theory so as
to make it look plausible, but I entirely disbelieve its truth. To its
vigorous and rigorous inventors the consideration that the nearness of the pillar-apostles to Jesus, and that the religious greatness of St. Paul, were good for very little if they could not so
much as prevent a hatred of this kind, will probably appear quite
insignificant; with me it has, I confess, serious weight. It would
need plain and strong facts to make me accept, in despite of this
consideration, the Tübingen theory. But no such facts are forth-
coming.

[The identification of the Balaam of the Apocalypse with Paul

[1] Paul is, in fact, 'der Apostate, der Irrlehrer, dessen als samaritanische
Ketzerei bezeichnetes falsches Evangelium höchst wahrscheinlich die Ent-
stehung der ganzen Sage von dem Magier Simon veranlasst hat.'—Baur,
Lehrbuch der christlichen Dogmengeschichte, p. 65.

requires us first to assume that the Tübingen theory is true. Now,
the evidence of Paul's own letters is against the theory. True,
there was difference between him and the older Apostles respecting the obligation of the Jewish law. They were narrower and
5   more timid than he was, and he tells us of his having once at
Antioch 'withstood Peter to the face because he was to be
blamed.' But he tells us, also, of his having come to a satisfactory
arrangement with the pillar-apostles, and of their having 'extended to him the right hand of fellowship.' The hardest word
10 he has for them is to call them 'apostles exceedingly.'[1] On the
other hand, quite distinct from the pillar-apostles whose action
it sought to force, is the real Judaising party whom Paul stigmatised as 'false brethren,' and to whom he 'will not give place by
subjection, no, not for an hour.'

15   [Again, of real antinomianism in morals among his Gentile
converts Paul clearly saw the danger and vehemently rebuked
the symptoms. He discountenanced, even, all unnecessary dis-
plays of liberalism and of superiority to prejudice, which might
offend and do harm. Now, the Peter of the pseudo-Clementine
20 Homilies controverts nothing that can be said to be Pauline. But
he attacks either Gnostic heresies, or else that antinomianism in
morals which is well known to have been rife in some of the
Gnostic sects. True, he represents his profane opponents as
questioning his authority, and as *withstanding* him; and the lan-
25 guage which he attributes to them is undoubtedly an adaptation
of Paul's language in the Epistle to the Galatians. This is the
whole and sole foundation of positive proof for the alleged
hatred between Peter and Paul. But what could be more natural,
than that the antinomian enemies of strictness of every kind
30 should have possessed themselves of phrases of Paul, the great liberal, and above all should have possessed themselves of his famous
rebuke of the narrower and more timid Peter, and turned it
against whoever blamed and restrained them; and that such an
employment and such employers of Paul's language are what the
35 Peter of the Homilies has in view? For my part, I feel convinced that this is the true explanation, and that the plausible

---

[1] τῶν ὑπερλίαν ἀποστόλων. II *Cor*. xi. 5, and xii. 11.

theory of the bitter and persistent hatred between St. Peter and St. Paul is quite erroneous. But if erroneous it is, how grave is the error! and in how serious a misconception of the beginnings of Christianity does it involve us! This must be my defence, if I appear to have dwelt too much on the untrustworthiness of the authors of this and similar theories, not enough on their learning and acuteness.

[In revising the present volume, the suspicion and alarm which its contents, like those of its predecessor, will in some quarters excite, could not but be present to my mind. I hope, however, that I have at last made my aim clear, even to the most suspicious. Some of the comments on *Literature and Dogma* did, I own, surprise me, in spite of a tolerably long experience of men's propensity to mistake things. Again and again I was reproached with having done, in that book, just what I had formerly blamed the Bishop of Natal for doing. But] *Literature and Dogma* had altogether for its object, and so too has the present work,—a work which clears, develops and defends the positions taken in *Literature and Dogma*,—to show the truth and necessity of Christianity, and also its charm for the heart, mind, and imagination of man, even though the preternatural, which is now its popular sanction, should have to be given up. To show this, is the end for which both books were written.

For the power of Christianity has been in the immense emotion which it has excited; in its engaging, for the government of man's conduct, the mighty forces of love, reverence, gratitude, hope, pity, and awe,—all that host of allies which Wordsworth includes under the one name of *imagination*, when he says that in the uprooting of old thoughts and old rules we must still always ask:—

> Survives *imagination*, to the change
> Superior? Help to virtue does she give?
> If not, O mortals, better cease to live!

Popular Christianity has enjoyed abundantly and with profit this help from the imagination to virtue and conduct. I have always thought, therefore, that merely to destroy the illusions of

popular Christianity was indefensible. Time, besides, was sure to
do it; but when it is done, the whole work of again cementing
the alliance between the imagination and conduct remains to be
effected. To those who effect nothing for the new alliance but
only dissolve the old, we take once more our text from Wordsworth, and we say:—

> Why with such earnest pains dost thou provoke
> The years to bring the inevitable yoke,
> Thus blindly with man's blessedness at strife?
> Full soon his soul will have its earthly freight;—

soon enough will the illusions which charmed and aided man's
inexperience be gone; what have you to give him in the place of
them?

[Dr. Colenso had nothing, and hence our dissatisfaction with
his work. But undoubtedly it is not easy to re-unite man's imagination with his virtue and conduct, when the tie between them
has been once broken. And therefore there will always be many
well-meaning people who say: Why meddle with religion at
all? why run the risk of breaking a tie which it is so hard to join
again? And the risk is not to be run lightly, and one is not always
to attack people's illusions about religion merely because illusions they are. But] at the present moment two things about the
Christian religion must surely be clear to anybody with eyes in
his head. One is, that men cannot do without it; the other, that
they cannot do with it as it is.

[And first, that they cannot do without it is shown by the certainty,—as Baur, with whom I am glad to agree at last, well says,
—by the certainty with which 'the predominance of an all-
denying unbelief does but call forth a keener craving for belief.'[1]
Nowhere did the old Christian belief seem to be so reasoned
down, laughed out of court, exploded and extinct as in France;
and in no country do we witness such a recrudescence, as liberals would say, of superstition, so formidable a clerical reaction.
In England the old Christian belief has never ceased to be a

---

[1] 'Die Herrschaft eines alles verneinenden Unglaubens ruft nur ein um
so heisseres Glaubensverlangen hervor.'

mighty power. Yet even here the voice of modern liberalism has of late more and more been raised to decry it and to foretell its speedy extinction; and the astonishing popularity of the American revivalists is the answer. Why is this so?

[It is so, because throughout the world there is a growing feel- 5
ing, that, whatever may have been amiss with the old religion, modern liberalism, though it confidently professed to have per- fect and sufficient substitutes for it, has not; and though it prom- ised to make the world get on without it, cannot. Even French- men are losing their long cherished belief in the gospel of the 10
rights of man and the ideas of 1789 as a substitute for it. Indeed, one has only to keep one's head clear and one's judgment impar- tial, to see that however poorly men may have got on when their governing idea was: *The fear of the Lord is the beginning of wisdom*, they can get on even less by the governing idea that *all* 15
men are born naturally free and equal. The barrenness and insuf- ficiency of the revolutionary formulas are visible to common sense as they lose the gloss of novelty. Either they are vague;— as when Michelet, for instance, talks of 'my idea, and Proud- hon's, of Justice, of Revolution, an idea the opposite of Chris- 20
tianity;' where the term *Christianity* has no doubt a plain enough meaning for us, but the terms *Justice* and *Revolution*, its sup- posed opposites, have not. Or if the formula is explained, it turns out to be something jejune, after all, which is meant;—as when Michelet tells us what Justice, the *pensée du siècle*, the thought 25
of the Age of Revolution, the opposite of Christianity is, and it is this: 'Unity of administration, gradual suppression of privilege, equal taxation.' But this is politics, it is merely what we call *ma- chinery;* and the 'thought of the age,' the idea of Justice and Revolution, the idea which is the opposite of Christianity, must 30
give us something more than this, or to replace Christianity it is quite ludicrously insufficient.

[All this most people are now beginning to see clearly enough; hence the reaction on which secularists so little counted. But indeed it is much more surprising that they should ever have 35
reckoned that their ideas of revolution and liberty, and of the spread of physical science dispelling a host of illusions, could at all do for the world what Christianity had done for it and serve

as a substitute for Christianity, than that they should now find
themselves to be out in their reckoning. For] Christianity enabled, or professed to enable, mankind to deal with personal conduct,—with an immense matter, at least three-fourths of human
5   life. And it seems strange that people should even imagine, either
that men will not demand something enabling them to do this,
or that the spread of physical science, and knowing that not the
sky moves but the earth, can in any way do it. And so the Secularists find themselves at fault in their calculations; and the best
10 scientific specialists are forward to confess, what is evident
enough, both that religion must and will have its claims attended to, and that physics and religion have, as Joubert says,
absolutely nothing to do with one another. Charlatans may
bluster; but, speaking in defence of the genuine men of science,
15 M. Réville declares of them that 'they willingly recognise the
legitimateness of the religious element in the human spirit, but
they say that to provide the satisfaction due to it is not a business
with which they are competent to deal.'[1]

It is true, all men of science are not thus sober-minded. Thus
20 we find a brilliant professor of mathematics, too early lost to us,
launching invectives which, if they are just, would prove either
that no religion at all has any right to mankind's regard, or that
the Christian religion, at all events, has none. Professor Clifford
calls Christianity 'that awful plague which has destroyed two
25 civilisations and but barely failed to slay such promise of good
as is now struggling to live amongst men.' He warns his fellow
men against showing any tenderness to 'the slender remnant of
a system which has made its red mark on history and still lives to
threaten mankind.' 'The grotesque forms of its intellectual be-
30 lief,' he sternly adds, by way of finish, 'have survived the discredit of its moral teaching.'

But these are merely the crackling fireworks of youthful para-
dox. One reads it all, half sighing, half smiling, as the declama-
tion of a clever and confident youth, with the hopeless inexpe-
35 rience, irredeemable by any cleverness, of his age. Only when

[1] Ils reconnaissent volontiers la légitimité de l'élément religieux de
l'esprit humain; mais ils disent qu'il ne rentre pas dans leur compétence de
lui fournir les satisfactions qu'il réclame.

one is young and headstrong can one thus prefer bravado to experience, can one stand by the Sea of Time, and instead of listening to the solemn and rhythmical beat of its waves, choose to fill the air with one's own whoopings to start the echo. But the mass of plain people hear such talk with impatient indignation, and flock all the more eagerly to Messrs. Moody and Sankey. They feel that the brilliant freethinker and revolutionist talks about their religion and yet is all abroad in it, does not know either that or the great facts of human life; and they go to those who know them better. And the plain people are not wrong. Compared with Professor Clifford, Messrs. Moody and Sankey are masters of the philosophy of history. Men are not mistaken in thinking that Christianity has done them good, in loving it, in wishing to listen to those who will talk to them about what they love, and will talk of it with admiration and gratitude, not contempt and hatred. Christianity is truly, as I have somewhere called it, 'the greatest and happiest stroke ever yet made for human perfection.' Men do not err, they are on firm ground of experience, when they say that they have practically found Christianity to be something incomparably beneficent. Where they err, is in their way of accounting for this, and of assigning its causes.

And here we reach our second point: that men cannot do with Christianity as it is. Something true and beneficent they have got hold of in it, they know; and they want to rely upon this, and to use it. But what men rely upon and use, they seek to give them-selves account of, they seek to make clear its right to be relied upon and used. Now, the old ways of accounting for Christian-ity, of establishing the ground of its claims upon us, no longer serve as they once did. Men's experience widens, they get to know the world better, to know the mental history of mankind better; they distinguish more clearly between history and legend, they grow more shy of recourse to the preternatural. I have quoted in the present volume the saying of Pascal: 'In good truth, the world is getting mistrustful, and does not believe things unless they are evident to it.'[1] But no one can more set this consid-

---

[1] En vérité, le monde devient méfiant, et ne croit les choses que quand il les voit.

eration at defiance than does Pascal himself in his account of
Christianity. Gleams of astonishing insight he has, as well as
bursts of unsurpassable eloquence; there is no writer on the
Christian religion who more than Pascal deserves a close study.
5 But the basis of his whole system is the acceptance, as positive history and literal matter of fact, of the story of Adam's fall. The
historical difficulty of taking this legend seriously, for us so decisive, Pascal hardly saw at all; but he saw plenty of other difficulty. Nothing, he observes, can be 'more contrary to the rules
10 of our miserable justice than to damn eternally a child born now
for a crime committed six thousand years before he came into
being.' Nevertheless Pascal accepts the story, because 'without
this mystery, the most incomprehensible of all mysteries, we are
incomprehensible to ourselves.' That is, he sees no other way
15 of explaining the mixture of grandeur and infirmity which he
finds in man,—of desire for happiness and of inability to reach
it. So that, if we put ourselves under Pascal's guidance, the necessary approach to our use of the salvation offered by the Christian religion is to believe the story of Adam's fall to be historical,
20 and literally true. And his famous figure of the wager is used by
Pascal to reconcile us the better to this belief. The chances are
such, he says, that we shall do well at all events to lay our stake
in favour of the story's truth. If we say we *cannot* believe it, let
us set to work to attain belief as others have attained it; and how
25 was this? 'By acting just as if they *did* believe it; by taking holy
water, having masses said, &c. *Quite naturally, that will make
you believe, and render you stupid!*[1]—But that is just what I am
afraid of.—And why; what have you to lose? What harm will
come to you from taking this course? You will be faithful, hon-
30 est, humble, grateful, charitable, sincere, a friend whom men
can trust.'

[1] *Naturellement même cela vous fera croire et vous abêtira.* The Port
Royal editors suppressed this wonderful sentence, and indeed the whole
passage which follows the words *and how was this?* What Port Royal sub-
35 stituted was the following: 'Imitez leurs actions extérieures, si vous ne
pouvez encore entrer dans leurs dispositions intérieures; quittez ces vains
amusements qui vous occupent tout entier.' Pascal's words were not restored until M. Cousin reverted to the original manuscript. See M. Havet's
careful and valuable edition of Pascal's *Pensées,* vol. i, pp. 152, 158.

Did ever a great reasoner reason so madly? And this is the man who saw that the world no longer believes things unless it has evidence of them! In the first place, there is no evidence that man is only comprehensible on the assumption that the story of Adam's fall is true. But even if it were so, man must still ask himself: *Is* the story true? And if it is not true, then the conclusion must be simply that man is not comprehensible. Now, sooner or later, as our experience widens, we must see that the story is not true; we must inevitably come to say to ourselves: 'It is all a legend! it never really happened, any of it!' It is no more real history than the Peruvian account of Manco Capac and Mama Ocollo, the children of the Sun, 'who appeared on the banks of the Lake Titicaca, sent by their beneficent parent, who beheld with pity the miseries of the human race, to instruct and to reclaim them.'[1] For a little while, even for a generation or two perhaps, man may, after he has begun to doubt the story's truth, still keep himself in the belief of it by 'taking holy water, rendering himself stupid;' but the time comes when he cannot. That a story will account for certain facts, that we wish to think it true, nay, that many have formerly thought it true and have grown faithful, humble, charitable, and so on, by thus doing, does not make the story true if it is not, and cannot prevent men after a certain time from seeing that it is not.

And on such a time we have now entered. The more we may have been helped to be faithful, humble and charitable by taking the truth of this story, and other stories equally legendary, for granted, the greater is our embarrassment, no doubt, at having to do without them. But we have to do without them none the less on that account. We may feel our hearts still vibrate in answer to the Old Testament telling us that the fear of the Lord is the beginning of wisdom, and to the New telling us that Jesus Christ saves his people from their sins. But this fear of the Lord, and this safety through Jesus Christ, can have Adam's fall for their fundamental basis and explanation no longer.

Cardinal Manning narrates the miraculous resuscitation of the Virgin Mary, and his argument for believing it is that the story is a beautiful one, and that it is a comfort and help to pious souls

---

[1] Robertson's *History of America*, book vi.

to think it true. Both may be freely conceded to him; but really as much may be said for the miraculous apparition of Cinderella's fairy godmother. The story is pathetic and beautiful, and it is a pleasure to kind souls to see the tables turned by enchant-
5   ment in favour of the poor little good Cinderella. But this does not make the story true. And if a story is unsubstantial in its foundation and character, no connecting of it with our affections, or with what does us good, can in the end prevent people from saying: 'But it is not true! it never really happened, any
10   of it!'

I heard Mr. Moody preach to one of his vast audiences on a topic eternally attractive,—salvation by Jesus Christ. Mr. Moody's account of that salvation was exactly the old story, to which I have often adverted, of the contract in the Council of
15   the Trinity. Justice puts in her claim, said Mr. Moody, for the punishment of guilty mankind; God admits it. Jesus intercedes, undertakes to bear their punishment, and signs an undertaking to that effect. Thousands of years pass; Jesus is on the cross on Calvary. Justice appears, and presents to him his signed under-
20   taking. Jesus accepts it, bows his head, and expires. Christian salvation consists in the undoubting belief in the transaction here described, and in the hearty acceptance of the release offered by it.

Never let us deny to this story power and pathos, or treat
25   with hostility ideas which have entered so deep into the life of Christendom. But the story is not true; it never really happened. These personages never did meet together, and speak, and act, in the manner related. The personages of the Christian Heaven and their conversations are no more matter of fact than the person-
30   ages of the Greek Olympus and their conversations. Sir Robert Phillimore seeks to tie up the Church of England to a belief in the personality of Satan, and he might as well seek to tie it up to a belief in the personality of Tisiphone. Satan and Tisiphone are alike not real persons, but shadows thrown by man's guilt
35   and terrors. Mr. Moody's audiences are the last people who will come to perceive all this; they are chiefly made up from the main body of lovers of our popular religion,—the serious and steady middle class, with its bounded horizons. To the more educated class above this, and to the more free class below it, the grave

beliefs of the religious middle class in such stories as Mr. Moody's story of the Covenant of Redemption are impossible now; to the religious middle class itself they will be impossible soon. Salvation by Jesus Christ, therefore, if it has any reality, must be placed somewhere else than in a hearty consent to Mr. Moody's story. Something Mr. Moody and his hearers have experienced from Jesus, let us own, which does them good; but of this something they have not yet succeeded in getting the right history.

Now, if one feels impatience with people who, like Professor Clifford, lightly run a-muck at an august thing, so a man who is in earnest must feel impatience with those who lightly allege this or that as the true foundation of it. People who offer us their stories of the contract in the Council of the Trinity, or of the miraculous resuscitation of the Virgin, are just like Mr. Ruskin telling us in his assured way: 'There is not a moment of any day of our lives, when nature is not producing picture after picture, and working still upon such exquisite and constant principles of such perfect beauty, *that it is quite certain it is all done for* us, *and intended for our perpetual pleasure.*' It is *not* quite certain, we have not a particle of certainty about it, and to say that it is certain is utterly fantastic. But whoever produces certainties to us, at any rate on the grave subject of religion, is bound to take care that they are serious ones; and yet on no subject is this less regarded.

There is no doubt that we touch here on a real fault both in Christians and in Christian theology; and that at Christianity's very first start in the world the heathen philosopher Celsus hit this fault, when he remarked on the κουφότης τῶν Χριστιανῶν. We must not translate κουφότης simply *levity*, for the seriousness of Christianity in morals has been its charm and its power. Ὅσα σεμνά! as St. Paul says,[1]—*whatever things are nobly serious!*— may here well stand for its motto. But the κουφότης Celsus meant was *a want of* intellectual *seriousness;* and the reproach of this was not altogether undeserved by the first Christians, while it has been abundantly deserved by Christian theology since. The first Christians misunderstood Jesus and had the multitude's appetite for miracles, the multitude's inexact observation and boundless

[1] *Philippians* iv. 8.

credulity. They it was who supplied the data which Christian theology took from them without question, and has ever since confidently built upon. But trained, critical, indifferent minds, which knew what evidence was and what popular beliefs were,
5 could not but be struck with the looseness in the joints of the Christian belief, with the slightness of evidence for its miraculous data. They *were* struck with them; and if the old civilisation had not been on the wane, if a supply of instructed, critical, cool, indifferent minds had continued, Christianity could not have es-
10 tablished itself in the precise form it did.

For its establishment in that form the extinction of the old civilisation was necessary;—to flood and drown all which this civilisation was, and thought, and knew, with the barbarian nations of the north, men of infantine and untrained mental habit.
15 The infancy of the world was renewed, with all its sweet illusions; and on this new world the popular Christian belief could lay hold freely. Professor Clifford execrates Christianity as an 'awful plague,' because its success thus involved the ruin of Roman civilisation. It was worth while to have that civilisation
20 ruined fifty times over, for the sake of planting Christianity through Europe in the only form in which it could then be planted there. Civilisation could build itself up again; but what Christianity had to give, and from the first did give in no small measure, was indispensable, and the Roman civilisation could
25 not give it. And Christianity's admixture of popular legend and illusion was sure to be cleared away with time, according to that profound saying of Jesus himself: 'There is nothing covered which shall not be uncovered, and hidden which shall not be known.'[1]

30 But the miraculous data supplied by the first Christians became, in the ruin of Roman civilisation, speedily consecrated; the looseness of the evidence for them soon escaped scrutiny. Theology, the exhibition of Christianity in a scientific and systematic way, took these data as an assured basis. Many theologians have
35 been very able men, and their reasonings and deductions have been very close and subtle. Still they have always had the defect

---

[1] Matthew x. 26.

of going seriously upon data produced and admitted with *a want of intellectual seriousness*. But science makes her progress, not merely by close reasoning and deduction, but also, and much more, by the close scrutiny and correction of the present commonly received data. And this scrutiny is just what theological science has never seriously given; and to listen to it, therefore, is, as we said in *Literature and Dogma*, like listening to Cosmas Indicopleustes the Christian cosmographer, or any other early Christian writer in a department of science, who goes upon data furnished by a time of imperfect observation and boundless credulity. Whatever acuteness the writer may manifest, yet upon these data he goes. And modern writers in other departments of science have now corrected their old data in them from top to bottom; half of these data they have clean abandoned, and the other half they have transformed. But theologians have not yet done so in their science of theology, and hence their unprofitableness.

Mr. Gladstone complains that objectors to the Athanasian Creed seem to forget, most of them, 'that theology is a science, and that it therefore has a technical language which is liable to be grossly misunderstood by those who have never made it the subject of study.' And this is a very usual complaint from our theologians. But the fact is, that their science is a science going gravely and confidingly upon the uncorrected data of a time of imperfect observation and boundless credulity, and that, therefore, the more formal and technical it gets, the more hollow it is. And the hollowness of the results exhibited by theologians is more apparent than the reason thereof; and a clear-headed man can often perceive that what the theologians say is futile, although he may never have been led to see that the untrustworthiness of their miraculous data is the real cause. [Dr. Littledale adjures people to 'study theology, instead of practically maintaining, as Dr. Arnold in all sincerity did, that the best preparation for laying down authoritative decisions in theology is to know nothing whatever about it.' But Dr. Arnold, who had a sound historical instinct, could tell at once, from the warnings of this instinct, that theology, which is a series of conclusions upon the history in the Bible, had apprehended that history all wrong;

that it was faulty, therefore, in its very base, and so could not
be a true theology, a science of the Christian religion, at all. And
most certainly it is not the best preparation for forming right
judgments in a true theology, to have one's head stuffed full of
5   a false.

[Moreover, this original vice of Christian theology seems to
have affected, where things religious are concerned, the whole
mental habit of those who receive it, and to have afflicted them
with a malady which cannot be better described than as the
10   κουφότης τῶν Χριστιανῶν, *want of intellectual seriousness* on the
part of lovers and defenders of Christianity. Men's experience
widens, they get a clearer sense of what fact is and what proof
is, they are more aware when they talk nonsense and more shy
of talking it; only where religion is concerned does this check of
15   sober reason seem quite to desert them, and levity to reign. We
have noticed Cardinal Manning's ground for believing the miraculous resuscitation of the Virgin Mary: that the story is so beautiful. But the same levity is shown by more cautious Catholics
discussing the Pope's infallibility, seeking to limit its extent, to
20   lay down in what sense he is really infallible and in what sense
he is not; for in no sense whatever is or can he be infallible, and
to debate the thing at all shows a want of intellectual seriousness.
The same when Lord Herries thinks to mend matters by saying,
that 'the Pope is the organ of the Church, and an Almighty
25   Power of infinite wisdom and of infinite truth established his
Church to teach all truth unto the end of the world, and as
such that Church must be infallible;' for there is plainly no such
thing existing as the said infallible Church, and it is a want of
intellectual seriousness to make believe that there is when there
30   is not. The same when Dr. Ward thinks to clear the doctrine
of the Real Presence, by talking of 'the divine substance in the
Host separable from all that group of visible and tangible phenomena which suggest the presence of bread.' All that this
acute mind effects, by thus gravely cheating itself with words, is
35   to illustrate the κουφότης τῶν Χριστιανῶν, the want of intellectual
seriousness found in Christians. The same, finally, when Mr.
Moody, the question being what Christian salvation positively
is, tells us his story about Justice and her contract. However

honest and earnest Mr. Moody may be, all we can say of a man who at the present juncture bases Christian salvation on a story like that, is that he shows a fatal want of intellectual seriousness.

[For] Protestantism has the same want of intellectual serious-ness as Catholicism, its advantage being, however, that it more possesses in itself the means of deliverance. But on this, the ad-vantage of Protestantism, we do not at the present moment in-sist; we rather point out the weakness, common to it and to Catholicism, of building confidently upon miraculous data lightly admitted. True, Catholicism has more levity in admitting new miraculous data; but Protestantism admits unreservedly one set of miraculous data and builds everything on them, because they are written in a book which, it says, cannot err; and this is levity. At the stage of experience where men are now arrived, it is evident to whoever looks at things fairly that the miraculous data of the Bible have not this unique character of trustworthi-ness; that they, like other such data, proceed from a medium of imperfect observation and boundless credulity. The story of the miraculous birth and resuscitation of Jesus was bred in such a medium; and not to see this, to build confidently on the story, is hardly more serious than to admit the story of the miraculous birth and resuscitation of the Virgin because it is so beautiful.

It is of the utmost importance to be perfectly honest here. M. de Laveleye[1] is struck, as any judicious Catholic may well be struck, with the superior freedom, order, stability, and reli-gious earnestness, of the Protestant nations as compared with the Catholic. But at the present moment the Protestant nations are living partly upon their past, partly upon their powers of self-transformation; great care is required to consult and use aright the experience which they offer. True, their religion has made them what they are, and their religion involved severance from Rome and involved the Protestant theology. But it would be a grave mistake to suppose that the secret of the Protestant nations lies in severance from Rome and in the received Protestant the-ology; or that, in now merely adopting those from them, a mod-

---

[1] See his excellent pamphlet: *Le Protestantisme et le Catholicisme*, Brus-sels, Muquardt.

ern nation could find freedom, order, stability, and religious
earnestness. The true force of Protestantism was its signal return
to the individual conscience,—to the method of Jesus. This
strengthened the man, this founded him on rock, this invigorated
5 his action upon all lines. It induced, too, separation from Rome
(so far as this was not due to causes political), and it induced the
received Protestant theology. But a man's conscience does not
necessarily tell him right on all points all at once; and now the
conscience of the Protestant nations is beginning to tell them that
10 in their theology of the sixteenth century it did not tell them
right. Conscience told them right in asserting its own general
supremacy as ultimate court of appeal; it did not tell them right
in its particular decision that the sixteenth century theology was
the true one. The secret of Protestantism's strength is undoubt-
15 edly its religion; but it has not at this moment a science of religion, or theology, to give to the Catholic nations, for it is working out its own anew. What it has to give them is the sincere,
uncompromising return to the method of Jesus, with the deep
and firm sense of reality which this return inspires. But if it
20 gives them this, it will have given to the Catholic nations what
enables them to do the rest for themselves.

It is the habit of increased intellectual seriousness, bred of a
wider experience and of a larger acquaintance with men's mental
history, which is now transforming religion in our country. In-
25 telligent people among the educated classes grow more and more
sceptical of the miraculous data which supply the basis for our
received theology. The habit is a conquest of the advancing
human race; it spreads and spreads, and will be on the whole and
in the end a boon to us. But many and many an individual it may
30 find unprepared for it, and may act upon him injuriously.
Goethe's saying is well known: 'All which merely frees our
spirit, without giving us the command over ourselves, is dele-
terious.'[1] It is of small use by itself alone, however it may be
indispensable, this one single current of intellectual seriousness;
35 of small use to those who are untouched by the great current
of seriousness about conduct. To a frivolous and materialised

---

[1] Alles was unsern Geist befreit, ohne uns die Herrschaft über uns selbst
zu geben, ist verderblich.

upper class, to a raw and sensual lower class, to feel the greater current may be more than a compensation for not feeling the lesser. They do now feel the lesser current, however; and it removes them farther than ever from the influence of the greater.

For fear of losing their religious convictions, the pious part of our people would fain shut off from themselves the intellectual current, which they fear might carry them away to shores of desolation. They may succeed for a longer or a shorter time. Their love of the old, and their fear of the new, alike give them energy; and we have repeatedly said that the nature of the debate as to the miraculous ground in Christianity is such, that the conviction of its unsoundness must form itself in a man's own mind, it cannot be forced upon him from without. It is true, what apologists are always urging, that there is no other example of such a success as that of the Christian religion, where the successful religion had an erroneous belief in miracles for its foundation. It is also true, what was well pointed out in the *Guardian*, that the rich crop of non-Christian miracles contemporary with the rise of Christianity, and which is often brought as proof of the hollowness of the Christian miracles, may naturally have been called up by the miracles of Christianity. The answer, no doubt, is, that no other religion with an unsound foundation of miracles has succeeded like Christianity, because no other religion had, in close conjunction with its unsound belief in miracles, such an element of soundness as the personality and word of Jesus. And the suggestion of non-Christian miracles by the Christian ones only proves a superior force somewhere in the Christian religion; and this it undoubtedly had, but not from its miracles. However, a religious man may still shut his eyes to all this, and may keep fast his old faith in the Christian miracles. But before very long the habit of intellectual seriousness will reach him also, and change him. Not a few religious people are even now gained by it against their will, and to their deep distress and bewilderment. So that, whether we look about us at the religious world or at the irreligious, the conclusion is the same: people cannot any longer do with Christianity just as it is.

The reader whom a work like the present has in view is not, I have often said, the man still striving to be content with the received theology. With him we do not seek to meddle. Neither

is it intended for a frivolous upper class in their religious insensibility, nor for a raw lower class in their religious insensibility, nor
for Liberal secularists at home or abroad, nor for Catholics who
are strangers, or very nearly so, to the Bible. Some or all of these
may perhaps come to find such a work useful to them one day,
and after they have undergone a change; but it is not directly
addressed to them. It is meant for those who, won by the modern
spirit to habits of intellectual seriousness, cannot receive what
sets these habits at nought, and will not try to force themselves
to do so; but who have stood near enough to the Christian religion to feel the attraction which a thing so very great, when
one stands really near to it, cannot but exercise, and who have
some familiarity with the Bible and some practice in using it.

Of such persons there are in this country, and in America also,
not a few. The familiarity with the Bible, the habit of using the
Bible, extends in Protestant countries throughout those large,
those very large, classes which have been religiously brought
up, and is invaluable to them. It is the excellent fruit which Protestantism gained by its return at the Reformation to the individual conscience,—to the method of Jesus. The Bible itself was
made the standard, and what the Bible really said. It matters not
that the Protestant's actual interpretation of the Bible has hitherto been little better than the Catholic's; he has still been conversant with the Bible, has felt its grandeur, has conceived the
just idea that in its right use is salvation. M. Sainte-Beuve, the
finest critical spirit of our times, conceived of the Bible so
falsely, simply from not knowing it, that he could cheerfully
and confidently repeat the Liberal formula: 'Unless we mean to
prefer Byzantinism to progress we must say goodbye *aux vieilles
Bibles*,—to the old Bibles.' Liberals, who think that religion in
general is an obstacle to progress, may naturally, however, be
ignorant of the virtue there is in knowing one's Bible. But Catholics, although they may love religion, are for the most part in
like case with its Liberal foes in not being aware what virtue
there lies in knowing the Bible. And therefore a Catholic, who
has once come to perceive the want of intellectual seriousness in
what his Church lays down, and in what he has been told of her
infallibility, thinks that there the thing ends, and that the Chris-

tian religion itself has as little intellectual seriousness as the dogmas of his Church. So we see how many Catholics break violently with religion altogether, and become its sworn enemies.
And even with Catholics who have been so near to it that they
cannot help feeling its attraction, what they feel is merely, when   5
the dogmas of their Church have lost credibility for them, a
vague sentiment at variance with their reason; capable, perhaps,
of making them view with dislike all who raise questions about
religion, but not capable of affording them any sure stay. Therefore Niebuhr might well say that 1517 ought to precede 1789;   10
and even the fanaticism of Exeter Hall can hardly assert too
roundly that the Catholic nations will never really improve until
they know the Bible better. For easily and always does a religious Protestant remain aware that religion is not at an end because the dogmas of a Church cannot stand. He knows that the   15
Bible is behind; and although he may be startled at for the first
time hearing that what creeds and confessions have for centuries
been giving as the sum and substance of the Bible is not its sum
and substance, yet he knows the vastness and depth of the Bible
well enough to understand that, after all, this may very likely   20
be quite true.

For such a reader is the present work meant;—for a reader
who is more or less conversant with the Bible, who can feel the
attraction of the Christian religion, but who has acquired habits
of intellectual seriousness, has been revolted by having things   25
presented solemnly to him for his use which will not hold water,
and who will start with none of such things even to reach what
he values. Come what may, he will deal with this great matter of
religion fairly.

It is the aim of the present volume, as it was the aim of *Litera-*   30
ture and Dogma, to show to such a man that his honesty will be
rewarded. Plenty of people there are who labour solely for the
diffusion of habits of intellectual seriousness, at whatever cost.
Perhaps they do well, perhaps ill; at all events I do not, in the
present volume and in its predecessor, write as one of them. I   35
write to convince the lover of religion that by following habits of
intellectual seriousness he need not, so far as religion is concerned, lose anything. Taking the Old Testament as Israel's sub-

lime establishment of the theme: *Righteousness is salvation!* taking the New as the incomparable elucidation by Jesus of what
righteousness is and how salvation is won, I do not fear comparing the power over the soul and imagination of the Bible,
taken in this sense,—a sense which is at the same time solid,—
with the like power in the old materialistic and miraculous sense
for the Bible, which is not.

The solidity itself is indeed an immense element of grandeur.
*To him that ordereth his conversation right shall be shown the
salvation of God!* Or conversely, and in modern phrase, the same
doctrine: *Nations and men, whoever is shipwrecked, is shipwrecked on conduct!* In vain do philosophical Radicals devise
fine new programmes which leave it out; in vain does France
trumpet the ideas of '89 which are to do instead. Whoever leaves
it out of his programme, whoever fancies that anything else
will do instead, is baffled and confounded by the sure event; experience keeps again and again sending him back to learn better,
like a school-boy with an ill-got lesson. France, which was in
such terror of Byzantinism and so resolved to have done with
'the old Bibles,' France, with all her eminent social instincts and
gifts, is she not, in her countless editions of M. Adolphe Belot's
novels, or M. Zola's, faring towards the real Byzantinism, a
Byzantinism from which 'the old Bibles,' perhaps, can alone save
her? For, as it is true that men are shipwrecked on conduct, so it
is true that the Bible is the great means for making men feel
this, and for saving them. It makes them feel it by the irresistible
power with which Israel, the Seer of the Vision of Peace, testifies
it; it saves them by the method and secret of Jesus.

[The indispensableness of the Bible and of Christianity, therefore, cannot be exaggerated. In morals, which are at least three-
fourths of life, to do without them is, as was said in *Literature
and Dogma*, exactly like doing in aesthetics without the art of
Greece. To do with 'the commonplaces of morality couched in
modern and congenial language,' which is what some of our
Liberal friends propose, answers precisely to doing with English, French, and German art in aesthetics. To do with the very
best and finest, in the way of morals, that has outside the Bible
been produced, answers to doing, in aesthetics, with Flemish and

Italian art. Every lover of art knows that perfection in art, salvation in art, will never be thus reached, will never be reached
without knowing Greece. So it is with perfection and salvation
in conduct, men's universal concern, *the way of peace;* they are
not to be reached without the Bible and Christianity. By the
Bible and Christianity, though not by what our missionaries now
offer as such, the non-Christian nations will finally be won, and
will come to regard their old religions much as a Christian, wide-
minded, reverent, and profound, would regard them now. So
will be fulfilled the word of Israel's Eternal: *My house shall be
called the house of prayer for all nations; there shall be one
Eternal, and his name one.*[1] And although we may willingly allow to Professor Rauwenhoff that the mind and life of our
Aryan race has deeply modified the religion of Semitic Israel
already, and will yet modify it much more, still that cannot prevent the root of the matter for us, in this immense concern of
religion, being in the Israel of the Bible, and he is our spiritual
progenitor:—*A Syrian ready to perish was thy father.*[2]]

Neither then in respect of the grandeur of the Bible and Christianity, nor in respect of their world-wide importance, will the
lover of religion, who brings habits of intellectual seriousness to
bear upon them, find that he has to change his notions. Nor will
he even have to revolutionise his phraseology. He will become
aware, indeed, that of the constitution of God we know nothing;
and that those who, like Christian philosophers in general, begin
by admitting this, and who add, even, that 'we are utterly powerless to conceive or comprehend the idea of an infinite Being,
Almighty, All-knowing, Omnipotent, and Eternal, of whose in-
scrutable purpose the material universe is the unexplained mani-
festation,'[3] but who then proceed calmly to affirm such a Being
as positively as if he were a man they were acquainted with in
the next street, talk idly. Nevertheless, admitting that all this cannot be affirmed about the God of our religion, but only that our
God is the Eternal not ourselves that makes for righteousness,
we yet know also that men inevitably use anthropomorphic lan-

[1] Isaiah lvi. 7; Zechariah xiv. 9.   [2] *Deuteronomy* xxvi. 5.
[3] Mr. R. A. Proctor, in the *Contemporary Review.*

guage about whatever makes them feel deeply, and the Biblical
language about God we may therefore freely use, but as approximative and poetical merely. To seek to discard, like some philosophers, the name of God and to substitute for it such a name
5   as the Unknowable, will seem to a plain man, surely, ridiculous.
For *Unknowable* is a name merely negative, and no man could
ever have cared anything about God in so far as he is simply unknowable. 'The Unknowable is our refuge and strength, a very
present help in trouble,' is what would occur to no man to think
10   or say. Men cared about God for the sake of what they knew
about him, not of what they did not. And they knew about him
that he was the Eternal not ourselves that makes for righteousness, and as such they gave him the name, *God*. It adds, indeed,
to our awe of God that although we are able to know of him
15   what so greatly concerns us, we know of him nothing more; but
simply to be able to know nothing of him could beget in us no
awe whatever.

Finally, he who most seizes the real significance of the Bible
and of Jesus, will be least disposed to cut himself off in religion
20   from his fellow-men, to renounce all participation in their religious language and worship. True, this language is approximative merely, while men imagine it to be adequate; it is *thrown out*
at certain realities which they very imperfectly comprehend. It
is materialised poetry, which they give as science; and there can
25   be no worse science than materialised poetry. But poetry is essentially concrete; and the moment one perceives that the religious language of the human race is in truth poetry, which it
mistakes for science, one cannot make it an objection to this
language that it is concrete. That it has long moved and deeply
30   engaged the affections of men, that the Christian generations
before us have all passed that way, adds immensely to its worth
as poetry. As the Catholic architecture, so the Catholic worship
is likely to survive and prevail, long after the intellectual child-
ishness of Catholic dogma and the political and social mischiefs
35   of the Roman system have tired out men's patience with them.
Catholic worship is likely, however modified, to survive as the
general worship of Christians, because it is the worship which,
in a sphere where poetry is permissible and natural, unites the
most of the elements of poetry.

Everything turns on its being at realities that this worship and its language are aimed. And its anthropomorphic language about God is aimed at a vast, though ill-apprehended, reality. So is its materialistic language about the death, the rising again, and the reign of Christ. [Baur says that the important thing is not whether Jesus really rose from the dead or no; the important thing is, Baur says, that his disciples believed him to have risen. Mr. Appleton, in a just and instructive review of the labours of Strauss, invites our approval for Strauss' early position that what is best in Christianity was not due to the individual Jesus, but was developed by the religious consciousness of humanity. But the religious consciousness of humanity has produced in Christianity not ideas, but imaginations; and it is ideas, not imaginations, which endure. The religious consciousness of humanity produced the doctrines of the Incarnation and of the Real Presence,—beautiful imaginations, but if Christianity depended upon them it would dissolve. It will live, because it depends upon] a true and inexhaustibly fruitful idea, the idea of death and resurrection as conceived and worked out by Jesus. *Baptized into Christ's death, if by any means we might attain to the resurrection from the dead*,[1] is the true, the just, the only adequate account of a Christian and his religion. The importance of the disciples' belief in their Master's resurrection lay in their believing what was true, although they materialised it. Jesus *had* died and risen again, but in his own sense not theirs. The strength of the Christian religion lies in its being founded on a truth; on a truth which hitherto Christendom has been able to apprehend only by materialising it, but which it will one day apprehend better, and which men could come to apprehend better only by passing through a materialistic stage. We can use their language because it is thrown out at an admirable truth; only it is not, as they suppose, their sense for their own language which is real while our sense is figurative, but it is our sense which is real, and theirs is merely figurative.

The freethinking of one age is the common sense of the next, and the Christian world will certainly learn to transform beliefs which it now thinks to be untransformable. The way will be

---

[1] *Romans* vi. 3; *Philippians* iii. 11.

found. And the new Christianity will call forth more effort in
the individual who uses it than the old, will require more open
and instructed minds for its reception; and this is progress. But
we live at the beginning of a great transition which cannot well
5 be accomplished without confusion and distress. I do not pretend to operate a general change of religious opinion, such as can
only come to pass through the operation of many labourers
working, all of them, towards a like end, and by the instrumen-
tality, in a very considerable degree, of the clergy. *One man's*
10 *life, what is it?* says Goethe; but even one man in his short term
may do something to ease a severe transition, to diminish violent shocks in it and bitter pain. With this end in view, I have
addressed myself to men such as are happily not rare in this
country, men of free and active minds, who, though they may be
15 profoundly dissatisfied with the received theology, are yet interested in religion and more or less acquainted with the Bible.
These I have endeavoured to help; and they, if they are helped,
will in their turn help others. To one people and race, and to
one sort of persons in it, and to one moment in its religious his-
20 tory, have I addressed myself; and if the attempt thus confessedly
partial has even a partial success, I am enough rewarded. Can
even a partial success of this kind be won? A calmer and a more
gradual judgment than that of the immediate present will decide. But however the ultimate judgment may go, whether it
25 pronounce the attempt here made to be of solid worth or not, I
have little fear but that it will recognise it to have been an attempt conservative, and an attempt religious.

Critical and Explanatory Notes

References to Arnold's diary-notebooks are drawn from H. F.
Lowry, K. Young, and W. H. Dunn, eds., *The Note-Books of Matthew Arnold* (London: Oxford University Press, 1952), supplemented by W. B. Guthrie, ed., *Matthew Arnold's Diaries: the Un-
published Items* (Ann Arbor: University Microfilms, 1959). Most
quotations from Arnold's letters to his publishers are drawn from
W. E. Buckler, ed., *Matthew Arnold's Books* (Geneva: Droz, 1958);
most quotations from his other letters are taken from the collected
edition by G. W. E. Russell, where they can be found under their
dates; the collection has been published in so many editions that page
references are not helpful. A very few quotations are from unpub-
lished letters; most of these can now be traced through Arthur Kyle
Davis's *Matthew Arnold's Letters: a Descriptive Checklist* (Char-
lottesville: The University Press of Virginia, 1968). Reference to
volumes in J.-P. Migne's *Patrologiae Cursus Completus: Patrologia
Graeca* and *Patrologia Latina* (Paris, 1857– and 1844–) have been
shortened to "Migne, *PG*" and "Migne, *PL*." *The Oxford Dictionary of the Christian Church* has been drawn upon more frequently
than the explicit references to it may indicate. Notes to cancelled
passages are placed in the same sequence as the notes to the final
text; when the parenthetical word "(variant)" appears, the note is
in explanation of a passage that will be found only in the Textual
Notes.

[A FEW WORDS ABOUT THE EDUCATION ACT]

The Elementary Education Act of 1870, sponsored by Arnold's
brother-in-law W. E. Forster, vice-president of the Committee of
Council on Education in Gladstone's government, received the royal
assent on August 9 and became effective immediately; the first Lon-

don school board election under the act was held on November 29. It was a compromise between the advocates of a state system and the voluntaryists and in many ways was a step in the dark, since no one actually knew the extent to which the prevailing voluntary system failed to reach the school-age population. The act provided that if the Education Department found a shortage of schools in any locality, it could cause a school board to be elected by the ratepayers and the board would establish needed schools from money raised through local taxation ("rates"). Denominational schools might continue; it was even expected (as Arnold's essay indicates) that there would be a determined effort on the part of the denominations to supply the needed schools and avoid the local establishment of nonsectarian board schools. Denominational schools, however, could not receive support from the rates; they did, of course, receive the Parliamentary grants offered to all inspected schools. All schools, whether voluntary or board, were obliged to place any religious instruction they wished to institute—and for board schools this must avoid all "religious catechism or religious formulary which is distinctive of any particular denomination," the Cowper-Temple clause in the act—at the beginning or the end of the school day and permit all students whose parents had conscientious objection to such instruction to absent themselves from it without penalty; this was the "conscience clause" to which Arnold referred. Schooling was to be compulsory only in places where the by-laws of the local school boards made it compulsory, and it was to be free only for children of parents found by the boards unable to pay. Section 16 of the act, to which Arnold refers in his final paragraph, provides that "if any dispute arises as to whether the school board have done or permitted any act in contravention of or have failed to comply with the said regulations, the matter shall be referred to the Education Department, whose decision thereon shall be final." Elementary education did not become universally compulsory until 1880; in 1891 it was made universally gratuitous in all schools, voluntary or board.—J. W. Adamson, *English Education, 1789–1902* (Cambridge, 1930), pp. 347–61.

Arnold's article, published in the first number of the short-lived *Educational Review* in January, 1871, though signed, remained hidden from modern scholars until discovered by Professor Roger L. Brooks, who published it in *Modern Philology* LXVI, 262–64 (February, 1969). The founding editor of the journal, J. S. Laurie, had been a school inspector and drew upon his former colleagues for much of the content of his first number. There is no record that Arnold received payment for it, nor it is mentioned in his pocket diaries or known correspondence.

(It should be added that though the Elementary Education Act was sponsored by Arnold's brother-in-law, it was not framed by Arnold's advice. "I am now more glad than I can say that [William] never consulted me about his bill in any manner," Arnold wrote to his mother early in 1872. "He would still have had his own bill, . . . and I should have been supposed to have abetted him out of enmity to the Dissenters. As it is, I can enjoy their heaping up of the epithets for themselves they have culled out of my writings, because they cannot go repeating them over without in some degree coming to perceive how terribly suiting they are.")

1:25. I.e., the clergy of the Church of England.

4:12. "National schools" are those of The National Society for Promoting the Education of the Poor in the Principles of the Established Church throughout England and Wales, the most numerous of the voluntary schools.

[A FRENCH ELIJAH]

The war between France and Germany in 1870–71 was a matter of especial interest to Arnold; he admired both nations and was much concerned to determine the spiritual and moral roots of the French catastrophe, as well as to observe the French reaction to the disaster. He and his wife passed through Paris en route to and from a short August holiday in Switzerland in 1871. "The ruin was far greater than I had any notion of, but the natural tendency of Paris to gaiety and splendour is indestructible, and the place is fast on the way to have all its old fascinations over again. The French are certainly much subdued, and that improves them greatly as to external manner; within, I fancy they deceive themselves and feed themselves on nonsense as much as ever," he wrote to his mother on August 18.

His pocket diary for 1871 records the receipt from the *Pall Mall Gazette* of four guineas in December and a letter to his mother on November 28 says: "I do not know whether you saw the thing I told you of in the Pall Mall, but it has appeared." These clues were sufficient to point to an unsigned article entitled "A French Elijah" on November 24 which is unmistakably Arnold's. The date of Arnold's letter rules out the anonymous article on "University Reform" published on November 30 and reprinted as Arnold's by Professor Fraser Neiman; it must also be condemned on stylistic grounds (see A. Dwight Culler in *Journal of English and Germanic Philology* LX, 337–38 [April, 1961] and the present editor in *Modern Language Quarterly* XX, 308 [September, 1961]).

Arnold's title may be explained by a sentence from *Literature and Dogma* published in the *Cornhill Magazine* the month before this article appeared: "To enable them to meet the terrible day, when the Eternal would avenge him of his enemies and make up his jewels, [the Hebrews] themselves needed, they knew, the voice of a second Elijah, a change of the inner man, *repentance*."—*Prose Works*, ed. Super, VI, 209. The schoolmaster in the play says of himself, in a passage Arnold quotes, "Je suis simple d'esprit et n'ai rien d'un prophète." Arnold's train of thought is that of a letter to his mother at the close of the war on January 31, 1871: "Whatever may be said of the harshness of such a sentence, it is yet true that [France's] fall is mainly due to that want of a serious conception of righteousness and the need of it, the consequences of which so often show themselves in the world's history, and in regard to the Graeco-Latin nations more particularly. The fall of Greece, the fall of Rome, the fall of the brilliant Italy of the fifteenth century, and now the fall of France, are all examples. Nothing gives more freshness and depth to one's reading of the Bible than the sense that this is so, and that this testimony is perpetually being borne to the book of righteousness, though the nation out of which it came was itself a political failure so utter and miserable. The qualities of the French genius, their lucidity, directness of intellect, and social charm, must always make themselves felt, as the far higher qualities of the Greeks did and do. But it is quite a question whether the practical military and political career of France may not be now ending, not again to revive, as that of Greece did after the Macedonian Conquest."

6:1–3. Charles Gounod's *Gallia, a Lamentation*, motet for soprano solo, chorus, orchestra, and organ, was first performed at Albert Hall, London, on May 1, 1871; its Paris première was October 29, 1871. It was based on the Lamentations of Jeremiah 1:1–2, 4, 12.

6:15. François Coppée (1842–1908) was a minor poet and dramatist whose work achieved considerable popularity. His *Fais ce que dois*, first presented on October 21, 1871, was published separately in 1871 and in a volume of his collected plays, *Théatre de François Coppée 1869–1872* (Paris, 1872). Arnold occasionally omits a few lines from passages he quotes and he italicizes passages for emphasis (none of the text is italicized in the original).

7:29. "Then shall the end come. When ye therefore shall see the abomination of desolation, spoken of by Daniel the prophet [9:27, 12:11], stand in the holy place."—Matthew 24:14–15.

10:27–30. Walter H. Pater, "The Poetry of Michelangelo," *Fortnightly Review*, XVI, 570 (November, 1871): "That strange interfusion of sweetness and strength is not to be found in those who claimed to be his [Michelangelo's] followers; but it is found in many of those who worked before him, and in many others down to our own time, in William Blake, for instance, and Victor Hugo, who, though not of his school, and unaware, are his true sons, and help us to understand him, as he in turn interprets and justifies them. Perhaps this is the chief use in studying old masters." The essay was reprinted in Pater's *The Renaissance*.

11:5–6. J. Joubert, *Pensées* (7th ed.; Paris, 1877), II, 366 (xxiv, §iv, 29), of Voltaire; quoted by Arnold in his essay on Joubert, *Prose Works*, ed. Super, III, 205:21.

11:15–17. Arnold listed the section on the Reformation from Jules Michelet's *Histoire de France* among the books he planned to read in 1869.—*Note-Books*, ed. Lowry, p. 585. In his essays on Renan, "Equality" and "Numbers" he repeated Michelet's judgment: " 'France did not want a reformation which was a moral one,' is Michelet's account of the matter: *La France ne voulait pas de réforme morale*."—See p. 44:31–33 and *Prose Works*, ed. Super, vol. VIII, X.

11:23–32. Agrippa d'Aubigné, *Histoire universelle*, ed. A. de Ruble (Paris, 1889), III, 130 (Book V, chapt. xviii). But Arnold was quoting from J. Michelet, *Histoire de France*, IX, chapt. xix (end), and Michelet somewhat paraphrased d'Aubigné. The battle of Moncontour, on October 3, 1569, in the French civil wars, was a defeat for the Huguenots, but Gaspard de Coligny, Admiral of France, their leader, was nevertheless able to conclude a favorable peace the following year. He was the first victim of the massacre of St. Bartholomew on August 24, 1572. L'Estrange's remark to Coligny is the opening verse of Psalm 73: "Truly God is good to Israel."

11:36–37. "Niebuhr might well say that 1517 ought to precede 1789," Arnold remarked in the Preface to *God and the Bible*, p. 393:10. Barthold Georg Niebuhr (1776–1831), German diplomat and historian of ancient Rome, was characterized by Arnold in his Preface to *Poems*, 1853, as the man of widest culture the age had produced.—*Prose Works*, ed. Super, I, 14. The fall of the Bastille on July 14, 1789, marked the beginning of the French Revolution. The Glorious Revolution of 1688 placed William and Mary on the throne of England in place of James II and laid the foundations of the mod-

ern British constitution. Luther's nailing of his theses on the church
door at Wittenberg on October 31, 1517, was the beginning of the
Reformation.

[A PERSIAN PASSION PLAY]

Arnold's surviving correspondence tells us nothing about when he
accepted an invitation to lecture before the Birmingham and Mid-
land Institute in the autumn of 1871 or what governed his choice of
subject. Three weeks before the lecture was delivered, he told his
mother that he had "been able to read a good deal and make some
preparation for it" at the same time that he saw the second installment of "Literature and Dogma" through proofs for the *Cornhill*.
After an afternoon walk into the Warwickshire countryside he had
been so fond of from his boyhood and a dinner-party with the members of the council of the Institute, he delivered his lecture on the
evening of October 16 in the Masonic Hall to an audience of nine
hundred people; nearly two hundred had been turned away. The
discourse took an hour and twenty minutes. "I am glad I did not
take their money, as it made me quite indifferent about pleasing
them so long as I gave them a lecture which satisfied myself; and I
did pretty well satisfy myself, though preparing the lecture bothered
me a good deal." There was an inevitable comparison of this audience with those he had been used to during his professorship of
poetry: "After Oxford, where there are comparatively so few people, and what there are overdone with lectures and languid in their
interest, an audience such as a place like Birmingham gives you is
very animating." He was indeed so pleased with his reception that
he made inquiry the following January about the possibility of delivering in Birmingham another lecture, perhaps this time, one may
speculate, on matters of public education which then so much occupied Birmingham. "As the moth is attracted to the flame, I am
rather drawn towards centres where ideas hostile to mine seem to
have it all their own way," he wrote to George David Boyle there.
The Birmingham newspaper made "rather a hash" of its resumé of
the Passion Play lecture, but "the Leamington people have heard
the fame of [it] and have asked me to repeat it there at my own fee;
I think it possible I may read it there about the middle of this month,
to get practise in reading and speaking to a large audience as much as
for any other reason," he told his mother on November 5, and on the

same day asked George Smith's consent to do so, since it was already in the printer's hands for the December number of the *Cornhill Magazine*. "I shall not take their money: but for Leamington, as for Birmingham, I have, from old Rugby days, the feelings of a neighbour, and should be glad to do its Institute a pleasure." He read the lecture from proof-sheets; "It was a much less interesting audience than the Birmingham one, but I read, I think, much better, and indeed a great part of the lecture I spoke without looking at my notes." For the publication in the *Cornhill* he was paid £30. When he was planning a third edition of *Essays in Criticism* in mid-March, 1875, he expressed to Macmillan his discontent with the amount of his profits from the first two editions; Macmillan proposed that there be an increase in price from six to nine shillings, justified by "some slight additional Essay," and Arnold determined upon "A Persian Passion Play," which he thought would "come in capitally"; it took its place between "Pagan and Mediaeval Religious Sentiment" and "Joubert."—Buckler, *Matthew Arnold's Books*, pp. 23–25, 71–73. It has been edited with the other *Essays in Criticism* of the first series by Sister Thomas Marion Hoctor (University of Chicago Press, 1968).

Arnold followed so often in Renan's footsteps that it is worth noting that here Renan followed in his with an essay on "Les Téaziés de la Perse," published in the *Journal des Débats*, July 9–10, 1878, and reprinted in *Nouvelles études d'histoire religieuse* (Paris, 1884), pp. 185–215. Arnold took advantage of the timely interest in the Oberammergau Passion Play to compare the Persian drama with that; Renan compared it rather with the medieval mystery plays.

12:1–2. The Passion Play at Oberammergau, customarily staged every tenth summer, was interrupted in 1870 by the Franco-German war, and resumed in 1871 from June 24 to September 24. (Hoctor)

13:22. "We walk by faith, not by sight."—II Corinthians 5:7.

14:3–5. Joseph-Arthur, comte de Gobineau, *Les Religions et les philosophies dans l'Asie centrale* (Paris, 1865). Gobineau had also written a four-volume *Essai sur l'inégalité des races humaines* (Paris, 1853–55). Professor F. E. Faverty describes Gobineau as "the most notorious of the advocates of Aryanism," though he finds no evidence that Arnold, for all his interest in racial theories, followed Gobineau here.—*Matthew Arnold the Ethnologist* (Evanston, Illinois, 1951), pp. 43, 228. Renan's "Les Téaziés de la Perse" (1878), a review of a new edition of Persian plays, drew heavily also on Gobineau.

14:32–15:8. Gobineau, pp. 145–46. Mirza-Ali-Mohammed, a lad

of about nineteen at this time (1843), claimed to be descended from the Prophet through the Imam Hussein.

15:9–18:30. Arnold summarizes part of Gibbon's chapt. 50 and Gobineau, pp. 363–66.

15:36–16:9, 23–28. Edward Gibbon, *The History of the Decline and Fall of the Roman Empire*, ed. J. B. Bury (London, 1898), V, 388 (chapt. 50).

17:9–14. Kurroglou lived in the latter half of the seventeenth century. Arnold quotes from Alexander Chodzko, *Specimens of the Popular Poetry of Persia* (London, 1842), p. 342. Chodzko reads "these footstools" and "thou hast made."

17:16–18:17, 21–26. Gibbon, V, 390–92 (chapt. 50).

18:35–19:2. Gobineau, pp. 453–54.

19:5–20:1. *Ibid.*, pp. 364, 367–70. Moharrem is the first month of the Muslim calendar.

20:2–37. *Ibid.*, pp. 374–79.

20:38–22:36. *Ibid.*, pp. 381–90, 393.

23:3–22. *Ibid.*, pp. 391–92.

23:23–24:6. *Ibid.*, pp. 396–97.

24:7–25:6. *Ibid.*, pp. 367, 371–75, 388–89, 396, 393–95.

25:8–26:15. *Ibid.*, pp. 384–85, 397–401.

26:16–27:14. *Ibid.*, pp. 440–42.

27:15–31:20. *Ibid.*, pp. 401–3, 406–12, 416, 421, 424–28, 430–33, 435.

31:24–32:3. Gibbon, *Decline and Fall*, ed. Bury, V, 391 (chapt. 50).

32:4–33:26. Gobineau, pp. 440, 444–49, 442–43, 390–91.

33:33–34:9. *Ibid.*, p. 366.

34:22–35:10. The story is told in the oldest life of Mohammed, but Arnold's source is not known. See A. Guillaume, *The Life of Muhammad*, a Translation of Ishaq's *Sirat Rasul Allah* (Lahore: Oxford University Press, 1955), pp. 151–52.

36:6–8. Ishmael was the son of Abraham and his Egyptian slave Hagar, Isaac the son of Abraham by his wife Sarah. When Isaac was born Sarah insisted that Hagar and Ishmael be cast out.—Genesis 16 and 21. It was predicted that both boys would be fathers to great nations.

37:16–23. *Decline and Fall*, ed. Bury, V, 392.

37:27–33. Simon Ockley, *The History of the Saracens* (London, 1857), pp. 351, 288, 412. (Hoctor)

38:2. Matthew 12:19; see p. 60:15–17n.

38:12–14. Gibbon, *Decline and Fall*, ed. Bury, V, 381.

38:34–36. In *St. Paul and Protestantism* and *Literature and Dogma*, *Prose Works*, ed. Super, VI, 115–16, 121, 299–301, 405–6, et passim.

39:11–12. Haggai 2:7.

39:17–18. Isaiah 45:5.

39:21–22. Matthew 11:29. Arnold wrote this passage (which is not in the language of the King James Version) near the beginning of his pocket diary for 1877.—*Note-Books*, ed. Lowry, p. 272.

[LA REFORME INTELLECTUELLE ET MORALE]

Arnold was in the councils of Charles Edward Appleton and his associates when they founded *The Academy* and his article on Obermann had the place of honor at the very beginning of the first number on October 9, 1869, as did his article on Sainte-Beuve in the second number a month later. Both these he may have contributed without compensation. Thereafter, despite Appleton's urging and offer of terms Arnold politely called "handsome," he contributed only one article, appropriate both to the *Academy*'s serious concern for continental books and to his own great interest in the spiritual and political fate of France after the war with Germany and the overthrow of the Second Empire. Ernest Renan's *La Réforme intellectuelle et morale* (i.e., "de la France") deals with that problem. Like Burke, Renan looked at France in the light of her history and in comparison with seventeenth-century England, and like Burke, Renan was essentially conservative. Arnold sensed the weaknesses of the book, as his essay makes clear, but some of Renan's basic principles come so close to Arnold's own that one almost wonders at not seeing sentences like the following quoted in his review: "Un pays n'est pas la simple addition des individus qui le composent; c'est une âme, une conscience, une personne, une résultante vivante" (p. 47) and "L'essentiel n'est pas que telle volonté particulière de la majorité se fasse; l'essentiel est que la raison générale de la nation triomphe" (p. 75). Arnold received two guineas (about one-fourth of what the *Pall Mall Gazette* would have paid) from *The Academy* for his article, which appeared on the first page of the number for February 15, 1872, and was promptly reprinted in America. He himself never republished it. As the notes make clear, he evidently read the book and wrote the essay in some haste. On March 25 he forwarded to Appleton a flattering letter he had received upon the article from Renan himself: "The good of writing in the *Academy* is that though the public do not see what you write, yet the half dozen eminent men, at Paris, Berlin, etc., about whom you particularly care, do, and much more certainly than if you put your notice in the *Times* or *Pall Mall*. Though I can scarce be a contributor as you would kindly wish, I say this much in your Organ's favour."—Diderik Roll-Hansen, "Matthew Arnold and the 'Academy,'" *PMLA* LXVIII, 387 (June, 1953). There are two references to the article in undated letters to his mother, one before and one after publication: "I have been going through Renan's new book on the Reform of France with great care, having promised, alas! to review it for the Academy: these short reviews are not worth doing, for it is shaping what one has to say about a book, and getting under way to say it, which costs time and labour, and not the going on at more or less length when one is started. Then reading this book took me back to Burke, and in short has occupied me more than what I shall write is worth. However I have nearly finished with it now." "I have had an interesting letter from Renan to thank me for my *Academy* article which he had seen: he says I may imagine the interest he read with it [*sic*] as I am 'the person living to whose judgment he attaches most weight.' That is pretty well: the letter is a sad and gloomy one as regards France."

40:2–15. "An Appeal from the New to the Old Whigs" (1791), nearly one-third through. At line 10 Arnold omits the sentence, "He is indeed convinced that the science of government would be poorly cultivated without that study."

41:5–6. "Reflections on the Revolution in France" (1790), about eight-ninths through.

41:7–13. *Ibid.*, about one-seventh through. Burke's expression was "profited of our example." Arnold has re-arranged his sentences and omitted some.

41:14. "A Letter to a Member of the National Assembly" (1791), not quite half-way through. Burke wrote: "Rousseau is their canon . . ."

41:19–24. Ernest Renan, *La Réforme intellectuelle et morale* (Paris, 1871), p. 7.

41:25–33. *Ibid.*, pp. 8, 70–72.

41:33–42:9. *Ibid.*, pp. 60–61, 65–66, 231 ("superficial jacobinism"), 82 ("vulgar republicanism"), 26 and 31 ("materialism"), 51–52, 81.

But Renan says it is "pas probable" that Prussia will be "entraînée à son tour dans la ronde du sabbat démocratique."

42:13. The International Working Men's Association, or "First International," was founded in London in 1864, where Marx quickly assumed the leadership. It reached its highest influence six or seven years later and was generally credited with inspiring, or encouraging, the revolutionary uprising of the Paris Commune in March, 1871. It soon divided into factions, however, and its Marxist wing disbanded in 1876, its Anarchist wing in 1881. The French kings were crowned at Rheims, the Prussian kings lived at Potsdam. See *La Réforme*, pp. 250–51.

42:14–19. The volume contains, in addition to the title piece which occupies about one third of its pages, "La Guerre entre la France et l'Allemagne" (published September 15, 1870), two open letters to D. F. Strauss (dated September 13, 1870, and September 15, 1871), three short articles "De la convocation d'une assemblée pendant le siége" (November 10, 13, and 28, 1870), a long essay on "La Monarchie constitutionnelle en France" (published November 1, 1869) and a lecture on "La Part de la famille et de l'État dans l'éducation" (dated April 19, 1869). The article on the war was a reasoned argument for the establishment of a European federation, a United States of Europe superior to all nationality.

42:25–26. A Paris correspondent summarized the title essay of Renan's book from proof sheets on December 12, 1871, p. 4, cols. 1–2 ("M. Renan on the Decay of France"). It is entirely an admiring summary, which does not mention the other essays in the volume.

43:6. Edgar Quinet (1803–75), French man of letters, was exiled from France for his republican opinions after the *coup d'état* of December 2, 1851. He remained abroad, in the latter decade a voluntary exile, until the overthrow of the Empire on September 4, 1870.

43:9–11. *La Réforme*, pp. 244–48.

43:16–18, 20. *Ibid.*, pp. 67–68.

43:35. *Ibid.*, p. 64.

44:5. *Ibid.*, p. 95.

44:5–11. George Sand, *Journal d'un Voyageur pendant la guerre* (Paris, 1871), pp. 30, 117.

44:11–13. "Ce qui nous a manqué, ce n'est pas le coeur, c'est la tête." "Le Français est bon, étourdi."—Renan, *La Réforme*, pp. 95, 50.

44:16–20. "Letter to a Member of the National Assembly," two-thirds through.

44:30–33. Arnold cited Michelet thus also in "A French Elijah," p. 11:15–17.

45:3–5. "La France est nécessaire comme protestation contre le pédantisme, le dogmatisme, le rigorisme étroit."—*La Réforme*, p. 178.

45:5–9. *Ibid.*, p. 204, in the second letter to Strauss. Renan does not go quite so far as Arnold suggests: "Comme vous, je me suis imposé, en qualité d'ancien clerc, d'observer strictement la règle des moeurs; mais je serais désolé qu'il n'y eût pas des gens du monde pour représenter une vie plus libre."

45:21–22. Psalm 103:7, Prayer-Book Version.

45:24. Gomer is a race mentioned in Genesis 10:2 as the eldest offspring of Noah's son Japheth. It was popularly identified in the nineteenth century with the Celts; see Arnold, *On the Study of Celtic Literature, Prose Works*, ed. Super, III, 292–93 and n. Vercingetorix was the Gallic chieftain who resisted Caesar's conquest of Gaul in 52 B.C., but was defeated, led in triumph at Rome, and executed there in 46 B.C.

45:27–32. *La Réforme*, pp. 153, 27.

45:33–46:4. Arnold discussed the impending disestablishment of the Church of Ireland in the final chapter of *Culture and Anarchy* and ridiculed the newspaper pretensions after the event in "A Recantation and Apology."—*Prose Works*, ed. Super, V, 193–99, 319–24.

46:5–6. For example: "La société que [la Révolution] rêva . . . est une sorte de régiment composé de matérialistes, et où la discipline tient lieu de vertu. La base toute négative que les hommes secs et durs de ce temps donnèrent à la société française ne peut produire qu'un peuple rogue et mal élevé."—*La Réforme*, p. 248.

46:11–16. *Ibid.*, pp. 254–56; see also p. 13.

46:29. Renan referred to "ce pédantisme rogue et jaloux qui nous déplaît parfois dans la Prusse" in his first open letter to Strauss.—*La Réforme*, p. 171.

46:29–33. *Ibid.*, p. xiii; and see pp. 236–37.

46:36–38. *Journal d'un Voyageur*, p. 31.

47:19–29. *La Réforme*, pp. xi, 120, 124, 179. The Italics are Arnold's. He has clearly misread one of these sentences, in which Renan in 1870 lamented the rupture between the two parts of the European race "dont l'union importait le plus au progrès de l'esprit humain"—"la grande maîtresse . . ." is Germany and "l'ingénieuse . . ." is France.

47:35–36. "Il est incontestable que, si on soumettait la question au peuple alsacien, une immense majorité se prononcerait pour rester unie à la France," and "L'Alsace est allemande de langue et de race, mais elle ne désire pas faire partie de l'État allemand," Renan wrote to Strauss, *La Réforme*, pp. 181, 198.

48:10. Sonnet "To a Republican Friend, 1848. Continued," line 4; published in *The Strayed Reveller, and Other Poems*, 1849.

48:11–13. "Même de nos jours, l'Allemagne a-t-elle un poëte comme M. Victor Hugo, un prosateur comme Mme. Sand, un critique comme M. Sainte-Beuve, une imagination comme celle de M. Michelet, un caractère philosophique comme celui de M. Littré?"—*La Réforme*, pp. x–xi.

48:20. "The serious" or "the excellent" is for Aristotle the principal ingredient of imaginative literature, which is "more philosophical and more serious than history."—*Poetics* 1451 b 6; and see his use of the word at 1448 a 2 and 1449 b 17.

48:21. *Aeneid* xii. 435.

48:28–29. *La Réforme*, p. 27.

49:2–4. See p. 48:11–13n.

49:6–8. "It is my most cherished conviction that this Anglo-American race is developing a finer organization than the stock from which it sprang. . . . Grant that is it the worthy mission of the current British literature to render style clear, simple, and convincing, it may yet be the mission of Americans to take that style and make it beautiful."—Thomas Wentworth Higginson, "On an Old Latin Text-Book," *Atlantic Essays* (Boston, 1871), pp. 337–38. Arnold jotted this passage in his pocket diary for December 19–22, 1871.—*Note-Books*, ed. Lowry, p. 163. In another essay in this volume (much of which is devoted to "culture" and "Americanism"), Higginson remarked: "I utterly reject the position taken by Matthew Arnold, that the Puritan spirit in America was essentially hostile to literature and art."—p. 59.

49:14–15. "Le sentiment des Vandales chastes devant les moeurs et le luxe de l'empire romain, une sort de fureur puritaine, la jalousie et la rage contre la vie facile de ceux qui jouissent."—*La Réforme*, p. 159.

49:17–18. *Ibid.*, p. 337, in the essay on "La Part de la famille et de l'État dans l'éducation."

49:21–29. *Ibid.*, pp. 293, 285, 278.

49:32–37. *Ibid.*, pp. 112–13, with omissions.

50:7. Renan was an unsuccessful candidate for the legislature in the general election of 1869; he alluded to his campaign in *La Ré-forme*, pp. 23, 30, and 186.

50:7–9. F. W. Riemer, *Mittheilungen über Goethe* (Berlin, 1841), II, 281, jotted in Arnold's pocket diary for January 28, 1871.—*Note-Books*, ed. Lowry, p. 150. Goethe quotes I Corinthians 7:31; Renan quotes the same scriptural passage in *La Réforme*, p. 61.

[ISAIAH XL–LXVI]

As England moved toward the solution of her elementary educa-tion problem, Arnold foresaw what he regarded as the danger of removing the study of the Bible from the schools altogether. "The Bible . . . is for the child in an elementary school almost his only contact with poetry and philosophy. . . . Even in the lowest classes the children in a German Protestant school begin learning verses of the Psalms by heart, and by the time a scholar reaches the top of the school he knows by heart a number of the finest passages from the Psalms and from the prophetical and historical books of the Old Testament, and nearly all the principal Gospel discourses and par-ables of the New. These have become a part of the stock of his mind, and he has them for life. What a course of eloquence and poetry (to call it by that name alone) is this in a school which has and can have but little eloquence and poetry! and how much do our elementary schools lose by not having such a course as part of their school programme." This passage in his report for 1868 upon the Wesleyan Training College at Westminster is echoed in other re-ports and in his letters. This frame of mind is undoubtedly what im-pelled him to try to make one of the greatest of the prophetical books available to school children by diminishing the difficulties that stood in the way of its being read with pleasure in the Authorized Version. Since, however, in adapting his version subsequently to the needs of a more general reading public, he omitted from his Intro-duction long and significant remarks on his notion of the place of good reading in the schools, the reader should be advised not to overlook these omitted passages as they are printed in the Textual Notes.

It is not clear when Arnold first approached Macmillan about his projected text-book, but by the end of December, 1871, plans for the printing were under way and the text was promised by Arnold for early in January. Proofs were reaching him in early February, and the printer's work was done by the end of April. *A Bible-Reading for Schools* was published at the price of one shilling on May 18, 1872; Arnold received his first copies from the publisher three days earlier. An edition of two thousand copies was exhausted by the latter part of September, with the help of a favorable review in *The Times* for September 19 (p. 4, col. 4), and a so-called "second edition" of a thousand copies was printed from stereotyped plates at that time and a "third edition" in October.—Buckler, *Matthew Arnold's Books*, pp. 119–21; *Athenaeum*, May 18, 1872, p. 632. The plates were used again for "fourth" and "fifth" editions in 1875 and 1889. To William Steward, a working man at Bedford with whom Arnold corresponded about the religious problem among the laboring classes, he forwarded a copy to show "that I am trying to help popular education in an untried, but, as I think, an important sort of a way." When Steward suggested that masterpieces of English literature might serve the same purpose, Arnold agreed; "but I think they will be read all the better, and with the more appreciation, if there is some such basis as that which this Bible reading proposes to give. And, after all, Isaiah is immensely superior to Milton's *Comus* in all the more essential qualities of a literary production, even as literature."—*Letters*, ed. Russell, May 30 and June 11, 1872.

As early as September 26, 1872, Macmillan raised the question of publishing the book at a higher price, finer in type and print, for general readers. But not until July 13, 1875, did Arnold feel ready to proceed. To the chapters already published he added, as appendix, four other passages from Isaiah that were associated by critics with the work of the "deutero-Isaiah," or at least dissociated from that of Isaiah of Jerusalem. The publication goal was Christmas day, and it seems to have been met by the narrowest of margins: the book was advertised as "nearly ready" in *The Athenaeum* for December 18, p. 819, and listed among the new books in that journal a week later (p. 879). The price was five shillings. In order to make it seem larger, Macmillan persuaded Arnold to begin the sequence of pagination with the beginning of the Introduction (a term he preferred to Arnold's "Preface").—Buckler, *Matthew Arnold's Books*, pp. 121–23.

A few years after its appearance M. E. Grant Duff spoke of the book in terms which drew from Arnold the remark that he had undertaken the work with a good deal of hope, but that it had produced very little result. He did, nevertheless, proceed with a version of the first thirty-nine chapters, which he published in 1883.

51:24–27. The Convocation of Canterbury, an assembly of clerics of the Church of England, in 1870 set up committees to undertake revision of the English translation of the Bible, principally in order to secure scholarly fidelity to the best texts. The revisers were instructed "to introduce as few alterations as possible into the text of the Authorized Version, consistently with faithfulness" and "to limit, as far as possible, the expression of such alterations to the language of the Authorized and earlier English versions." The Revised Version of the New Testament was published in 1881, of the Old Testament in 1885. Neither supplanted the Authorized Version in popular favor.—*Oxford Dictionary of the Christian Church*. The early deliberations of the revisers provided a background for some of the humor of *Literature and Dogma*.

52:11 (variant). Wordsworth, *The Excursion*, I, 135–36, 166–69 (where Wordsworth reads "Nourished" and "gave"). Goldsmith, *The Traveller*, lines 178, 138, 401–2. Arnold, "Report on the Wesleyan Training College at Westminster for the Year 1868," *Reports on Elementary Schools*, ed. F. Sandford (London, 1889), pp. 295–97; ed. F. S. Marvin (London, 1908), pp. 262–63. Isaiah 26:18.

52:22–25. The prophet Isaiah, traditionally author of the entire Old Testament book that bears his name, carried on his prophetic work at the court of the kings of Judah in the last third of the eighth century B.C. It has long been generally agreed, however, that Chapters 40–66 were written during the last years of the Babylonian captivity, which came to an end with the conquest of Babylon by Cyrus in 539 B.C., and these chapters are sometimes referred to as the "second Isaiah" or "deutero-Isaiah." More modern critics separate this section into a "second Isaiah" (Chapts. 40–55) and a slightly later "third Isaiah" (Chapts. 56–66) written after the return of the Jews to Palestine.

52:30–31. St. Jerome made this statement in the Preface to his translation of Isaiah, in the Prologue to his Commentary on Isaiah, and in a letter to Paulinus on the study of Scripture.—Migne, *PL*, XXVIII, 771; XXIV, 18; XXII, 547. All three passages, and the one from St. Augustine's *Confessions*, are cited in Wilhelm Gesenius, *Der Prophet Jesaia, übersetzt und mit einem vollständigen philologisch-kritischen und historischen Commentar begleitet* (Leipzig, 1821), I, 41.

52:31–32. St. Augustine inquired of St. Ambrose, bishop of Milan, what parts of Holy Scripture would best prepare him for baptism, and was told to read Isaiah—"presumably," says Augustine, "because he foreshadowed more clearly than the others the Gospel and the calling of the Gentiles." "But," he continued, "I could not understand him when I began to read, and supposing that the whole would be like the part I read, I set him aside with a view to trying again when I became more expert in the tongue of Our Lord."—*Confessions* IX, v.

52:36–53:1. Gesenius, *Jesaia*, I, 39.

53:23–54:15. Arnold's version, where it differs from the Authorized Version, reads:

2. A grievous vision is declared unto me! the robber robbeth, and the spoiler spoileth. Go up, O Elam! . . .

5. Prepare the table, watch the watch, eat, drink.—*Rise, ye princes, anoint the shield!*

7. And if he see a train of couples of horsemen, a train of asses, a train of camels, let him hearken diligently with much heed.

8. And he cried as a lion: My Lord, . . .

9. And, behold, there cometh a train of men, with couples of horsemen! And he answered . . .

10. O my threshing-ground and thou son of my floor! that which . . .

54:36. Heinrich von Ewald (1803–75), a native of Göttingen, was professor at the university there for most of his life, apart from a decade at Tübingen (where he was quite at odds with the "Tübingen school" of higher critics led by F. C. Baur). He was a lively teacher and a very significant philologist, historian, and critic of the Bible.

55:38. John Keble (1792–1866), having preceded Thomas Arnold as an undergraduate at Corpus Christi College, Oxford, was his contemporary and close friend as fellow of Oriel College. They drifted apart when Keble a decade or so after Matthew Arnold's birth became a moving spirit among the Tractarians and Dr. Arnold took the broad church line with equal vigor. But while Matthew Arnold was a pupil at Winchester he called on his godfather at his parish nearby. Keble was elected professor of poetry at Oxford twenty-six years before Matthew Arnold.

56:18–24, 28–31. See Ewald, *Commentary on the Prophets of the Old Testament*, tr. J. Frederick Smith (London, 1875–81), IV, 348 (with the reference to Jeremiah 29:22), 353.

57:17–18. An English version of A. H. L. Heeren's *Historical Researches into the Politics, Intercourse, and Trade of the Principal Nations of Antiquity* was published in three volumes at Oxford in 1833.

57:22–24. Arnold here accepts the interpretation of Cheyne rather than Ewald, *Prophets*, IV, 274 ("For your sakes I send to Babel and throw into groaning their harps, and the rejoicing of the Chaldeans into sighing.")

57:34–58:4. Ewald, *Prophets*, IV, 353–54. "I am holier than thou" is from Isaiah 65:5.

59:3. Thomas Kelly Cheyne (1841–1915) was a fellow of Arnold's college, Balliol, from 1868 to 1882. During his undergraduate years he had studied with Ewald at Göttingen. He was one of the earliest English scholars to support the historical criticism of the Bible with adequate scholarship. As a reviewer for *The Academy* he wrote both on the present book and on Arnold's later version of *Isaiah of Jerusalem*, defending, in the former review, his own "setting religion in the earth" (see p. 62:19) on the ground that " 'noble and consecrated expressions' are sometimes, as in this passage, entirely wrong, and commonly among the chief obstacles to understanding the Scriptures. [Mr. Arnold] has pointed this out in part with great force in the case of the New Testament (*Literature and Dogma*, pp. [289–90]); how is it that he misses the mark in the Old?"—*Academy* IX, 163 (February 19, 1876); see also XXIV, 410–11 (December 22, 1883). Cheyne's *Book of Isaiah Chronologically Arranged. An amended version, with historical and critical introductions and explanatory notes* (London, 1870) had a somewhat more literary aim than his scholarly version with commentary that appeared ten years later; like Arnold's version, it was published by Macmillan. When Arnold added four passages (21:1–10, 13:2–14:23, chaps. 34–35 and 24–27) from the earlier part of Isaiah to his translation of chaps. 40–66, he was following Cheyne's opinion in 1870; see Ewald, *Prophets*, II, 342–43.

59:8–14. *The Psalms Chronologically Arranged. An amended version with historical introductions and explanatory notes by Four Friends*. London and Cambridge: Macmillan and Co., 1867. The text, as Arnold indicates, was mainly the Prayer Book Version. In 1870 this book appeared in a second edition and, with the notes abbreviated, in the Golden Treasury series. The "Four Friends" included Alexander W. Potts and Francis E. Kitchener.

59:31–32. Among the schools Arnold inspected was the Jews' Free School in London. His speech at a banquet for the school on May 21, 1884, will be printed in the Appendix to vol. X of this edition of his works.

60:15–17. In Matthew 12:19. Arnold used the phrase in "Lines Written in Kensington Gardens" (1852): "The will to neither strive nor cry" (line 41), and in the Preface to *Essays in Criticism* (1865), *Prose Works*, ed. Super, III, 286:10.

60:17–19. The passage is echoed in John 12:38 and Romans 10:16.

61:9–10. See the instruction of Convocation to the revisers of the English Bible, p. 51:24–27n.

61:20–21. See p. 62:16–17.

61:23. Robert Lowth (1710–87), bishop of London and Arnold's predecessor as professor of poetry at Oxford by a little more than a century, analyzed the poetic style of Hebrew sacred poetry in his lectures from that chair and published a pioneering version and commentary on Isaiah in 1778. The edition used here is *Isaiah: a New Translation; with a Preliminary Dissertation and Notes*, by Robert Lowth. From the tenth English edition. Boston, Mass., 1834.

61:24. Campegius Vitringa (c. 1659–1722), Dutch scholar, published a commentary on Isaiah in two folio volumes, 1714–20. Abenezra, or Ibn Ezra (1092–1167), medieval rabbi, was the earliest scholar to sense the problem of the different authorship of the two principal parts of the Book of Isaiah.

61:31–34. Sebastian Castellio (1515–63), Calvinist theologian, aimed at classical elegance in his Latin translation of the Bible (Basel, 1551). See Lowth, *Isaiah*, p. xxviii.

61:35–37. *Ibid.*, p. lix.

62:3–12. These passages are Isaiah 40:2, 14; 47:8; 53:4, 10; 56:1.

62:16–17. Cheyne, p. v.

62:18–20, 25–28. Isaiah 42:4, 53:1, 7; (variant) 42:3.

63:8–11. Isaiah 53:8.

64:16. Horace *Carmina* III, ii, 31–32.

64:35–36. Isaiah 42:4.

65:6–7. The Septuagint is a Greek translation of the Old Testament made at Alexandria in the second century B.C. The Vulgate is St. Jerome's Latin translation of the Bible, made at the end of the fourth century A.D. Martin Luther's translation of the Bible from the original tongues into German appeared in 1522 (N.T.) and 1534 (O.T.)

67:21. Ahaz was king of Judah c. 735–715 B.C.; the prophet Isaiah flourished during his reign. See p. 52:22–25n.

68:12 (variant). J. H. Newman, "The Protestant Idea of Antichrist," *Essays Critical and Historical* (London, 1888), II, 184. The beast, the scarlet woman (*Revelation* 17:3–8) and Antichrist (I John 2 and 4) were Protestant symbols for the Church of Rome.

68:23–29. "Maximen und Reflexionen," *Werke* (Weimar, 1907),

XLII (2), 192, jotted in Arnold's pocket diary at the end of 1871.—
Note-Books, ed. Lowry, p. 168.

69:26–29. Ewald, *Prophets of the Old Testament*, IV, 255–56.

70:24–25. *Ibid.*, IV, 292–97.

70:25–28. Gesenius, *Iesaia*, III, 121–22.

71:16. "There's a good time coming" took on a proverbial com-
plexion in the nineteenth century. It was the opening line of a poem
by Charles Mackay, published as "Wait a Little Longer" in his *Voices
from the Crowd* (1846); later the title was changed to "The Good
Time Coming." Each of its eight stanzas begins: "There's a good
time coming, boys, / A good time coming." Arnold used the expression again in the Preface to *Higher Schools and Universities in Germany*, p. 111:7–8.

71:28. The perhaps legendary Licinian laws, proposed by the
tribune C. Licinius Calvus Stolo in 377 B.C. and passed ten years later,
were said to have ended the struggle between patricians and plebe-
ians in Rome.

72:1–3. "All men ever have, and ever will complain, that the bur-
dens, crosses, satieties of this life, do much surpass the conveniences
and comforts of it."—"The Profitableness of Godliness," *Theological
Works*, ed. A. Napier (Cambridge, 1859), I, 216.

[SAVINGS BANKS IN SCHOOLS]

"Savings Banks in Schools" is an anonymous article in *The Pall Mall
Gazette* for November 22, 1873, first attributed to Arnold by Pro-
fessor Fraser Neiman and published by him in *Essays, Letters, and
Reviews by Matthew Arnold* (Cambridge: Harvard University
Press, 1960), pp. 194–98. Arnold was paid £4.4.0 for the article. A
memorandum in his pocket diary for November 11 reads: "Send
Savings Bank."

73:19–20. J. P. Eckermann, *Gespräche mit Goethe*, ed. E. Castle
(Berlin, 1916), I, 323 (March 21, 1830), jotted in Arnold's pocket
diary at the end of 1866 and four times thereafter, the last at the
beginning of 1870.—*Note-Books*, ed. Lowry, pp. 38, 43, 67, 114, 120.

73:26–74:11. F. Laurent, *Conférence sur l'épargne*. Nouvelle édi-
tion, précédée du rapport du Jury, qui a décerné, pour la première
fois, la prix Guinard à la *Conférence sur l'épargne*. Bruxelles: Typo-
graphie Bruylant-Christophe & Compagnie, 1875. The report of the
jury, from which (pp. i–ii) Arnold draws his information about the

bequest, is dated February 3, 1873. Dr. Jean-Baptiste Guinard died on May 28, 1867. François Laurent (1810–87), professor of civil law at the University of Ghent, was a liberal historian and writer upon questions of the relation of church and state, between which he favored entire separation.

74:8–9. Émile-Louis-Victor de Laveleye (1822–92), Belgian man of letters and economist, was one of the editors of the *Revue des Deux Mondes* and a prolific writer on a variety of subjects, including public instruction.

74:12–75:22. Laurent, *Conférence* (1875), pp. iii, v–vii, ix–xi, xvi, 32, 39.

74:37. The communes are the municipalities; the communal schools are the public elementary schools.

75:22–76:2. Laurent, *Conférence* (1875), pp. 22–23, xi, 11, 23.

76:3–6, 24–77:5. *Ibid.*, pp. 8–9.

77:13–19. *Ibid.*, pp. 6–7.

77:20–32. *Ibid.*, pp. 10, 15.

77:33–34. John 12:25.

78:2–7. Laurent, *Conférence* (1875), p. 27.

78:11. Count Pellegrino Rossi (1787–1848), Italian born but naturalized in France in 1833, held the chair of political economy at the Collége de France, returned to Italy in 1845 as envoy from Guizot's government and became first minister to Pius IX in 1848. He was author of many of the constitutional reforms in the papal states, but was assassinated by the radicals at the beginning of the revolution of that year.

78:12–13. The "Salles d'asile" are public nurseries for children of working women; they provide day care and appropriate instruction from the ages of two to six.

[A SPEECH AT WESTMINSTER]

"I am miserable, because I have to-morrow to make an address to the Association of Westminster Teachers," Arnold wrote to Lady de Rothschild on December 5, 1873. "I found they would be mortified if I refused, but I am so little used to speaking that the prospect quite upsets me. Think of me with pity about four o'clock to-morrow afternoon."—*Letters*, ed. Russell. The address was essentially a reply to the attack of John Morley on the Elementary Education Act of 1870. Morley's *The Struggle for National Education*—initially three articles in the *Fortnightly Review* (of which Morley was editor) in August–October, 1873, then augmented as a book published on November 1—was aimed at removing all religious instruction and sectarian government from the public elementary schools (which by definition of the act included all schools that were inspected by the Education Department and received a parliamentary grant, whether governed by religious boards or elected local school boards); the immediate focus of the attack was the clause that permitted local boards to pay from the rates pupil fees for indigent pupils in sectarian schools if the parents chose such schools. Morley and Arnold were friends; indeed one sees in the book suggestions that Morley had been reading Arnold, for on the same page (70) he criticizes those bishops of Gloucester and Winchester Arnold had made sport of in *Literature and Dogma* (Ellicott for brutal hostility to the workingmen's movement to improve their wages, Wilberforce for "denouncing dissent as a co-equal cause with beerhouses in producing rural immorality"). But on the issue of Church establishment and religious instruction they were poles apart. Arnold's ms was basis for the report in *The Pall Mall Gazette* on December 9 and the lecture was published in *Macmillan's Magazine* for February 1874; Arnold received 2½ gns. from the *Gazette*, 10 gns. from *Macmillan's*.

79:14–20. Morley cited many of the inspectors' reports in support of his assertion that "the teachers are bad," "the schools are . . . too small to support an efficient system," and "only one child in sixty-three . . . received even a decent amount of primary instruction."— *National Education*, pp. 34, 48, and *Fortnightly Review* XX, 152 (August, 1873).

80:10–20. Julie Annevelle, "L'instruction publique aux États-Unis d'Amérique," *Bibliothèque universelle et revue suisse* XLVIII n.s., 451–69 (November, 1873). The author claims "une expérience assez longue des écoles américaines et de la jeunesse qu'elles façonnent."

80:20–31. Annevelle, pp. 451, 452n. The figure for Maine is true "dans quelques villes"; ninety-four per cent of the schoolmasters of Michigan "ne sont nullement préparés pour leur vocation," which may not be quite the same as "unfit for their function."

80:35–81:9. Annevelle, pp. 458–59 (with omissions), 454.

81:9–15. *National Education*, pp. 28–29. "Instruction enough for this" refers to "profit by professors' lectures," not (as Arnold's paraphrase might be misunderstood to suggest) "shaving at a barber's."

81:15. Richard Porson (1759–1808), regius professor of Greek at Cambridge, had a reputation for learning almost legendary.

81:21–82:13. Annevelle, pp. 454 (Arnold omits "Latin" after "political economy" on her list), 455–56 (where he adds "physiology" and "political economy" from the previous list), 462–63, 459n (*"fine French scholars"*). *Télémaque* (1699) was a narrative in prose of the imaginary adventures of Telemachus, written by François de la Mothe-Fénelon for the instruction of his pupil the Duke of Burgundy.

82:18. The "classical and commercial academies" were private and inadequate schools that made their appeal to the lower middle class, which could not afford the large "public" secondary schools and were moreover unable to judge the quality of education. See Arnold's *Popular Education of France* and *A French Eton, Prose Works*, ed. Super, II, 22, 281, 297, 310.

82:36–83:6. Morley, *National Education*, p. 3, jotted in Arnold's pocket diary for January 8, 1874.—*Note-Books*, ed. Lowry, p. 207. For Morley's sympathy with the state of the laboring class, see pp. 68–70.

83:27–36. Annevelle, p. 464.

84:25–26. See *Schools and Universities on the Continent, Prose Works*, ed. Super, IV, 230–31, 243.

84:27–31. Morley, *National Education*, p. 41. He has been quoting newspaper advertisements for schoolmasters in the sectarian schools, including one in which the teacher was "to act as clerk and *sexton* [hence "digging graves" in Morley's comment]; harmonium, singing, and sewing required. House and £ 50, and two-thirds of government grant."

85:5. Forster defended the religious impartiality of the Elementary Education Act in a speech at Liverpool on November 25, 1873.

85:19. James Guinness Rogers (1822–1911), pastor of the Clapham Congregational Church on Gratton Square from 1865 to 1900, was a friend and political ally of Gladstone's and one of the most influential Nonconformists in England.

86:22–23. For the Revised Code, see p. 87:18–20n.

86:30–34. Joshua Girling Fitch (1824–1903) moved from the principalship of the Borough Road Training College to an inspectorship under the Education Department in 1863. Arnold refers to his article, "Statistical Fallacies Respecting Public Instruction," which corrected a pamphlet upon which Morley had partially based his attack. Morley deleted that portion of his work when he published it as a book and substituted Fitch's article for his own planned fourth part in the *Fortnightly Review* XX, 614–28 (November, 1873). For

Fitch's praise of the schools, see p. 624. Fitch made much the same comment as Arnold respecting the misuse of inspectors' reports—that they were intended for teachers and school managers as guides to improvement, not for a general public as full and impartial estimates of the quality of instruction at large.

86:34–36. Anthony John Mundella (1825–97), English-born son of an Italian political refugee, became a hosiery manufacturer in Nottingham and was member of Parliament for Sheffield from 1868 until his death. He knew something of German education from frequent visits to his firm's branch factory at Chemnitz, became a public advocate of education reform, was a warm supporter of Forster's Elementary Education Act and in 1880 sponsored the supplementary act which made education universally compulsory in England. He was vice-president of the Committee of Council on Education (i.e., ministerial head of the Education Department) in Gladstone's government of 1880–85. Arnold alludes here to a speech Mundella made in the House of Commons on March 18, 1870, quoted by Morley, *National Education*, p. 25.

87:11–16. See Arnold's earnest recommendation of a modern municipal structure in *Schools and Universities on the Continent, Prose Works*, ed. Super, IV, 306–7.

87:18. Edwin Abbott Abbott, D. D., was the headmaster of the City of London School from 1865–89.

87:18–20. The Revised Code promulgated by Robert Lowe in 1862 provided that grants to schools would be in proportion to the number of students who, having attended a certain minimum number of days, passed the Education Department's examinations in reading, writing, and arithmetic. This was described as "payment by results" or "free trade in education." Arnold's opposition to the code was repeatedly expressed in his inspectoral reports and most importantly in the anonymous article, "The Twice-Revised Code," *Fraser's Magazine* LXV, 347–65 (March, 1862), which he published despite fear that he was risking his inspectoral post in doing so. See *Prose Works*, ed. Super, II, 212–43 and notes.

87:21. The code of 1871, laid down by W. E. Forster to give effect to the Elementary Education Act of the preceding year, provided for examination in the three primary studies according to six stages or "standards" and introduced several other studies as options for the more advanced students.

87:29–30. "The Church-Porch," lines 333–34.

88:18. "The teachers of the primary and secondary schools [of

Zurich] . . . unite with the whole body of teachers of the higher schools of the canton to form a School Synod, having for its business the promotion of education in the canton, and to convey the wishes and proposals of the teaching body to the authorities."— *Schools and Universities on the Continent, Prose Works*, ed. Super, IV, 283.

88:30–37. Arnold made this point in his general report as school inspector for the year 1872, and, at greater length, in his report for 1874.—*Reports on Elementary Schools*, ed. F. R. Sanford (London, 1889), pp. 163–64, 182–84.

89:7–9. Mark 4:26–27 (Arnold's version?)

[HIGHER SCHOOLS AND UNIVERSITIES IN GERMANY]

Arnold's republication of the chapters on Germany from his *Schools and Universities on the Continent* was intended, as he said in his new Preface, to illuminate the recently debated and still current problem of England's handling of Irish university education. The University of Dublin had in fact only one college, Trinity, a Protestant foundation dating from the reign of Queen Elizabeth I. The Queen's University, with colleges in Cork, Galway, and Belfast, was established in 1847 as a non-sectarian institution equally available to all faiths, but it was not satisfactory to the Roman Catholic hierarchy, which set up a university of its own in Dublin, initially with John Henry Newman as rector. This university, however, lacked the power to grant degrees and was without either endowment or financial support from Parliament. Hence the continued Catholic discontent which Gladstone hoped to answer with his Irish University Education bill in 1873.

The position of the Roman Catholics throughout Europe in the 1870's was extraordinarily complex. Two months before the Pope lost his temporal power altogether to the Italian monarchy, the first Vatican Council defined the dogma of papal infallibility; one of its most earnest advocates was Henry Edward Manning, archbishop of Westminster, himself a convert like Newman from the Church of England clergy. Reaction against the dogma led to the splitting off from the Roman Catholic Church of a considerable group in Germany, Switzerland, and the Lowlands who called themselves the Old Catholics. Meanwhile, Germany, in consequence of the war with France in 1870–71, found herself united under the King of

Prussia into a federation of states of which most followed the Prussian lead even in areas where they had constitutional autonomy; and Prussia, as a Protestant state, strongly suspected the Catholic Church of opposition to this union which gave her a hegemony over the Catholic German states.

The Prussian government's endowment of Roman Catholic universities within its state system was a consequence of Prussia's acquisition in 1815, after the Napoleonic wars, of large Catholic provinces, principally on the Rhine. The University of Bonn was founded in 1818. Provision was made for Catholic education and religious practice through a bureau in the Prussian government. But Bismarck's consciousness of Catholic opposition to German unification led him to embark on the so-called *Kulturkampf* to define the separate functions of church and state, through the passage in the Prussian legislature in May, 1873, and in the two succeeding years, of a series of increasingly stringent laws restricting the sphere of Catholic activity. At the end of the decade, he retreated from his position, but not before the expulsion of the religious orders gave the occasion for Hopkins' magnificent poem "The Wreck of the Deutschland" (1875–76). These developments were for the most part in the future, of course, when Arnold wrote his Preface. The essay itself, independent of unforeseeable developments in Prussia, is Arnold's most lucid statement of his conception of the relation between Church and State.

Arnold's determination to republish the German chapters of *Schools and Universities on the Continent* was made before he left on a prolonged continental tour on February 15, 1873, and proofs followed him abroad. He promised on March 6 that he would send Macmillan the new Preface within the week. But it remained undone; when November came round he begged for a postponement until January.—Buckler, *Matthew Arnold's Books*, pp. 112–14. It was still before him when he described his occupations to Lady de Rothschild on December 5. There is in the latter part of the Preface an allusion to an article by Renan published in the *Revue des Deux Mondes* as late as February 15, 1874. "I have just finished the new preface to my account of German schools," he wrote in an undated letter to his sister Mrs. Forster, "and have at last accomplished comparing Bismarck's policy towards R. Catholicism with ours in Ireland —a thing I have long wished to do and I think it will interest people and perhaps produce some effect." *Higher Schools and Universities in Germany* was advertised for "next week" in *The Athenaeum* for February 28, p. 279, and as "just ready" on March 7, p. 315, at the price of six shillings. Sales were disappointing; in December, 1875, Macmillan paid off £25 in lieu of royalties on the rest of the edition, which seems not to have been exhausted until the end of 1881.—Buckler, *Matthew Arnold's Books*, pp. 25, 114.

90:11–12. Gladstone's Irish University Education Bill, viewed as the third great measure of his government for the alleviation of Irish grievances (after the disestablishment of the Protestant Episcopalian Church of Ireland in 1869 and the land tenure reform of 1870), was introduced on February 13, 1873. It provided for the combination of the Queen's University (three non-sectarian colleges at Belfast, Cork, and Galway; but the last was to be abolished), Trinity College (Protestant Episcopalian), the Roman Catholic University, Magee College (a small Presbyterian institution) and perhaps other educational institutions at the higher level, into a single university, from which religious tests were barred and certain controversial disciplines were withdrawn. There would be a large measure of government support and the new university would be controlled by a council selected on a complicated formula that was meant to ensure representation from all groups and a large measure of self-government. The bill was defeated at its second reading on March 11 by a vote of 287 to 284.

90:22–24. Arnold's informant may well have been Georg Bunsen, son of Dr. Arnold's friend the former Prussian ambassador to England; a letter from Arnold to him on June 10, 1872, inquires about some aspect of Prussian education as it developed since Arnold's tour in 1865.

92:13. The German word *Wissenschaft*, or *wissenschaftlich*, has much broader connotations than the English *science* or *scientifically*. In his lecture on "Literature and Science" (1882) Arnold quoted with approval Friedrich Wolf's definition: "I call all teaching *scientific* which is systematically laid out and followed up to its original sources."—*Prose Works*, ed. Super, vol. X.

92:25–32. Arnold's best-known statement of this principle is in "The Function of Criticism at the Present Time" (1864), *Prose Works*, ed. Super, III, 269–71.

94:5–6. On January 27, 1874, for example, public meetings under the auspices of the Protestant Educational Institute were held at St. James's Hall and Exeter Hall to express sympathy with the German government in its struggle against Ultramontanism. Exeter Hall as a name was synonymous with the more evangelical Protestantism of England.

94:7–9. In a speech before the Prussian Parliament, Bismarck cited what he claimed were official British memoranda on the Irish Catholics to show a parallel to the plotting of the Ultramontanes in Germany. "Who is trying to find Prince Bismarck new excuses, drawn from the condition of our Irish affairs, for a disastrous policy which we have long abandoned in Ireland, though some few silly politicians would like to be nibbling at it again?"—*Spectator* XLVI, 687 (May 31, 1873).

94:18–21. The Church of Ireland (Protestant Episcopalian) was disestablished by an Act of July 26, 1869. The term "Catholic emancipation" usually refers, however, to the removal of civil disabilities from the Roman Catholics in 1829.

94:23–25. Gladstone's Irish University Education Bill professed to set up a teaching university as well as an examining university, but in order to avoid sectarian misgivings respecting rights of conscience, it was to be without chairs in theology, philosophy, and modern history.

94:26–27. "In point of fact, this measure was one of indirect endowment of the Roman Catholic Church," claimed Sir Michael Hicks Beach in the debate on the second reading of the bill on March 3, 1873.—*Times*, March 4, p. 8, col. 1. In the new Conservative administration of 1874 Hicks Beach became chief secretary for Ireland.

94:36–95:2. Bartholomew Woodlock, rector of the Catholic University of Dublin, quoted by [James Lowry Whittle], "The Ministry and University Education in Ireland," *Quarterly Review*, American ed., CXXXIV, 144 (January, 1873). The article is on Arnold's reading-list for 1873.—*Note-Books*, ed. Lowry, p. 588.

95:10–12. In the debate on the bill on March 6, 1873, Robert Lowe, chancellor of the exchequer, made the distinction between the term "college," which implied a teaching provision, and "university," which implied, in addition to a teaching function, the power of giving degrees. There was every room for competition among teachers, but the degree-granting power should be made as nearly a monopoly as possible, he said, to prevent debasement by competitive underbidding. *The Times* remarked in a leading article: "His argument, if it was worth anything, could be carried to the length suggested, by Mr. [Gathorne] Hardy, of making the University of London the single Examining Board of the United Kingdom—a result which the representative of that University [Lowe sat in Parliament for the University of London] might not ungracefully advocate, but which is not likely to be approved by the independent judgment of others." —March 7, p. 9, col. 2.

95:30–32. See, for example, the statement of the Irish correspondent to *The Times:* "No inconsiderable section of the Irish community has a real grievance. . . . Their demands ought to be complied with, so far as they are just, . . . [but] we cannot recede from the fixed lines of our recent policy, and cannot endow Catholicism as such, by the endowment of purely Roman Catholic Colleges."—February 6, 1873, p. 7, col. 3. In introducing the Irish University Education Bill, Gladstone said: "Denominational endowment [i.e., by the government], whether applied to a University or to a College, in Ireland would be in opposition to the uniform and explicit declarations which have been made ever since this question assumed a new position six or seven years ago by, I believe, every member of the Government, and, as I can safely assert, by myself."—*Times*, February 14, p. 4, col. 5.

95:33–37. See p. 96:32–97:33n.

96:6–9. Leading article, August 18, 1873, p. 9, col. 4, jotted in Arnold's pocket diary for August 5–7.—*Note-Books*, ed. Lowry, p. 198.

96:15. The Dublin correspondent of *The Times* quoted *The Nation* (Dublin) of February 22 as saying: "The Catholics of Ireland demand, and need, and must have a Catholic University, or—call it what we may—a great central national institution which shall be for them the equal in every respect of Trinity College, and which shall fulfill for them the ends which Trinity has so well and proudly fulfilled for our Protestant fellow-countrymen. To pretend that they will ever be satisfied with less would be uncandid and deceptive."—*Times*, February 24, 1873, p. 6, col. 2.

96:32–97:33. The "anti-popery" bills introduced in the lower house of the Prussian legislature in January, 1873, by Dr. Adalbert Falk, minister of ecclesiastical affairs, abolished seminaries for Roman Catholic boys preparing for the priesthood and required them to attend the ordinary secondary schools and the universities, where they would go through a regular course of university studies like candidates for the other learned professions and submit to the university examinations rather than to examination by the bishops, as had been permitted them since 1850. No one might be nominated to a living by his bishop without the consent of the state.—*Times*, January 14, 1873, p. 12, col. 3. The resistance of the Roman Catholic bishops was countered by severe penalties imposed by civil courts, on which, to be sure, Catholic laymen were represented.

97:37–98:1. Richard Southwell Bourke, after 1867 sixth Earl of

Mayo, was chief secretary for Ireland in the Conservative administrations of the Earl of Derby in 1852, 1858, and 1866–68. Archbishop Patrick Leahy and Bishop John Derry, delegated by the Irish Catholic archbishops and bishops to enter into negotiations with the Government respecting a charter and endowment for the Catholic University of Ireland, approached Lord Mayo on October 23, 1867. Subsequent negotiations led to a memorandum from the bishops, dated March 31, 1868, setting forth their notion of the constitution and government appropriate to such a university, which was so far from what the Government was prepared to offer that the matter was dropped.—House of Commons, *Sessional Papers*, 1867–68, LIII, 779–94.

98:24–25. Arnold repeatedly uses this definition of the State, which he attributes to Burke; but the words apparently are not Burke's. See *Prose Works*, ed. Super, II, 294n.

98:35. The italicized phrase comes from Arnold's argument for the establishment of a minister of education in England, in the final chapter of *Schools and Universities on the Continent* (1868), reprinted on p. 220 of the book to which this is the Preface. See *Prose Works*, ed. Super, IV, 314. The Public Schools Act of 1868, following upon the report of the Clarendon Commission set up in 1861 to inquire into the condition of nine so-called "public schools" (i.e., the largest and best of the endowed secondary schools), compelled seven of the nine to reform their governing bodies "in order" (as the Commissioners' report said) "to render them thoroughly suitable and efficient for the purpose and duties they are designed to fulfil."—J. W. Adamson, *English Education, 1789–1902* (Cambridge, 1930), pp. 255–56.

99:37–38. Arnold coupled "Millism"—a "somewhat degenerated and inadequate form of Hellenism" or rationalism—with "Mialism" —"a sub-form of Hebraism, . . . a somewhat spurious and degenerated form"—in the Preface to *St. Paul and Protestantism* in April, 1870, and again in *Friendship's Garland* a year later. "Mialism" was the earlier coinage, in the Preface to *Culture and Anarchy* (1869), from which, however, it disappeared in the second edition (1875).— *Prose Works*, ed. Super, VI, 125–26, 420; V, 46, 534–35. Mill died on May 8, 1873. "Philosophical radicalism" is of course Benthamite Utilitarianism.

100:28–29. The black death is the relatively modern name given to the catastrophic plague which swept Europe in 1347–51 and, in lesser manifestations, later in the century. The sweating sickness was a febrile disease, almost immediately fatal, that swept England periodically from 1485 to 1578. Neither one is clearly identifiable in modern medicine and there was at the time no remedy or preventive.

100:34–35. The Old Catholics withdrew from the Roman Catholic Church because they declined to accept the dogma of papal infallibility. The Prussian state intervened to prevent the expulsion of Old Catholic priests from their parishes by the Roman Catholic bishops and the Swiss government provided that a vote of the community might turn over a Roman Catholic church edifice to the Old Catholics, who were especially strong, for example, in Geneva.

103:21. The motto of the weekly newspaper of the Dissenters, *The Nonconformist*, was "The Dissidence of Dissent and the Protestantism of the Protestant Religion," an expression taken from Burke's speech *On Conciliation with the Colonies*, one-fourth through. Arnold ridiculed the motto in the first chapter of *Culture and Anarchy.—Prose Works*, ed. Super, V, 101.

104:2. François de la Mothe-Fénelon (1651–1715), French theologian and archbishop of Cambrai under Louis XIV, was described by Arnold in "Eugénie de Guérin" as "the ideal saint; . . . a nature of ineffable sweetness and serenity, a nature in which struggle and revolt is over, and the whole man (so far as is possible to human infirmity) swallowed up in love."—*Prose Works*, ed. Super, III, 87.

104:3. Thomas Ken (1637–1711), bishop of Bath and Wells under James II and a man of great sanctity, was author of a manual of devotion and of the well-known hymn, "Awake, my soul, and with the sun." Thomas Wilson (1663–1755), bishop of Sodor and Man, wrote the *Maxims of Piety and of Christianity* Arnold was so fond of quoting in *Culture and Anarchy* and in his religion writings. In *St. Paul and Protestantism* Arnold linked Wilson and Ken with George Herbert as types of Christian righteousness at its best, preeminent over the worthies of Puritanism.—*Prose Works*, ed. Super, VI, 104.

104:4–7. Arnold makes the same point in the Preface to *Culture and Anarchy.—Prose Works*, ed. Super, V, 244.

104:23–24. "Let every one of us please his neighbour for his good to edification."—Romans 15:2. "To the weak became I as weak, that I might gain the weak: I am made all things to all men, that I might by all means save some."—I Corinthians 9:22.

104:26–27. I Corinthians 11:16. The Authorized Version reads: "But if any man seem to be contentious, we have no such custom, neither the churches of God."

105:7. Arnold first used this phrase to define the critical function at the end of his second lecture *On Translating Homer* and quoted it again at the beginning of his lecture on "The Function of Criticism at the Present Time."—*Prose Works*, ed. Super, I, 140; III, 258.

105:10–12. "It belongs to parliaments to establish true religion and to punish false," said John Pym in the parliamentary debate of January 27, 1628–29, that ended in a formal protest against the Roman Catholic and Arminian interpretations of the Thirty-Nine Articles. See Daniel Neal, *History of the Puritans* (New York, 1844), I, 292 (Part II, chapt. iii, three-fourths through). Arnold jotted the remark in his pocket diary for December 16, 1871.—*Note-Books*, ed. Lowry, p. 163.

105:22–23. John Goodwin, expelled from his benefice at St. Stephen's, Coleman Street, London, in 1845, as a heretic, engaged in pamphlet warfare with the Presbyterians on the issue of their dominance and their power of expelling clergy who disagreed with them. —Neal, *History of the Puritans*, II, 45 (Part III, chapt. viii, one-third through). Arnold jotted two passages from Goodwin upon *The Divine Authority of the Scriptures* at the end of his pocket diary for 1874.—*Note-Books*, ed. Lowry, p. 221. The Independents were the 17th-century Congregationalists.

105:29–30. The Savoy Declaration of Faith and Order was promulgated by a conference of Independent ministers meeting at the Savoy Palace in 1658. Arnold took his quotation from Neal's *History of the Puritans*, II, 179 (Part IV, chapt. iii, latter part). The first Baptist Confession of Faith, drawn up by seven congregations in London in 1644–46, stated: "It is the magistrates' duty to tender the liberty of men's consciences."—Henry Bettenson, ed., *Documents of the Christian Church* (2nd ed.; London: Oxford University Press, 1967), p. 249.

106:17. Ritualism was a movement for the increase of ceremony within the Church of England that led to some notable prosecutions before the Privy Council against what were viewed as extreme practices.

107:9–10. See p. 103:21n.

107:33–38. The question of "religious profession," which had been proposed as part of the census of 1861, was stricken out by the Liberal government at that time in response to protests of the Nonconformists, led in the House of Commons by Edward Baines. See Arnold, *Prose Works*, ed. Super, V. 60:36n. The strength of the resistance in 1860 was so great as to induce the government to leave the question out of the Census Bill of 1870 (which authorized the census of 1871), and an amendment to introduce it was negatived on July 26.

109:2–6. The Pope apparently works on Arnold's principle for the reform of a nation, not by flattery but by pointing out what the nation, given its temperament, most needs. Arnold's conviction that the defeat of France in 1871 was a punishment for her lack of regard for feminine virtue is implied as early as *Literature and Dogma.*— *Prose Works*, ed. Super, VI, 390–92. See also the essay on Renan's "La Réforme intellectuelle et morale de la France," p. 45.

109:22–24. *Moralium* VIII. ii; Migne, *PL*, LXXV, 803.

109:25. The dogma of papal infallibility was defined in the first Vatican Council on July 18, 1870; the pope was Pius IX.

110:12–21. Arnold jotted in his pocket diary for 1873 two passages from anonymous articles in the *Pall Mall Gazette* which he attributed to Stephen. The first, from a review of John Morley's *Struggle for National Education* (London, 1873) published November 20, p. 12, reads: "The Dissenting rate-payer has a real grievance, a substantial grievance, even though compromises may be devised to moderate its oppressiveness." The second, from a leading article of December 4, p. 1, is the passage here quoted, though with the order of the sentences reversed.—*Note-Books*, ed. Lowry, pp. 199–200. See also Arnold's "A Speech at Westminster," pp. 82–83.

110:23–24. "Plead thou singly the blood of the covenant, the ransom paid for thy proud stubborn sinful soul," wrote John Wesley in his sermon on "Justification by Faith," *Works* (London, 1872), V, 64.

110:32–33. In the Dublin ed. of 1866, XI, 367. The italics are Arnold's.

111:21. The cult of Juggernaut, at the town of Puri on the Bay of Bengal in India, involves the dragging of the statue of this avatar of Vishnu on an unwieldy cart by thousands of pilgrims every summer. It was popularly supposed that large numbers of the pilgrims ritually hurled themselves to their deaths beneath the wheels of the cart.

112:12–14. Ephesians 4:3, 4:13; II Corinthians 13:11; Philippians 3:16.

112:16–19. For the Savoy Confession, see p. 105:29n. Arnold took this passage from Daniel Neal's *History of the Puritans*, II, 178 (Part IV, chapt. iii, latter part); he jotted it in his pocket diary for January 20, 1874.—*Note-Books*, ed. Lowry, p. 208.

112:22–25. *Pensées*, sect. xiv, 871; *Oeuvres*, ed. L. Brunschvicg (Paris, 1921), XIV, 312. Jotted in Arnold's pocket diary for January 4, 1874.—*Note-Books*, ed. Lowry, p. 206.

113:20–21. Positions explicitly affirmed in the Thirty-Nine Articles: "The Bishop of *Rome* hath no jurisdiction in this Realm of *England*" (Art. 37), and "The Romish Doctrine concerning Purgatory, Pardons, Worshipping and Adoration, as well of Images as of Reliques, and also invocation of Saints, is a fond thing vainly invented, and grounded upon no warranty of Scripture, but rather repugnant to the Word of God" (Art. 22).

114:13. For the Old Catholics, see p. 100:34n.

116:13. "Caesarism and Ultramontanism" was the title of a paper read by Archbishop Manning on December 23, 1873, and printed in *The Times* next day, p. 7, cols. 1–4. It was directed primarily against the action of the Prussian government in the Falk laws and that of Bavaria with respect to Dr. Döllinger, professor at the University of Munich and a leader of the Old Catholic movement. The essence of Caesarism he defined as "the absolute dominion of man over man: the power of life and death, including supreme power over liberty and goods, and extending to the whole life of man, political and religious, social and domestic," whereas Ultramontanism is "the liberty of the soul divinely guaranteed by an infallible Church; the proper check and restraint of Caesarism, as Caesarism is the proper antagonist of the sovereignty of God."

117:25–31. *Autobiography*, chapt. ii, paragraph 2 and second from end. Arnold jotted these passages in his pocket diary for 1873, the year of Mill's death and the publication of the *Autobiography*. It seems likely that Arnold has misunderstood Mill's point in the latter passage, which speaks of the "general abstinence (except among a few of the stricter religionists) from professing any high principles of action at all, except in those preordained cases in which such profession is put on as part of the costume and formalities of the occasion." In context, Mill seems to be distinguishing the religionists for their professions only, not for what they perform.

118:1–9. Ernest Renan, "La Crise religieuse en Europe," *Revue des Deux Mondes*, 3rd pér., I (February 15, 1874), 776–77, jotted in Arnold's pocket diary for February 18.—*Note-Books*, ed. Lowry, p. 210.

118:16–18. Joseph Chamberlain used "*a free Church in a free state*" as a new Liberal slogan in "The Liberal Party and Its Leaders," *Fortnightly Review* XX, 295 (September, 1873).

119:19. Gustave de Molinari (1819–1911) was a Belgian economist and prolific journalist in both his native country and France.

120:10–17. Ruggero Bonghi (1826–95) became minister of public instruction in Italy a few months after the publication of Arnold's Preface (September, 1874–March, 1876). He delivered his speech on the Faculty of Theology in the Chamber of Deputies on April 29, 1872. See *Discorsi parlamentari di Ruggero Bonghi* (Rome, 1918), I, 382–98 (and especially p. 389).

122:13–18. Arnold is quoting his own argument in *The Popular Education of France;* he quoted it again in *Culture and Anarchy.— Prose Works*, ed. Super, II, 198; V, 193. For "the nation in its collective and corporate character," see p. 98:24n.

122:26. When Gladstone's Liberal government was defeated on the Irish University Education Bill in March, 1873, Disraeli declined to form a government. Gladstone appealed to the nation at the beginning of the next session by dissolving Parliament in January, 1874. The Tories were returned in a clear majority early in February and Disraeli became Prime Minister.

122:31–37. See "Our Liberal Practitioners," the final chapter of *Culture and Anarchy.—Prose Works*, ed. Super, V, 193–208.

123:10–11. Dr. Johnson reported that Hume made this acknowledgment to a clergyman in the bishopric of Durham.—Boswell, *Life of Johnson*, 1766 and 1777.

123:26–28. "A Letter to a Noble Lord," three-fifths through. Arnold jotted this expression in his pocket diary for July 17, 1869, and seven times thereafter in the next decade, as well as in one of his "General Note-Books."—*Note-Books*, ed. Lowry, p. 105, etc. He cited it in the "Dedicatory Letter" to *Friendship's Garland* (1871). —*Prose Works*, ed. Super, V, 353.

124:11–14. Isaac Barrow, "Of a Peaceable Temper and Carriage," ¶1, *Theological Works*, ed. Alexander Napier (Cambridge, 1859), II, 401, quoted in Arnold's pocket diary for January 12, 1874.— *Note-Books*, ed. Lowry, p. 207.

124:20–21. Ephesians 5:21.

124:24–25. "Servus servorum dei," *servant of the servants of God*, has been the formula of superscription of papal documents from the eleventh century. It was first applied to himself by St. Gregory the Great in 591.

126:20–24. Edward Aldam Leatham, M. P. for Huddersfield, Yorkshire, was a radical Liberal devoted to Church Disestablishment. *The Spectator* objected to his "tone . . . of juvenile levity," his "flippant and jubilant tone" in a speech at Huddersfield on Septem-

ber 27, 1873.—"Mr. Leatham on the Liberal Prospects," XLVI, 1235
(October 4, 1873). The term "drunken Helot" is "in allusion to the
statement (Plutarch *Lycurgus* xxviii) that Helots [i.e., the class of
serfs in ancient Sparta] were, on certain occasions, compelled to appear in a state of intoxication, in order to excite in the Spartan youth
repugnance to drunken habits."—*N.E.D.*

126:25–28. Joseph Chamberlain (1836–1914), mayor of Birmingham and chairman of its first school board, was Liberal candidate
for Parliament from the industrial city of Sheffield in the election
of 1874, but was defeated by J. A. Roebuck and A. J. Mundella.
Speaking in Sheffield on January 1, he proclaimed himself in favor
of "free schools, free labour, free land, and a free Church." "He
contended that the Church as an organization, with some great and
distinguished exceptions, was always on the side of power and privilege, and opposed to the poor and oppressed. . . . The priest, parson,
squire, the land, and the Church, the aristocracy of birth and the
plutocracy of commerce, would be banded together to stem the tide
of democracy and roll back the current of advancing popular
thought."—*Times*, January 2, 1874, p. 10, cols. 2–3.

126:36–37. See p. 123:26n.

127:14–15. John Carvell Williams (1821–1907) became secretary
to the British Anti-State Church Association (later the Liberation
Society) in 1847, three years after its founding by Edward Miall.
Alexander Gordon, in the *D.N.B.*, describes him as "for over half a
century . . . 'the chief strategist of the nonconformist force, in its
steady advance upon the privileged position of the Church of England.' " He wrote a great deal for Miall's newspaper, *The Nonconformist*, and himself founded the monthly *Liberator* in 1853.

127:19. "And thou, child, shalt be called the prophet of the Highest: for thou shalt go before the face of the Lord to prepare his ways;
. . . To give light to them that sit in darkness and in the shadow of
death, to guide our feet into the way of peace."—Luke 1:76, 79 (the
prophecy of Zacharias respecting his son John the Baptist).

128:8. The advowson, or right of naming the incumbent to a parish church or "living," remained a property right, capable of sale
like any other property right, and it was often in private hands.
Despite attempts to remedy its worst evils, agents were still adver-
tising for sale not only the advowson, but the limited right to make
the next appointment—an arrangement tantamount to purchasing
the position outright for oneself or a friend. A special inducement in
such advertisements was the advanced age of the current incumbent,
whose early demise might then confidently be counted upon.

128:36–129:1. *The Times*, February 6, 1873, p. 9, col. 3 (leading article). *The Times* describes them as "justly and implacably hostile."

129:9–16. Plato *Gorgias* 521 E–522 A and 464 D–E, partially quoted in Arnold's pocket diary for February 24, 1873.—*Note-Books*, ed. Lowry, p. 196.

129:24–25. Leading article, February 10, 1874, p. 9, col. 1, jotted in Arnold's pocket diary for February 21.—*Note-Books*, ed. Lowry, p. 210.

129:29–32. From Lowe's address at Sheffield, September 4, 1873; reported next day in *The Times*, p. 3, col. 3, and *The Pall Mall Gazette*, p. 1. Jotted in Arnold's pocket diary for August 10, 1873.—*Note-Books*, ed. Lowry, p. 199.

129:34–35. *The Times*, in a leading article on the speech in which Lowe acknowledged his re-election as member of Parliament for the University of London, mentions Lowe's description of Disraeli as "a political 'teratologist,' always absorbed in the study of faraway monstrosities and occupied in the search for them."—February 4, 1874, p. 10, col. 1.

130:1–5. Plato *Gorgias* 521 D. Jowett's translation reads: "I am the only politician of my time." Arnold jotted the Greek in his pocket diary for September 26, 1872, and February 23, 1873.—*Note-Books*, ed. Lowry, pp. 183, 196.

[ROMAN CATHOLICS AND THE STATE]

This letter in the *Pall Mall Gazette* of April 8, 1875, supplements the Preface to the 1874 edition of *Higher Schools and Universities in Germany* and was published with that work in vol. XII of the De-Luxe edition of Arnold's *Works* in 1903–4; it had not been republished in Arnold's lifetime. One of his pocket diaries contains the memorandum on March 21, 1875, repeated the next day: "P.M.G. letter." He received 5 gns. in payment for it.

131:3–5. See p. 94:15–17.

133:7. One might hazard a guess that this distinguished Scotch Liberal was Arnold's friend M. E. Grant Duff.

133:15. John Dobree Dalgairns (1818–76), of Scottish descent, was associated with Newman at Oxford and Littlemore and was received into the Roman Catholic Church a few days before Newman. He was superior of the Brompton Oratory from 1863 to 1865 and a scholar in the history of mysticism and devotion.

133:20. Alexander Bain (1818–1903), Scottish utilitarian psychologist and logician, was early a contributor to the *Westminster Review* and an associate of John Stuart Mill. He was professor of logic and English at the University of Aberdeen from 1860 to 1880. Bain and Arnold both received the LL.D. degree at the University of Edinburgh in April, 1869, and journeyed southward by train together the next day.—Bain, *Autobiography* (London, 1904), p. 292.

135:17–18. The *Fortnightly Review*, edited by John Morley, was rationalist and liberal in its doctrines, of the school of John Stuart Mill. For Moody and Sankey, who were conducting their meetings in London at this time, see p. 372. The two positions are those Arnold elsewhere calls Secularist and Nonconformist.

136:5–15. Both Myles O'Reilly and Lyon Playfair spoke in the House of Commons debate on primary education in Ireland on March 5, 1875 (*Times*, March 6, p. 6, cols. 3–6), and the *Times* was severely critical of Irish denominational demands for education in a leading article of March 8, p. 9, cols. 2–3 (an article quoted by Arnold in his pocket diary for March 14—*Note-Books*, ed. Lowry, p. 228). O'Reilly replied to the *Times* in a letter to the editor published March 16, p. 8, col. 3: "Far from objecting to the training of teachers, and certificates being required for teachers, . . . the great majority of managers asked . . . that as we have conscientious objections to availing ourselves of the existing Training School, . . . we should be allowed with our own money to establish Training Schools for teachers, subject to every condition of efficiency required by the State, and which shall receive payment, as in England, strictly by results; that is, for each certificated teacher whom they shall train and who shall continue to teach in a National School." Playfair (1818–98) had been professor of chemistry at the University of Edinburgh (1858–69) and represented the universities of Edinburgh and St. Andrews in Parliament from 1868 to 1885. O'Reilly (1825–80) was M. P. for Longford from 1862 to 1879.

[GOD AND THE BIBLE]

"I really *hate* polemics," Arnold wrote to the editor of the *Contemporary Review* as he forwarded proofs of the second installment of *God and the Bible*. (On the other hand, he is said to have responded to an inquiry about his health, "I *thrive* on religious exegesis."—A. C. Benson, *The Leaves of the Tree* [New York, 1911], p. 409.) Initially, he told the readers of the fourth edition of *Literature and Dogma* at the beginning of 1874, he intended to discuss the principal objections raised against that book in a supplementary chapter at the end of it, but he found he had neither space nor time to do so; "I propose, therefore, to notice objections . . . elsewhere."—*Prose Works*, ed. Super, VI, 564. These objections were mainly, as he understood them, his refusal to affirm a personal God and his use of the Fourth Gospel. He approached James T. Knowles, editor of the *Contemporary Review* (to which Arnold had not previously contributed) about the middle of March respecting a series of articles in which he proposed to deal with them much as he replied to the critics of "Culture and Its Enemies" in the articles that later became *Culture and Anarchy.* The single difference was that in this case he had already agreed to publish his articles as a book with Smith, Elder, and from the beginning made this understanding clear to Knowles.

The articles were subject to the same sort of irritating delays in the writing that had plagued the earlier series, and like "Anarchy and Authority" grew significantly under his hand. He initially hoped to have the first ready by the middle of April, for the May number. But he had agreed to look over the English essays for the Indian Civil Service; these fell due on April 15, and he thought then that by deferring his beginning until the June number he would be able to complete his series in three successive installments. "But again I must postpone the fulfillment of my promise," he wrote to Knowles on May 6. "My schools keep me so busy day after day that I cannot get the collectedness necessary for giving literary form to what I have to say; all I can do is to keep on reading and thinking about my subject, and, I hope, ripening myself to treat it easily and satisfactorily when I do treat it." He hoped to have the first installment now before his summer holiday; instead, he worked on it during a vacation at Fox How, but it was still unfinished when he returned home to Cobham, and was not completed until the week of September 7–14. "Do not let the printers change my stopping or put capitals where I do not," he instructed Knowles. ("Your printers are excellent," he remarked when he saw the proofs of the first article.) "I am amused to see Strahan's handbill stuck in all the magazines and book-stalls, announcing Gladstone and me as his two attractions this month," Arnold wrote to his sister when the first number appeared in the *Contemporary.*

At this point he hoped to finish with the question of a personal

God in the November number and with his use of the Fourth Gospel in December (or perhaps December and January). His free time was preoccupied, however, by revising the French translation of *Literature and Dogma* and he missed the December number; when he sent his third article on December 15, he still planned to complete the series in one more number, but as the subject was "no less than the N. T. Canon in General and the 4th Gospel in particular," he begged a few extra pages, rather than running on into a fifth article. Knowles urged him not to crowd himself; he did plan a fifth article for April, then left his notes and memoranda on a train and deferred Part V until the May number. "It will really be the last, but may extend to 30 pages," he wrote. It was not; the most important and original part of what he had to say about the Fourth Gospel required two more installments, in July and September, 1875. Even these had expanded as he worked on them; as late as May 29 he was promising Knowles the "concluding part" by June 16. Payments from the *Contemporary* were £24.10s, £22, £25.10s, £27, £25, and (for the final pair) £51.10s. "I owe you a debt of gratitude for the aid you have given to these papers by putting them into the Contemporary: it has been of real service to them," Arnold told Knowles.

Proofs of the book began to arrive while Arnold was at Fox How early in August, 1875. Draft passages of the Preface are jotted at the end of his pocket diary for that year. Publication was planned for the end of October and actually took place on November 12, at a price of nine shillings. Arnold sent copies to, among others, Renan, Réville, Rauwenhoff, and the author of *Supernatural Religion*. Two thousand copies were printed, of which 500 were sold to Macmillan for publication in New York. The success of *Literature and Dogma* led Arnold to form high expectations for the new book; a thousand copies were gone by Christmas, then sales fell off. In the summer of 1878 he returned to the publisher George Smith part of "the £100 you advanced to me when I calculated that 'God and the Bible' was about to pass into that second edition which has never arrived for it, poor thing."—Buckler, *Matthew Arnold's Books*, p. 159; see also pp. 98–99, 26–28. American sale was better, but did Arnold little good: James R. Osgood of Boston printed an edition of 1500 copies and these, or others printed from the same electrotypes, supplemented Macmillan's copies and held the American market (under the imprint of Osgood, then of Henry Holt & Co., then of Macmillan) until the collected American edition of Arnold was published in 1883; Osgood paid Arnold nothing for the copyright. The success of the abridged "popular edition" of *Literature and Dogma* in 1883 led Arnold and his London publishers to bring out a similar edition of *God and the Bible* on November 17, 1884, at the price of half a crown; this was the only other edition of the book published in England in Arnold's lifetime.

Yet on the whole Arnold was proud of this book, and with some justice. Though the first article gave him "horrid trouble" and proved a "trying subject" that "made many people very angry," he considered the second part "not bad": "I have been able to keep it in an easier and lighter tone than was possible for the first part. . . . Really the question is between not having the Bible studied and prized at all, in some ten years time, or having it studied and prized with new ideas and on new grounds." By the time the third article was ready, he told Knowles: "No man can be trusted to judge his own things, but it is my own notion that in this last article there is some of the best prose I have ever written"—almost the same language he used ten years later when he promised to send Charles Eliot Norton a copy of the popular edition: "In preparing it for the press I seem to find some chapters in it to be the best prose I have ever succeeded in writing."—*Letters*, ed. Russell (October 8, 1884). (But no other of his writings was so extensively revised on stylistic grounds in its successive editions, and especially in the transition from periodical to book.) Certainly its original title does it an injustice; it is far more than a "review of objections" to *Literature and Dogma*. Like the lectures *On the Study of Celtic Literature*, it is a remarkable demonstration of Arnold's ability to master a technical literature for which he seems at first sight ill equipped; the application of a quick mind and sharp intelligence to the learning of the biblical critics, and especially of the Germans, is a striking display of scholarly and historical criticism at its best. Some at least of the credit must go to the massive work which did more than any other to bring the German higher criticism before the British public, W. R. Cassels' two-volume *Supernatural Religion*, published anonymously early in 1874 and referred to by Arnold in his first article and throughout; Cassels' work is pedantic and amorphous, but it must have made clear that a purely belletristic approach would no longer be adequate for an English audience and it undoubtedly provided a challenge to Arnold to do better with the same materials. "It will more and more become evident how entirely religious is the work I have done in *Literature and Dogma*," he wrote to his sister Frances on October 2, 1874. "The enemies of religion see this well enough already. It is odd that while

I was in my recent article blaming a new book, *Supernatural Religion*, for being purely negative in its Bible criticism, Morley in the *Fortnightly* was praising the book for this very thing, which he says is all we want at present, and contrasting my book unfavourably with it as not insisting enough on the negative side and on disproof." As he told Huxley, however, when the latter commented upon *God and the Bible*, "[You] put the saddle on the right horse, and made me indebted to Spinoza and not to the Germans. It makes me rather angry to be affiliated to German Biblical critics; I have had to read masses of them, and they would have drowned me if it had not been for the corks I had brought from the study of Spinoza."— W. H. G. Armytage, "Matthew Arnold and T. H. Huxley," *Review of English Studies*, IV n.s., 350 (October, 1953). Again and again he asserted his intention to provide an affirmative antidote "against negative criticism of the Bible, both German and of home production, although, of course, I do not mean to say that the subject will be treated from the point of view of the ordinary defenders of the Bible against innovators," as he told his sister in November, 1874. He made clear his aim again in what he wrote on May 23, 1876, to Édouard Reuss about Reuss's own writings: "En lisant, il y a quelques années, votre histoire de la théologie chrétienne au siècle apostolique, j'ai rencontré pour la première fois un livre tout animé de l'esprit nouveau, complètement dégagé du système d'exégèse traditionnelle, et en même temps un livre religieux, plein d'un amour profond pour ces vérités qui ont longtemps fait, et qui feront, je crois, toujours, la vie et le bonheur de l'âme humaine. Dans vos récentes publications bibliques je vois les résultats de l'érudition moderne . . . traités avec le sentiment qu'il s'agit non seulement d'abattre les erreurs traditionnelles, mais de tirer de la Bible plus de fruit encore que par le passé."—André Koszul, "Une lettre inédite de Matthew Arnold," *Revue de littérature comparée* III, 654 (October, 1923). Allied with this motive of a positive approach to biblical criticism, as he told Fontanès while he was planning the articles, was "discussion of the evidence respecting the Fourth Gospel and its character, in reply to the Tübingen critics," and to the success of this (running counter, as it did, to the general temper of biblical criticism in Arnold's day) one may cite the testimony of a Cambridge scholar lecturing at the turn of the century: "For my own part I have found Matthew Arnold's remarks . . . to be much the most illuminating investigation of the origin and character of the Gospel according to St. John which has yet appeared. . . . Most literary people do not know how well equipped he was for the work. He had the habit and experience of literary criticism, and an excellent knowledge not only of the works of modern theologians, but—what is of much more importance—of the ancient sources also. Few professed theologians know how to quote as well as Matthew Arnold from Eusebius or *Philosophumena*."—F. Crawford Burkitt, *Two Lectures on the Gospels* (London, 1901), pp. 54–56, 67.

P. 140, epigraph: *Goethes Unterhaltungen mit dem Kanzler Friedrich von Müller*, ed. C. A. H. Burkhardt (3rd ed.; Stuttgart, 1904), p. 71 (September 18, 1873). Müller's word was "Revolutionärem" ("the revolutionary," not "revolutionaries").

141:1–16. Polycarp's martyrdom at Smyrna in 167(?) in the reign of Marcus Aurelius is mentioned in Arnold's essay on that monarch, *Prose Works*, ed. Super, III, 143. The story Arnold tells here comes from chapt. ix of the *Martyrium Polycarpi*, a letter written in the name of the church of Smyrna describing the event, the earliest preserved account of a Christian martyr's death. The Epistle of Polycarp to the Philippians is preserved partially in Greek and entire in a Latin translation. Its authenticity is flatly denied by the author of *Supernatural Religion*, Part II, Chapt. ii (see p. 147:37n), but has been defended by subsequent scholars, including J. B. Lightfoot, *The Apostolic Fathers. Part II: Ignatius and Polycarp* (3 vols.; London, 1885), where both the *Martyrium* and the Epistle are translated.

142:9–11. Leading article against ritualism in *The Times*, February 25, 1871, p. 9, col. 5, jotted in Arnold's pocket diary for November 9, 1873.—*Note-Books*, ed. Lowry, p. 184.

142:26–27. "Literature and Dogma," *Dublin Review*, XX n.s., 357–80 (April, 1873).

143:9–10 (variant). J. Llewelyn Davies, "Mr. Matthew Arnold's New Religion of the Bible," *Contemporary Review* XXI, 842–66 (May, 1873). L. W. E. Rauwenhoff, "Matthew Arnold" [review of *Literature and Dogma*], *Theologisch Tijdschrift* (Leiden) VII, 287–347 (May–June, 1873). Albert Réville, "Literature and Dogma," *Academy* IV, 327–30 (September 1, 1873). Charles Secrétan, "Littérature et Dogme," *Bibliothèque universelle et revue suisse* XLIX n.s., 342–59 (February, 1874).

144:24–26. See Arnold's reference to William Steward, *Hindrances to the Advancement and Contentment of the Working Classes* (1872) in *Literature and Dogma*, *Prose Works*, ed. Super, VI, 148, 150.

145:2, 10–12. Joseph Chamberlain (1836–1914), later a well-known politician and cabinet minister, was chairman of the National Education League of Birmingham from 1868 and became mayor of the city in 1873. He was a Unitarian and Utilitarian—devoted to the cause of municipal sanitation and services and to national education, but hostile to the Elementary Education Act of 1870. George Dawson (1821–76) was a very popular preacher in a nonsecetarian chapel erected for him in Birmingham in 1847. Robert William Dale (1829–95), associated with the Congregationalist chapel in Carr's Lane, Birmingham, from 1852 and its pastor from 1859, was an influential and scholarly theologian and co-worker with Chamberlain in municipal reform and educational policy. Jesse Collings (1831–1920) became a partner in a Birmingham industrial firm in 1864 and in 1868 published the pamphlet which led to the immediate formation of the National Education League for the advocacy of free, compulsory, non-sectarian elementary education.—*D.N.B.* The Birmingham League opposed Forster's Education Act of 1870 because it continued to depend heavily on the voluntary (and hence sectarian) support of education; the rival National Education Union's program was more nearly in accord with the act as it was passed. Shiloh was the seat of the ark of the covenant and the tabernacle from the time of Joshua until the days of Samuel. When David had the ark brought south to Jerusalem, he "danced before the Lord with all his might. . . . And as the ark of the Lord came into the city of David, Michal Saul's daughter [and David's wife] looked through a window, and saw king David leaping and dancing before the Lord; and she despised him in her heart."—II Samuel 6:14, 16. The Lord, through Samuel, earlier commanded King Saul to destroy the Amalekites utterly, and "slay both man and woman, infant and suckling, ox and sheep, camel and ass." Saul, however, spared the king of the Amalekites, Agag, and the more valuable cattle. Thereupon Samuel proclaimed the Lord's displeasure and himself "hewed Agag in pieces before the Lord in Gilgal."—I Samuel 15.

145:3–4. "Le Dieu des bonnes gens" is an early song of Pierre-Jean de Béranger, who was a great favorite of Arnold in his Oxford years; he took Béranger's works with him on his Swiss holiday in September, 1848, but expressed weariness with them.—Arnold, *Letters to A. H. Clough*, ed. H. F. Lowry (London, 1932), pp. 92–93. The refrain of Béranger's poem is: "Le verre en main, gaîment je me confie / Au Dieu des bonnes gens."

145:27–32. "Does anyone, if he simply and naturally reads his consciousness, discover that he has any rights at all? For my part, the deeper I go in my own consciousness, and the more simply I abandon myself to it, the more it seems to tell me that I have no rights at all, only duties; and that men get this notion of rights from a process of abstract reasoning, inferring that the obligations they are conscious of towards others, others must be conscious of towards them, and not from any direct witness of consciousness at all."—*Culture and Anarchy, Prose Works*, ed. Super, V, 201. For "the method and secret and sweet reasonableness of Jesus Christ," see *Literature and Dogma, ibid.*, VI, 284–301 *et passim.* Arnold jotted his sentence "Man sincere . . . life" at the end of his pocket diary for 1873.—*Note-Books*, ed. Lowry, p. 201.

146:16–19. In *Literature and Dogma* Arnold cited Littré as authority for the statement that all human impulses can be traced to "two elementary instincts, the instinct of self-preservation and the reproductive instinct," and elsewhere quoted as axiomatic Pope's proposition that "happiness is our being's end and aim."—*Prose Works*, ed. Super, VI, 174, 195. The latter conviction was one of his chief grounds for disagreement with Carlyle; see his lecture on Emerson (1883) in *Discourses in America, Prose Works*, ed. Super, vol. X.

146:21. "Fight the good fight of faith, lay hold on eternal life."—I Timothy 6:12 (6:19). "Seek ye first the kingdom of God." —Matthew 6:33, Luke 12:31.

146:34. The British Association for the Advancement of Science, founded in 1831, holds annual meetings open to the general public as well as to scientists and is concerned with the promotion of research in all scientific fields except medicine and with the dissemination of scientific knowledge.

147:7. For the phrase "investigators of truth" see the quotation from *Supernatural Religion*, p. 148:15–18n.

147:8–13. See *Literature and Dogma, Prose Works*, ed. Super, VI, 238, 363.

147:20–28. Arnold's witty attack on the first volume of J. W. Colenso's *The Pentateuch and Book of Joshua Critically Examined* was an essay in *Macmillan's Magazine* VII, 241–56 (January, 1863) called "The Bishop and the Philosopher." It was his earliest venture into direct theological controversy. The parts of the essay that deal with the philosopher Spinoza were incorporated into Arnold's discussion of Spinoza in *Essays in Criticism* but he never reprinted the parts on Colenso. For Colenso on the "prayer of Ram," etc., see Arnold, *Prose Works*, ed. Super, III, 47.

147:28–32. W. R. Greg, whom Arnold knew as a neighbor of the Arnold family home in the Lake District, published a reply to the essay on Colenso, "Truth *versus* Edification," *Westminster Review*, American ed., LXXIX, 265–72 (April, 1863). Arnold had laid it down as the function of a good book of Biblical criticism that it either instruct the learned by adding to their learning or edify the many by giving them insights into the true moral and spiritual values of Scripture; Colenso's, he said, merely deprived the masses of all confidence in the values of Scripture, while his "learning" was the naïveté of profound ignorance. Greg, on the other hand, vigorously affirmed the edifying value of critical books like Colenso's that demolish false dogmas in which the masses of Christians are brought up under the instruction of their ignorant clergy. Though Greg's article was anonymous, he sent Arnold a copy over his own name and republished it both in his *Literary and Social Judgments* in 1868 and as a separate pamphlet in 1869. Greg's *Creed of Christendom: its foundations contrasted with its superstructure*, first written between 1845 and 1848, was published in one volume in 1851; it was much amplified for a two-volume third edition in 1873 and reached an eighth edition by 1883. In a review of recent works upon the Bible in his introduction to the third edition, Greg accused Arnold in *Literature and Dogma* of a complete reversal of his position of 1863 and of having joined the camp of Colenso; Greg's very words of praise for Arnold show how little he grasped the force of Arnold's criticism: "It is . . . impossible to regard his work, trenchantly iconoclastic though it indisputably is, as otherwise than conceived in the interest, and imbued with the spirit of sincere religion. Many will describe Mr. Arnold as having run a ruthless and sacrilegious tilt against the Bible. I should say rather that he had lifted it off one pedestal to put it on another—with much reverence, and perhaps a little condescension."—I, xxv.

147:37–38. *Supernatural Religion: an Inquiry into the Reality of Divine Revelation*, published anonymously in 1874, was written from much the same motives as Arnold's *Literature and Dogma*. It was frequently revised and went through numerous editions into the present century. The author, variously guessed at for many years, was Walter Richard Cassels (1826–1907), a retired merchant from India, entirely self-educated in theological matters.

148:5–6. "The leaves of the tree [of life] were for the healing of the nations."—Revelation 22:2.

148:15–18. The author of *Supernatural Religion* devoted several paragraphs of his Introduction to "the immense personal importance of Truth in regard to Religion—the necessity of investigating, before accepting, dogmas. . . . [We must dismiss] preconceived ideas . . . and [seek] only the Truth."—(3rd ed.; London, 1874), I, xviii–xx. And in his Conclusions, parts of which Arnold here quotes, he proclaims, "The only thing absolutely necessary for man is Truth."—II, 491.

148:27–35. *Ibid.*, II, 483, 489–90. The author of *Supernatural Religion* of course denies the truth of miracle and denies John's authorship of the Fourth Gospel.

148:37. Galvanic action, named after the Bolognese physiologist Luigi Galvani (1737–98), who experimented with the phenomenon, is the twitching of the muscles of a lifeless body caused by the application of an electrical stimulus to the nerves. "No doubt some appearance of life is still kept up in the Protestant churches by the galvanic operations of wealthy divines; but really and truly Protestantism in England, as well as in Germany, is a corpse."—"Literature and Dogma," *Dublin Review* XX n.s., 357–58 (April, 1873).

150:33–151:3. For Arnold's illustration of the Trinity as "the three Lord Shaftesburys" and for his criticism of William Thomson, archbishop of York, Samuel Wilberforce, bishop of Winchester, and Charles John Ellicott, bishop of Gloucester and Bristol, in *Literature and Dogma*, see *Prose Works*, ed. Super, vol. VI, Index. See also Textual Notes to this passage. "Mr. Arnold knows that large masses of his countrymen will regard the language we have quoted [to illustrate the most Blessed Trinity by the 'three Lord Shaftesburys'] as blasphemous and disgusting. Under these circumstances is there in using such language and using it needlessly, any sweetness at all? . . . It does not require very exalted powers of reasoning to discover when one is simply impudent. And we really do think that Mr. Arnold is able to see so far. We must, therefore, with, however, all possible sweetness, say he is somewhat to blame. Conscious impudence is, after all, a drawback in a professor of culture."—"Literature and Dogma," *Dublin Review* XX n.s., 361–62 (April, 1873).

151:11–15. In a review of *Literature and Dogma*, *Guardian*, June 11, 1873, p. 781.

151:19–20. See p. 141:1–16.

151:36. For the liberal's characterization of popular Christianity as "a degrading superstition," see *Literature and Dogma*, *Prose Works*, ed. Super, VI, 358–59.

152:25–26. Archbishop William Thomson was a personal acquaintance of Arnold's, and like Arnold a member of the Athenaeum Club. While still an undergraduate at Oxford he practically completed a treatise on logic published in 1842 (when he was twenty-three) as *Outlines of the Laws of Thought*, which early brought him a reputation. He figured in *Literature and Dogma* for his lecture on "Design in Nature," delivered for the Christian Evidence Society on April 25, 1871.

153:2. Bishop Samuel Wilberforce, who died in 1873, is best remembered today, and not to his advantage, for his debate with T. H. Huxley on Darwinism. Arnold describes a meeting with him at a house party of Lady de Rothschild's in letters to his mother on January 28 and February 2, 1864. For the bishop's remarks in Convocation in February, 1871, on the "Westminster Scandal," which Arnold ridiculed in *Literature and Dogma* and which he quotes here, see *Prose Works*, ed. Super, VI, 466.

153:14–15. Arnold is using the figurative language of the Duke of Somerset which he ridiculed in *Literature and Dogma*, *Prose Works*, ed. Super, VI, 238: "There is . . . one unassailable fortress to which [the authority of religion] may retire—faith in God."

153:29–31. See p. 142:9–11.

154:2. At this point Arnold originally included some scathing remarks upon Gladstone's eulogy of Wilberforce, but dropped them at the request of Knowles, who protested that Gladstone was a contributor to the same number of the *Contemporary* and could not with propriety be ridiculed in its columns. "I have altered the passage you disliked," Arnold wrote to Knowles on September 21, 1874, as he returned the proofs. "I have left out from 'The astonishing' down to 'He was not the universal bishop, he', inclusive; and for these last words I have substituted 'The late Bp. of Winchester was'— so that it goes on 'a man of a sympathetic temper' &c. There is therefore no mention of Gladstone left, nor any quotation of his words. It is natural you should not like to have so strong a remark on a contributor, but Gladstone's speech did, I must say, deserve the severest criticism."

154:15–16. "Except a man be born of water and of the Spirit, he cannot enter into the kingdom of God."—John 3:5.

154:17. Bishop Ellicott's lifetime work was a series of commentaries on the Epistles of St. Paul, and he was chairman of the company of scholars that revised the English translation of the New Testament. He associated himself with Bishop Wilberforce in the debate in Convocation over the "Westminster Scandal," but Arnold also ridiculed the solemn piety with which he had affirmed his belief in "the blessed truth that the God of the universe is a PERSON."— See *Prose Works*, ed. Super, VI, 466, 483.

154:23–25. Arnold said of Frederick Denison Maurice (1805–72) in *Literature and Dogma* that "in theology [that pure and devout spirit] passed his life beating the bush with deep emotion and never starting the hare."—*Prose Works*, ed. Super, VI, 383. One expression of the offense Arnold's remark gave to Maurice's friends is in the Preface Thomas Hughes wrote for Maurice's posthumous *The Friendship of Books* (London, 1880), pp. ix–xxi.

155:14–156:3. Arnold here summarizes the argument of *Literature and Dogma*, chapt. i, sects. 4–5; *Prose Works*, ed. Super, VI, 189–201. See also the Index to that volume, *s.v.* "God."

156:17–26. Davies, "Mr. Arnold's New Religion," *Contemporary Review* XXI, 857–58 (May, 1873). Arnold here misquotes Isaiah 57:15 ("high and holy One" for "high and lofty One") precisely as he did in every edition of *Literature and Dogma;* see *Prose Works*, ed. Super, VI, 187 and Textual Notes.

157:10–11. "I count all things but loss for the excellency of the knowledge of Christ Jesus my Lord: for whom I have suffered the loss of all things, and do count them but dung, that I may win Christ, . . . That I may know him, and the power of his resurrection, and the fellowship of his sufferings, being made conformable unto his death."—Philippians 3:8, 10.

157:19–20. Arnold first used this etymology in *On the Study of Celtic Literature* (1866) and repeated it in *Literature and Dogma* (1871); see *Prose Works*, ed. Super, III, 331 and VI, 171. That the root meaning of "shining" may be behind the Latin *deus* is accepted by Georg Curtius, *Principles of Greek Etymology*, tr. A. S. Wilkins and E. B. England (London, 1875), I, 292.

157:20–23. Richard Whately, *Elements of Logic* (new ed.; Boston, Mass., 1851), p. 197; Book III, sect. 8, end. Sextus Pompeius Festus, a late second-century Roman scholar, epitomized the now lost *De significatu verborum* of Verrius Flaccus, a tutor in the household of Augustus; for his explanation, as Arnold gives it, see Sexti Pompei Festi *De verborum significatu quae supersunt* ed. W. M. Lindsay (Leipzig, 1913), p. 393. A comparable etymology of "sycophant" is suggested in Plutarch *Solon* xxiv; both are discredited by modern lexicographers as a mere guess.

158:3–4 (variant). Psalm 31:1 or 71:1 (Prayer Book Version).

158:12–25. George Lord Lyttelton, "On Undogmatic and Unsectarian Teaching," *Contemporary Review* XXIV, 67–74 (June, 1874); Arnold quotes from pp. 74, 69. Lyttelton, a personal acquaintance of Arnold's and a member of the Clarendon Commission to study the great public schools and the Taunton Commission to study other secondary education (the latter of which sent Arnold

to the Continent in 1865), believed that teaching in the schools could
not be "unsectarian" and "undogmatic" and feared that the attempt
to make it so would merely exchange "the strong and solid meat of
the Gospel whereon saints and heroes have been reared, for the
skimmed-milk and water, not fit even for babes—the mere froth on
the surface of the wells of salvation—the boneless, pulpy, unsatisfy-
ing substitute, which is offered to us by the shallow sciolists and
apostles of modern Unsectarianism." Arnold's comment appeared in
the *Contemporary* four months after Lyttelton's article: he had
asked James Knowles on August 7 to forward a copy to him at Fox
How, where he was working on the first part of his series of articles.

159:36–160:2. Jakob Frohschammer, "Strauss on the Old and the
New Faiths," *Contemporary Review* XXII, 45 (June, 1873); Arnold,
however, saw these passages quoted in a footnote to an article on
"Inductive Theology," *British Quarterly Review* LIX, 61n (January, 1874), where they are offered as a reply to Arnold's definition
of God. He jotted them in his pocket diary for January 23 and 25,
1874.—*Note-Books*, ed. Lowry, p. 208. Frohschammer spoke not of
"the deeper elements of personality" but of "a deeper consideration
of the essential elements of personality."

160:7–17. Albert Réville, review of *Literature and Dogma*, *Academy* IV, 329 (September 1, 1873). Réville's words are "discovered
the nature to be impersonal," and in view of Arnold's use of "nature"
in the next paragraph it may be assumed that "discovered the action"
in lines 17 and 27 was a misprint; see Textual Notes. Réville, four
years younger than Arnold, was a French Protestant theologian,
until 1873 pastor of the Walloon church in Rotterdam. Larousse's
Dictionnaire universelle describes him as a member of the most
advanced school of French Protestantism, one of the first to pronounce against the dogma of literal inspiration of the Bible and
against faith in the supernatural. His handling of *Literature and
Dogma* was sympathetic, and he subsequently reviewed *God and the
Bible* also, *Academy* VIII, 618–19 (December 18, 1875).

160:20–24. "Dr. Strauss' Confession," *Edinburgh Review*, American ed., CXXXVIII, 282 (October, 1873), somewhat abbreviated.
The *Wellesley Index to Victorian Periodicals* names G. H. Curteis
as author. On p. 279 the reviewer refers in passing to "taking religion at its very lowest estimate—that of Mr. M. Arnold—as 'morality
touched with emotion.' "

160:27–28. Réville, p. 329.

161:6–8, 15–16. *Ibid.*

161:28 (variant). Arnold repeats the self-depreciating concluding paragraphs of *Literature and Dogma*. The description of himself as without systematic philosophy—one he often quoted—is adapted from Frederic Harrison, "Culture: a Dialogue," *Fortnightly Review* VIII, 608 (November, 1867).

162:27. Apis and Anubis were Egyptian gods represented in the form of a bull and a jackal.

162:31–33. An echo of a passage from Goethe which Arnold quotes or alludes to frequently elsewhere: "Jeglicher das Beste, was er kennt, / Er Gott, ja seinen Gott benennt, / Ihm Himmel und Erden übergibt, / Ihn fürchtet, und wo möglich liebt."—"Gott, Gemüth und Welt," lines 23–26; *Werke* (Weimar, 1888), II, 216. See Arnold, *Note-Books*, ed. Lowry, p. 39, and *Prose Works*, ed. Super, V, 83; VI, 10, 372.

162:37. Article I: "There is but one living and true God, everlasting, without body, parts, or passions; of infinite power, wisdom, and goodness; the Maker, and Preserver of all things both visible and invisible. And in unity of this Godhead there be three Persons, of one substance, power, and eternity; the Father, the Son, and the Holy Ghost."

163:17–20. See Joshua 10:12–14; Matthew 3:17 (Mark 1:11, Luke 3:22).

163:30–35. In a review of *Literature and Dogma, Guardian*, June 11, 1873, p. 780. The Bampton lectures are a series of lectures on matters of Christian theology delivered at Oxford by an English divine designated annually (in the twentieth century less frequently) under an endowment set up by John Bampton (d. 1751). James Bowling Mozley (1813–78), an undergraduate at Oriel while Newman and Keble were there, shared the views of the Tractarians but remained a High Church Anglican. His Bampton lectures *On Miracles* were delivered and published in 1865. In 1871 he became regius professor of divinity at Oxford and a doctor of divinity.

164:1–2. *Supernatural Religion* (3rd ed.; London, 1874), I, 1–211 (Part I, "Miracles."). The author introduces Mozley's views early and late in his discussion.

164:8–9. David Friedrich Strauss, *Das Leben Jesu für das deutsche Volk bearbeitet, Gesammelte Schriften* (Bonn, 1877), III, 206 ("Einleitung: 26. Plan des Werkes," last paragraph). Strauss (1808–74) was only twenty-eight when he completed his first *Leben Jesu*, a monumental study of the evidence concerning the life of Jesus, in which all supernatural elements were ascribed to the creative force of myth. (The book from which Arnold quotes is a much later, quite different work.) Strauss's subsequent career was rather polemical than scholarly, and his final book, published in 1872, *Der alte und der neue Glaube*, is essentially a negation of Christianity. Though he was at Tübingen only a short time, he is commonly associated with the Tübingen school of higher criticism.

164:13–18. Arnold repeats what he has said in chapt. v, sect. 3 of *Literature and Dogma*, *Prose Works*, ed. Super, VI, 246.

165:5–19. *Supernatural Religion* (1874), I, 78–94 (Part I, chapt. iii, sect. 3). The passages quoted from Mill (I, 80–81) are in *A System of Logic*, Book III, chapt. xxv, sect. 2; that from Paley (I, 89) is in his *View of the Evidences of Christianity*, ed. R. Whately (London, 1859), pp. 16–17 ("Preparatory Considerations").

167:4–6. Matthew 27:52–53.

167:14–18. Acts 9:5, 7 (22:9).

167:23–24. Luke 1:20–22, 62–64.

167:28–31. Mark 10:46–52; Matthew 20:29–34. See also Luke 18:35–42. One "reconciler," Augustus Neander, faced with the fact that Luke says Jesus cured one blind man on entering Jericho, Mark one blind man on leaving it, and Matthew two blind men on leaving it, supposes that "two blind men were cured, one at the entrance, the other at the outlet, of the town. (It was a common thing for blind beggars to sit at the gates.) This supposition, and a subsequent blending of the two narratives, would account not only for Matthew's mentioning *two* blind men, but also for the discrepancy in Mark and Luke as to the spot of the cure."—*Life of Jesus Christ*, tr. J. McClintock and C. E. Blumenthal (New York, 1870), p. 346n.

168:30–32. John 2:13–17; Matthew 21:12–13 (Mark 11:15–17, Luke 19:45–46).

169:2–5. Perhaps a slightly unfair reference to Neander, *Life of Jesus Christ* (New York, 1870), p. 168.

169:13–26. On June 5, 1874, the *Times* (p. 5, col. 6) gave a circumstantial account of the melancholy death of a Mrs. Liskeard on Mont Blanc before the eyes of her husband on their wedding tour. The report was categorically denied three days later (p. 7, col. 1). Meanwhile two correspondents recalled a parallel incident early in August, 1870; one of them, indeed, identified the newlyweds of 1870 as a couple named Mark, of Liskeard, Cornwall (June 6, p. 8, col. 3; June 8, p. 9, col. 2).

170:27–30. "He brought out of water, by his creative energy, a substance (wine), which is naturally the joint product of the growth of the vine, and of human labour, water being only one of the co-operating factors; and thus substituted his creative power for various natural and artificial processes. But we are not justified in inferring that the water was changed into *manufactured wine;* but that, by his direct agency, he imparted to it powers capable of producing the same effects; that he *intensified* (so to speak) the powers of water into those of wine. Indeed, this latter view of the miracle conforms better to its spiritual import than the former."—Neander, *Life of Jesus Christ*, p. 167.

171:1–2. Matthew 17:24–27.

171:16–24. See, for example, D. F. Strauss, *The Old Faith and the New*, tr. M. Blind (3rd ed.; London, 1874), pp. 58–59 (sect. 20), or *Life of Jesus*, tr. George Eliot (2nd ed.; London, 1892), pp. 540–46 (Part II, chapt. x, sect. 107). Strauss in the latter volume links Jesus' walking on the water to the Israelites' crossing the Red Sea dry-shod and to Elisha's dividing the River Jordan by a stroke of his mantle (p. 504; Part II, chapt. ix, sect. 101). The cursing of the fig-tree presents no Old Testament analogue for Strauss, but he takes it as a dilation of the statements by John the Baptist and Jesus that the tree that bears no good fruit is cast into the fire, and of the parable of the barren fig-tree (p. 533; Part II, chapt. ix, sect. 104). The transfiguration is narrated in Matthew 17:1–9, Mark 9:2–10, Luke 9:28–36; the walking on the Lake of Gennesaret in Matthew 14:24–33, Mark 6:47–53, John 6:16–21; the cursing of the barren fig-tree in Matthew 21:18–20, Mark 11:12–14, 20–21.

171:35. For the feeding of the multitude, see Matthew 14:15–21, 15:32–38; Mark 6:35–44, 8:1–9; Luke 9:12–17; John 6:5–14.

172:9–13. Arnold used, for this gospel, the edition of Hilgenfeld (see p. 258:33n). Hilgenfeld treats as two versions of the "Gospel according to the Hebrews" that used by the Nazaraeans and that used by the Ebionites, and gives the passage Arnold refers to here, from the later, on p. 34. The only source for this gospel is Epiphanius, *Against Heresies*, book xxx; here, in the description of Jesus' baptism, along with the account of the familiar miracles, occurs the statement, "And immediately a great light shone round about the place." —E. Hennecke, *New Testament Apocrypha*, ed. W. Schneemelcher; tr. ed. R. McL. Wilson (London: Lutterworth Press, 1963), I, 157. This light is discussed in *Supernatural Religion* (3rd ed., 1874), I, 320–23.

173:3. Vergil *Aeneid* vi, 426.

173:9–10. It was Carlyle who christened social science and polit-

452 Critical and Explanatory Notes

ical economy "the Dismal Science" in "The Nigger Question" (1849) and *Latter Day Pamphlets*, No. 1 (1850); *Works* (Centenary ed.; New York, 1898), XXXIX, 354; XX, 44.

173:19–21. T. H. Huxley, "On the Hypothesis that Animals are Automata, and Its History," *Fortnightly Review* XXII, 555–80 (November, 1874), an address delivered at the meeting of the British Association for the Advancement of Science at Belfast and later reprinted in *Science and Culture* and in *Collected Essays* (New York, 1897), I, 199–250. An earlier lecture on Descartes' *Discourse on Method*, delivered to the Cambridge YMCA on March 24, 1870, was published in *Macmillan's Magazine* XXII, 69–80 (May, 1870) and reprinted in *Lay Sermons* and in *Collected Essays*, I, 166–98; here Huxley spoke of Descartes as spiritual ancestor of modern ways of thinking, both in philosophy and in science, leading equally to the critical idealism of Kant and to the materialism which lies at the heart of modern physical science.

173:23–24. "Qu'on me donne de la matière & du mouvement, dit Descartes, & je vais créer un monde."—Antoine Thomas, *Éloge de René Descartes* (Paris, 1765), p. 36. Arnold jotted two passages from this monograph in his pocket diary for February 28 and March 8, 1874.—*Note-Books*, ed. Lowry, p. 210. "Des Cartes, speaking as a naturalist, and in imitation of Archimedes, said, give me matter and motion and I will construct you the universe."—Coleridge, *Biographia Literaria*, beginning of chapt. xiii. The doctrine may be derived from *Le Monde* or from *Les Principes de la Philosophie* but the sentence is perhaps not Descartes'.

173:24–25. *Pensées*, sect. ii, nos. 77–79; *Oeuvres de Pascal*, ed. L. Brunschvicg (Paris, 1921), XII, 98–99.

174:20–21. *Méditations touchant la première philosophie*, no. 2, paragraph 7; *Oeuvres philosophiques*, ed. F. Alquié (Paris, 1967), II, 418–19. See *Discourse on Method*, part II (I, 586). Descartes' *Discourse on Method* (1637), an account of how he arrived at his method of scientific reasoning, is somewhat refined in the *Méditations* four years later. Arnold was reading both in 1874, when he quoted from them sixteen times in his pocket diaries. The *Discourse on Method* was on his reading-list as early as 1845 as he prepared for the Oriel fellowship examination.

174:21–23. *Méditations*, no. 2, paragraph 1; *Oeuvres philosophiques*, II, 414. See *Discourse on Method*, part IV (I, 602).

174:27–28. *Méditations*, no. 5, final paragraph; *Oeuvres philosophiques*, II, 479.

174:36–37. Descartes, *Méditations*, no. 5, final paragraph; *Oeuvres philosophiques*, II, 479; jotted in Arnold's pocket diary for October 25, 1874.—*Note-Books*, ed. Lowry, p. 219.

175:1–3. "Abrégé des six Méditations," paragraph 3, or *Méditations*, no. 3, paragraph 2, 4; *Oeuvres philosophiques*, II, 400 or 431–32. See *Discourse on Method*, part IV (I, 604, 610).

175:14–16. Joseph Butler, *Analogy of Religion, Works*, ed. W. E. Gladstone (Oxford, 1896), I, 6 (Introduction, paragraph 5), quoted by Arnold in *Literature and Dogma*, chapt. x, sect. 2; *Prose Works*, ed. Super, VI, 367.

175:17–22. *Méditations*, no. 1, ¶2; *Oeuvres philosophiques*, II, 405.

175:34 (variant). Arnold iterates once more Harrison's witty criticism of him; see p. 161:28n.

175:35–176:1. *Méditations*, no. 2, fifth paragr. from end; *Oeuvres philosophiques*, II, 426–27.

176:19–23. "Archimède, pour tirer le globe terrestre de sa place et le transporter en un autre lieu, ne demandait rien qu'un point qui fût fixe et assuré. Ainsi j'aurai droit de concevoir de hautes espérances, si je suis assez heureux pour trouver seulement une chose qui soit certaine et indubitable."—*Méditations*, no. 2, ¶2; *Oeuvres philosophiques*, II, 414. "Et remarquant que cette vérité: *je pense, donc je suis* [*Ego cogito ergo sum*], était si ferme et si assurée, que toutes les plus extravagantes suppositions des sceptiques n'étaient pas capables de l'ébranler, je jugeai que je pouvais la recevoir, sans scrupule, pour le premier principe de la philosophie que je cherchais."—*Discourse on Method*, part IV; *ibid.*, I, 603.

176:24–28. *Méditations*, no. 2, ¶4; *Oeuvres philosophiques*, II, 415–16.

176:31–35. John Locke, *An Essay Concerning Human Understanding*, Book IV, chapt. ix, paragraph 3.

177:11–14. *Méditations*, no. 2, ¶9; *Oeuvres philosophiques*, II, 420–21. The word "understands" is added to the list a few lines after the sentence Arnold quotes.

178:8–10. *Méditations*, no. 3; *Oeuvres philosophiques*, II, 438, 445, 448.

178:10–15. *Ibid.*, II, 437–38.

178:36–179:3. *Ibid.*, II, 445–46.

179:7–10. Samuel Clarke, *A Discourse Concerning the Being and Attributes of God* (new ed.; Glasgow, 1823), pp. 7, 46 (propositions 1, 8), summarized in Arnold's pocket diary for January 21–22, 1874. —*Note-Books*, ed. Lowry, p. 208. Clarke (1675–1729), whose mode of reasoning was in the tradition of Descartes, was regarded as the principal English metaphysician in the quarter of a century following the death of Locke.

179:10–15. Locke, *Human Understanding*, Book IV, chapt. x, ¶¶3, 1.

179:15–19. "Est aliquid, quod, sive essentia sive substantia sive natura dicatur, optimum et maximum est et summum omnium quae sunt."—St. Anselm, *Monologion*, chapt. iii; *Opera omnia*, ed. F. S. Schmitt (Edinburgh, 1946), I, 16.

180:28–30. François de la Mothe-Fénelon, *Traité de l'existence et des attributs de Dieu*, Part II, chapt. ii, arguments 2 and 3. Arnold jotted a sentence from Fénelon's Cartesian argument in his pocket diary for August 8, 1874.—*Note-Books*, ed. Lowry, p. 216.

181:29 (variant). See p. 388:30–33.

182:21. "It is possible that general investigation of languages will one day enable us . . . to find for transitions of meaning general human laws and analogies, which will then be naturally of the greatest importance to philosophic etymology and for philosophy in general. How interesting would it be for example if the generally received principle that the abstract proceeds from the concrete [*abstracta ex concretis*] were to be tested by a multitude of examples from the most different languages!"—Georg Curtius, *Grundzüge der griechischen Etymologie* (3rd ed.; Leipzig, 1869), pp. 90–91; tr. A. S. Wilkins and E. B. England (London, 1875), I, 116. In his diary for July 12, 1874, Arnold jotted another form of this proposition: "Abstracte Begriffe erst durch die Länge der Zeit und Aufklärung aus concreten enstanden sind. Adelung."—*Note-Books*, ed. Lowry, p. 214. And two years earlier he copied from Renan's *De l'origine du langage* (Paris, 1858), p. 128: "C'est une chose bien digne de réflexion que les termes les plus abstraits dont se serve la métaphysique aient tous une racine matérielle."—*Note-Books*, p. 180.

183:8–20. Curtius, 3rd ed., p. 350; tr. Wilkins and England, I, 469. The "verb substantive" is the verb *to be*.

183:26–33. Curtius, 3rd ed., p. 285; tr. Wilkins and England, I, 379.

184:1–3. Curtius, 3rd ed., pp. 199–200; tr. Wilkins and England, I, 260–61.

184:6–8. Émile Littré, founder, editor and frequent writer for the *Revue de philosophie positive*, of which Arnold was often a reader, published his *Dictionnaire de la langue française* in four volumes from 1863 to 1872. It aimed at recording the shifts in meanings of

words from the twelfth century down, and gave illustrative quotations from the pre-sixteenth-century period. Arnold jotted parts of
the entries for "métaphysique" and for "substance" in his pocket
diary for June 28–August 2, 1874.—*Note-Books*, ed. Lowry, pp. 214–
15. Here in *God and the Bible* he draws upon the etymological discussion at the end of the article upon the verb *être*.

186:13–18. Brian Walton, *Biblia Sacra Polyglotta* (London, 1657),
I, 236–37 (Exodus 3:14).

186:19–23. Arnold jotted the quotation from Wilhelm Gesenius
at the end of his pocket diary for 1874.—*Note-Books*, ed. Lowry, p.
222. He was using a Latin version of the *Hebrew Lexicon of the
Old Textament, s.v.* Jahve.

186:23–24. Moritz M. Kalisch, *A Historical and Critical Commentary on the Old Testament.* London, 1858.

188:10, 16–17. "Dum ergo incomprehensibilis intelligitur, per ex-
cellentiam nihilum non immerito vocitatur."—Joannis Scoti Erigenae
De divisione naturae III. xix, jotted in Arnold's pocket diary for
July 20, 1874.—*Note-Books*, ed. Lowry, p. 215.

189:7. The Declaration of the Rights of Man, adopted by the revolutionary National Assembly on August 26, 1789, was proclaimed
(as its Preamble declares) "en présence et sous les auspices de l'Être
suprême."

191:20–23. Henry Dunn, *Facts, Not Fairy-Tales: Brief Notes on
. . . "Literature and Dogma"* (London, 1873), p. 30.

191:31–32. The opening words of Psalms 14 and 53. This was the
text upon which St. Anselm built his *Proslogion*.

191:32–33. This is a central axiom of *Literature and Dogma;* see
Arnold, *Prose Works*, ed. Super, VI, 144, 373, 393, 401.

192:3–4. Dunn, *Facts, Not Fairy-Tales*, p. 31.

192:16–17. An ancient, and presumably correct, etymology of
the Latin "aeternus" makes it a contraction of the word "aevum"
("era," "age," "aeon") with the ending "-ternus." Its meaning in
Latin is essentially the same as in English.

193:37–39. This too is a central concept of *Literature and Dogma;*
see Arnold, *Prose Works*, VI, 152, 189, 243, 316, 408.

194:6. *Discourse on Method*, Part IV; *Oeuvres philosophiques*, ed.
F. Alquié (Paris, 1963), I, 604.

194:14, 20–23. Descartes, *Principes de la Philosophie*, "Préface,"
¶5 and Part I, ¶10, 14.—*Oeuvres*, ed. C. Adam and P. Tannery (Paris,
1964), IX (2), 10, 29, 31; and see p. 196:6–15.

195:17–19. See p. 160:20–24.

196:6–15. Descartes, *Méditations*, no. 3, ¶¶22–23; *Oeuvres philosophiques*, II, 445. Anselm *Proslogion* ii–iv; tr. M. J. Charlesworth (Oxford: Clarendon Press, 1965), pp. 116–21.

196:37–197:3. *Méditations*, no. 6, ¶2; *Oeuvres philosophiques*, II, 481.

196:33. J. S. Mill explains "the argument from design," which was common in the eighteenth century, as "the ordinary argument for [the existence and nature of] a Deity, from marks of design in the universe, or, in other words, from the resemblance of the order in nature to the effects of human skill and contrivance."—"Coleridge," one-sixth through.

200:24. Eduard von Hartmann (1842–1906), German philosopher, published his three-volume *Philosophie des Unbewussten* in 1869.

200:26–27. Psalm 37:11 (i.e., 36:11, Vulgate version), "the meek shall delight themselves," echoed in Matthew 5:5.

200:38–201:2. "Lettres écrites à un provincial," no. 1, ¶11; *Oeuvres*, ed. L. Brunschvicg (Paris, 1914), IV, 124; jotted in Arnold's pocket diary for November 9, 1873.—*Note-Books*, ed. Lowry, p. 200.

201:28–31. See p. 175:14–16.

202:15. "By the waters of Babylon we sat down and wept, when we remembered thee, O Sion."—Psalm 137:1 (Prayer Book Version).

202:15–23. See pp. 147:10–13, 148:27–30.

202:23–24. Psalm 120:5 (Prayer Book Version).

203:4–7. For example, when the reviewer of *Literature and Dogma* deduces the meaning of sacrifice to the pre-historic Hebrews from its meaning as anthropologists observe it in other races, he asserts; "No law is more certain than that similar effects are produced by similar causes."—"The Bible As Interpreted by Mr. Arnold," *Westminster Review*, American ed., CI, 151 (April, 1874). This article is the first in the April number. In January, 1875, Arnold speculated that it was written by the author of *Supernatural Religion*, perhaps because of the *Westminster's* warm reception of that book (American ed., CII, 97–99 [July, 1874]), but two months later remarked that the latter "has had the kindness to inform me that he is not identical with the *Westminster* Reviewer." See Textual Notes. The earliest notice of *Literature and Dogma* by the *Westminster* was a long section in its article on current theological and philosophical literature in April, 1873 (American ed., XCIX, 262–63), in which Arnold drew the highest praise on all counts except his style. When this reviewer remarked that the Book of Ecclesiastes was "by no means so early as the 5th century B.C.," Arnold in later editions changed his dating of that book to the fourth century; see *Prose Works*, ed. Super, VI, 207:14–16 and Textual Notes. He did not alter his dating of the Book of Proverbs in response to the reviewer's statement that he was wrong there too (*ibid.*, VI, 205:29–32).

203:20–204:7. *Westminster Review* CI, 152, 151, 152, paraphrased.

204:8–11. *Supernatural Religion* (3rd ed., 1874), II, 483; (variant) II, 490–91. See p. 148:27–35.

204:14. Mark 5:39, Luke 8:52.

204:18–24. *Westminster Review* CI, 154. See John 8:58, 10:17. The Authorized Version reads "that I might take," but the *Westminster* reads "may take."

204:28–30. Matthew 8:10, Luke 7:9; Matthew 15:26, Mark 7:27.

204:34–35. Luke 21:20–28, 23:28–30.

205:8–10. Albert Réville remarked that Arnold's religious theory "does not err either by excess of vigor or excess of rigor."—*Academy* IV, 329 (September 1, 1873).

206:4–13. *Westminster Review* CI, 150.

207:17. Sir John Lubbock (1834–1913), later Baron Avebury, was a banker, a Liberal M. P., and a scientist of merit in zoology and botany; "his interest in the new science of anthropology led him to travel to many centres in Europe where there was news or promise of fresh evidence of man's antiquity."—*D.N.B.* By the time Arnold wrote, Lubbock had published *Prehistoric Times* (1865) and *The Origin of Civilization* (1870). He and Arnold were house guests of M. E. Grant Duff at Hampden, in the Chilterns, in mid December, 1871, and a month later Arnold received a presentation copy of the new edition of Lubbock's *Prehistoric Times*. Edward Burnett Tylor (1832–1917) did more than any other man in his day to gain recognition for anthropology as a serious science. His books, by the time Arnold wrote, included *Researches into the Early History of Mankind* (1865) and *Primitive Culture* (1871).

207:23–28. In his lectures *On the Study of Celtic Literature* Arnold made an early excursion into philology: "The name of [the Scythians'] father and god, Targitavus, . . . *Shining with the targe*, the Greek Hercules, the Sun, contains in the second half of his name, *tavus*, 'shining,' a wonderful cement to hold times and nations together. *Tavus*, 'shining', from 'tava'—in Sanscrit, as well as Scythian, 'to burn' or 'shine,'—is *Divus*, *dies*, *Zeus*, Θεός, *Dêva*, and I know not how much more." Though he appended in a footnote to this passage Lord Strangford's comment that there was no connection between the root of *tavus* and the root of the words for god, Arnold in

Literature and Dogma repeated his affirmation with a slight qualification: "Strictly and formally the word 'God,' so some philologists tell us, means, like its kindred Aryan words, *Theos*, *Deus*, and *Dêva*, simply *shining* or *brilliant*. In a certain narrow way, therefore, this would be (if the etymology is right) the one exact and scientific sense of the word."—*Prose Works*, ed. Super, III, 331–32; VI, 171. Although Arnold's best authority on etymology, Georg Curtius, denies the connection of the Greek word Θεός with the Sanscrit *Dêvas* and the Latin *deus*, he does derive the two latter, like the Greek name Zeus, from the root which means "shine."—*Griechische Etymologie* (3rd ed.; Leipzig, 1869), pp. 466, 222; tr. Wilkins and England (London, 1875–76), II, 122; I, 292.

208:6–29. For his account of the union of Hellenic national life under an Apolline religion, Arnold depends heavily upon Book I, chapt. iv of Ernst Curtius, *History of Greece*, tr. A. W. Ward (London, 1868), a volume he reviewed in the *Pall Mall Gazette* on October 12, 1868 (see *Prose Works*, ed. Super, V, 257–65). The vale of Tempe, at the foot of Mount Olympus in northern Greece, was the site of early shrines of Apollo; according to Curtius, the Dorians in their prehistoric migration from that part of Greece brought their Apolline conceptions to the shrine of the god at Delphi, on the slopes of Parnassus in central Greece; the two were joined by a sacred road known as the Pythian Way, used for religious processions even in historic times. The actual derivation of the name "Phoebus" (as of "Apollo") is uncertain; "Zeus," according to Ernst Curtius, "merely means the heavens, the aether, the luminous abode of the Invisible."—*History of Greece*, Book I, chapt. ii.

208:32–34. Curtius, *History* (London, 1869), II, 83; quoted by Arnold in his review of that volume, *Pall Mall Gazette*, April 28, 1871, p. 11. See *Prose Works*, ed. Super, V, 271:19–21.

209:4. For Arnold on the religious temper of Pindar, Aeschylus and Sophocles in "Pagan and Mediaeval Religious Sentiment," *St. Paul and Protestantism*, and *Literature and Dogma*, see *Prose Works*, ed. Super, III, 231; VI, 21, 178.

209:27–28. This line of thinking led Arnold to his famous dictum, in "The Study of Poetry" (1880), that "the future of poetry is immense, because in poetry, where it is worthy of its high destinies, our race, as time goes on, will find an ever surer and surer stay. . . . The strongest part of our religion to-day is its unconscious poetry." —*Prose Works*, ed. Super, vol. IX.

209:36–37. "The Lovers" is a short Platonic dialogue, probably not genuine. Arnold quotes from 138 A: "So this is the message, it seems, of the Delphic inscription—that one is to practise temperance and justice."—tr. W. R. M. Lamb (Loeb Classical Library).

210:15–21. Phryne, the most exquisite and most prosperous Athenian courtesan of her day (late fourth century, after the Macedonian conquest of Athens), was the model for the most famous work of the greatest Greek painter, Apelles' Aphrodite rising from the sea. She also modelled the Cnidian Aphrodite for the sculptor Praxiteles, who was in love with her and executed a statue of her in gold to be set up at Delphi. Eleusis, near Athens, was the ancient seat of the "mysteries" of Demeter, rites in honor of the goddess of grain that probably derived from the legend of the loss of her daughter Persephone to the god of the underworld for six months of each year.

210:28–30. Pindar, fragment 137 (in Bergk's numbering), preserved by Clement of Alexandria.

211:1–2. The Book of Daniel, traditionally ascribed to a prophet Daniel of the Babylonian exile in the sixth century B.C., is now commonly believed to date from about 168–65 B.C., and to have been written "to encourage the reader during the persecutions of the Jews at the hands of Antiochus Epiphanes," king of Syria of the ruling family established by one of Alexander's generals.—*Oxford Dictionary of the Christian Church*.

212:15–213:23. All quotations are from the Prayer Book Version, but with the numbering of the Authorized Version and with "the Eternal" substituted for "the Lord."

213:24–30. *Westminster Review* CI, 150–51, paraphrased.

215:20–216:9. *Ibid.*, 151–52, 150 (in part summarized), 150 (summarized), 151, 152. The sentence at 216:2–3 is most closely represented in the article by "The Jewish idea of righteousness . . . consisted largely, if not chiefly, of piety, enthusiastic devotion, and attention to religious ceremonial" (p. 151). When Barak the Israelite and his army defeated the forces of Sisera, captain of the host to the Canaanite king of Hazor, Sisera took refuge in the tent of Jael, wife of Heber the Kenite, "for there was peace between Jabin the king of Hazor and the house of Heber the Kenite. And Jael went out to meet Sisera, and said unto him, Turn in, my lord, turn in to me; fear not." Thereupon, while he slept in his weariness, she "took a nail of the tent, and took an hammer in her hand, and went softly unto him, and smote the nail into his temples, and fastened it into the ground. . . . So he died."—Judges 4:17–18, 21. The glorification of Jael by Barak and the prophetess Deborah is in Judges 5:24–31.

216:30–32. *Westminster Review* CI, 150.

217:11–14, 26–28. The work of Xenophanes of Colophon, a late sixth-century exile from Ionia living in Sicily, survives only in fragments. Arnold cites nos. 15 and 18 (2) in J. M. Edmonds' arrangement, the former preserved by Clement of Alexandria, the latter by Stobaeus.—*Greek Elegy and Iambus* (Loeb Classical Library), I, 201, 203.

218:1–2. "And the earth was without form, and void; and darkness was upon the face of the deep. And the Spirit of God moved upon the face of the waters."—Genesis 1:2.

218:13–21. The *Westminster* reviewer cited "Abraham's all but consummated sacrifice of Isaac" (Genesis 22) as evidence that the custom of human sacrifice had once, in pre-historic times, existed, though now grown rudimentary from disuse.—CI, 151. In II Chronicles 20:7 Jehoshaphat, addressing God, refers to "Abraham thy friend" and James remarks in his Epistle (2:21, 23): "Was not Abraham our father justified by works, when he had offered Isaac his son upon the altar? . . . He was called the Friend of God." In Genesis 20:5 Abimelech, who had taken Abraham's wife from him, sought to shield himself from God's vengeance by pleading, "In the integrity of my heart and innocency of my hands have I done this," and the Lord allowed the plea. See p. 211:23–25.

218:34. Acts 17:27.

219:14–15. See p. 212:18–19.

219:25–28. Jerusalem was destroyed by the Babylonian king Nebuchadnezzar about 586 B.C. and many of the Jews were carried into exile in Babylon. They were restored to their home after the fall of Babylon to Cyrus the Great, king of Persia, in 539. The Persians in their turn were driven from Palestine by the Macedonians under Alexander the Great in 332. After Alexander's death the land was disputed between the dynasties established by two of his generals, Ptolemy in Egypt and Seleucus in Syria, with the latter prevailing. Antiochus IV of Syria, who reigned 175–163 B.C., an almost fanatical devotee of Hellenic culture, established an altar of Zeus in the Temple at Jerusalem, and thereby stirred up the revolt led by Judas Maccabaeus in 167. The Jews came under Roman domination with Pompey's destruction of Jerusalem in 63 B.C. and were ruled, under Roman overlordship, by Herod the Great and his son Herod Archelaus. The brother of the latter, Herod Antipas, commanded the execution of John the Baptist.

220:4–5. "Thus saith the Lord, Keep ye judgment, and do justice." —Isaiah 56:1. Gabriel in a vision announced to Daniel the duty of his people "to finish the transgression and to make an end of sins, and to make reconciliation for iniquity, and to bring in everlasting righteousness."—Daniel 9:24.

220:28–31. See *Prose Works*, ed. Super, VI, 372–73. The reference is to Abraham Kuenen, *The Religion of Israel*, tr. A. H. May (London, 1874–75), I, 225–27, 308–17.

220:31–35. See Armand-Pierre Caussin de Perceval, *Essai sur l'Histoire des Arabes* (Paris, 1847), II, 326–32 (the Moàllaca of Imroulcays, who died about 540 A.D.), 352–61, 366–73, 384–92, 521–27, 531–36.

221:2. "The most shameful custom among the Babylonians is this: every woman of the land is required once in her lifetime to sit in the temple of Aphrodite (or Mylitta, as the Assyrians call her) and have intercourse with a stranger."

221:10–12. Kuenen, tr. May, I, 361.

222:8–22. "Modern Culture," *Quarterly Review*, American ed., CXXXVII, 205–20 (October, 1874), an article on works by Carlyle, Arnold, Symonds, and Pater that the *Wellesley Index* attributes to W. J. Courthope. Arnold alludes especially to pp. 208, 210.

223:2–3. Darwin discussed the matter in chapt. v of *The Descent of Man* (1871).

223:14. See *Prose Works*, ed. Super, VI, 174.

223:19–21. Pascal, *Pensées*, sect. ii, no. 93; *Oeuvres*, ed. L. Brunschvicg (Paris, 1921), XIII, 20–21, slightly modified by Arnold. Arnold inserted this quotation as a footnote in *Literature and Dogma* in the Fourth Edition of 1874. See *Prose Works*, ed. Super, VI, 183.

223:30–31. "Honor thy father and mother; which is the first commandment with promise."—Ephesians 6:2. The "promise" is "that thy days may be long upon [or "in"] the land which the Lord thy God giveth thee."—Exodus 20:12. This is the Fifth Commandment in the Anglican Prayer Book, the Fourth in the Roman Catholic usage.

226:1–5. "God is simply *the stream of tendency by which all things seek to fulfil the law of their being*," a power "not ourselves." —*Literature and Dogma, Prose Works*, ed. Super, VI, 189, 181.

226:19–20. Exodus 20:14, the Seventh Commandment in the Anglican Prayer Book, the Sixth in the Roman Catholic usage.

227:3–4. "Religion . . . is ethics heightened, enkindled, lit up by feeling; the passage from morality to religion is made when to morality is applied emotion. And the true meaning of religion is thus, not simply *morality*, but *morality touched by emotion*."—*Literature and Dogma, Prose Works*, ed. Super, VI, 176.

228:18–21. "Je me souviens . . . surtout de Haymarket et du

Strand le soir. Sur cent pas, on heurte vingt filles; quelques-unes vous demandent un verre de gin; d'autres disent: 'Monsieur, c'est pour payer mon terme.' Ce n'est pas la débauche qui s'étale, mais la misère, et quelle misère! La déplorable procession dans l'ombre des rues monumentales fait mal au coeur; il me semblait voir un défilé de mortes. Voilà une plaie, la vraie plaie de la société anglaise."— Hippolyte Taine, *Notes sur l'Angleterre* (Paris, 1872), p. 39 (four-fifths through chapt. i). The Bois de Boulogne is one of the larger Paris parks. Arnold must have been reading Taine's book about the time he wrote to Ernest Fontanès on August 15, 1873: "Le Celte pur, l'Irlandais, est chaste; le Celte latinisé, le Français, est tout autre chose. Selon Ste. Beuve, Proudhon disait que "la France était tournée toute entière vers la fornication"; et c'est là, en effet, votre plaie; or, à cet égard, l'Irlande offre aux autres pays un exemple vraiment admirable, ses fautes sont ailleurs."—*Letters*, ed. G. W. E. Russell.

228:23–27. Mill, *Autobiography*, chapt. vii, sixth paragraph, in Mill's discussion of his personal relations with Mrs. Taylor. The *Autobiography* was published in 1873; Arnold read it that year and jotted some passages in his pocket diary.—*Note-Books*, ed. Lowry, pp. 197–98, 204.

229:7 (variant). See p. 226:32–33.

229:8–15. On April 7, 1830, Goethe was speaking to Müller about the Greek idealization of the male and the development of Platonic love. "Die Knabenliebe sei so alt wie die Menschheit, und man könne daher sagen, sie liege in der Natur, ob sie gleich gegen die Natur sei. Was die Kultur der Natur abgewonnen habe, dürfe man nicht wieder fahren lassen, es um keinen Preis aufgeben. So sei auch der Begriff der Heiligkeit der Ehe eine solche Kulturerrungen-schaft des Christentums und von unschätzbarem Wert, obgleich die Ehe eigentlich unnatürlich sei."—C. A. H. Burkhardt, ed., *Goethe's Unterhaltungen mit dem Kanzler Friedrich von Müller* (3rd ed.; Stuttgart, 1904), p. 174. The conversations were first published in 1870, and "Goethe & Müller" appears in Arnold's diary among the books to be read in 1874.—*Note-Books*, ed. Lowry, p. 589.

229:26–27. See p. 226:32–33.

230:4–9. Charles Secrétan, "Littérature et Dogme," *Bibliothèque universelle et revue suisse* XLIX n.s., 346 (February, 1874), summarized, not quoted. The article devotes nearly ten of its seventeen pages to translating passages of the book, which in the reviewer's opinion "abonde en aperçus précieux," and expresses "un point de vue un peu étroit, mais intéressant."

230:27. "Extra-belief" is Arnold's translation of the German word *Aberglaube*, a term that means "superstition," but without the pejorative connotation of "superstition."—*Literature and Dogma, Prose Works*, ed. Super, VI, 212.

231:20–23. "Behold, one like the Son of man came with the clouds of heaven, and came to the Ancient of days, and they brought him near before him. . . . And judgment was given to the saints of the most High; and the time came that the saints possessed the kingdom. . . . And many of them that sleep in the dust of the earth shall awake, some to everlasting life, and some to shame and everlasting contempt."—Daniel 7:13, 22; 12:2. The Greek words for "judgment" and "resurrection" in the Septuagint version of Daniel and in the New Testament are "crisis" and "anastasis." But see p. 251:9n.

232:2–3 (variant). Psalm 37:17, 24, Prayer Book Version.

232:20–23, 32–233:3, 5–6. "Mr. Arnold's Sublimated Bible," *Spectator* XLVII, 1257 (October 10, 1874), an article on the first installment of *God and the Bible*. The question Arnold answers from Butler the *Spectator* asked only with respect to Wordsworth.

233:4. Wordsworth, "Tintern Abbey," lines 122–23. Wordsworth wrote "never did betray."

233:8–16. Joseph Butler, Sermon XV, "Upon the Ignorance of Man," ¶11; *Works*, ed. W. E. Gladstone (Oxford, 1896), II, 268. Arnold's "If things afford to man" sums up Butler's "If the make and constitution of man, the circumstances he is placed in, or the reason of things affords," and Butler wrote "inviolable practice" and "neither the dangers nor." The italics are Arnold's, and except for the italics he wrote the passage, exactly as he quotes it here, in his second "general note-book."—*Note-Books*, ed. Lowry, p. 518. Arnold goes on here to allude to his two lectures on "Bishop Butler and the Zeit-Geist," delivered at Edinburgh on January 4 and 7, 1876, and published in *Last Essays on Church and Religion, Prose Works*, ed. Super, vol. VIII. When Arnold first published this passage, of course, the lectures on Butler were still in the future; he did not revise his language respecting them until he published the Popular Edition; see Textual Notes.

233:33–35. "Pour tenter l'épreuve sous l'impulsion du mobile intéressé dont le Dr. Arnold fait le ressort universel, conformément à la tradition de l'école anglaise, il faudrait croire au préalable à l'efficacité du renoncement pour procurer le bonheur. Disons mieux: l'expérience commencée sous de tels auspices raterait certainement de la façon la plus honteuse."—Secrétan, "Littérature et Dogme,"

p. 347. But later on the same page the reviewer explains Arnold's failure to understand human motives thus: "L'éducation morale de l'auteur s'est faite évidemment sur le terrain de la religion et non sur le terrain de l'utilitarisme. Le fond de ses idées est d'un kantien beaucoup plus que d'un empirique."

234:8–9. Arnold quoted this sentence from St. Augustine in *Literature and Dogma, Prose Works*, ed. Super, VI, 192:36–38. I have not found the source.

234:9–11. *Pensées*, §vii, no. 425; *Oeuvres de Pascal*, ed. L. Brunschvicg (Paris, 1921), XIII, 321.

234:11–13. "Happiness, or the *Summum bonum*, the utmost scope of human desire, . . . the highest good, the chiefest desirable thing." —Sermon V: "The Profitableness of Godliness," *Theological Works*, ed. Alexander Napier (Cambridge, 1859), I, 221.

234:13–15. Butler, Sermon XII, "Upon the Love of Our Neighbour," ¶20; *Works*, ed. Gladstone (1896), II, 224; quoted in *Literature and Dogma, Prose Works*, ed. Super, VI, 192:31–32.

234:16–18. *Literature and Dogma* was the subject of discussion in the Unitarian weekly, *The Inquirer*, on February 15 and 22 and March 15, 1873.

234:28–235:7. *Westminster Review* CI, 154, 155, 153. For an example of the expression "the secret of the Eternal," see Psalm 25:14: "The secret of the Lord is with them that fear him; and he will shew them his covenant."

235:12–15. "Modern Culture," *Quarterly Review*, American ed., CXXXVII, 210.

235:19–21. Augustine *Retractiones* I. xiii. 3, jotted in Arnold's pocket diary for September 6, 1868.—*Note-Books*, ed. Lowry, p. 82.

235:22–25. L. W. E. Rauwenhoff, "Matthew Arnold," *Theologisch Tijdschrift* (Leiden) VII, 337 (May–June, 1873). Rauwenhoff's 61-page article on *Literature and Dogma* is filled with the most enthusiastic praise of the book, which he summarizes at length. He and Abraham Kuenen (whom Arnold had praised in *Literature and Dogma*) were among the co-editors of the *Theologisch Tijdschrift*. Arnold's attention may have been drawn to this article by a summary of it in *The Academy* IV, 209 (June 2, 1873). "Mon livre a été fort critiqué, mais il produit son effet," Arnold wrote to Ernest Fontanès on August 15, 1873; "la plupart des articles de revue s'occupent de billevesées; seule, une revue hollandaise, *Le Journal théologique* de Leyden, a traité à fond le livre et la thèse qui y est soutenue."—*Letters*, ed. Russell.

235:27. Paul thus described the infant sect of Christianity, II Corinthians 6:9.

236:18–19. "Hast thou appealed unto Caesar? unto Caesar shalt thou go," were Festus' words to Paul, Acts 25:12.

237:1–238:14. *Prose Works*, ed. Super, VI, 266, 268–69, 271. The phrase "on which so much thought is by many bestowed," added by Arnold when he published *God and the Bible* in book form, is not in *Literature and Dogma*, and p. 237:13 reads "be really settled." Arnold dropped all this discussion (chapt. vi, sects. 3–4) from the Popular Edition of *Literature and Dogma*, partly, no doubt, because he had so much amplified it here.

238:15–16. *Westminster Review* CI, 155.

238:16–22. *Supernatural Religion* (3rd ed., 1874), II, 450, 462–64. Though Arnold does not quote precisely, the expressions "dogmatic mysticism," "artificial dialogues," "prolix discourses," "sublime morality" and "simple eloquence" belong to his source.

239:9–11. *Ibid.*, II, 489–90.

239:17–18. The reviewer in *The Spectator* XLVII, 947 (July 25, 1874) called the book "learned and able." But Arnold might not be displeased with the quotation of another reviewer's judgment: "It abounds with acuteness, it overflows with reading: except 'intelligence,' in Goethe and Matthew Arnold's sense, it has every characteristic of a first-rate book; indeed, perhaps it would be one, except that it is not a book at all."—W. H. Simcox, "Supernatural Religion," *Academy* VI, 281 (September 12, 1874).

239:39. See Arnold's "Introduction," parts i–ii.

240:22–36. The author of *Supernatural Religion* replied promptly to this statement by Arnold, as well as to the earlier allusion to his work (p. 147), in a Preface to his sixth edition dated March 15, 1875. See complete ed. (3 vols.; London, 1879), I, lxxx–lxxxiii.

241:8–10. *Supernatural Religion* (3rd ed., 1874), II, 489–90.

241:10–11. See p. 153:14–15 and n.

241:33–38. Matthew 23:26, Mark 7:20; Matthew 16:25 (10:39, Mark 8:35, Luke 9:24, 17:33); Matthew 11:29.

242:13. Preface to the New Testament, *Die deutsche Bibel* (Weimar, 1929), VI, 10. See *Literature and Dogma*, *Prose Works*, ed. Super, VI, 271:22–23.

242:17–18. For Strauss's discussion of the artistic merits of the Fourth Gospel (which Arnold had already cited in *Literature and Dogma*, *Prose Works*, ed. Super, VI, 271), see *Das Leben Jesu für das deutsche Volk bearbeitet*, *Gesammelte Schriften* (Bonn, 1877),

III, 178–83. Strauss quotes Baur's praise of the "reine Geistigkeit" of the Gospel.

242:26–29. Criticism is "a disinterested endeavour to learn and propagate the best that is known and thought in the world," "the endeavour, in all branches of knowledge, theology, philosophy, history, art, science, to see the object as in itself it really is."—Arnold, "The Function of Criticism at the Present Time," *Prose Works*, ed. Super, III, 283, 258.

243:1–3. "In our day, the great chastener and corrector of all investigation, and of the whole business of inference from the known to the unknown, is scientific inquiry into the facts of nature; but though its influence, great already, is destined to be much greater, it is altogether modern. Englishmen have for long had, not indeed an adequate, but a valuable substitute for it in their law of evidence. . . . The system evolved had many defects, some of which have been removed; but even in its unimproved state it produced a certain severity of judgment on questions of fact which has long been a healthy characteristic of the English mind."—H. S. Maine, "Mr. Fitzjames Stephen's Introduction to the Indian Evidence Act," *Fortnightly Review* XIX, 67 (January, 1873). And see p. 280:5–8n.

244:38–245:1. Arnold alluded to this wish of Themistocles in *The Popular Education of France*, *Prose Works*, ed. Super, II, 136:17. So too did Carlyle in *Sartor Resartus*, Book I, chapt. vii, near the end.

245:10–14. *De Imitatione Christi* I. xxiii. 2, quoted twice in *Literature and Dogma*, *Prose Works*, ed. Super, VI, 192, 350. The *Imitation* reads *essemus* for *simus*.

245:14–17. *Ibid.*, III. l. 7, jotted in Arnold's pocket diaries for 1866, 1869, and 1871.—*Note-Books*, ed. Lowry, pp. 39, 110, 147.

246:7. "I Daniel understood by books," where "by books" translates ἐν ταῖς βίβλοις.

247:17. The Thora, or Torah, is the Pentateuch, the "books of the law."

248:35–38. Josiah was king of Judah, slain in 609 B.C. after a reign of thirty-one years (II Kings 22:1, 23:29 and II Chronicles 34:1, 35:23–24). The rival monarchy of Israel, of which Ahab was king in the mid ninth century, fell with the destruction of Samaria by Sargon of Assyria in 722 B.C. Because of the wickedness of Josiah's grandfather, the Lord said: "Behold, I am bringing such evil upon Jerusalem and Judah, that whosoever heareth of it, both his ears shall tingle. And I will stretch over Jerusalem the line of Samaria, and the plummet of the house of Ahab: and I will wipe Jerusalem as a man wipeth a dish, wiping it, and turning it upside down."—II Kings 21:12–13. The kingdom of Judah fell before Nebuchadnezzar of Babylon about 586 B.C. The words of the Lord in Deuteronomy 31–32 correspond with the promise of vengeance in II Kings 21, and therefore may have been written about the same time.

249:17–251:3. This account in general follows that of Édouard Reuss, *Histoire du canon des Saintes-Écritures* (2nd ed.; Strasbourg, 1863), pp. 2–13. Jerome's use of the term *Hagiographa* is mentioned on p. 205.

249:22–24. The Pentateuch was the only part of the Old Testament accepted by the Samaritans, whose version differs slightly from that of the Jews.

250:29–31. The revolt under Judas Maccabaeus began in 167 B.C. (see p. 219:25n); Jerusalem fell to the armies of Titus, future emperor of Rome, in 70 A.D. The translation of the Hebrew scripture into the Greek of the so-called Septuagint was completed at Alexandria not long after the Maccabaean revolt. It does not preserve the old Hebrew order of the books (see p. 252:15–20).

251:5–6. The Book of Enoch is a heterogeneous collection of writings dating probably from the last two centuries before Christ and known principally only through an Ethiopic translation of the Aramaic original. Arnold quoted a few passages from it in *Literature and Dogma, Prose Works*, ed. Super, VI, 284.

251:9–11. See p. 231:20–23. In the commonly-used Greek version of Daniel by Theodotion, the word "anastasis" does not occur; in another version it appears in its verb form, but not as a noun.

251:22. Mount Moriah was the hill of Jerusalem on which the Temple was built, according to II Chronicles 3:1.

252:3–7. See Reuss, *Histoire du canon* (2nd ed.; Strasbourg, 1863), p. 12.

253:24–27. Numerous ecclesiastical councils were held at Carthage over a span of three centuries, from 251 to 534. Arnold alludes in particular to two of those presided over by St. Aurelius, bishop of Carthage and friend of St. Augustine.

253:30–34. "The grass withereth, the flower fadeth: but the word of our God shall stand for ever."—Isaiah 40:8. This passage is quoted in I Peter 1:23–25. Eusebius' Greek is quoted by Reuss, *Histoire du canon*, p. 21.

253:36–39. According to the *New Catholic Encyclopedia* (*s.v.* Bible: III. Canon), the synod of 397 does not list the Epistle to the Hebrews as Pauline, though it does regard the book as canonical.

But Arnold here follows Reuss, *Histoire du canon*, pp. 218–220; the difference is in the interpretation of an ambiguity in the Latin of the synod.

254:1–4. Migne, *PG*, XXVI, 1176–77.

254:12–13. St. Jerome's Latin version of the Bible, the Vulgate, is the authoritative text in the Roman Catholic church. It was commissioned by Pope Damasus in 382 and completed about 404.

254:22. Edward Bouverie Pusey (1800–1882), regius professor of Hebrew at Oxford, was the pillar of the Tractarian movement; after Newman's conversion to Roman Catholicism he was the most forceful champion of conservative orthodoxy within the Church of England. The revision of the Authorized Version of the Bible was at the moment Arnold wrote being undertaken by the Anglican Church, but not with Pusey's participation.

254:26–29. *Epistola ad Dardanum* ¶3; Migne, *PL*, XXII, 1103.

254:29–30. *De viris illustribus* cap. i; Migne, *PL*, XXIII, 609.

254:30–32. *Ibid.*, cap. ii; Migne, *PL*, XXIII, 609.

254:32–255:1. *Ibid.*, cap. iv; Migne, *PL*, XXIII, 615.

255:1–4. *Ibid.*, cap. ix; Migne, *PL*, XXIII, 623. All these Latin passages are quoted (with slight differences) in Reuss, *Histoire du canon*, pp. 208–211 and (exactly as Arnold gives them) in B. F. Westcott, *History of the Canon of the New Testament* (5th ed.; London, 1881), pp. 452–53.

255:5–17. Arnold's observations on St. Jerome are based on Reuss, *Histoire du canon*, pp. 211–12.

255:21–26. The canon of the Council of Carthage in 397 lists, between the Psalms and the Minor Prophets, "Salomonis libri quinque" (i.e., Proverbs, Ecclesiastes, Song of Solomon, Wisdom, and Ecclesiasticus). See Reuss, *Histoire du canon*, p. 218.

255:34–256:1. *Contra epistolam Manichaei* cap. v; Migne, *PL*, XLII, 176. Quoted by Reuss, *Histoire du canon*, p. 215.

256:12. The dean of Carlisle, Francis Close (1797–1882), was a popular preacher but narrow controversialist of the Evangelical wing of the Church of England.

256:32. For Eusebius, see p. 259. Origen was an Alexandrian theologian of the early third century, a hundred years earlier than Eusebius. He was much concerned to affirm the integrity and inspiration of the Scripture against the Marcionites (see p. 257:34n). Arnold here draws on Reuss, *Histoire du canon*, pp. 142–44, 158–59.

257:5–7. Christopher Wordsworth, bishop of Lincoln, speaking in the House of Lords on August 4, 1874; see *The Times*, August 5, p.

4, col. 3; jotted in Arnold's pocket diary for August 4.—*Note-Books*, ed. Lowry, p. 216.

257:34. The heretic Marcion (d. *c.* 160) had as his central thesis that "the Christian gospel was wholly a Gospel of Love to the absolute exclusion of Law"; the God of Jesus was entirely unlike the God of the Old Testament, whom it was Christ's purpose to overthrow. Marcion accepted as canonical only ten epistles of St. Paul and an edited version (which purported to be Pauline) of the Gospel of St. Luke (so that Arnold's statement at p. 258:14 is misleading). His heresy was the chief threat to the Church doctrine for some fifty years; it gradually died out in the third century.—*Oxford Dictionary of the Christian Church*. The Pastoral Epistles are those to Timothy (I & II) and Titus. See Reuss, *Histoire du canon*, pp. 76–79.

258:10. The Alogi denied the divinity of Christ as the Logos (as presented in St. John's Gospel) and of the Holy Ghost. Some at least attributed the Fourth Gospel and the Apocalypse to the Gnostic heretic Cerinthus, who flourished about the year 100.

258:30–32. II Thessalonians 2:2.

258:33–35. Adolph Hilgenfeld, *Novum Testamentum extra canonem receptum*, fascicle IV: *Evangeliorum secundum Hebraeos &c* (Leipzig, 1866), p. 69, quoting Tertullian *On Baptism*, chapt. xvii.

259:2–6. Quoted in English by Westcott, p. 420, in French by Reuss, p. 161.

259:19–20. Quoted in English by Westcott, p. 358.

259:34–35. Jerome's Preface to the translation of the four Gospels, addressed to Pope Damasus; Migne, *PL*, XXIX, 527–28.

260:2–5. Irenaeus *Contra haereses* III. xi. 8, in Migne, *PG*, VII, 885. Irenaeus was a native of Smyrna who became bishop of Lyons, France, about 178.

260:9–10. Ignatius was bishop of Antioch (d. *c.* 107). Justin Martyr was a Christian teacher who suffered martyrdom at Rome under Marcus Aurelius, *c.* 165. His "First Apology on Behalf of Christians" is to be dated about 150. For Polycarp, see p. 141:1n.

260:10–261:18. For discussion of the Canon of Muratori and the fragments of Apollinaris see Westcott (5th ed., 1881), pp. 211–20, 227–28, Reuss, *Histoire du canon*, pp. 100–109, and *Supernatural Religion* (3rd ed.; 1874), II, 237–48, 185–91. The fragment was found by Muratori in the Ambrosian Library, whither it is presumed to have come from Bobbio, the monastery about forty miles northeast of Genoa founded by St. Columban in 612.

261:19–23. The alleged fragments of Apollinaris are preserved in the Paschal Chronicle, a Byzantine chronicle compiled in the first half of the seventh century. Eusebius lists the works of Apollinaris in his *Ecclesiastical History* IV. xxvii.

261:36–37. Arnold presumably alludes to this passage of Joseph Butler's *Analogy of Religion* (II, vii, 29): "It plainly requires a degree of modesty and fairness, beyond what every one has, for a man to say, not to the world, but to himself, that there is a real appearance of somewhat of great weight in this matter, though he is not able thoroughly to satisfy himself about it; but it shall have its influence upon him, in proportion to its appearing reality and weight. It is much more easy, and more falls in with the negligence, presumption, and wilfulness of the generality, to determine at once, with a decisive air, There is nothing in it."—*Works*, ed. W. E. Gladstone (Oxford, 1896), I, 327–28.

262:8–11. The Epistle of Barnabas, so called because it was early attributed to the Apostle Barnabas, probably dates from Alexandria about the last third of the first century or the early second century. It is preserved in the Codex Sinaiticus of the New Testament (see p. 266:12n) and elsewhere. Arnold alludes to the passage, "Let us take heed lest as it was written we be found 'many called but few chosen.' "—4:14.

262:12. Matthew 20:16, 22:14.

262:16–25. Arnold draws in part upon Tischendorf's indignant ridicule of Volkmar and Strauss in his *Origin of the Four Gospels*, tr. W. L. Gage (Boston, Mass., 1867), pp. 160–61 and notes. Gustav Volkmar, a professor at Zurich and follower of the Tübingen school, published an edition of the *Epistle of Barnabas* in 1864 (*Index lectionum in literarum Universitate Turicensi*; for the view Arnold cites, see p. 16, or his *Einleitung in die Apokryphen* [Tübingen, 1860], II, 105). Strauss lent his support ("ohne Zweifel," as Arnold quotes him) in *Das Leben Jesu für das deutsche Volk bearbeitet*, *Gesammelte Schriften* (Bonn, 1877), III, 69. Eduard Zeller was editor of Strauss's collected works. The author of *Supernatural Religion* takes the view that the allusion is to II Esdras 8:3.—(3rd ed., 1874) I, 236–49.

262:29–30. Orders in Council are administrative rules issued by the Crown on the advice of the Privy Council. The Committee of Council on Education and the Education Department, under which Arnold held his inspectorship, were created, not by Parliament, but by an Order in Council.

263:1–4. Neander's argument and motive Arnold takes from Baur,

Kritische Untersuchungen, pp. 340–41. Baur cites Neander's *Geschichte der christlichen Religion und Kirche* (2nd ed.), II, pt. i, 512f. Neander was a conservative critic.

263:4—10. C. C. J. Bunsen, *Hippolytus and His Age* (London, 1852), II, 135–36, 137. Westcott says, "The attempt to identify [*the Epistle to the Alexandrians*] with that *to the Hebrews* is not supported by the slightest external evidence."—(5th ed., 1881), p. 218, n. 1.

263:36–38. *I.e.*, the Epistle of Barnabas and the Muratorian Canon.

264:23. Clement was bishop of Rome at the end of the first century and author of the Epistle of Clement to the church at Corinth.

264:30–265:1. John 3:24, quoted by Eusebius *Ecclesiastical History* III. xxiv. 11. Eusebius does expressly mention the Fourth Gospel as his source. But Arnold seems to be making a concession to the opponents of *Supernatural Religion* on a minor point, while he agrees with the major position of that work. "When . . . , in early writings, we meet with quotations closely resembling, or we may add, even identical with passages which are found in our Gospels, the source of which, however, is not mentioned, nor is any author's name indicated, the similarity or even identity cannot by any means be admitted as evidence that the quotation is necessarily from our Gospels, and not from some other similar work now no longer extant, and more especially not when in the same writings there are other quotations from apocryphal sources different from our Gospels."—(3rd ed., 1874), I, 213.

264:35–36. Justin Martyr *Dialogus cum Tryphone Judaeo* cap. ciii, in Migne, *PG*, VI, 717; quoted in *Supernatural Religion* (3rd ed., 1874), I, 291n.

264:37. Justin Martyr *Apologia I* cap. lxvii, in Migne, *PG*, VI, 429; quoted in *Supernatural Religion* (3rd ed., 1874), I, 295n. In this sentence Justin speaks of the "memorabilia" of the apostles and the "written accounts" of the prophets.

265:10–14. For these ancient and fragmentary gospels Arnold has gone to the edition of Hilgenfeld; see p. 258:33n. The Ebionites were a severely ascetic sect of early Jewish Christians of whom we know very little, and that chiefly from the early writings against heresies. Epiphanius says that the Ebionites "receive the Gospel according to Matthew. . . . And they call it 'according to the Hebrews.'" The Gospels according to the Egyptians and according to the Twelve are mentioned (from Origen) in Hilgenfeld, p. 43.

265:19–23. Hilgenfeld, pp. 7–9.

265:24–26. See p. 172:12–13.

265:26–27. Hilgenfeld, pp. 17, 29, from Jerome *de viris illustribus* cap. ii (Migne, *PL*, XXIII, 611–13). See I Corinthians 15:7.

265:28–29. Hilgenfeld, pp. 18, 29, from Jerome, *loc. cit.*, cap. xvi (Migne, *PL*, XXIII, 633). The Greek version is from Ignatius *Epistola ad Smyrnaeos* cap. iii (Migne, *PG*, V, 709). It is quoted by Reuss, *Histoire du canon* (2nd ed.; 1863), p. 25.

265:32: Hegesippus was a second-century church historian, surviving for the most part only in fragments quoted by Eusebius.

265:34–266:1. The so-called "Protevangelium of James," mentioned by Origen and dating probably from the second century, survives almost entire in Greek. The description of Jesus' birth in a cave is in chapts. xviii–xix, and is mentioned in Justin's *Dialogue with the Jew Tryphon*, cap. lxxviii (Migne, *PG*, VI, 657). See Tischendorf, *Origin of the Four Gospels*, p. 133; Reuss, *Histoire du canon*, p. 57, and *Supernatural Religion* (3rd ed., 1874), I, 310–13.

266:2–5. Hilgenfeld, pp. 17, 27, with both versions of the Greek, Jerome's Latin, and the array of Fathers alluded to by Arnold. The saying is cited also by Strauss, *Leben Jesu . . . bearbeitet, Gesammelte Schriften* (Bonn, 1877), III, 176.

266:6–12. "Since therefore they are going to say that Christ is David's son, David himself prophesies, fearing and understanding the error of the sinners, 'The Lord said to my Lord sit thou on my right hand until I make thy enemies thy footstool.' . . . See how 'David calls him Lord' and does not say Son."—*Epistle of Barnabas* 12:10–11 (tr. K. Lake, Loeb Classical Library). See Psalm 110:1 and the use made of it by Jesus in Matthew 22:43–45, Mark 12:35–37, Luke 20:41–44. Arnold discusses this use in *Literature and Dogma, Prose Works*, ed. Super, VI, 234–35. He is at one with the author of *Supernatural Religion* (3rd ed., 1874), I, 253–55, in denying the validity of Tischendorf's assertion that the Epistle of Barnabas alludes to the Gospel passages. Arnold presumably used the edition of Barnabas by A. Hilgenfeld, *Novum Testamentum extra canonem receptus* (Leipzig, 1866), fascicle II.

266:12. Constantin Tischendorf (1815–74), a most meticulous textual critic of the New Testament, was the discoverer in 1859 of the Codex Sinaiticus in the monastery of St. Catherine on Mount Sinai, one of the earliest manuscripts of the New Testament, dating, as it does, from the late fourth century. In Arnold's day, the Codex Sinaiticus was housed in the Imperial Library at St. Petersburg; now it is in the British Museum. Arnold's criticism of Tischendorf's handling of the *Epistle of Barnabas* is directed against his *Origin of the Four Gospels*, pp. 156–62, and against Tischendorf's own popularization of this treatise, *When Were Our Gospels Written* (New York, 1867), pp. 97–102. On Arnold's reading list for 1875 appeared "Tischendorff on Canon."—*Note-Books*, ed. Lowry, p. 589.

266:29–30. *Epistle of Barnabas* 4:3.

267:21–23. The First Epistle of Clement, datable about 96 A.D., is actually preserved in the Codex Alexandrinus, one of the earliest manuscripts of the Bible (fifth century). Arnold in *Literature and Dogma* treats its omission from the New Testament canon as almost accidental.—*Prose Works*, ed. Super, VI, 160.

267:24–25. Jerome *De viris illustribus* cap. xv; Migne, *PL*, XXIII, 633. Arnold may have found the passage also in *Supernatural Religion* (3rd ed., 1874), I, 295.

267:31–32. *Epistle of Clement* 18:2–17.

267:33–34. I.e., the version made in Alexandria by (it was said) seventy scholars; the Septuagint.

268:18–19. Justin Martyr *Apology I* cap. xv–xvii, in Migne, *PG*, VI, 349–53; discussed in *Supernatural Religion*, I, 346–59.

268:22–23. Justin *Apology I* cap. xvii, in Migne, *PG*, VI, 354; cf. Matthew 22:21, Mark 12:17, Luke 20:25. So far as the sentence beginning "Render unto Caesar" is concerned, Justin's version is like that in the Gospels; the difference comes in the question Jesus asked before he gave that advice ("Whose image and superscription is this" against "Whose image does the coin bear?").

268:34–38. *Epistle of Clement* 13:2, Migne, *PG*, I, 236; cf. Matthew 5:7, 6:14, 7:12, 2 and Luke 6:31, 36–38. The parallels and discrepancies are shown in *Supernatural Religion*, I, 223–24, which gives the Greek as Arnold quotes it.

269:5–9. Justin *Apology I* cap. xxxiv, lii, in Migne, *PG*, VI, 381–84, 405; cf. Micah 5:2 and Matthew 2:6, Zechariah 12:10 and John 19:37. See also p. 357:1–2n.

270:9. For Irenaeus see p. 260:2–5n.

271:12–14. *Prose Works*, ed. Super, VI, 269.

271:14 (variant). Marcus Aurelius *Meditations* III, 14 (Jeremy Collier's translation); quoted by Arnold in his essay on Marcus Aurelius, *Prose Works*, ed. Super, III, 138.

272:1–3. The youthful philosopher was C. E. Appleton, first editor of *The Academy*, to which Arnold was an occasional contributor. His letter to Arnold apparently does not survive, but Arnold's reply to it, dated November 22, 1874, is published in Diderik Roll-Hansen,

"Matthew Arnold and the 'Academy,'" *PMLA* LXVIII, 391–92 (June, 1953). Appleton pursued the matter in a pair of articles devoted to Arnold's writings on religion, "A Plea for Metaphysic," *Contemporary Review* XXVIII, 923–47 (November, 1876), and XXIX, 44–69 (December, 1876).

272:17–24. A notice of John Fiske's thousand-page *Outlines of Cosmic Philosophy, based on the Doctrine of Evolution, with Criticisms on the Positive Philosophy* (Boston, 1875) remarks: "The potent word just now is Evolution, and the purpose of Mr. Fiske's book is to expound to us the law of Evolution as laid down by Mr. Spencer;—the most sublime achievement, in Mr. Fiske's opinion, of modern science. Here it is: 'Evolution is . . .'"—*North American Review* CXX, 201 (January, 1875). Professor F. A. Dudley points out that in 1871 Arnold remarked to the geologist John W. Judd, "I cannot understand why you scientific people make such a fuss about Darwin. Why it's all in Lucretius!" And when Judd replied that Lucretius merely guessed what Darwin proved, Arnold "mischievously rejoined 'Ah! that only shows how much greater Lucretius was,—for he divined a truth, which Darwin spent a life of labour in groping for.'"—J. W. Judd, *The Coming of Evolution* (Cambridge, 1910), pp. 3–4.

273:16. Matthew 16:18. The words appear in no other Gospel. Baur makes his comment in his *Geschichte der christlichen Kirche* (3rd ed.; Tübingen, 1863), I, 75.

273:27–28. Luke 5:6.

273:37–274:3. See Luke 23:33, 39–43. Albert Schwegler (1819–57) was a scholar whose studies of the early Christian church were dominated by the views of Baur and the Tübingen school.

274:9–12. John 21:6–11.

274:27–37. "The disciple whom Jesus loved" was John, so described in John 19:26. For John and Peter at Jesus' tomb, see John 20:2–10; for Jesus' remark to Peter, John 21:22–23.

275:35–36. "I have had to read Baur: 'Untersuchungen über die kanonischen Evangelien,' with its 620 pages of horrid German and horrid print, right through," Arnold told Charles Appleton on November 16, 1873.—Diderik Roll-Hansen, "Matthew Arnold and the 'Academy,'" *PMLA* LXVIII, 386 (June, 1953).

276:6–9. "Ich will kein besonderes Gewicht darauf legen, dass, wie der sächsische Anonymus meint, mit dem Worte: πυτεῖν ἐπάνω ὄφεων, speciell auf ein im Leben des Paulus thatsächlich vorgekommenes Ereigniss Apg. 28, 3 f. hingedeutet ist," and "Wie man auch diesen äussern Umstand nehmen mag, dass die Bergrede bei Lucas, wenn auch nicht zu einer Thalrede (wie sie der sächsische Anonymus nennt), doch zu einer Feldpredigt geworden ist, in jedem Fall kann man in der ganzen Behandlung der Bergrede bei Lucas, gegenüber der Gestalt, die sie bei Matthäus hat, nur eine Degradation sehen."—*Kritische Untersuchungen*, pp. 441, 457. The allusion is to an anonymous book published in Leipzig in 1845, *Die Evangelien, ihr Geist, ihre Verfasser und ihr Verhältniss zu einander.*

276:15–16. The Leipzig publisher Bernhard Tauchnitz published as Vol. 1000 in his Collection of British Authors (1869) an edition of the New Testament in the Authorized Version with an introduction by Constantin Tischendorf and a record of variant readings from the Sinaitic, Vatican, and Alexandrine MSS. The first two of these manuscripts date probably from the fourth century, the last from the fifth century.

276:27–277:4. Baur, *Geschichte der christlichen Kirche* (3rd ed.; Tübingen, 1863), I, 74–75. Having supported himself by the view of fellow scholars like Volkmar and Hilgenfeld that the Marcionite version of Luke contained, along with Marcion's perversions, some readings that are actually closer to the original than the canonical text, Baur says simply: "I believe on good ground that the reading of Luke 16:17 is among these."

277:5–15. See Matthew 5:18, Luke 16:17. Marcion, a notorious Gnostic heretic of the middle of the second century, was accused by Tertullian and Epiphanius of altering the text of the Gospel of St. Luke to accord with his theology. The alteration at Luke 16:17 is recorded in Tertullian *Against Marcion* IV. xxxiii; Migne, *PL*, II, 472. Arnold might have found it mentioned in Édouard Reuss, *History of the Sacred Scriptures of the New Testament* (5th ed., 1874), § 246; tr. E. L. Houghton (Edinburgh, 1884), p. 255.

277:30–32. *Kritische Untersuchungen*, pp. 549–50, 553–54.

278:7–8. "The so-called *Tendenz* criticism of the Tübingen school (Baur, Schwegler, Ritschl, Hilgenfeld, Köstlin, . . .), which apprehends and explains the relation of the Gospels to one another essentially on the basis of their theological bias, has proved itself inadequate to solve the problem conclusively, even were there higher warrant for its premises."—Reuss, *History of the New Testament*, §185; tr. Houghton, p. 184. In the passage on the Third Gospel which Arnold cites, Baur says: "Wie die Anlage und Tendenz des Lukasevangeliums nur aus seinem Verhältniss zum Matthäusevangelium begriffen werden kann, so gibt auch der Judaismus des letz-

tern den besten Massstab zur Bestimmung seines paulinischen Char-
akters."—*Geschichte der christlichen Kirche* (Tübingen, 1863), I,
73.

278:18–24. Baur, *Kritische Untersuchungen*, pp. 586–87.

279:13–16. Baur, *Kritische Untersuchungen*, p. 571. Adolph Hilgenfeld (1823–1907), who taught at the University of Jena, was a
historical scholar of the early Christian church who adopted the
principles of the Tübingen school but was less radical than they.
He replied to Baur's theory about the second Gospel in *Das Markus-
Evangelium, nach seiner Composition, seiner Stellung in der Evan-
gelien-Literatur, seinem Ursprung und Charakter dargestellt.* Leipzig,
1850.

279:16–18. This is the doctrine of Volkmar's *Die Religion Jesu
und ihre erste Entwickelung.* Leipzig, 1857.

279:20–26. Both words are translated "iniquity" in the Authorized Version of Matthew 7:23 and Luke 13:27. Strauss makes the
claim Arnold quotes in *Das Leben Jesu . . . bearbeitet, Gesammelte
Schriften* (Bonn, 1877), III, 158, and on the preceding page asserts
that Luke placed Jesus' sermon on the Plain in order to remove the
implied parallel between Jesus on the Mount and Moses the Jewish
lawgiver on Mount Sinai.

280:5–8. H. S. Maine, *Lectures on the Early History of Institutions* (3rd ed.; London, 1880), p. 48 (two-thirds through Lecture
II). And see p. 243:1–3n.

280:22–24. See Tischendorf's Preface to his *Origin of the Four
Gospels,* tr. W. L. Gage (Boston, 1867), pp. 19, 16.

280:25–30. Heymann Steinthal, the philologist, on W. D. Whit-
ney of Harvard, quoted by F. Max Müller, "My Reply to Mr.
Darwin," *Contemporary Review* XXV, 313 (January, 1875). This
article immediately followed the third installment of *God and the
Bible.* Müller was of course an old friend of the Arnold family.

280:30–34. Theodor Mommsen (1817–1903) became professor at
the University of Berlin in 1858. He edited the entire corpus of extant Roman inscriptions and was author of a history of Rome that
is still read. He delivered his address upon formally assuming the
rectorate on October 15, 1874: "Freilich also sind wir stolz darauf
Deutsche zu sein, und wir haben dessen auch kein Hehl. Unter allen
Prahlereien ist keine leerer und falscher als die Prahlerei mit deutscher
Bescheidenheit. Wir sind durchaus nicht bescheiden, und wir wollen
es weder sein noch also heissen."—*Reden und Aufsätze* (Berlin,
1905), p. 5.

281:11–14. *Goethes Unterhaltungen mit dem Kanzler Friedrich von Müller*, ed. C. A. H. Burkhardt (Stuttgart, 1904), pp. 150–51 (August 23, 1827); jotted at the front of Arnold's pocket diary for 1875.—*Note-Books*, ed. Lowry, p. 224.

281:15–18. *Ibid.*, p. 97 (January 15, 1824), jotted in Arnold's pocket diary with the preceding.

282:18–20. Sir William Harcourt (1827–1904), like his friend Fitzjames Stephen one of the writers for the *Saturday Review*, was a prosperous barrister and from 1869 professor of international law at Cambridge. He turned to politics with his election as Liberal member of Parliament for Oxford in 1868, and was more than once in open opposition to his chief, Gladstone. He became solicitor-general, with a knighthood, at the end of 1873, but the defeat of the Liberals at the beginning of 1874 put him out of office. In January, 1875, he successfully urged Lord Hartington to accept the leadership of the Liberal party which Gladstone was willing to resign.

283:11–13. "Diesen Kampf [the challenge of the problem of the Fourth Gospel] aufgenommen und auf eine Weise durchgefochten zu haben, wie noch selten kritische Kämpfe durchgefochten worden sind, ist der unvergängliche Ruhm des verewigten Dr. Baur . . . So scharf er nachzuweisen suchte, dass es nicht als geschichtliche Quelle gelten könne, so eifrig suchte er seinen idealen Gehalt, seine künstlerische Vollendung in's Licht zu setzen."—D. F. Strauss, *Das Leben Jesu . . . bearbeitet, Gesammelte Schriften* (Bonn, 1877), III, 136–37.

283:31–284:8. Baur, *Kritische Untersuchungen*, pp. 114–16.

284:9–17. *Ibid.*, pp. 143, 145, 154.

284:18–29. *Ibid.*, pp. 159, 243–47, 87.

285:13–19. The text and a version of this part of the Canon of Muratori are given in *Supernatural Religion* (3rd ed., 1874), II, 383–84.

285:31–286:4. This position is summarized in Strauss, *Das Leben Jesu . . . bearbeitet, Gesammelte Schriften*, III, 96. The Paschal Controversy of about 170 A.D., one of many on the date of celebrating Easter, was the debate between the Asiatic churches, which followed the Jewish practice of celebrating the Passover on Nisan 14, whatever the day of the week, and the other Christian churches, which celebrated Easter always on the Sunday following Nisan 14, if that should fall on a weekday. There was further dispute whether it was the Last Supper or the Crucifixion that took place on the Passover.

285:36. In Migne, *PG*, XLI, 909–10.

286:31–287:16. John 2:6, 3:25 (where the Authorized Version

reads "and the Jews"), 2:13 and 11:55, 19:40, 42; see *Supernatural Religion* (3rd ed., 1874), II, 416. Richard Cobden (1804–1865), a Manchester industrialist and Liberal politician, was leader of the free trade movement in England. (Variant) John 5:1.

287:17–288:25. John 1:6 (cf. Matthew 3:1), 11:49, 51, and 18:13, 15. Strauss (III, 98) points out a good many of the indications that the author of the Fourth Gospel was not a Palestinian Jew, including the misplacing of Bethany beyond Jordan (the reading of the Sinaitic MS; the Authorized Version reads "Bethabara beyond Jordan") and the blunder about Caiaphas' term of office; the instances Arnold mentions are also to be found in *Supernatural Religion* (3rd ed., 1874), II, 417–20, 426–27. Willesden is a suburb northwest of London through which Arnold regularly passed when he lived at Harrow; the Trent flows across England a good deal to the north. Similarly, Bethany is a village on the outskirts of Jerusalem, the home of Mary, Martha, and Lazarus; it is not at all "beyond Jordan."

288:26–289:18. See *Supernatural Religion*, II, 414–15: "The philosophical statements with which the Gospel commences, it will be admitted, are anything but characteristic of the Son of thunder, the ignorant and unlearned fisherman of Galilee who, to a comparatively advanced period of life, continued preaching in his native country to his brethren of the circumcision."

289:15. The "Book of Elkesai" (or, as Arnold calls it, "Elxai") was an apocalyptic writing held sacred by an ascetic sect of Jewish Christians east of the Jordan at the end of the first century or beginning of the second. Most of our knowledge of the Elkesaites comes from Hippolytus' *Philosophumena* (see p. 295:19–21) and Epiphanius' work against heresy.

289:18. "Gnosticism" was a complex religious movement of the second century, based on the redemptive power of specially revealed knowledge of God ("gnosis"), transmitted by secret tradition from the Apostles or directly revealed to the founder of the sect. Valentinus, a native of Egypt, in the middle of the second century seceded from the Church to found the heretical Gnostic sect of Valentinians. Basilides, a Gnostic who taught at Alexandria in the middle of the second century, claimed to possess a secret tradition transmitted from St. Peter. Both writers survive only in fragments.

290:21. For Origen see p. 256:32n.

290:24. "And I saw the dead, small and great, stand before God; and the books were opened: and another book was opened, which is the book of life: and the dead were judged out of those things which were written in the books, according to their works. . . . And whosoever was not found written in the book of life was cast into the lake of fire."—Revelation 20:12, 15. The Book of Revelation was also attributed to the Apostle John.

292:12–17. *Prose Works*, ed. Super, VI, 272.

292:19–22. The author of *Supernatural Religion* summarizes Ewald's theory of John's relation to the Fourth Gospel—which is much like Arnold's—in order to refute it.—II, 433–34.

292:22–23. "[Es scheint] nichts übrig zu bleiben, als das johanneische Evangelium entweder ganz oder gar nicht als apostolisch anzuerkennen."—*Leben Jesu . . . bearbeitet, Gesammelte Schriften*, III, 130.

293:13–18. The views of Friedrich Schleiermacher in his lectures on the life of Christ and of Christian Hermann Weisse in his *Die Evangelienfrage in ihrem gegenwärtigen Stadium* (1856) are summarized by Strauss, III, 26, 129.

293:18–27. "Unserm Apostel am ende eines langen lebens die worte wie er sie vom verklärten Christus sich tausendfach zugerufen gefühlt hatte leichter auch wohl schon in dieser verklärteren gestalt beim zeichnen des bildes des einst lebenden sich wiederholen."— Ewald, *Die johanneischen Schriften übersetzt und erklärt* (Göttingen, 1861), pp. 38–39.

294:1–3. See Tischendorf, *Origin of the Four Gospels*, p. 47.

294:7–17. *Ibid.*, pp. 70–71 and note; *Supernatural Religion* (3rd ed., 1874), II, 306–7 (with Justin's Greek); Justin *Apology I* cap. lxi, in Migne, *PG*, VI, 420.

294:14 (variant). Hilgenfeld, *Evangeliorum secundum Hebraeos* etc., p. 72, citing Origen *Commentary on John* XX. 12 (Migne, *PG*, XIV, 600).

295:2 (variant). *Supernatural Religion*, II, 312–13, with a barrage of footnote references to the works of the Tübingen critics. Baur's view is that the first part of Justin's remark (from its similarity of language) is akin to the passage from Matthew and to one in the Gospel According to the Hebrews. The resemblance of the latter part of Justin's remark to the Fourth Gospel, then, need not lead to the inference that the Fourth Gospel was Justin's source; "it is just as possible, indeed decidedly more probable, that both [Justin and the author of the Fourth Gospel] drew from a common source. For if Justin had the passage from John directly before his eyes, why would he not have taken his version of Christ's words from it also?"—*Kritische Untersuchungen*, p. 352.

295:19–21. *Origenis philosophumena sive omnium haeresium refutatio.* E codice Parisino nunc primum edidit E[mmanuel] Miller. Oxonii, 1851.

295:24–29. Photius, a ninth-century patriarch of Constantinople, in his *Bibliotheca* describes a booklet against thirty-two heresies, written by Hippolytus. Hippolytus is generally referred to as "bishop of Rome" and may have been a schismatic in view of his attack on St. Callistus, the successor to Zephyrinus in the chair of St. Peter. But Bunsen calls him "Bishop of Portus"—i.e., of the Port of Rome, near ancient Ostia—, partly on the authority of the passage in the *Chronicon Paschale.*

295:30–33. *Chronicon Paschale,* ed. L. Dindorf (Bonn, 1832), vols. 16–17 of B. G. Niebuhr's *Corpus Scriptorum Historiae Byzantinae.* The Quartodecimans were heretics of the middle and late second century who dated Easter from the celebration of the Jewish Passover on the fourteenth day of the first moon after the vernal equinox, whether the day was Sunday or not (see p. 285:31n).

295:33–296:1. C. C. J. Bunsen, *Hippolytus and His Age* (2nd ed.; London, 1854), I, 335; see also I, 382–84. Bunsen was a friend of Dr. Arnold's, and dedicated the second volume of *Hippolytus* to his memory. For Bunsen on the Canon of Muratori in the first edition of this book, see p. 263:4–10.

296:17–19. The *Philosophumena* may be found in Migne, *PG,* XVI. This passage is in col. 3306.

296:29–297:3. *Supernatural Religion* (3rd ed., 1874), II, 52–54, 69–73.

297:24. Friedrich Schleiermacher (1768–1834) was a Protestant pastor in Berlin and one of the first professors of theology at the new University of Berlin. He was a reconciler of the views of the conservatives and the higher criticism; his stress upon feeling, rather than dogma, made many of the questions raised by the latter matters of indifference to him. Both Arnold and his father had a high regard for Schleiermacher. See p. 293:17.

298:10. Migne, *PG,* XVI, 3206.

298:11–13. *Supernatural Religion,* II, 248n. The Naasseni or Ophites and the Peratae are the first two groups of heretics discussed in the *Philosophumena;* the expression, "the Catholic snake" is found in the discussion of the latter group, Migne, *PG,* XVI, 3174.

298:20–22. Migne, *PG,* XVI, 3139, 3174.

298:22–24. *Ibid.,* cols. 3178, 3146; see John 10:7, 9.

298:24–27. *Ibid.,* col. 3174.

298:27–30. *Ibid.*, col. 3158.

298:30–299:3. *Ibid.*, col. 3139.

299:3–6. *Ibid.*, col. 3142.

300:8. See John 10:1–16, 26–27.

300:14–16. See p. 298:22–24.

300:21–24. The Latin is quoted in *Supernatural Religion*, II, 243.

300:25–29. *Ibid.*, II, 257.

301:1–4. *Ibid.*, II, 8–9, 336–40; see Matthew 11:28, John 10:27.

301:4–9. *Ibid.*, II, 325, 329; see John 14:2 and, for the passage in Irenaeus, Migne, *PG*, VII, 1223.

301:10–25. *Ibid.*, I, 258–59, 268. William Cureton's *Syriac Epistles of Ignatius* was published in London in 1845. The expression "the prince of this world" (John 12:31, 14:30, 16:11) may be found in Migne, *PG*, V, 660, 693.

301:15–18. John 6:69.

301:25–27. *Supernatural Religion*, II, 260–61; see John 6:51–56. The passage from Ignatius is in Migne, *PG*, V, 693.

302:6–16. *Supernatural Religion*, II, 341. The passage may be found in Migne, *PG*, II, 444, or in *Clementis Romani quae feruntur Homiliae*, ed. A. R. M. Dressel (Göttingen, 1853). It was Dressel who in 1838 discovered a second manuscript of the *Homilies*; the only other manuscript breaks off a little beyond the middle of the nineteenth Homily (out of twenty).

303:8–11. *Supernatural Religion*, II, 322–23.

303:24–25. Scholten's theory is alluded to in *Supernatural Religion*, II, 410.

304:4. Joseph Barber Lightfoot (1828–89), Hulsean professor of divinity at Cambridge in succession to C. J. Ellicott (and after 1879 bishop of Durham), was associated with Ellicott in the revision of the English version of the New Testament, was editor of the Clementine epistles and other writings of the Apostolic Fathers, and author of a long critique of *Supernatural Religion* which appeared concurrently with Arnold's *God and the Bible* in the *Contemporary Review*. In the first installment of this critique, Lightfoot said: "Mr. Matthew Arnold, alluding to an eccentric work of rationalizing tendencies written by an English scholar, and using M. Renan as his mouthpiece, expresses the opinion that 'an extravagance of this sort could never have come from Germany where there is a great force of critical opinion controlling a learned man's vagaries, and keeping him straight.' I confess that my experiences of the critical literature of Germany have not been so fortunate."—Lightfoot, "Supernatural Religion," *Contemporary Review* XXV, 17 (December, 1874); see Arnold on Charles Forster's *The One Primeval Language* in "The Literary Influence of Academies," *Prose Works*, ed. Super, III, 243–44.

305:19–23. This may be a summary of *Supernatural Religion*, II, 462–64, 467–68.

305:24–25. "Ars est celare artem," a Latin proverb brought into English at least as early as the sixteenth century.

306:25–26. "I can see as far into a millstone as another man" is a proverb recorded as early as the mid-sixteenth century, and often used ironically, as here.

307:7. The parallel with Plato's treatment of Socrates (see also p. 324:16) may have been suggested to Arnold by Renan's discussion of the Fourth Gospel in his *Vie de Jésus* (28th ed.; Paris, 1899), pp. 520, lxxix. He compares, for historical veracity respecting the life of Socrates and of Jesus, the *Memorabilia* of Xenophon to the Synoptics and the Dialogues of Plato to the Fourth Gospel. Of the long discourses in the last he remarks: "Ce sont des pièces de théologie et de rhétorique, sans aucune analogie avec les discours de Jésus dans les Évangiles synoptiques, et auxquels il ne faut pas plus attribuer de réalité historique qu'aux discours que Platon met dans la bouche de son maître au moment de mourir."—p. 520.

307:32–308:4. There are minor alterations from the Authorized Version, in which Arnold follows the Greek; the most significant is the connective word at the beginning of the italicized passage, where the Authorized Version reads "And herein" and Arnold reads, with the Greek, "For herein."

309:5. "To be on all fours" with something is to present an exact analogy with something; presumably it derives from the image of a dog running smoothly on four legs, not limping on three.—*N.E.D.*

309:6–9. Arnold substitutes phrases from John 10:1, 3, 2 for phrases in the basic passage, 10:7–9.

310:26–28. John 4:23.

311:18. The article ("*the* two days") is in the Greek but not in the Authorized Version; the "and went" of the latter is not in the Vatican or Sinaitic manuscript and so Arnold omits it.

311:24–25. John 6:24–25.

312:21–25. *Prose Works*, ed. Super, VI, 274. The Second Isaiah, or "Deutero-Isaiah," is the portion of the Book of Isaiah (chapts. 40–66) written during the Babylonian exile of the Jews, more than a century after the earlier chapters. Arnold prepared a school edition of the "Deutero-Isaiah," the Preface to which is printed in this volume. (Today, the "Second Isaiah" is commonly held to include chapts. 40–55 and a "Third Isaiah" of even later date is assigned chapts. 56–66.)

313:27. See *Literature and Dogma, Prose Works*, ed. Super, VI, 266.

313:31–34. This is much what Baur says in *Kritische Untersuchungen*, p. 227.

315:29. "Paraclete" is translated "Comforter" in the Authorized Version of John 14:26.

316:13. Arnold's longest discussion of St. Paul's doctrine of "necrosis" (dying) is in *St. Paul and Protestantism, Prose Works*, ed. Super, VI, 46–54.

316:38. Arnold follows the reading of the Alexandrine MS, but only partially that of the Vatican.

317:21–23. Romulus, having founded Rome and put it on the path to glory, was translated to heaven during a severe thunderstorm as the city's guardian deity, Quirinus.—Plutarch *Romulus* xxvii–xxviii; Livy I. xvi. The Cretan Epimenides, sent into the country to recover a stray sheep, fell asleep at noonday in a cave and remained asleep for fifty-seven years; when he awoke, unaware that he had taken more than a short nap, he was bewildered by finding others in possession of his father's farm and house. This archetypal Rip Van Winkle continued to live in the high esteem of the Hellenic world to the age of 154 (or perhaps 299) years.—Diogenes Laertius I. x. King Arthur after his wounding in the great battle in the west was conveyed by three queens in a boat to the Vale of Avalon, whence he will arise to rule Britain again in her hour of greatest need.— Malory, *Morte Arthur*, Book XXI, chapts. v–vii.

318:12. Louis de Rouvroy, duc de Saint-Simon (1675–1755) was an assiduous writer of memoirs that have been published fragmentarily and entirely posthumously. They were subjects of two of Sainte-Beuve's *Causeries du lundi*. James Boswell recorded in his diaries the conversations of Samuel Johnson which have made his *Life of Johnson* so vivid.

319:12–13. John 20:9.

319:35–38. Arnold uses the version he had published for use in schools, but with "the Eternal" substituted for "the Lord."

322:3–6. For Aberglaube, or "extra-belief," see p. 230:27n. Arnold discusses Jesus' method ("inwardness"), secret ("self-renouncement") and temper of mildness and sweet reasonableness in *Literature and Dogma, Prose Works*, ed. Super, VI, 284–301.

324:23–32. Baur, *Kritische Untersuchungen*, pp. 382–86.

325:2–5. The absence of this *logion* from the gospels was pointed out by Strauss, *Das Leben Jesu ... bearbeitet, Gesammelte Schriften* (Bonn, 1877), III, 176.

325:31 (variant). John 4:44. Two of the *logia* Arnold used in his first (*Contemporary Review*) version of this passage were to be found in other gospels as well as in John, and therefore did not properly illustrate his point.

326:17–23. It was on much this ground that Renan in his *Life of Jesus* denied that the discourses in the Fourth Gospel had historical validity, whereas he would concede some authenticity to the facts narrated.—lxxviii–lxxx. Arnold is therefore in part answering Renan and in part advancing on him. But he does not couple his name with those of the Tübingen school, presumably because he honored Renan's claim to be applying the method of literary criticism to his subject. Indeed, Arnold must have been heartily in accord with the aims and methods Renan announced in the concluding pages of the Introduction to his *Vie de Jésus*.

326:26–28. Justin *Apologia I* cap. xiv, in Migne, *PG*, VI, 349.

329:27–28. Tertullian *De Praescriptionibus adversus Haereticos* cap. vii; Migne, *PL*, II, 22.

329:37. Eusebius is reporting Clement of Alexandria's account of how John came to write his gospel.

332:24–28. See p. 305:19–23.

333:33. Philo of Alexandria (c. 20 B.C.–c. 50 A.D.) was a prolific Jewish writer in Greek whose "allegorical interpretation of Scripture ... enabled him to discover much Greek philosophy in the Old Testament. . . . He accorded a central place in his system to the Logos who was at once the creative power which orders the world and the intermediary through whom men know God. . . . Philo's influence was especially strong in the Alexandrine school of theology. Clement and Origen used him freely. . . . His influence on the Logos doctrine of the Fourth Gospel and of the Apologists, notably St. Justin, has often been alleged, but in recent times the differences between the Christian and the Philonic conceptions have been very widely admitted."—*Oxford Dictionary of the Christian Church*.

334:6–10. Arnold uses his own recently published version of Isaiah.

334:29. The doctrine of the Real Presence is the doctrine that the Body and Blood of Christ are actually present in the Sacrament of the Eucharist, not present only figuratively or symbolically.—*Oxford Dictionary of the Christian Church*.

337:32–34. "Do you see of what sort of the soul's food is? It is a word of God, continuous, resembling dew, embracing all the soul and leaving no portion without part in itself."—III. 169; tr. G. H. Whitaker (Loeb Classical Library), I, 415. Thomas Mangey's two-volume folio edition was published in London in 1742.

339:30–31. See p. 326:30–327:1.

347:28. See p. 329:27.

348:30–31. "Who being the brightness of his glory, and the express image of his person, and upholding all things by the word of his power, when he had by himself purged our sins, sat down on the right hand of the Majesty on high."—Hebrews 1:3.

349:20–24, 350:5–7. See pp. 171–72.

351:25–28. For purposes of his argument, Baur does indeed so regard them. The Fourth Gospel, he says, is so concerned to mould all events into the service of a dominant idea that it "cannot be a historical gospel in the same sense in which the Synoptics, despite all the unhistorical elements they may reveal, are to be regarded as historical gospels."—*Kritische Untersuchungen*, p. 238.

352:18–22. A summary of Baur's discussion of the Fourth Gospel in *Geschichte der christlichen Kirche* (3rd ed.; Tübingen, 1863), I, 148–72.

353:7. Arnold jotted parts of Baur's argument on this point, including the Greek quotation from the Paschal Chronicle, in his pocket diary for April 3–5, 1873.—*Note-Books*, ed. Lowry, p. 198; *Kritische Untersuchungen*, pp. 353, 340–42, 335–36.

353:18. For the Paschal controversy, see p. 285:31n.

353:30–31. The dispute between the English and the Scottish churches over the day for celebrating Easter was conducted in the Synod of Whitby, A.D. 664. Wilfrid's language seems to echo that of Polycrates as reported in Eusebius, in the assertion that John celebrated the Last Supper on the 14th day of Nisan. See p. 285:31n.

353:35. Victor became Pope in 189.

354:9–14. See *Kritische Untersuchungen*, pp. 338–39.

354:25–29. For Michelet see pp. 11:15n and 379:19n.

355:20–21. "Then Moses called for all the elders of Israel, and said unto them, Draw out and take you a lamb according to your families, and kill the passover. And ye shall take a bunch of hyssop, and dip it in the blood that is in the bason, and strike the lintel and the two side posts with the blood that is in the bason."—Exodus 12:21–22. For Jesus and "the blood of sprinkling," see Hebrews 12:24.

355:27–356:4. Baur, *Geschichte der christlichen Kirche*, I, 152, 163; *Kritische Untersuchungen*, pp. 216–19, 272–73.

356:29–31. See pp. 357:31–358:2 for translation.

357:1–2. The "Greek Bible" referred to is the Septuagint. The Authorized Version of the Old Testament is translated from the Hebrew and does not show the difference between Zechariah and John which Arnold alludes to. Justin Martyr quotes the Greek text of Zechariah 12:10 as "they shall look on whom they pierced" (*Apology I* cap. lii, in Migne, *PG*, VI, 405), and the passage Arnold alludes to in Revelation reads: "And every eye shall see him, and they also which pierced him"—1:7. Pierre Sabatier, whose monumental work was published posthumously in three folio volumes, 1743–49, was a French Benedictine scholar; his "virtually exhaustive collection of the material for the Old Latin (i.e. pre-Vulgate) text of the Bible" is only now being superseded.—*Oxford Dictionary of the Christian Church*. See p. 267:33n.

358:18–20. The Peratae are reported as quoting this passage by Hippolytus *Philosophumena* V cap. xvii; Migne, *PG*, XVI, 3178. See p. 298:11–13n.

358:29–31. Fragment IV of Apollinaris (see p. 261:19n), printed in J. K. T. Otto, *Corpus Apologetarum Christianorum Saeculi Secundi* (Jena, 1872), IX, 487. The fragment is preserved in the Paschal Chronicle. Otto's account of Melito's part in the controversy (drawn largely from Eusebius) is at IX, 399–400.

358:32–34. In Migne, *PG*, CXXIV, 283–84. Theophylact was an eleventh-century Byzantine exegete, an archbishop among the Bulgarians.

359:16. "They which shall be accounted worthy to obtain that world . . . are equal unto the angels; and are the children of God, being the children of the resurrection (τῆς ἀναστάσεως υἱοὶ ὄντες)."—Luke 20:35–36.

> "For thou art gone away from earth,
> And place with those dost claim,
> The Children of the Second Birth,
> Whom the world could not tame."
>
> —Arnold, "Stanzas in Memory of the Author of 'Obermann,'" lines 141–44.

360:10–12. For Basilides, see p. 289:18; for Marcion, see p. 277.

360:26–29. "Forasmuch as many (πολλοί) have taken in hand to set forth in order a declaration (διήγησιν) of those things which are most surely believed among us, even as they delivered them unto us, which from the beginning were eyewitnesses, and ministers of the word; it seemed good to me also, having had perfect understanding of all things from the very first, to write unto thee in order, most excellent Theophilus, that thou mightest know the certainty of those things, in which thou hast been instructed."—Luke 1:1–4.

362:31–38. Johann Jakob Griesbach (1745–1812), professor at the University of Jena, with his edition of the New Testament laid the foundations of all subsequent work on the Greek text. Arnold quotes from his *Synopsis Evangeliorum Matthaei Marci et Lucae* (3rd ed.; Halle, 1809), p. ix ("Praefatio editionis secundae").

365:3–8. "Il est bien peu admissible qu'en l'an 69, du vivant de l'apôtre Jean ou peu après sa mort, quelqu'un ait usurpé son nom sans son consentement pour des conseils et des réprimandes aussi intimes. . . . Sans nier les doutes qui restent sur presque toutes ces questions d'authenticité d'écrits apostoliques, vu le peu de scrupule qu'on se faisait d'attribuer à des apôtres et à de saints personnages les révélations auxquelles on voulait donner de l'autorité, nous regardons comme probable que l'Apocalypse est l'ouvrage de l'apôtre Jean, ou du moins qu'elle fut acceptée par lui et adressée aux Églises d'Asie sous son patronage."—Ernest Renan, *L'Antechrist* (Paris, 1873), p. 370–71. Renan discusses the question at greater length in his "Introduction," pp. xxi–xliii, and adduces the "authoritative tone" of the work on pp. xxii–xxiii.

366:17–21. Jerome makes the statement in *De viris illustribus* cap. xix. Routh points out that Jerome's source is undoubtedly Eusebius' quotation of a work of Quadratus, but that the crucial claim that Quadratus himself saw such people is lacking in Eusebius.—*Reliquiae Sacrae*, ed. M. J. Routh (Oxford, 1846), I, 71, 74.

367:14. "Even with Lourdes and La Salette before our eyes, we may yet say that miracles are doomed; they will drop out, like fairies or witchcraft, from among the matters which serious people believe."—*Literature and Dogma*, chapt. viii; *Prose Works*, ed. Super, VI, 324. At Lourdes, in southwestern France, the Blessed Virgin appeared eighteen times, between February 11 and July 16, 1858, to a poor fourteen-year-old girl, Bernadette Soubirous. Near La Salette, in the diocese of Grenoble, the Blessed Virgin appeared on September 19, 1846, to a shepherdess of fifteen and her companion, a shepherd boy of eleven. Both apparitions were confirmed as certain by the ecclesiastical authorities, churches were built at the shrines, and miraculous cures were effected. Lourdes, especially, is the object of vast numbers of pilgrims.

368:36–37. *Irenaei Quae Supersunt Omnia*, ed. Adolphus Stieren (Leipzig, 1848), I, 408. The editor's note insists that Irenaeus must have meant the expression "mortui resurrexerunt" to be understood quite literally—that people actually dead had been brought back to life.

369:22. Sir Matthew Hale, chief justice of the king's bench under Charles II (1671–76), while an assize justice at Bury St. Edmunds in 1662 presided over the trial of two old widows as witches, and expressed himself as having no doubt at all of the existence of witches, as proved by Scriptures, by acts of Parliament, and by general consent. Sir Thomas Browne was a witness for the prosecution.

370:4. Randle Cotgrave's *Dictionarie of the French and English Tongues* (1611), under "giant," quotes the proverb: "A dwarf on a giant's shoulder sees farther of the two," which he explains as: "We, having the aid of our ancestors' knowledge, understand somewhat more than they did." The figure, in precisely this sense, was used by Bernard of Chartres in the twelfth century.

370:14–15. "The salvation of the righteous is of the Lord."— Psalm 37:39. "Righteousness tendeth to life."—Proverbs 11:19.

370:16–17. Matthew 16:25, Mark 8:35, Luke 9:24.

372:18. The title of the *Spectator*'s article on the first installment of *God and the Bible* was "Mr. Arnold's Sublimated Bible." See pp. 232–33.

372:20–21. Dwight Lyman Moody (1837–99), a lay evangelist who turned from a promising career as shoe salesman in Chicago to active work in the YMCA and in slum missions, and Ira David Sankey (1840–1908), his organist and hymn-leader, conducted a very successful two-year series of evangelistic revivals in Britain, beginning at York in the summer of 1873, moving through Scotland, Ireland, and the industrial midlands, and ending with four months in London in the spring and summer of 1875; they left England just about the time Arnold wrote these words. (Arnold himself heard Moody preach; see p. 384.) They held their 285 meetings in the five principal sections of London and are believed to have attracted a total audience there of over two and a half million people. They received considerable notice in the public press, including a leading article in the *Times*, March 16, 1875, p. 9, cols. 5–6.—*D.A.B.* The Salvation Army was founded in 1878, officially named in June, 1880.

374:17–18. F. C. Baur, *Geschichte der christlichen Kirche* (3rd ed.; Tübingen, 1863), I, 26–28, a subtle discussion of the "poor, who have nothing and yet have everything."

374:18–19. The puzzling parable of the unjust steward (Luke 16:1–13) is treated at length by Baur, *Kritische Untersuchungen*, pp. 450–54. His point is essentially that the steward acted prudently according to his worldly lights; the righteous should show equal prudence respecting their "everlasting habitations."

375:14–17. "Die Ursache ihres feindlichen Hasses gegen den Apostel war nicht blos seine Verwerfung des Gesetzes, sondern, da er mit seiner gesetzlosen Lehre auch kein wahrer Apostel sein konnte, die Anmassung, mit welcher er, der Apostate, der Irrlehrer, . . . die Auctorität eines Apostels sich angeeignet und statt die Gabe des heiligen Geistes zu besitzen, nur mit dämonischer Magie sein Spiel getrieben haben sollte."—F. C. Baur, *Lehrbuch der christlichen Dogmengeschichte* (3rd ed., Leipzig, 1867), pp. 65–66. Arnold jotted most of the passage he quotes at the end of his pocket diary for 1873.—*Note-Books*, ed. Lowry, p. 204. The term "pillar-apostles" comes from Paul's own account of his relations with Peter (Galatians 2:9): "James, Cephas [i.e., Peter], and John, who seemed to be pillars."

375:18. See Revelation 2:13–16. Baur, in his *Geschichte der christlichen Kirche*, I, 80, raises the question of the identity of the followers of Balaam, "who taught Balac to cast a stumbling-block before the children of Israel, to eat things sacrificed unto idols, and to commit fornication," and concludes that the passage was intended to characterize the Pauline Christians.

375:19–20. The *Homilies* attributed to Pope Clement I of Rome are an account of a fictitious visit by Clement to Judaea, where he is welcomed by St. Peter and witnesses St. Peter's debate with the scandalous impostor Simon Magus. The Clementine Homilies are of uncertain date, perhaps of the third century, but the Tübingen school took them to be early and a genuine account of the conflict between the Twelve and St. Paul, who was, they maintained, figured forth by Simon Magus.—See Baur, *Geschichte der christlichen Kirche*, I, 85–93. Perhaps Peter's language in Homily XVII, cap. xix, was suggested by Paul's language in Galatians 2:11.

376:5–10. See Galatians 2:11, 9. The Authorized Version translates Arnold's "apostles exceedingly" as "the very chiefest apostles."

376:10–14. See Galatians 2:4–5.

377:14–16. For example, F. W. Newman begins his review of *Literature and Dogma:* "It is but a few years since Mr. Matthew Arnold gave scandal to sincere men, by strictures on Bishop Colenso, whom he censured for foolishly telling to the vulgar what it was better for the wise to keep to themselves. . . . In the present book Mr. Arnold has made a clean breast of it, and in his preface declares that the time has come to speak out. He does not explain why such utterances were premature ten or twenty years ago. It is easy to understand that *he* was not then ripe; but as the times were ripe, and other men were ripe, they did not deserve his rebuke: and we must accept this book as virtually an apology to Bishop Colenso, though his name, we believe, is not found in it."—*Fraser's Magazine* VIII n.s., 114 (July, 1873). See also the Introduction to the third edition of W. R. Greg's *The Creed of Christendom* (London, 1874), pp. xxii–xxiii: "In 1863 [Mr. Arnold] published . . . two attacks singularly unmeasured and unfair, upon the Bishop of Natal, condemning that dignitary with the utmost harshness and severity for having blurted out to the common world his discoveries that the Pentateuch is often inaccurate, and, therefore, as a whole, could not possibly be inspired; that much of it was obviously unhistorical, legendary, and almost certainly not Mosaic. . . . And now the critic himself comes forward to do precisely the same thing in a far more sweeping fashion, and in a far less tentative and modest temper." For Arnold's criticism of Colenso see p. 147:20–28n.

377:31–33. Lines 12–14 of a sonnet beginning "The pibroch's note, discountenanced or mute," no. 7 in the "Yarrow Revisited" series.

378:7–10. "Ode: Intimations of Immortality,"lines 124–27. Wordsworth wrote "thy blessedness" and "thy Soul."

378:27–29. *Geschichte der christlichen Kirche* (3rd ed.; Tübingen, 1863), I, 7.

379:3–4. Moody and Sankey; see p. 372:20–21.

379:10–11. I.e., the ideals of the French Revolution of 1789.

379:14–15. Psalm 111:10, Proverbs 9:10.

379:15–16. Americans will be reminded of their version of the "ideals of 1789" in the Preamble to the Declaration of Independence (1776).

379:19–21, 25–28. Jules Michelet (1798–1874) was author of a long and vivid history of France, of strong Republican principles. Pierre Joseph Proudhon (1809–65), socialist and revolutionary economist, was obliged to flee from France temporarily upon the publication of his *De la Justice dans la Révolution et dans l'Église* (1858), a bitter attack on the Church and other existing institutions. Arnold jotted both quotations from Michelet at the beginning of one of his pocket diaries for 1875.

379:28–29. For Arnold on "machinery"—and "what is freedom but machinery?"—see *Culture and Anarchy, Prose Works*, ed. Super, V, 96–100 *et passim.*

380:7–8. The famous proposition of Galileo that was held to be the chief threat to orthodoxy on the part of science in the seventeenth century; see Arnold's essay on "Dr. Stanley's Lectures on the Jewish Church," *Prose Works*, ed. Super, III, 67–69.

380:12–13. "Il faut que les idées spirituelles et morales entrent les premières dans la tête, car si elles y trouvaient la place prise par les dogmes de la physique, elles ne pourraient plus s'y faire jour. L'esprit alors habitué à se contenter de notions grossières en refuserait de meilleures."—Joubert, *Pensées* (Paris, 1877), II, 242 (titre xix, no. 47).

380:15–18. Albert Réville, "Les Sciences naturelles et l'orthodoxie en Angleterre," *Revue des Deux Mondes*, 3d pér., VIII, 393 (March 15, 1875). The essay takes its start from Huxley's *Lay Sermons* and John Tyndall's British Association address.

380:23. William Kingdon Clifford (1845–79) became professor of applied mathematics at University College, London, at twenty-six and a fellow of the Royal Society at twenty-nine, having modestly refused an earlier nomination. He wrote on metaphysics and morals as well as mathematics and theory of science.

381:2. A familiar metaphor of Arnold's: "Our fathers water'd with their tears / This sea of time whereon we sail."—"Stanzas from the Grande Chartreuse," lines 121–22.

381:16–18. In *Literature and Dogma*, *Prose Works*, ed. Super, VI, 232–33.

381:34–36. See pp. 200–201.

382:9–14. *Pensées*, sect. vii, no. 434; *Oeuvres de Pascal*, ed. L. Brunschvicg (Paris, 1921), XIII, 348–49. Arnold has slightly abbreviated Pascal.

382:20–39. *Pensées*, sect. iii, no. 233; *ibid.*, XIII, 147, 153–54. Arnold used Ernest Havet's second edition of the *Pensées* (2 vols., Paris, 1866).

383:11–15. William Robertson's *History of America* was first published in 1777. The passage Arnold quotes is near the beginning of Book VI (9th ed., London, 1800, III, 127).

383:30–32. Psalm 111:10 and Proverbs 9:10; Matthew 1:21.

384:11–23. For Dwight Lyman Moody, see p. 372:20. For the contract in the Council of the Trinity see Arnold's summary of the language of the (Calvinistic) Westminster Assembly of Divines in *St. Paul and Protestantism*, *Prose Works*, ed. Super, VI, 11–12. The phrase "hearty consent" (p. 385:5) is part of this language (see VI, 12:17).

384:30–31. Sir Robert Phillimore (1810–85) was the highest ecclesiastical judge in England from 1867 to 1875, years when matters of ritual and doctrine were especially troublesome. He was a learned scholar in the law.

384:33. Tisiphone was one of the three Furies, goddesses in classical mythology who punished murder and other serious crimes both during the lifetime of the guilty person (through madness and a tortured conscience) and after death.

385:15–19. *Modern Painters*, Part II, sect. III, chapt. i, paragraph 1, jotted in Arnold's pocket diary for February 25, 1874.—*Note-Books*, ed. Lowry, p. 210. Ruskin wrote: "producing scene after scene, picture after picture, glory after glory," and "principles of the most perfect beauty."

385:27–28. Celsus' polemic against Christianity, *True Discourse*, presumably written about 178–80, is largely preserved in the reply to it by Origen, who devotes several chapters at the end of the third book of his treatise *Contra Celsum* to Celsus' charge that the Christians sought to seduce man by "vain hopes" (κούφαις ἐλπίσι).

385:31. "Whatsoever things are honest" is the Authorized Version.

386:11–17. This summary of western history in the infancy of Christianity parallels that in "Obermann Once More," lines 121–72. The sentence at l. 15 ("The . . . illusions") occurs in the jottings of the "Yale MS": Tinker and Lowry, *Commentary*, p. 270.

387:7–11. "Cosmas Indicopleustes, a Christian navigator of Justinian's time [c. 535–47], denies that the earth is spherical, and asserts it to be a flat surface with the sky put over it like a dish cover. The Christian metaphysics of the same age applying the ideas of substance and identity to what the Bible says about God, Jesus, and the Holy Spirit, are on a par with this natural philosophy."—*Prose Works*, ed. Super, VI, 346.

387:31–35. R. F. Littledale, "Church Parties," *Contemporary Review* XXIV, 319 (July, 1874), in a passage of advice to the Broad Church party. Littledale was himself a high churchman. The passage in the *Contemporary* reads: "practically arguing, as Dr. Arnold did in all seriousness, that the main qualification for pronouncing authoritative decisions . . ."

388:18–21, 23–27. Arnold alludes especially to the correspondence on the Vatican Decrees in the *Times* of mid-November, 1874. William Constable-Maxwell (1804–76), tenth Baron Herries, was a leading Roman Catholic Scottish peer. Arnold quotes, with insignificant modification, from his letter to the *Times* on November 17, 1874, p. 7, col. 3. The first Vatican Council in 1870 declared that infallibility attached to the Pope's definitions *ex cathedra* in matters of faith and morals. Many Englishmen held this to have been a personal triumph for Archbishop Manning, who was one of the leaders of the prevailing party at the Council. Manning became a cardinal in March, 1875.

388:30. William George Ward (1812–82) had been bursar at Balliol College while Arnold was an undergraduate there. He became a convert to Roman Catholicism in 1845, was made a Doctor of Philosophy by the Pope in 1854, and was editor of the *Dublin Review* from 1863 to 1878. He was a sharp and intolerant polemicist on behalf of a conservative Catholicism. Arnold jotted this quotation near the end of one of his pocket diaries for 1875. See p. 181:29 (variant).

390:4. "Whosoever heareth these sayings of mine, and doeth them, I will liken him unto a wise man, which built his house upon a rock: And the rain descended, and the floods came, and the winds blew, and beat upon that house; and it fell not: for it was founded upon a rock."—Matthew 7:24–25; see also Luke 6:48.

390:31–33. "Maximen und Reflexionen," *Werke* (Weimar, 1907), XLII (2), 174, jotted in Arnold's pocket diary for November 13, 1870, and June 27, 1871.—*Note-Books*, ed. Lowry, pp. 138, 155, which records a comment of Arnold's not in the pocket diary: "Anti-Colenso."

391:10–13. See, for example, *Prose Works*, ed. Super, VI, 257.

391:17–21. Perhaps the following sentence from the review of *Literature and Dogma:* "That in numberless cases natural events have been mistaken for miracles,—that, in some cases, actual fraud has been committed, we regard as not only certain, but as what might be expected to happen; just as, to use a somewhat hackneyed but not unfair illustration, the existence of real coins and bank-notes leads to the formation of false coins and forged notes."—*Guardian*, June 11, 1873, p. 780.

392:25–30. Arnold jotted Sainte-Beuve's view of the "vieilles Bibles" and the choice between Byzantinism and progress at the end of his pocket diary for 1875, with the heading "Sainte-Beuve in 1867" and the comment "half true." He drew it from Bernard Othenin, Vicomte d'Haussonville's *Saint-Beuve: sa vie et ses oeuvres* (Paris, 1875), pp. 301–2, or from the periodical version of the same work, *Revue des Deux Mondes*, 3d pér., VII, 593 (February 1, 1875). The draft of the passage from *God and the Bible* in which he cites Sainte-Beuve (pp. 392:7–393:9, 399:24–27) is jotted a few pages earlier in the same diary.—*Note-Books*, ed. Lowry, pp. 236–38.

393:10. B. G. Niebuhr (1776–1831) was best known for his epoch-making history of Rome, a landmark in scientific historical research.

This remark is also quoted in "A French Elijah," p. 11:36–37.

393:11. Exeter Hall, a building in the Strand used for religious and philanthropic assemblies, came to stand for a certain type of fundamental Evangelicalism.

394:9–12. Psalm 50:23. The "modern phrase" is Arnold's, from *Literature and Dogma*, *Prose Works*, ed. Super, VI, 386.

394:21–22. Adolphe Belot (1829–90), a very popular dramatist and novelist whose romances did indeed carry on their title-pages "50th edition" or even "62nd edition," drew the comment in Larousse's *Dictionnaire universel* that though he had even less repute than talent, he managed to get himself talked about. Arnold's addition of Zola's name in the Popular Edition is in keeping with his other references to Zola; Zola (born 1840) was only beginning to make his mark when *God and the Bible* was first published.

394:30–33. See *Prose Works*, ed. Super, VI, 198–99.

395:4. "Thou shalt go before the face of the Lord to prepare his ways; To give knowledge of salvation unto his people by the remission of their sins, Through the tender mercy of our God; whereby the dayspring from on high hath visited us, To give light to them that sit in darkness and in the shadow of death, to guide our feet into the way of peace."—Luke 1:76–79 (of John the Baptist).

395:12–15. L. W. E. Rauwenhoff, "Matthew Arnold," *Theologisch Tijdschrift* VII, 338–39 (May-June, 1873).

395:26–30. "The Past and Future of Our Earth," *Contemporary Review* XXV, 92, (December, 1874); the article reads "Omnipresent," not "Omnipotent." Richard Anthony Proctor (1837–88) was a lecturer and popular writer on astronomy.

396:5–9. This passage amplifies Arnold's earlier protest against Herbert Spencer's use of "The Unknowable" as a term for God; see *Literature and Dogma*, *Prose Works*, ed. Super, VI, 200. "The Unknowable is our refuge & strength Ps. xlvi, 1," Arnold jotted at the end of his pocket diary for 1875.

397:5–7. "Was die Auferstehung an sich ist, liegt ausserhalb des Kreises der geschichtlichen Untersuchung. Die geschichtliche Betrachtung hat sich nur daran zu halten, dass für den Glauben der Jünger die Auferstehung Jesu zur festesten und unumstösslichsten Gewissheit geworden ist. In diesem Glauben hat erst das Christenthum den festen Grund seiner geschichtlichen Entwicklung gewonnen. Was für die Geschichte die nothwendige Voraussetzung für alles Folgende ist, ist nicht sowohl das Factische der Auferstehung Jesu selbst, als vielmehr der Glaube an dasselbe."—*Geschichte der christlichen Kirche* (3rd ed.; Tübingen, 1863), I, 39–40. Arnold jotted part of this passage in his pocket diary for November 1, 1874. —*Note-Books*, ed. Lowry, p. 219.

397:8–11. C. E. Appleton, "Strauss as a Theologian," *Contemporary Review* XXIV, 234–53 (July, 1874); see in particular p. 238.

Textual Notes

[A FEW WORDS ABOUT THE EDUCATION ACT]

EducR. "A Few Words about the Education Act," *Educational Review* I, 17–21 (January, 1871). Not reprinted by Arnold.

[A FRENCH ELIJAH]

PMG "A French Elijah," *Pall Mall Gazette*, November 24, 1871, p. 10. Anonymous. Not reprinted by Arnold.
7:31. de profond *PMG; corrected from Coppée.*

[A PERSIAN PASSION PLAY]

Cornh. "A Persian Passion Play," *Cornhill Magazine* XXIV, 668–87 (December, 1871).
Ev.Sat. "A Persian Passion Play," *Every Saturday*, 3rd ser. I, 1–8 (January 6, 1872). Not collated.
Lit. "A Persian Passion Play," *Littell's Living Age* CXII, 3–16 (January 6, 1872). Not collated.
Ecl. "A Persian Passion Play," *Eclectic Magazine*, n.s. XV, 157–71 (February, 1872). Not collated.
75e.* Essays in Criticism | By | Matthew Arnold | formerly Professor of Poetry in the University of Oxford | and Fellow of Oriel College | Third Edition | *Revised and Enlarged* | London | Macmillan and Co | 1875 | [*All rights reserved*]
"A Persian Passion Play," pp. 259–307.

* For 75 read 1875, etc.

80. Passages from | the Prose Writings | of | Matthew Arnold | London | Smith, Elder, & Co., 15 Waterloo Place | 1880 | [*All rights reserved*]

    Also issued with the imprint: New York | Macmillan and Co., | 1880

83e. Essays in Criticism | By | Matthew Arnold | New York | Macmillan and Co. | 1883

    "A Persian Passion Play," pp. 223–64.

84e. Essays in Criticism | By | Matthew Arnold | New Edition | London | Macmillan and Co. | 1884.

    From the stereotyped plates of 83e; not collated.

87. Essays in Criticism | By | Matthew Arnold. | *Copyright Edition.* | In two volumes. | Vol. II. | Leipzig | Bernhard Tauchnitz | 1887. | *The Right of Translation is reserved.*

    "A Persian Passion Play," II, 46–101. This edition has no textual authority and is not collated.

One passage appears in 80: 37:24–38:31 (pp. 303–5, headed "The Imams").

12:14. ecclesiastics there present   *Cornh.*

13:13. Catholic; but   *Cornh.*

13:27. relate. For the   *Cornh.*

15:13–14. cousin, and the first who, after his wife, believed   *Cornh.*

15:16. captains; he   *Cornh.*

15:20–21. death Ali was   *Cornh.*

15:30–31. accepted the   *Cornh.*

16:14. Sunis; the   *Cornh.*

19:12. Damascus; the   *Cornh.*

21:6. the very smallest   *Cornh.*, 75e; the smallest   83e

21:16, 25. simple; the . . . *sakou;* this   *Cornh.*

22:9. skin, and flags and   *Cornh.*

22:13, 16–17, 23. Cashmere; there . . . everywhere; the . . . them; the   *Cornh.*

22:31–32. part is about to require him to   *Cornh.*

23:24. boys; but the children   *Cornh.*

24:28. family speak   *Cornh.*, 75

24:30. peace   *mispr.* 83e

26:21, 25. Hussein; the . . . starts; Fatima   *Cornh.*

26:33. thine own   *Cornh.*

27:9. are these   *Cornh.*

27:32. thirst; one   *Cornh.*

28:29. go out,   *Cornh.*

29:7. martyrdom; O my   *Cornh.*

29:18. eyes run with   *Cornh.*

31:2. victorious; he   *Cornh.*

32:11. gone; to   *Cornh.*

33:5. tableau, of which I have already spoken, of   *Cornh.*

33:6. caliph; the   *Cornh.*

33:25. out of life,   *Cornh.*

33:33. *no* ¶   *Cornh.*

34:19. than just indicate;   *Cornh.*

35:18. the wonders which   *Cornh.*

36:1–2. has not. Therefore, to get the sort of power which all this gives, popular Christianity is apt to treat the Bible as if it was just like the Koran; and because of this sort of power, among the   *Cornh.*

36:3–5. missionaries are said to be much more   *Cornh.*

36:20–21. religion; but   *Cornh.*

36:35–36. and formal, and needed   *Cornh.*

37:2, 4. renewing; it . . . remained; it   *Cornh.*

37:30. instead of clutching   80

37:31. them; so of Hussein it was   *Cornh.*

38:3, 10. Islam; the . . . touching; his   *Cornh.*

38:15. and of their   80

38:16–18. children; there, too, are the beauty and . . . youth; all follow   *Cornh.*; children. There, too, are lovers and their story, lovers lit with the beauty and . . . youth; all follow   80

38:19–20. for him; their tender pathos flows into his and enhances it, till there arises   *Cornh.*

38:35. of Christ possess, I have often elsewhere   *Cornh.*

39:4. which may yet   *Cornh.*

39:11. that Christ   *Cornh.*

[LA REFORME INTELLECTUELLE ET MORALE]

Acad.   Review of *La Réforme intellectuelle et morale de la France.* Par Ernest Renan. *The Academy* III, 61–64 (February 15, 1872). Not reprinted by Arnold.

Ev.Sat.   "Matthew Arnold on M. Renan," *Every Saturday,* 3rd ser. I, 316–19 (March 23, 1872). Not collated.

48:1. even   *Acad.; corrected by ed.*

49:27. *avec sa violence,*   *Acad.; corrected from Renan*

[ISAIAH XL–LXVI]

72.* *A Bible-Reading for Schools.* | The Great Prophecy | of |
Israel's Restoration | (Isaiah, Chapters 40–66) | *Arranged
and Edited for* | *Young Learners* | By | Matthew Arnold,
D. C. L.,| Formerly Professor of Poetry in the University
of Oxford; | and Fellow of Oriel College. | London: | Mac-
millan and Co. | 1872 | [*All Rights reserved.*]

    Reprinted ("Second Edition," etc.) September and Oc-
tober, 1872; 1875; 1889. The Preface was unchanged in
these reprints.

75i. Isaiah | XL–LXVI | with the | Shorter Prophecies Allied to
It | *Arranged and Edited* | *With Notes* | By | Matthew Ar-
nold | Formerly Professor of Poetry in the University of
Oxford | and Fellow of Oriel College | London | Macmillan
and Co. | 1875 | [*All rights reserved*]

80. Passages from | the Prose Writings | of | Matthew Arnold |
London | Smith, Elder, & Co., 15 Waterloo Place | 1880 |
[*All rights reserved*]

    Also issued with the imprint: New York | Macmillan and
Co., | 1880

One passage appears in 80: 71:11–18 (pp. 26–27, headed "Exhilaration of Hebrew Prophecy").

Title: Preface 72; Introduction 75i

Epigraph: "Israel shall be saved in the Lord with an everlasting salvation." 72

51:1–2. in this little book cannot 72

51:3. enabling English school-children to 72

51:28. universally or almost universally received 72

52:11–18. ¶And why is the attempt made? It is made because of my
conviction of the immense importance in education of what is
called *letters;* of the side which engages our feelings and imagination. Science, the side which engages our faculty of exact knowledge, may have been too much neglected; more particularly this
may have been so as regards our knowledge of nature. This is probably true of our secondary schools and universities. But on our

---

* For 72 read 1872, etc.

schools for the people (by this good German name let us call them,
to mark the overwhelmingly preponderant share which falls to
them in the work of national education) the power of letters has
hardly been brought to bear at all; certainly it has not been brought
5   to bear in excess, as compared with the power of the natural sciences. And now, perhaps, it is less likely than ever to be brought
to bear. The natural sciences are in high favour, it is felt that they
have been unduly neglected, they have gifted and brilliant men
for their advocates, schools for the people offer some special facili-
10 ties for introducing them; on the other hand, the Bible, which
would naturally be the great vehicle for conveying the power of
letters into these schools, is withdrawn from the list of matters
with which Government inspection concerns itself, and, so far,
from attention. At the same time, good compendiums for the
15 teaching of the natural sciences in schools for the people are coming forth; and the advantage to any branch of study of possessing
good and compendious text-books it is impossible to overrate. The
several natural sciences, too, from their limited and definite character, admit better of being advantageously presented by short
20 text-books than such a wide and indefinite subject-matter,—nothing less than the whole history of the human spirit,—as that which
belongs to letters; and this inherent advantage men of skill and talent, like the authors of the text-books I speak of, are just the people to turn to the best account. So that at the very time when the
25 friends of the natural sciences have the public favour with them
in saying to letters: "Give place, you have had more than your
share of attention!" their case is still further improved by their being able to produce their own well-planned text-books for physics,
and then to point to the literary text-books now in use in schools
30 for the people, and to say to the friends of letters: "And this is
what you have to offer! this is what you make such a fuss over!
this is what you keep our studies out in the cold for!" And in truth,
while for those branches of study which belong partly to letters,
partly to science,—language, geography, history,—our schools for
35 the people have no text-books meriting comparison with the new
text-books in physics, the schools are in worse plight still when
we come to their means of acquainting their scholars with *letters*
strictly so called, with poetry, philosophy, eloquence. A succession of pieces, not in general well-chosen, fragmentary, presented
40 without any order or plan, and very ill comprehended by the
pupil, is what our schools for the people give as *letters;* and the

effect wrought by letters in these schools may be said, therefore, to be absolutely null.

It is through the apprehension, either of all literature,—the entire history of the human spirit,—or of a single great literature, or of a single great literary work, as a connected whole, that the real power of letters makes itself felt. Our leading secondary schools give the best share of their time to the literature of Greece and Rome. We shall not blame them for it; this literature is, indeed, only a part of the history of the human spirit, but it is a very important part. Yet how little, let us remark, do they conceive this literature as a whole! how little, therefore, do they get at its significance! how little do they *know* it! how little does it become a power, in their hands, towards wide and complete knowledge! But though in our secondary schools the scholar is not led to apprehend Greek and Latin literature as a whole, he is (and this is a very important matter) led and often enabled to lay hold of single great works, or connected portions of great works, of that literature, as wholes. Even supposing that the *Iliad* and *Odyssey* and *Aeneid* and *Oresteia* are seldom entirely read at school, yet we must admit that portions of the *Iliad, Odyssey* and *Aeneid*, and single plays of the *Oresteia*, do form important wholes by themselves, and that all the upper scholars in our chief schools have read them. What these scholars read or learn of English literature may be no more than what the scholars in our schools for the people read or learn of it,—short single pieces, or else bits detached here and there from longer works. But the last book of the *Iliad*, or the sixth book of the *Aeneid*, or the *Agamemnon*, are considerable wholes in themselves, and these and other wholes of like beauty and magnitude they do read. And all their training has been such as to help them to understand what they read; they have always been hearing and learning (far too much so, many people think) about the objects and personages they meet with in it; Helicon and Parnassus are far more familiar names to them than Snowdon or Skiddaw; Troy and Mycenae than Berlin or Vienna; Zeus and Phoebus than the gods of their own ancestors, Odin and Thor. So they are brought into "the presence and the power of greatness," as Wordsworth calls it, in these indisputably great works and great wholes; and when they are so brought, they may, if they attend, "perceive" it; they have the equipment of notions and of previous information qualifying them to perceive it. Now to know what Greece is, as a factor in the history of the human spirit, is one thing; to take in and enjoy the *Agamemnon* is another. But each is *a whole;* the two wholes are of a very different degree of value, nevertheless the second is a whole, and a worthy whole, as well as the first; and the apprehension of it leads, however rudimentarily, towards the first, and towards the whole of which the first is itself but a part. For it tends,—how much we cannot exactly determine, not much in one case, in another more than we could have believed possible,—it does tend, as Wordsworth again says, in lines which if not exactly good verse are at any rate good philosophy, to

> "Nourish imagination in her growth,
> And give the mind that apprehensive power,
> Whereby she is made quick to recognise
> The moral properties and scope of things."

In general, the scholars in our schools for the people come in contact with English literature in a mere fragmentary way, by short pieces or by odds and ends; and the power of a great work as a whole they have, therefore, no chance of feeling. But attempts are now sometimes made to acquaint them with some whole work, which is supposed to be clear and simple, such as, for instance, Goldsmith's *Deserted Village* or his *Traveller*. The *Deserted Village* and the *Traveller*, works of a very different rank from the same author's *Vicar of Wakefield*, may be called good poems, but they are good poems amongst poetry of the second or even the third order, and it would be absurd to speak of feeling the power of poetry through them as one feels it through the *Agamemnon*. But besides this, the modern literatures have so grown up under the influence of the literature of Greece and Rome, that the forms, fashions, notions, wordings, allusions of that literature have got deeply into them, and are an indispensable preparation for understanding them; now this preparation the scholars in our secondary schools, we have seen, have; all their training is such as to give it them, and it has thus passed into all the life and speech of what are called the cultivated classes. The people are without it; and how much of English literature is, therefore, almost unintelligible to the people, or at least to the people in their commencements of learning,—to the children of the people,—we can hardly perhaps enough convince ourselves. What the people can understand is such speech as:

> "He sees his little lot the lot of all;"

but how small a proportion do lines like these bear, in Goldsmith's poetry, to lines like:
>"The pregnant quarry teem'd with human form;"

or:

>"See opulence, her grandeur to maintain, 5
>Lead stern depopulation in her train;"

and everything of this kind falls on the ear of the people simply as words without meaning. Such diction is a reminiscence, bad or good, of Latin literature with its highly artificial manner; and such has been the influence of classical antiquity that this sort of diction, 10 and the sort of notions that go with it, pervade in some shape or other nearly all our literature,—pervade works of infinitely higher merit than these poems of Goldsmith. And wherever this sort of diction and of notions presents itself, the people, one may say generally, are thrown out. A preparation is required which they have 15 not had.

Only one literature there is, one great literature, for which the people have had a preparation,—the literature of the Bible. However far they may be from having a complete preparation for it, they have some; and it is the only great literature for which they 20 have any. Their bringing up, what they have heard and talked of ever since they were born, have given them no sort of conversance with the forms, fashions, notions, wordings, allusions, of literature having its source in Greece and Rome; but they have given them a good deal of conversance with the forms, fashions, notions, word- 25 ings, allusions, of the Bible. Zion and Babylon are their Athens and Rome, their Ida and Olympus are Tabor and Hermon, Sharon is their Tempe; these and the like Bible names can reach their imagination, kindle trains of thought and remembrance in them. The elements with which the literature of Greece and Rome conjures, 30 have no power on them; the elements with which the literature of the Bible conjures, have. Therefore I have so often insisted, in reports to the Education Department, on the need, if from this point of view only, for the Bible in schools for the people. If poetry, philosophy, and eloquence, if what we call in one word 35 *letters*, are a power, and a beneficent wonder-working power, in education, through the Bible only have the people much chance of getting at poetry, philosophy, and eloquence. Perhaps I may here quote what I have at former times said: "Chords of power are touched by this instruction which no other part of the instruc- 40 tion in a popular school reaches, and chords various, not the single

religious chord only. The Bible is for the child in an elementary
school almost his only contact with poetry and philosophy. What a
course of eloquence and poetry (to call it by that name alone) is
the Bible in a school which has and can have but little eloquence
5   and poetry! and how much do our elementary schools lose by not
having any such course as part of their school-programme. All
who value the Bible may rest assured that thus to know and possess the Bible is the most certain way to extend the power and
efficacy of the Bible."

10   I abstain from touching here on the political and ecclesiastical
causes which obstruct such a use of the Bible in our popular
schools. A cause more real is to be found in the conditions which at
present rule our Bible-reading itself. If letters are a power, and if
the first stage in feeling this power is, as we have seen, to appre-
15   hend certain great works as connected wholes, then it must be
said that there are hardly any means at present for enabling young
learners to get at this power through the Bible. And for two reasons. The Catholics taunted the Reformers with their *Bible-Babel;*
and indeed that grand and vast miscellany which presents itself
20   to us between the two covers of the Bible has in it something overpowering and bewildering. And its mass has never been grappled
with, and separated, and had clear and connected wholes taken
from it and arranged so that learners can use them, as the literature of Greece and Rome has. The Bible stands before the learner
25   as an immense whole; yet to know the Bible as a whole, to know it
in its historical aspect and in its connexion, to have a systematic
acquaintance with its documents, is as great an affair as to know
Greek literature as a whole; and we have seen how far our best
education is from accomplishing this. But our best education does
30   at any rate prepare the way for it, by presenting to the learner
great connected wholes from Greek literature, like the *Agamemnon,* and does give the learner every help for understanding them;
nothing or next to nothing of this kind has been done for the
Bible. This is one reason why the fruitful use of the Bible, as lit-
35   erature, in our schools for the people, is at present almost impossible. The other reason lies in the defects of our translation, noble
as it is; defects which abound most in those very parts of the Bible
which, considered merely as literature, might have most power.
Grant that we had definite wholes taken out of those parts of the
40   Bible which exhibit its poetry and eloquence most conspicuously;
grant that these wholes were furnished with all the explanations

and helps for the young learner with which a Greek masterpiece is furnished; he would still again and again be thrown out by finding what he reads, though English, though his mother tongue, though always rhythmical, always nobly sounding, yet fail to be intelligible, fail to give a connexion with what precedes and follows, fail, as we commonly say, to *make sense*. This is a more serious matter than we might perhaps think. To be thrown out by a passage clean unintelligible, impairs and obscures the reader's understanding of much more than that particular passage itself; the entire connexion of ideas is broken for him and he has to begin again; and after several such passages have occurred in succession, he often reads languidly and hopelessly where he had begun to read with animation and joy; or, at any rate, even if the beauty of single phrases and verses still touches him, yet all grasp on his object as a whole is gone. But we have seen that it is by being apprehended *as a whole*, that the true power of a work of literature makes itself felt.

An ounce of practice, they say, is better than a pound of theory; and certainly one may talk for ever about the wonder-working power of letters, and yet produce no good at all, unless one really puts people in the way of feeling this power. The friends of physics do not content themselves with extolling physics; they put forth school-books by which the study of physics may be with proper advantage brought near to those who before were strangers to it; and they do wisely. For any one who believes in the civilising power of letters and often talks of this belief, to think that he has for more than twenty years got his living by inspecting schools for the people, has gone in and out among them, has seen that the power of letters never reaches them at all and that the whole study of letters is thereby discredited and its power called in question, and yet has attempted nothing to remedy this state of things, cannot but be vexing and disquieting. He may truly say, like the Israel of the prophet: "We have not wrought any deliverance in the earth!" and he may well desire to do something to pay his debt to popular education before he finally departs, and to serve it, if he can, in that point where its need is sorest, where he has always said its need was sorest, and where, nevertheless, it is as sore still as when he began saying this, twenty years ago. Even if what he does cannot be of service at once, owing to special prejudices and difficulties, yet these prejudices and difficulties years are almost sure to dissipate, and it may be of service hereafter.

The object, then, is to find some literary production of the highest order, which in our schools for the people can be studied and apprehended as a connected whole. It has been made out, I think, that we must go to the Bible for this; so the object will be to
5   find in the Bible some whole, of admirable literary beauty in style and treatment, of manageable length, with defined limits; to present this to the learner in an intelligible shape, and to add such explanations and helps as may enable him to grasp it as a connected and complete work. Evidently the Old Testament offers
10 more suitable matter for this purpose than the New. Its documents exhibit Hebrew literature in its perfection, while the New Testament does not pretend to exhibit the Greek language and literature in their perfection; the contents of the New Testament, moreover, almost entirely purport to be a plain record of events, or
15 else to be epistles, and do not the least give themselves out as aspiring to the literary characters of poetry, rhythm, and eloquence; many parts of the Old Testament, on the other hand, do bear, and profess to bear, these characters. To the Old Testament, then, we had better go for what we want; and I think it is clear that noth-
20 ing could more exactly suit our purpose than what the Old Testament gives us in the last twenty-seven chapters of the Book of Isaiah. The Hebrew language   72

52:20–21. on the English translation, which nowhere perhaps rises to 72

52:22. Book. Then, whatever may   72

53:7–18. ¶But how to present these chapters to a young learner so that he may apprehend them? Evidently, as they stand in   72

53:20. take a passage, not in this series of chapters, but yet evidently by its subject belonging to them,—let us take the 21st   72

54:18. ¶Now the learner in our schools for the people, who has   72

54:23. as a learner would   72

54:30. correcting. It must be   72

54:33–34. veneration; and we are dealing with it not for the benefit of the learned, but for the benefit of our schools for the people,
35 where we have not much readiness for change to expect, but rather much resistance to innovation. As to arrangement, therefore, we must not cut and carve too freely; a book, for instance, like *The Psalms Chronologically Arranged, by Four Friends,*—with its Psalter turned, so to speak, inside out, with its re-distribution, its novel
40 lettering, its interpolation of headings in archaic English by the Four Friends,—one can hardly imagine a book like this, useful as

it really is, coming at present into general use in schools; the
changes it makes are too glaring and radical. We have not even
ventured to detach from their place, and to print with the last
twenty-seven chapters, those earlier chapters of the Book of Isaiah,
the 13th with the 14th down to the end of the 23rd verse, the 21st   5
down to the end of the 10th verse, the chapters from the beginning
of the 24th to the end of the 27th, and the 34th and 35th chapters;
though these chapters are certainly connected by their subject
with the concluding series, are boldly printed with them by recent translators, and should at any rate be read in connexion with   10
them by every student who wishes to apprehend the concluding
series fully. But this concluding series forms a connected whole
by itself, even as it now stands in our Bibles; by itself it does give
us, in strictness, what we want; and to take other separated chapters out of their place, and print them in a new order, might fairly   15
enough be called tearing the Book of Isaiah to pieces and recom-
posing it by private authority; and a book for elementary schools
ought not to lay itself open to a reproach of this kind. The same is
to be said of the novel way of dividing, organising, and presenting
72

54:36. Professor Ewald,   72
54:37–55:1. but for our purpose it changes   72
55:15. on the same . . . middle. And it had   72
55:23. to unskilled learners the series of chapters I had chosen,   72
55:28, 29, 35. as we have . . . So we might . . . as we have   72
56:13. thing; even   72
56:14–15. wrong, if its words . . . sense, I have almost always left them
unaltered. Sometimes, however, when the right   72
56:16. either markedly clearer or markedly higher   72
56:17. corrected; but only if both the correction seemed certain,
and the gain in clearness, or in beauty, or in both, undeniable.   72
56:31. Professor Ewald   72
57:3–4. though, I believe, not   72
57:5. clear, I without hesitation feel bound to abstain from change.
It   72
57:13. So in verse   72
57:16, 22, 34. out; we . . . one; whereas . . . midst;" now,   72
57:36. Professor Ewald   72
58:8. in the processions   72
58:10. is strictly limited;   72
58:17–18. different. Possibly too, as has been already said, a body of

Bible-revisers acting . . . ought to take   72

58:20. error. Perhaps they ought; but it is clear that no private translator, taking such latitude, could have any hope of getting his work
admitted into schools for the people. And the reader in these
5   schools we want to benefit, not the learned. And our object   72

58:21–23. of the Bible . . . indispensable; we want to enable him to
72

58:25, 31. way; by . . . intact; and   72

59:5. which Oxford   72

59:6–7. studies,—Mr. Cheyne writes for teachers, and his object is
scientific,   72

59:7–8. exactness. This is well, and it is a line a translator may very
properly and usefully take; only then he should not talk of governing himself, in making changes, by "the affectionate reverence
15   with which the Authorised Version is so justly regarded," for his
changes are such as to get rid of the effect and sentiment of this
version entirely. But how   72

59:9–10. mean their book for religious   72

59:14. Professor Ewald;   72

59:22–23. expression, *The Lord?* And *Jehovah* is in any   72

59:26–27. which the French versions use,   72

59:28. *Lord;* in disquisition   72

59:33–36. rendering. But for English school-children, and, indeed,
for all English people using the Bible except with a special scientific purpose, *The Lord* is surely   72

59:37. consecrated; the   72

59:38. meaning contained in the original   72

60:1. this original more adequately; but,   72

60:5. Bible must retain,   72

60:7. and firmly fixed there.   72

60:13. 43rd chapter,   72, 75i; *corrected by ed.*

60:14. rendering; *He*   72

60:16. seems to us best of   72

60:17. made it familiar.   72

60:17–21. reason, it is with extreme reluctance that we alter any
signally familiar wording; the change in the first clause of the
53rd chapter is the only such change I can recall, and it will hardly
be believed what a struggle it cost me to make it. Considerations
of clearness, and of the sense and connexion of the whole, are in
40   the last resort to govern us; now, to make the prophet say, as one
of the sinful people, *Who believed what we heard?* instead of

making him say, as a prophet of God, *Who hath believed our report?* suits much better in connexion with what immediately follows, where he manifestly speaks as one of the sinful people. Undoubtedly, in our series of chapters, he speaks in both capacities; but it seems too baffling that he should speak in the one capacity in the first verse of a chapter, and then in the other capacity in the five verses which instantly follow. Add to this, that the meaning we have adopted joins the verse in a very striking way to the intimately connected last verse of the preceding chapter. Still, we tried at first to keep the old wording, *Who believed our report?* explaining in a note that *our report* meant not the report *we gave* but the report *we had*. This, however, evidently takes all clearness out of the expression; so in deference, first, to the sense and connexion of the whole, and then to clearness, we finally were driven to the change made. All this is mentioned to shew what deference we really feel to be   72

60:26. *air;* get   72

60:36–37. *not in* 72

61:2, 15, 23–24. style; the . . . rhythm? the . . . respect; he,   72

62:1–2. air; else   72

62:12–13. is not perfecting but   72

62:14–17. too, Mr. Cheyne may be rendering   72

62:18. writes: "He shall bring forth *religion truthfully,*" instead of "He shall bring forth *judgment unto truth;*" but he must not imagine that he is here making a trifling change in the wording of the old version, for he destroys its character altogether. When he writes: "He shall not   72

62:20. doctrine," he must   72

62:35. it; and   72

63:8, 11. and from judgment was . . . stricken."   72, 75i; *corrected from Cheyne.*

63:17. we at least   72

63:27–30. is perfectly clear and . . . so we have kept it; but it is certainly not at all the sense of the original, and public . . . correctors would be right in changing it. But   72

63:32. original; for   72

63:35–36. reason to change.   72

63:37, 39. ambiguous; it . . . punishments; it   72

64:2. readily. Mr. Cheyne makes no change at all; he ought to have made a change. Lowth   72

64:12, 21. future; they . . . render; the   72

64:31–32. *receive;*" but the present is   72

64:35. change; for example: "The   72

64:36. we have   72

65:7–8, 13. poetical; *coasts,* . . . preferable; but sometimes remoteness   72

65:22, 23, 26. we have . . . we have . . . we have   72

65:27. talk, like Mr.   72

65:28. to us   72

65:31, 37, 38. we have . . . we have . . . we have   72

66:3. If we are . . . we could   72

66:4–6. we answer that two or three more school-generations will have gone before this revision comes, and even then it will not give us what for our special purpose we want,—one self-contained   72

66:8. we will . . . we think   72

66:10–11. harm; and we are   72

66:14, 16. makes us . . . binds us,   72

66:19. gratifying as to   72

66:23. Bible; that   72

66:28. ¶We must   72

66:28–29. explanations. This little book is meant for the young, and has no business to discuss,   72

66:31. in it which   72

66:33. using it, and from putting it into the hands of children. The   72

67:5. striking; now,   72

67:11. handled were mere   72

67:25, 36. admit; even . . . before; whether   72

68:7, 9. scope far, far beyond . . . scope is far, far the more   72

68:9–11. The secondary . . . historical application. *not in* 72

68:12–14. critic; but we must make a distinction. There is a substratum of history and literature in the Bible which belongs to science and schools; there is an application of the Bible and an edification by the Bible which belongs to religion and churches. Some people say the Bible altogether belongs to the Church, not the school. This is an error; the Bible's application and edification belong to the Church, its literary and historical substance to the school. Other people say, that the Bible does indeed belong to school as well as Church, but that its application and edification are inseparable from its literature and history. This is an error, they *are* separable. And though its application and edification are what matter to a man far most (we say so in all sincerity), are what he mainly lives by, yet it so happens that it is just in this application and edification that religious differences arise. For things do really lend themselves to far greater diversity in the way of application of them, and edification by them, than in the way of their pri-   5 mary historical and literary interpretation. To take an example which will come home to all Protestants: Dr. Newman, in one of those charming Essays which he has of late rescued for us, quotes from the 54th chapter of Isaiah the passage beginning, *I will lay thy stones with fair colours and thy foundations with sapphires,*   10 as a prophecy and authorisation of the sumptuosities of the Church of Rome. This is evidently to use the passage in the way of appli-cation. Protestants will say that it is a wrong use of it; but to Dr. Newman their similar use of passages about the beast, and the scar-let woman, and Antichrist, will seem equally wrong; and in these   15 cases of application who shall decide? But as to the historical sub-stratum, the primary sense of the passage Dr. Newman quotes, what dissension can there be? who can deny that in the first in-stance, however we may apply them afterwards and whether this after-application be right or wrong, the prophet's words apply to   20 the restored Zion? Then it is said, that those who lay stress on this primary application of the words of the Bible reject and disparage the secondary. So far from it, that the secondary application of the 53rd chapter of Isaiah to Christ both *is* incomparably more im-portant than its now obscure primary historical application, and   25 will be admitted by every sound critic to be so. But, finally, it is said that the historical and literary substratum in the Bible is, then, relatively unimportant. And this belief   72

68:15. we answer,   72
68:16. —that absolutely, at any rate, it is of   72
68:33–34. *more;* and besides it belongs to school, and can be taught and learned without offering   72
69:8–11. and Ewald. Professor Ewald exhibits in   72
69:14–15. historical. For the literary and historical investigation   72
69:37. readers to Biblical   72
70:2–3. to Christ,   72
70:4. application; who   72
70:24–25. Professor Ewald . . . Professor Ewald's   72
70:34. suspicion; a   72
70:37. ¶We have . . . but our attempt is   72
70:38. One or two words of yet   72

71:1. have yet to be added. References, except to the passages quoted from the Bible, are hardly ever given in our notes; they are written for readers who in general will have no book of reference but their Bible. A variety   72

71:5–6. those who are not ripe for weighing conflicting interpretations, and whose one great need is a clear   72

71:7. whole. I hope that teachers who use the book will above all things attend to making their pupils seize the connexion of sense; and that to this end they will require the chapter or chapters read to be always prepared beforehand, the notes studied, and the connexion in some sort grasped by the pupil. The notes contain some words which the pupil will probably not understand, and which will have to be explained to him,—words like *nomad*, for instance, or *elliptical*. It would have been pedantic and tedious to avoid them and to use circumlocutions; but a teacher will know at a glance which they are, and will take care that the pupil is not suffered to be thrown out by them, or to get rid of the obligation to learn his lesson beforehand and to master its sense. The lesson in class will then be of double value to him: the strict preparation of the class-lesson beforehand, so universally insisted upon in our secondary schools, is an excellent discipline which our elementary schools, partly from bad habits of teaching, partly from want of books, are too much without. The seizing the connexion of sense, the apprehending *a whole*, is another discipline nearly unknown to them, and, as I have urged in the early part of this preface, most salutary. It would be possible that every child of twelve or thirteen years of age, who leaves the highest class in an elementary school, should have read this series of chapters and received a clear sense of their contents as a whole. It is not at all likely that a discipline so novel should at once be introduced on this wide scale; but could it be so, it seems to me that the fresh life and spring given to popular education would almost be such as to regenerate it. If I say this, and if I add no apologetic   72

71:8. annotating, it is not   72

71:11. great work pass into the popular mind   72, 80

71:12. but the series of chapters at the end of the Book of Isaiah, the chapters containing the great prophecy of Israel's restoration,— have, as has Hebrew prophecy in general, but to a still higher degree than anything else in Hebrew prophecy, one quality   80

71:14–15. life of the people is   72, 80

71:15–16. joy. If ever . . . for which they long,   72, 80

71:19. conditions; it   72
71:32. better. The pupil in our schools for the people, who began   72
71:35–37. whole; if but for a few pupils out of many this could happen, yet, even so, what access to a new life, almost unknown to
   their class hitherto! what   72
72:3. comfort;" there   72
72:19. (in . . . 6) *not in* 72

[SAVINGS BANKS IN SCHOOLS]

PMG   "Savings Banks in Schools," *Pall Mall Gazette*, November
   22, 1873, p. 12. Anonymous. Not reprinted by Arnold.
75:27. 3,787   *PMG; corrected from Laurent*

[A SPEECH AT WESTMINSTER]

PMG   "Mr. Matthew Arnold on English Schools," *Pall Mall Gazette*, December 9, 1873, p. 7. A summary of the lecture,
   made presumably from Arnold's manuscript.
Macm.   "A Speech at Westminster," *Macmillan's Magazine* XXIX,
   361–66 (February, 1874). Not reprinted by Arnold.
79:1–3. *Arnold's note*
84:31. graves. The teacher is left to his own business." That   *PMG*
87:16–17. parish. Before saying, therefore, Have school boards
   everywhere, it would be well to say, Have municipalities everywhere. The other   *PMG*

[HIGHER SCHOOLS AND UNIVERSITIES IN GERMANY]

74.*   Higher Schools and | Universities in | Germany | By | Mat-
   thew Arnold, D.C.L. | *Formerly Foreign Assistant Commis-
   sioner to the Schools Enquiry Commission* | London | Mac-
   millan and Co. | 1874 | *All rights reserved*
   Preface to the Second Edition, pp. v–lxx

* For 74 read 1874, etc.

92.   A French Eton | or | Middle-class Education and the State |
             To Which Is Added | Schools and Universities in France |
             Being Part of a Volume on 'Schools and Universities | on
             the Continent' Published in 1868 | By | Matthew Arnold |
             London | Macmillan and Co. | and New York | 1892 | *All
             rights reserved*
                  Preface to the Second Edition (1874), pp. 135–217. This
                  edition has no textual authority and is not collated.
90:3.   [*Publisher's footnote in* 92:] This Preface originally appeared
             in 1874, when the portion of *Schools and Universities on the Con-
             tinent*, dealing with Germany, was first published separately. The
             Preface was dropped from subsequent editions, but is now re-
             printed, as it contains much matter which is of interest in view of
             present discussions on educational matters (1892).
93:4. is generally   74; *corrected by editor*
95:24. the children   74; *corrected by editor*
114:11. make   74; *corrected by editor*

[ROMAN CATHOLICS AND THE STATE]

PMG   "Roman Catholics and the State," *Pall Mall Gazette*, April
             8, 1875, pp. 2–3. Not reprinted by Arnold.

[GOD AND THE BIBLE]

Cont.   "Review of Objections to 'Literature and Dogma,' " *Con-
             temporary Review* XXIV, 794–818 (October, 1874) [pp.
             141–173:18 in this edition]; XXIV, 981–1003 (November,
             1874) [pp. 173:19–202]; XXV, 279–304 (January, 1875)
             [pp. 203–236]; XXV, 499–526 (March, 1875) [pp. 237–71];
             XXV, 963–88 (May, 1875) [pp. 272–304]; XXVI, 326–51
             (July, 1875) [pp. 305–337]; XXVI, 676–702 (September,
             1875) [pp. 338–73].
75g.*   God & the Bible | *a Review of* | *Objections to 'Literature &
             Dogma'* | By | Matthew Arnold | Formerly Professor of
             Poetry in the University of Oxford | and Fellow of Oriel

                         * For 75 read 1875, etc.

College | London | Smith, Elder, & Co., 15 Waterloo Place |
1875 | [*The right of translation is reserved*]

    Also issued with the imprint: Macmillan and Co. | New
York | 1875

76.   God and the Bible. | A | Review of Objections to "Litera-
ture | and Dogma." | By | Matthew Arnold, D.C.L., | For-
merly Professor of Poetry in the University of Oxford |
and Fellow of Oriel College. | [*orn. monogram*] | Boston: |
James R. Osgood and Company, | Late Ticknor & Fields,
and Fields, Osgood, & Co. | 1876.

    Also issued with the imprints: New York | Henry Holt
and Company | 1876 and: New York | Macmillan and
Co. | 1879

    This edition has no textual authority and is not collated.

80.   Passages from | the Prose Writings | of | Matthew Arnold |
London | Smith, Elder, & Co., 15 Waterloo Place | 1880 |
[*All rights reserved*]

    Also issued with the imprint: New York | Macmillan and
Co., | 1880

83g.   God & the Bible | a Review of | Objections to 'Literature &
Dogma' | By | Matthew Arnold | Formerly Professor of
Poetry in the University of Oxford | and Fellow of Oriel
College | New York | Macmillan and Co. | 1883

84.   God and the Bible | a Sequel to 'Literature and Dogma' |
By | Matthew Arnold | Formerly Professor of Poetry in
the University of Oxford | and Fellow of Oriel College |
Popular Edition | London | Smith, Elder, & Co., 15 Water-
loo Place | 1884 | [*The right of translation is reserved*]

    The following passages appear in 80: 201:24–202:8 (pp. 243–44,
headed "The Stream of Tendency"); 215:15–216:11 (pp. 260–62,
headed " 'Cogitavi Vias Meas' "); 219:5–220:5 (pp. 252–53, headed
"Greece and Israel"); 223:24–226:20 (pp. 253–58, headed "The Decalogue by Evolution"); 368:21–369:30 (pp. 234–36, headed "Miracles
Going Out"); 369:31–370:8 (p. 227, headed "The Reproach of Presumption"); 370:9–372:17 (pp. 320–23, headed "The New Religious
Prospect"); 372:18–373:28 (pp. 323–25, headed "Reproach of a Sublimated Christianity"); 380:20–381:22 (pp. 216–18, headed "Professor Clifford"); 384:11–385:8 (pp. 215–16, headed "Messrs. Moody
and Sankey"); 390:22–391:4 (pp. 227–28, headed "Intellectual Seriousness"); 397:35–398:18 (p. 226, headed "Object of 'Literature and

Dogma' ").

The papers in *Cont.* are not divided into sections or chapters.

Title: Review of Objections to 'Literature and Dogma.' *Cont.*;
God & the Bible, A Review of Objections to 'Literature & Dogma.'
75g, 83g

140, Epigraph. *not in Cont.*

141:1. Modern scepticism will not   *Cont.*, 75g, 83g

141:3. authentic; nevertheless a   *Cont.*

141:4. Smyrna before   *Cont.*

141:12–13. heathen multitudes that filled   *Cont.*

141:25. it now cries   *Cont.*

141:28. critic execrated by our popular religion and by its votaries
might   *Cont.*

142:2. which this religion   *Cont.*

142:7. popular religion,   *Cont.*; popular theology,   75g, 83g; popular theory,   84

142:8. do not set   *Cont.*

142:9–24. *not in 84*

142:10. this current theology   *Cont.*

142:20–21. our official theology   *Cont.*

142:24. strictures of official theology on   *Cont.*

142:26. exception must be   *Cont.*

142:30. *no* ¶ To retort upon   84

143:8. of official theology; there   *Cont.*

143:9–10. deserving, some of them, our high respect, others, not our
high respect only but our warm gratitude also; all of them, our
careful attention. Eminently of this sort were the criticisms by Mr.
Llewellyn Davies in this REVIEW [in the *Contemporary Review*,
75g, 83g], by Professor Rauwenhoff in the Theological Review of
Leyden, by M. Albert Réville in the *Academy*, by M. Charles
Secrétan in the *Revue Suisse* [the Swiss Review   75g, 83g]. But
nothing   *Cont.*, 75g, 83g

143:10. author's set vindication   *Cont.*, 75g, 83g

143:13. should we think   *Cont.*, 75g, 83g

143:17. is all that   *Cont.*, 75g, 83g

143:18. should in general wish   *Cont.*, 75g, 83g

143:19. let me recall   *Cont.*

143:20–146:19. win sure and safe grounds for the continued use and
enjoyment of the Bible. The Bible has   84

143:34–35. I sought . . . I myself   *Cont.*

143:38. is my object. . . . seemed to me that   *Cont.*

144:6. Jesus; now   *Cont.*

144:7, 11, 13. to me . . . I sought . . . which I   *Cont.*

144:24. passions; as one hears   *Cont.*

144:27. secure, and favourable   *Cont.*

144:30. religion, for many   *Cont.*

144:31. too; and we   *Cont.*

144:32–33. it. [*no* ¶] And a . . . kind will grow   *Cont.*

145:2. League; not   *Cont.*

145:8. turn preserved   *Cont.*

145:11. before the ark,   *Cont.*

145:15. *no* ¶   *Cont.*

145:32. enjoyment; but such   *Cont.*

145:36. thinking, that   *Cont.*

145:38. continued prevalence and   *Cont.*

146:1. and that   *Cont.*

146:2. continued acceptance and   *Cont.*

146:9. down *the truth* as it is called. For   *Cont.*

146:10. that the truth,   *Cont.*

146:15. in our hands   *Cont.*

146:18–19. happiness to exercise influence, to excite emotion and joy. And the   *Cont.*

146:19–20. been enjoyed and enjoyed deeply; its   *Cont.*, 75g, 83g

146:22–23. They regarded   *Cont.*

146:24, 26. wish them to . . . lead people to   *Cont.*, 75g, 83g

146:27–150:5. *not in* 84

146:29–35. *not in Cont.*

147:1–2. said wonderful things far over the heads of his hearers, and that   *Cont.*

147:3. precious; now   *Cont.*

147:7. that as the   *Cont.*

147:10. systems, therefore the Bible   *Cont.*

147:21. in Dr. Colenso's treatment   *Cont.*

147:26. from Tully's Offices,   *Cont.*

147:28. circumstances, a ground quite comically   *Cont.*

148:1–2. occasion to speak of this work at more length, but   *Cont.*

148:16. know the truth, and . . . know the truth about   *Cont.*

148:39. Tully's Offices, his   *Cont.*

149:1. him, much more in the   *Cont.*

149:15–16. what we have . . . what we have   *Cont.*

149:19. vain; we   *Cont.*

149:24. *no* ¶   *Cont.*

149:26. here: if　*Cont.*

149:36. said at first in publishing . . . On its first　*Cont.*

149:38. written, the religious　*Cont.*

150:1. scandal. It　*Cont.*

150:3. theology; it　*Cont.*

150:6. *no* ¶ Into the　*Cont.*; ¶Into the　75g, 83g

150:6–7. readers of this sort the book has fallen,　*Cont.*, 75g, 83g

150:7. abroad, and they have　*Cont.*, 75g, 83g

150:9. the current theology,　*Cont.*

150:10–12. from it. [*no* ¶] But many and grave objections have been alleged against the book which has done them this service.　*Cont.*, 75g, 83g

150:13–17. Its . . . Gospel.　*not in Cont.*

150:14–15. have been severely . . . have been taken　75g, 83g

150:17–19. What are they to think of these objections, or at　*Cont.*

150:22–23. are they to　*Cont.*, 75g, 83g

150:24. suppose them; and yet　*Cont.*

150:24–25. ear to them, if　*Cont.*

150:29. *no* ¶　*Cont.*, 75g, 83g

150:30. difficulties, I propose　*Cont.*; difficulties, we propose　75g, 83g

150:31. with the reproaches and　*Cont.*, 75g, 83g

150:33–154:38. *not in* 84

150:36. the incessant use　*Cont.*

151:9–14. of my English . . . found me . . . censured me. . . . by my mention . . . by my remarks . . . upon me . . . I cannot　*Cont.*

152:9. indulgence due, however, from　*Cont.*

152:14. amongst us, in　*Cont.*

152:15–16. than I do. . . . fill me　*Cont.*

152:23. manner. Private considerations are not, in general, matter with which to trouble the public, but where they come in to fix a rule for literary conduct they may be mentioned. Personal acquaintance, if it is at all friendly or intimate, excludes in my opinion the right of public ridicule and attack. For many years I have been on terms of at least friendly acquaintance with the Archbishop of York; to say in print what was offensive to him I should think as inexcusable as to say it in his company. I believe that I have in my book said nothing of him that can be offensive. Logical and　*Cont.*

152:29–31, 33–34. Certainly I believe that . . . I believe . . . I say . . . I see . . . I say　*Cont.*

152:37. has chosen   *Cont.*

153:1. us. My personal acquaintance with the late Bishop of Winchester was of that very slight kind which imposes no restraint upon public criticism. I feel more   *Cont.*

153:2. speaking of him now that   *Cont.*

153:3, 6. I should . . . I quoted,   *Cont.*

153:7. fault which in   *Cont.*, 75g, 83g; *corrected by ed.*

153:25. to objects which   *Cont.*

153:29. *no* ¶ The . . . the popular Christianity   *Cont.*

153:39. treated at the   *Cont.*

154:2. The late Bishop of Winchester was   *Cont.*

154:3. energy, professing to be   *Cont.*

154:6–8. I have . . . discredit a position such as that which he assumed, I cannot   *Cont.*

154:14. us; real   *Cont.*

154:17–18. ¶With the Bishop of Gloucester and Bristol I had, when 'Literature and Dogma' was published, no personal acquaintance whatever. I respect him as one of   *Cont.*

154:21, 23, 25–26. which I have . . . I ought, . . . say a word of remark . . . I cannot . . . seems to me   *Cont.*

154:29. agitation; on   *Cont.*

154:34–36. them, and to Mr. . . . . to have had such   *Cont.*

154:37–38. I have . . . myself to my main   *Cont.*

155:5. *literary*,—that is, the language of   *Cont.*

155:8–10. error. Those who could follow us would have, we said, for their reward, this: they would feel once more, or they would feel   25
for the first time, what it was the object of our book to inspire,—an enthusiasm for the Bible. They would be able to use it, enjoy it, live by it. But much to which we were led by those two considerations with which we set out has been violently impugned; what we have now to do is   *Cont.*   30

155:10–11. profit from those considerations to examine   *Cont.*

155:12. whether we ought to give   *Cont.*

155:14–16. impugned our definition of God. And   *Cont.*

155:17, 20. complain; for . . . impossible; and yet   *Cont.*

155:21. hardly ever regarded, but   *Cont.*

156:4. *no* ¶   *Cont.*

156:13. everything; unless   *Cont.*

156:17. that I admit   *Cont.*

156:26. approximative. I answer: *Cont.*

156:32–33. more close and precise   *Cont.*, 75g, 83g

157:5–6, 9. all: first, . . . righteousness; secondly   *Cont.*

157:12. method and secret of   *Cont.*, 75g, 83g

157:16. the word 'God.' Until   *Cont.*, 75g, 83g

157:18–19. to the word no more   *Cont.*, 75g, 83g

157:31. to a cheating impostor of any sort. The   *Cont.*, 75g, 83g

157:36. *no* ¶   *Cont.*

158:3–4. certain. 'In thee, O Shining, have I put my trust! O Shining, thou   *Cont.*

158:7. satisfaction; but   *Cont.*

158:12. ¶Lord Lyttelton lately published in this Review [in the *Contemporary Review*   75g, 83g]   *Cont.*, 75g, 83g

158:26–27. if he examines . . . he will find that   *Cont.*, 75g, 83g

158:29. series; now,   *Cont.*

158:34. universal acceptance.   *Cont.*

158:37. *not in Cont.*

159:3. word God its strict etymological   *Cont.*, 75g, 83g

159:5–6. good, we have any right.   *Cont.*

159:8–9. the final proposition: *Cont.*, 75g, 83g

159:9–10. That inconclusiveness,   *Cont.*

159:14–15. this word 'God,' we   *Cont.*, 75g, 83g

159:20. *no* ¶   *Cont.*, 75g, 83g

159:22–23. God, they admit; and . . . as this to them and to us experience proves.   *Cont.*

159:24. shows us   *Cont.*

159:25. righteousness; yet   *Cont.*

159:27–28. but is, so . . . see, an eternal   *Cont.*, 75g, 83g

159:32. name, *God*, the   *Cont.*, 75g, 83g

159:35. *no* ¶   *Cont.*, 75g, 83g

159:36. is personal and   *Cont.*, 75g, 83g

160:17. discovered the action to   *Cont.*, 75g, 83g, 84; *corrected from Réville.*

160:25. going further   *Cont.*

160:27. the action of God   *Cont.*, 75g, 83g, 84; *corrected from Réville.*

160:31, 36. the nature of   *all edd.*

160:39. religion; it   *Cont.*

161:1, 4. we; we object . . . cannot; and   *Cont.*

161:15. says of us 'decidedly   *Cont.*

161:19. theologians offer to give, and   *Cont.*

161:28. pretension, by our very want of 'a philosophy based on principles interdependent, subordinate and coherent'; because we   *Cont.*, 75g, 83g

161:31. it was so   *Cont.*

161:32. no ¶   *Cont.*

161:36–37. We for our part are by   *Cont.*, 75g, 83g

162:2–3. love, and which may be attributed   *Cont.*

162:3. without our failing   *Cont.*

162:4. meant by thinking and loving; and they may   *Cont.*

162:9. authors that live . . . ourselves; we   *Cont.*

162:12. personification; being   *Cont.*

162:13. and . . . sex,   *not in Cont.*, 75g, 83g

162:20, 26. loves; naturally . . . animals: we   *Cont.*

162:30. and outwardly or inwardly has made God in the image   *Cont.*

162:31. All we can then do is to   *Cont.*

162:35. weakness and inserting its contrary, and by   *Cont.*, 75g, 83g

163:8. no ¶   *Cont.*

163:9–10. metaphysical grounds, of which we will speak presently and from . . . of miracles. Interferences   *Cont.*

163:15–17. If . . . explained.   *not in Cont.*

163:28. recollect that half a dozen   *Cont.*, 75g, 83g

163:31–32. Mr. Mozley's   *Cont.*; that we ought . . . if we could, 75g, 83g

163:33–34. expect this of me 'would   *Cont.*; expect this of us 'would 75g, 83g

164:2. Mr. Mozley's . . . Lectures; he   *Cont.*

164:3. I am sure he has   *Cont.*; Sure we are that he has   75g, 83g

164:4. but it ought   *Cont.*, 75g, 83g

164:5–7. For our part, although we . . . in our opinion,   75g, 83g

164:6. Mr. Mozley's   *Cont.*

164:19–21. ¶If I were to claim commendation for anything in 'Literature and Dogma,' I should be disposed to claim it, above all, for the brevity and moderation with which the subject of miracles is treated. It is   *Cont.*

164:22. spend far too much   *Cont.*

164:23. on; for the thesis,   *Cont.*

164:26–27. relied on. We   *Cont.*

164:33. commonly employ that   *Cont.*

164:35. exaggerate vainly the   *Cont.*

165:7. and he quotes   *Cont.*

165:25. miracles   *Cont.*, 75g, 83g; miracle   84

165:30. that they were not   *Cont.*

165:35. inclination either   *Cont.*

165:38. ourselves over again, whenever   *Cont.*

166:11. themselves; and from   *Cont.*

166:17. Delphi, the arms dedicated in the temple miraculously went forth of themselves, and two local   *Cont.*

166:33–34. *not in Cont.;* [i. 175] *added by ed.*

167:3. know, we say, by experience, how   *Cont.*

167:4. at the Crucifixion,   *Cont.*

167:7. we put it   *Cont.*

167:12. we say, by   *Cont.*

167:22. *no* ¶   *Cont.;* Pedasus is   *Cont.,* 75g, 83g

167:23. miraculous blindness   *Cont.*

167:26. thrice; the discrepancy   *Cont.*

167:27. we say,   *Cont.*

167:34, 36. Jericho; or . . . it; and   *Cont.*

168:7–169:38. *not in* 84

168:13. fail; it   *Cont.*

168:29. to Christ clearing   *Cont.*

168:31. career, the synoptics put   *Cont.*

168:37. act came at   *Cont.*

169:2, 6. at all; the . . . surprising; but   *Cont.*

169:8–11. Crumble with them sooner or later it will; what may convince them, at once and for ever, of its hollowness, and save them much . . . of mind? The application   *Cont.*

169:14, 21. Alps, they . . . fact! people   *Cont.*

169:31. make scales fall   *Cont.*

169:33–34. reports; the . . . induction, but   *Cont.*

170:5. They do us   *Cont.*

170:20. Let him accustom himself   *Cont.,* 75g, 83g

170:34. but suggested that   *Cont.,* 75g, 83g

170:35. one-horse brougham.   *Cont.,* 75g, 83g

171:6. her vegetables.   *Cont.,* 75g, 83g

171:19. explanation; it   *Cont.*

171:23. miracles, such as the walking on the Lake of Gennesaret or the cursing of the barren fig-tree, Strauss's   *Cont.,* 75g, 83g

171:27–28. adopted. [*no* ¶] But every   *Cont.,* 75g, 83g

171:30–31. as that of Peter's fish is ridiculous; yet a   *Cont.*

172:1. for but one or two, will   *Cont.*

172:6. Galilee: here,   *Cont.*

172:6–7. fact which started   *Cont.*

172:13. far as I   *Cont.*

172:16. the little original nucleus   *Cont.,* 75g, 83g

172:25. has by this achieved   *Cont.*

172:26–27. which inevitably some day or other would cost [would have cost   75g, 83g] him   *Cont.*, 75g, 83g

173:4. *metaphysics*, essence,   *Cont.*

173:10. even here we will ask the   *Cont.*, 75g, 83g

173:11. so unsophisticated a companion,   *Cont.*, 75g, 83g

173:15. things; now the   *Cont.*

173:19. discourse the other day at   *Cont.*, 75g, 83g

174:4. who had   *Cont.*, 75g, 83g, 84; *corrected by ed.*

174:11. true; he   *Cont.*

174:17. unsettlement, of impatience   *Cont.*

174:19. his premises?   *mispr. Cont.*

174:21, 23, 31. true; *Je . . .* doubt;—what . . . reasons;—what   *Cont.*

174:29. conceive thoroughly and   *mispr. Cont.*

174:34–175:11. *not in* 84

174:34. *no* ¶ Will . . . said that here is an opening,   *Cont.*

174:36–37. *not in Cont.*

175:8–9. good; we   *Cont.*

175:12. ¶At any rate, that first and greatest rule of Descartes, never to receive   *Cont.*, 75g, 83g

175:23. will seem   *Cont.*

175:28–29. plagued; indeed,   *Cont.*

175:29. they are   *Cont.*, 75g, 83g

175:34–35. as people told us. But probably this was from [this limited character of our doubting arose from   75g, 83g] our want of philosophy and philosophical principles, which is so notorious, and which is so often and so uncharitably cast in our teeth. Descartes could   *Cont.*, 75g, 83g

176:7–8. scrupulous. For we all of us, as many as . . . find our need   *Cont.*

176:36. to it, and it is   *Cont.*

177:4. fundamental maxim of   *Cont.*

177:5–6. others seem to derive . . . for this reason, the philosopher   *Cont.*

177:11. tells us: "A   *Cont.*

177:13. wishes, which does not wish, which imagines   *Cont.*

177:14. good; but he does not   *Cont.*

177:15–16. which convey the fundamental   *Cont.*

177:19. terms; and   *Cont.*

177:36–37. translate it in order to be able   *Cont.*

178:8–10. 'We . . . says: *not in Cont.*

178:18–20. lays down that of *substances* we   *Cont.*

178:26. doubt; it   *Cont.*

178:33–34. have an Infinite Being, eternal, immutable, all-knowing, all-powerful, and having   *Cont.*

178:37–38. is something that   *Cont.*

179:25–26. propositions that there is an essential   *Cont.*

179:28. cause must have been   *Cont.*, 75g, 83g

179:33. us; for he   *Cont.*

179:34. promise us something   *Cont.*, 75g, 83g

180:6. for us. And perhaps this may be so; but [so. But   75g, 83g] *Cont.*, 75g, 83g

180:17. he would start with   *Cont.*

180:23, 38. discover; but . . . else; the   *Cont.*

181:13–14. but we use   *Cont.*, 75g, 83g

181:16. means a stepping   *Cont.*, 75g, 83g

181:23–24. organization; but perhaps   *Cont.*

181:29. in *being*. In the same way, again, our difficulties about the Real Presence may vanish; in [vanish. In   75g, 83g] bread there is an [is, perhaps, an   75g, 83g] essence or substance separable from
20   what the theologians call "that group of visible and tangible phenomena which suggest the presence of bread," in other words, from that assemblage of certain atoms in a certain combination which we think is the bread; and in the Sacred Host this essence or substance is not substance of bread but divine substance. All this   *Cont.*, 75g, 83g

181:36. race; and   *Cont.*

182:5. is. Such a . . . find; and in these   *Cont.*, 75g, 83g

182:14. really was.   *Cont.*, 75g, 83g

182:30–31. Let . . . rate.   *not in Cont.*

182:34. information; but   *Cont.*

183:7. our everlasting   *Cont.*, 75g, 83g

183:8–9. *eimi, eis* or *ei, esti,*   *Cont.*

183:15. to Renan   *Cont.*, 75g, 83g

183:18. Here . . . last!   *not in Cont.*

183:20. *esti,* an Indo-European   *Cont.*

183:21. get thus much was delightful, but   *Cont.*

183:34–35. This . . . discovery.   *not in Cont.*, 75g, 83g

183:35. entity, am, be and   *Cont.*, 75g, 83g

184:1. all; as   *Cont.*

184:6. Mr. Littré   *mispr. Cont.*

184:13. men's way   *Cont.*

184:16–17. But we *Cont.*

184:31. same; he *Cont.*

184:35. now it alone *Cont.*

185:9. grow; the *Cont.*

185:16. found. Sometimes, *Cont.;* found: *plus.* Sometimes, 75g, 83g

185:24. ¶Nor were these *Cont.,* 75g, 83g

185:32, 36. *be;* literally, . . . *exists;* that *Cont.*

186:8. said: God *is,* God *exists,* or in [*exists.* In 75g, 83g] other words, God *breathes,* God *steps forth.* *Cont.,* 75g, 83g

186:9. *no ¶ Cont.*

186:12. (I will *Cont.*

186:14. Polyglott *Cont.,* 75g, 83g

186:23. the same effect *Cont.*

186:28. *no ¶ Cont.*

186:36. operation, nothing *Cont.,* 75g, 83g

187:1. which do . . . from which *Cont.,* 75g, 83g

187:3–4. to tell us something about the nature *Cont.*

187:5. we noticed, *Cont.*

188:27, 35–36, 39. means; and . . . breath;" a true . . . conditions; but surely *Cont.*

189:15. perfumer; for *Cont.*

189:16–18. speaking of the breathing of . . . speaking of the breathing of *Cont.,* 75g, 83g

189:26. way through them, 75g, 83g

190:4–5. that they have *Cont.;* us, that they operate. [*end of sentence*] *Cont.,* 75g, 83g

190:11. ether; that common *Cont.*

190:14. may call *Cont.,* 75g, 83g

190:15, 28. ether; that is . . . constitution; but *Cont.*

190:32–35. bodies. Men abstract, say, from a number of brave and self-denying actions which have come within their experience, the quality which in these actions strikes them; some [them. Some men 75g, 83g] abstract inexactly and ill what they thus perceive, others exactly and well. But whether they abstract it exactly or inexactly,   35 alike they talk of the *being* of what they have thus abstracted; alike they say that virtue and duty have [courage and duty have 75g, 83g] *growing* or being, alike they assert *Cont.,* 75g, 83g

190:35. that virtue and duty *Cont.*

190:38. of their own constitution. *Cont.*

191:5. *forth;* that is, *Cont.*

191:17–192:27. *not in* 84

191:17. verified. Mr. Dunn,—whom we   *Cont.*

191:31. *no* ¶ Some . . . operates: *The*   *Cont.*

192:11. *no* ¶   *Cont.*

192:27. *no* ¶ Men become   84

192:29. *being,* they   *Cont.*

192:36–37. But, long   *Cont.*, 75g, 83g

192:37. they dimly and obscurely are conscious   *Cont.*, 75g, 83g

193:10. *no* ¶   *Cont.*

193:11. But this does   *Cont.*, 75g, 83g

193:19. the Eternal that makes   *Cont.*

193:28. primitives. What is the conclusion of the whole matter with
    them? [about them?   75g, 83g] It is this. They were   *Cont.*, 75g,
    83g

193:31. bodily constitution, but   *Cont.*

193:32. by a figure our own bodily   *Cont.*

193:37. that when   *Cont.*, 75g, 83g

193:39–194:30. *not in* 84

194:8–9, 11, 19. breathe, and . . . have; but it . . . alive, and . . . true;
    and   *Cont.*

194:35. can enter and   *Cont.*

194:36–195:2. either mean breathe and grow, or else they mean op-
    erate. But when   *Cont.*, 75g, 83g

195:6–8. *être.* But being, *être, are* breathing and growing. And then,
    Cont.

195:6. *être.*" But they are unaware   75g, 83g

195:7. which simply mean   75g, 83g

195:13. operation; and this   *Cont.*

195:14. about the origin and production of things,   *Cont.*, 75g, 83g

195:16–17. *no* ¶ Now the *Edinburgh*   *Cont.*

195:18. existing things must   *Cont.*, 75g, 83g, 84; *corrected from*
    Edinburgh Review *and p. 160:22*

195:19–32. *not in* 84

195:20. in *things.   Cont.*, 75g, 83g; *corrected by ed.*

195:29. operation; and   *Cont.*

195:32. other; and he   *Cont.*; other. He   75g, 83g

195:33. and that he must   *Cont.*

196:6. ¶And that favourite and   *Cont.*

196:10–11. exist, for existence is a   *Cont.*

196:13. being; but   *Cont.*; this idea quite   *Cont.*, 75g, 83g

196:15. it; all   *Cont.*

196:16–17. moment we regard it steadily and with an exact remembrance of what our words mean. The deception comes from the
words *perfect Cont.*

196:18. are aware;— *Cont.*

196:23–25. imperfection? But after examining *is* and *be,* we are sure
that no man has a clear idea of an infinite substance, knowing and
thinking, and [thinking. And   75g, 83g] the idea which he thus
describes is an idea which, . . . wherein he really has it, he may . . .
to himself. *Cont.,* 75g, 83g

196:26. immensely magnified and *Cont.*

196:27. no ¶ *Cont.*

196:34. power,—all that we can *Cont.*

197:1. idea, and we *Cont.*

197:5. knowledge and power, *Cont.,* 75g, 83g

197:7–8. great, but confused. And granting *Cont.,* 75g, 83g

197:12–32. *not in Cont.*

197:12–13. people insist that perfect ideas *must* have being   75g, 83g

197:22. to nature? or   75g, 83g; to nature; or   84

197:33 ¶Or let us *Cont.*

197:34. The fallacy lies *Cont.*

197:35. by which . . . designed. *not in Cont.*

198:26. which . . . well, *not in Cont.,* 75g, 83g

199:5–6. So we had to *Cont.,* 75g, 83g

199:8, 17–18. loves; and . . . thousands; and *Cont.*

199:20. no ¶ *Cont.*

199:22–23, 26, 29. one; people . . . them; no . . . them; but *Cont.*

199:34–35. preternatural beings of *Cont.,* 75g, 83g

199:35. inevitable; and *Cont.*

199:36. being supposed *Cont.*

200:2. long. And an *Cont.*

200:4. better for them. If *Cont.;* better for them. But if   75g, 83g

200:17. to say that we *Cont.*

200:24. Bible once *Cont.*

200:28. say again as *Cont.*

200:34. it, many of us, if *Cont.;* it, more and more amongst us, if
75g, 83g

200:35. require one first   75g, 83g

200:36. will or no, this *Cont.*

201:5–6. learned, repels (for . . . not repel we *Cont.,* 75g, 83g

201:26, 29, 31, 35. I say that, . . . I say that . . . I do not . . . I maintain,
80

201:27. religion upon   *Cont.*

201:30. built upon   *Cont.*

202:1. solid, serious, awe-inspiring, and   80

202:2. be the same   *Cont.*

202:6. things fulfil   *Cont.*, 75g, 83g

202:7–8. in it new elements of a religion hopeful,   *Cont.*

202:8. degree serious, hopeful, solemn, and   80

202:11. commanding. This was what we attempted in 'Literature and Dogma,' and the whole value of that book depends, we repeat, on whether we attempted it successfully.   *Cont.*

202:12. if the reader of 'Literature and Dogma' has   *Cont.*

202:19. reading their grand   *Cont.*

202:23. race, let him say: *Cont.; hath dwelt   mispr.* 75g, 83g, 84

202:24–25. *peace!* and let him remember   *Cont.*

202:28–29. In what remains,   *Cont.*

203:1–3. ¶Conjectures are dangerous things, but they form themselves and visit us whether one will or no. And we cannot help entertaining the conjecture that the criticism upon "Literature and Dogma" in the *Westminster Review* was written by the author of "Supernatural Religion." At any rate the character which marks both the criticism in the Review and that in "Supernatural Religion" is the same,—a mechanical character. Criticism with this character is very rife among German critics of the Bible, and it has its conveniences. For negative purposes it is   *Cont.*

203:5. an uniform   *Cont.*

203:11, 13. falsely; if . . . it; if   *Cont.*

203:18. growth; no,   *Cont.*, 75g, 83g

203:20–21. This . . . follows:—   *not in Cont.;* ¶This mechanical character strongly marked a criticism in the *Westminster Review* upon *Literature and Dogma.* The reviewer's line ran as follows:— 75g, 83g

203:22. *no* ¶ "Israel's first   *Cont.*

203:29. We say that the world   *Cont.*; We, again, say that the world 75g, 83g

204:1. Bible. But Israel   *Cont.*

204:3. says the *Westminster* Reviewer,   *Cont.*, 75g, 83g

204:11. race." No, this salvation must come of that "true and noble faith which is the child of reason. All that we do know of the regulation of the universe being so perfect and wise, all that we do not know must be equally so. Faith in the perfect ordering of all things is independent of revelation." ¶On   *Cont.*

204:23. proving, for that they   *Cont.*

204:24–26. Men . . . born.   *not in Cont.*, 75g, 83g

204:26. this sort of   *Cont.*

204:27–29. have said of . . . and to the Canaanitish   *Cont.*

204:32. tendency. The first   *Cont.*

205:12. and it does   *Cont.*, 75g, 83g

205:36. Bible, at any rate not the   *Cont.*

205:37. Testament,—that the God   *Cont.*

206:1–2. and must establish in spite of it, if we   *Cont.*, 75g, 83g

206:3. righteousness. First, however, it may be well to set clear what by this assertion we mean, and what we do not mean.   *Cont.*

206:4. ¶For the *Westminster* Reviewer objects   *Cont.;* ¶The *Westminster* Reviewer objects   75g, 83g

206:9. which makes   *Cont.*, 75g, 83g, 84; *corrected from Westminster*

206:11. is his *à priori*   *Cont.*

206:13–14. not mean— . . . us to mean—   *Cont.*

206:21–22. world. I . . . only God. I   *Cont.*

207:7. itself; and the *Westminster* Reviewer holds this just as much as we do. How, then,   *Cont.*

207:9. *no* ¶   *Cont.*

207:12–13. was the pressure of them upon   *Cont.;* was the pressure upon   75g, 83g

207:20, 25. interesting; but . . . religion; in   *Cont.*

207:26. for God, *The*   *Cont.*, 75g, 83g

207:27. of the most   *Cont.*

207:31. them; his religion does not   *Cont.*

207:32. us. It practically concerns   *Cont.*

207:38. religion; and no   *Cont.*

208:1. from the very first   *Cont.*, 75g, 83g

208:4. ¶Let us at present say no more of Bible-religion, and   *Cont.;* ¶Let us for a moment leave Bible-religion, and   75g, 83g

208:16. sanctuary soon . . . as the common centre   *Cont.*

208:17. religion. We   *Cont.*

208:21. Hellas, and at Delphi where the hardy and serious tribes of the Dorian Highlands made their influence felt, Apollo was   *Cont.*, 75g, 83g

208:22–23. effort; he   *Cont.*

208:26. air—now risen; they   *Cont.*

208:30. *no* ¶   *Cont.*

208:35. pupils; and   *Cont.*

208:36. to man's consciousness,— *Cont.*, 75g, 83g

208:38–209:2. *righteousness*, words which remained written up in the temple at Delphi, were thus . . . of its religion. *Cont.*

209:4, 14, 20. itself; from . . . last; there . . . ceased; bribes *Cont.*

209:23–24. predominance of a *Cont.*

209:26–27. Still these *Cont.*

209:29. ceased to inspire *Cont.*

209:32–33. human nature; but a religion *Cont.*

209:36–37. *not in Cont.*

210:4. effaced in life;— *Cont.*, 75g, 83g

210:8–10. in which it appears . . . righteousness; many *Cont.*

210:10. life of activity *mispr. Cont.*

210:12. remains; in *Cont.*; remains. In 75g, 83g

210:17. witnessed with transport and *Cont.*, 75g, 83g

210:27. Biblical—the strain of Job, *Cont.*

210:33. *not in Cont.*

211:6. with them, therefore; with their *Cont.*

211:10–11. their natural [*mispr.*] life is coming to an *Cont.*, 75g, 83g

211:16–19. of their history, to those beginnings of their national life which may not inaptly correspond to the beginnings . . . life—to that time when *Cont.*

211:21. Such a point in *Cont.*

211:22. race is given us, sufficiently for our purpose, by the *Cont.*

212:4–5. between Abraham, at *Cont.*

212:10–11. face of these documents—Israel's *Cont.*

212:14, 20. *no* ¶ *Cont.*

212:23. on that theme, but *Cont.*

212:24–25. righteous," says David, "but the ungodly and him that delighteth in wickedness doth his soul abhor." "Unto *Cont.*

212:31. hands. "Put thou thy trust in the Eternal and be *doing good.*" "If I incline unto *wickedness* with my heart, the Eternal will not hear me." No; for this is the *Cont*, 75g, 83g; [*footnotes:*] Ps. xxxvii.3. Ps. lxvi.18. 75g, 83g

212:34–36. *not in Cont.*

213:1. *no* ¶ *Cont.*

213:3. ceremonies? "Come ye *Cont.*

213:6. what evil and wickedness is, what *Cont.*

213:13–14. way that points . . . what we all mean *Cont.*

213:15. evil; it *Cont.*

213:24. ¶But the *Westminster* Reviewer says *Cont.*, 75g, 83g

213:28. they allege *Cont.*

213:31. *no ¶ Cont.*

213:33–36. *not in Cont.*

214:4. Hellas; they *Cont.*

214:4–5. old-fashioned words inscribed in the temple *Cont.*

214:14–15. of the most profound . . . the national consciousness, *Cont.*, 75g, 83g

214:16. philosophy, the isolated *Cont.*

214:20. a courtezan *Cont.*; a courtesan 75g, 83g

214:25. that to him were entrusted the oracles of God, to [that to 75g, 83g] him our religion *Cont.*, 75g, 83g

214:29–30. intelligible to us, to stand *Cont.*

214:32–34. And . . . life. *not in* 84

214:32. Now these *Cont.*

214:34. life; or, if Mr. Gladstone pleases (and perhaps it really does add a little dignity to the thing), let us say seventy-five per cent. It matters *Cont.*

215:3. waifs and fragments from *Cont.*

215:7–8. find him impressed, *Cont.*, 75g, 83g

215:11–12. fascinated, that is enough. *Cont.*; and . . . revelation. *not in Cont.*; the revelation. *not in* 75g, 83g

215:13–216:11. *not in* 84

215:13. *no ¶ Cont.*; intuition with him, *Cont.*

215:14–17. out. "I called . . . testimonies."* But the Vulgate is here shorter and more forcible: *Cogitavi . . . Tua.* Israel *Cont.*

215:19, 22. conduct; and . . . *origine;*" even *Cont.*

215:20. "Sacrifices work a *Cont.*, 75g, 83g; *corrected from* Westminster *and* 80

215:21–22. says one of my critics; 80

215:23. hung about him traces *Cont.*; hung, we are told, about Israel traces 80

215:26. but still, may Israel answer, still, *Cont.*; so. But still, Israel can 80

215:28–29. pursues our critic, 80

215:30. still that conception *Cont.*

215:33–34. Sisera.—True, and yet for all that: *Cogitavi . . .*—Israel's God is a *Cont.*; Sisera.' 'Israel's God,' this objector 80

215:37. *not in* 80

216:1. this crude conception *Cont.*; soothed.' True, Israel may again answer; but nevertheless, with all this mixture, and with this crude anthropomorphic conception 80

216:3. enthusiasms, *Cont.*

216:7. cries our anti-Israelitish critic,   80

216:8. addressed; what a commentary is afforded   80

216:10. faith, he did not walk by it aright, it did not   80

216:12. ¶The *Westminster* Reviewer   *Cont.*, 75g, 83g

216:18–19. the *Westminster* Reviewer   *Cont.*, 75g, 83g

216:20. We . . . however.   *not in Cont.*, 75g, 83g

216:33. pieces of experience,   *Cont.*

217:7–8. the sun—hope   *Cont.*

217:14–15. of oxen. Even when   *Cont.;* of oxen. And even when 75g, 83g

217:17. *no* ¶ Then arose names   *Cont.*

217:18. or Deus, God, the *Shining*.   *Cont.*, 75g, 83g

217:20. use the *Westminster* Reviewer's   *Cont.*, 75g, 83g

217:29. at the point   *Cont.*

218:4–7. In . . . experience.   *not in* 84

218:5. half-recollections   *Cont.*

218:8. *no* ¶ From that primitive time were handed   *Cont.;* ¶From the older religions were handed   75g, 83g

218:15. by the cradle   *Cont.*

218:18. victims;" the God   *Cont.*

218:22. one true religion of Israel, the religion of   *Cont.*

218:27–28. Hellas, as we   *Cont.*

218:35. also; but   *Cont.*

219:6–7. after . . . Israel,   *not in* 80

219:7. moment of unison with   *Cont.*

219:12. as often as we   80

219:16. Israel, on the contrary, advanced   *Cont.*, 75g, 83g; For Israel advanced   80

219:23. it went on   *Cont.*

219:36. *not in Cont.*

220:11–13. had a special turn, a bent, a gift for these ideas. How else *Cont.*

220:16. sending angels.   *Cont.*

220:21. their being   *mispr. Cont.*, 75g

220:26–27. wrong; and therefore they act imprudently. But they really   *Cont.*

220:28–29. noticed Professor   *Cont.*

220:33. of the Arabs . . . will find them   *Cont.*

220:36. by the book of the   *Cont.*

221:3. *no* ¶   *Cont.*

221:4. English; we   *Cont.*

221:4–5. a religious revival in Hebrew religion *sic in all edd.*

221:12. to Jahveh. Why Jahveh, and not Baal? Why should they die rather than renounce Jahveh? These questions were laid before them by the very circumstances of their position. For those who endeavoured to answer them a new light was thrown on Jahvism." And so, we are *Cont.*

221:15. ¶*And so?*—but *Cont.*

221:26–222:6, 34. *not in* 84

221:27. religion; suppose *Cont.*

221:36. *not in Cont.*

222:3. paramount; and *Cont.*

222:7–9. to have a *Westminster* Reviewer on one's hands, there comes a *Quarterly* Reviewer besides, *Cont.*, 75g, 83g

222:10–11. some reflexions [animadversions 75g, 83g] on our reasoning faculty, which are probably just, *Cont.*, 75g, 83g

222:15–16. the *Quarterly* Reviewer says *Cont.*, 75g, 83g

222:19–20. says the *Quarterly* Reviewer:—"The origin of the moral perceptions in man *Cont.*, 75g, 83g; says the reviewer, 'many doubt whether the origin of the moral perceptions is due to intuition, but the origin of the moral perceptions in man 84; *Quarterly Rev. reads* perception

222:22. inheritance. Which ever conclusion a man accepts, it is plain that he must satisfy himself with reasoning, which amounts to no more than probability." *Cont.*

222:23. the *Quarterly* Reviewer that, *Cont.*, 75g, 83g; purposes. whether he assigns *Cont.*

223:11. unaffected by it is religion. *Cont.*

223:13. to so many *Cont.*, 75g, 83g; bugbear; neither *Cont.*

223:16. is still less acceptable *Cont.*

223:24. ¶Suppose 80

223:31. I say 80

223:36. them. And *Cont.*, 75g, 80, 83g

224:5. attachment; and *Cont.*

224:12–14. expostulated, and entreated, . . . their way was best; some *Cont.*

224:15. for their parents *Cont.*, 75g, 80, 83g

224:18. *no* ¶ *Cont.*

224:23. when the reformers solicited 80

224:25. or less faint in *Cont.*

224:28–29. majority; and *Cont.*

224:35. twilight and ante-natal *Cont.*

225:4. are formed. *Cont.*, 75g, 80, 83g

225:5. I say, 80

225:12. us. And *Cont.*, 75g, 80, 83g

225:20. as by our supposition *Cont.*

225:27. disasters are *Cont.*, 75g, 80, 83g

225:33. he that first, *Cont.*, 75g, 80, 83g

226:6. was, he would soon *Cont.*, 75g, 80, 83g

226:8–9. and greater happiness. 80

226:21. ¶We might *Cont.*

226:27. him. But let us leave Christianity for the present out of the
10   question. We have undertaken to show that even supposing moral
        perceptions and habits to arise by evolution and inheritance, this
        makes no difference to religion, and that we may still with pro-
        priety speak of the intuition of moral perceptions, and of Israel, in
        especial, having had this intuition. So for the purpose of bringing
15   this out, let us, after hearing *Cont.*

226:28. take him in *Cont.*

226:29. There he touches *Cont.*, 75g, 83g

226:34–35. ask the *Quarterly* Reviewer to consider this saying of
        Israel, led *Cont.*, 75g, 83g

227:1. of his history, *Cont.*, 75g, 83g

227:1–2. consummated by the well-known *Cont.*

227:3–7. in the latter.* *Cont.*; Religion . . . religion. *not in Cont.*

227:4. Now, this may 75g, 83g

227:9. sexes are originally *Cont.*; sexes were originally 75g, 83g

227:10. as for everybody *Cont.*, 75g, 83g

227:19–20. with emotion are those who have most bent for it, most
        feeling, *Cont.*

227:25. religion, and that *Cont.*

227:26. the special matter *Cont.*, 75g, 83g

227:26–28. and in . . . religion. *not in Cont.*; and in others of 75g,
        83g

227:29. a bent or *Cont.*, 75g, 83g

228:2–3. rules establishing them, on the supposition . . . following,
        take a long *Cont.*

228:4. up; there *Cont.*

228:7–11. and reinforces . . . reality. *not in Cont.*

228:12. *no* ¶ But then, again, a *Cont.*

228:32–33. much it may . . . it must be *Cont.*

229:2–4. And . . . progress? *not in Cont.*

229:4–5. the accent of clear *Cont.*, 75g, 83g

229:6–7. Love is invaluable. *He knows not that the dead are there,*

and that her guests are in the depths of hell. Cont., 75g, 83g; marks
. . . religion. *not in Cont.*, 75g, 83g

229:8. *no* ¶ Cont.

229:10–11. divorce, and his reason is this:—"What *Cont.*

229:18–21. Man's . . . Israel. *not in Cont.*; And such was *Cont.*

229:25. that emancipation of this sort was,— *Cont.*

229:28. *no* ¶ *Cont.*; the *Quarterly* Reviewer will *Cont.*, 75g,
83g

229:31. And the *Westminster* Reviewer will *Cont.*, 75g, 83g

229:33. from other nations of *Cont.*

229:36. *not in Cont.*, 75g, 83g

230:1–2. ¶Finally, a very different writer from the *Westminster* Reviewer—M. Charles Secrétan, in the *Revue Suisse*—is at one with
the *Westminster* Reviewer in denying *Cont.*, 75g, 83g

230:3. ground *Cont.*

230:5, 16. says M. Charles Secrétan, . . . is M. Charles Secrétan's:
Cont., 75g, 83g

230:25. that it would certainly all happen. *Cont.*

230:26. ¶Jesus Christ, *Cont.*, 75g, 83g

230:28–29. now; neither will we now ourselves set *Cont.*, 75g, 83g

230:35. forward; it *Cont.*

231:4–5. less. If *Cont.*

231:9–11. ¶But admitting the idea of these truths being in human
nature and in experience—and this we suppose the reader of "Literature and Dogma" to do,—we say . . . of the Old Testament is to
Cont.

231:12–15. against . . . mankind *not in Cont.*; by the inspiration of
Cont., 75g, 83g

231:16. to them *Cont.*

231:21. Days requisite for it, and *Cont.*

231:23. this is, in *Cont.*

231:31. *no* ¶ *Cont.*

231:36. of M. Charles Secrétan. *Cont.*, 75g, 83g

231:37. *not in Cont.*

232:1. not really an *Cont.*; not really,' says M. Secrétan, 'an 75g,
83g

232:2–3. verify."—*The Eternal upholdeth the righteous; though he
fall he shall not be cast away, for the Eternal upholdeth him with
his hand. I have been* Cont.; verify; the contrary is true.' Let Israel
answer. *The Eternal . . . I have been* 75g, 83g

232:4. *forsaken.—*"The contrary is true."—*I* Cont.; *myself have
seen the ungodly in* Cont., 75g, 83g

232:6–12. 'Experience,' . . . But   *not in* 84

232:6. "Experience offers   *Cont.*

232:8. What . . . Israel?   *not in Cont.*

232:12. disappointment   *Cont.*

232:12–13. that this truth is a   *Cont.*, 75g, 83g

232:20–21. ¶The *Spectator* asks: . . . that Israel meant what he said when he   *Cont.*, 75g, 83g

232:22. that he did not speak literally when he   *Cont.*, 75g, 83g

232:32. no ¶   *Cont.;* The *Spectator* asks,   *Cont.*, 75g, 83g

232:34. *not in Cont.; note 1 includes* Ps. xxxvii, 24   *in* 75g, 83g

233:5. asks the *Spectator*,   *Cont.*, 75g, 83g

233:8. in the sermon   *Cont.*

233:9–10. says Butler,   *not in Cont.*

233:18. law he is   *Cont.*

233:21. Butler, as we hope one day to show, is   *Cont.*, 75g, 83g

233:28–30. as we are . . . to us; . . . our obligations   *Cont.*, 75g, 83g

233:31. ¶From our   *Cont.*, 75g, 83g

233:33–34. reproached with making   *Cont.;* school"—(the *Westminster* Reviewers will hear with astonishment what company they have been keeping!)—"self-interest   *Cont.*, 75g, 83g

234:3, 5. happiness; and *pleasure* and . . . not; we   *Cont.*

234:9–11. Pascal:— . . . happiness,'   *not in Cont.*

234:15–16. It cannot be gainsaid; to reject . . . perversions of the truth, is   *Cont.*

234:16–23. From . . . doomed.   *not in* 84

234:22. spite of its   *Cont.*

234:24. make an impression   *Cont.*

234:27–28. The *Westminster* Reviewer complains   *Cont.*, 75g, 83g

234:33–34. Again, we must not   *Cont.*

234:34–35. in the dealings of Jesus with the possessed because the *Cont.*

235:1. represented dealing with them also.   *Cont.*

235:5. and the *Westminster* Reviewer objects   *Cont.*, 75g, 83g

235:10. God; speaking   *Cont.;* as the *Westminster* reviewer   *Cont.*, 75g, 83g

235:12–21. *not in* 84

235:18. and thinks the   *Cont.*

235:22–23. ¶The mention of the Fourth Gospel reminds us that Professor Rauwenhoff lays down that   *Cont.;* ¶We have just now appealed to the Fourth Gospel. Professor Rauwenhoff lays down that   75g, 83g

235:24–25. from that Gospel   *Cont.,* 75g, 83g

235:29. their criticisms   *Cont.*

235:30–31. treat them as certain.   *Cont.;* treat it as certain.   75g, 83g

235:31–32. We have hitherto had little of such discussions, but the vogue for them will   *Cont.;* Discussions . . . frequent in this country, but . . . for such discussions will   75g, 83g

235:33–34. What we think of such discussions, and of their fundamental character, we have said   *Cont.;* What we think of this class . . . its fundamental character, we have said   75g, 83g

235:36. well; and perhaps, too,   *Cont.*

235:37. *not in Cont.,* 84

236:1. our use of the   *Cont.*

236:2–3. Gospel. The method, . . . and the sweet reasonableness of Jesus   *Cont.,* 75g, 83g

236:4. but from that . . . receive important   *Cont.,* 75g, 83g

236:5–10. no ¶ So in conclusion, we will speak of the discussions of the Canon of the New Testament, and in particular we will deal with the Fourth Gospel, and with the criticisms   *Cont.;* ¶The question   75g, 83g

236:12–16. We will take the external evidence, the questions of dates and texts, first. But   *Cont.*

236:17–18. school; so we will try   *Cont.*

237:4. to remark as   *Cont.,* 75g, 83g

237:8–9. on which . . . bestowed,   *not in Cont.*

237:11. observations   *mispr. Cont.,* 75g, 83g

237:20. no ¶   *Cont.*

237:21. of these recorders   *Cont.,* 75g, 83g, *and Literature and Dogma;* of the recorders   84

237:29–238:1. with his head   *Cont.*

238:2. have invented the insistence [*mispr.* insistance   *Cont.*] on internal   *Cont.,* 75g, 83g

238:9. instance upon   *mispr. Cont.*

238:15. Critics like the *Westminster* Reviewer will not   *Cont.,* 75g, 83g

238:16. Religion" (who has had the kindness to inform me that he is not identical with the *Westminster* Reviewer), far   *Cont.*

239:9–27. He . . . Chorus.   *not in* 84

239:9. unlearned. To the professional Biblical critics on the Liberal side he is almost the ideal of what an "able critic" in Biblical matters, a "profound critic," ought to be. He huddles up, as we have seen, into a page   *Cont.*

239:14. to what, in the eyes of these critics, is the real matter of Liberal Biblical criticism—a negative   *Cont.*

239:15–19. documents. And if the professional theological critic of the *Westminster Review* is delighted, and pronounces that here the right line is taken indeed, the bulk of what may be termed the lay world of Liberalism is not less moved to admiration. Its members say to   *Cont.*

239:21. Liberal philosophers, Liberal editors, Liberal newspapers, *Cont.*

240:3–4. supplies a . . . for our present purpose.   *Cont.*

240:5. poems; some   *Cont.*

240:9. almost sure   *Cont.*

240:12. turn it to   *Cont.*

240:12–13. dealing with Homer and his critics, we say,   *Cont.*

240:14–15. where the interest, whether it is engaged with the disquisitions or with the poetry, remains always what may be called an intellectual one.   *Cont.*

240:16–17. Bible, where the interest changes, according as we make it consist in discussing the Bible's mode of composition, or in feeling and applying the Bible, from intellectual to practical, and *vice versâ.*   *Cont.*

240:31. he is practically   *Cont.*

240:36. happen. But this conclusion we suppose our reader to have had forced upon him by his own reflection and experience; therefore he does not require to have it demonstrated to him as a case of complete induction, nor indeed do we believe that it can be so demonstrated, or that it can be irresistibly pressed upon any mind which has not been led to it by its own experience and reflection. So, too, we suppose   *Cont.*

240:37–38. be willing enough . . . say of the condition . . . us; for *Cont.*

240:39. inclined to reject the Bible,   *Cont.;* inclined to reject the Bible-testimony,   75g, 83g

241:1. to its personages and documents   *Cont.*

241:5–12. Whereas . . . begins.   *not in* 84

241:7. over; or,   *Cont.*

241:12–13. begins; his work is to   *Cont.;* begins. His work, with us, is to   75g, 83g

241:32–38. In . . . that   *not in* 84

241:38. If we lose   84

241:39. these; all   *Cont.;* of the veil   *Cont.,* 75g, 83g

242:16. its chief rejectors *Cont.*

242:27. of our minds *Cont.*

242:29. this might be . . . really was. We had not, *Cont.*

242:33–34. reporters capable of rendering *Cont.*

242:35–243:3. ¶Sir Henry Maine gives it as his opinion that the English law of . . . judges of evidence. In England, then, the evidence as to ∴ . . well judged. *Cont.*

243:9. Testament, this criticism *Cont.*, 75g, 83g

243:12–13. criticism; the *Cont.*

243:17–22. Great . . . is. *not in 84*

243:21. employed simply to draw forth the truth *Cont.*

243:22. as it really *Cont.*

244:2. them; they *Cont.*

244:7–8. speciality. 83g

244:10. Of . . . enough. *not in Cont.*

244:11. true, and a truth *Cont.*, 75g, 83g

244:19–20. curious; we *Cont.*

244:21. who were in *Cont.*

244:24. use. He will trust *Cont.*

244:25. if we take *Cont.*

244:29. but to put him in a way *Cont.*

244:32–245:19. *not in 84*

245:3. into one small piece of paper, how *Cont.*

245:9. let the reader of "Literature and Dogma" share *Cont.*

245:20. ¶But let us come *Cont.*, 75g, 83g

245:23. reader may wish, before *Cont.*

245:24. together, in *Cont.*

245:25. what he is to think of *Cont.*

245:28. Testament, but *Cont.*

245:33–34. *Greek not in Cont.*

246:2. Scriptures; and, *Cont.*

246:8. era to listen to late and *Cont.*, 75g, 83g

246:18. *and the prophets,* *Cont.*, 75g, 83g

246:23. importance; the *Cont.*

246:27. Scriptures, or the Law, *Cont.*

246:36–37. II Maccabees ii. 13 *not in Cont.*

247:12. which our *Cont.*

247:15–16. the same as ours, *Cont.*

247:32. dawn; in *Cont.*

248:6. ¶This *Cont.*

248:7. Nehemiah, had its *Cont.*

248:8. In his discovery   *Cont.*

248:23–25. to it."* Here we have, in all probability, Deuteronomy; as
a summary and an edifying redaction, from [as an edifying summary, from   75g, 83g] the   *Cont.*, 75g, 83g

248:34–38. *not in Cont.*

248:38. and the house of   75g, 83g

249:6. and . . . people.   *not in Cont.*

249:14–15. It was the "testimony," . . . which was given   *Cont.*

249:22. Thora; and this   *Cont.*

249:26. For prophecy   *Cont.*

249:34–35. third instalment of [division of   75g, 83g] the Bible had
the name of Ketubim,   *Cont.*, 75g, 83g

249:36. *n. 1 not in Cont.*

250:2. are the "remaining writings" mentioned   *Cont.*, 75g, 83g

250:5–6. At their head was   *Cont.*, 75g, 83g

250:14. works like   *Cont.*, 75g, 83g

250:21–22. writings," cannot certainly, after we   *Cont.*, 75g, 83g

250:25. somewhat lower character   *Cont.*

250:39. Ecclesiasticus—all the   *Cont.*

251:9. time. *Resurrection*,   *Cont.*; time, and spoke its language.
Resurrection,   75g, 83g

251:12. excellent; we   *Cont.*

251:19–20. But there came the end   *Cont.*, 75g, 83g

251:26–27. weak points, like   *Cont.*, 75g, 83g

251:27–28. Solomon; they   *Cont.*

251:30. But it extended   *Cont.*, 75g, 83g

251:38. *not in Cont.*

252:2. and were by   *Cont.*, 75g, 83g

252:5. Canon; but   *Cont.*

252:14. of the Vulgate,   *Cont.*

253:15. was manifestly not   *Cont.*

253:16. Scriptures answering to   *Cont.*

253:17–18. if . . . fashion   *not in Cont.*

254:4. is, probably, 365.   *Cont.*

254:5. among Greek   *Cont.*

254:24. of the Anglican Church . . . , was speaking of   *Cont.*, 75g,
83g

255:9–10. Synods presently did.   *Cont.*, 75g, 83g

255:11. in favour of it,   *Cont.*

255:20–21. amidst the invasions and miseries of the general break-up
which was then   *Cont.*, 75g, 83g

255:28. know well enough, although   *Cont.*

255:34. "*I receive the   Cont.*, 75g, 83g

256:12. the Dean of Carlisle wrote   *Cont.*, 75g, 83g

256:15–16. just; nay,   *Cont.*

256:28–29. which everyone accepted. [*no* ¶] And   *Cont.*

257:3. Carlisle does,   *Cont.*, 75g, 83g

257:34–35. Marcion rejected St. . . . Titus, while he admitted the others.   *Cont.*, 75g, 83g

258:6. because they really were not genuine.   *Cont.*, 75g, 83g

258:16. circumstances, ask to be satisfied about the authenticity   *Cont.*

259:1. a great churchman,   *Cont.*, 75g, 83g

260:19. others have supposed   *Cont.*

260:28. in Rome."   *Cont.*, 75g, 83g

261:1. own times"   *Cont.*, 75g, 83g; own time'   84

261:6–7. a time rather before A.D. 187 than after it; that is,   *Cont.*

261:16, 22, 30. time; and this theory . . . them; but . . . theory; and   *Cont.*

261:34–35. Dogma," formerly indisposed to the Bible, but now   *Cont.*

262:30. to have it called   *Cont.*, 75g, 83g

262:32. rare; but at   *Cont.*

263:37. of Christ as   *Cont.*

264:3. circumstance; and   *Cont.*

264:9. of those only.*   *Cont.*

264:13. St. Matthew certainly does   *Cont.*

264:15–16. own that almost certainly the Bishop   *Cont.*

264:35–36. ἅ φημι *and* συντετάχθαι   *not in Cont.*

265:2. we should be   *Cont.*

265:12. mentioned. There were   *Cont.*

265:15. *no* ¶   *Cont.*

265:16, 21–22. our Matthew . . . our Matthew   *Cont.*

265:25–26. mentioned by us in this review; *Cont.;* mentioned by us in our first chapter;   75g, 83g

265:32. from other old   *Cont.*, 75g, 83g

265:34–35. authentic; like the story of the birth   *Cont.*

266:1–2. art; or like the saying of Christ,   *Cont.*

266:3. Apostolic Constitutions,   83g;   Apostolical Constitutions, *Cont.*, 75g, 84

266:12. is what Tischendorf does all through   *Cont.*, 75g, 83g

266:18. merited; but   *Cont.*

266:23–26. attacking side. The writer of   *Cont.*

266:28. Psalm; for   *Cont.*

266:29–33. Scripture, and he refers, let us add, to the apocryphal
Book of Enoch as *Scripture* too. In the first case, he may have been
quoting oral tradition merely; in the second he was quoting some
Cont.

267:5–6. recognize the author.   *Cont.*

267:11–12. *Canon* habitually quoted in   *Cont.*

267:15. have quoted them   *Cont.*

267:16. in which, as is now alleged, they quote   *Cont.*

267:25. Scripture; it   *Cont.*

268:22. saying   *Cont.*, 84; sayings   75g, 83g

268:22–23. famous words, *Render to Caesar*, &c., were quoted by
Justin; words so   *Cont.*

268:26–27. Gospels; but even the words, as   *Cont.*

268:28. writers quoted   *Cont.*

268:34–35. compare with Matthew and   *Cont.*

269:18–20. that at the end of the first century, and nearly up to the
last quarter of the second century, there existed   *Cont.*, 75g, 83g

269:22–23. Scriptures, and that their occasional variations from
Cont.

269:24–25. sometimes more, sometimes less, are yet no greater than
such as may be   *Cont.*

269:27. Their variations   *Cont.*

269:38. Gospels; and   *Cont.*

270:1–2. that through all of them there is the same sort of variation,
inexplicable   *Cont.*

270:4–13. It . . . proved it.   *not in Cont.*

270:13–271:9. *not in* 84

270:13. *no* ¶ This, . . . has done;   *Cont.*

270:17, 19–20, 21. investigation; he . . . desired; his . . . inadequate;
his   *Cont.*

270:31. a critic, whose   *Cont.*

270:34. necessary; what   *Cont.*

270:35–36. to re-arrange and re-settle   *Cont.*

270:38. is well calculated.   *Cont.*

271:1. when we have to sum   *Cont.*

271:14. *account.* Our reader may take this as true, and now go on to
his main business—the learning how to profit by the life and words
40   contained in the record. But no, not quite yet; before we may thus
set him free, another, a final task is imposed on us—the establish-

ment of what we have said about the Fourth Gospel. With what joy shall we release him, after that, from a kind of disquisition always trying to get itself rated above its real importance, and to interest us beyond our real needs! "Don't go too far in your books, and overgrasp yourself. Alas, you have no time left to peruse your   5 diary, to read over the Greek and Roman history; come, don't flatter and deceive yourself; look to the main chance, to the end and design of reading, and mind life more than notion. I say, if you have a kindness for your person, drive at the practice and help yourself, for that is in your own power."   10

What would Marcus Aurelius have said if he could have seen the lists of references in "Supernatural Religion?"   *Cont.*

272:1–278:35. *not in* 84

272:7–11. when we approach the consideration of the Fourth Gospel, and are confronted by   *Cont.*

272:16. one, we   *Cont.*

273:2–3, 7, 20. words; it . . . one; he . . . inference; and   *Cont.*

273:25. *no* ¶   *Cont.*

273:30. the immense result   *Cont.*

273:37. *no* ¶   *Cont.*

274:5. who composedly builds   *Cont.*

274:23. *no* ¶   *Cont.*

274:25–26. Gospel still wishes to pass   *Cont.*

274:27. Scholten this is   *Cont.*

275:12. or even probable one,   *Cont.*

275:32. who are put   *Cont.*

276:4. him, *this is*   *Cont.*

276:22. *as to cause his*   *Cont.*

276:25–26. reasoning. Yet how   *Cont.*

276:29. this he has told us again and   *Cont.*

277:32. things, to   *Cont.*

277:33. sort of proof does   *Cont.*

278:4–5. that they were really   *Cont.*

278:6. are; but   *Cont.*

278:13. words before them.   *Cont.*

278:15–17. Mark's . . . extent.   *not in Cont.*

278:18. *no* ¶ It is . . . with his proof   *Cont.*

278:26, 30. methodically; but . . . words; but   *Cont.*

278:37. plausibility. Now, the truth is, that on very many questions like the above, which German   *Cont.*, 75g, 83g

278:38. *not in Cont.*

279:1. of the Bible raise,   *Cont.*, 75g, 83g

279:2–3. all; the   *Cont.*

279:7. demonstration is out of   *Cont.*

279:12. admitting of demonstration   *Cont.*, 75g, 83g; admitting demonstration   84

279:30. does nor seriously   *mispr.* 75g

279:32–33. probability. But it is not the necessity of a certain construction for certain texts which determines [creates   75g, 83g] probability. It is absurd, as we have seen, to take such a necessity for granted. The probability of the thesis that our Four Gospels   *Cont.*, 75g, 83g

279:35. on the certainty   *Cont.*

279:36. them; it   *Cont.*

279:38. our inference from   *Cont.*, 75g, 83g

280:2–3. for discovering . . . is not?   *not in Cont.*

280:5–12. Now . . . research;   *not in* 84

280:5–6. *no* ¶ "Nowhere else . . . world," says Sir Henry Maine, *Cont.*

280:12. *no* ¶ Now, much   84

280:12–14. research; much may be said in praise of Germany's superiority in these respects. Yet,   *Cont.*, 75g, 83g

280:14–16. learning and study . . . them, for want   *Cont.*, 75g, 83g

280:16–17. lose all balance of judgment! Hear   *Cont.*, 75g, 83g

280:17–281:23. Hear . . . counter-weight.   *not in* 84

281:5. give it him.   *Cont.*

281:10–11. do with culture. "What   *Cont.*

281:12. higher notion of   *Cont.*

281:30–35. *not in Cont.*

282:12–20. One . . . basis.   *not in* 84

282:15. an article   *Cont.*

282:28. proper, whether or no   *Cont.*; proper. Whether or no   75g, 83g

282:30. already. The old   *Cont.*, 75g, 83g

282:31. way. But the result   *Cont.*, 75g, 83g

283:3. us, *wide is the*   *Cont.*, 75g, 83g

283:8. possess it very seldom.   *Cont.*

283:10. critics, of Ferdinand   *Cont.*

283:17–18. end, and, with a . . . art, freely   *Cont.*

283:29, 31. legend; they . . . example:* the   *Cont.*

284:9. comes   *Cont.*

284:13. unbelieving; the   *Cont.*

284:17. heathen, not, as is   *Cont.*

284:22. life; presently,   *Cont.*

284:27–28. nothing mere history, but idea moulding   *Cont.*, 75g, 83g

284:29. *motived;* to   *Cont.*

284:37. *no* ¶ Baur would have   *Cont.*

285:3. Baur's theory is not,   *Cont.*

285:10–11. It is already mentioned in the Canon   *Cont.;* It is given us in the already mentioned Canon   75g, 83g

285:21. died in 220, we   *Cont.*

285:22. "perceiving that in   *Cont.*

285:24. *friends*, and being   *Cont.*

286:2. wrote it after   *Cont.*

286:3. year 170, to develop   *Cont.*

286:20–21. know the Oriental languages, and where,   *Cont.*, 75g, 83g

286:24. not busy ourselves   *Cont.*

286:35–36. purifying;"* "after this was *a feast of the Jews;*" "now *the*   *Cont.*

286:36–287:1. 'they wound . . . *bury;*'   *not in Cont.*

287:34. office; an   *Cont.*

288:9. and who has   *Cont.*

288:14. Trent;" a   *Cont.*

288:17. three early and   *Cont.*

288:33. transported in a moment from   *Cont.*

288:35. of the birds and   *Cont.*

288:36. recourse; and in the   *Cont.*

289:15–16. Elxai.* In the introduction to the Fourth Gospel Gnostic ideas are handled with   *Cont.*

289:23. produced; it   *Cont.*

289:29–30. not hold the pen himself, but that others held it, and guarantee   *Cont.*

289:31–33. 'This . . . say again: *not in Cont.*

289:37–38. *not in Cont.*

290:5–6. supplied the materials for it, the expression   *Cont.*

290:7. *no* ¶   *Cont.*

290:13. to give his treasure to the   *Cont.*

290:14–15. provide . . . publish   *Cont.*, 83g; provides . . . publish 75g

290:16. by one hand—   *Cont.*

290:18–19. talent, of soul also, a theologian; a   *Cont.*

290:36. ἵνα ὑμεῖς   *Cont.*

291:33–34. not; they   *Cont.*

291:36. *no* ¶   *Cont.*

291:36–37. of our Lord, . . . and he has new   *Cont.*

292:2. of his own,   *Cont.*, 75g, 83g

292:8. to place and plant his   *Cont.*

292:9–10. them; he   *Cont.*

292:12. we said in   *Cont.*

292:25. No, say these   *Cont.*

292:28. there were other   *mispr. Cont.*

292:37. happened; things   *Cont.*

293:4. truth; the   *Cont.*

293:6. *no* ¶   *Cont.*

293:11. The other hand   *Cont.*

293:18–19. Professor Ewald supposes   *Cont.*

293:24. St. John's "glorified   *Cont.*, 75g, 83g

293:28. fashion; but,   *Cont.*

294:8. written in the   *Cont.*

294:14. be born from above* he [*footnote:*] *The word ἄνωθεν may quite well mean *again*. Origen, referring in Greek to the famous story, *Domine quo vadis? Vado Romam iterum crucifigi*, uses ἄνωθεν for *iterum*: ἄνωθεν μέλλω σταυρωθῆναι. But ἄνωθεν cannot well mean *again* in one place in a chapter [in a composition   75g, 83g], and *from above* ('I am from above') in other places in the same composition. *Born* [in all other places. *Born*   75g, 83g] *from above*, however, is merely the fuller description of being *born again*.   *Cont.*, 75g, 83g

294:16–17. into the womb of his mother   *Cont.*

294:25–26. source; certainly, if   *Cont.*

294:34. quoted, and exactly.   *Cont.*

295:2. advance, and we need hardly say that the author of "Supernatural Religion" follows suit. But   *Cont.*, 75g, 83g

295:9–10. be a fancy-piece,   *Cont.*

295:11–12. judgment they surely are, . . . probable that   *Cont.*

295:17–18. as free inventions.   *Cont.*

295:19. back much farther than   *Cont.*, 75g, 83g

296:29–297:30. *not in* 84

296:35. We follow the rendering   *Cont.*

297:7–8. often mixes   *Cont.*

297:15–16. "Philosophumena" wields   *Cont.*

297:23. year 125, had   *Cont.*

297:24–25. wildly when, in   *Cont.*

297:33. The line commences   *Cont.*

298:3. Epiphanius; their   *Cont.*

298:15. *no* ¶   *Cont.*

298:17. Scripture; but   *Cont.*

298:22. certain words which   *Cont.*

298:36. for   *om.* 83g

299:16. sacred; it   *Cont.*

299:20. Secondly, that Baur and   *Cont.*

299:24. against this being   *Cont.*, 75g, 83g

299:24–26. And this is the point that mainly   *Cont.*; And this is the point which mainly   75g, 83g

301:4. voice."* Baur maintained . . . [p. 302:4–16 *and footnote*] . . . verbal difference. Irenaeus relies   *Cont.*

301:8. and confirmed this   *Cont.*, 75g, 83g

301:34. *All edd. misread* xvi *for* xix

301:37. [the first]   *added by ed.*

302:3–17. suppose. [*no* ¶] We may say,   *Cont.; see note to p. 301:4*

302:17–19. like, that not a word of Ignatius   *Cont.*

302:22–23. *sheep;* that the pseudo-Clementine Homilies were composed in the third or fourth century; that Hermas, author   *Cont.*

302:25. episcopate,—all   *Cont.*

302:25–26. bring many ingenious   *Cont.*, 75g, 83g

302:33–34. Synoptics, they . . . authority, tradition   *Cont.*

303:5. between 130 and   *Cont.*

303:10–11. Scriptures admitted and the Scriptures disputed. In the first   *Cont.*

303:19. the good Bishop of   *Cont.*, 75g, 83g

303:20–21. existed in the time   *Cont.*

303:24. then there is   *Cont.*

303:35. See the German translation of Dr. Scholten's treatise, *Der Cont.; initials added by ed.*

304:4–11. We . . . altogether.   *not in* 84

304:12. evidence in the case of the   *Cont.*

305:12. gradation,   *Cont.*

306:8. later edition   *mispr.* 84

306:17. (which is hardly likely)   *Cont.*

306:37–307:1. presenting materials in   *Cont.*

307:6–7. effect, freely   *Cont.*

307:7–8. of Plato; and the writer   *Cont.*

307:24. by John. He has   *Cont.*

307:28–29. real. [*no* ¶] No artist of   *Cont.*

308:7–8. reapers; the   *Cont.*

308:12. make long, continuous   *Cont.*

308:13, 20. fashion; he . . . importance; the   *Cont.*

309:5. *no ¶   Cont.*

309:16. follows them, and ought   *Cont.*

309:16–17. from it. "I am   *Cont.*

309:28. *no ¶   Cont.*

309:35. x.8, 9. *all edd.; corrected by editor*

310:4, 9. here; but . . . do. Arise, . . . hence. I   *Cont.*

310:14. of the fifteenth   *Cont.*, 75g, 83g

310:29. hence. I   *Cont.*

310:37. *not in Cont.*

311:5–6. is an incongruity. But the writer had in   *Cont.*

311:16. *no ¶   Cont.*

311:32. offered; but   *Cont.*

312:8–9. an author . . . but   *not in Cont.*

312:10–11. does not compose thus negligently.   *Cont.*

312:24. in the Second Isaiah   *Cont.*, 75g, 83g

312:30. it; and   *Cont.*

312:33. *verse* 23 *added to note by ed.*

312:34. *reference to Isaiah not in Cont.*

313:5. the sense of   *Cont.*

313:6–7. put this mechanical   *Cont.*

313:8. who put it   *Cont.*

313:22. of the first which   *Cont.;* of the first-mentioned saying which   75g, 83g

313:23–26. to the second? In the first, . . . theme; in the second, . . . inventor of the first have [first saying have   75g, 83g] . . . prophecy of the second?   *Cont.*, 75g, 83g

313:27. for us our   *Cont.*, 75g, 83g

313:28. Gospels; and it is   *Cont.*

313:34, 314:6, 315:8–9. believer's conscience   *Cont.* [*at 315:35,* consciousness]

313:36. St. Paul; but   *Cont.*

314:10. of the Synoptics carries it.   *Cont.*

314:11–12, 21. clearly; if . . . Jesus; and this,   *Cont.*

314:27. was said by   *Cont.*, 75g, 83g

314:30. to these a third: *Cont.*

314:34. *ref. to* vii.33 *not in Cont.*

315:2–3. nearest approach possible   *Cont.*, 75g, 83g

315:22. A disciple asks   *Cont.*

315:25. and I will love him,   *not in Cont.*, 75g, 83g; *from John* xiv: 21.

315:27. afraid; *I go   Cont.*

315:33, 35. gives us, no . . . gives it us as   *Cont.*, 75g, 83g

315:36. *ref. to verse* 21 *added by ed.*

316:8. *no* ¶ *Cont.;* an one,   *Cont.*, 75g, 83g

316:10. with it that he left us in   *Cont.*

316:12. could leave us   *Cont.*

316:15–16. in the believer's conscience.   *Cont.;* which, while fully accepting   *Cont.*, 75g, 83g

316:17–18. have a spiritual   *Cont.*

316:28. be no doubt   *Cont.*

316:32. by the other   *Cont.*

316:35. lament, but the world shall rejoice; ye shall be   *Cont.*

317:2. from you."* The *ye shall see me* of the primitive theme here finishes by becoming *I will see you;* and the whole   *Cont.*

317:6–7. resurrection of Jesus.   *Cont.*, 75g, 83g

317:9. themes we have   *Cont.*, 75g, 83g

317:13. the words by   *Cont.*

317:17. *no* ¶ *Cont.*, 75g, 83g; after him, Christ's   *Cont.*

317:23. return; their   *Cont.*

317:34. something Jesus said,   *Cont.*

318:1, 3. themselves tell us . . . themselves tell us   *Cont.*, 75g, 83g

318:2. happened; only   *Cont.*

318:21. *no* ¶ *Cont.*

318:25. report; the sayings, as   *Cont.*

318:27. had said   *Cont.*

319:4–6. spoken exactly as he is reported, if he had really thus laid *Cont.;* spoken merely as he is here reported, if what he said had had . . . thus laid   75g, 83g

319:7–8. phrase is, what was going to happen, the   *Cont.*

319:10–11. the simple truth,   *Cont.*

319:15. of a literal   *Cont.*

319:16. place; but   *Cont.*

319:17–18. that . . . subject,   *not in Cont.*

320:3–4. On . . . again.'   *not in Cont.*, 75g, 83g

320:4. say: *On the   Cont.*, 75g, 83g

320:6. them; as, for instance,   *Cont.*

320:9–10. is a locution of   *Cont.*

320:11. *The . . . again,   not in Cont.*, 75g, 83g

320:15–16. *third day he will raise us up."*   *Cont.*

320:18. lay one finger   *mispr. Cont.*

320:18–19. upon the central *logion*, serving as foundation for   *Cont.*

320:20. Let us combine   *Cont.*

320:22. in some degree   *Cont.*

320:25. *no* ¶   *Cont.;* with him is   *Cont.*

320:26. effort, the eternal effort,   *Cont.*, 75g, 83g

320:37–38. and again, . . . 33.   *not in Cont.*

321:5–6, 8. crucify; nevertheless, . . . work; I   *Cont.*

321:9–15. All . . . fruit.   *not in Cont.*

321:16. so shall the   *Cont.*

321:18. *thus it behoved Christ to suffer, and to rise*   Cont.; *thus it was written that Christ should suffer, and* should *rise*   75g, 83g

321:21. So they did also with   *Cont.;* And they did also with   75g, 83g

321:21–22. 'I go . . . Father;   *not in Cont.*

321:26. in his resuscitation   *Cont.*

321:30. *no* ¶   *Cont.;* so. *It behoved that in his*   *Cont.*

321:34–36. For . . . Jesus.   *not in Cont., nor refs. to* Luke xviii. 31–33, John xii. 24.

321:37. The . . . followed.   *not in Cont.*

322:11. *no* ¶   *Cont.*

322:26–27. much that is precious; he   *Cont.*

322:31. ¶Once more. Baur's . . . the consummately artistic   *Cont.*

323:12–13. why he, then, may   *Cont.*, 75g, 83g

323:15. But the whole   *Cont.*, 75g, 83g

323:17. pronounced   *Cont.*, 75g, 83g

323:20, 29. him; but had his theory . . . soul; it   *Cont.*

324:1–2. as an instrument whom he might use for his   *Cont.*

324:3–4. unconsciously, and we can perceive . . . so; if   *Cont.*

324:8–9. as he speaks from   *Cont.*

324:14. throw himself, more or less, into   *Cont.*

324:15. and with verisimilitude,   *Cont.*, 75g, 83g; and verisimilitude, 84

324:23, 28. Baur has . . . argues,   *Cont.*

324:24. replying that in   *Cont.*

324:33. *no* ¶   *Cont;* have no backwardness   75g, 83g

324:38. done; St. Paul   *Cont.;* done. St. Paul   75g, 83g

325:8. different: *I try not mine own self (for I am conscious of nothing to myself, yet am I not hereby justified), but he that trieth me is the Lord.** Imagine [*footnote:*] *I Cor. iv. 3, 4.   *Cont.*, 75g, 83g

325:14–15. Jesus; where   *Cont.*

325:27. *no* ¶   *Cont.*

325:31. them: '*A prophet has no honour in his own country.—My* Cont.

325:34. *labours.—The poor ye have always with you, but me ye have not always.—The servant* [footnote:] John xii. 8. *Cont.; The night . . . work. not in Cont.*

326:17. can have made the *Cont.*

326:29. testimony, by no means so familiar, *Cont.*

326:32. xviii, 36. *om. erroneously in* 75g, 83g, 84

327:2. given; they *Cont.*

327:15–16. each other, join . . . and so frame *Cont.*, 75g, 83g

327:17–18. ours; and, indeed, . . . world learnt to *Cont.*

327:19. and . . . composed. *not in Cont.*

327:20. no ¶ *Cont.;* on . . . hand, *not in Cont.*

327:21. to the Semitic *Cont.*

327:22. was natural. *Cont.*

327:24–25. himself; and the form of the utterances of Jesus there can be no doubt that the First Gospel *Cont.*

328:1, 5. them; the editor . . . it; he *Cont.*

328:11. the more simple and practical 75g, 83g

328:27. no ¶ *Cont.*

328:33. smell *tendence, Cont.*

328:35. *all edd. read* xvi. 27 *for* xvi. 28

329:10. was announced by *Cont.*

329:18, 33. speculation; the . . . *logia;* he *Cont.*

330:1. to change *Cont.;* to charge *mispr.* 75g, 83g, 84

330:18–19. freely inventing it all. But *Cont.*, 75g, 83g

331:8. connection; so *Cont.*

331:37. xii, 46 *mispr.* xii, 6 *in* 75g, 84. *All edd. erroneously place* xii, 47 *before* vi, 47

332:8. Only a criticism which *Cont.*

333:6. from Jesus; and, *Cont.*, 75g, 83g

333:12–13. incredible that *Cont.*

333:25. ¶It is certain that *Cont.*, 75g, 83g

333:26–27. not from him but from his editor. *Cont.*, 75g, 83g

333:32–34. such as philosophers . . . theology, *not in Cont.*

334:9. *of the Gentiles, Cont.*, 75g, 83g, 84; *corrected from Arnold's version of Isaiah*

334:26. objection; one *Cont.*

334:28–34. To this . . . materialism. *not in Cont.*

335:1–2. hearers; nine-tenths of what Jesus *Cont.*

335:4. did; and if *Cont.*

335:5. bread from heaven, *not in Cont.*

335:13–14. word; they appropriate what they can of it, and get *Cont.*

335:29. Evangelist had a   *Cont.*

336:14–15. eat?"* Jesus answered: *Cont.*

336:34. *verse* 35 *om. all edd.*

337:8. now stagger us.   *Cont.*

337:9. ¶Again, it is   *Cont.*

337:13. is most natural   *Cont.*

337:18. is utterly inconceivable that after saying, "Labour not for the meat that perisheth, but for the meat that endureth unto ever-lasting life," Jesus should have added, "which the Son of man will give unto you, for him hath the Father sealed, even God."* [*foot-note:** John vi. 27.] It is utterly inconceivable that after saying, "It is   *Cont.*

337:21. he should have   *Cont.*

337:23–24. These additions are inconceivable from . . . manner of them are   *Cont.*

337:26. notions and   *Cont.*

337:28. clauses. ¶We have been far longer than we could wish; nev-ertheless let us be allowed to trace in yet one or two more instances this way of proceeding by the combination, the repetition, the am-plification and development of his data, which is so characteristic of our Evangelist, and so necessary to be seized by whoever would read his Gospel aright. Then we will sum up and conclude.   *Cont.*

337:29–36. For . . . poet.   *not in Cont.*

338:9. to help them to see   *Cont.*

338:14. Testament is really   *Cont.*

338:18–19. is, many important elements   *Cont.*

338:21. throwing it aside   *Cont.*

338:27–28. of the Fourth Gospel is impossible.   *Cont.*

338:34–35. criticism of every passage in the Fourth   *Cont.*

339:9. things which made   *Cont.*

339:10. plausible, and to extricate   *Cont.*

339:11–340:19. *not in* 84

339:15. particular *logion* was spoken and   *Cont.*

339:16. belongs. The main   *Cont.*

339:18. his stock of *logia*.   *Cont.*

339:23–25. stop short of this, then by setting aside our . . . untrust-worthy we simply leave to   *Cont.*

339:29–30. belonged, had in   *Cont.*

339:37. curiosity we may   *Cont.*

340:12. instance; we will take   *Cont.*

340:20. point, then, as   *Cont.*, 75g, 83g; point as   84

340:24–25. He had a   *Cont.*

340:30–341:13. Almost . . . Jews.   *not in* 84

340:37. its true place,   *Cont.*

341:6. go with the *logia* of the sixteenth   *Cont.*

341:14–16. quite sure [absolutely sure   75g, 83g] of finding the . . . for any *logion* of this kind; the safe   *Cont.*, 75g, 83g

341:28. ¶It is   *Cont.*

341:34–37. *not in* 84

342:13–14. between what is really probable, and what can only be called plausible.   *Cont.*

342:15–343:17. *not in* 84

342:24. certain; and   *Cont.*

342:27. to the world.   *Cont.*

343:6. Gentiles;" "Go ye and teach all nations;" "One [*footnote:*] Matt. xxviii. 19;   *Cont.*

343:27. proceeded; the   *Cont.*

343:28. is in the   *Cont.*

343:30–31. The . . . mentioned.   *not in* 84

343:30–32. no ¶ The governing word of the chapters, and one or two of their primitive themes, we have formerly mentioned.   *Cont.*

343:32. of their primitive   75g, 83g

343:32–33. Besides these, which we showed   *Cont.*, 75g, 83g; These we showed   84

343:33–35. sayings giving the true doctrine of Jesus himself about his resurrection,   *Cont.*

343:35–344:12. resurrection.   84; there . . . Evangelist.   *not in* 84

343:36. *not in* 84

344:12. Other sayings have in like manner their primitive theme. And if the reader   84

344:15–18. On . . . developments.   *not in* 84

344:17–18. how much is repetition,   *Cont.*

344:19–20. under the heads or themes indicated all the sayings for each, and   *Cont.;* under . . . for each theme, and   75g, 83g; under heads all the sayings on each theme, and   84

344:22. show him how true   *Cont.;* show him at least how true 75g, 83g

344:28–29. *logia* about the new commandment, making the   *Cont.*, 75g, 83g

345:13–14. All these we   *Cont.;* having . . . theme   *not in Cont.*, 75g, 83g

345:15. of his long   *Cont.*, 75g, 83g; of this long   84

345:21. take, as the primitive   *Cont.;* take another theme, the primitive   75g, 83g

345:22. disciples' requests   *Cont.,* 75g, 83g

345:23. these words: *Cont.*

345:24. with them all the   *Cont.*

346:5. is not the least in the   *Cont.*

346:12. it. First of all, we   *Cont.,* 75g, 83g

346:14–15. Gentiles, or as our Evangelist naturally calls [Evangelist calls   75g, 83g] them, the Greeks, present at the last Passover he [that he   75g, 83g] kept, and desirous   *Cont.,* 75g, 83g

346:27. large, of the reign of   *Cont.*

346:31. Gentiles."* To bring   *Cont.*

347:2. their mouth [*mispr. Cont.*] before him; he shall see of the travail of his soul and be satisfied; he shall justify many."* Texts [*footnote:*] Isaiah lii. 14 [*for* 15]; liii. 11.   *Cont.*

347:10–11. the strangers desiring to   *Cont.;* the strangers desirous to 75g, 83g

347:15–16. of this theme and of one other: *That they may be one as we are one!** It is [*footnote:*] **ἵνα ὦσιν ἕν καθὼς ἡμεῖς.* See John xvii. 11, 21–23.   *Cont.,* 75g, 83g

347:21, 25. *no* ¶ Jesus checked ... ¶But   *Cont.*

347:26–27. whole history of Christianity,   *Cont.*

347:29. how was Jesus precisely related   *Cont.;* precisely how was Jesus related   75g, 83g, 84;   *corrected by ed.*

348:7–8. personages, Wisdom and Word of God, *Sophia* and *Logos*. *Cont.*

348:11. of his calling himself the   *Cont.,* 75g, 83g

348:16. is possible   *Cont.,* 75g, 83g

348:21–22. It is possible; possible that our   *Cont.,* 75g, 83g

348:23. had this [had thus much   75g, 83g] to go upon, as well as *logia* like "Before Abraham was, I am," and "I and the Father are one."* At any [*footnote:*]* John viii. 58, and x. 30.   *Cont.,* 75g, 83g

348:32. xx. 34   *mispr.* 83g

348:34. Perhaps, however,   75g, 83g

348:34–38. *not in Cont.*

349:5. Jesus never theosophized.   *Cont.*

349:16. exceed considerably in amount   *Cont.,* 75g, 83g

349:21. said in the first of these papers that   *Cont.*

349:31. only distrusts the final result!   *Cont.,* 75g, 83g

349:33. and hint of   *Cont.*

349:34. The ... followed. *not in Cont.*

350:3. seize this hint *Cont.*

350:5. no ¶ We have remarked *Cont.*

350:9–10. Perhaps ... Lazarus. *not in Cont.*

350:12. disquisition, every detail has been *Cont.*

350:17–18. us attempt this juxtaposition. *Cont.*

350:19–20. as Jesus construed and connected it, had *Cont.*

350:21–22. glory."* *The hour is come, that the Son of Man should be glorified.*† At this [*footnote:*] †John xii. 23; comp. xi. 4 *Cont.*, 75g, 83g

350:24–25. of Jesus, the introduction and *Cont.*

350:28. at that moment *Cont.*, 75g, 83g

350:34. Martha imagines *Cont.*

350:36–351:1. Vain ... dawn! *not in Cont.*, 75g, 83g

351:1–2. but the correction *Cont.;* slowly to deepen, not *Cont.*, 75g, 83g

351:6–10. The *logion* ... then. *not in Cont.*, 75g, 83g

351:11. that very *logion* *Cont.*, 75g, 83g; which points to *Cont.*

351:13. grew up, probably, *Cont.*

351:15. ideal,—the raising of Lazarus. This *logion*, *Cont.*

351:16–17. *logion*, with the ... *again;* with the *Cont.*, 75g, 83g

351:18. *him;* with some saying of Jesus about his glory, such as, *The hour is come that the Son of Man should be glorified*, were the materials *Cont.*, 75g, 83g

351:20–23. *Sed* ... large. *not in 84*

351:30. exercise; a *Cont.*

351:31. pressure, too, on the sayings of *Cont.*, 75g, 83g

351:32–33. his. Sometimes *Cont.*

352:9–10. the original of ... to the agony in *Cont.*

352:14. of knowledge he lacks, not *Cont.*

352:15–16. The Tübingen critics are confident that the truth of Baur's theory about *Cont.*

352:19. any heed of *Cont.*

352:24. no ¶ *Cont.*

352:27. they represent *Cont.*, 75g, 83g

353:16. puts this *Cont.*, 75g, 83g; put this 84

353:17. have been written by *Cont.*

353:20–23. Passover; and Rome and the Christian Church at large adopted its view. There was, *Cont.*

354:9–10. aim at marking, and with a *Cont.*

354:11–12. about the days *Cont.*

354:15. He cannot   *Cont.*

354:19. it is for want,   *Cont.*

354:24. narrative; but   *Cont.*

354:28–29. well, but   *Cont.*

354:34–35. to bring in this piece   *Cont.*

355:1. contradicting the Synoptics,   *Cont.*

355:16. plant probably something   *Cont.*, 75g, 83g

355:33. Baur; the   *Cont.*

356:5. *no* ¶ The argument   *Cont.*

356:9. of Christ's side,   *Cont.*, 75g, 83g

356:18–19. with the form in   *Cont.*, 75g, 83g

356:20. Exodus: "Ye   *Cont.;* Exodus; which latter passage runs: 'Ye
75g, 83g

356:25. *no* ¶   *Cont.*

357:4. *look on whom they*   *Cont.*, 75g, 83g

357:5. proves nothing   *Cont.*

357:6. Gospel; passages   *Cont.*

357:7. which had a   *Cont.*, 75g, 83g; which had had a   84

357:8. have said above,   *Cont.*

357:11–12. nails, the Greek verb of the Messianic Psalm would
Cont.

357:14. also; a different   *Cont.*

357:15. *no* ¶ We do not deny   *Cont.*

357:17–18. Evangelist; it was a   *Cont.*

357:20. become with him the nucleus   *Cont.*

357:29. do. Now, he   *Cont.*, 75g, 83g

358:12–13. fancy-piece, but a document full of   *Cont.*

358:15. *no* ¶   *Cont.*

358:15–16. inventions because they seem   *Cont.*

358:17–18. like them; as, for example, the saying to the Jews   *Cont.*

358:19. Its . . . But   *not in Cont.*

358:23. *no* ¶   *Cont.*

358:30–31. with the note.   *Cont.;* in . . . Sardis.   *not in Cont.*

358:28–359:6. always there. With some such thought as this, Jesus
pursued his lofy treatment   *Cont.*

359:5. Jesus then did but   75g, 83g

359:10. *no* ¶   *Cont.*

359:12. resurrection, a visible   *Cont.*

359:15. happiness and reward to   *Cont.*

359:20. have already said,   *Cont.*

359:24. ¶Thus to the best of our ability have we made good our thesis, that the Fourth Gospel is no fancy-piece but an invaluable help towards a right understanding of Jesus and of the line taken by him. But we do not require our reader, even, to be   *Cont.;* ¶But we do not require our reader, even, to be   75g, 83g

359:25–26. about admitting sayings as genuine.   *Cont.*

359:35. study of this Gospel,   *Cont.*

359:37. *not in Cont.*

360:7–10. other three Gospels. [*no*¶] As we accept   *Cont.*

360:11. early part of   *Cont.*, 75g, 83g

360:16. Matthew,* but the   *Cont.*

361:2. facts that   *Cont.*

361:4. *no* ¶   *Cont.*

361:5–6. first coming forth formed   *Cont.*

361:12–13. And we know that there were many other accounts besides these,   *Cont.*

361:20–21. being quoted as they are now given in our Gospels. *Cont.*

361:22. *no* ¶ So little were they documents sacred   *Cont.*

361:24. went on along after   *mispr.* 75g, 83g

362:25. data from the original   *Cont.*

362:29–38. *not in Cont.*

363:1. ¶In the chief   *Cont.*

363:11–12. absence of it we ought to resign   *Cont.*

363:16. for every Epistle,   *Cont.*

363:18. *no* ¶   *Cont.*

363:19. survive and float . . . though their context   *Cont.*, 75g, 83g

363:20. lost; here   *Cont.*

363:29–30. would have amply served   *Cont.*

363:34. To us   *Cont.*, 75g, 83g

364:15. used it,*   *Cont.*

364:19. *no* ¶   *Cont.*

364:24. so identifying him.*   *Cont.*

366:13. evidence of eye-witnesses—   *Cont.*, 75g, 83g

366:15. *no* ¶ Such evidence is remarkably   *Cont.*

366:16. miraculous part in the commencements of Christianity. Sometimes   *Cont.*

366:17. getting it, but   *Cont.*

366:19–20. with their eyes   *Cont.*, 75g, 83g

367:7. that improved   *Cont.*

367:13. people who came a . . . or the people   *Cont.*

367:14. Lourdes or La Salette   *Cont.*

367:17. recommended, to the   *Cont.*, 75g, 83g

367:21. certain points   *Cont.*

367:22–23. not yet lost, and which … out of sight afterwards.   *Cont.*

367:24. genuine doctrine of   *Cont.*, 75g, 83g

367:25. could possess; so   *Cont.*, 75g, 83g

367:31. happen. It is true,   *Cont.*

368:1. it; at   *Cont.*

368:10. *no* ¶   *Cont.*

368:18. seem to drop from   *Cont.*, 75g, 83g

368:19. is to hold   *Cont.*

368:21. *no* ¶   *Cont.*

368:23. I repeat,   80

368:28–29. was sure, as soon   *Cont.*

368:31. long ago over.   *Cont.*, 75g, 83g

369:1. tries to explain   *Cont.*

369:5. assertions like this   80

369:11. and Epiphanius and others, as well as   80

369:12. even for him, the *Time Spirit* is   *Cont.*, 75g, 83g

369:20. as the last century has seen the extinction,   *Cont.*

369:22–23. Hale affirmed to have   *Cont.*

369:31. *no* ¶   *Cont.*

370:1. witchcraft; nay,   *Cont.*

370:8. Yet this itself, surely,   *Cont.*

370:9. to take the legendary   *Cont.*

370:16. investing the secret   *Cont.*

370:18. can make it feel   *Cont.*

370:20–21. is by leading men to   *Cont.*

370:22. again the religion   *Cont.*

370:31. inspire. What Jesus,   *Cont.*, 75g, 80, 83g

370:34. *not in* 80

371:3. *no* ¶   *Cont.*

371:4–5. Messias-ideal, the ideal of happiness and salvation, of the old Israel; to disengage   *Cont.*; Messias-ideal of his time, the ideal of happiness and salvation of the Jewish people; to disengage   75g, 80, 83g

371:14. author. For him himself, his own   *Cont.*

371:21–22. inclines many persons   *Cont.*

371:24–25. laughs; nevertheless,   *Cont.*

371:27. are a leaven set up in the world,   *Cont.*

371:32. as he did.   *Cont.*

371:34. notions of the   *Cont.*

372:1. which Jesus strove   *Cont.*

372:3. application, and judges   *Cont.*

372:5. to promise ourselves   *Cont.*, 75g, 83g

372:10–11. in which we can   *Cont.*

372:12–13. ourselves. This will stand us in stead   *Cont.*

372:14. fails us. And here again,   *Cont.*

372:15. may be to us,   *Cont.*

372:20. that of Messrs. Moody and   *Cont.*, 75g, 80, 83g

372:21. Sankey. Insensibly to lift us   *Cont.*

372:22–23. The parable   *Cont.*, 75g, 80, 83g

372:25–26. was cast out.*   *Cont.*, 75g, 80, 83g; Here, as usual, the Tübingen critics perceive *tendence.*   *Cont.*

372:32. whose lucidity was so   *Cont.*, 75g, 80, 83g

372:33. much that was   *Cont.*

372:34–35. and meant to mark,   *Cont.*, 75g, 80, 83g

373:1. popular religion the religion of Jesus had to   80

373:8. What could have been   *Cont.*, 75g, 80, 83g

373:9. such fastidious   *Cont.*

373:11–12. guests are all to stay and fall to. Popular   *Cont.*

373:13. almost as it were by accident,   *Cont.*

373:14–15. falls under the   *Cont.*

373:16. how many of those guests are   *Cont.*, 75g, 80, 83g

373:17. and to follow   80

373:19. *no* ¶ The delinquent is   *Cont.; no* ¶ The conspicuous delinquent, however, is   80

373:20. and to be taken   80; ¶In the   80

373:21. how utterly those   *Cont.*, 75g, 80, 83g

373:24. was inevitable.   *Cont.;* was, indeed, inevitable.   80

373:28. rise above it.   *Cont.*

374:1–377:16. *not in* 84

374:1. [i.e., preceding] *inserted by ed.*

377:16. The present volume is a sequel to the popular edition of *Literature and Dogma* published last year. It is meant to reproduce, in a somewhat condensed and much cheaper form, a work, *God and the Bible,* which the objections to *Literature and Dogma* called forth. ¶*Literature and*   84

377:17–19. —a work . . . *Dogma,*—   *not in* 75g, 83g

377:20. and its power and charm for   75g, 83g

377:22. was the end   75g, 83g

377:34–35. *no* ¶ Popular Christianity, drenched in the preternatural, has enjoyed abundantly this help of the imagination to   75g, 83g

378:8. bring on the   75g, 83g, 84; *corrected from Wordsworth*

378:14–22, 26–380:2. *not in* 84

378:22. ¶At the   84

380:2. ¶Christianity enabled,   84

380:7–8. or that revolution, and equality, and knowing that   75g, 83g

380:8–9. so the revolutionists find   75g, 83g

380:19. true, all specialists are not equally sober-minded.   75g, 83g

380:20. ¶We find   80; a brilliant mathematician, Professor Clifford, launching   75g, 80, 83g

380:21. they were just,   80

380:23–24. He calls   75g, 80, 83g

380:30. he scornfully adds   80

381:16–17. as in *Literature and Dogma* I have called   75g, 80, 83g

382:26. &c.; *quite*   75g, 83g

383:24. we are now entering.   75g, 83g

383:26. and others equally   75g, 83g

385:12. who gravely offer us about Christianity their   75g, 83g

385:21. fantastic. However, Mr. Ruskin is talking only about the beauties of nature; and here, perhaps, it is an excuse for inventing certainties that what one invents is so beautiful. But religion is to govern our life. Whoever produces   75g, 83g

385:22. us on the subject of   75g, 83g

385:23. is this so little   75g, 83g

385:25. ¶And there is   75g, 83g

386:11. *no* ¶   75g, 83g

386:31. became in this manner speedily   75g, 83g

387:12. And Christian writers in   75g, 83g

387:15. But Christian theologians   75g, 83g

387:31–389:4. Dr. . . . For   *not in* 84

389:4. ¶Protestantism has   84

389:6. deliverance. On this,   75g, 83g

389:21–22. the magical birth   75g, 83g

389:25. and even religious   75g, 83g

389:32. the received Protestant theology.   75g, 83g

390:5. on all lines. It induced separation   75g, 83g

390:14. true one. Protestantism's secret is undoubtedly   75g, 83g

390:21. do all the rest for   75g, 83g

390:28. and spreads; it cannot but be, and will be, on the   75g, 80, 83g

390:36. frivolous and sensual   75g, 80, 83g

391:37–38. whom the present work has . . . is not the man   75g, 83g

392:5. find the work useful   75g, 83g

392:7. aimed at them. It   75g, 83g

392:13. some acquaintance with   75g, 83g

392:14. and probably in   75g, 83g

392:15–17. with the Bible extends . . . throughout those large classes which   75g, 83g

393:16–17. startled on first hearing   75g, 83g

393:23. who is conversant with   75g, 83g

393:28–29. values. If there are but ten people in the world who deal with religion fairly, he is resolved to be one of those ten.   75g, 83g

393:38. as Israel's magnificent   75g, 83g

394:2. as the perfect elucidation   75g, 83g

394:3. comparing even the   75g, 83g

394:10–11. modern phrase: *Nations*   75g, 83g

394:21–22. in her forty and fifty editions of M. Adolphe Belot's novels, faring   75g, 83g

394:29–395:18, 36. *not in* 84

395:19. ¶Thus neither in respect of   75g, 83g

395:23–24. will be aware, indeed,   75g, 83g

395:30. but then proceed   75g, 83g

396:5–6. ridiculous. For *God*,—the name which has so engaged all men's feelings,—is at the same time by its very derivation a positive name, expressing that which is the most blessed of boons to man, Light; whereas *Unknowable* is a . . . negative. And no man   75g, 83g

396:13. gave him that name for what gives light and warmth, *God*. It   75g, 83g

396:38. unites the most   75g, 83g; unites most   84

397:2. aimed. Its   75g, 83g

397:5–17. Baur . . . upon   *not in* 84

397:17–18. The language is aimed at a true and   84

398:18. To one country and nation, and   75g, 83g

398:21–22. rewarded. May even that partial success be looked for? A   75g, 83g

398:24. however that judgment may   75g, 83g

Index

A reference to a page of text should be taken to include the notes to that page.